American Women in Science

A Biographical Dictionary

American Women in Science

A Biographical Dictionary

Martha J. Bailey

ABC-CLIO

Denver, Colorado
Santa Barbara, California
Oxford, England

Library of Congress Cataloging-in-Publication Data

Bailey, Martha J.
    American women in science: a biographical dictionary / Martha J. Bailey
    Includes bibliographical references and index.
    1. Women scientists—United States—Biography—Dictionaries. 2. nus. I. Title.
    Q141.B25 1994 509.2'273—dc20   [B] 94-10096

ISBN 0-87436-740-9

00 99 98 97 96 95   10 9 8 7 6 5 4 3 2

ABC-CLIO, Inc.
130 Cremona Drive, P.O. Box 1911
Santa Barbara, California 93116-1911

This book is printed on acid-free paper ⊗.
Manufactured in the United States of America

Contents

Preface

This book focuses on American women scientists—primarily in the physical and natural sciences—in the nineteenth and early twentieth centuries. Only women who began their careers prior to 1950 are included, and even a few who began as early as the eighteenth century. Like the pioneer women who joined in the great westward migration, nineteenth-century women scientists and other women who contributed to the development of science were also pioneers. They were the first females to receive academic degrees in science, the first to be appointed to faculties, or the first to be hired by science-oriented companies and government agencies. They prepared illustrations, classified specimens, prepared bibliographies, or wrote popular treatments of scientific subjects. "The pioneer first generation of women who attended college in the late nineteenth century left an unparalleled record of achievement in the profession and in social reform."[1]

Researching American Women in Science

Although some early women scientists, such as Lucy Braun, Gladys Emerson, and Margaret Mead, are well known, the contributions of countless others remain obscure. It is difficult to find data on these women because, during the times in which they lived, pioneer women scientists did not have the same opportunities that men had for advanced education, research grants, peer review, travel, participation in scientific societies, and recognition for their work. In addition, there have been few of them compared to the number of men scientists; for instance, only 4.2 percent of the women in federal government (versus 10.3 percent of the men) were classified as technical, scientific, and professional in 1938.[2] Even today women comprise only one in four scientists and one in twenty-five engineers in the United States.[3]

In many cases only scraps of information could be found. For example, there are several photographs of Agnes Quirk in the files of the National Archives, and Margaret Rossiter's book includes her photograph.[4] The references that were consulted, however, provide little or no biographical information on Quirk; they reveal only that she coauthored one U.S. Department of Agriculture publication.

Significant dates, such as birth, death, marriage, and occupation dates, were often omitted, not for lack of research, but for lack of clear documentation. While this information surely is recorded somewhere, it cannot be found without a tremendous amount of difficulty. It is hard to know where to begin when researching women, who, based on our cultural tradition, generally take a spouse's name, but not always. In an obituary a woman may be listed under her first, second, third, or subsequent husband's name, or under her maiden name. Further inconsistencies in the records hindered inclusion of various facts. Omissions should not be viewed as oversights, but rather as testimony to the elusiveness of information on professional women in the late nineteenth and early twentieth centuries.

There are numerous publications on women scientists, but most biographical guides are worldwide in scope. This volume concentrates specifically on American women in the sciences, and the initial problem in preparing this book was identifying the names of these women. *American Men and Women of Science* (formerly *American Men of Science*)[5] was consulted because it has been the primary source for identifying American scientists since the publication of its first edition in 1906. The earlier editions focused on male members of the field; few women were included. *Notable American Women*[6] and the *Dictionary of American Biography*[7] were also used as starting points for research. Caroline Herzenberg's *Women Scientists from Antiquity to the Present*[8] provided a checklist of women and identified sources for information about them. John Barnhart's *Biographical Notes upon Botanists*[9] proved an excellent source for identifying women who were employed by federal and state agencies. Patricia Siegel's *Women in the Scientific Search*[10] and Marilyn Ogilvie's *Women in Sciences: Antiquity through the Nineteenth Century*[11] supplied the names of several women. The numerous other titles that were consulted are listed in the bibliography.

The listings in *American Men and Women of Science* are brief, and it sometimes is not clear what criteria were used for selecting the women who are included. The first two editions of the reference book are particularly puzzling. Harriet M. Miller was an amateur ornithologist and naturalist who wrote popular books for both adults and children under the pseudonym Olive Thorne Miller. She is listed in both the first and second editions. Nellie Doubleday wrote popular books on natural science that were published by her husband's publishing firm, and she also is listed in the first two editions. Margaret Rossiter discusses further the question of criteria for inclusion.[12] The first seven editions of the book starred the names of "outstanding" scientists. There are some puzzling selections here, too. Susanna Phelps Gage's name was starred with her husband's, Simon H. Gage, who also was an embryologist. Susanna Gage, however, officially was unemployed. Stephen Visher's *Scientists Starred 1903–1943 in "American Men of Science"* provides a lengthy analysis of the selection of "stars."[13]

Other recent publications that include some information on American women are Margaret Rossiter's *Women Scientists in America*,[14] *Uneasy Careers and Intimate Lives*,[15] G. Kass-Simon's and Patricia Farnes' *Women of Science*,[16] and Londa Schiebinger's *The Mind Has No Sex?*[17] Laura Shapiro, in *Perfection Salad*,[18] describes the development of the home economics discipline, particularly in the areas of foods and nutrition.

Although initially it was difficult to identify women scientists, many names surfaced during the research, and deciding who was to be *excluded* became a problem. The people who were selected fall into the following categories:

- Women listed in the first three editions of *American Men and Women of Science* or whose names were starred in any of the first seven editions
- Women listed in other sources who started their employment prior to 1950
- Women selected for recognition in their respective fields, such as election to the National Academy of Sciences
- Women scientists who could be identified as working as professionals for federal or state agencies
- Other women who contributed to the development of various sciences in the nineteenth and early twentieth centuries (some worked for companies, museums, arboreta, or associations; some opened cooking schools that later were incorporated into college home economics departments; and some were authors or artists)

Notes

1. Barbara Sicherman. "College and Careers: Historical Perspectives on the Lives and Work Patterns of Women College Graduates." In *Women and Higher Education of American History,* edited by John M. Faragher and Florence Howe. New York: W. W. Norton & Company, 1988, 134–136.

2. Margaret W. Rossiter. *Women Scientists in America: Struggles and Strategies to 1940* Baltimore: Johns Hopkins University Press, 1982, 223.

3. *Women and Minorities in Science and Engineering.* Washington, DC: National Science Foundation, 1988, 15.

4. Rossiter, op. cit., 62.

5. *American Men and Women of Science.* New York: R. R. Bowker, 1906– . (Formerly *American Men of Science).*

6. E. T. James, ed. *Notable American Women 1607–1950: A Biographical Dictionary.* Cambridge: Harvard University Press, 1971; Barbara Sicherman et al., eds. *Notable American Women: The Modern Period: A Biographical Dictionary.*Cambridge: Harvard University Press, 1980.

7. *Dictionary of American Biography.* New York: Scribner's. 1928–1981.

8. Caroline L. Herzenberg. *Women Scientists from Antiquity to the Present: An Index.* West Cornwall, CT: Locust Hill Press, 1986.

9. John H. Barnhart. *Biographical Notes upon Botanists.* Boston: G. K. Hall and Company, 1965.

10. Patricia J. Siegel and Kay T. Finley. *Women in the Scientific Search: An American Bio-Bibliography 1724–1979.* Metuchen, NJ: Scarecrow Press, 1985.

11. Marilyn B. Ogilvie. *Women in Science: Antiquity through the Nineteenth Century: A Biographical Dictionary with Annotated Bibliography.* Cambridge: MIT Press, 1986.

12. Rossiter, op. cit., 107.

13. Stephen S. Visher. *Scientists Starred 1903–1943 in "American Men of Science."* Baltimore: Johns Hopkins Press, 1947.

14. Rossiter, op. cit.

15. P. G. Abir-Am and D. Outram, eds. *Uneasy Careers and Intimate Lives: Women in Science 1789–1979.* New Brunswick, NJ: Rutgers University Press, 1987.

16. G. Kass-Simon and Patricia Farnes, eds. *Women of Science: Righting the Record.* Bloomington: Indiana University Press, 1990.

17. Londa Schiebinger. *The Mind Has No Sex? Women in the Origins of Modern Science.* Cambridge: Harvard University Press, 1989.

18. Laura Shapiro. *Perfection Salad: Women and Cooking at the Turn of the Century.* New York: Farrar, Straus & Giroux, 1986.

Acknowledgments

The author expresses her thanks to Emily R. Mobley, Dean of Libraries, Purdue University, who encouraged and supported the project. She thanks the numerous librarians and archivists who searched for references about and photographs of the women who are included in this book. The research was supported partially by the Purdue University Libraries and by the Thomas S. Wilmeth Fund of the Libraries.

Introduction

The *study of* women scientists is hampered by a definition of terms. Since women were not admitted to graduate degree programs until late in the nineteenth century, it is difficult to determine at what point they could be designated *women scientists.* The term *scientist* was coined in 1840 by Englishman William Whewell as a substitute for the terms *savant, philosopher,* and *scientific man.*[1] "Until the twentieth century, science was populated almost exclusively by men, and thus the phrase 'men of science' was almost equivalent to the non-sex-linked tag 'scientist.'"[2] Margaret Rossiter's studies of the persons in all fields of science who were listed in *American Men and Women of Science*[3] prior to 1940 indicates that women scientists were concentrated in biology, medicine, psychology, and mathematics.[4]

Selecting criteria for women scientists is problematic. One cannot apply the same criteria—research and publication—to women scientists that apply to men scientists because, during the periods in which they lived, women did not have the same opportunities for education, employment, travel, membership in scientific societies, and peer participation. Due to the social conventions of the day, women received only rudimentary education, and few middle-class women worked for wages. When women secured academic degrees, they were almost exclusively employed as instructors or research assistants in colleges or as technicians in government agencies.

Science was a family endeavor. Women often would work with fathers, brothers, or husbands in laboratories or museums with little or no salaries; therefore, they generally did not build long lists of prestigious appointments and publications. It is difficult to assess the contributions of a woman to a father's or husband's research and publications.

H. F. Mozans, in *Women in Science,* refers to the wives and daughters of scientists as "inspirers and collaborators."[5] Jane Colden, often mentioned as the first American woman scientist, worked with her father, Cadwalladar Colden, on his botanical collection. Other early eighteenth-century women scientists working with their families were Martha Logan, who operated a nursery business with her son in Charleston, South Carolina,[6] and Eliza Pinckney, who experimented with new plants on her plantation.[7] In the nineteenth century, Maria Fernald was recognized for her own work as an entomologist as well as for the assistance she gave her husband in his research. Arvilla Ellis, however, is known only for her contributions to publishing her husband's research.[8]

Several women scientists were widows or had husbands with incapacitating illnesses. Flora Patterson and Agnes Chase both were widows and both were employed by the U.S. Department of Agriculture. After she was widowed, Mary Brandegee obtained a medical degree and became a curator of the botanical collection at the California Academy of Sciences. After her husband's death, Wanda Farr continued the research on which they had collaborated, eventually leading to the discovery of cellulose.

Numerous women continued to work after marriage, and often wives and husbands were employed at the same location. Katherine Bitting and A. W. Bitting worked for the same employers throughout their careers. Ellen Richards and Robert Richards both were members of the faculty of Massachusetts Institute of Technology. Likewise, Anna Comstock and John Comstock both were faculty members at Cornell University. In the first few editions of *American Men and Women of Science,* many women were listed under their husbands' names. Ellen Richards is listed as "Mrs. Robert Richards"; her name is starred but his is not. Anthropologist Margaret Mead retained her maiden name over several marriages.

Despite their virtual anonymity, women in the nineteenth century wrote texts on natural history, chemistry, and botany that enjoyed great popularity; for instance, Almira Phelps wrote on botany and Mary Treat on natural history. Other women trained themselves to be experts—Helen Michael, for instance, was recognized as an expert in the fledgling discipline of chemical analysis of plants.

Education

Coeducational colleges originated in the Midwest when Oberlin College in 1837 began admitting women and African Americans. In 1885 Bryn Mawr College became the first to establish a graduate program for women.[9]

Land-grant institutions, which often were coeducational, were established by the Morrill Act of 1862. The early curricula were based on the prevailing ideas of the sciences that were pertinent to scientific agriculture. The ranking with regard to importance to agriculture at the time was as follows:

1.) Chemistry
2.) Geology and meteorology
3.) Botany and horticulture, zoology and biology, and entomology[10]

Negro Land-Grant Colleges in the 17 Southern states were established under the Second Morrill Act of 1890. Mississippi already had established Alcorn University in 1871 under the Morrill Act of 1862, and South Carolina and Virginia likewise had shared their funds since 1872 with black colleges in their states.[11]

The data on the number of academic degrees received by women in the early years are sparse. Margaret Rossiter's study of women scientists listed in the first three editions of *American Men and Women of Science* (1906, 1910, and 1921) indicates that 98 institutions granted baccalaureate degrees to 439 women prior to 1920. The primary fields of study were botany, zoology, psychology, medical sciences, and mathematics.[12] Many of these degree recipients were graduates of women's colleges.

Since the turn of the century, the number of women who have received doctorates has continued to increase, but the proportion of women to men receiving doctorates dropped between 1950 and 1970 and did not again reach the high levels of the 1920s and 1930s until the late 1970s. The explanation for this drop is that many men doctoral students received financial support from the G. I. Bill, a source that few women students could use. The number of women doctorates has risen since 1970, but the number of men has dropped considerably. These data account for the proportionate increase in the number of women Ph.D.s since the 1970s.[13]

Women scientists continue to be concentrated in the life and social sciences. In the 1970s women received one-fifth of the doctorates in the life sciences but less than one-tenth in the physical sciences.[14] This trend continued into the 1980s. In 1985 more than four-fifths of women scientists were in either life sciences, psychology, or social sciences.[15]

Sources for Employment

*T*he *following* paragraphs provide background information on opportunities for employment for women scientists primarily in the late nineteenth and early twentieth centuries.

Academic Institutions

Educational institutions traditionally have been the primary employer of women scientists. The trend continues today. Although only 25 percent of all scientists are women, about 59 percent of those women are employed in academe.[16] Numerous women are employed in administrative, professional, and non-tenure track teaching positions. Women scientists often teach introductory-level courses or are employed in colleges that do not emphasize research and publication, both of which limit opportunities for study.

In the nineteenth century both men and women taught in academic institutions before they completed their own academic degrees. Mary Woolman was asked to join the faculty of Teachers' College, Columbia University, based on her book and lectures on practical sewing. She later completed a degree in textile chemistry and continued on the faculty. Martha Van Rensselaer, who established the first accredited home economics program at Cornell in 1900, did not receive her own undergraduate degree until 1909.

When women were not admitted to American universities, they tried to enter European schools, particularly in Germany and Switzerland. Several American women scientists received doctorates from the University of Zurich, including botanists Emily L. Gregory and Julia Snow.

Women scientists often were assigned to home economics departments instead of biology or chemistry departments. In coeducational colleges, unmarried women faculty members were placed in charge of women's dormitories. Marion Talbot, although a prominent scientist whose name was starred in *American Men and Women of Science,* also was dean of women at the University of Chicago from 1895 to 1925. In the 1890s Emily L. Gregory, although she had a doctorate from the University of Zurich, was unable to secure employment. She accepted a position at Barnard College to teach botany without a salary because she had an independent income.[17]

Some women faculty members were not listed in faculty rosters in order to avoid controversy with boards of trustees, alumni, and other faculty members. Anna Comstock at Cornell was appointed an assistant professor in 1889, demoted to lecturer due to objections from the trustees, and then promoted again to assistant professor in 1913 and finally to professor in 1920.

Some women faculty members, however, were recognized in their lifetimes for their achievements. In addition to being the first woman science student at Massachusetts Institute of Technology, Ellen Richards was the first woman faculty member. She remained at the level of instructor of sanitary chemistry for 40 years, although she received international recognition for her work. Mary Swartz Rose of Teachers' College, Columbia University, was recognized as a pioneer in the field of nutrition in what was one of the outstanding departments in the United States at that time. Nettie Stevens at Bryn Mawr College was recognized as an independent codiscoverer of the determination of sex by chromosomes. Margaret Ferguson at Wellesley College developed the leading undergraduate program in the nation for the study of plant science. Florence Sabin at Johns Hopkins was an outstanding woman scientist in the medical field in the first half of the twentieth century.

Federal Agencies

Although it seems incongruous that Victorian women would seek employment in the federal government, numerous middle-class women were forced to do so by economic conditions in the late nineteenth century. The Treasury Department is credited with officially hiring women in 1861 to clip and count paper money—at about half the salary male clerks received. Several years later, after the department purchased mechanical paper cutters, women employees were moved to other clerical tasks.[18] By 1868 women also were employed in the U.S. Postal Service and the Coast Survey.[19]

Margaret Rossiter's study of the women listed in the third edition of *American Men and Women of Science* indicated that in 1921 about 63 percent of the women scientists who worked for the federal government were employed by the Department of Agriculture. She quotes Women's Bureau Bulletin no. 53, a 1925 study that indicated that the department employed about 72 percent of the women scientists working in the federal government at that time.[20] Women scientists were concentrated in the Division of Plant Industry and in the Bureau of Home Economics,[21] and they also were employed at regional research laboratories scattered across the country.

The first woman scientist employed by the Department of Agriculture was Effie A. Southworth, later Effie Spalding, who served as an assistant pathologist in the Bureau of Plant Industry from 1888 to 1893, when she left to attend graduate school. In 1896 a second woman scientist, Flora Patterson, was hired to supervise the herbarium in the division of vegetable pathology; she retired in 1923. Mary Pennington joined the staff of the Bureau of Chemistry in 1905. She was appointed chief of the food research laboratory when it was established in 1908, but she left the department in 1919 to work in industry.

Eloise Gerry was hired by the Forest Products Laboratory at Madison, Wisconsin, in 1910 and spent her entire career there. Angie Beckwith worked for the Forest Service in Washington, D.C., starting in 1908. Audrey Richards, who joined the division in 1917, was appointed pathologist in charge (but not chief) of the Forest Products Laboratory from 1929 to 1943.

Agnes Chase had an interesting career in the Department of Agriculture. Largely self-educated, she was promoted through the ranks and in 1936 appointed the principal scientist in charge of systematic agrostology (study of grasses). Her name was starred in the fifth, sixth, and seventh editions of *American Men and Women of Science*.

Louise Stanley was the highest ranking woman scientist in the federal government when she was appointed the first chief of the Bureau of Home Economics in 1923. Alice Evans was the preeminent woman scientist in the federal government prior to World War II due to her pioneering studies on the common origin of brucellosis in both cattle and humans. She was employed by the Department of Agriculture from 1910 until 1918, when she transferred to what is now the Public Health Service.

Very few women were employed in professional positions in other federal agencies prior to 1900. Maria Mitchell worked on contract as a "computer" (performer of calculations) for the Coast Survey from 1849 to 1868. Mary Jane Rathbun was employed by the National Museum starting in 1887. Matilda Stevenson worked with her husband at the Bureau of Ethnology and was hired in 1890 after his death to assemble his notes and catalog specimens. In 1896 the Geological Survey started hiring women, such as Florence Bascom, on a contract basis rather than as full-time employees.

State Agencies

Since the development of experiment stations and extension services was closely tied to land-grant institutions, some women found employment in these agencies. The impetus for establishing agricultural experiment stations in the mid–nineteenth century was farm groups petitioning their state legislatures to provide reliable information on soil analysis and fertilizers to improve crops.[22] The first state to establish an experiment station was Connecticut. The station originally was located at Wesleyan University under W. O. Atwater in 1875, but two years later it was moved to Yale University.

The Hatch Act of 1887 provided each state and territory with $15,000 per year for research.[23] This marked the first significant federal research aid to states and universities. Many states also appointed a state chemist to oversee the testing of fertilizers and other products. This person often was a chemistry professor at the state agricultural college.[24]

The extension service was established in 1914 under the Smith-Lever Act. Prior to that many states held "farmers' institutes" to educate farmers on crops, wives on homemaking, and children on vocational skills,[25] all with an emphasis to keep families on the farm. The Smith-Lever Act provided funds for both women's programs and vocational education, funds that women faculty members in home economics departments could utilize.[26]

Employment of women in state agencies paralleled the situation in the federal government. Traditionally the areas of food and nutrition, child care, textiles, and other areas of domestic science were assigned to women. Some continued to work in laboratories and herbaria handling routine analyses and classifications.

African-American women were concentrated in home economics in order to teach in public schools or to work as home demonstration agents for the African-American community.[27] The first African-American woman agent was Annie Peters, who was employed in Okfuskee County, Oklahoma, in 1912.[28]

Edith Patch was head of the Department of Entomology at the Maine Agricultural Experiment Station from 1904 to 1937. Since the office included faculty status, she was one of the first women faculty members at the University of Maine. Mary Murtfeldt, an entomologist and botanist, was hired by the state entomologist office of Missouri in 1868 and served as the acting state entomologist from 1888 to 1896. Very few women were employed by state agencies prior to 1900, but in the 1890s experiment stations in some states hired women in laboratories.

Some examples of women who worked for state agencies are Frances N. Clark, California Fish and Game Division; Lela A. Ewers, Ohio Division of Conservation; Martha Koehne, Ohio Department of Health; Ruth D. Svihla, Louisiana Department of Conservation; and Elsie G. Whitney, New York State Museum.

Authors and Artists

In the nineteenth century there was a popular demand for elementary textbooks on chemistry, botany, and other sciences to be used by both men and women who attended classes and lectures at museums, lyceums, and chautauquas. Almira Phelps and Eliza Andrews wrote books on botany for the general public. Mrs. Phelps sold more than a quarter million copies of her book, *Familiar Lectures on Botany*, between 1820 and 1870.[29] Charlotte Taylor wrote articles on entomology that were published in *Harper's New Monthly Magazine*. Mary Treat wrote popular books and articles on natural history.

The science of home economics was not established as a formal discipline until the 1890s, although books on housekeeping and cooking date back to previous centuries (in fact, recipes and menus have been found on cuneiform tablets). Catharine Beecher, Christine Frederick, Helen Campbell, and Mary Terhune, who wrote under the pseudonym Marion Harland, were popular authors of books on housekeeping.

There actually was a person named Fannie Farmer who taught cooking in Boston and published cookbooks. Other early authors, some of whom also operated cooking schools, were Mary Lincoln, Lizzie Kander,[30] Maria Parloa, Mary Randolph,[31] Sarah Rorer, and Irma

Rombauer.[32] Adelle Davis was the food guru of the 1950s, writing and giving interviews on radio and television.

Many women scientists were recognized as scientific artists, particularly before the development of photography. Lucy Say illustrated texts written by her husband, naturalist Thomas Say. Agnes Chase obtained a position as a botanical illustrator with the U.S. Department of Agriculture and developed expertise on grasses. Maria Bachman was an associate of John Audubon and assisted in preparing his paintings. Sarah P. Lemmon specialized in watercolors of the flora of the Pacific slopes. Graceanna Lewis was known for her paintings of birds. Mary Walcott wrote *North American Wildflowers*, a book that included her paintings. Anna Comstock studied wood engraving in order to illustrate her husband's publications; later she completed her college education so her illustrations and her own publications would be scientifically accurate. Kathryn M. Sommerman[33] was an artist and entomological assistant for the Illinois Natural History Survey and later worked as an entomologist for the U.S. Department of Agriculture. Herbert Osborn and W. R. Walton[34] mention other scientific artists who could not be identified.

Museums, Arboreta, and Herbaria

Women were employed by museums and herbaria to classify and prepare specimens and to set up exhibits. Martha Maxwell was unique in that she was self-employed as a taxidermist and museum owner. She was so well known that sets of stereo cards were published that illustrated her craft at the Centennial Exposition of 1876.[35]

Mary Brandegee was a curator at the California Academy of Sciences. She and her husband founded the journal *Zoe,* which was published from 1883 to 1893. She was succeeded as curator by Alice Eastwood, who is remembered for her work to reestablish museum collections after the San Francisco earthquake of 1906. Elizabeth Britton suggested the founding of the New York Botanical Garden, and her husband was the first director. Although she did not have a doctorate, Elizabeth Britton was one of the most famous women scientists in the United States in the 1890s.

Horticulture and landscape architecture were areas that were slow to develop into professions. Kate Sessions was the founder of Balboa Park in San Diego. Beatrix Farrand was one of the first women landscape architects in the United States. Natalie Bowen, who used the pseudonym Natalie Gomez, was a professional gardener and horticulturist who was known as a horticultural writer.[36] Louisa King wrote ten popular books on gardening. Theodora Hubbard was associated with the journal *Landscape Architecture* and wrote several books on landscape and city planning.

Editors and Librarians

A number of women were editors of scientific journals. Clara Cummings was on the editorial staff of *Plant World*, Annie Gravatt and Helen Hart were with *Phytopathology*, Mary Swartz Rose was with *Journal of Nutrition*, and Lucy Braun was on the editorial staff of *Wild-Flower*.

Women often became librarians in government agencies, associations, and museums. Entomologist Mabel Colcord[37] worked in the entomology library of the U.S. Department of Agriculture. Mary Day was the librarian of Gray Herbarium from 1893 to 1924. Eunice Oberly, the librarian for the Bureau of Plant Industry, has a prize named in her honor. All three women were noted for their contributions to scientific bibliography.

Business and Industry

Few women worked in industry as professionals prior to World War I. Mary Pennington owned her own analytical laboratory in 1901 and worked for several companies. Jane Rollman was the head chemist for Pevely Dairy Company in St. Louis.[38] Anne Swift worked for Eastman Kodak from 1918 to 1922.[39] Cynthia Westcott entered private practice as a plant pathologist in 1933 after she was unable to obtain professional employment. Kate Sessions operated a nursery business from 1885 to 1940. Adelia McCrea was a research mycologist with Parke, Davis & Company from 1919 through 1942. Betty Sullivan was chair of the board for Experience, Inc. in 1973. Entomologist Janet Rapp was appointed assistant director of research for Archem Corporation in 1949. Wanda Farr, the discoverer of cellulose, worked for American Cyanamid Company and for Celanese Corporation of America in the 1940s. Katherine Blodgett, who worked for General Electric, developed nonreflecting glass, and Edith Clarke designed large electric power systems at General Electric in the 1930s and 1940s.

Associations and Societies

Perhaps the most serious barrier encountered by early women scientists was denial of contact with colleagues in the "invisible colleges" and informal networks at scientific meetings. In the nineteenth century meetings of scientific societies were exclusively a male privilege. The few women members did not attend either due to the prevailing notions of propriety or more often because meetings were held in men's clubs that did not admit women.

Lucy Say was elected a member of the Academy of Natural Sciences of Philadelphia in 1841, but she did not attend any meetings. Late in the nineteenth century women were admitted as members of some societies and gradually were elected to offices, including that of president.

Several women were employed by associations and societies as secretaries or editors, and a few worked as scientists. Mary Reid, a botanist, worked for the U.S. Golf Association. Later she worked as a plant physiologist for the Department of Agriculture and for the Public Health Service.[41] Bertha Cady was a naturalist for the National Girl Scouts from 1924 to 1936. Katherine G. Bitting was employed as a scientist by the National Canners Association and the Glass Container Association. Physicist Mary Warga was executive secretary of the Optical Society of America from 1959 to 1972.

Explorers

A phenomenon of the nineteenth century was English ladies traveling to all corners of the world gathering scientific specimens for museums or supporting themselves by their publications and public lectures. Mary Kingsley and Isabella Bishop probably were the best known of these Englishwomen.[42] Some American women had similar pursuits. Ynes Mexia collected botanical specimens in Mexico. Grace Seton explored with her husband, naturalist Ernest Thompson Seton, and wrote popular treatments of their studies.[43] Mary Akeley collected specimens of wild animals for American natural history museums.[44] Archaeologist Annie Peck was the first person to climb several mountains in the Andes.

Current Employment

One result of the legislation on equal opportunity in employment has been increased opportunities for diverse careers for women in the past 20 years. Academe, however is still the primary employer of women scientists. In 1981 the distribution of employment for women scientists and engineers was 59 percent in colleges and universities, 19 percent in business and industry, 6 percent in hospitals and clinics, 5 percent in the federal government, 5 percent in nonprofit organizations, 3 percent in other government agencies, and 3 percent in elementary and secondary schools.[46]

Employment of women scientists and engineers increased 250 percent (18 percent per year) between 1976 and 1986 compared with 84 percent (6 percent per year) for men.[47] "Between 1976 and 1986, employment of women scientists and engineers grew fastest in the industrial sector, rising at an annual rate of 17 percent."[48] On the other hand, employment of women in academia, primarily in four-year colleges and universities, dropped from 28 percent in 1977 to 21 percent in 1986, while academia was the fastest growing sector of employment for men.[49]

Women have not yet attained pay scales equal to those of men. Salaries for women scientists and engineers averaged 75 percent of those for men in 1986, but women's salaries in the life sciences were only 70 percent of those for men.[50]

Notes

1. Robert V. Bruce. *Launching of Modern American Science 1846–1876.* New York: Knopf, 1987.
2. Nathan R. Cole. "Women in Science." *American Scientist* 69 (July–August 1981): 385.
3. *American Men and Women of Science.* New York: R. R. Bowker, 1906– . (Formerly *American Men of Science).*
4. Margaret W. Rossiter. *Women Scientists in America: Struggles and Strategies to 1940.* Baltimore: Johns Hopkins University Press, 1982, 223–225.
5. H. F. Mozans. "Women as Inspirers and Collaborators in Science." In *Women in Science.* New York: D. Appleton and Company, 1913; reprint MIT Press, 1979.
6. E. T. James, ed. *Notable American Women 1906–1950: A Biographical Dictionary,* vol 2. Cambridge: Harvard University Press, 1971, 419.
7. Ibid., vol. 3, 69.
8. "In the Death of Mrs. Arvilla Ellis . . ." *Science* 10 (11 August 1899): 191.
9. Joseph N. Kane. *Famous First Facts and Records in the United States.* New York: Ace Books, 1974.
10. Alan I. Marcus. *Agricultural Science and the Quest for Legitimacy: Farmers, Agricultural Colleges, and Experiment Stations, 1870–1890.* Ames: Iowa State University Press, 1985, 19.
11. Edward D. Eddy. "The Negro Land-Grant Colleges." In *Colleges for Our Land and Time: The Land-Grant Idea in American Education.* New York: Harper & Brothers, 1957.
12. Rossiter, op. cit., 11.
13. *Climbing the Ladder: An Update on the Status of Doctoral Women Scientists and Engineers.* Washington, DC: National Academy Press, 1983, 2.1.
14. Ibid., 1.1.
15. *Women and Minorities in Science and Engineering.* Washington, DC: National Science Foundation, 1988, 6.
16. *Climbing the Ladder . . . ,* 4.2.
17. Rossiter, op. cit., 17.
18. Cindy S. Aron. *Ladies and Gentlemen of the Civil Service: Middle-Class Workers in Victorian America.* New York: Oxford University Press, 1987, 70.

19. Gladys L. Baker. "Women in the U.S. Department of Agriculture." *Agricultural History* 50 (1976): 191.
20. Rossiter, op. cit., 224–227.
21. Baker, op. cit., 196.
22. Bruce, op. cit., 80.
23. Ibid., 317.
24. Marcus, op. cit., 42–44.
25. Roy V. Scott. *The Reluctant Farmer: The Rise of Agricultural Extension to 1914.* Urbana: University of Illinois Press, 1970.
26. Rossiter, op. cit., 200.
27. Jeanne Noble. "Higher Education of Black Women in the Twentieth Century." In *Women and Higher Education in American History,* edited by John M. Faragher and Florence Howe. New York: Norton, 1988, 90.
28. Alfred C. True. "A History of Agricultural Extension Work in the United States 1785–1923." Miscellaneous Publication 15 (1928): 189. Washington, DC: U.S. Department of Agriculture.
29. Bruce, op. cit., 79.
30. *Notable American Women* (1971).
31. Ibid.
32. Barbara Sicherman et al., eds. *Notable American Women: The Modern Period: A Biographical Dictionary.* Cambridge: Harvard University Press, 1980.
33. *American Men and Women of Science,* 8th ed., 1949.
34. Herbert Osborn. *Fragments of Entomological History, Including Some Personal Recollections of Men and Events.* Columbus, OH: The author, 1927–1946; W. R. Walton. "Entomological Drawings and Draftsmen." Entomological Society of Washington *Proceedings* 23 (1921): 93–94.
35. William C. Darrah. *The World of Stereographs.* Gettysburg, PA: The author, 1977.
36. John H. Barnhart. *Biographical Notes upon Botanists.* Boston: G. K. Hall and Company, 1965.
37. Osborn, op. cit.
38. Barnhart, op. cit.
39. Ibid.
40. Elizabeth M. O'Hern. "Women Scientists in Microbiology." *Bioscience* 23 (September 1973): 539.
41. Barnhart, op. cit.
42. Stanley J. Kunitz, ed. *British Authors of the Nineteenth Century.* New York: H. W. Wilson Co., 1936.
43. *Notable American Women* (1980).
44. Ibid.
45. *Women and Minorities . . . ,* 15.
46. *Climbing the Ladder . . . ,* 4.2.
47. *Women and Minorities . . . ,* viii.
48. Ibid., 9.
49. Ibid.
50. Ibid., 14.

Sophie Bledsoe Aberle
Bernice Ackerman
(Amy) Elizabeth Adams
Elizabeth Cabot Cary Agassiz
Ruth Florence Allen
Margaret Altmann
Eliza Frances Andrews
Grace Andrews
Gladys Amelia Anslow
Helen Woodard Atwater
Pauline Morrow Austin

Aberle, Sophie Bledsoe

(1899–)

anthropologist and nutritionist

Education: A.B., Stanford University, 1923, M.S., 1925, Ph.D. in genetics, 1927; M.D., Yale University, 1930

Employment: Assistant histologist, Stanford University, 1924–1925, assistant embryologist and neurologist, 1925–1926; instructor in anthropology, Institute of Human Relations, Yale University, 1927–1930, Sterling fellow, School of Medicine, 1930–1931, instructor, 1930–1934; associate in research, Carnegie Institute, 1934–1935; superintendent of Pueblo Indians, Bureau of Indian Affairs, and secretary, Southwest Superintendents Council, 1935–1944; division of medical science, National Research Council, 1944–1949; special research director, University of New Mexico, 1949–1954; chief nutritionist, Bernalillo County Indian Hospital, 1953–1966; member of staff, Department of Psychiatry, Medical School, 1966–1969, member of staff, Law School, University of New Mexico, 1970–

Married: 1940

*S*ophie Aberle is one of the few Native Americans working in the field during the early twentieth century. She has enjoyed a remarkable career that has encompassed working as an anthropologist, a physician, a nutritionist, and a psychiatrist. Starting about 1935, when she held a position with the Bureau of Indian Affairs, Sophie Aberle became visible as an advocate for her people in all areas of their lives, including health, education, culture, and living conditions. The list of her activities is extensive: member of the upper Rio Grande drainage basin committee; consultant for the health committee of the All Indian Pueblo Council; member of New Mexico Nutrition Committee; member of White House Conference on Children in Democracy; chair of the board of directors for the Southwest Field Training School for Federal Service; member of the committee of maternal and infant mortality; acting executive director of the Commission on Rights, Liberties and Responsibilities of American Indians; director of a survey of Indian Education for the Bureau of Indian Affairs; consultant to the All Indian Pueblo Council on computer assisted instruction program; consultant for Stanford University's study of Indian education; and consultant for the bilingual/bicultural project of the Bernalillo School District. She served on the board of directors of numerous organizations such as Planned Parenthood, the county YWCA, and the Bernalillo County Indian Hospital. She was the first woman member of the National Science Board (the policymaking body for the National Science Foundation), serving on the board from 1950 to 1957. She has lived a long, very eventful life. She was a member of the American Association for the Advancement of Science and the American Medical Association. She was listed in the 1992–1993 edition of *American Men and Women of Science*.

Bibliography: *American Men and Women of Science* 5–18; Herzenberg, Caroline L., *Women Scientists from Antiquity to the Present; International Directory of Anthropologists;* O'Neill, Lois S., *The Women's Book of World Records and Achievements*.

Ackerman, Bernice
(1924–)
meteorologist

Education: B.S., University of Chicago, 1948; M.S., 1955, Ph.D. in geophysical science, 1965
Employment: Meteorologist and hydrologist, U.S. Weather Bureau, 1948–1953; research associate in cloud physics, University of Chicago, 1953–1965, assistant professor of meteorology, 1965–1967; associate professor, Texas A&M University, 1967–1970; associate meteorologist, Argonne National Laboratory, 1970–1972; senior meteorologist in cloud physics, meso-meteorology, and boundary layer, Illinois State Water Survey, 1972–1978, principal scientist, 1978–1989, head of meteorology section, 1980–1989

Bernice Ackerman has been a major participant in a field that was the exclusive domain of men until World War II—meteorology. At that time the government started training women to work as meteorologists and hydrologists to free men for other work. Some of the women were members of the U.S. Navy's Women Accepted for Voluntary Emergency Services (WAVES) and others were civilian employees. Although she was a member of the WAVES, the sources do not indicate that Ackerman started her meteorological career there. At any rate, she has excelled in her profession and holds many firsts. She was the first woman weather forecaster in the United States, the only woman research meteorologist in the Cloud Physics Laboratory at the University of Chicago, and the first woman meteorologist at Argonne National Laboratory. She received her undergraduate degree after leaving the WAVES and worked for the U.S. Weather Bureau for several years before returning to the University of Chicago to complete her master's degree. She stayed at Chicago as a research associate while completing her doctorate. Later she joined the staff of Argonne National Laboratory, where she stayed two years before moving to the Illinois State Water Survey. She was a fellow of the American Association for the Advancement of Science and a fellow of the American Meteorological Society. She was also a member of the American Geophysical Union. Her name was listed in the 1992–1993 edition of *American Men and Women of Science.*

Bibliography: American Men and Women of Science 10–18; Herzenberg, Caroline L., *Women Scientists from Antiquity to the Present;* O'Neill, Lois S., *The Women's Book of World Records and Achievements.*

Adams, (Amy) Elizabeth
(1892–1962)
zoologist

Education: A.B., Mount Holyoke College, 1914; University of Chicago, 1916; A.M., Columbia University, 1918; honorary fellow, Yale University, 1922–1923, Ph.D. in zoology, 1923; University of Edinburgh, 1930–1931
Employment: Assistant in zoology, Mount Holyoke College, 1914–1915, instructor, 1915–1917, 1918–1919, associate professor, 1919–1928, professor, 1928– ? , acting head of department three times, acting dean, 1926–1927, department chair, 1947–1953

*E*lizabeth Adams was a notable scientist in that her name was starred in the sixth and seventh editions of *American Men and Women of Science* and she was elected a fellow of the New York Academy of Sciences. The zoology department at Mount Holyoke, where Elizabeth Adams spent her entire career, was rated highly due to her teaching and research. For example, in Margaret Rossiter's *Women Scientists in America,* a study of women listed in the sixth edition (1938) of *American Men and Women of Science,* most of the women zoologists had received their degrees from Mount Holyoke. Elizabeth Adams's reputation was so solid that even in the 1930s she was successful in obtaining grants from numerous sources such as the Bache Fund of the National Academy of Sciences, Sigma Xi, the American Association for the Advancement of Science, several committees of the National Research Council, and the Rockefeller Foundation; all were for sums of less than $5,000, however. Particularly in women's colleges at that time, research funds, facilities, and faculty time were scarce or nonexistent, a situation that was difficult for women who were strongly oriented to research. Adams's areas of research were experimental embryology and endocrinology, and at the same time she held increasingly responsible administrative appointments. She was a member of several scientific societies, including the Endocrine Society and the Society for Experimental Biology and Medicine.

Bibliography: American Men and Women of Science 6–11; Herzenberg, Caroline L., *Women Scientists from Antiquity to the Present;* Rossiter, Margaret W., *Women Scientists in America;* Visher, Stephen S., *Scientists Starred 1903–1943 in "American Men of Science."*

Agassiz, Elizabeth Cabot Cary
(1822–1907)
naturalist

Education: At home
Employment: Operated private schools in her home; president of Radcliffe College, 1894–1903
Married: Louis Agassiz, 1850, died 1873

*E*lizabeth Agassiz was known for her work as an educator, notably in the founding of Radcliffe College, where she served at the first president. Although she had little formal education, as was the custom at the time, she developed an interest in natural history and is known for her work in recording her husband's scientific research. Since her health was considered delicate, she was not sent to school as a child but was educated at home. She met her husband, naturalist Louis Agassiz, when he visited the United States in 1846 from Switzerland. She married him in 1850 after he had received an appointment at Harvard University as the chair of natural history at Lawrence Scientific School. He had three children (ages 9 to 14) from his previous marriage who lived with them, but Elizabeth had no children of her own. In order to help support the family, she opened schools in her home at various times during their marriage.

From 1865 to 1866, Elizabeth Agassiz accompanied her husband on the Thayer expedition to Brazil to study the fauna. She also went on a deep-sea dredging venture, the Hassler Expedition, along the Atlantic and Pacific coasts of the Americas from 1871 to 1872, serving as the official recorder for her husband. During their marriage she had taken notes on most of her husband's lectures, and her notes on Brazilian society and Agassiz's lectures were the basis of a successful book on which they collaborated—*A Journey in Brazil* (1868). She assisted her husband in 1873 in the planning and management of the coeducational Anderson School of Natural History, which was both a summer school and marine laboratory.

Elizabeth Agassiz's contribution to science was that she preserved, interpreted, and popularized her husband's ideas. She received all of her information from her association with her husband. She published *Actae, A First Lesson in Natural History* (1859) under his direction, but based on her extensive notes. In collaboration with her stepson Alexander, she prepared a revised edition known as *Seaside Studies in Natural History* (1865) as a textbook and field guide. Alexander supplied the drawings of specimens. She also wrote a

biography of her husband, *Louis Agassiz: His Life and Correspondence* (1885), which, although it has proven to be an important source for recording his ideas for posterity, provides little information about her own life and contributions to his work. Later she turned her attention to her earlier interest in educating girls and women. Lucy A. Paton prepared a biography of her, *Elizabeth Cary Agassiz: A Biography* (1919), which includes a photograph.

Bibliography: Barr, Ernest S., *An Index to Biographical Fragments in Unspecialized Scientific Journals;* Herzenberg, Caroline L., *Women Scientists from Antiquity to the Present;* James, E. T., ed., *Notable American Women 1607–1950;* Mozans, H. J., *Women in Science; National Union Catalog;* Ogilvie, Marilyn B., *Women in Science;* O'Neill, Lois S., *The Women's Book of World Records and Achievements;* Rossiter, Margaret W., *Women Scientists in America;* Siegel, Patricia J. and Kay Thomas Finley, *Women in the Scientific Search;* Uglow, Jennifer S., *International Dictionary of Women's Biography.*

Allen, Ruth Florence
(1879–1963)
plant pathologist

Education: A.B., University of Wisconsin, 1905, A.M., 1907, Ph.D., 1909
Employment: Assistant botanist, University of Wisconsin, 1905–1910; instructor, Michigan State College, 1910–1914; instructor and assistant professor, Wellesley College, 1914–1918; associate pathologist, Bureau of Plant Industry, U.S. Department of Agriculture, 1918–1929, pathologist, 1929–1936

Ruth Allen was a long-term employee of the U.S. Department of Agriculture (USDA) in Washington, D.C., and her name has been kept before the public by an award that still is given today, the Ruth Allen Award. After several years of employment on the faculties of Michigan State and Wellesley, she joined the USDA in

1918 as a plant pathologist. There she distinguished herself as the most cited author in her field of cereal disease and cytology. Many women employed by the USDA enjoyed lifetime employment with the agency, but Ruth Allen was not that fortunate. During the Depression years, jobs were scarce and salaries were meager even for single women; married women often had little hope for employment. Ruth Allen's salary was reduced each year until 1936, when her position no longer was funded. She "retired" shortly after, at the age of 58, and moved to Berkeley, California, where she died in 1963. Her heirs in 1965 gave funds in her memory to the American Phytopathological Society to establish the Ruth Allen Award for outstanding contributions by any man or woman to the science of plant pathology. The award is presented annually during the society's meeting and consists of a certificate and cash prize. She was a member of the American Association for the Advancement of Science, the Botanical Society of America, and the American Phytopathological Society.

Bibliography: *American Men and Women of Science* 3–11; Barnhart, John H., *Biographical Notes upon Botanists;* Herzenberg, Caroline L., *Women Scientists from Antiquity to the Present; National Union Catalog;* Rossiter, Margaret W., *Women Scientists in America.*

Altmann, Margaret
(b. 1900)
biologist

Education: Ph.D. in rural economics, University of Bonn, 1928; Ph.D. in animal breeding, Cornell University, 1938

Employment: Farm manager, Germany, 1921–1930; dairy researcher, German government, 1928–1929; German Agriculture Ministry lecturer, 1929–1931, Agricultural Council specialist, 1932–1933; assistant in animal breeding, Cornell University, 1933–1938, research associate in psychobiology, 1938–1941; associate professor of biology and animal husbandry and department chair, Hampton Institute, 1941, professor of animal husbandry and genetics, 1941–1956; visiting lecturer of psychology, University of Colorado, 1958; visiting professor of psychology and biology, Kenyon College, 1959; professor of psychology, University of Colorado, 1959–1969; emeritus professor

Concurrent Position: Big game researcher, Biology Research Station, 1948–1956

Margaret Altmann was one of the first women who worked in the area of agricultural animal sciences. This field seemed to be nearly the exclusive domain of male scientists at the time she was employed, but it currently is more open for women, especially in veterinary science. After receiving a doctorate and working for several agencies of the German government, she came to the United States, where she was granted a doctorate in animal breeding. Although the sources do not give the reasons for her leaving Germany, she perhaps was just part of the immigration movement of the 1930s, when so many scientists left Germany for the United States. While at Cornell she held a position as a psychobiologist. She then moved to Hampton Institute, where she held the position of department chair as a professor of animal husbandry and genetics. She then accepted a position at the University of Colorado as a professor of psychology, retiring in 1969. She held a concurrent position as a big game researcher at the Biology Research Station—even today this typically is considered a male profession. It is a credit to Margaret Altmann's expertise and persistence that she succeeded in two male-dominated areas of research. She was a member of the American Association for the Advancement of Science and the Genetics Society of America.

Bibliography: *American Men and Women of Science 7–12; National Union Catalog.*

Andrews, Eliza Frances
(1840–1931)
author and botanist

Education: A.B., La Grange Female College (Georgia), 1857
Employment: Schoolteacher, 1873–1903

*E**liza Andrews** was an author and self-taught botanist who published two widely popular textbooks on botany. Although she did not experience the devastation of property and family finances that many people in the South did during the war and Reconstruction, she wrote several magazine articles during the period expressing her views of the situation. In 1873, however, the family became impoverished after her father's death. She taught school for a number of years; this included teaching botany for six years in a public high school. She turned to writing novels about the Civil War and its aftermath during this period. These romantic novels reveal her distaste for the postwar social structure and the limited sphere prescribed for women. Her best known work was the diary, *The War-Time Journal of a Georgia Girl* (1908). This is based on a diary she started in 1864 and continued until a few months after the war's end. It has been compared by historians with the diary of Mary B. Chesnut. During this period Andrews embraced the socialist cause, and listed herself as a socialist for several years in *Who's Who in America.* After retiring from teaching, she spent much of her time in the serious study of botany, an interest she had continued intermittently from childhood. She eventually gained considerable competence in the subject and wrote two books: *Botany All the Year Round* (1903) and *A Practical Course in Botany* (1911). The latter was translated for use in French schools.

Bibliography: Barnhart, John H., *Biographical Notes upon Botanists;* James, E. T., ed., *Notable American Women 1607–1950.*

Andrews, Grace
(1869–1951)
mathematician

Education: B.S., Wellesley College, 1890; A.M., Columbia University, 1899, Ph.D. in mathematics, 1901

Employment: Assistant in mathematics, Barnard College, Columbia University, 1900–1902; assistant treasurer, Wesleyan University, 1903–1926; missions service of her church, 1926–1951

Grace Andrews deserves recognition as a mathematician listed in the first edition of *American Men and Women of Science*. Since only two women mathematicians were starred in that edition, just having the name listed for four editions would constitute an honor in itself. Although no personal information could be located, she received her undergraduate degree after age 30; she may have taught school, the occupation of many women who later obtained baccalaureate degrees. Wellesley College was producing many women scientists during the period she attended. Her graduate degrees were obtained about ten years later, and there is no indication of her employment during the interim period. Many women scientists of her era worked only briefly in their professions. Grace Andrews followed this pattern by teaching at Barnard for three years before obtaining an administrative position in the treasurer's office at Wesleyan University. Before the development of calculating machines, many women mathematicians worked as "computers" for insurance companies and other businesses or handled similar calculations in colleges. She spent the latter part of her life in missions service of her church and as treasurer and director of the board of the Kosmos Club of Brooklyn, a social and cultural club.

Bibliography: *American Men and Women of Science* 1–4; Siegel, Patricia J. and Kay Thomas Finley, *Women in the Scientific Search.*

Anslow, Gladys Amelia
(1892–1969)
physicist

Education: A.B., Smith College, 1914, A.M., 1917; Ph.D., Yale University, 1924
Employment: Demonstrator, physics department, Smith College, 1914–1915, assistant, 1915–1917, instructor, 1917–1924, assistant professor, 1924–1930, associate professor, 1931–1936, professor, 1936–1958, chair of the graduate school, 1941–1958

Gladys Anslow was rated as an outstanding teacher and researcher in the early twentieth century, when many women's colleges did not have adequate facilities for research in physics. During that period it was common practice for both men and women to have a master's degree as their final certificate, particularly in the physical sciences and engineering. Many completed their graduate education while they were teaching in academia; Gladys Anslow received the doctorate only seven years after her master's degree. She spent her entire career at Smith College, and she received an honorary degree from the college in 1950 acknowledging her contributions. She received the Presidential Certificate of Merit in 1948 for her work with the Office of Scientific Research and Development in 1944 and 1945. She was elected to Phi Beta Kappa and Sigma Xi, she was elected a fellow of the American Physical Society, and she was also a member of the American Academy of Arts and Sciences, the American Association of Physics Teachers, the Optical Society of

America, and the Society for Applied Spectroscopy. Her areas of research were mass spectroscopy, fast neutron ionization, quantitative chemical spectroscopy, ultraviolet absorption spectroscopy of biological materials, ultraviolet vacuum spectroscopy, and nuclear structure problems.

Bibliography: *American Men and Women of Science* 6–11; Debus, A. G., ed., *World Who's Who in Science;* Herzenberg, Caroline L., *Women Scientists from Antiquity to the Present;* Rossiter, Margaret W., *Women Scientists in America.*

Atwater, Helen Woodard
(1876–1947)
home economist

Education: B.L., Smith College, 1897
Employment: Expert, scientific assistant, and later in charge of editorial work, Office of Home Economics, U.S. Department of Agriculture, 1909–1923; editor of *Journal of Home Economics,* 1923–1940

Helen Atwater's contribution to science was in writing and editing publications of the U.S. Department of Agriculture (USDA) to emphasize to rural women the importance of scientific information in food preparation; as editor of the *Journal of Home Economics,* she brought the young field of home economics to scientific prominence. Her father, Wilbur O. Atwater, was a pioneer in agricultural and food chemistry. After graduating from Smith College, Helen spent the next nine years as her father's assistant at Wesleyan University in preparing and writing many of his papers. After his death in 1907, she prepared a bibliography of his writings on nutrition. In her work in the Office of Home Economics, she wrote extensively on nutrition and food preparation in editions of the *Yearbook of Agriculture* and in the *Farmers' Bulletin* series. She also wrote a book entitled *Home Economics: The Art and Science of Homemaking* (1929). She left the USDA in 1923 to become the first full-time editor of the *Journal of Home Economics,* published by the American Home Economics Association. Due to her many personal contacts with scientists, Atwater was able to develop high standards in both the subject matter and writing of papers published in the journal, which contributed to improving both the stature and the understanding of the field. Her own articles and editorials were models of excellent writing. She received an honorary degree from Smith College in 1943, and in 1948 the American Home Economics Association established the Helen Atwater International Fellowship Award in her memory.

Bibliography: *American Men and Women of Science* 3–7; James, E. T., ed., *Notable American Women 1607–1950; National Union Catalog;* Siegel, Patricia J. and Kay Thomas Finley, *Women in the Scientific Search.*

Austin, Pauline Morrow
(1916–)
meteorologist

Education: B.A., Wilson College, 1938; M.A., Smith College, 1939; Ph.D. in physics, Massachusetts Institute of Technology, 1942
Employment: Computer, Radiation Laboratory, MIT, 1941–1942, member of the staff, 1942–1945, research staff, 1946–1953; lecturer, Wellesley College, 1953–1955; senior research associate, MIT, 1956–1979
Married: 1941

Pauline Austin has received recognition as a meteorologist and at one time was the director of weather radar at Massachusetts Institute of Technology. She was a major participant in a profession that until World War II was almost exclusively a male domain. Pauline Austin was one of the first women identified as a meteorologist. Her association with MIT started with the position of "computer" in the Radiation Laboratory in 1941, the year she was married. At that time, several women, both civilians and military personnel, were trained under government auspices at the Radiation Laboratory to perform the work men formerly had handled. The sources do not indicate whether she was part of this government-sponsored effort or whether she was just fulfilling requirements for her doctorate. She continued as a member of the research staff until 1979, except from 1953 to 1955, when she was a lecturer at Wellesley College. Meanwhile she had two children, thus combining career and family. She received several honors, including an honorary doctorate from Wilson College in 1964 and election as a fellow of the American Meteorological Society. She served as associate editor of the *Journal of Applied Meteorology.* Her areas of research were radar scattering cross sections, propagation of electromagnetic waves in the atmosphere, and precipitation physics. Her name was listed in the 1992–1993 edition of *American Men and Women of Science.*

Bibliography: American Men and Women of Science 8–18; Herzenberg, Caroline L., *Women Scientists from Antiquity to the Present;* O'Neill, Lois S., *The Women's Book of World Records and Achievements.*

Zonia Baber
Maria Martin Bachman
Anna Medora Baetjer
Florence Winger Bagley
Catherine Hayes Bailey
Florence Augusta Merriam Bailey
Nora Stanton Blatch Barney
Charlotte Cynthia Barnum
Florence Bascom
Esther Lord Batchelder
Grace Elizabeth Bates
Angie Maria Beckwith
Catharine Esther Beecher
Ruth Fulton Benedict
Ruth Rogan Benerito
Isabel Bevier
Katherine Eliza Golden Bitting
Eleanor Albert Bliss
Katharine Burr Blodgett
Katharine Blunt
Rachel Littler Bodley
Mary Ann Allard Booth
Alice Middleton Boring
Louise Arner Boyd
Hazel Elisabeth Branch
Mary Katharine Layne Brandegee
Annette Frances Braun
(Emma) Lucy Braun
Mary Bidwell Breed
Anne M. Briscoe
Elizabeth Gertrude Knight Britton
Matilda Moldenhauer Brooks
Nellie Adalesa Brown
Rachel Fuller Brown
Elizabeth Thompson Bunce
Martha Bunting
Mary Ingraham Bunting
Katharine Jeannette Bush
Mary Emma Byrd
Esther Fussell Byrnes

Baber, Zonia
(b. 1862)
geographer

Education: B.S., University of Chicago, 1904
Employment: Principal, private school, 1886–1888; critic teacher, Cook County Normal School, 1888–1890, head, department of geography, 1890–1899; associate professor and head of geography and geology department, School of Education, University of Chicago, 1901–1921, principal, Elementary School, School of Education, University of Chicago, 1901–1921; emeritus associate professor

Zonia Baber was recognized as a pioneer in developing a rational basis for teaching geography and as a member of some early professional societies. Her name was listed in the first edition of *American Men and Women of Science,* one of the few women geographers who was listed by this reference. Her career paralleled the pattern of many women of her age, that of teaching school for a number of years before obtaining an undergraduate degree; in fact, she was teaching at the University of Chicago at the time she received her degree, another practice common at that time. She was noted for the quality of the curriculum of her geology department at the university. She was a member of several professional societies and was noted as one of the founders of the Chicago Geographic Society, which she served as president. At the fiftieth anniversary of the society, Zonia Baber was recognized as the person who suggested its founding.

Bibliography: American Men and Women of Science 1–4; Siegel, Patricia J. and Kay Thomas Finley, *Women in the Scientific Search.*

Bachman, Maria Martin
(1796–1863)
nature painter

Education: No formal education
Employment: No formal employment
Married: John Bachman, 1848

Maria Bachman was one of the artists who provided backgrounds for the paintings of ornithologist and artist John James Audubon. Maria's husband, John Bachman, was a pastor by profession and a leading amateur naturalist in South Carolina who corresponded with American naturalists John Bartram and Cadwalladar Colden. Audubon and his staff lived at the Bachman house when they were in Charleston, and two of Audubon's sons married two of John Bachman's daughters. John first was married to Maria's sister Harriet, who bore him 14 children, 9 of whom survived to adulthood. As the unmarried aunt, Maria supervised the household due to Harriet's poor health, and after her sister's death, Maria married John Bachman. Although there is no record of any formal schooling, she was known to be expert in music, literature, and drawing. She trained in natural science and preferred botany and entomology to the study of animals. She is credited with the watercolor backgrounds in the second and fourth volumes of Audubon's *Birds of America*. The ornithologist's usual method was to paint the bird first, place it on an unadorned branch, and then either paint the background himself or give the canvas to Maria or either of his other two assistants to complete. He especially admired Maria's paintings of insects in the backgrounds. John Bachman collaborated with Audubon on *The Quadrupeds of North America* (1845–1854), and Maria was responsible for much of the editing and compiling of the manuscript. She also contributed drawings of reptiles to John E. Holbrook's *North American Herpetology* (1836–1842). There is a photograph of Maria Bachman in Lois Arnold's *Four Lives in Science*.

Bibliography: Arnold, Lois B., *Four Lives in Science;* Herzenberg, Caroline L., *Women Scientists from Antiquity to the Present;* Hollingsworth, Buckner, *Her Garden Was Her Delight;* James, E. T., ed., *Notable American Women 1607–1950;* Kass-Simon, G. and Patricia Farnes, *Women of Science;* Siegel, Patricia J. and Kay Thomas Finley, *Women in the Scientific Search.*

Baetjer, Anna Medora
(b. 1899)
physiologist and toxicologist

Education: A.B., Wellesley College, 1920; Sc.D. in physiology, physiological hygiene, and industrial health, Johns Hopkins University, 1924

Employment: Assistant, School of Hygiene and Public Health, Johns Hopkins University, 1923–1924, instructor, 1924–1927, associate, 1927–1945, assistant professor, 1945–1950, environmental medicine, 1950–1952, associate professor, 1952–1961, professor, 1962–1970; emeritus professor

*A*nna Baetjer was known for her work as a physiologist and toxicologist in the department of industrial or occupational hygiene in the School of Hygiene and Public Health at Johns Hopkins University. She was a pioneer in the field of occupational health. When she first was associated with the university during the 1920s and 1930s, the School of Hygiene and Public Health suffered severe budget cuts that resulted in the loss of a number of her colleagues, but she was able to retain her position. She was a member of numerous commissions and committees— a consultant for the preventive medicine division of the Office of Surgeon General of the Army (beginning in 1947), a member of the board of trustees of the Mellon Institute from 1958 and vice chair of the board from 1964 to 1970, and from 1966 to 1970 a member of the advisory committee on safety of pesticide residues in foods to the Food and Drug Administration. She was elected president of the American Industrial Hygiene Association in 1951, and she received the Cummings Memorial Award in 1964. She also received the Kehoe Award of the American Academy of Occupational

Medicine (1976) and the Stokinger Award of the American Conference of Government Industrial Hygienists (1980). She received honorary degrees from Woman's Medical College of Pennsylvania (1953), Wheaton College (1966), and Johns Hopkins University (1979). She also was a member of the American Physiological Society and the American Public Health Association. Among her many publications are chapters contributed to the monographs *Preventive* *Medicine and Public Health* (1965) and to *Women in Industry: Their Health and Efficiency* (1946).

Bibliography: *American Men and Women of Science* 6–16; Debus, A. G., ed., *World Who's Who in Science*; Herzenberg, Caroline L., *Women Scientists from Antiquity to the Present*; Rossiter, Margaret W., *Women Scientists in America*; *Who Was Who in America*.

Bagley, Florence Winger
(1874–1952)
psychologist

Education: A.B., University of Nebraska, 1895, A.M., 1898; Cornell University, 1898–1901
Employment: Assistant in psychology, University of Nebraska, 1896–1898
Married: William C. Bagley, 1901

Florence Bagley was listed in the first and second editions of *American Men and Women of Science*. It is not always clear what criteria were used in selecting people to be included in the first few editions of that reference. There were few women in the field of psychology, and almost any one of them could have been chosen. According to the custom at the time, she was listed officially as Mrs. W. C. Bagley (Florence Winger). Also in line with the times, she was not officially employed after her marriage in 1901. The profession of psychology was in its infancy in the late nineteenth century, and some biographies list people as working in both psychology and philosophy. This is the case for Florence Bagley, since she was a member of the Western Philosophical Association. She did publish scientific papers after her marriage; one was in the distinguished *American Journal of Psychology* (1902) on Fechner's color rings. Her area of research was on the esthetics of color, and she continued her research after her marriage. Her husband's research was in the area of educational psychology; he was director of the school of education at the University of Illinois.

Bibliography: *American Men and Women of Science* 1–2; Siegel, Patricia J. and Kay Thomas Finley, *Women in the Scientific Search*.

Bailey, Catherine Hayes
(1921–)
plant geneticist

Education: B.A., Douglass College, 1942; Ph.D. in fruit breeding, Rutgers University, 1957
Employment: Technical assistant, Agricultural Experiment Station, Rutgers University, 1948–1954, research associate, 1954–1957, assistant professor of pomology, 1957–1966, associate research professor, 1966–1972, professor, 1972–1980

Catherine Bailey has been noted for her work on developing new varieties of fruit. After working about six years for the Agricultural Experiment Station at Rutgers University (the New Jersey Agricultural Experiment Station), she joined the faculty as a research professor. Her research involves developing new cultures of peaches, nectarines, apples, and pears—all crops that would be important to New Jersey fruit growers. The most recent project she lists is inheritance of season of ripening in progenies from certain early ripening peach varieties and selections. She has been a member of numerous professional societies, including the American Society for Horticultural Science, the American Pomological Society, the Torrey Botanical Club, and the International Society for Horticultural Science. Her name was listed in the 1992–1993 edition of *American Men and Women of Science.*

Bibliography: *American Men and Women of Science* 9–18; Herzenberg, Caroline L., *Women Scientists from Antiquity to the Present;* O'Neill, Lois S., *The Women's Book of World Records and Achievements.*

Bailey, Florence Augusta Merriam
(1863–1948)
ornithologist

Education: A.B., Smith College, 1921 (attended 1882–1886)
Employment: Author
Married: Vernon Bailey, 1899

Florence Bailey was a popularizer of natural history who specialized in ornithology. Her first book was *Birds through an Opera Glass* (1889), which was comprised of revised versions of articles she had contributed as a student to *Audubon Magazine.* In 1894 she published *My Summer in a Mormon Village,* in 1896 *A-Birding on a Bronco,* and in 1898 *Birds of Village and Field.* The latter is a book for beginners in ornithology and one of the first popular American bird guides. Her brother, Clinton Hart Merriam, was the first chief of the U.S. Biological Survey, and her husband was its chief naturalist. She joined her husband on the majority of his field trips, observing the birds about which she wrote. She also wrote chapters on birds in some of her husband's books, notably *Wild Animals of Glacier National Park* (1918) and *Cave Life of Kentucky* (1933). Her *Handbook of Birds of the Western United States* (1902) was a standard work for many years. She wrote the first comprehensive report on the bird life of the Southwest in *Birds of New Mexico* (1928), published by the New Mexico Department of Game and Fish. For this she became in 1931 the first woman to receive the Brewster Award of the American Ornithologists' Union. In 1933 the University of New Mexico awarded her an honorary LL.D. degree. She was the first woman member of the American Ornithologists' Union (an associate member only) in 1885. In 1901 she became the first woman regular member, and in 1929 she was elected the first woman fellow. Harriet Kofalk has written her biography, *No Woman Tenderfoot: Florence Merriam Bailey, Pioneer Naturalist* (1989). This contains numerous photographs of the Baileys at home and in the field. She was listed as Mrs. Vernon Bailey in the second through fifth editions of *American Men and Women of Science.*

Bibliography: Abir-Am, P. G. and Dorinda Outram, eds., *Uneasy Careers and Intimate Lives; American Men and Women of Science* 2–7; Debus, A. G., ed., *World Who's Who in Science; Dictionary of American Biography;* Herzenberg, Caroline L., *Women Scientists from Antiquity to the Present;* James, E. T., ed., *Notable American Women 1607–1950;* McHenry, Robert, ed., *Famous American Women; National Cyclopedia of American Biography; National Union Catalog;* Ogilvie, Marilyn B., *Women in Science;* O'Neill, Lois S., *The Women's Book of World Records and Achievements;* Rossiter, Margaret W., *Women Scientists in America;* Rossiter, Margaret W., "Women Scientists in America before 1920"; Siegel, Patricia J. and Kay Thomas Finley, *Women in the Scientific Search.*

Barney, Nora Stanton Blatch
(1883–1971)
civil engineer

Education: B.S., Cornell University, 1905
Employment: Draftsman, American Bridge Company, 1905–1906; New York City Board of Water Supply, 1907; engineer, husband's company, 1908–1909; assistant engineer and chief draftsman, Radley Steel Construction Company, 1909–1912; real estate developer, Long Island, 1914–1922; real estate developer, Greenwich, Connecticut, 1923–1971
Married: Lee de Forest, 1908, divorced 1912; Morgan Barney, 1919, died 1943

Nora Barney was notable as the first woman to receive a degree in civil engineering from Cornell University. The granddaughter of Elizabeth Cady Stanton, a pioneer in the women's rights effort, she also was active in the women's movement, especially from 1912 to 1914. She had organized a woman suffrage club while a student at Cornell. Upon graduation she worked as a draftsman for several companies before attending courses in electricity and mathematics at Columbia University in order to obtain a position as a laboratory assistant for Lee de Forest, the American inventor who developed the radio vacuum tube. After their marriage, she continued working in the manufacturing part of the business. Although she realized the company was not financially secure, her husband refused to break with his partners. The company soon failed, and the marriage could not survive their professional and personal problems. They filed for divorce soon after the birth of their daughter, Harriet, in 1909; the divorce was final in 1912. Nora Barney continued working as an engineer for several companies. She sued the American Society of Civil Engineers (ASCE) in 1916, without success, to retain her membership. She was the first woman member of the ASCE, but she was dropped from the society when she passed the age limit for junior status. She had two children, Rhoda and John, with her second husband. After her second marriage, she concentrated on real estate development. She continued to be politically active during her life; and she was even investigated in 1950 by the House Committee on Un-American Activities, although she was not called to testify. Throughout her life she insisted that women seek full legal and professional, as well as political, equality. Her photograph was included the April 1971 issue of the journal *Civil Engineering* and in Margaret Rossiter's *Women Scientists in America.* The photographs show her participating in political campaigns in 1911 and 1913, respectively.

Bibliography: Herzenberg, Caroline L., *Women Scientists from Antiquity to the Present;* Rossiter, Margaret W., *Women Scientists in America;* Sicherman, Barbara et al., *Notable American Women.*

Barnum, Charlotte Cynthia
(1860–1934)
mathematician

Education: A.B., Vassar College, 1881; Johns Hopkins University, 1890–1892; Ph.D. in mathematics, Yale University, 1895
Employment: Teacher, private school, 1881–1882, public school, 1883, 1885–1886; computer, Yale Observatory and "Dana's Mineralogy," 1883–1887; teacher of astronomy, Smith College, 1889–1890; teacher of mathematics, Carleton College, 1895–1896; computer, Massachusetts Mutual Life Insurance Company, 1898; Fidelity Mutual Life Insurance Company, Philadelphia, 1900–1901; U.S. Naval Observatory, 1901; Tidal Division, U.S. Coast and Geodesic Survey, 1901–1908; editor, biological survey, U.S. Department of Agriculture, 1908–1913; editor and proofreader, scientific publications, Yale University, 1914–1926
Concurrent Position: Assistant editor, *Webster's International Dictionary*, 1886–1890, 1897

Charlotte Barnum's quality of work earned her listing in the first edition of *American Men and Women of Science* and she continued to be listed until her death. Charlotte Barnum's varied experience in academia, business, and government probably reflects the lack of professional opportunities for women during that time. She taught in public and private schools for several years after receiving her undergraduate degree. She then worked as a "computer" for Yale University while assisting in the preparation of an unabridged dictionary and teaching astronomy at Smith College for a year. After receiving her doctorate, she taught mathematics at Carleton College for a year, worked as a computer until 1913, and then returned to editing scientific publications, this time at Yale. She was one of the earliest members of the American Mathematical Society, which she joined in 1894. In the fifth edition of *American Men and Women of Science* she lists her research interests as functions having lines or surfaces of discontinuity, tides and currents, annuities, and social legislation, which summarize her professional career.

Bibliography: *American Men and Women of Science* 1–5; Siegel, Patricia J. and Kay Thomas Finley, *Women in the Scientific Search.*

Bascom, Florence
(1862–1945)
geologist

Education: A.B., B.L., University of Wisconsin, 1882, B.S., 1884, A.M., 1887; Ph.D., Johns Hopkins University, 1898

Employment: Instructor, geology and petrology, Ohio State University, 1893–1895; lecturer and associate professor of geology, Bryn Mawr College, 1895–1906, professor, 1906–1928; geological assistant, U.S. Geological Survey, 1896–1901, assistant geologist, 1901–1909, geologist, 1909–1932, emeritus professor

Florence Bascom has been recognized as one of the most notable geologists and the foremost woman geologist of her time. Her name was starred in the first seven editions of *American Men and Women of Science.* A survey in 1903 by Stephen Visher rated her the only woman among 100 notable geologists in America. She enjoyed many firsts—she was the first woman to receive a doctorate from Johns Hopkins University and she was the first American woman to receive a doctorate in geology. She was the first woman vice president of the Geological Society of America. Since her father was the president of the University of Wisconsin, she received her earlier education in geology at that institution. In the 1880s she introduced the microscopic study of minerals in the United States. She enrolled in Johns Hopkins when the school offered graduate courses for women, but she received her doctorate in 1898 by a special dispensation because women were not officially admitted until 1907. After teaching for two years at Ohio State University, she moved to Bryn Mawr College, where she remained until retirement. The school had no facilities for

geological research, but Florence Bascom secured rock and mineral specimens and expanded her course into a full major. She soon was accepting graduate students from all over the country and from Europe, and until the mid-1930s a majority of the American women geologists came from Bryn Mawr. As a teacher and researcher she adhered to high standards and insisted that her students do likewise. Bascom pioneered again by becoming the first woman employed as an assistant for the U.S. Geological Survey (USGS). Usually she spent her summers working for the USGS with the assistance of her students. She became the authority on the crystalline rocks of the Piedmont province from the Susquehanna River to Trenton, New Jersey. She was the first woman to be elected a fellow of the Geological Society of America (1894). She retired from teaching in 1928 due to poor health, but she continued working for the USGS for several years. Her photograph was included in an article in *American Mineralogist* 31 (1946): 168–172 and in Lois Arnold's *Four Lives in Science.* The former includes a bibliography of her publications.

Bibliography: *American Men and Women of Science* 1–7; Arnold, Lois B., *Four Lives in Science*; Debus, A. G., ed., *World Who's Who in Science*; *Dictionary of American Biography*; Herzenberg, Caroline L., *Women Scientists from Antiquity to the Present*; James, E. T., ed., *Notable American Women 1607–1950*; Kass-Simon, G. and Patricia Farnes, *Women of Science*; Mozans, H. J., *Women in Science*; *National Union Catalog*; Ogilvie, Marilyn B., *Women in Science*; O'Neill, Lois S., *The Women's Book of World Records and Achievements*; Rossiter, Margaret W., *Women Scientists in America*; Rossiter, Margaret W., "Women Scientists in America before 1920"; Siegel, Patricia J. and Kay Thomas Finley, *Women in the Scientific Search*; Visher, Stephen S., *Scientists Starred 1903–1943 in "American Men of Science."*

Batchelder, Esther Lord
(b. 1897)
chemist

Education: B.S., Connecticut College, 1919; A.M., Columbia University, 1925, Ph.D. in chemistry, 1929

Employment: Chemist, East Malleable Iron Company, 1919–1920, and Henry Souther Engineering Company, 1920–1924; assistant in chemistry, Columbia University, 1924–1925, food chemist, 1925–1929; nutrition specialist for the journal *Delineator*, 1929–1932; assistant professor of nutrition, Washington State University, 1932–1934, and University of Arizona, 1934–1936; head of home economics department, Rhode Island State College, 1936–1942; human nutrition branch, U.S. Department of Agriculture, 1942–1956, director of clothing and housing research division, 1956–1965

Esther Batchelder was a long-term employee of the U.S. Department of Agriculture (USDA) who was recognized as expert in the field of nutrition. Her career discounts the impression many people today have that all women who taught in early home economics programs had limited education. She had a graduate degree from Columbia University, which at the time had an international reputation for the quality of its nutrition program. She certainly was not typical of most women chemists in that she was employed by two manufacturing companies in the years following her undergraduate degree. When she was employed by the journal *Delineator*, she wrote a series of pamphlets on nutrition, such as "Eating To Gain or Lose Weight" (1930) and "Feeding Children from First Grade through College" (1931). She was employed by the USDA more than 20 years before retiring as a division head. After retirement Esther Batchelder continued to work as a consultant in home economics in Bristol, Connecticut. She was a member of the food mission to Germany in 1947 and to Japan in 1949. She received a Distinguished Service Award from the USDA in 1954, and she was a trustee of Connecticut College starting in 1936. She was a member of the American Home Economics Association, American Public Health Association, and American Association of Textile Chemists and Colorists.

Bibliography: *American Men and Women of Science* 5–11; Debus, A. G., ed., *World Who's Who in Science*; Herzenberg, Caroline L., *Women Scientists from Antiquity to the Present*; *National Union Catalog*.

Bates, Grace Elizabeth
(1914–)
mathematician

Education: B.S., Middlebury College, 1935; Sc.M., Brown University, 1938; Ph.D. in mathematics, University of Illinois, 1946
Employment: High school teacher, 1935–1936, 1938–1943; instructor in mathematics, Sweet Briar College, 1943–1944; Mount Holyoke College, 1946–1947, assistant professor, 1947–1952, associate professor, 1952–1956, professor, 1956–1979; emeritus professor

Grace Bates is recognized for her work as a mathematician at a distinguished women's college, Mount Holyoke. She worked as a high school teacher for a year after receiving her undergraduate degree and again taught after receiving her master's degree. She then moved to Sweet Briar College for one year before joining the faculty at Mount Holyoke, where she remained until retirement. After receiving her doctorate from the University of Illinois, she was promoted to assistant professor, then associate and full professor. Grace Bates was the coauthor of two books, *The Real Number System* (1960) and *Modern Algebra, Second Course* (1963). She also contributed papers on algebra and probability theory to technical journals. Among the honors she received was an honorary degree from Middlebury College (1972). She is a member of numerous professional societies, including the American Mathematical Society and the Mathematical Association of America. The latest edition of *American Men and Women of Science* lists her research interests as modern algebra, free loops and nets and their generalizations, probability, and mathematical statistics. Her name was listed in the 1992–1993 edition of *American Men and Women of Science.*

Bibliography: *American Men and Women of Science* 8–18; Debus, A. G., ed., *World Who's Who in Science;* Herzenberg, Caroline L., *Women Scientists from Antiquity to the Present; National Union Catalog.*

Beckwith, Angie Maria
(b. 1881)
plant pathologist

Education: A.B., University of Michigan, 1904; University of Chicago, 1904–1905
Employment: Assistant in biological laboratory, Vassar College, 1906–1908; expert xylotomist (wood specialist), U.S. Forest Service, 1908–1910; scientific assistant, later junior pathologist, Bureau of Plant Industry, U.S. Department of Agriculture, 1910–1940s

Angie Beckwith was one of the first women employed by the U.S. Forest Service, a division of the Department of Agriculture (USDA). At the time Angie Beckwith was entering college, women's colleges and land grant colleges were among the few academic institutions who admitted women as students. She last was listed in the seventh edition (1944) of *American Men and Women of Science* when she was about 64 years old, still listing the USDA as her employer. One of the privileges that USDA women enjoyed, even in the early years, was that they were permitted to publish the results of their research in their own names. Angie Beckwith lists one paper—"Life History of the Grape Rootrot Fungus, 'Roesleria Hypogaea' "—in *USDA Journal of Agricultural Research* 27 (1924): 609–616. She was a member of several professional associations, including the American Association for the Advancement of Science and the American Phytopathological Society. Her areas of research were rubus and grape diseases and control of insect pests and plant diseases.

Bibliography: *American Men and Women of Science* 3–7; Barnhart, John H., *Biographical Notes upon Botanists; National Union Catalog.*

Beecher, Catharine Esther
(1800–1878)
author and educator

Education: Private school
Employment: Schoolteacher, 1821–1871

Catharine Beecher was noted for her work in promoting education for women and for introducing domestic science into the American school curriculum. She wrote several books on domestic economy, one in collaboration with her sister, Harriet Beecher Stowe. She founded several schools designed to meet the educational needs of women, and campaigned vigorously to reform education for women to provide opportunities for training both teachers and homemakers.

She was active in the women's suffrage movement.

The first school she founded was the Hartford Female Seminary in Hartford, Connecticut, in 1823. This had an innovative curriculum that included calisthenics in a course of physical education. In 1832 she opened the Western Female Institute in Cincinnati, Ohio, but due to financial difficulties and her poor health the school closed five years later. She devoted the rest of her life to developing educational facilities in the Midwest and promoting equal educational opportunities for women. In 1852 she founded the American Woman's Educational Association to recruit and train teachers for schools on the frontier. She also campaigned vigorously to interest the public in establishing normal schools in the newly settled regions of the West. She supported herself by her writings on women's suffrage and on education. She wrote *A Treatise on Domestic Economy* (1841), *Miss Beecher's Domestic Receipt Book* (1846), which went through five editions between 1846 and 1872, and the *American Woman's Home* (1869), the latter in collaboration with her sister. These works provided practical instruction on cooking, family health, infant care, children's education, and proper home management. Her other books were *The Duty of American Women to Their Country* (1845), *The Evils Suffered by American Women and American Children* (1846), *Physiology and Calisthenics for Schools and Families* (1856), *Calisthenic Exercises, for Schools, Families and Health Establishments* (1860), *Woman Suffrage and Woman's Profession* (1871), and *Educational Reminiscences and Suggestions* (1874). Her biography is *Catharine Beecher: A Study in American Domesticity* (1973) by Kathryn K. Sklar.

Bibliography: Abir-Am, P. G. and Dorinda Outram, eds., *Uneasy Careers and Intimate Lives*; James, E. T., ed., *Notable American Women 1607–1950*; McHenry, Robert, ed., *Famous American Women*; Macksey, Joan and Kenneth Macksey, *The Book of Women's Achievements; National Union Catalog*; Rossiter, Margaret W., *Women Scientists in America*; Rossiter, Margaret W., "'Women's Work' in Science, 1880–1910"; Shapiro, Laura, *Perfection Salad*.

Benedict, Ruth Fulton
(1887–1948)
anthropologist

Education: A.B., Vassar College, 1909; Ph.D., Columbia University, 1923
Employment: Lecturer in anthropology, Columbia University, 1924–1930, assistant professor, 1930–1936, associate professor, 1936–1948, professor, 1948
Married: Stanley R. Benedict, 1914, died 1936

Ruth Benedict originated the controversial concept of patterns of culture, which combined anthropology with sociology, psychology, and philosophy. She was recognized as the country's leading anthropologist, the first American woman to become the prominent leader of a learned profession. Her name was starred in the fifth, sixth, and seventh editions of *American Men and Women of Science.* She was president of the American Ethnological Society from 1927 to 1929 and the American Anthropological Association from 1947 to 1948. She was editor of the *Journal of American Folk-Lore* from 1923 to 1940.

After receiving her undergraduate degree, she taught school for a few years and then married. Becoming bored with charitable work, she enrolled in the New School for Social Research at Columbia University, where she received her doctorate in anthropology in 1923. She made her first field trip in 1922 to the Serrano Indians and spent subsequent summers studying other tribes. At Columbia she was employed as a lecturer at a minimum salary on an annual appointment. During this time her marriage was failing, and the couple separated. She published some poetry to express her thoughts under the pseudonym Anne Singleton. She was appointed assistant professor in 1931 and began to evolve the concept of the patterns of culture. During World War II she worked for the Office of War Information in overseas intelligence and foreign morale. This was a new departure for anthropologists, that of analyzing complex modern societies from a distance through interviews and reading the national literature. She made numerous field trips to study Native American tribes (particularly the Zuni), to Japan, and to New Guinea. These studies were reported in her books *Concept of the Guardian Spirit in American Culture* (1923), *Patterns of Culture* (1934), *Zuni Mythology* (1935), *Race: Science and Politics* (1940), and *The Chrysanthemum and the Sword: Patterns of Japanese Culture* (1946). The publication of the latter book brought her such renown that Columbia promoted her to the rank of full professor in what proved to be the last year of her life. In 1947 the Office of Naval Research gave her a large grant to establish and direct a program entitled Research in Contemporary Cultures.

Bibliography: *American Men and Women of Science* 5–7; Debus, A. G., ed., *World Who's Who in Science;* Herzenberg, Caroline L., *Women Scientists from Antiquity to the Present;* James, E. T., ed., *Notable American Women 1607–1950;* Macksey, Joan and Kenneth Macksey, *The Book of Women's Achievements; National Union Catalog;* O'Neill, Lois S., *The Women's Book of World Records and Achievements;* Rossiter, Margaret W., *Women Scientists in America;* Rossiter, Margaret W., "Women Scientists in America before 1920"; Siegel, Patricia J. and Kay Thomas Finley, *Women in the Scientific Search;* Uglow, Jennifer S., *International Dictionary of Women's Biography;* Visher, Stephen S., *Scientists Starred 1903–1943 in "American Men of Science."*

Benerito, Ruth Rogan
(1916–)
polymer chemist

Education: B.S., Sophie Newcomb College, 1935; M.S., Tulane University, 1938; Ph.D. in chemistry, University of Chicago, 1948

Employment: Instructor in chemistry, Randolph-Macon Women's College, 1940–1943; assistant professor, Tulane University, 1943–1953; physical chemist, Southern Regional Research Center, U.S. Department of Agriculture, 1953–1958, head of colloidal chemistry investigation, 1958–1961, head of physical chemistry group, 1961–1986

Married: 1950

Ruth Benerito has been a pioneer in the development of wash-and-wear fabrics. She was a scholar at Bryn Mawr College from 1935 to 1936 and taught at Randolph-Macon Women's College for several years after receiving her master's degree from Tulane University. She moved to Tulane University, where she remained for several years after receiving her doctorate in 1948. She was a scholar at the University of Chicago from 1946 to 1947. She then spent the next 30 years or more at the Southern Regional Research Center, U.S. Department of Agriculture (USDA), in New Orleans, and one of the center's specialties is cotton and synthetic fabrics, due to the textile industry in that region. Ruth Bencrito has had a successful career with the USDA as head of several divisions at New Orleans. She has received numerous awards for her work, including the Federal Woman Award in 1968, Southern Chemist Award in 1968, the Garvan Medal in 1970, and the Southwest Regional Award of the American Chemical Society in 1972. She received an honorary degree from Tulane in 1981. She was listed in the 1992–1993 edition of *American Men and Women of Science*. She has been a member of the American Association for the Advancement of Science, the American Chemical Society, and the American Association of Textile Chemists and Colorists.

Bibliography: *American Men and Women of Science* 10–18; Herzenberg, Caroline L., *Women Scientists from Antiquity to the Present*; O'Neill, Lois S., *The Women's Book of World Records and Achievements*.

Bevier, Isabel
(1860–1942)
home economist

Education: Ph.B., College of Wooster, 1885, Ph.M., 1888; Harvard University, 1888; Wesleyan University, 1894; Massachusetts Institute of Technology, 1898
Employment: High school teacher, 1885–1888; professor of natural science, Pennsylvania College for Women, 1888–1897; professor of chemistry, Lake Erie College, 1898–1899; head, department of household science, University of Illinois, 1900–1922; vice chair of home economics extension, 1929–1930; emeritus professor

*I*sabel Bevier was an educator who was noted for her contributions to the young profession of home economics. She was hired at the University of Illinois in 1900 to reinstate the home economics program that earlier had been formed by Louisa Gregory (q.v.). Although other land grant institutions had organized their courses on a cooking school format, she insisted on providing a scientific basis for the curriculum at the University of Illinois. She named her new department Household Science, with the early curriculum built around food, shelter, and clothing. She had taught languages in high schools, but after several years her interest shifted to the natural sciences. She attended science classes at several universities, and studied food chemistry while attending MIT. When the University of Illinois invited her to join the faculty, she had the opportunity to put into practice her concepts of the liberal education proper for women.

She originated the idea of using the thermometer for meat cooking in 1907; the following year she established a house on the campus as a laboratory for study. She left the University of Illinois for two years to become chair of the home economics department at the University of California, Los Angeles, returning to the University of Illinois in 1929 as professor of home economics and vice chair of the home economics extension. She was elected the second president of the new American Home Economics Association, and served in that capacity from 1910 to 1912. She also was a member of the American Chemical Society and the American Public Health Association. She received honorary doctorates from Iowa State (1920) and the College of Wooster (1936), and the home economics building at the University of Illinois was named for her. One of the books she wrote was *Home Economics in Education* (1924). She was listed in the first edition of *American Men and Women of Science.*

Bibliography: *American Men and Women of Science* 1–6; Herzenberg, Caroline L., *Women Scientists from Antiquity to the Present;* James, E. T., ed., *Notable American Women 1607–1950;* McHenry, Robert, ed., *Famous American Women; National Union Catalog;* Rossiter, Margaret W., *Women Scientists in America;* Rossiter, Margaret W., "Women Scientists in America before 1920"; Rossiter, Margaret W., "'Women's Work' in Science, 1880–1910"; Siegel, Patricia J. and Kay Thomas Finley, *Women in the Scientific Search.*

Bitting, Katherine Eliza Golden
(1869–1937)
botanist, food researcher

Education: B.S., Purdue University, 1890, M.S., 1892
Employment: Assistant botanist, Indiana Experiment Station, 1890–1893; instructor in biology, Purdue University, 1893–1901, assistant professor, 1901–1905; microanalyst, U.S. Department of Agriculture, 1907–1913; microanalyst, National Canners Association, 1913–1918; bacteriologist, Glass Container Association, 1919–1923
Married: A. W. Bitting, 1904

Katherine Bitting was a distinguished botanist and microanalyst, specializing in molds and microorganisms involved in the preparation and preservation of food. She was listed in the first edition of *American Men and Women of Science* under her maiden name, Golden. While she was on the staff of the Indiana Experiment Station, she worked closely with pioneer botanist J. C. Arthur. She succeeded in making the transfer from the research laboratory to the faculty, a feat that few women of her day were able to accomplish. Her husband also was a member of the Purdue faculty when they married, and they continued to work for the same employers throughout their marriage, publishing extensively on joint research. In 1935 the couple received honorary degrees from Purdue. When the university contacted A. W. Bitting about granting him an honorary degree, he insisted that his wife deserved the honor more than he did. After his wife's death in 1937, Mr. Bitting arranged for the publication of her book, *Gastronomic Bibliography*, which still is a basic reference for food research. He presented the 2,500-volume memorial collection of the books listed in the bibliography to the Library of Congress. She was a member of the American Association for the Advancement of Science, Botanical Society of America, and

the American Society for Microbiology. There is an obituary and photograph in the *Proceedings* of the Indiana Academy of Science 48 (1939): 3–4, and the papers of J. C. Arthur, housed in the Arthur Herbarium, Purdue University, contain information concerning her work.

Bibliography: American Men and Women of Science 1–5; Barnhart, John H., *Biographical Notes upon Botanists*; Herzenberg, Caroline L., *Women Scientists from Antiquity to the Present*; Mozans, H. J., *Women in Science*; *National Union Catalog*; Rossiter, Margaret W., *Women Scientists in America*; Rudolph, Emanuel D., "Women in Nineteenth Century American Botany"; Siegel, Patricia J. and Kay Thomas Finley, *Women in the Scientific Search.*

Bliss, Eleanor Albert
(1899–1987)
bacteriologist

Education: A.B., Bryn Mawr College, 1921; Sc.D., Johns Hopkins University, 1925
Employment: Fellow in medicine, Johns Hopkins University, 1925–1935, faculty
1936–1952; professor of biology and dean of graduate school, Bryn Mawr, 1952–1966;
director, 1945–1952, advisor to U.S. Army Chemical Corps, 1945–1950; member of board,
University of Pennsylvania, 1954–1959

Eleanor Bliss was an authority on the use of sulfa drugs, and she discovered group F, a minute hemolytic streptococcus of the serological group. After serving on the faculty of Johns Hopkins University for 16 years, she accepted an appointment as professor of biology and dean of the graduate school at Bryn Mawr College. Although some might consider this a step down in the profession, Bryn Mawr has had a solid reputation in research since its founding and was one of the first colleges to offer graduate courses for women. Eleanor Bliss's research on sulfa drugs was on the front line of research at the time—sulfa drugs were used extensively for the first time during World

War II, primarily to treat the wounds of service people, but today many have been replaced by more effective medications. Eleanor Bliss took a leave of absence from Bryn Mawr to work with the Chemical Corps during the war years. In addition to numerous papers on the topic, she published *Clinical and Experimental Use of Sulfanilamide, Sulfapyridine and Allied Compounds* (1939). She was elected a fellow of the American Academy of Microbiology and of the American Association for the Advancement of Science. She was a member of several professional societies, including the American Society of Bacteriologists and the American Association of Immunologists. She received an honorary degree from Drexel University in 1956.

Bibliography: Debus, A. G., ed., *World Who's Who in Science;* Herzenberg, Caroline L., *Women Scientists from Antiquity to the Present;* Ireland, Norma O., *Index to Scientists of the World;* McNeil, Barbara, ed., *Biography and Genealogy Master Index 1986–90, Cumulation,* vol. 1; Rossiter, Margaret W., *Women Scientists in America.*

Blodgett, Katharine Burr
(1897–1979)
physicist

Education: A.B., Bryn Mawr College, 1917; S.M., University of Chicago, 1918; Ph.D. in physics, Cambridge University, 1926
Employment: Research physicist and chemist, General Electric Company, 1918–1924, 1926–1962

Katharine Blodgett invented nonreflecting glass, developed methods for constructing films of infinitesimal thickness, developed a device for measuring the thickness of films within one micro-inch, and invented a new kind of smoke screen. After receiving her master's degree, she was hired by General Electric, where she worked with Irving Langmuir in the research laboratory, the first woman to work in the company's labs. Through Langmuir's influence, she was able to obtain a position at Cavendish Laboratory, which resulted in her being the first woman to receive a Ph.D. in physics from Cambridge. After her return from Cambridge, she worked with Langmuir on problems with tungsten filaments in lamps. These simple statements of her work mask the magnitude of her accomplishments. It was virtually impossible for women scientists to find professional-level jobs in corporations at that time. Some were hired during World War I due to a shortage of personnel, but few were able to retain their positions when the war was over. Many of her papers were coauthored with Langmuir, who later received a Nobel Prize, and her name was starred in the seventh edition of *American Men and Women of Science.* She received numerous awards, including the Garvan Medal in 1951, and received honorary degrees from Elmira College (1939), Brown University (1942), Western College (1942), and Russell Sage College (1944). She was elected a fellow of the American Physical Society and was a member of the Optical Society of America. There are photographs of Katharine Blodgett in *Current Biography, Women of Science,* by G. Kass-Simon and Patricia Farnes, and in the journal *Chemtech* 6 (1976): 738–743.

Bibliography: American Men and Women of Science 6–11; *Current Biography;* Debus, A. G., ed., *World Who's Who in Science;* Goff, Alice C., *Women Can Be Engineers;* Herzenberg, Caroline L., *Women Scientists from Antiquity to the Present;* Kass-Simon, G. and Patricia Farnes, *Women of Science;* Mozans, H. J., *Women in Science;* O'Neill, Lois S., *The Women's Book of World Records and Achievements;* Rossiter, Margaret W., *Women Scientists in America;* Siegel, Patricia J. and Kay Thomas Finley, *Women in the Scientific Search;* Visher, Stephen S., *Scientists Starred 1903–1943 in "American Men of Science";* Yost, Edna, *American Women of Science.*

Blunt, Katharine
(1876–1954)
home economics educator and nutritionist

Education: A.B., Vassar College, 1898; Massachusetts Institute of Technology, 1902–1903; Ph.D. in organic chemistry, University of Chicago, 1907

Employment: Assistant in chemistry, Vassar College, 1903–1905; instructor, Pratt Institute, 1907–1908; instructor, Vassar, 1908–1913; assistant professor of home economics, University of Chicago, 1913–1918, associate professor, 1918–1925, professor, 1925–1929; department chair, 1918–1929; president, Connecticut College for Women, 1929–1945

Katharine Blunt's contribution to science was as a leading home economics educator and nutritionist. After she joined the department of home economics at the University of Chicago, she began to serve as the informal chair of the department, and the position was officially recognized in 1925. Katharine Blunt developed a curriculum with a scientific basis for training professionals. The faculty and graduates included many outstanding researchers; their work contributed to making home economics a valid profession and a proper university subject. Her major field was nutrition, and her scholarly work appeared regularly in significant journals. She published several books, including *Ultra-Violet Light and Vitamin D in Nutrition* (1930). Blunt served as president of the American Home Economics Association from 1924 to 1926. In 1929 she was named the third president of what is now Connecticut College, the first woman to hold the post (at that time it was a women's college). She used her administrative skills to develop a curriculum there that met the highest standards of teaching and scholarship. She was awarded honorary degrees by Connecticut College, University of Chicago, Mount Holyoke College, and Wesleyan University. She also was a member of the American Chemical Society and the American Society of Biological Chemists. There are photographs of her in *Current Biography* and the *National Cyclopedia of American Biography*.

Bibliography: American Men and Women of Science 2–8; Current Biography; Herzenberg, Caroline L., Women Scientists from Antiquity to the Present; Ireland, Norma O., Index to Scientists of the World; National Cyclopedia of American Biography; National Union Catalog; Rossiter, Margaret W., Women Scientists in America; Sicherman, Barbara et al., Notable American Women; Siegel, Patricia J. and Kay Thomas Finley, Women in the Scientific Search.

Bodley, Rachel Littler
(1831–1888)
chemist and botanist

Education: Diploma, Wesleyan Female College, Cincinnati, 1849; Polytechnic College, Philadelphia, 1860–1862

Employment: Teacher of natural sciences, Wesleyan Female College, 1849–1860; professor of chemistry, Women's Medical College, Philadelphia, 1865–1873, dean 1874–1888

Rachel Bodley, who did not have a medical degree, served as dean of the Women's Medical College in Philadelphia for 14 years. Although her primary interest was in botany, she was appointed the first woman chemist on the staff of the Women's Medical College; during the early 1880s she gave six lectures on "household chemistry" at Philadelphia's Franklin Institute. She developed expertise in sea plants, and she spent her summer trips adding to her collection. The college grew in stature during her tenure as dean, and many of the graduates became successful physicians. She was especially interested in preparing women as medical missionaries, because as a young woman her health had been considered too delicate to undertake this type of work. She was a charter member of the American Chemical Society and a vice president of the association. It was her suggestion that American chemists honor the centennial of Joseph Priestley's discovery of oxygen by holding a meeting in 1874, and the American Chemical Society was established as a direct result of this meeting. She was elected to membership in the Academy of Natural Sciences of Philadelphia in 1871 and the New York Academy of Sciences in 1876. The college presented her with an honorary M.D. in 1879 in recognition for her contributions to the school. She also published a study on the number of Women's Medical College graduates who combined marriage with a career in medicine.

Bibliography: Elliott, Clark A., *Biographical Dictionary of American Science;* Harshberger, John W., *The Botanists of Philadelphia and Their Work;* Herzenberg, Caroline L., *Women Scientists from Antiquity to the Present;* James, E. T., ed., *Notable American Women 1607–1950; National Union Catalog;* Ogilvie, Marilyn B., *Women in Science;* Rossiter, Margaret W., *Women Scientists in America;* Rossiter, Margaret W., "Women Scientists in America before 1920"; Siegel, Patricia J. and Kay Thomas Finley, *Women in the Scientific Search;* Uglow, Jennifer S., *International Dictionary of Women's Biography.*

Booth, Mary Ann Allard
(1843–1922)
microscopist

Education: Wilbraham Academy and private teachers
Employment: No formal employment

Mary Booth had a distinguished career as a microscopist in research, although she did not seem to be employed. She lectured before many scientific societies in the United States and Canada, illustrating her talks with stereopticon slides that she prepared. Her name was acknowledged in several textbooks of the period for her assistance in their preparation. She developed her skills during years of chronic illness. She had a well-equipped laboratory and a large collection of microscopical slides in her home. She was credited with possessing the largest private collection of parasites in the country, and many of the species had never been photographed before. Photography was in its infancy at this period, and numerous women learned to use cameras both as hobbyists and professionals. Mary Booth was known for her work in making photomicrographs of germ-bearing fleas of rats for stereo slides during the campaign against bubonic plague in San Francisco (1907 to 1909). She gathered a large collection of parasite specimens and produced award-winning photomicrographs that earned her medals from the New Orleans Exposition (1885), the St. Louis Exposition (1904), and the San Francisco Exposition (1915). She was editor of *Practical Microscopy* from 1900 to 1907 and was elected a fellow of both the Royal Microscopical Society and the Royal Photographic Society. She also was a member of the American Association for the Advancement of Science and American Microscopical Society. Her name was included in the first three editions of *American Men and Women of Science,* and her photograph was in the *National Cyclopedia of American Biography.*

Bibliography: *American Men and Women of Science* 1–3; Debus, A. G., ed., *World Who's Who in Science;* Herzenberg, Caroline L., *Women Scientists from Antiquity to the Present; National Cyclopedia of American Biography;* Siegel, Patricia J. and Kay Thomas Finley, *Women in the Scientific Search.*

Boring, Alice Middleton
(1883–1955)
zoologist

Education: B.A., Bryn Mawr College, 1904, M.A., 1905, Ph.D., 1910; fellow, University of Pennsylvania, 1905–1906; University of Wurzburg and Naples Zoological Station, 1908–1909

Employment: Instructor in biology, Vassar College, 1907–1908; instructor in zoology, 1911, University of Maine, assistant professor, 1911–1913, associate professor, 1913–1918; assistant professor of biology, Peking Union Medical College, 1918–1920; professor of zoology, Wellesley College, 1920–1923; professor of zoology, Yenching University, 1923–1950; part-time professor of zoology, Smith College, 1951–1953

*A*lice *Boring* distinguished herself as a researcher, although she spent a major portion of her career outside the United States. She spent about ten years on the faculties of Vassar and the University of Maine, attaining the position of associate professor at the latter institution. Except for brief interludes in the United States, Alice Boring remained in China from 1918 through 1950 teaching and conducting research. During this time she witnessed civil war, revolution, the Japanese occupation, World War II (involving her internment and repatriation), and the creation of a new socialist society in China. She continued to publish scientific papers during this period and made significant contributions to the literature on the taxonomy of Chinese amphibians and reptiles. Her early research had involved cytology and genetics, and she seemed to be headed for a traditional career in academia. After her first two-year term in China, she made it her mission in life to stay in that country to teach. She immediately involved herself in Chinese educational and political causes. She was repatriated from China in 1943 after spending two years with British and American citizens in a concentration camp, but she eagerly returned to the country she loved in 1946 for four additional years. She contributed to science by teaching several generations of Chinese students and by collecting original data on the fauna of China.

Bibliography: *American Men and Women of Science 6–9*; Herzenberg, Caroline L., *Women Scientists from Antiquity to the Present*; *National Union Catalog*; Ogilvie, Marilyn B., *Women in Science*; Rossiter, Margaret W., *Women Scientists in America*; Rossiter, Margaret W., "Women Scientists in America before 1920."

Boyd, Louise Arner
(1887–1972)
geographer and explorer

Education: Private schools
Employment: Scientific explorations of polar regions

*L*ouise Boyd contributed to science by sponsoring and leading expeditions of scientifically trained personnel who made significant contributions to our knowledge of the Arctic. During World War II she was a consultant to the U.S. War Department due to her experience in exploring the polar regions. Since the Danes and the Norwegians had conducted the primary polar research, her files of notes, maps, photographs, botanical specimens, and so on were the only sources available. She was a wealthy woman who first saw polar ice on a vacation with friends in 1926. She sponsored six additional trips to arctic regions, primarily to east Greenland. Although she was not a scientist, she provided the best equipment available to the scientists who accompanied her, and she consulted with the staff of the American Geographical Society in selecting both the scientists and the equipment. She trained herself to be an expert photographer and developed skill in collecting botanical specimens. She was the first woman to reach the North Pole by flight in 1955 and became the first woman councilor of the American Geographical Society in 1960. She wrote two books—*Fiord Region of East Greenland* (1935), which gives the scientific results of her 1931 and 1933 trips, and *Polish Countrysides* (1937), which records her trip to Warsaw for the International Geographical Congress of 1934. She was a delegate to this congress, representing the U.S. government and the American Geographical Society. She had exceptional leadership skills, which made her the only woman to achieve an outstanding position in arctic exploration. When she was in residence in California, however, she led the life of a socialite, wearing the latest fashions and entertaining lavishly. She always wore a hat and was always called Miss Boyd. She received honorary degrees in 1939 from both University of California and from Mills College. Her biography is included in *Women of the Four Winds* (1985) by Elizabeth F. Olds, which provides detailed descriptions of her first three expeditions. Her photo appears in *Current Biography*.

Bibliography: *Current Biography*; Debus, A. G., ed., *World Who's Who in Science*; Herzenberg, Caroline L., *Women Scientists from Antiquity to the Present*; Ireland, Norma O., *Index to Scientists of the World*; *National Union Catalog*; Rossiter, Margaret W., *Women Scientists in America*.

Branch, Hazel Elisabeth

(b. 1886)

entomologist

Education: A.B., University of Kansas, 1908, A.M., 1912; Ph.D. in entomology, Cornell University, 1921

Employment: Preceptress, Collegiate Sisters of Bethany, 1914–1918; assistant in biology, Cornell, 1918–1922; professor, Fairmont College, 1922–1926; professor of zoology, Wichita State University, 1926–1956; emeritus professor

Hazel Branch was recognized by her peers to be a significant contributor to the field of entomology. This is confirmed by her inclusion in Herbert Osborn's *Fragments of Entomological History*, a who's who of the field of entomology for the period. After her employment as a preceptress at a small college, Branch worked at Cornell University for four years while she completed the requirements for a doctorate in entomology; Cornell had an outstanding reputation at that time for the quality of its programs in the natural sciences. During this period she also was a researcher for the New York Milk Conference Board (1920–1921), which probably was located at the university. She then was employed by another small college before receiving an appointment at Wichita State University. It is significant that she was appointed at the level of professor; a woman who had lesser credentials would have been hired at a lower level. She was on the faculty of Wichita State for 30 years and was elected emeritus professor when she retired in 1956. She was elected president of the Kansas Academy of Science in 1930 and was a member of the Entomological Society of America and the American Public Health Association as well as a fellow of the American Association for the Advancement of Science. A photograph was included in Osborn's book.

Bibliography: American Men and Women of Science 4–11; *National Union Catalog;* Osborn, Herbert, *Fragments of Entomological History; Who Was Who in America.*

Brandegee, Mary Katharine Layne

(1844–1920)

botanist

Education: M.D., University of California, San Francisco, 1878

Employment: Curator of botany, California Academy of Sciences, 1883–1893

Married: Hugh Curran, 1866, died 1874; Townshend S. Brandegee, 1889

Mary Brandegee was one of the outstanding women botanists in the United States in the nineteenth century and was a leading authority on California plants. After her husband, Hugh Curran, died in 1874, she moved to San Francisco and obtained an M.D. degree from the University of California. She became interested in materia medica and started learning about plants of medicinal value, later expanding her interest to plants in general. She practiced medicine for a few years, but joined the California Academy of Sciences in 1879 and began working with the herbarium, becoming curator in 1883. Since the University of California, San

Francisco, had not yet established an herbarium, her position as curator was one of the most strategic in botany for a woman in the United States.

She married Townshend Brandegee, a civil engineer and plant collector, in 1889. In the 1880s she had established a series of *Bulletins* for the California Academy of Sciences, serving as editor. The Brandegees founded the journal *Zoe,* which they published from 1890 to 1908. In 1898 they moved to San Diego, where they built their own botanical library and herbarium. They returned to San Francisco in 1906 when Mr. Brandegee accepted a position as honorary curator at the University of California. They spent the rest of their lives at the herbarium, without salary, giving their library and collection of over 75,000 specimens to the university. A guide to their collections was published in *American Midland Naturalist* 27 (1942): 772–789 and a bibliography of their papers appeared in the University of California *Publications in Botany* 13 (1926): 155–178.

Bibliography: Abir-Am, P. G. and Dorinda Outram, eds., *Uneasy Careers and Intimate Lives;* Barnhart, John H., *Biographical Notes upon Botanists;* Bonta, Marcia M., *Women in the Field;* Herzenberg, Caroline L., *Women Scientists from Antiquity to the Present;* James, E. T., ed., *Notable American Women 1607–1950;* Ogilvie, Marilyn B., *Women in Science;* Rudolph, Emanuel D., "Women in Nineteenth Century American Botany"; Siegel, Patricia J. and Kay Thomas Finley, *Women in the Scientific Search.*

Braun, Annette Frances
(1884–1978)
entomologist

Education: A.B., University of Cincinnati, 1906, A.M., 1908, Ph.D. in zoology, 1911
Employment: Assistant in zoology, University of Cincinnati, 1911–1916; private research, 1916–1978

*A*nnette Braun was an eminent entomologist and a leading authority on Lepidoptera, particularly Microlepidoptera. After receiving her doctorate, she was engaged in research at the University of Cincinnati for about five years before she left that position to engage in private research. The quality of her work is confirmed by her inclusion in Herbert Osborn's *Fragments of Entomological History,* a who's who of entomology of that period. A further indication of her reputation is that she was elected vice president of the Entomological Society of America in 1926 and also elected a fellow of the society. She and her sister Lucy Braun (q.v.) maintained a garden famous for its unusual plants at their home in Cincinnati. She continued to publish significant work well into her sixties, and she lived to the age of 94. One of her contributions was a 110-page text on Microlepidoptera, "Elachistidae of North America (Microlepidoptera)," published as *Memoir* 13 of the American Entomological Society in 1948. Her photograph in Osborn's book, centered on the page surrounded by photographs of eight men, reveals an attractive middle-aged woman with a gentle expression. The ratio of men to women on the page is not representative, because there were few women scientists at that time.

Bibliography: *American Men and Women of Science* 3–11; Bonta, Marcia M., *Women in the Field; National Union Catalog;* Osborn, Herbert, *Fragments of Entomological History.*

Braun, (Emma) Lucy
(1889–1971)
botanist

Education: A.B., University of Cincinnati, 1910, A.M. in geology, 1912, Ph.D. in botany, 1914

Employment: Assistant in geology, University of Cincinnati, 1910–1913, assistant in botany, 1914–1917, instructor in botany, 1917-1923, assistant professor of botany, 1923–1927, associate professor of botany, 1927–1946, professor of plant ecology, 1946–1948; emeritus professor

Lucy Braun was instrumental in developing the scientific discipline of ecology in the United States. She took early retirement from the University of Cincinnati to devote her time to fieldwork, particularly in Ohio. In the 1920s and 1930s she cataloged the flora of the Cincinnati area and compared it with the flora of the same region 100 years earlier. One of the first studies of its type in the United States, this provided a model for comparing changes in flora over a span of time. She published *An Annotated Catalog of the Spermatophytes of Kentucky* (1943), *Deciduous Forests of Eastern North America* (1950), *The Woody Plants of Ohio* (1961), *Monocotyledoneae* (1967), and various studies on plants new to science in Ohio and Kentucky. She was editor of the *Wild-Flower*, the journal of the New England Wild Flower Preservation Society. She was the first woman president of the Ecological Society of America in 1950 and the first woman president of the Ohio Academy of Science, serving from 1933 to 1934. She received the Mary Soper Pope Medal for achievement in the field of botany in 1952, a Certificate of Merit in 1956 from the Botanical Society of America, and an honorary degree from the University of Cincinnati in 1964. She and her sister Annette Braun (q.v.) were among several sets of sisters who were listed in *American Men and Women of Science*.

Bibliography: Abir-Am, P. G. and Dorinda Outram, eds., *Uneasy Careers and Intimate Lives; American Men and Women of Science 3–11*; Barnhart, John H., *Biographical Notes upon Botanists*; Bonta, Marcia M., *Women in the Field*; Herzenberg, Caroline L., *Women Scientists from Antiquity to the Present; National Union Catalog*; Sicherman, Barbara et al., *Notable American Women*; Siegel, Patricia J. and Kay Thomas Finley, *Women in the Scientific Search.*

Breed, Mary Bidwell
(1870–1949)
chemist

Education: A.B., Bryn Mawr College, 1894, A.M., 1895; University of Heidelberg, 1895–1896; Ph.D., Bryn Mawr, 1901

Employment: Assistant, chemistry laboratory, Bryn Mawr College, 1894–1895; head, science department, Pennsylvania College for Women, 1897–1899; assistant professor of chemistry and dean of women, Indiana University, 1901–1906; head of Read Hall University of Missouri, 1906–1912; associate head, private school, 1912–1913; dean of Margaret Morrison College, Carnegie Institute of Technology, 1913–1929

Mary Breed was one of the numerous women in the late nineteenth and early twentieth centuries who went to Europe to obtain advanced instruction in the sciences, particularly to Germany and Switzerland. She was the first woman to participate in scientific research at the University of Heidelberg, and she worked in both inorganic and organic chemistry. She received her doctorate at Bryn Mawr College, one of the first institutions in the United States to grant graduate degrees to women. After she completed her degree, she was employed at several colleges, and at Indiana University she served as dean of women while teaching in the chemistry department. (It was a common situation for women faculty members to be appointed head of the women's dormitory or dean of women while carrying a full load of teaching, which left little time for research. The problem was not resolved until the 1930s and 1940s when the position of dean of women became an administrative appointment rather than an adjunct of a faculty position.) Later as dean of Margaret Morrison College of the Carnegie Institute, Mary Breed was instrumental in raising the standing of the institution from a trade school to a fully qualified college. She was listed in the first edition of *American Men and Women of Science.*

Bibliography: *American Men and Women of Science* 1; Siegel, Patricia J. and Kay Thomas Finley, *Women in the Scientific Search.*

Briscoe, Anne M.
(1918–)
biochemist

Education: B.A., Adelphi College, 1942; A.M., Vassar College, 1945; Ph.D. in physical chemistry, Yale University, 1949

Employment: Assistant chemist, University of Maine, 1942–1943; Vassar College, 1943–1945; physiological chemist, Yale, 1946–1947; fellow, University of Pennsylvania, 1949–1950; associate biochemist, medical college, Cornell University, 1950–1954, assistant professor, 1954–1955; research associate, school of medicine, University of Pennsylvania, 1956; associate biochemist, Columbia University, 1956–1972; assistant professor of medicine, college of physicians and surgeons, Columbia University, 1972–1987

Married: 1955

Anne Briscoe has been a distinguished researcher and faculty member in biochemistry, with a primary emphasis on medical research. She has held positions with numerous prestigious employers, including the medical college of Cornell University, the University of Pennsylvania School of Medicine, and the college of physicians and surgeons of Columbia University. She has been active as a consultant for the Veterans Administration Hospital, Castle Point, New York. While her primary focus was on research, she has lectured in the School of General Studies of Columbia University, the School of Nursing at Harlem Hospital Center, and Antioch College's Physicians Assistance Program at Harlem Hospital Center. She was a special lecturer at Columbia beginning in 1987. She has been very active professionally, serving as president of the Association for Women in Science (1978). She has been recognized for her work by being elected a fellow of the American Institute of Chemists and a fellow of the New York Academy of Sciences. She also has been a member of the American Chemical Society and the American Society for Clinical Nutrition. Her research has focused on metabolism of calcium and magnesium in human subjects. She was listed in the 1992–1993 edition of *American Men and Women of Science.*

Bibliography: *American Men and Women of Science* 10 18; Herzenberg, Caroline L., *Women Scientists from Antiquity to the Present.*

Britton, Elizabeth Gertrude Knight
(1858–1934)
bryologist

Education: New York City Normal College (later Hunter College), 1875
Employment: Critic teacher, New York City Normal College, 1875–1882, assistant in natural science, 1882–1885
Married: Nathaniel L. Britton, 1885

Elizabeth Britton was one of the prominent women scientists of the 1890s, although she did not have a doctorate. She added data on mosses to the scientific literature, and she contributed to public service by working toward the establishment of the New York Botanical Garden and the preservation of endangered species. After she graduated from Hunter College, she remained at the school until 1885, originally as a critic teacher in the model school and then as an assistant in natural science. She brought out her first scientific paper in March 1883, and her first paper on mosses in September that same year. She became the unofficial curator of the moss collection at Columbia College

after her marriage. Her husband was a geologist at Columbia College, but he became so interested in botany that he moved to the botany department the year following their marriage, becoming an internationally acclaimed botanist in his own right. They shared their fieldwork completely but published independently of each other.

At Elizabeth Britton's suggestion, the Torrey Botanical Club and interested citizen groups established the New York Botanical Garden in 1891; her husband was appointed the first director in 1896. In 1912 she was appointed honorary curator of mosses. She was one of the primary founders of the Wild Flower Preservation

Society of America in 1902. Through lectures and publications she attempted to push conservation measures through the New York legislature. Although she did not publish any books, she produced 346 scientific papers. She was editor of the *Bulletin* of the Torrey Botanical Club from 1886 to 1889 and was known for her sharply worded reviews of papers she thought represented sloppy scientific work. She was the principal founder of the Sullivant Moss Society in 1898 and was the first president of the society, serving from 1916 to 1919. (It was renamed the American Bryological Society in 1949.) There were 15 species of plants and the moss genus Bryobrittonia named in her honor, and in 1935 a double peak in Puerto Rico's Luquillo National Park was given the name of Mount Britton. She was the only woman among the 25 charter members of the Botanical Society of America in 1893. Her name was starred in the first five editions of *American Men and Women of Science,* but she was listed as Mrs.

N. L. Britton or Mrs. Nathaniel L. Britton. Her husband's name also was starred. There are photographs of the couple in the journal *Chronica Botanica* 1 (1935): 308.

Bibliography: Abir-Am, P. G. and Dorinda Outram, eds., *Uneasy Careers and Intimate Lives; American Men and Women of Science 1–5;* Barnhart, John H., *Biographical Notes upon Botanists;* Bonta, Marcia M., *Women in the Field;* Herzenberg, Caroline L., *Women Scientists from Antiquity to the Present;* James, E. T., ed., *Notable American Women 1607–1950;* Mozans, H. J., *Women in Science; National Cyclopedia of American Biography; National Union Catalog;* Ogilvie, Marilyn B., *Women in Science;* Rossiter, Margaret W., *Women Scientists in America;* Rudolph, Emanuel D., "Women in Nineteenth Century American Botany"; Siegel, Patricia J. and Kay Thomas Finley, *Women in the Scientific Search;* Visher, Stephen S., *Scientists Starred 1903–1943 in "American Men of Science."*

Brooks, Matilda Moldenhauer
(b. 1890)
physiologist

Education: A.B., M.S., University of Pittsburgh, 1913; Ph.D., Radcliffe College, 1920
Employment: Bacteriologist, research institute, National Dental Association, 1917; assistant biologist, U.S. Public Health Service, 1920–1924, associate biologist, 1924–1926; research associate in physiology, University of California, Berkeley, 1927–?
Married: Sumner Brooks 1917

Matilda Brooks was recognized for developing a treatment for cyanide and carbon dioxide poisoning. She was one of the few early women scientists who seem to have devoted her entire career to research. After spending about six years with the U.S. Public Health Service, she moved to the University of California, Berkeley, as a research associate. She was a member of the Marine Biological Laboratory Corporation in Woods Hole, an honor that few women

had enjoyed at that time. She received numerous distinguished grants, such as the Bache grant of the National Academy of Science, the Naples research grant of the National Research Council, the Permanent Science Foundation grant, and the American Philosophical Society grant—although earlier, in the 1930s, the Naples Table committee had refused to give her funds because the members felt some of her work had been inadequate. She was a member of several professional societies, such as the American Physiological Society, the Society of General Physiologists, and the Cooper Ornithological Society. Although her long-term research had involved respiration, in 1976 she listed her primary interest as effects of solar light and ultraviolet light on sugar production and the four basic acids. Her photograph is included in *Current Biography*.

Bibliography: *American Men and Women of Science* 4–14; *Current Biography;* Herzenberg, Caroline L., *Women Scientists from Antiquity to the Present*; Ireland, Norma O., *Index to Scientists of the World*; O'Neill, Lois S., *The Women's Book of World Records and Achievements*; Rossiter, Margaret W., *Women Scientists in America*.

Brown, Nellie Adalesa
(1877–1956)
plant pathologist

Education: A.B., University of Michigan, 1901
Employment: High school teacher, 1901–1905; scientific assistant, Bureau of Plant Industry, U.S. Department of Agriculture, 1906–1910, assistant pathologist, 1910–1925, associate pathologist, 1925–1941

*N*ellie Brown was one of a group of women scientists who were employed by the U.S. Department of Agriculture (USDA) before many women were employed as professionals by the federal government. She followed the pattern of many women of her time in that, after receiving her undergraduate degree, she taught school (in Michigan and Florida) for several years before joining the USDA. During her tenure the Bureau of Plant Industry was the largest single employer of women scientists in the federal government. This situation remained until the Bureau of Home Economics was established in the 1930s. It was not uncommon for the agency to employ women who had received only undergraduate degrees because women were unable to be accepted for advanced work in many colleges. The women in the Bureau of Plant Industry enjoyed the privilege of publishing their work under their own names. Nellie Brown was the author or coauthor of 14 publications during her career, a fairly average number for that period. She was a member of the American Association for the Advancement of Science and the American Phytopathological Society. In her photograph on file in the National Archives, she appears to be a delicate and very attractive woman. It is a studio portrait, and she is in a relaxed pose, wearing an afternoon or Sunday frock rather than a lab coat. She was listed in the third through seventh editions of *American Men and Women of Science.*

Bibliography: *American Men and Women of Science 3–7;* Barnhart, John H., *Biographical Notes upon Botanists;* Herzenberg, Caroline L., *Women Scientists from Antiquity to the Present; National Union Catalog;* Rossiter, Margaret W., "'Women's Work' in Science, 1880–1910."

Brown, Rachel Fuller
(1898–1980)
biochemist

Education: A.B., Mount Holyoke College, 1920; M.S., University of Chicago, 1921, Ph.D. in chemistry, 1933

Employment: Teacher, private school, 1921–1924; assistant chemist, New York State Department of Health, 1926–1929, assistant biochemist, 1929–1936, senior biochemist, 1936–1951, associate biochemist, 1951–1964, research scientist, 1964–?

Rachel Brown's contribution to science was being the codiscoverer of the fungicide nystatin. She spent her entire career at the division of laboratories and research of the New York State Department of Health. She was not interested in chemistry in high school, but when she matriculated to Mount Holyoke College, which had an excellent chemistry department, she changed to a double major of history and chemistry. When she had completed her thesis for her doctorate, her major professor delayed in approving it. Since she was out of funds and already was promised the position in New York, she left the University of Chicago without the diploma. Seven years later, after she had produced some interesting work, her professor approved the thesis. Rachel Brown's early work at the state laboratory focused on pneumococci. Later, when patients started developing severe side effects from the overprescribing of new antibiotics, she and coworker Elizabeth Hazen (q.v.), a microbiologist, patented the fungicide nystatin. Instead of personally using the funds from licensing the patent, they formed a foundation to use the money for scholarships and research. All royalties were used to further research in the natural sciences. A portion was designated to provide advanced training for the staff at the state laboratory where they worked. Later the two women isolated another antibiotic, phalamycin. Their joint biography is *The Fungus Fighters: Two Women Scientists and Their Discovery* (1981) by Richard S. Baldwin.

Bibliography: *American Men and Women of Science 8–11;* Herzenberg, Caroline L., *Women Scientists from Antiquity to the Present;* Ireland, Norma O., *Index to Scientists of the World;* Siegel, Patricia J. and Kay Thomas Finley, *Women in the Scientific Search;* Uglow, Jennifer S., *International Dictionary of Women's Biography;* Yost, Edna, *Women of Modern Science.*

Bunce, Elizabeth Thompson

(1915–)

geophysicist

Education: A.B., Smith College, 1937, M.A., 1949
Employment: Instructor in physics, Smith College, 1949–1951; research assistant, Woods Hole Oceanographic Institute, 1951–1952, associate scientist, physics and geophysics, 1952–1975, senior scientist, 1975–1980; emeritus scientist

Elizabeth Bunce is the first American woman to become chief scientist on a major oceanographic expedition at Woods Hole. When she began working, few women were permitted to engage in oceanographic exploration—perhaps for fear of their safety, since comparatively few women are as physically strong as men, or perhaps it was taboo at the time for men and women to work together in such close quarters. She started her career at Smith College, but soon joined Woods Hole as a research assistant, progressing through the ranks to associate scientist, senior scientist, and then emeritus scientist. In recognition for her work she was elected a fellow of the Geological Society of America and received an honorary degree from Smith College in 1971. Her other professional memberships include the Society of Exploration Geophysics, the American Geophysical Union, and the American Association of Petroleum Geologists. Her name is listed in the 1992–1993 edition of *American Men and Women of Science,* where she mentions marine seismology and underwater acoustics as her research interests.

Bibliography: American Men and Women of Science 11–18; Herzenberg, Caroline L., *Women Scientists from Antiquity to the Present;* O'Neill, Lois S., *The Women's Book of World Records and Achievements.*

Bunting, Martha

(b. 1861)

biologist

Education: B.L., Swarthmore College, 1881; B.S., University of Pennsylvania, 1890; Bryn Mawr College, 1891–1893; Marine Biological Laboratory, Woods Hole, 1891–1892; Ph.D., Bryn Mawr College, 1895; Columbia University, 1898–1899; Woods Hole, 1899
Employment: Instructor in biology, Goucher College, 1893–1897; high school teacher, 1897–1898, 1900–1910; research assistant, University of Pennsylvania, 1910–1916, 1918–1919, fellow by courtesy, 1919–1924, 1926–1927, 1930–1931

Martha Bunting's work was considered significant enough to have her name included in the first edition of *American Men and Women of Science.* Her education and career were typical of women of her generation, but it is difficult today to see its significance. She received a doctorate from Bryn Mawr College, one of the few colleges at the time that granted advanced degrees to women.

She spent more than ten years as a high school teacher even after she received a Ph.D. from a prestigious college. She spent over ten years as a fellow by courtesy at the University of Pennsylvania, rather than receiving a permanent appointment (even the appointments there were sporadic, with gaps of several years in some instances). She was engaged in war relief work from 1916 to 1918; many women scientists of her day were unable to receive continuous employment or research funding in order to produce a significant body of research. She was a member of the American Association for the Advancement of Science and the Academy of Natural Sciences of Philadelphia. She mentions a long list of research interests: photozoology; sex cells in Hydractinia and Podocoryne; otoliths and the geotropic functions of Astacus; life cycle and binary fission in Tetramitus rostratus, Perty; and cork tissues in the roots of rosaceous genera.

Bibliography: *American Men and Women of Science* 1–7; Harshberger, John W., *The Botanists of Philadelphia and Their Work;* Siegel, Patricia J. and Kay Thomas Finley, *Women in the Scientific Search; Who Was Who in America.*

Bunting, Mary Ingraham
(b. 1910)
microbiologist

Education: A.B., Vassar College, 1931; A.M., University of Wisconsin, 1932, Ph.D., 1933

Employment: Assistant agricultural bacteriologist and agricultural chemist, University of Wisconsin, 1933–1935; department of biology, Bennington College, 1935–1937; instructor in physiology and hygiene, Goucher College, 1937–1938; research fellow, Yale University, 1938–1941; fellow, Wellesley College, 1946–1947; research assistant, Yale University, 1948–1952, lecturer in microbiology, 1952–1955; dean of Douglass College of Rutgers University, 1955–1960; president of Radcliffe College, 1960–1972; assistant to president, Princeton University, 1972–1975; consultant

Concurrent Positions: Commissioner, Atomic Energy Commission, 1964–1965; member of the national science board of the National Science Foundation, 1965–1970

Married: John Bunting, 1937, died 1954

Mary Bunting had two distinguished careers, the first as a renowned scientist and the second as an effective academic administrator. She received appointments at distinguished academic institutions, including Wellesley College and Yale University. In Elizabeth O'Hern's article, "Women Scientists in Microbiology," she is listed as one of the outstanding women microbiologists for her significant contributions to microbial genetics. She started on her second career by accepting a position as dean of Douglass College of Rutgers University, the women's college of the school. She was appointed president of Radcliffe College, where she stayed for 12 years before joining Princeton University as assistant to the president. This might seem to be a backward step, but Princeton is a large institution with a distinguished history in education. She then returned to her first career as a scientist by accepting a position with the Atomic Energy Commission. Her election to the national science board indicates how highly she was rated by her fellow scientists: the science board is the governing body of the National Science Foundation, one of the major sources for scientific grants. She was a member of the American Society for Microbiology. In addition to her career in science, she was the mother of four. *Current Biography* includes her photograph.

Bibliography: *American Men and Women of Science* 6–15; *Current Biography*; Herzenberg, Caroline L., *Women Scientists from Antiquity to the Present*; O'Hern, Elizabeth M., "Women Scientists in Microbiology"; O'Neill, Lois S., *The Women's Book of World Records and Achievements*.

Bush, Katharine Jeannette
(1855–1937)
marine zoologist

Education: Ph.D., Yale University, 1901
Employment: Assistant, zoology department, Yale University Museum, 1879–1888; assistant, U.S. Fish Commission, 1881–1888; U.S. National Museum, 1891–1892, 1894–1898

Katharine Bush was the first woman to be granted a doctorate in zoology from Yale University. She spent her entire career at Yale in the zoological laboratories of the Peabody Museum. She obtained the equivalent of an undergraduate education by working with Addison E. Verrill; Yale did not admit women students at the time. She was the coauthor of many of Verrill's papers of that period on the subject on mollusks and annelids. Her own papers contain thorough descriptions and accurate drawings of marine invertebrates, especially mollusks, annelids, and echinoderms. She started working in the museum writing labels and preparing catalogs. In 1883 she published her first original paper in the *Proceedings* of the United States National Museum. In 1885 she was a special student in Yale's Sheffield Scientific School, and in 1901 she was awarded her doctorate at Yale. When she was paid, it was from grants provided by the United States Fish Commission, which supported the systematic classification of a large collection of sea animals obtained on

sea expeditions in the late nineteenth century by both the government and private individuals. Jeanne E. Remington published a biography, "Katharine Jeannette Bush: Peabody's Mysterious Zoologist," in *Discovery* 12 (1977): 3–8. Her name was listed in the first edition of *American Men and Women of Science*. Margaret Rossiter's *Women Scientists in America* includes a photograph of Katharine Bush taken about 1890 at Woods Hole; she was dressed in the standard attire of a high-necked pastel frock with a hat, rather than a lab coat. She was a member of the American Society of Naturalists and the American Society of Zoologists.

Bibliography: *American Men and Women of Science* 1–5; Debus, A. G., ed., *World Who's Who in Science*; Herzenberg, Caroline L., *Women Scientists from Antiquity to the Present*; Mozans, H. J., *Women in Science*; Rossiter, Margaret W., *Women Scientists in America*; Siegel, Patricia J. and Kay Thomas Finley, *Women in the Scientific Search*.

Byrd, Mary Emma
(1849–1934)
astronomer

Education: A.B., University of Michigan, 1878; Harvard College Observatory, 1882–1883
Employment: High school principal, 1879–1882; first assistant, observatory of Carleton College, 1883–1887; director, Smith College observatory, 1887–1906, professor of astronomy, 1898–1906; lecturer, Hunter College, 1913–1914

Mary Byrd was the first professor of astronomy at Smith College, and her name was included in the first edition of *American Men and Women of Science.* After receiving her undergraduate degree, she was employed as a high school principal for several years; this was a typical pattern for women of her era. She then studied astronomy by working for the Harvard College Observatory. (At the time that she was studying, most training in astronomy was given by observatories rather than colleges.) She taught astronomy at Carleton College and served as first assistant in the observatory. She moved to Smith College as director of the observatory and its first professor of astronomy. A dedicated feminist, she abruptly resigned from Smith in 1906 in protest of the college's accepting grants from the Rockefeller and Carnegie Foundation. (She felt that the college should not accept funds from the robber barons Rockefeller and Carnegie.) She accepted a position in the astronomical department of Hunter College, at that time called the Normal College of the City of New York. Her primary research was the application of pillar micrometers to the problem of determining the position of comets. She received her greatest satisfaction from teaching, however, and she published two manuals as teaching aids. Carleton College awarded her an honorary degree in 1904. There is biographical information in the paper "Mary E. Byrd" by Louise B. Hobitt, published in *Popular Astronomy* 42 (1934): 496–498.

Bibliography: American Men and Women of Science 1–5; Davis, Herman S., "Women Astronomers (1750–1890)"; Kass-Simon, G. and Patricia Farnes, *Women of Science;* Rossiter, Margaret W., *Women Scientists in America;* Siegel, Patricia J. and Kay Thomas Finley, *Women in the Scientific Search.*

Byrnes, Esther Fussell
(1867–1946)
biologist

Education: A.B., Bryn Mawr College, 1891, A.M., 1894, Ph.D., 1898; Marine Biological Laboratory, Woods Hole, 1891
Employment: Demonstrator in biology, Vassar College, 1891–1893; Bryn Mawr College, 1895–1897; senior instructor in physiology and biology teacher, girls high school, 1898–1932

*E*sther Byrnes was recognized by her contemporaries as an expert in marine science; her name was included in the first edition of *American Men and Women of Science*. Although she received all of her collegiate education at Bryn Mawr College and she taught briefly at both Bryn Mawr and Vassar, she spent the remainder of her career teaching in a girl's high school in Philadelphia, a pattern in education that lasted until World War II. A large number of women who possessed advanced degrees spent the majority of their careers teaching in public and private schools, particularly in biology and chemistry. Many had received credentials from prestigious academic institutions, such as Yale, Harvard, the University of Chicago, or Bryn Mawr. Esther Byrnes specialized in marine science, and her studies were considered important by her fellow scientists. Her research focused on cytology, maturation and fertilization, and limb muscles and limb regeneration in amphibia. In 1926 she was granted a sabbatical leave from the high school to tutor the princesses of the Japanese royal family. Later she served as director of the Mount Desert Biological Laboratory. The quality of her research was recognized by her election as a fellow of the New York Academy of Sciences sometime before 1906. She also was a member of professional societies such the American Association for the Advancement of Science, the American Society of Naturalists, and the American Society of Zoologists.

Bibliography: *American Men and Women of Science* 1–7; Siegel, Patricia J. and Kay Thomas Finley, *Women in the Scientific Search.*

Bertha Louise Chapman Cady
Mary Whiton Calkins
Helen Stuart Campbell
Annie Jump Cannon
(Estella) Eleanor Carothers
Emma Perry Carr
Rachel Louise Carson
Vera Katherine Charles
(Mary) Agnes Meara Chase
Cornelia Maria Clapp
Eugenie Clark
Edith Clarke
Edith Jane Claypole
Edith Gertrude Schwartz Clements
Mildred Cohn
Jane Colden
Elizabeth Florence Colson
Anna Botsford Comstock
Esther Marly Conwell
Jacquelin Smith Cooley
Gerty Theresa Radnitz Cori
Juliet Corson
Gertrude Mary Cox
Elizabeth Caroline Crosby
Clara Eaton Cummings
Susan Cunningham

Cady, Bertha Louise Chapman
(1873–1956)
entomologist

Education: A.B., A.M., Ph.D., Stanford University, 1923; also attended University of Chicago, University of California, and Columbia University

Employment: High school teacher, 1900–1907; assistant in nature study, University of Chicago, 1907–1909; with department of biology, California State Teachers College, 1918; lecturer, Stanford University, 1921–1923; naturalist, National Girl Scouts, 1924–1936

Concurrent Positions: Lecturer and field secretary, Social Hygiene Association, 1914–1924; secretary, Coordinating Council on Nature, 1928–1930

Bertha Cady was an important contributor to science in her long-term association with the nature study movement. While teaching biology at the high school level, she was the director of nature study for the high schools in Oakland, California. She was about 30 years old, but there was no information on her activities prior to that time. She then was an assistant in nature study in the school of education at the University of Chicago and later taught in the biology department at California State Teachers College. She obtained employment as a naturalist for the Girl Scouts, and during that time she served as secretary of the Coordinating Council on Nature. Prior to this she worked as lecturer and field secretary of the Social Hygiene Association. Also during this period, as a member of the National Tuberculosis Association, she served as the director of the department of nature study (1929–1936). Bertha Cady was a member of the advisory science board for the American School of the Air for the Columbia Broadcasting Company. She was president of the American Nature Study Society from 1926 to 1929. She published several books on nature study, including *Animal Pets: A Study in Character and Nature Education* (1930) and *Nature Guide for Schools, Volunteer Organizations, Camps, and Clubs* (1930). She listed her research interests as natural history and child and adolescent psychology.

Bibliography: American Men and Women of Science 4–8; National Union Catalog; Rossiter, Margaret W., *Women Scientists in America*.

Calkins, Mary Whiton
(1863–1930)
psychologist

Education: B.A., Smith College, 1887, M.A., 1887; Harvard University, 1890–1895
Employment: Instructor in Greek, Wellesley College, 1887–1890, instructor in psychology, 1890–1897, associate professor of psychology and philosophy, 1897–1898, professor of psychology and philosophy, 1898–1929, research professor, 1928–1930

Mary Calkins was a pioneer in the profession of psychology. In recognition of her stature in the profession, her name was included in the first edition of *American Men and Women of Science,* and it was starred in the first four editions. In a study conducted by Stephen Visher in 1903, in a field of 50 prominent American psychologists she was ranked first in distinction among the three women in the group. Although she fulfilled all of the requirements for a doctorate in psychology, Harvard would not grant a Ph.D. to a woman, and Mary Calkins refused to accept Radcliffe College's offer of the degree. In 1891 she established a psychology laboratory at Wellesley, the first in any women's college and one of the early ones in the country. She also conducted experimental research in dreams, emotions, and memory. Her work on the conscious self was not popular at the time, but psychologists today working in the field of personality acknowledge her contributions. Her chief interest in philosophy was in metaphysics. She did distinguished work in psychology and philosophy, publishing 68 papers in psychology and 37 in philosophy. Her books are *The Persistent Problems of Philosophy* (1907) and *A First Book in Psychology* (1909). She was the first woman elected president of the American Psychological Association (1905) and of the American Philosophical Association (1918). She received an honorary degree from Columbia University in 1909 and one from Smith College in 1910. She was involved in social issues in her private life, supporting pacifist issues and often voting the Socialist ticket.

Bibliography: American Men and Women of Science 1–4; Bryan, Alice I. and Edwin G. Boring, "Women in American Psychology"; Dictionary of American Biography; Herzenberg, Caroline L., Women Scientists from Antiquity to the Present; James, E. T., ed., Notable American Women 1607–1950; McHenry, Robert, ed., Famous American Women; National Cyclopedia of American Biography; National Union Catalog; Ogilvie, Marilyn B., Women in Science; O'Neill, Lois S., The Women's Book of World Records and Achievements; Rossiter, Margaret W., Women Scientists in America; Rossiter, Margaret W., "Women Scientists in America before 1920"; Siegel, Patricia J. and Kay Thomas Finley, Women in the Scientific Search; Visher, Stephen S., Scientists Starred 1903–1943 in "American Men of Science."

Campbell, Helen Stuart
(1839–1918)
home economist and author

Education: Private schools
Employment: Teacher, Raleigh Cooking School, North Carolina, 1878; mission cooking school and diet kitchen, Washington, D.C., 1880; literary and household editor, *Our Continent* magazine, 1882–1884; lecturer in household science and social science, University of Wisconsin, 1895; professor of home economics, Kansas State Agricultural College, 1897–1898
Married: Grenville M. Weeks, ca. 1860, later divorced

Helen Campbell was one of the many women who established cooking schools, and she later taught in some of the very early home economics departments in colleges. In about 1862 she started publishing children's stories under her married name. She also published adult novels under the names Campbell Wheaton and Helen Stuart Campbell; she continued to use the latter name for the rest of her life.

During the 1870s she became active in the young home economics movement. She began teaching in 1878 in the Raleigh Cooking School. While there she wrote a textbook, *The Easiest Way in House-Keeping and Cooking* (1881). She helped found a mission cooking school and diet kitchen in Washington, D.C., in 1880. In New York she was literary and household editor of *Our Continent* magazine from 1882 to 1884. Among her other books on domestic science were *American Girls Home Book of Work and Play* (1882) and *Household Economics* (1896). She was invited to give a series of lectures at the University of Wisconsin in 1895 on household science and social science. In 1897 she was appointed professor of home economics at Kansas State, but ill health forced her to resign in 1898 to return to her free-lance writing and lecturing. She was noted also for her books on social issues. These include *The Problem of the Poor* (1879), *Prisoners of Poverty* (1887), *Prisoners of Poverty Abroad* (1889), and *Women Wage Earners* (1893). She produced little after 1900.

Bibliography: James, E. T., ed., *Notable American Women 1607–1950; National Cyclopedia of American Biography; National Union Catalog;* Shapiro, Laura, *Perfection Salad.*

Cannon, Annie Jump
(1863–1941)
astronomer

Education: B.S., Wellesley College, 1884, M.A., 1907; special student, Radcliffe College, 1895–1897
Employment: Astronomer, Harvard College Observatory, 1896–1940, curator of astronomical photographs, 1911–1938, William Cranch Bond Astronomer, Harvard University, 1938–1940

*A*nnie Cannon was a distinguished astronomer and probably the best-known woman astronomer in the first half of the twentieth century. Her name was starred in the second through sixth editions of *American Men and Women of Science*. She became interested in astronomy at Wellesley while studying under Sarah Whiting (q.v.), but she spent several years at home with her parents enjoying the social life before returning to Wellesley as a postgraduate student. She became an assistant at the Harvard College Observatory in 1896 as part of the team with Williamina Fleming (q.v.) and Antonia Maury (q.v.). Her own specialty was the study of stellar spectra. She succeeded Mrs. Fleming as curator of the observatory's astronomical photographs and in 1938 was appointed William Cranch Bond Astronomer at Harvard University. This was one of the first appointments for a woman by the Harvard corporation. Although she did not create the concept or invent the methodology for studying stellar spectra, she simplified and perfected the system. She was one of the pioneers in the photographic study of stellar variability. She discovered 277 variable stars and five new stars. She produced such a huge volume of data that she was popularly called the Census Taker of the Stars. Her major publications were *The Henry Draper Catalogue* (1918–1924) and *The Henry Draper Extension* (1925–1949). She also published over 90 lesser catalogs and shorter papers. No other astronomer or group of astronomers has yet matched the sheer bulk of Annie Cannon's output in the field of spectral classification.

She received the Nova Medal of the American Association of Variable Star Observers in 1922, the Draper Medal of the National Academy of Sciences in 1931, and the Ellen Richards Prize of the Society to Aid Scientific Research by Women in 1932. She received six honorary degrees, including one from the University of Groningen in 1921 and one from Oxford University in 1925, becoming the first woman to receive honorary degrees from these two universities. She was elected to membership in such honorary societies as the American Philosophical Society of Philadelphia and the American Academy of Arts and Sciences of Boston. In 1933 she established the Annie J. Cannon Prize of the American Astronomical Society to be awarded triennially to a woman who demonstrates distinguished service to astronomy. The prize was to be a brooch for the recipient to wear rather than a ceremonial medal. She supported woman suffrage and was a member of the National Woman's Party. Her photograph was included in *Women of Science*.

Bibliography: American Men and Women of Science 2–6; Current Biography; Debus, A. G., ed., World Who's Who in Science; Dictionary of American Biography; Dictionary of Scientific Biography; Herzenberg, Caroline L., Women Scientists from Antiquity to the Present; James, E. T., ed., Notable American Women 1607–1950; Kass-Simon, G. and Patricia Farnes, Women of Science; Macksey, Joan and Kenneth Macksey, The Book of Women's Achievements; Mozans, H. J., Women in Science; National Union Catalog; Ogilvie, Marilyn B., Women in Science; O'Neill, Lois S., The Women's Book of World Records and Achievements; Rossiter, Margaret W., Women Scientists in America; Rossiter, Margaret W., "Women Scientists in America before 1920"; Rossiter, Margaret W., "'Women's Work' in Science, 1880–1910"; Siegel, Patricia J. and Kay Thomas Finley, Women in the Scientific Search; Uglow, Jennifer S., International Dictionary of Women's Biography; Visher, Stephen S., Scientists Starred 1903–1943 in "American Men of Science"; Yost, Edna, American Women of Science.

Carothers, (Estella) Eleanor
(1882–1957)
zoologist

Education: Nickerson Normal College, Kansas; B.A., University of Kansas, 1911, M.A., 1912; Ph.D., University of Pennsylvania, 1916
Employment: Assistant in zoology, University of Pennsylvania, 1914–1926, lecturer, 1926–1933; research associate, University of Iowa, 1935–1941

Eleanor Carothers' contribution to science was her work on the cytological basis of heredity. Her name was starred in the fourth through the seventh editions of *American Men and Women of Science*. She received her undergraduate degree from the University of Kansas at the age of 28. Since she attended a normal college, it is possible that she taught in public schools prior to attending Kansas. She was a member of the University of Pennsylvania's scientific expeditions to the southern and southwestern states in 1915 and 1919, which would have been an honor for a woman at that time. She specialized in orthopteran genetics and cytology, and her work contributed both data and explanations to the question of the cytological basis of heredity. Her findings were published in important journals, such as the *Journal of Morphology* and the *Biological Bulletin*. She was one of seven women cited as primary investigators by Thomas H. Morgan in *The Mechanism of Mendelian Heredity* (1915). She was awarded the Ellen Richards Research Prize of the Naples Table Association in 1921. She was elected to membership in the National Academy of Sciences and in the Academy of Natural Sciences of Philadelphia. She published *The Segregation and Recombination of Homologous Chromosomes as Found in Two Genera of Acrididae (Orthoptera)* in 1917. Several sources list her name in error as Eleanor E. Carothers.

Bibliography: *American Men and Women of Science* 3–9; Herzenberg, Caroline L., *Women Scientists from Antiquity to the Present; National Union Catalog;* Ogilvie, Marilyn B., *Women in Science;* Rossiter, Margaret W., *Women Scientists in America;* Rossiter, Margaret W., "Women Scientists in America before 1920"; Siegel, Patricia J. and Kay Thomas Finley, *Women in the Scientific Search;* Visher, Stephen S., *Scientists Starred 1903–1943 in "American Men of Science."*

Carr, Emma Perry
(1880–1972)
chemist

Education: Ohio State University, 1898–1899; Mount Holyoke College, 1901–1904; B.S., University of Chicago, 1905, Ph.D. in physical chemistry, 1910; Queen's University, Belfast, 1919; University of Zurich, 1925, 1929–1930
Employment: Instructor in chemistry, Mount Holyoke College, 1905–1908, associate professor, 1910–1913, professor and department chair, 1913–1946; emeritus professor

Emma Carr was recognized for developing an ambitious research program in chemistry that was conducted by undergraduates and by a limited number of master's degree candidates. Due to her initiative, Mount Holyoke became one of the first American research centers to make use of ultraviolet spectrophotometry to determine the structure of complex organic molecules. Later she and her students made fundamental contributions to the understanding of the causes of selective absorption of radiant energy. Emma Carr continued the tradition of the strong chemistry department at Mount Holyoke started by its founder, Mary Lyon, who was herself a chemistry teacher. She was linked so closely with Mount Holyoke for 65 years that it is impossible to think of her without thinking of the college. As professor and chair of the department, she built a program that integrated teaching and research. Although she was burdened with heavy administrative responsibilities, she was considered to be a fine teacher at all levels of the curriculum. She received grants in the 1930s and 1940s from the National Science Foundation and the Rockefeller Foundation to investigate simple unsaturated hydrocarbons using ultraviolet spectrophotometry. She was a cooperating expert in charge of absorption spectra data for the International Critical Tables. She received numerous grants and prizes during her career. She was chosen in 1937 to be the first recipient of the Garvan Medal of the American Chemical Society. She was elected a fellow of the American Physical Society and also was a member of the American Chemical Society and the Optical Society of America. She received honorary degrees from Allegheny College in 1939, Russell Sage College in 1941, and Mount Holyoke College in 1952. There is a photograph of Emma Carr in the journal *Chemtech* 6 (1976): 738–743 and in *Current Biography*.

Bibliography: *American Men and Women of Science* 6–11; *Current Biography*; Debus, A. G., ed., *World Who's Who in Science*; Herzenberg, Caroline L., *Women Scientists from Antiquity to the Present*; Kass-Simon, G. and Patricia Farnes, *Women of Science*; *National Cyclopedia of American Biography*; O'Neill, Lois S., *The Women's Book of World Records and Achievements*; Rossiter, Margaret W., *Women Scientists in America*; Rossiter, Margaret W., "Women Scientists in America before 1920"; Sicherman, Barbara et al., *Notable American Women*; Siegel, Patricia J. and Kay Thomas Finley, *Women in the Scientific Search*.

Carson, Rachel Louise
(1907–1964)
biologist and conservationist

Education: A.B., Pennsylvania College for Women, 1929; A.M., Johns Hopkins University, 1932

Employment: Zoology staff, University of Maryland, 1931–1936; biologist, Bureau of Fisheries, 1936–1949, editor-in-chief, 1949–1952; resigned to write full time

Rachel Carson was prominent in the conservation movement in the United States in the mid-twentieth century. Her books still enjoy great popularity and are still reprinted today. Although she did not coin the word *ecology*, her name is synonymous with it. She displayed writing skills even as a child, but her interest in natural history prompted her to major in science in college. After graduating magna cum laude with a degree in zoology, she taught at the University of Maryland for a few years. From 1929 to 1936 she also taught in the Johns Hopkins summer school and undertook postgraduate studies at the Marine Biological Laboratory in Woods Hole, Massachusetts. Due to increased financial responsibilities to support her mother and nieces, she accepted a position in 1936 as an aquatic biologist with the Bureau of Fisheries. She was one of the first two women to be hired by the bureau in a professional position. She supplemented her income by writing magazine articles on natural history subjects in addition to writing numerous publications on conservation for the bureau. In 1940, when the Bureau of Fisheries merged with the Biological Survey to form the United States Fish and Wildlife Service, one of the stated purposes of the new department was conservation. Rachel Carson then was promoted in rank, and in 1947 she became editor-in-chief of the bureau's publications. She produced 12 government pamphlets on "Conservation in Action" concerning national wildlife refuges. In these pamphlets she argued for a national policy for conserving natural resources.

The publication of *The Sea around Us* (1951) won her recognition as a writer. It became a best-seller, won a National Book Award, and was translated into 30 languages. The same year she received a Guggenheim Foundation fellowship, which allowed her to take a year's leave from the bureau. She resigned the following year, able to realize enough money from her writing to build a cottage by the sea in Maine.

The book for which she is best known is *Silent Spring* (1962), which was one of the first efforts to point out the dangers of using insecticides, notably DDT. It has been given a major share of the credit for initiating the environmental movement, and it was a best-seller, as were her other books. It also raised a national controversy and aroused public opinion. Although she was suffering from deteriorating health due to cancer, she threw herself into the campaign to influence legislation. By 1962 state legislatures had introduced over 42 bills to curtail the use of insecticide, but she died before any substantive results were achieved.

Although she received a vast amount of publicity from her books, Rachel Carson never considered herself a crusader; she viewed herself as a scientist and a writer. She received numerous awards for her work, including the 1952 John Burroughs Medal, the 1954 Gold Medal of the New York Zoological Society, and the 1963 Conservationist of the Year Award of the National Wildlife Federation. Her other books were *Under the Sea Wind* (1941) and *The Edge of the Sea* (1956). There are several biographies, including Paul Brooks's *Rachel Carson at Work: The House of Life* (1985, c. 1972). There are photographs in Joan Marlow's *The Great Women* and in G. Kass-Simon's and Patricia Farnes's *Women of Science: Righting the Record*.

Bibliography: Bonta, Marcia M., *Women in the Field*; Debus, A. G., ed., *World Who's Who in Science*; Herzenberg, Caroline L., *Women Scientists from Antiquity to the Present*; Kass-Simon, G. and Patricia Farnes, *Women of Science*; McHenry, Robert, ed., *Famous American Women*; Marlow, Joan, *The Great Women*; *National Union Catalog*; O'Neill, Lois S., *The Women's Book of World Records and Achievements*; Rossiter, Margaret W., *Women Scientists in America*; Rossiter, Margaret W., "Women Scientists in America before 1920"; Sicherman, Barbara et al., *Notable American Women*; Siegel, Patricia J. and Kay Thomas Finley, *Women in the Scientific Search*; Uglow, Jennifer S., *International Dictionary of Women's Biography*.

Charles, Vera Katherine
(1877–1954)
mycologist

Education: Mount Holyoke College; A.B., Cornell University, 1903
Employment: Mycologist, Bureau of Plant Industry, U.S. Department of Agriculture, 1903–1942

Vera Charles was among the first dozen or so women who were hired by the U.S. Department of Agriculture in professional positions in the late nineteenth and early twentieth centuries. She was the expert on mushrooms in the government agencies. She coauthored Bulletin 175, "Mushrooms and Other Common Fungi," with Flora Patterson (q.v.) in 1915 and was the single author of the revised publication in 1917 and 1931. These were widely known and highly regarded by her contemporaries. She had expert knowledge of Fungi Imperfecti, but this was not reflected in her publications. One of her primary interests was Florida fungi, and she spent several winters there making mycological collections. Prior to the enactment of the Plant Quarantine Act in 1912, Vera Charles inspected a large portion of the imported plants received in the department. She

continued working as a collaborator for the division of mycology and disease survey for several years after she retired until failing eyesight forced her to give up her microscopic studies. She wrote one book, *Introduction to Mushroom Hunting* (1931), and she published a chapter, "The Mycologist," in the book *Careers for Women* (1935) by Catherine Filene. A brief biography and a list of her scientific publications is printed in the journal *Mycologia* 47 (1955): 263–265. Her photograph is on file at the National Archives.

Bibliography: Baker, Gladys L., "Women in the U.S. Department of Agriculture"; Barnhart, John H., *Biographical Notes upon Botanists; National Union Catalog;* Siegel, Patricia J. and Kay Thomas Finley, *Women in the Scientific Search.*

Chase, (Mary) Agnes Meara

(1869–1963)
botanist and suffragist

Education: Public school
Employment: Assistant in botany, Field Museum of Natural History, 1901–1903; meat inspector, Chicago stockyards, U.S. Department of Agriculture, 1901–1903, botanical artist, Bureau of Plant Industry, 1903–1907, assistant systematic agrostologist, 1907–1923, assistant botanist, 1923–1925, associate botanist, 1925–1936, senior botanist, 1936–1939; custodian of grasses, National Herbarium, 1939–1963
Married: William I. Chase, 1888, died 1889

*A*gnes Chase was an expert on grasses, and her name was starred in the fifth, sixth, and seventh editions of *American Men and Women of Science.* While working for a periodical in Chicago, she married the editor, William I. Chase, in 1888, but he died the following year. As a widow working at various jobs to pay off their debts, she became interested in botany and helped illustrate several publications for the Field Museum. After transferring to Washington, D.C., with the U.S. Department of Agriculture (USDA) in 1903, she began her collaboration with A. S. Hitchcock, a specialist in agrostology (grasses). In 1936 she succeeded Hitchcock as the principal scientist in charge of systematic agrostology, and she became a senior botanist. Her contribution to science was expanding the data on grasses, particularly those of the Northern Hemisphere. She updated and augmented the collections of the grass herbarium that was originally part of the United States National Herbarium of the USDA and was returned to the Smithsonian Institution in 1912. She donated her own personal agrostological library to the Smithsonian.

She was the author of more than 70 research publications. She wrote *First Book on Grasses* (1922) and *Index to Grass Species* (1962), a bibliographic register of types. She was also responsible for the 1950 revised edition of the *Manual of Grasses of the United States* (miscellaneous publication 200).

She was active in various reform movements, including women's rights, prohibition, and socialism. At one time she was jailed for participating in a women's rights march. She retired in 1939 but continued her work at the National Herbarium for the rest of her life. Although she had little formal education, she was regarded as an expert on grasses. The Botanical Society of America awarded her a certificate of merit in 1956. In 1958 the University of Illinois awarded her an honorary degree, and the Smithsonian Institution named her its eighth honorary fellow. A bibliography of her publications is included in the journal *Taxon* 8 (1959): 145–151, along with a biography and a photograph. There is later biographical sketch in *Taxon* 27 (1978): 373–374.

Bibliography: Abir-Am, P. G. and Dorinda Outram, eds., *Uneasy Careers and Intimate Lives; American Men and Women of Science* 2–11; Baker, Gladys L., "Women in the U.S. Department of Agriculture"; Barnhart, John H., *Biographical Notes upon Botanists;* Bonta, Marcia M., *Women in the Field;* Herzenberg, Caroline L., *Women Scientists from Antiquity to the Present; National Union Catalog;* Ogilvie, Marilyn B., *Women in Science;* Rossiter, Margaret W., *Women Scientists in America;* Rudolph, Emanuel D., "Women in Nineteenth Century American Botany"; Sicherman, Barbara et al., *Notable American Women;* Siegel, Patricia J. and Kay Thomas Finley, *Women in the Scientific Search;* Visher, Stephen S., *Scientists Starred 1903–1943 in "American Men of Science."*

Clapp, Cornelia Maria
(1849–1934)
zoologist

Education: Mount Holyoke Seminary, 1868–1871; Anderson School of Natural History, 1874; Ph.B., Syracuse University, 1888, Ph.D., 1889; Ph.D., University of Chicago, 1896
Employment: Teacher, private school, 1871; teacher, Mount Holyoke Seminary, 1872–1896; professor of zoology, Mount Holyoke College, 1896–1916

Cornelia Clapp was rated one of the top zoologists in the country during her lifetime. For over 40 years she was one of the primary participants in the development of Mount Holyoke Seminary and College. She had received the Ph.B. and Ph.D. degrees from Syracuse University after qualifying by examination. When Mount Holyoke made the transition from a seminary to a college, Cornelia Clapp took a three-year leave in order to obtain a doctorate at the University of Chicago. When she returned to Mount Holyoke, she was promoted to the rank of professor. When the Marine Biological Laboratory at Woods Hole opened in 1888, she was one of the first participants. Thereafter she spent most summers at Woods Hole as an investigator, teacher, librarian, corporation member, and trustee. She was the only woman trustee there during her lifetime, and she took an active role in gaining opportunities for women to study science. Since she preferred fieldwork to writing, she prepared few publications. She was known for the quality of her teaching, and she influenced hundreds of young women through her teaching methods and enthusiasm. Her name was starred in the first five editions of *American Men and Women of Science.* In a study conducted in 1903 she was rated among the top 150 zoologists in the country, as reported in Stephen Visher's *Scientists Starred 1903–1943 in "American Men of Science."* She was a member of the American Association for the Advancement of Science and the American Society of Zoologists. Mount Holyoke presented her with an honorary degree in 1921 and named its new science building for her in 1923.

Bibliography: Abir-Am, P. G. and Dorinda Outram, eds., *Uneasy Careers and Intimate Lives; American Men and Women of Science 1–5;* Elliott, Clark A., *Biographical Dictionary of American Science;* Herzenberg, Caroline L., *Women Scientists from Antiquity to the Present;* James, E. T., ed., *Notable American Women 1607–1950;* McHenry, Robert, ed., *Famous American Women;* Mozans, H. J., *Women in Science; National Union Catalog;* Ogilvie, Marilyn B., *Women in Science;* Rossiter, Margaret W., *Women Scientists in America;* Rossiter, Margaret W., "Women Scientists in America before 1920"; Siegel, Patricia J. and Kay Thomas Finley, *Women in the Scientific Search;* Visher, Stephen S., *Scientists Starred 1903–1943 in "American Men of Science."*

Clark, Eugenie
(1922–)
zoologist

Education: B.A., Hunter College, 1942; M.S., New York University, 1946, Ph.D. in zoology, 1950

Employment: Research assistant in ichthyology, Scripps Institute of Oceanography, 1946–1947; New York Zoological Society, 1947–1948; animal behavior, American Museum of Natural History, 1948–1949, research associate, 1950–1954; executive director of marine biology, Cape Haze Marine Laboratory, 1955–1966; associate professor of biology, City University of New York, 1966–1967; associate professor, University of Maryland, 1969–1973, professor of zoology, 1973–

Concurrent Positions: Fulbright scholar, Egypt, 1951; Saxton fellow and Breadloaf Writer's fellow, 1952; independent research on the behavior of sharks at numerous international locations, 1954–

Married: Ilias Konstantinu, 1950

*E*ugenie Clark has been one of the foremost marine biologists in the world, and she has successfully combined scientific research with imparting scientific information to the general public. After a series of short-term appointments at important research institutes, she was employed as executive director of marine biology at a research facility for more than ten years. She then joined the faculty of the University of Maryland. She was a member of the board of trustees, National Parks and Conservation Association, from 1975 to 1983 and member of the board of directors, National Aquarium. She has received numerous awards, such as the Cousteau Award in 1973, the Gold Medal of the Society of Women Geographers in 1975, and the Lowell Thomas Award of the Explorers Club in 1986. In addition to her scientific articles, she has been able to explain complex scientific work to the general public in sources such as *National Geographic* magazine. She received recognition for her writing also, with a Breadloaf Writer's fellowship in 1952. She has been a member of the American Society of Ichthyologists and Herpetologists and the Society of Women Geographers. An expert on sharks, her research has involved the reproductive behavior of fishes, morphology and taxonomy of plectognath fishes, and Red Sea fishes. She is the mother of four children. Her name was included in the 1992–1993 edition of *American Men and Women of Science.*

Bibliography: *American Men and Women of Science* 9–18; Debus, A. G., ed., *World Who's Who in Science;* Herzenberg, Caroline L., *Women Scientists from Antiquity to the Present;* Ireland, Norma O., *Index to Scientists of the World;* O'Neill, Lois S., *The Women's Book of World Records and Achievements.*

Clarke, Edith
(1883–1959)
electrical engineer

Education: A.B., Vassar College, 1908; University of Wisconsin, 1911–1912; M.S., Massachusetts Institute of Technology, 1919

Employment: High school teacher, 1909; Marshall College, 1910–1911; computer, American Telephone and Telegraph (AT&T), 1912–1918; General Electric Company (GE), 1920–1921; physics teacher, Constantinople Woman's College, 1921–1922; engineer, GE, 1922–1945; professor of electrical engineering, University of Texas, Austin, 1947–1956

Edith Clarke was recognized as an expert in the design of large power stations while working for the General Electric Company. Her primary contribution was as a mathematician and theorist—she designed systems that were based on solid mathematical principles. She was the first woman to teach electrical engineering in a university in the United States. After receiving her undergraduate degree, she taught mathematics at a high school and a college for several years before deciding to switch to engineering. She studied civil engineering at the University of Wisconsin for one year, and she received the first master's degree in electrical engineering granted by MIT to a woman. No one would hire her as an engineer, however. Her work as a "computer" at AT&T had involved supervising a group of women performing computations for research engineers in an era before the development of the electronic calculator and computer. After teaching abroad for one year, she was hired by GE as an engineer. Her work focused on large electrical power systems. She developed calculating devices that allowed the prediction of system reactions to extraordinary events without solving the same sets of equations repeatedly. She patented such a calculating device in 1925.

She authored numerous articles that were recognized for their high merit; two of them received prizes from the American Institute of Electrical Engineers (AIEE). Her book, *Circuit Analysis of A-C Power Systems* (1943, 1950), became a standard graduate text. After retiring from GE, she was offered a position at the University of Texas as professor of electrical engineering. Here she conducted an active program of graduate student research and publications. She was the first woman elected a fellow of the AIEE in 1948, and she received the Society of Women Engineers' Achievement Award in 1954. She received a great deal of publicity during her lifetime due to her unique position at GE, but interest in her intensified after she was appointed a professor at Texas.

Bibliography: Goff, Alice C., *Women Can Be Engineers;* Herzenberg, Caroline L., *Women Scientists from Antiquity to the Present;* Kass-Simon, G. and Patricia Farnes, *Women of Science;* O'Neill, Lois S., *The Women's Book of World Records and Achievements;* Rossiter, Margaret W., *Women Scientists in America;* Sicherman, Barbara et al., *Notable American Women;* Siegel, Patricia J. and Kay Thomas Finley, *Women in the Scientific Search.*

Claypole, Edith Jane
(1870–1915)
physiologist

Education: Ph.B., Buchtel College, 1892; M.S., Cornell University, 1893; Massachusetts Institute of Technology (MIT), 1894; Woods Hole Biological Laboratory, 1895–1896; M.D., University of California, Los Angeles, 1904

Employment: Instructor in physiology and histology, Wellesley College, 1894–1899; pathologist, 1902–1911, University of California, Los Angeles, research associate, 1912–1915

Edith Claypole was well regarded as a pathologist when she died in 1915. She and her identical twin sister, Agnes Claypole Moody (q.v.), were unique in that they both pursued careers in science. After completing her graduate work, Edith taught physiology and histology at Wellesley from 1894 to 1899, and during two of those years she served as acting head of the zoology department. She started her medical course work at Cornell and MIT but moved to Los Angeles to care for her mother and continued her education on a parttime basis. She worked as a pathologist in Pasadena and Los Angeles, at first part time, while she completed her degree. In 1912 she joined the Department of Pathology at the University of California as a volunteer. She then was appointed a research associate. During the period in which she lived, various areas of medicine were favored as careers for women. (A comparatively large number of women had careers in anatomy, pathology, and other areas of medicine. Apparently women were able to find employment in medicine more consistently than in the other sciences.) Agnes Claypole's research was in the area of blood and tissue histology and pathology. She was noted for her work on lung pathology and on typhoid immunization. She died of typhoid fever, contracted during her research on the typhoid bacillus. She published several papers in scientific journals. She was elected a fellow of the Southern California Academy of Histology. She and her sister were both listed in the first edition of *American Men and Women of Science.* There is a photograph of the sisters in Margaret Rossiter's *Women Scientists in America.*

Bibliography: American Men and Women of Science 1–2; Barr, Ernest S., *An Index to Biographical Fragments in Unspecialized Scientific Journals;* Herzenberg, Caroline L., *Women Scientists from Antiquity to the Present;* Mozans, H. J., *Women in Science; National Cyclopedia of American Biography; National Union Catalog;* Ogilvie, Marilyn B., *Women in Science;* Rossiter, Margaret W., *Women Scientists in America;* Siegel, Patricia J. and Kay Thomas Finley, *Women in the Scientific Search.*

Clements, Edith Gertrude Schwartz
(1874–1971)
botanist

Education: A.B., University of Nebraska, 1898, Ph.D. in languages and ecology, 1906
Employment: Assistant in botany, University of Nebraska, 1904–1907; instructor, University of Minnesota, 1909–1913; research ecologist, Carnegie Institution of Washington, 1918–1941; illustrator and author
Married: Frederic E. Clements, 1899

Edith Clements was an ecologist and author. After she completed her undergraduate degree, she was a teaching fellow in German at Nebraska. Her husband, Frederic E. Clements, who became a distinguished ecologist, persuaded her to take up the study of botany. She was the first woman to receive a doctorate from the University of Nebraska. When her husband accepted a position as head of the botany department at the University of Minnesota, for two years Edith Clements was employed as an instructor. During their summer vacations, they studied the vegetation of Colorado. On the slopes of Pike's Peak they established a place for ecological investigations. This later developed into the Alpine Laboratory under the Carnegie Institution, with Frederic Clements as director in addition to his appointment in 1917 as research associate. Somewhat later Edith's contributions to ecological research were recognized officially by her appointment as field assistant at the Carnegie Institution. Autumn and winter months were spent at headquarters in Washington, D.C., the desert laboratory in Tucson, Arizona, and the coastal laboratory at Santa Barbara, California. She illustrated their publications with original drawings in pen and ink or watercolor. Her expertise as a painter of wildflowers was recognized by *National Geographic* magazine, which published her articles, "Wildflowers of the West" (1927) and "The Flower Pageant of the Midwest" (1939). She coauthored several books with her husband, including *Rocky Mountain Flowers* (1914), *Flowers of Mountain and Plain* (1915), and *Flower Families and Ancestors* (1928). She was the sole author of *Adventures in Ecology: Half a Million Miles from Mud to Macadam* (1960). She was listed in *American Men and Women of Science* as Mrs. Frederic E. Clements until the eleventh edition. In *Women Scientists in America* Margaret Rossiter quoted an anonymous statement that called the couple the most illustrious husband and wife team since the Curies. There is a photograph in the *National Cyclopedia of American Biography*.

Bibliography: Abir-Am, P. G. and Dorinda Outram, eds., *Uneasy Careers and Intimate Lives; American Men and Women of Science* 3–11; Barnhart, John H., *Biographical Notes upon Botanists;* Herzenberg, Caroline L., *Women Scientists from Antiquity to the Present; National Cyclopedia of American Biography; National Union Catalog;* Rossiter, Margaret W., *Women Scientists in America; Who Was Who in America.*

Cohn, Mildred
(1913–)
biochemist

Education: A.B., Hunter College, 1931; A.M., Columbia University, 1932, Ph.D. in chemistry, 1938

Employment: Junior science aide, National Advisory Committee on Aeronautics, 1932–1935; biophysical assistant in isotopes, medical college, George Washington University, 1937–1938; biophysicist, medical college, Cornell University, 1938–1941, research associate, 1941–1946; biochemist, school of medicine, Washington University, St. Louis, 1946–1957, associate professor, 1958–1960; associate professor, medical school, University of Pennsylvania, 1960, professor of biophysics and physical biochemistry, 1960–1978, Benjamin Bush professor, 1978–1982; career investigator, American Heart Association, 1964–1978; emeritus professor

Married: 1938

Mildred Cohn is the only woman who has had a lifetime career as an investigator with the American Heart Association. She was awarded the Garvan Medal in 1963 and was elected to membership in the National Academy of Sciences in 1971. She was awarded the National Medal of Science in 1983. She was a senior member of the Institute for Cancer Research from 1982 to 1985 and was president of the American Society of Biological Chemists in 1978–1979. She was employed continuously in research until 1958, when she was appointed associate professor at Washington University and later at the University of Pennsylvania. Her research has focused on metabolic studies with stable isotopes, mechanisms of enzymatic reactions, and electron spin and nuclear magnetic resonance. She has been a member of several professional societies, including the American Philosophical Society, the American Academy of Arts and Sciences, the American Chemical Society, and the Biophysical Society.

Mildred Cohn published a brief autobiography in *Annual Review of Biophysics and Biomolecular Structure* 21 (1992): 1–24, which includes a photograph. She mentions that, since she and her husband had three children, she found it very convenient to arrange her research around her family responsibilities and activities. This would not have been possible if she were a faculty member. Her name was included in the 1992–1993 edition of *American Men and Women of Science.*

Bibliography: American Men and Women of Science 7–18; Herzenberg, Caroline L., *Women Scientists from Antiquity to the Present*; O'Neill, Lois S., *The Women's Book of World Records and Achievements.*

Colden, Jane
(1724–1766)
botanist

Education: No formal education
Employment: No formal employment
Married: William Farquhar, 1759

*J*ane Colden is recognized as the first woman in the United States to be distinguished as a botanist. Her father was naturalist Cadwalladar Colden, who corresponded with the leading naturalists of his day, including Linnaeus. Taught by her father, she learned to take botanical impressions and to prepare descriptions in English, but she never learned Latin. By 1757 she had prepared a catalog of over 300 local species of flora and had exchanged specimens and seeds with several colonial and European botanists. As her father's interests turned to other subjects, he planned that she would take over his botanical activities, including the correspondence. At the time of few scientific journals, correspondence with other collectors and with university professors was the primary source for data. Jane Colden mastered the Linnaean classification system and published a paper, "Description," in *Essays and Observations, Physical and Literary* of the Edinburgh Philosophical Society 2 (1770): 5–7. Her work never seems to have been accepted on a par with that of her father and other American male botanists. However, Sir Joseph Banks later purchased her manuscript on New York flora; this was deposited in the British Museum, and a portion of it was published in 1963. While her drawings are now considered poor, her descriptions are thought to be thorough and accurate, as if they were taken from living plants. It is not known whether the drawings extant represent her best work. After she married in 1759, there is no indication that she continued her interest in botany. One review of her work was published in "Biographical Notes VIII: Jane Colden and the Flora of New York" by James Britten in *Journal of Botany* 33 (1895): 12–15.

Bibliography: Abir-Am, P. G. and Dorinda Outram, eds., *Uneasy Careers and Intimate Lives;* Bonta, Marcia M., *Women in the Field; Dictionary of American Biography; Dictionary of Scientific Biography;* Herzenberg, Caroline L., *Women Scientists from Antiquity to the Present;* Hollingsworth, Buckner, *Her Garden Was Her Delight;* James, E. T., ed., *Notable American Women 1607–1950;* Kass-Simon, G. and Patricia Farnes, *Women of Science;* Ogilvie, Marilyn B., *Women in Science;* Rossiter, Margaret W., *Women Scientists in America;* Rossiter, Margaret W., "Women Scientists in America before 1920"; Siegel, Patricia J. and Kay Thomas Finley, *Women in the Scientific Search;* Vare, Ethlie Ann and Greg Ptacek, *Mothers of Invention.*

Colson, Elizabeth Florence
(1917–)
anthropologist

Education: A.B., University of Minnesota, 1938, A.M., 1940; A.M., Radcliffe College, 1941, Ph.D. in social anthropology, 1945

Employment: Assistant social science analyst, War Relocation Authority, 1942–1943; research assistant in anthropology, Harvard University, 1944–1945; director, Rhodes-Livingstone Institute of Social Research, Northern Rhodesia, 1947–1951; senior lecturer, social anthropology, Manchester University, England, 1951–1953; associate professor of anthropology, Goucher College, 1954–1955; associate professor, African studies, Boston University, 1955–1959; professor of anthropology, Brandeis University, 1959–1963; visiting professor, Northwestern University, 1963–1964; professor of anthropology, University of California Berkeley, 1964–1984; emeritus professor

*E*lizabeth Colson has investigated social change in central Africa and in the northwest United States, and some of her work seems to be a forerunner of the current work on African Americans. Her research interest has been a longitudinal study of the Gwembe Tonga and Zambia. She was elected to the National Academy of Sciences in 1977. She has had unique appointments as director of an institute in Northern Rhodesia and as a senior lecturer at Manchester University in England. In common with many anthropologists, she has had a variety of jobs in academia, institutes, fellowships, and special projects. She received the Morgan Lectureship at the University of Rochester (1973), the Rivers Memorial Medal of the Royal Anthropological Institute (1982), and the Malinowski lectureship of the Society of Applied Anthropology. She was elected an honorary fellow of the Royal Anthropological Institute, a fellow of the American Anthropological Association, and a fellow of the American Association for the Advancement of Science. She has been a member of the American Association of African Studies, the American Academy of Arts and Sciences, and the Association of Social Anthropologists. She received honorary degrees from Brown University in 1979 and the University of Rochester in 1985. Her name was listed in the 1992–1993 edition of *American Men and Women of Science.*

Bibliography: *American Men and Women of Science* 9–18; Herzenberg, Caroline L., *Women Scientists from Antiquity to the Present*; O'Neill, Lois S., *The Women's Book of World Records and Achievements.*

Comstock, Anna Botsford
(1854–1930)
entomologist and naturalist

Education: B.S., Cornell University, 1885; Cooper Union
Employment: Assistant to husband, 1878–1899; assistant professor, extension department, Cornell University, 1899–1900, lecturer, 1900–1913, assistant professor, 1913–1920, professor, 1920–1922; emeritus professor
Married: John Henry Comstock, 1878

*A*nna Comstock was a leader in the nature study movement at the university level in the early twentieth century. At first she worked only with her husband in his laboratory and provided the diagrams for his lectures. In 1881 she enrolled in Cornell to complete her undergraduate degree, which she had started prior to her marriage. She taught herself wood engraving so she could illustrate her husband's textbooks. In 1888 she was initiated into Sigma Xi, the national honor society of the sciences, for her superior illustrations; she was one of the first four women to be so honored. Her primary contribution was, as part of the nature study movement that began in New York State in 1895, to teach nature study in rural schools. She prepared leaflets for classroom use, lectured before teachers' institutes, and lobbied the State Education Department.

Anna Comstock was the first woman to attain professorial status at Cornell when she was appointed assistant professor in 1899. Due to objections from the trustees on having a female professor, she was demoted to lecturer in 1900, but she was promoted again to assistant professor in 1913 and to professor in 1920. Her major work was *The Handbook of Nature-Study* (1911), which went through 24 editions by 1939; it was reprinted in 1988. She was listed in the first four editions of *American Men and Women of Science* as Mrs. J. H. Comstock. Her photograph was included in Herbert Osborn's *Fragments of Entomological History.*

Bibliography: Abir-Am, P. G. and Dorinda Outram, eds., *Uneasy Careers and Intimate Lives; American Men and Women of Science 1–4;* Bonta, Marcia M., *Women in the Field;* Debus, A. G., ed., *World Who's Who in Science;* Herzenberg, Caroline L., *Women Scientists from Antiquity to the Present;* James, E. T., ed., *Notable American Women 1607–1950;* Kass-Simon, G. and Patricia Farnes, *Women of Science;* McHenry, Robert, ed., *Famous American Women; National Cyclopedia of American Biography; National Union Catalog;* Ogilvie, Marilyn B., *Women in Science;* Osborn, Herbert, *Fragments of Entomological History;* Rossiter, Margaret W., *Women Scientists in America;* Rossiter, Margaret W., "'Women's Work' in Science, 1880–1910";* Siegel, Patricia J. and Kay Thomas Finley, *Women in the Scientific Search.*

Conwell, Esther Marly
(1922–)
physicist

Education: B.A., Brooklyn College, 1942; M.S., University of Rochester, 1945; Ph.D. in physics, University of Chicago, 1948
Employment: Instructor in physics, Brooklyn College, 1946–1951; technical staff, Bell Telephone Laboratories, 1951–1952; engineering specialist, General Telephone and Electronics Laboratory (GTE), 1952–1963, manager of physics department, 1963–1972; principal scientist, Xerox Laboratories, 1972–1980, research fellow, 1980–
Married: Abraham Rothberg, 1945

*E*sther Conwell, a solid-state theorist, has published over 100 papers on the properties of semiconductors. She has headed research departments at both GTE and Xerox. She received the Society of Women Engineers achievement award in 1960 and was elected to both the National Academy of Engineering (in 1980) and the

National Academy of Sciences (in 1990). After a brief tenure as an instructor at Brooklyn College, she has spent her career in corporate research, often at a managerial level. She joined the technical staff at Bell for one year, then moved to GTE, where she rose through the ranks to manager of the physics department. After a year as the Abby Rockefeller Mauze Professor at the Massachusetts Institute of Technology, she served as principal scientist for Xerox from 1972 to 1980, when she was appointed a research fellow. Her papers have been published in leading scientific journals. They describe how semiconductors can be affected by subjecting the substances to outside perturbations like high electric fields. She is the author of *High-Field Transport in Semiconductors* (1967). She has been elected a fellow of the American Physical Society, and she also is a member of the Institute of Electrical and Electronics Engineers. Her research interest has been on quasi i-d conductors. She married in 1945, and the couple had one son, Lewis. Her name was included in the 1992–1993 edition of *American Men and Women of Science.*

Bibliography: *American Men and Women of Science* 8–18; Debus, A. G., ed., *World Who's Who in Science;* Herzenberg, Caroline L., *Women Scientists from Antiquity to the Present;* Kass-Simon, G. and Patricia Farnes, *Women of Science;* O'Neill, Lois S., *The Women's Book of World Records and Achievements.*

Cooley, Jacquelin Smith
(b. 1883)
botanist

Education: A.B., Randolph-Macon College, 1906; M.S., Virginia Polytechnic Institute, 1911; Ph.D., Washington University, St. Louis, 1914
Employment: Assistant plant pathologist, Virginia Experiment Station, 1911–1912; scientific assistant, assistant pathologist, associate pathologist, and senior pathologist, U.S. Department of Agriculture, 1912–1951
Married: 1914

Jacquelin Cooley represents the many women who were able to rise through the ranks in the U.S. Department of Agriculture (USDA) research departments long before many government agencies would hire women scientists as professional employees. In her case she had very good credentials; she received her doctorate after she joined the agency. Apparently the agency was very supportive in allowing employees, including women, time to obtain advanced degrees. The department that employed her was the Bureau of Plant Industry, which later changed its name several times but not its policies. (Although it seems strange that so many women were employed by the USDA, it was the largest single employer of women professionals in the 1920s in the federal government, and it offered the most benefits for women. There were employment possibilities for women botanists in state experiment stations and associated state offices. The same situation existed in the federal government, where data was coming in from states to be verified and classified, as well as the data from federal agricultural regulations.) Jacquelin Cooley was a well-qualified botanist who authored or coauthored at least 12 publications in her career. She was a member of the American Association for the Advancement of Science and the Botanical Society of America.

Bibliography: *American Men and Women of Science* 3–11; Barnhart, John H., *Biographical Notes upon Botanists; National Union Catalog.*

Cori, Gerty Theresa Radnitz
(1896–1957)
biochemist

Education: M.D., German University of Prague, 1920
Employment: Assistant, Karolinen Children's Hospital, 1920–1922; assistant pathologist, Roswell Park Memorial Institute, 1922–1925, assistant biochemist, 1925–1931; research, medical school, Washington University, St. Louis, 1931–1947, professor of biochemistry, 1947–1957
Married: Carl F. Cori, 1920

Gerty Cori was the first American woman to be awarded a Nobel Prize for medicine and physiology in 1947. Her husband, Carl Cori, was one of the cowinners for his work on glycogen. They met while they were both in medical school and were married when she completed her degree. They emigrated to the United States when Carl received an appointment at Roswell Park Memorial Institute in Buffalo. Gerty also received a staff appointment; the two had time to pursue their own research interests in addition to their routine duties. Since their interest was in normal carbohydrate metabolism and its regulation, rather than cancer, he accepted an appointment at Washington University as chair of the department of pharmacology. The university had rules against employing married couples in the same department; Gerty Cori did not have a job, but she collaborated with her husband while receiving a token salary between 1931 and 1947. She did not receive a full professorial appointment until they were awarded the Nobel Prize. She was only the third woman to be a corecipient of the prize in medicine and physiology. The work for which they received the prize was the effect of hormones on the rate of conversion of glycogen to glucose in the overall processes of the body's carbohydrate metabolism. Their laboratory in St. Louis became the focal point for all researchers interested in carbohydrate metabolism. In later work they demonstrated that a human heritable disease can stem from a defect in an enzyme. Gerty Cori first was diagnosed with bone marrow disease in 1947, but she continued to work in spite of extreme pain until she died ten years later. She received the Garvan Medal and was elected to the National Academy of Sciences in 1948. She had one son, Carl T. Her photograph was included in *Chemtech* 6 (1976): 738–743. There are photographs in *Current Biography,* Sharon McGrayne's *Nobel Prize Women in Science, Biographical Memoirs* of the National Academy of Sciences, Olga Opfell's *Lady Laureates,* and G. Kass-Simon's and Patricia Farnes' *Women of Science: ' Biographical Memoirs.*

Bibliography: *American Men and Women of Science* 6–10; Debus, A. G., ed., *World Who's Who in Science; Current Biography; Dictionary of Scientific Biography;* Herzenberg, Caroline L., *Women Scientists from Antiquity to the Present;* Kass-Simon, G. and Patricia Farnes, *Women of Science;* McHenry, Robert, ed., *Famous American Women;* National Academy of Sciences, *Biographical Memoirs;* Opfell, Olga S., *The Lady Laureates;* Perl, Teri, *Math Equals;* Rossiter, Margaret W., *Women Scientists in America;* Sicherman, Barbara et al., *Notable American Women;* Siegel, Patricia J. and Kay Thomas Finley, *Women in the Scientific Search;* Uglow, Jennifer S., *International Dictionary of Women's Biography;* Yost, Edna, *Women of Modern Science.*

Corson, Juliet
(1841–1897)
cooking school educator

Education: No formal education
Employment: Lecturer on cooking, Free Training School for Women and for another charitable group, 1874–1875; owner, New York Cooking School, 1876–1892

Juliet Corson was a pioneer in the cooking school movement. Although she did not have any special background in cooking, she started giving lectures on the subject for several charitable groups and continued lecturing in mission schools and orphanages even while operating her own school. In 1873 the Women's Educational and Industrial Society of New York, of which Miss Corson was a member, opened a Free Training School for Women where subjects such as sewing, bookkeeping, and proofreading were taught. When a cooking class was added in 1874, Miss Corson gave the lectures while a chef cooked. The next year she started cooking classes for another charitable group. In 1876 she opened the New York Cooking School, initially in her own home. She added a course in plain cooking the following year for workingmens' families and to train young women to earn their living as cooks. The school was incorporated in 1878. She wrote a series of pamphlets on inexpensive menus, starting with "Fifteen Cent Dinners for Families of Six" (1877). In addition to numerous articles, she wrote the *New Family Cook Book* (1885), *Miss Corson's Practical American Cookery and Household Management* (1886), and *Family Living on $500 a Year* (1887), the latter of which outlined a complete domestic budget. She retired from teaching in 1892 due to poor health.

Bibliography: James, E. T., ed., *Notable American Women 1607–1950;* McHenry, Robert, ed., *Famous American Women; National Union Catalog;* Shapiro, Laura, *Perfection Salad.*

Cox, Gertrude Mary
(1900–1978)
statistician

Education: B.S. in mathematics, Iowa State University, 1929, M.S. in statistics, 1931; University of California, Berkeley, 1931–1933

Employment: Assistant, statistical laboratory, Iowa State University, 1933–1939, research assistant professor, 1939–1940; professor and head, department of experimental statistics, North Carolina State College, 1940–1944, Institute of Statistics, 1944–1949, department of biostatistics, 1949–1960; head, Research Triangle Institute, statistics research division, 1960–1965; consultant

Gertrude Cox was the prominent woman statistician in the United States during her career. Her forte was the design of experiments, and she utilized each generation of computers as it became available. Her other skill was fund-raising, and she spent her last 11 years at North Carolina State College administering the Institute of Statistics. After she graduated from high school, she spent several years training to become a deaconess in the Methodist Episcopal Church; this training included a period of caring for children in a Montana orphanage. Later she enrolled at Iowa State to obtain a degree in social science, but she switched to mathematics because she enjoyed the courses. She received her B.S. in 1929 and, in 1931, the first master's degree in statistics that was given by Iowa's mathematics department. She studied psychological statistics at Berkeley for two years before returning to Iowa State to assist in the new Statistical Laboratory. She was appointed to the faculty in 1939, but in 1940 she left to accept the newly created position of head of the department of experimental statistics at North Carolina State. She obtained sizable grants for a program in statistics and later organized the department of experimental statistics, with programs in training and consulting. In 1945 she organized and became director of the Institute of Statistics, which combined the teaching of statistics at the University of North Carolina and at North Carolina State. Although the institute originally was funded by General Education Board grants, she obtained funds from the Rockefeller Foundation to support a program in statistical genetics and one from the Ford Foundation for a joint program in dynamic economics with the London School of Economics. She was instrumental in establishing strong statistical programs throughout the South. In 1960 she was appointed head of the Statistics Section of the Research Triangle Institute at Durham, North Carolina, from which position she retired in 1965. After her retirement she consulted for government agencies, trade associations, and other groups. She was the coauthor of *Experimental Designs* (1950) and was editor of the journal *Biometrics* from 1945 to 1955. She was president of the American Statistical Association in 1956 and of the Biometric Society in 1968–1969. She was one of the founders of the latter. She received many awards during her career, including election to the National Academy of Sciences in 1975 and selection for an honorary degree from Iowa State in 1958. Cox Hall at North Carolina State was named in her honor in 1970, and in 1977 a Gertrude M. Cox Fellowship Fund was established for outstanding graduate students in statistics. Her photograph and list of publications were included in the *Biographical Memoirs* of the National Academy of Sciences.

Bibliography: Grinstein, Louise S. and Paul J. Campbell, eds., *Women of*

Mathematics; Herzenberg, Caroline L., *Women Scientists from Antiquity to the Present;* National Academy of Sciences, *Biographical Memoirs; National Union Catalog;* O'Neill, Lois S., *The Women's Book of World Records and Achievements.*

Crosby, Elizabeth Caroline
(b. 1888)
anatomist

Education: B.S., Adrian College, 1910; M.S., University of Chicago, 1912, Ph.D. 1915
Employment: Principal and school superintendent, 1915–1920; instructor in anatomy, University of Michigan, 1920–1926, assistant professor, 1926–1929, associate professor, 1929–1936, professor of anatomy and consulting neurosurgeon, 1936–1960; emeritus professor

*E*lizabeth Crosby was recognized as one of the leading anatomists of her time by receiving a star in the seventh edition of *American Men and Women of Science.* After completing her doctorate at the University of Chicago, she worked as a public school administrator in Michigan before receiving an appointment as instructor at the University of Michigan. There she rose steadily through the ranks to professor in 1936. This was a significant accomplishment because she did not have a medical degree. (In academic circles there is much discussion on the relative quality of the doctor of philosophy degree and the medical degree.) In 1958 she received an honorary M.D. from the University of Groningen in the Netherlands. She presented many distinguished lectureships at the University of Pittsburgh, Yale University, Mayo Clinic, Tulane University, and Emory University. After her retirement, she was an emeritus professor at the University of Alabama. She received the Galen Award in 1956 for preclinical medical teaching. She coauthored several books: *The Comparative Anatomy of the Nervous System* (1936), *Correlative Neurosurgery* (1955), and *The Correlative Anatomy of the Nervous System* (1962). She received several awards in recognition for her studies on the comparative neurology of vertebrates. She received honorary degrees from six universities, including Smith College (1968), Woman's Medical College of Pennsylvania (1968), and the University of Michigan (1970). Although she did not marry, she had a foster daughter, Kathleen.

Bibliography: *American Men and Women of Science* 5–12; Debus, A. G., ed., *World Who's Who in Science;* Herzenberg, Caroline L., *Women Scientists from Antiquity to the Present;* Rossiter, Margaret W., *Women Scientists in America;* Siegel, Patricia J. and Kay Thomas Finley, *Women in the Scientific Search;* Visher, Stephen S., *Scientists Starred 1903–1943 in "American Men of Science.";* Who Was Who in America.

Cummings, Clara Eaton
(1855–1906)
cryptogamic botanist

Education: Wellesley College, 1876–1878; University of Zurich, 1887
Employment: Curator of botanical museum, Wellesley College, 1878–1879, instructor in botany, 1879–1887, associate professor of cryptogamic botany, 1887–1903; Hunnewell Professor of Cryptogamic Botany, 1903–1906

Clara Cummings was recognized as a specialist in cryptogamic (spore-producing) flora, and her name was included in the first edition of *American Men and Women of Science.* She entered Wellesley in 1876, the second class after it opened, and attended the school until 1878. She did not obtain a degree, but she remained associated with the botany department throughout her career, first as curator of the botanical museum (1878–1879) and then as instructor in botany (1879–1887). After a period of study in Zurich, she returned to the college as associate professor of cryptogamic botany, a position she held from 1887 to 1903. In 1903 she was appointed Hunnewell Professor of Cryptogamic Botany in recognition of the specialized work in which she had reached distinction. She was recognized for her work on the lichens of Alaska and Labrador, which represents important additions to the systematics of that group. She was the chief editor of "Decades of North American Lichens" and

of "Lichens Boreali." With the latter, she initiated a system of distributing dried specimens of plants among collectors. She was associate editor of the journal *Plant World,* and she served as vice president in 1904 of the Society for Plant Morphology and Physiology. She was the author of *Catalogue of Musci and Hepaticae of North America, North of Mexico* (1885), which covers mosses and liverworts. She was elected a fellow of the American Association for the Advancement of Science.

Bibliography: Abir-Am, P. G. and Dorinda Outram, eds., *Uneasy Careers and Intimate Lives; American Men and Women of Science* 1; Barnhart, John H., *Biographical Notes upon Botanists;* Barr, Ernest S., *An Index to Biographical Fragments in Unspecialized Scientific Journals;* Herzenberg, Caroline L., *Women Scientists from Antiquity to the Present;* Mozans, H. J., *Women in Science; National Union Catalog;* Ogilvie, Marilyn B., *Women in Science;* Rossiter, Margaret W., *Women Scientists in America;* Rudolph,

Emanuel D., "Women in Nineteenth Century American Botany"; Siegel,

Patricia J. and Kay Thomas Finley, *Women in the Scientific Search.*

Cunningham, Susan
(1842–1921)
astronomer

Education: Vassar College, 1866–1867; Harvard University, 1874, 1876; Princeton University, 1881; Cambridge University, 1877–1879, 1882, 1887; Williams College, 1883–1884

Employment: Instructor of mathematics, Swarthmore College, 1869–1872, assistant professor, 1872–1874, professor of mathematics and astronomy, 1874–1906; emeritus professor

Susan Cunningham was recognized for her work as director of the Swarthmore Observatory, and her name was included in the first three editions of *American Men and Women of Science.* After attending Vassar for two years, she joined the staff at Swarthmore as an instructor and rose to professor of mathematics and astronomy. Although she did not receive a formal academic degree, she spent 20 summers at a succession of schools to increase and keep current her knowledge of mathematics and astronomy. It may seem strange that she did not complete a degree in 30 years of teaching, but this was not an unusual situation. Women's colleges did not hold formal classes during summer; the only way to complete a degree was to take a leave of absence to enroll as a regular student. In the early years it was common for people to enroll in specific lectures or laboratories both here and abroad; this was especially true for people in astronomy, since most training was given at observatories rather than colleges. At the time of her retirement, Susan Cunningham was the only faculty member who had served Swarthmore College since its founding. Swarthmore awarded her an honorary doctorate in 1888. She was a member of the Astronomical Society of the Pacific and the British Astronomical Association.

Bibliography: *American Men and Women of Science* 1–3; Davis, Herman S., "Women Astronomers (1750–1890)"; Herzenberg, Caroline L., *Women Scientists from Antiquity to the Present*; Mozans, H. J., *Women in Science*; Rossiter, Margaret W., *Women Scientists in America*; Siegel, Patricia J. and Kay Thomas Finley, *Women in the Scientific Search.*

Gertrude Crotty Davenport
Adelle Davis
Olive Griffith Stull Davis
Dorothy Day
Mary Anna Day
Frederica Annis DeLaguna
Freda Detmers
Lydia Marie Adams DeWitt
Gladys Rowena Henry Dick
Mary Cynthia Dickerson
Helen Walter Dodson
Nellie Blanchan De Graff Doubleday
June Etta Downey
Katherine Dunham

Davenport, Gertrude Crotty
(1866–1946)
zoologist

Education: B.S., University of Kansas, 1889; Radcliffe College, 1892–1894
Employment: Instructor in zoology, University of Kansas, 1889–1892; microscopic methods, biological laboratory, Cold Spring Harbor Laboratory, 1898–1903
Married: Charles B. Davenport, 1894

Gertrude Davenport was representative of the many wives who assisted their husbands in their research. Both she and her husband were included in the first edition of *American Men of Science*. In eight editions she was listed as either Mrs. C. B. Davenport or Mrs. Charles B. Davenport, according to the convention of the day. She does not seem to have been employed officially after 1903, but she generally was recognized as a significant contributor to her husband's work. Margaret Rossiter, in *Women Scientists in America*, lists them as one of the notable couples in science before 1940. Gertrude Davenport was educated at the University of Kansas and studied at Radcliffe until she married in 1894. After her husband was appointed director of the Carnegie Station for Experimental Evolution at Cold Spring Harbor, New York, she worked on microscopic methods in the biological laboratory and served on the women's auxiliary board. She was a member of the American Society of Zoologists, of which her husband was president in 1907 and 1929. As the other biographies indicate, many of the wives of researchers were in charge of recording data, preparing illustrations, and preparing manuscripts for publication as well as serving as unpaid lab assistants. Gertrude Davenport listed her own research as embryology of the turtle, variation in Sargartia and starfish, variations in organisms, and heredity in humans. Her husband's research was in experimental evolution.

Bibliography: American Men and Women of Science 1–8; Herzenberg, Caroline L., *Women Scientists from Antiquity to the Present;* Rossiter, Margaret W., *Women Scientists in America;* Rossiter, Margaret W., "Women Scientists in America before 1920"; Siegel, Patricia J. and Kay Thomas Finley, *Women in the Scientific Search.*

Davis, Adelle
(1904–1974)
writer and lecturer on food and health

Education: Purdue University, 1923–1925; B.A. in household science, University of California, Berkeley, 1927; M.S. in biochemistry, University of Southern California, 1939
Employment: Supervisor of nutrition, Yonkers public schools, 1928–1930; private consulting practice in nutrition, 1931–1958
Married: George E. Leisey, 1946, divorced 1953; Frank V. Sieglinger, 1960

*A*delle Davis was a food guru in the late 1960s and was considered the country's foremost crusader for good nutrition in the 1970s. She contributed to the health food movement that thrived on publicity about pesticide residues and food additives. She advocated for many years the use of organic fruits and vegetables, whole wheat bread, milk, wheat germ, brewer's yeast, and other nutritious foods. It was not until the emergence of the natural foods movement and consumerism in the 1970s that she became a celebrity on the lecture circuit and on television talk shows. Although she had a solid background in nutrition, her books were marred by incorrect citations to the scientific literature and lack of evidence to support her sometimes dangerous advice. She wrote a number of books, four of which were popular and sold millions of copies. These were *Let's Cook It Right* (1947), *Let's Have Healthy Children* (1951), *Let's Eat Right To Keep Fit* (1954), and *Let's Get Well* (1965). Some examples of theories for which she was criticized were her recommendations of massive daily doses of vitamins A, D, and E; her assertion that magnesium offered useful treatment for epilepsy; her assertion that a mother's drinking skim milk during pregnancy might lead to the development of cataracts in her baby; and her criticism of the pasteurization of milk. During the 1969 White House Conference on Food, Nutrition, and Health, the panel on deception and misinformation named Adelle Davis probably the nation's most harmful single source of false nutrition information. She had such a solid following by the popular media that criticism by scientific nutritionists had little effect on her reputation.

She was born Daisie Adelle Davis, but she later dropped her first name. After receiving her degree from Berkeley, she took additional instruction at Bellevue and Fordham hospitals in New York and supervised nutrition in the Yonkers, New York, public schools. She attended Teachers' College, Columbia University, for further postgraduate education but left before the school term was over to travel to Europe. She returned to California, where she worked as a consulting nutritionist in several clinics. While completing her degree in biochemistry, she began building up her private consulting practice. She turned to writing books for the general public in order to obtain a wider distribution of her theories. By 1958 she gave up her private consulting practice to concentrate on writing and lecturing. Other books she wrote include *Vitality through Planned Nutrition* (1942) and *Exploring Inner Space* (1961). She received an honorary degree from Plano University in 1972. She had two adopted children, George and Barbara Leisey. Her photograph was published in *Current Biography.*

Bibliography: Current Biography; National Union Catalog; Sicherman, Barbara et al., Notable American Women.

Davis, Olive Griffith Stull
(b. 1905)
herpetologist

Education: A.B., Smith College, 1926; A.M., University of Michigan, 1928, Ph.D. in herpetology, 1929
Employment: Teaching fellow, Syracuse University, 1926–1927; professor of biology, Virginia State Teachers College, Fredericksburg, 1929–1930; National Research Council fellow, Museum of Comparative Zoology, Harvard University, 1930–1931; technician,

Purdue University, 1943, assistant, 1943–1953, assistant professor of veterinary anatomy, histology, and embryology, 1953–1961, associate professor of veterinary anatomy, 1961–?; agent for poultry pathology, Bureau of Animal Industry, U.S. Department of Agriculture, 1943–1950
Married: Loy E. Davis, 1930

*O*live Davis was one of the few women who could be identified as working in veterinary medicine at the college level in the 1950s. Women were not admitted to veterinary science programs in numbers until the 1960s. Probably the increased emphasis in veterinary work on household pets brought more women into the profession, or at least it convinced college administrators that jobs were available for women.

Olive Davis was educated as a herpetologist and was a fellow in the zoology museums at the Universities of Michigan and Harvard. It is surprising that she was promoted to assistant professor at Purdue University as early as 1953. She also was employed by the U.S. Department of Agriculture (USDA) as an agent for poultry pathology. She was a member of the American Society of Ichthyologists and Herpetologists, the Association of Veterinary Anatomists, and the World Association of Veterinary Anatomists. She listed her research interests as the taxonomy, physiology, and distribution of snakes; poultry pathology; avian leukosis; and cancer research. She was listed as Olive Stull in the fifth, sixth, and seventh editions of *American Men and Women of Science,* but as Olive Davis in the later editions.

Bibliography: American Men and Women of Science 5–11.

Day, Dorothy
(b. 1896)
plant physiologist

Education: A.B., Wellesley College, 1919; M.S., University of Wisconsin, 1925, Ph.D. in plant physiology, 1927; University of Chicago, 1929; Cornell University, 1942–1943
Employment: Instructor in botany and bacteriology, Hood College, 1921–1924; assistant instructor in botany, University of Wisconsin, 1924–1926; instructor in botany and bacteriology, Mills College, 1927–1928, assistant professor, 1928–1929; assistant professor of botany, Smith College, 1929–1937, associate professor, 1937–1942; assistant, Cornell University, 1942–1943; plant physiologist, California Central Fibre Corporation, 1943–1944; research associate, University of Minnesota, 1944–1946; microbiologist, biological laboratories, Quartermaster Corps, 1946–1949; mycologist, industrial testing laboratory, Naval Shipyard, Philadelphia, 1949; associate professor of biology, MacMurray College, 1950–1952; microbiological consultant, Alaska Research Laboratories, 1952–1954; professional associate, Bio-Sci Information Exchange, 1954–1955; teacher, public schools, 1955–1957; lecturer in biology, Westminster College, 1957–1958; visiting professor of botany, Brigham Young University, 1958 and 1960

Dorothy Day had an intriguing career that encompassed academe, government agencies, and corporations. She held many jobs during her career. After serving on the faculty of Smith College for about 12 years, she averaged about 2 years at each of the succeeding positions she held. Some of the variety in her employment could be attributed to the opportunities for women scientists that opened during World War II. She taught at Hood, Mills, Smith, Cornell, MacMurray, Westminster, and Brigham Young. Among the more intriguing assignments were jobs as a microbiologist for the Quartermaster Corps and as a mycologist for the Philadelphia Naval Shipyard. She served as a microbiological consultant for the Alaska Research Laboratories before working for an information service, the Bio-Sci Information Exchange. She taught public school for a few years before returning to college teaching. She was a member of the American Association for the Advancement of Science, the Botanical Society of America, the American Society of Plant Physiologists, and the Society for Industrial Microbiology. Her research interests were plant physiology, nutrition, and tissue culture.

Bibliography: *American Men and Women of Science* 7–11.

Day, Mary Anna
(1852–1924)
librarian

Education: Academy of Lancaster, Massachusetts
Employment: Public school teacher, 1871–1880; public librarian, 1887–1892; librarian, Gray Herbarium of Harvard University, 1893–1924

Mary Day's contribution to science was that she compiled a massive bibliography on the subject of botany and she edited the publications of the Gray Herbarium for 30 years. Although she did not have a background in science, she was employed as the librarian of the Gray Herbarium of Harvard University. After teaching school for ten years and working as a public librarian for six years, she wrote to the librarian of Harvard University inquiring whether a position was open. The librarian for the Herbarium had moved to another library, and Mary Day accepted the position in 1893. Her first assignment was to verify some 5,000 bibliographical references for the supplement to the *Synoptical Flora of North America.* After that introduction to the literature, she became expert in botanical bibliography. For about 20 years she edited and compiled the *Card Index of the Genera, Species, and Varieties of American Plants,* a publication issued in the form of cards that were distributed to about 18 subscribers throughout the world. The first 20 issues (1894–1903) were prepared by the library of the U.S. Department of Agriculture, and Mary Day continued to issue it for another 20 years. The index was brought out in quarterly issues consisting of 1,000 to 2,500 cards each; this was a massive undertaking involving indexing more than 130 scientific serials and monographs published worldwide in several languages. She was involved in the editorial work on the majority of contributions from the Herbarium that appeared during a 30-year period. She prepared and published for the New England Botanical Club a "List of

Local Floras of New England" and "Herbariums of New England." For many years she prepared the index for the journal *Rhodora*. Her biography and photograph were included in *Rhodora* 26 (1924): 41–47.

Bibliography: Barnhart, John H., *Biographical Notes upon Botanists*; Herzenberg, Caroline L., *Women Scientists from Antiquity to the Present*; Rossiter, Margaret W., *Women Scientists in America*.

DeLaguna, Frederica Annis
(b. 1906)
anthropologist

Education: B.A., Bryn Mawr College, 1927; Ph.D. in anthropology, Columbia University, 1933

Employment: Assistant, American section, University of Pennsylvania Museum, 1931–1934; associate soil conservationist, Pima Reservation, U.S. Department of Agriculture, 1935–1936; lecturer, Bryn Mawr College, 1938–1941, assistant professor, 1941–1942, associate professor, 1942–1949, professor, 1949–1975; emeritus professor

Concurrent Position: Research associate, University of Pennsylvania Museum, 1935

*F*rederica DeLaguna's major accomplishment was that she led the first survey to the Pacific Eskimo cultures. In 1929, soon after receiving her undergraduate degree, she participated as an assistant in Eskimo archaeology in an expedition to Greenland sponsored by the Danish government. This was the beginning of a long career involving trips to the Arctic regions to study the people there. Throughout the 1930s Frederica DeLaguna led anthropological expeditions to Alaska and the Yukon, primarily for the University of Pennsylvania Museum, as an expert on Eskimo and Paleolithic art. She joined the faculty of Bryn Mawr College in 1938, rising to the rank of professor. She had a concurrent appointment as a research associate of the University of Pennsylvania Museum starting in 1935. She was one of the first fellows of the Arctic Institute of North America, and she was elected to membership in the National Academy of Sciences in 1975. Grants are a major source for funding archaeological projects, and

Frederica DeLaguna was proficient in securing funding from the Rockefeller Foundation, the Viking Fund, Inc., and the Danish government, among other sources. She served as a lieutenant commander in the U.S. Naval Reserve from 1942 to 1945. Her experience in the Arctic region was invaluable during World War II, since most exploration had been conducted by the Danes and Norwegians. When Greenland and Alaska became strategic points in protecting mainland North America, her data and observations could be used by the American and Canadian armed forces. Her areas of research were archaeology and ethnology of North America.

Bibliography: *American Men and Women of Science* 5–13; Debus, A. G., ed., *World Who's Who in Science*; Herzenberg, Caroline L., *Women Scientists from Antiquity to the Present*; *International Directory of Anthropologists*; O'Neill, Lois S., *The Women's Book of World Records and Achievements*.

Detmers, Freda
(1867–1934)
plant pathologist

Education: B.S., Ohio State University, 1887, M.S., 1891, Ph.D., 1912
Employment: Assistant botanist, Ohio Experiment Station, 1890–1893; instructor in botany, Ohio State University, 1907–1914, assistant professor, 1914–1918, assistant botanist, experiment station, 1918–1923, systematist, 1923–1929; curator, herbarium in the botany department, University of Southern California, 1929–1934

Freda Detmers was among the first women scientists identified as being employed by a state experiment station before securing a position as a faculty member. After receiving her undergraduate degree from Ohio State, she was an assistant botanist on the staff of the Ohio Experiment Station for three years while she was studying for her master's degree. After an interval of several years she was hired in 1907 as an instructor of botany at Ohio State, being promoted to assistant professor seven years later. Although she had meanwhile completed her doctorate, she returned to the staff of the Experiment Station as an assistant botanist, rising to the position of systematist in 1923. She left Ohio State in 1929 for an appointment as the curator of the herbarium in the botany department of the University of Southern California. Her career was fairly typical for women botanists of that period. Many were hired to handle the routine analyses in state experiment stations. Few were able to secure a position on the faculty of land grant institutions, and few women faculty members at any academic institution were able to rise above the rank of assistant professor. (There seemed to be an unwritten rule that women could teach only as lecturers, instructors, or assistant professors.) Freda Detmers listed her research interests as general taxonomic work and weed control, which would indicate fairly routine work conducted in an analytical laboratory. She was listed in two sources as Frederica Detmers.

Bibliography: American Men and Women of Science 3–6; Barnhart, John H., *Biographical Notes upon Botanists;* Herzenberg, Caroline L., *Women Scientists from Antiquity to the Present; National Union Catalog;* Rossiter, Margaret W., *Women Scientists in America.*

DeWitt, Lydia Marie Adams
(1859–1928)
pathologist

Education: Michigan State Normal School, 1896; University of Michigan, 1895–1898, M.D., 1898, B.S., 1899; University of Berlin, 1906
Employment: Schoolteacher, 1878–1894; demonstrator in anatomy, University of Michigan, 1896–1897, assistant in histology, 1898–1902, instructor, 1902–1910; pathologist, Washington University, St. Louis, 1910–1912; instructor in pathology, University of

Berlin, 1908–1910; assistant professor, University of Chicago, 1912–1918, associate professor, 1918–1928

Concurrent Position: Assistant city pathologist and bacteriologist, St. Louis Department of Health, 1910–1912

Married: Alton D. DeWitt, 1878, died 1921

Lydia DeWitt was known for her pioneering studies in the chemotherapy of tuberculosis. Her name was starred in the first three editions of *American Men and Women of Science*. She was included in a study of 25 outstanding American anatomists conducted by Stephen Visher in 1903; there were only two women anatomists in the study. Following the pattern of many women of her generation, Lydia DeWitt taught school for about 17 years before she studied at a normal school and then received a medical degree at age 40. Her husband also was a teacher, and he held positions as superintendent in several school systems. She had demonstrated skill in research while obtaining her medical education, and she spent the next 11 years working in the areas of anatomy, histology, and pathology. She founded the Women's Research Club at the University of Michigan in 1902 after she was denied membership in men's scientific clubs. While she was employed in St. Louis, she served as assistant city pathologist and bacteriologist in the St. Louis Department of Health. She was coauthor of several publications on improved bacteriological procedures in public health practice. She was invited to join the Sprague Memorial Institute at the University of Chicago in 1912. Here she examined the effects of dyes linked to such metals as copper, gold, and mercury on tuberculosis. Her experiments in using dyes such as trypan red, methylene blue, and basic fuchsin to treat tuberculosis were not successful, but the meticulous methods she reported in a series of scientific papers on "The Biochemistry and Chemotherapy of Tuberculosis" served as a model for later experimenters who treated the disease with quite different chemical agents. She received an honorary degree from the University of Michigan in 1914, and she was elected president of the Chicago Pathological Society for 1924–1925. She was also a member of the American Medical Association, the American Association of Pathologists, and the American Society of Tuberculosis. She and her husband separated about the time she received her medical degree; they had two children, Clyde and Stella. Her photograph was included in the *National Cyclopedia of American Biography*.

Bibliography: *American Men and Women of Science* 1–4; Hall, Diana Long, "Academics, Bluestockings, and Biologists"; Herzenberg, Caroline L., *Women Scientists from Antiquity to the Present*; James, E. T., ed., *Notable American Women 1607–1950*; *National Cyclopedia of American Biography*; Ogilvie, Marilyn B., *Women in Science*; Rossiter, Margaret W., *Women Scientists in America*; Siegel, Patricia J. and Kay Thomas Finley, *Women in the Scientific Search*; Visher, Stephen S., *Scientists Starred 1903–1943 in "American Men of Science."*

Dick, Gladys Rowena Henry
(1881–1963)
microbiologist and physician

Education: B.S., University of Nebraska, 1900; M.D., Johns Hopkins University, 1907; University of Berlin, 1910
Employment: Schoolteacher, 1900–1901; physician, 1907–1909; researcher, University of Chicago, 1911–1953
Married: George F. Dick, 1914

Gladys Dick and her husband were celebrated for their joint research on the prevention and treatment of scarlet fever. In 1923 they proved that the hemolytic streptococci was the causative agent. They developed the Dick test, a skin test to indicate susceptibility to or immunity from scarlet fever. The test involved injection of a solution into the arm; development of a local redness of the skin indicated susceptibility. The test also was applied to pregnant women as an indication of the likelihood of their developing puerperal infection.

After she received her undergraduate degree in 1900, Gladys Dick spent three years persuading her mother to allow her to enroll in medical school. She taught high school biology for one year and enrolled in graduate courses at the University of Nebraska. During her internship at Johns Hopkins, she was involved in research on experimental cardiac surgery and blood chemistry. She met her future husband and collaborator while working at the University of Chicago. After a short time in private practice as a physician, she joined her husband at the McCormick Memorial Institute for Infectious Diseases. At that time scarlet fever was endemic to North America and Europe; it struck children, causing crippling complications and a mortality rate of up to 25 percent. The couple took the unprecedented action of patenting their methods of toxin and antitoxin preparation in order to protect the quality of the preparations. In the late 1920s they won a lengthy lawsuit against one company for patent infringement and improper toxin manufacture. The antibiotics that were developed during World War II superseded the use of their test; however, the significance of their research cannot be overlooked even today. They were contenders for the Nobel Prize in medicine in 1925, but no prize was awarded that year. She and her husband received the Cameron Prize of the University of Edinburgh in 1933 and the Mickel Prize from the University of Toronto in 1926. Gladys Dick's later research involved polio. She was coauthor of the book *Scarlet Fever* (1938). She received an honorary degree from the University of Nebraska in 1925 and from Northwestern University in 1928. When she was 49 years old she and her husband adopted two children, Roger and Rowena. Her photograph was included in the *National Cyclopedia of American Biography.*

Bibliography: Herzenberg, Caroline L., *Women Scientists from Antiquity to the Present; National Cyclopedia of American Biography;* O'Hern, Elizabeth M., "Women Scientists in Microbiology"; O'Neill, Lois S., *The Women's Book of World Records and Achievements;* Rossiter, Margaret W., *Women Scientists in America;* Sicherman, Barbara et al., *Notable American Women;* Siegel, Patricia J. and Kay Thomas Finley, *Women in the Scientific Search.*

Dickerson, Mary Cynthia
(1866–1923)
zoologist

Education: University of Michigan, 1886–1891; Woods Hole Biological Laboratory, 1894, 1897–1898, 1905–1906; B.S., University of Chicago, 1897

Employment: High school biology teacher, 1891–1895; head of department of zoology and botany, Normal School, Providence, Rhode Island, 1897–1905; instructor in zoology, Stanford University, 1907–1908; curator in department of woods and forestry, American Museum of Natural History, 1908–1910, assistant curator and curator of herpetology, 1910–1923

Mary Dickerson's contribution to science was in editing major publications aimed at the general public that were issued by the American Museum of Natural History. Her career followed the pattern of many women of her generation. After attending the University of Michigan, she taught high school biology for a time. Receiving her undergraduate degree from the University of Chicago and attending sessions at Woods Hole qualified her for a position as head of the department of zoology and botany at the Normal School and later at Stanford. She joined the staff of the American Museum of Natural History as a curator and later became editor of their journals *American Museum Journal* and *Natural History*. (The positions of curator in museums and herbaria were often choice jobs for women scientists. They probably were rated above that of teaching because they presented opportunities to publish and to participate in expeditions.) She wrote two books: *Moths and Butterflies* (1901) and *The Frog Book: North American Toads and Frogs* (1906). She was elected a fellow of the New York Academy of Sciences and was a member of several other professional societies. Her research centered on the morphology, ecology, and life histories of amphibians and reptiles.

Bibliography: *American Men and Women of Science* 2–3; *National Union Catalog.*

Dodson, Helen Walter
(b. 1905)
solar astronomer

Education: A.B., Goucher College, 1927; A.M., University of Michigan, 1932, Ph.D. in astronomy, 1934

Employment: Assistant statistician, State Department of Education, Maryland, 1927–1931; instructor in astronomy, Wellesley College, 1933–1937, assistant professor, 1937–1945; associate professor of astronomy and mathematics, Goucher College, 1945–1950; astronomer, McMath-Hulbert Observatory, University of Michigan, 1949–1957, professor of astronomy and associate director, 1957–?

Concurrent Position: Staff member, Paris Observatory and Radiation Laboratory, Massachusetts Institute of Technology, 1943–1945

Married: Edmond L. Prince, 1956

Helen Dodson spent 50 years observing solar activity, particularly the outbreak of solar flares. After working for five years as an assistant statistician for a Maryland state agency, she returned to college to earn her doctorate in astronomy. She was on the astronomy faculty of Wellesley and then Goucher before joining the staff of the McMath-Hulbert Observatory at the University of Michigan. She was appointed professor of astronomy and associate director of the observatory in 1957. She held joint appointments with the Paris Observatory and with the Radiation Laboratory, Massachusetts Institute of Technology. She spent the summers of 1934 and 1935 as an assistant astronomer at the Maria Mitchell Observatory in Nantucket, Massachusetts. She received an honorary degree from Goucher College in 1952. Among her awards was the Annie Jump Cannon Prize of the American Astronomical Society (1954). She was elected a fellow of the American Astronomical Society and held memberships in the American Association for the Advancement of Science and the American Geophysical Union. Although she was not associated with glamorous observatories such as Yale or Harvard, she made a solid contribution in solar research. She was able to work in her major field of astronomy continuously after receiving her doctorate, an accomplishment many women scientists have been unable to realize. Her research interests were solar physics, especially solar prominences and flares; solar radio astronomy; and solar terrestrial relationships. She was listed in some sources as Helen Prince.

Bibliography: *American Men and Women of Science* 6–13; Debus, A. G., ed., *World Who's Who in Science;* Herzenberg, Caroline L., *Women Scientists from Antiquity to the Present;* O'Neill, Lois S., *The Women's Book of World Records and Achievements.*

Doubleday, Nellie Blanchan De Graff
(1865–1918)
nature writer

Education: Private schools
Employment: No formal employment
Married: Frank N. Doubleday, 1886

Nellie Doubleday was one of the women authors who wrote popular treatments of scientific subjects for the general public. Her books were immensely popular during her lifetime. She used the pseudonym Neltje Blanchan for her nature books, which were published by her husband's company, Doubleday, Doran & Company. She became interested in writing after her marriage to Frank Doubleday, who was manager of *Scribner's Magazine* before founding his own publishing company. She wrote *The Piegan Indians* (1889), concerning a Blackfoot tribe of the northern plains, before turning to nature writing. First she wrote two books on birds: *Bird Neighbors* (1897) and *Birds That Hunt and Are Hunted* (1898). Both were attractively bound and contained numerous colored photographs of mounted birds, but they reflect some unusual attitudes of the time, such as the need to kill certain species of hawks. Next she wrote two flower books: *Nature's Garden* (1900), a volume on wildflowers, and *The American Flower Garden* (1909), on designing and maintaining various types of gardens. In 1917 she compiled sections from her previous books as *Birds Worth Knowing* and included 48 color plates. She was considered one of the notable women writers on birds, and she was listed in the first two editions of *American Men and Women of Science* (as Mrs. F. N. Doubleday). The Doubledays were shocked when they read the proofs of Theodore Dreiser's first novel, *Sister Carrie* (1900). The firm brought out a small printing with no advertising, and fewer than 500 copies were sold. In later life Dreiser blamed Nellie Doubleday as the person responsible for suppressing the printing. She died in Canton, China, while she and her husband were on a special mission for the Red Cross. The couple had three children: Felix, Nelson, and Dorothy.

Bibliography: *American Men and Women of Science* 1–2; Barnhart, John H., *Biographical Notes upon Botanists;* Herzenberg, Caroline L., *Women Scientists from Antiquity to the Present;* James, E. T., ed., *Notable American Women 1607–1950; National Cyclopedia of American Biography; National Union Catalog;* Siegel, Patricia J. and Kay Thomas Finley, *Women in the Scientific Search.*

Downey, June Etta
(1875–1932)
psychologist

Education: B.A., University of Wyoming, 1895; M.A. in philosophy and psychology, University of Chicago, 1898, Ph.D. in psychology, 1907
Employment: Instructor in English and philosophy, University of Wyoming, 1898–1905, professor of English and philosophy, 1905–1915, professor of philosophy and psychology, 1915–1932, department head, 1907–1932

June Downey was the first woman to head a department of psychology in a state university, and she was honored for her development of the Individual Will-Temperament Test in personality testing. She spent her entire career at the University of Wyoming and contributed to the growth and development of that school by serving on important university committees. In 1915 June Downey was one of the few faculty members in the school who had a doctorate and was engaged in research. She was principal of the Department of University Extension from 1908 to 1916, and she chaired the graduate committee for many years. She came from a pioneer Wyoming family. Her father was one of the founders of the university, and he was president of the board of regents. After she received her undergraduate degree, she taught public school for one year before attending the University of Chicago, where she received her master's degree in philosophy and psychology. She taught English and philosophy upon her return to Wyoming. Her interest in psychology was sparked during a 1901 summer session at Cornell, where she first observed experimental procedures. She was not associated with a particular school of psychological thought. She had many interests in research, but she was known for her work on the analysis of personality through handwriting. This involved studies of automatic phenomena, muscle reading, the reading and writing of mirror script, writing under distraction, the retention of writing skill after lapse of practice, handwriting disguise, and pen lapses.

These studies resulted in development of the Individual Will-Temperament Test with which her name is associated. The test does not result in a total score; the scores are plotted on a graph, resulting in a "will-profile" for each case. The work is summarized in the books *Graphology and Psychology of Handwriting* (1919) and *The Will-Temperament and Its Testing* (1924). Among her other interests were creativity, voluntary and involuntary motor controls, imagery, and esthetics. Her work earned her international recognition. The university had few graduate students at the time, but she was able to secure the enthusiastic assistance of undergrads in conducting her research. She was one of the first women elected to the Society of Experimentalists, a select group of 50 eminent psychologists, and her name was starred in the fourth edition of *American Men and Women of Science.* Among her honors were membership on the council of the American Psychological Association (1923–1925) and election as a fellow of the American Association for the Advancement of Science. She published 7 books and about 70 scholarly papers plus 29 literary books and articles. Her literary publications included short stories, poems, and plays. She wrote the song "Alma Mater" for the university in 1898. A biography with bibliography and photograph were published in the *Journal of General Psychology* 9 (1933): 351–364.

Bibliography: *American Men and Women of Science* 4; Bryan, Alice I. and Edwin G. Boring, "Women in American

Psychology"; Herzenberg, Caroline L., *Women Scientists from Antiquity to the Present*; James, E. T., ed., *Notable American Women 1607–1950*; McHenry, Robert, ed., *Famous American Women*; Ogilvie, Marilyn B., *Women in Science*; Rossiter, Margaret W., *Women Scientists in America*; Siegel, Patricia J. and Kay Thomas Finley, *Women in the Scientific Search*; Visher, Stephen S., *Scientists Starred 1903–1943 in "American Men of Science."*

Dunham, Katherine
(1909–)
anthropologist

Education: B.S., M.A., Ph.D., University of Chicago
Employment: Choreographer and dancer in films, stage productions, and musical theater, and owner of dance studios, 1931–1967; artist in residence at the Performing Arts Training Center, Southern Illinois University at Edwardsville, 1967–1972
Married: Jordis McCoo, 1931, divorced 1939; John Pratt, 1939, died 1986

atherine Dunham has been an anthropologist whose research has been reported more often in stage and film performances than in scientific papers. In the 1940s and 1950s she was a popular dancer who performed with her troupe throughout the world. She started dancing in high school, and she gave dance lessons to pay for her studies at the University of Chicago. She studied modern dance and ballet, and she formed a black dance group, later the Chicago Negro School of Ballet. In her studies in anthropology, she chose fieldwork in the Caribbean, where she studied African-based ritual dance as well as the role of dance in popular culture. In a trip to Jamaica, the Maroon people accepted her as one of the "lost peoples" of Africa whose mission was to instruct her people in their rituals. In Haiti she was initiated into the Vaudun and performed in the public dance. She used these formal studies of Caribbean, African, and African-American dance in her choreography and in the performances of her dance troupes. Her Ph.D. thesis was titled "Dances of Haiti." She continued to maintain contacts with the academic world by giving lectures with demonstrations at Yale, Chicago, the Royal Anthropological Society of London, and other learned groups. When she was appearing on Broadway in 1941, she lectured to the Anthropology Club of the Yale University Graduate School on the practical application of primitive materials to the theater. She has held academic positions as a visiting professor at Case Western Reserve, artist in residence at Southern Illinois University at Edwardsville and the University of California, Berkeley, as well as professor and professor emerita at Edwardsville. In the 1930s she was part of the dance program of the Works Project Administration (WPA) in Chicago. She founded her first dance troupe in 1939, and the company appeared in the stage production of "Cabin in the Sky" in New York in 1940. In the 1940s and 1950s the troupe appeared in several movies in addition to continuing to perform onstage and on television. She considered herself to be a better choreographer than dancer, although she was critically acclaimed as a dancer.

From 1940 to 1963, when she was touring and performing, Katherine Dunham continued to conduct anthropological investigations. She took her dancers into villages and neighborhoods so they could understand the cultural and social contexts of the dances they performed. Throughout her career, she has worked with the National Association for the Advancement of Colored People and the Urban League to end segregation in accommodations and audiences in the cities in which her company performed. In the early years they were denied hotel accommodations in several parts of the world in addition to the United States because they were black. She developed the Performing Arts Training Center of Southern Illinois University at Edwardsville starting in 1967. There is also the Katherine Dunham Museum nearby to house artifacts and art objects from her world travels. In addition to her scientific publications, she wrote an account of her anthropological studies in Jamaica in *Katherine Dunham's Journey to Accompong* (1946) and an autobiography, *A Touch of Innocence* (1959). She has won many awards, including the Albert Schweitzer Music Award in 1979, the Kennedy Center Award in 1983, and the Distinguished Service Award of the American Anthropological Association in 1986. There is a description of her dance technique and a list of performances in the book *Katherine Dunham: Reflections on the Social and Political Contexts of Afro-American Dance* (1981) by Joyce Aschenbrenner, and it includes a brief biography. The sources consulted do not agree on many biographical details. For example, her date of birth is given variously as 1905, 1909, and 1910, and there is no agreement on the dates of her degrees from the University of Chicago.

Bibliography: *Current Biography;* Herzenberg, Caroline L., *Women Scientists from Antiquity to the Present;* McHenry, Robert, ed., *Famous American Women;* O'Neill, Lois S., *The Women's Book of World Records and Achievements.*

Alice Eastwood
Sophia Hennion Eckerson
Fannie Pearson Hardy Eckstorm
Tilly Edinger
Rosa Smith Eigenmann
Gertrude Belle Elion
Charlotte Elliott
Florence May Hawley Ellis
Gladys Anderson Emerson
Katherine Esau
Alice Catherine Evans

Eastwood, Alice
(1859–1953)
botanist

Education: Public schools
Employment: High school teacher, Denver, 1879–1890; curator of botany, California
Academy of Sciences, 1892–1950

*A**lice Eastwood** was one of the most
knowledgeable systematic botanists
of her time. She was curator of
botany at the California Academy of
Sciences for more than 50 years and was a
specialist on the flowering plants of the
Rocky Mountains and the California coast.
Her name was starred in the first seven
editions of *American Men and Women of
Science.* In a study of 100 prominent
American botanists in 1903, reported by
Stephen Visher in *Scientists Starred
1903–1943 in "American Men and Women of
Science,"* she was one of two women who
were included. While teaching in Denver,
she acquired an extensive knowledge of
botany by exploring various areas of
Colorado. She was invited in 1892 to join
Mary Brandegee (q.v.), curator of botany at
the California Academy of Sciences, and
later succeeded her as curator. Both were
members of a group of prominent botanists
who were working in California at the turn
of the century. In 1893 she published, at her
own expense, *Popular Flora of Denver,
Colorado.* In 1905 she wrote *A Handbook of*

the Trees of California. In 1932 she and J. T.
Howell founded and edited the journal
Leaflets of Western Botany. This was an
important outlet for the active research that
was being conducted in the western United
States. She founded the California Botanical
Club and directed its activities thereafter. In
addition to her work at the Academy, she
was able to perform extensive fieldwork in
California and she added hundreds of
specimens to the collection.

After the San Francisco earthquake and
fire of 1906, she spent several years
rebuilding the botanical collections at the
California Academy of Sciences. She
verified the descriptions of specimens by
visits to the British Museum, the Royal
Botanic Gardens, the Natural History
Museum at Paris, Harvard University, the
New York Botanical Garden, and the
National Herbarium. Between 1912 and her
retirement, over 340,000 specimens were
added to the herbarium. One of her goals
was to verify the classification of tropical
and subtropical exotics grown in California.
She also was responsible for developing the

Academy's vast botanical library, which included many volumes she contributed from her personal collection.

She published about 300 papers, including semipopular articles on California. Among the honors she received was being elected honorary president of the Seventh International Botanical Congress in Stockholm in 1950. She was a member of the American Association for the Advancement of Science, the Botanical Society of America, and the Ecological Society of America. A bibliography of her publications was included in the *Proceedings of the Academy* (1949): xv–xxiv. Carol G. Wilson wrote a biography, *Alice Eastwood's Wonderland: The Adventures of a Botanist* (1955).

Bibliography: Abir-Am, P. G. and Dorinda Outram, eds., *Uneasy Careers and Intimate Lives; American Men and Women of Science 1–8;* Barnhart, John H., *Biographical Notes upon Botanists;* Bonta, Marcia M., *Women in the Field;* Debus, A. G., ed., *World Who's Who in Science;* Herzenberg, Caroline L., *Women Scientists from Antiquity to the Present;* Hollingsworth, Buckner, *Her Garden Was Her Delight; National Union Catalog;* Ogilvie, Marilyn B., *Women in Science;* Rossiter, Margaret W., *Women Scientists in America;* Rossiter, Margaret W., "Women Scientists in America before 1920"; Rudolph, Emanuel D., "Women in Nineteenth Century American Botany"; Sicherman, Barbara et al., *Notable American Women;* Siegel, Patricia J. and Kay Thomas Finley, *Women in the Scientific Search;* Visher, Stephen S., *Scientists Starred 1903–1943 in "American Men of Science."*

Eckerson, Sophia Hennion
(d. 1954)
botanist and plant physiologist

Education: A.B., Smith College, 1905, M.A., 1907; Ph.D., University of Chicago, 1911
Employment: Assistant plant physiologist, University of Chicago, 1911–1915, instructor, 1916–1920; microchemist, State College of Washington, 1914; Bureau of Plant Industry, U.S. Department of Agriculture, 1919–1922; University of Wisconsin, 1921–1923; plant microchemist, Boyce Thompson Institute for Plant Research, 1923–1940

*S*ophia Eckerson received recognition for her work as a scientist when her name was starred in the sixth and seventh editions of *American Men and Women of Science.* Her specialties were plant physiology and microchemistry. She received her doctorate from the University of Chicago at a time when many prominent women scientists were members of the faculty, and she was apparently one of the outstanding graduates of the school. She secured a position as a member of the plant physiology staff at the same university and then taught as an instructor for five years. She moved briefly to Washington State before joining the U.S. Department of Agriculture (USDA) in the Bureau of Plant Industry for three years. (In the 1920s the USDA employed more women scientists in professional positions than any other federal agency. The majority of these women were members of the Bureau of Plant Industry.) After working briefly for the University of Wisconsin, she joined the Boyce Thompson Institute for Plant Research, where she stayed until retiring in 1940. Boyce Thompson was a prestigious research institute; there was great competition for both men and women to be hired there. Her selection and continued employment during the Depression years confirm her reputation as an outstanding scientist. She served as chair of the physiology section of the Botanical Society of America in 1935.

Bibliography: *American Men and Women of Science* 6–8; Barnhart, John H., *Biographical Notes upon Botanists;* Hall, Diana Long, "Academics, Bluestockings, and Biologists"; Herzenberg, Caroline L., *Women Scientists from Antiquity to the Present; National Union Catalog;* Rossiter, Margaret W., *Women Scientists in America;* Siegel, Patricia J. and Kay Thomas Finley, *Women in the Scientific Search;* Visher, Stephen S., *Scientists Starred 1903–1943 in "American Men of Science."*

Eckstorm, Fannie Pearson Hardy
(1865–1946)
writer and ornithologist

Education: A.B., Smith College, 1888
Employment: Superintendent of schools, 1889–1891; reader of scientific manuscripts for the publisher D. C. Heath, 1892
Married: Rev. Jacob A. Eckstorm, 1893, died 1899

Fannie Eckstorm was recognized as an author who wrote popular books on ornithology for the general public, and she was one of several women writers whose names were included in early editions of *American Men and Women of Science.* These women authors had significant roles in popularizing science at the turn of the century. She was an authority on the history, folk songs, and Native Americans of Maine. Her father was one of the largest fur traders in Maine, and he greatly influenced her interest in the wilderness and its people. While a student at Smith, Fannie Eckstorm founded a college Audubon Society. In 1891, while working as a school superintendent, she contributed two series of articles to the sportsmen's magazine *Forest and Stream* on the rights of native hunters and preserving the state's big game. She then spent a year as a reader of scientific manuscripts for a publisher. After her marriage, she wrote numerous articles on ornithological subjects for magazines such as *Auk* and *Bird-Lore.* She published two books in 1901: *The Bird Book,* a children's text, and *The Woodpeckers.* The remainder of her books were on the subjects of folk songs and ballads, and Native American history, language, and legend. She was recognized as an authority on both the wildlife and the people of Maine, and she published several articles on the history and legends of the Native Americans there. She received an honorary degree from the University of Maine in 1929. Her name was included in the first and second editions of *American Men and Women of Science.*

Bibliography: *American Men and Women of Science 1–2; Dictionary of American Biography;* Herzenberg, Caroline L., *Women Scientists from Antiquity to the Present;* James, E. T., ed., *Notable American Women 1607–1950;* McHenry, Robert, ed., *Famous American Women; National Union Catalog;* Siegel, Patricia J. and Kay Thomas Finley, *Women in the Scientific Search.*

Edinger, Tilly
(1897–1967)
paleontologist

Education: University of Heidelberg and University of Munich, 1916–1918; Ph.D. in natural philosophy, University of Frankfurt, 1921

Employment: Research assistant in paleontology, University of Frankfurt, 1921–1927; curator, vertebrate collection, Senckenberg Museum of Frankfurt, 1927–1938; translator, 1939; research associate, Museum of Comparative Zoology, Harvard University, 1940–1967

Tilly Edinger was the first person to perform systematic work on the study of fossil brains. She proved that the brain's evolution could be studied directly from fossils. She worked for a number of years as curator of vertebrate collection, without pay, in the museum in Frankfurt, Germany. Five years after the Nazis came to power, she was forced to flee the country due to her Jewish heritage. She came to Harvard because the school had designated funds for the temporary employment of displaced European scholars. She spent the rest of her life at Harvard's Museum of Comparative Zoology. She published the first of her major works while still in Germany; this was *Die Fossilen Gehirne* (1929). Her second book, *The Evolution of the Horse Brain* (1948), was published while she was at Harvard. She recognized that the evolution of the brain must be studied directly from the fossils and that mammals' brains are uniquely suited to such study. She theorized that the evolution

of the brain was more complex than other paleontogists had stated. Her father was a famous medical researcher who helped found the science of comparative neurology. She was not a passive follower in her father's footsteps; she planned to become a geologist until she found there were no employment opportunities for women. She then switched to vertebrate paleontology and ranked among the major figures in her field in the twentieth century. She virtually established the field of paleoneurology, the study of fossil brains. She was elected president of the Society of Vertebrate Paleontology for the 1963–1964 term. She received honorary degrees from Wellesley College in 1950, the University of Giessen in 1957, and the University of Frankfurt in 1964.

Bibliography: James, E. T., ed., *Notable American Women 1607–1950;* Siegel, Patricia J. and Kay Thomas Finley, *Women in the Scientific Search.*

Eigenmann, Rosa Smith

(1858–1947)

ichthyologist

Education: Business college, San Francisco; Indiana University, 1880–1882; Harvard University, 1887–1888
Employment: No formal employment
Married: Carl H. Eigenmann, 1887

Rosa Eigenmann was recognized as the first American woman to attain prominence in ichthyology. Her career began in 1880 when she read a paper on the identification of a new species of fish before the San Diego Society of Natural History that impressed America's leading ichthyologist, David S. Jordan, who visited the meeting. In the same year she had published her first scientific paper, and she was the first woman member of the society. She had been working as a reporter for her brother's newspaper, but she went to Indiana University in Bloomington, Indiana, to study under Jordan. There she married a fellow student, Carl Eigenmann. They conducted research at the Museum of Comparative Zoology at Harvard, where their primary interest was in the collections of fishes gathered during the Thayer Expedition in Brazil and the Hassler Expedition around South America. She was a special student in cryptogamic botany while they were at Harvard. They continued their work on freshwater fishes of South America and western North America at the San Diego Society of Natural History, where he was appointed curator.

In 1891 they returned to Indiana, where he was appointed professor of zoology. The Eigenmanns were considered authorities on South American fishes; Rosa published 20 papers independently of those she coauthored with her husband. After 1893 she continued to edit his manuscripts but no longer collaborated in the research and did not accompany her husband on his scientific travels and expeditions due to family responsibilities. The couple had five children, Margaret, Charlotte, Theodore, Adele, and Thora. One was retarded and another became mentally ill. In spite of her short career, Rosa Eigenmann has been recognized as the first American woman to attain prominence in ichthyology.

Bibliography: Herzenberg, Caroline L., *Women Scientists from Antiquity to the Present;* James, E. T., ed., *Notable American Women 1607–1950;* Mozans, H. J., *Women in Science;* Ogilvie, Marilyn B., *Women in Science;* Rossiter, Margaret W., *Women Scientists in America;* Rossiter, Margaret W., "Women Scientists in America before 1920"; Siegel, Patricia J. and Kay Thomas Finley, *Women in the Scientific Search.*

Elion, Gertrude Belle

(1918–)

biochemist

Education: A.B., Hunter College, 1937; M.S., New York University, 1941
Employment: Laboratory assistant in biochemistry, school of nursing, New York Hospital, 1937; assistant organic chemist, Denver Chemical Company, 1938–1939; teacher of

chemistry and physics, 1941–1942; analyst in food chemistry, Quaker Maid Company, 1942–1943; research chemist in organic chemistry, Johnson & Johnson, 1943–1944; senior research biochemist, Burroughs Wellcome Research Laboratories, 1944–1967, assistant to director, chemotherapy division, 1963–1967; head of experimental therapy, Burroughs Wellcome Company, 1967–1983; emeritus scientist

Concurrent Positions: Consultant, chemotherapy study section, U.S. Public Health Service, 1960–1964; adjunct professor of pharmacology and experimental medicine, Duke University, 1971–1983, research professor, 1983–; adjunct professor of pharmacology, University of North Carolina, 1973–

Gertrude Elion was awarded the Nobel Prize in physiology and medicine in 1988 and the Garvan Medal in 1968. She has been an acknowledged leader in the field of purine antimetabolites for the treatment of cancer. She has been one of the few scientists in the cancer research field and one of the few Nobel Prize winners in science who does not have a doctorate. She graduated from Hunter College summa cum laude, but 15 schools rejected her applications for a graduate assistantship because she was a woman. She held marginal jobs for several years until her great potential was recognized at Burroughs Wellcome, where she was employed in 1944 due to the shortage of men scientists during World War II. Prior to that she worked for several companies for short periods, taught school briefly, and completed her master's degree. She has proven to be an outstanding organic chemist, pharmacologist, and administrator and director of research in industry. For many years she was the only woman holding a top post in a major pharmaceutical company. She has been renowned for her chemotherapy research, in which she has synthesized and studied drugs used to treat leukemia and to ensure successful organ transplants. She developed the first drug that attacks viruses. Her research was the basis for the development of AZT, the first drug approved by the Food and Drug Administration for AIDS patients.

She helped change the way that pharmaceuticals are discovered. She and her collaborators developed drugs to interrupt the life cycle of abnormal cells while leaving healthy cells unharmed. Unlike many pharmaceutical companies, Burroughs Wellcome encouraged its scientists to publish their findings once patents had been registered, and her department head allowed her to publish in her own name. She published more than 225 papers. She enrolled in classes toward her doctorate at Brooklyn Polytechnic Institute for two years. The college required her to enroll full time, but she refused to quit her job, quitting school instead. She has received honorary degrees from several universities and received numerous awards. She was elected to the National Academy of Sciences in 1990, and she was awarded the National Medal of Science in 1991. She was elected a fellow of the American Academy of Pharmaceutical Scientists. She has been a member of the American Chemical Society, the New York Academy of Sciences, and the American Society of Biological Chemists. Her photograph was included in Sharon McGrayne's *Nobel Prize Women in Science.* Her name was listed in the 1992–1993 edition of *American Men and Women of Science.*

Bibliography: American Men and Women of Science 9–18; Herzenberg, Caroline L., *Women Scientists from Antiquity to the Present;* Kass-Simon, G. and Patricia Farnes, *Women of Science;* McGrayne, Sharon B., *Nobel Prize Women in Science;* O'Neill, Lois S., *The Women's Book of World Records and Achievements.*

Elliott, Charlotte
(1883–1974)
plant physiologist

Education: A.B., Stanford University, 1907, A.M., 1913; Ph.D. in plant physiology, University of Wisconsin, 1918

Employment: High school teacher, 1907–1908; instructor in biology and geography, South Dakota State Normal School, 1908–1912; teacher, Brookings State College, 1914–1916; scientific assistant, Bureau of Plant Industry, U.S. Department of Agriculture, 1918–1922, assistant pathologist, 1922–1923, associate pathologist, 1923–1940, pathologist, 1940–1946

*C*harlotte Elliott was one of the many women who found employment with the U.S. Department of Agriculture (USDA), the largest employer of women in the federal service. After receiving her undergraduate degree, she taught public school for two years and taught in two small colleges while obtaining her master's degree. She received her doctorate from the University of Wisconsin in 1918, the same year she accepted a position with the USDA. She was employed in the agency's Bureau of Plant Industry, in which the majority of USDA women were concentrated. With the outbreak of World War I, a woman with a doctorate would have been a welcome addition to many research facilities, and she rose steadily in rank in the agency. She retired in 1946 at the level of pathologist. One advantage of working for the bureau was that the managers permitted all of the researchers,

both men and women, to publish under their own names rather than under the name of the chief scientist or the department head. She published five papers in the *USDA Journal of Agricultural Research* and one in the *Farmers Bulletin* series. In addition, she wrote *Manual of Bacterial Plant Pathogens* (1930, 1951). She was president of the Botanical Society of Washington in 1942. Her research interest was bacterial and fungus diseases of plants. Her photograph is on file at the National Archives.

Bibliography: *American Men and Women of Science* 3–11; Barnhart, John H., *Biographical Notes upon Botanists;* Herzenberg, Caroline L., *Women Scientists from Antiquity to the Present; National Union Catalog;* Rossiter, Margaret W., *Women Scientists in America;* Rossiter, Margaret W., "'Women's Work' in Science, 1880–1910."

Ellis, Florence May Hawley
(1906–)
anthropologist

Education: A.B., University of Arizona, 1927, M.A., 1928; Ph.D. in anthropology, University of Chicago, 1934

Employment: Research associate, Arizona State Museum, 1928–1929; instructor in anthropology, University of Arizona, 1929–1933; faculty, University of New Mexico, 1934–1954, professor, 1954–1971; emeritus professor

Married: Donovan Senter, 1936, divorced 1947; Bruce Ellis, 1949

florence Ellis has been known for her pioneer work on the dating of ceramics of the Southwest. She published her first papers in the 1920s, becoming one of the first women to establish herself in the study of early American culture. She originally enrolled as a history major at the University of Arizona, but she found there were too many dates to remember and switched to anthropology. Her master's thesis featured ceramics from three closely successive stages found in excavated sites near her home town of Miami, Arizona. She was not only able to separate the sequential stages but to suggest the possible Mexican relationship. After receiving her master's degree, she taught at Arizona in the anthropology department and continued her research. In addition to her skill at dating ceramics, she developed expertise in tree-ring dating (dendrochronology). Due to her special skills, she was on loan half time to the University of Chicago to teach dendrochronology from 1937 to 1941. After receiving her doctorate, she accepted a position at the University of New Mexico, where she remained until her retirement. Fortunately for her, very little work had been reported on the history and prehistory of the Native Americans of New Mexico. In the 1960s and 1970s she assisted in the definition of ancient tribal areas for most of the New Mexico and Arizona Pueblo tribes

and for the Navajos. In the 1950s she had a major role in the Wetherill Mesa project to establish relationships between prehistoric culture and living peoples. She did extensive work in ethnography and ethnology, particularly in Pueblo and Navajo ethnography. She had close relationships with many Native Americans, who often permitted her to investigate areas that were closed to other ethnologists due to religious principles. In addition to scientific papers, she has published four books: *The Significance of the Dated Prehistory of Chetro Ketl, Chaco Canyon, N. M.* (1934), *Field Manual of Prehistoric Southwestern Pottery Types* (1936), *Tree Ring Analysis and Dating in the Mississippi Drainage* (1941), and *A Reconstruction of the Basic Jemez Pattern of Social Organization* (1964). She was elected president of the American Society of Ethnohistory in 1970. She and her first husband had a daughter, Andrea. A brief biography and photograph are included in G. Kass-Simon's and Patricia Farnes' *Women of Science.*

Bibliography: *American Men and Women of Science* 9–13; Debus, A. G., ed., *World Who's Who in Science;* Herzenberg, Caroline L., *Women Scientists from Antiquity to the Present;* Kass-Simon, G. and Patricia Farnes, *Women of Science; National Union Catalog.*

Emerson, Gladys Anderson
(1903–1984)
nutritionist and biochemist

Education: B.S. in physics and chemistry, A.B. in history and English, Oklahoma College for Women, 1925; M.A. in history, Stanford University, 1926; Ph.D. in nutrition and biochemistry, University of California, Berkeley, 1932

Employment: Assistant at Stanford, 1925–1926; social sciences teacher, 1926–1929; assistant at Iowa State College, 1930–1931; research associate, Institute for Experimental Biology, University of California, Berkeley, 1933–1942; head of department of nutrition, Merck Institute of Therapeutic Research, 1942–1957; professor and chair, department of home economics, University of California, Los Angeles, 1957–1961; professor of nutrition and head of division, School of Public Health at Los Angeles, 1962–1970; emeritus professor

Concurrent positions: Member of advisory board, Quartermaster Food & Container Institute, 1948–1949; research associate, Sloan-Kettering Institute of Cancer Research, 1950–1953; member of food and nutrition board, National Research Council, 1959–1964

Gladys Emerson was recognized as the co-isolator of vitamin E while at the University of California, Berkeley, in the late 1930s. As an undergraduate, she received a joint degree in both science and history. After receiving a master's degree in history, she taught school for several years. Changing directions in her career, she obtained a fellowship at the University of California, Berkeley, where she received a doctorate in nutrition and biochemistry in 1932. She received an appointment as a research associate at the Institute for Experimental Biology at Berkeley, where she started the research that resulted in isolating vitamin E from wheat germ oil. In 1942 she joined the Merck Institute of Therapeutic Research as head of the department of nutrition. At the University of California, Los Angeles she became professor and head of the department of home economics and then professor of nutrition and head of the division of the School of Public Health at Los Angeles. She held concurrent positions as a member of the advisory board for the Quartermaster Food & Container Institute (1948–1949), research associate at Sloan-Kettering Institute of Cancer Research (1950–1953), and member of the food and nutrition board of the National Research Council (1959–1964). She was associate editor of the *Journal of Nutrition* from 1952 to 1956. She received the Garvan

Medal in 1952. She was a fellow of the American Association for the Advancement of Science, the American Institute of Nutrition, and the New York Academy of Sciences. Her areas of research were amino acids, vitamin E, and vitamin B complex. There is a photograph in the journal *Chemtech* 6 (1976): 738–743 and in Edna Yost's *Women of Modern Science*.

Bibliography: *American Men and Women of Science* 6–15; Debus, A. G., ed., *World Who's Who in Science*; Herzenberg, Caroline L., *Women Scientists from Antiquity to the Present*; *National Union Catalog*; O'Neill, Lois S., *The Women's Book of World Records and Achievements*; Uglow, Jennifer S., *International Dictionary of Women's Biography*; Vare, Ethlie Ann and Greg Ptacek, *Mothers of Invention*; Yost, Edna, *Women of Modern Science*.

Esau, Katherine
(1898–)
botanist

Education: College of Agriculture, Moscow, 1916–1917; College of Agriculture, Berlin, 1919–1922; Ph.D., University of California, Davis, 1931

Employment: Plant breeder, Spreckels Sugar Company, 1924–1928; assistant, University of California, Davis, 1928–1931, instructor, 1931–1937, assistant professor, 1937–1943, associate professor, 1943–1949, professor, 1949–1965; emeritus professor

Concurrent Positions: Junior botanist, agricultural experiment station, University of California, Davis, 1931–1937, assistant botanist, 1937–1943, associate botanist, 1943–1949, botanist, 1949–1968

Katherine Esau has been recognized for her work on the effects of viruses on plants. Her family originally lived in the Ukraine, but after World War I they emigrated to Germany, where she attended an agricultural school. Instead of returning to Russia, the family came to the United States in 1922 to settle in Reedley, California, which had a large Mennonite population. After working at several odd jobs, she was hired by Spreckels Sugar Company as a plant breeder. She then accepted an assistantship at University of California, Davis, where she received her doctorate in 1931. She was appointed to a joint position of faculty member and botanist with the agricultural experiment station. She was elected to membership in the National Academy of Sciences in 1957. In 1963 she moved to the Santa Barbara campus of the University of California to continue collaborative research on the phloem. It should be noted that, although her expertise was recognized by the university, her advancement in faculty rank was exactly at six-year intervals. When she was elected to the National Academy of Sciences, her office was still in a university garage where the botany department was housed at Davis. She was president of the Botanical Society of America in 1951, and she was elected to the Swedish Royal Academy of Sciences in 1971. She has been the author of several books: *Plant Anatomy* (1953, 1965), *Anatomy of Seed Plants* (1960, 1977), *Plants, Viruses, and Insects* (1961), *Vascular Differentiation in Plants* (1965), and *Viruses in Plant Hosts* (1968). She has been an authority on the structure and ontogeny of phloem, food-conducting tissue of plants, and plant-host virus relationships. A biography and photograph were included in *Plant Science Bulletin* 31 (1985): 33–37. She was listed in the 1992–1993 edition of *American Men and Women of Science.*

Bibliography: Abir-Am, P. G. and Dorinda Outram, eds., *Uneasy Careers and Intimate Lives; American Men and Women of Science* 6–18; Debus, A. G., ed., *World Who's Who in Science;* Herzenberg, Caroline L., *Women Scientists from Antiquity to the Present;* O'Neill, Lois S., *The Women's Book of World Records and Achievements;* Rossiter, Margaret W., *Women Scientists in America;* Uglow, Jennifer S., *International Dictionary of Women's Biography.*

Evans, Alice Catherine
(1881–1975)
microbiologist

Education: B.S., Cornell University, 1909; M.S. in bacteriology, University of Wisconsin, 1910

Employment: Public school teacher, 1901–1905; dairy bacteriologist, Bureau of Animal Industry, U.S. Department of Agriculture (USDA), at agricultural experiment station,

Madison, Wisconsin, 1910–1913, bacteriologist, USDA, Washington, D.C., 1913–1918; Public Health Service, 1918–1945

*A*lice Evans was the foremost woman scientist in the federal government prior to World War II. Her work on brucellosis is cited as one of the outstanding achievements in medical science in the first quarter of the twentieth century. She taught public school for four years before enrolling in 1905 in a two-year nature study course for rural teachers at Cornell. She continued taking courses at Cornell to earn her undergraduate degree, then went to the University of Wisconsin, where she received a master's degree in bacteriology in 1910. She accepted a position in the dairy division of the USDA's Bureau of Animal Industry in 1910 and worked at the agricultural experiment station in Madison, Wisconsin. She transferred to the new research laboratories of the dairy division in Washington, D.C., in 1913 to study bacterial contamination of milk products. This work led to her pioneering studies on the common origin of brucellosis in both cattle and humans; prior to that the assumption was that these were two separate diseases. The human form at that time was called undulant fever. Many scientists and physicians would not accept her conclusions and refused to support her campaign for the pasteurization of milk. It was unthinkable that a pure product such as unpasteurized milk could cause disease, and she was a woman scientist who did not have a doctorate or a medical degree.

Transferring to the U.S. Public Health Service in 1918, she worked on epidemic meningitis, influenza, and streptococcal infections. By that time her theories on brucellosis were gaining wide acceptance because human brucellosis was being reported throughout the world and from diverse animal sources. (In the 1930s the dairy industry was forced to pasteurize all milk.) In 1928 she became the first woman elected president of the Society of American Bacteriologists. In 1975 she was elected an honorary member of the American Society for Microbiology. She received an honorary M.D. from the Woman's Medical College of Pennsylvania in 1934 and an honorary Sc.D. from Wilson College in 1936. There are photographs in *Current Biography* and Margaret Rossiter's *Women Scientists in America.*

Bibliography: American Men and Women of Science 4–11; Baker, Gladys L., "Women in the U.S. Department of Agriculture"; Current Biography; Herzenberg, Caroline L., Women Scientists from Antiquity to the Present; Kass-Simon, G. and Patricia Farnes, Women of Science; O'Hern, Elizabeth M., "Women Scientists in Microbiology"; O'Neill, Lois S., The Women's Book of World Records and Achievements; Rossiter, Margaret W., Women Scientists in America; Sicherman, Barbara et al., Notable American Women; Siegel, Patricia J. and Kay Thomas Finley, Women in the Scientific Search.

F

Fannie Merritt Farmer
Wanda Kirkbride Farr
Beatrix Cadwalader Jones Farrand
Margaret Clay Ferguson
Maria Elizabeth Smith Fernald
Adele Marion Fielde
Kathryn Ferguson Fink
Elizabeth Florette Fisher
Williamina Paton Stevens Fleming
Alice Cunningham Fletcher
Irmgard Flugge-Lotz
Katharine Foot
Mary Louise Foster
Katharine Stevens Fowler-Billings
Christine McGaffey Frederick
Kate Furbish
Caroline Ellen Furness

Farmer, Fannie Merritt
(1857–1915)
teacher of cooking and dietetics

Education: High school; Boston Cooking School, 1887–1889
Employment: Assistant principal, Boston Cooking School, 1889–1894, head of school, 1894–1902; owner, Miss Farmer's School of Cookery, 1902–1915

Fannie Farmer was the most famous of several women who founded early cooking schools and published cookbooks. Her contribution was in helping to create the profession of homemaking. She was a teacher of cooking and dietetics and the author of *The Boston Cooking-School Cook Book.* At the age of 16 she suffered paralysis in her left leg, probably the result of polio; this prevented her from completing her education beyond high school. During the 1880s, when her father had difficulty supporting the family, she became a mother's helper in the home of a family friend. While there she became proficient in cooking, and she enrolled in the Boston Cooking School, an institution established in 1879 by the Woman's Education Association of Boston. (In 1903 the Boston Cooking School formed the basis of the department of home economics at Simmons College.) After completing the course, she stayed on as an assistant principal, becoming head of the school in 1894. In 1902 she resigned her position to open her own school, Miss Farmer's School of Cookery. In contrast to the Boston Cooking School's goal of training women to earn their livings as cooks or to teach cooking in public and private schools, Fannie Farmer concentrated on teaching housewives and society girls. Her popular weekly demonstration lectures were reported in the local newspaper and reprinted in others throughout the United States. Later she began concentrating on diets for the sick and the convalescent. She gave short courses to nurses in hospitals, trained hospital dietitians, and lectured at the Harvard Medical School. She considered her book *Food and Cookery for the Sick and the Convalescent* (1904) her most important work.

She is famous for publishing *The Boston Cooking-School Cook Book,* which first appeared in 1896. It surpassed the *Boston Cook Book* of Mary Bailey Lincoln (q.v.) in popularity, and editions still are published today. It marked a new approach to cookbook writing in emphasizing the nutritional values of foods and in giving exact measurements. She published numerous other books, but the *Boston* was her most popular one. For ten years she and her sister contributed a monthly page on cooking in the *Woman's Home Companion.* After Fannie Farmer's death in 1915, her school continued to operate until 1944.

Bibliography: James, E. T., ed., *Notable American Women 1607–1950;* McHenry, Robert, ed., *Famous American Women; National Cyclopedia of American Biography; National Union Catalog;* O'Neill, Lois S., *The Women's Book of World Records and Achievements;* Shapiro, Laura, *Perfection Salad;* Vare, Ethlie Ann and Greg Ptacek, *Mothers of Invention.*

Farr, Wanda Kirkbride
(b. 1895)
cytologist

Education: B.S., Ohio University, Athens, Ohio, 1915; A.M., Columbia University, 1918
Employment: Assistant in botany, Ohio University, 1915–1916; instructor, Kansas State College, 1917–1918; instructor, Agricultural and Mechanical College of Texas, 1918–1919; research associate, Barnard Free Skin and Cancer Clinic, St. Louis, 1926–1927; instructor, Shaw School of Botany, St. Louis, 1928; investigator in plant physiology, Boyce Thompson Institute, 1928–1929; associate cotton technologist, U.S. Department of Agriculture, 1929–1936; director of cellulose laboratory, Boyce Thompson, 1936–1940; research chemist, American Cyanamid Company, 1940–1943; Research Division, Celanese Corporation of America, 1943–1954, research consultant, 1954–?; associate professor of botany, University of Maine, consultant, 1975–?
Married: Clifford H. Farr, 1918, died 1928; Roy C. Faulwetter, 1928

Wanda Farr discovered the source for cellulose in research she and her first husband had started several years previously. She had planned to study medicine when she attended college, but her family refused to permit it because her health was somewhat frail. She then decided to study science. She completed her undergraduate degree in three years and went to Columbia University for her master's degree. There she met Clifford Farr, who was completing his doctorate. He told friends that when he saw the quality of slides she prepared he knew he had to make Wanda Kirkbride a member of his family. She interrupted her master's program to teach at Kansas State while he was teaching at Texas A&M. The two were married and moved to Washington, D.C., where he was on special assignment to the U.S. Department of Agriculture (USDA) during World War I. She obtained a position in the botany department when they returned to Texas, but she combined independent research with family responsibilities (a son, Robert) while her husband was teaching at Iowa. When they moved to St. Louis, she obtained a position at the Barnard Free Skin and Cancer Clinic, where she assisted in research on living cells of animal organisms. This applied to the couple's research on living plant cells. When Clifford

Farr died in 1928, she was invited by the university to continue his classes because she was so familiar with his work. She was able to continue their research on root hairs of plants under her own name with a grant from the Bache Fund.

After working briefly for Boyce Thompson, she moved to the USDA to perform research on cotton. This research applied to her individual project on root hairs, which led to her discovery of the source for cellulose. She later obtained significant appointments at Boyce Thompson and two chemical companies, American Cyanamid and Celanese Corporation. Wanda Farr was extremely fortunate to be able to continue her husband's research under her own name after his death. Perhaps because she had a young son to support, employers gave her appointments with significant responsibilities, although she did not have a doctorate. Since her first husband had been a well-known botanist, her contemporaries questioned how much original work she actually contributed. She was able to overcome this prejudice and continue her work. She was elected a fellow of the Royal Microscopical Society and was a member of professional societies such as the Botanical Society of America and the Torrey Botanical Club. Several references list her maiden name as Kirkbridge.

Bibliography: Abir-Am, P. G. and Dorinda Outram, eds., *Uneasy Careers and Intimate Lives; American Men and Women of Science* 5–11; Barnhart, John H., *Biographical Notes upon Botanists;* Debus, A. G., ed., *World Who's Who in Science;* Herzenberg, Caroline L., *Women Scientists from Antiquity to the Present;* Ireland, Norma O., *Index to Scientists of the World;* Vare, Ethlie Ann and Greg Ptacek, *Mothers of Invention;* Yost, Edna, *American Women of Science.*

Farrand, Beatrix Cadwalader Jones
(1872–1959)
landscape architect

Education: Private tutors
Employment: Self-employed, 1897–1959
Married: Max Farrand, 1913, died 1945

Beatrix Farrand was the foremost American woman landscape architect in the twentieth-century United States. Since there were no schools of landscape architecture in the 1890s—Harvard University did not start its program in landscape architecture until 1900—at the age of 20 she apprenticed herself with Charles S. Sargent, the founder and first director of the Arnold Arboretum. She began taking private landscape commissions in 1897. Most of her work was done for private clients. She also did extensive commissions for Princeton University, Vassar College, the University of Chicago, and Oberlin College. Her most famous work was the remodeling of the house and grounds at Dumbarton Oaks, an estate in Washington, D.C., over a period of approximately 20 years. The plans for this estate were described in *Plant Book for Dumbarton Oaks* (1980), edited by Diane K. McGuire. Beatrix married Max Farrand, who was chair of the Yale University history department. After he was appointed director of research at the Huntington Library in San Marino, California, they still maintained their home principally at Bar Harbor, Maine. She traveled constantly for assignments in Maine, New York, and Washington, supervising her staff working at the various sites. She had started her career at a time when people became interested in improving their living quarters, and when the captains of industry were amassing great wealth and spending it on large houses, estates, and other signs of largesse. Since her family was socially prominent, she was able to obtain wealthy clients such as J. P. Morgan. Her own designs combined the best elements of baroque and English landscape gardening.

Beatrix Farrand was the only woman member of the American Society of Landscape Architects when it was founded in 1899. She received the New York Botanical Garden Distinguished Service Award in 1952 and the Garden Club of America Medal of Achievement in 1947. She published the *Reef Point Gardens Bulletin* from 1946 to 1956, Reef Point being the name of her estate at Bar Harbor, where she had an herbarium and experimental gardens of native flora. She tore down her house when the town of Bar Harbor refused to protect the property from real estate development, and shortly before her death, she gave her library and herbarium to the University of California at Berkeley. Biographical information and photographs are included in *Beatrix Farrand's American Landscapes: Her Gardens and Campuses* (1985) by Diana Balmori and others and in *Horticulture* 63 (1985): 32–45 and *Landscape Architecture* (January 1977): 69–77.

Bibliography: Barnhart, John H., *Biographical Notes upon Botanists; Dictionary of American Biography;* James, E. T., ed., *Notable American Women 1607–1950.*

Ferguson, Margaret Clay
(1863–1951)
botanist

Education: Wellesley College, 1889–1891; B.S., Cornell University, 1899, Ph.D. in botany, 1901

Employment: Teacher and principal, public schools, 1877–1888; private school, 1892–1893; instructor of botany, Wellesley College, 1894–1896, 1901–1904, associate professor, 1904–1906, head of botany department, 1904–1930, research professor, 1930–1932, director of botany greenhouses and gardens, 1922–1932

Margaret Ferguson was recognized as one of the most productive women botanists of her time. As head of the department at Wellesley, she trained more women botanists than anyone else. She was listed in the first edition of *American Men and Women of Science,* and her name was starred in the second through seventh editions. After teaching school and obtaining a limited amount of education, she became a special student at Wellesley in botany and chemistry. She taught school again before returning to Wellesley as an instructor in botany. She completed her formal education at Cornell, receiving her doctorate in 1901. In her research at Cornell,

she initiated important work on the reproductive process and life history of a species of native pine. This was published in the *Proceedings* of the Washington Academy of Sciences in 1904 and gained wide attention. The study was one of the first to give a detailed analysis of the functional morphology and cytology of a pine native to North America. Returning to Wellesley in 1901, she rose in rank to professor and head of the department in 1904. As department head, she helped make it one of the leading undergraduate centers in the nation for the study of plant science. She emphasized laboratory work and the importance of chemistry and physics to botanical studies. She was able to combine research with her teaching and administrative responsibilities and to secure funds to build new college greenhouses and a botany building.

During the 1920s the focus of her research and advanced courses shifted to genetics, based on her study of *Petunia*. Although she retired in 1932, she continued her research until 1938. She was elected the first woman president of the Botanical Society of America in 1929, and she was elected a fellow of the New York Academy of Sciences in 1943. She received an honorary degree at Mount Holyoke College's centennial in 1937. Wellesley honored her by naming for her the greenhouses that she had designed and directed.

Bibliography: Abir-Am, P. G. and Dorinda Outram, eds., *Uneasy Careers and Intimate Lives; American Men and Women of Science 1–8;* Barnhart, John H., *Biographical Notes upon Botanists;* Herzenberg, Caroline L., *Women Scientists from Antiquity to the Present; National Union Catalog;* Ogilvie, Marilyn B., *Women in Science;* Rossiter, Margaret W., *Women Scientists in America;* Rossiter, Margaret W., "Women Scientists in America before 1920"; Rudolph, Emanuel D., "Women in Nineteenth Century American Botany"; Sicherman, Barbara et al., *Notable American Women;* Siegel, Patricia J. and Kay Thomas Finley, *Women in the Scientific Search;* Visher, Stephen S., *Scientists Starred 1903–1943 in "American Men of Science."*

Fernald, Maria Elizabeth Smith
(1839–1919)
entomologist

Education: Maine Wesleyan Seminary and Female College
Employment: Preceptress, Maine Wesleyan Seminary and Female College
Married: Charles H. Fernald, 1862

Maria Fernald was known for her own work, although her husband was an entomologist at Massachusetts State College. She not only assisted her husband in gathering specimens and working with his students but also started a card index of coccidae, which was a bibliographical and synonymical list for coccidae species worldwide. This was published as *Catalogue* *of the Coccidae of the World* (1903) by the Hatch Experiment Station. The publication represents only one section of a catalog of Tortricidae that she prepared and gave to the college. It was the first known card index on entomology to exist at the time. She graduated from the first class of the Maine Wesleyan Seminary and Female College, where she afterward was employed as a preceptress. Her life was typical of her time; there were few educational opportunities for women. She worked with her husband on his research and even was involved in his teaching and laboratory work. It is truly remarkable that she received brief obituaries not only in Herbert Osborn's *Fragments of Entomological History* but also in the prominent scientific publication, the *Journal of Economic Entomology* 13 (1920): 153, which includes notes on her publications. The sources mention a son, H. T. Fernald, who also was a scientist. Her photograph is on file in the National Archives.

Bibliography: *National Union Catalog;* Osborn, Herbert, *Fragments of Entomological History.*

Fielde, Adele Marion
(1839–1916)
biologist

Education: New York State Normal School, 1860
Employment: Public school teacher, 1860–1905; missionary in Siam and China, 1866–1899; lecturer, Woods Hole Biological Laboratory, 1900–1907

*A*dele Fielde was one of the few female scientists who went to a foreign country as a teacher or missionary. She was one of the most unusual persons listed in the early editions of *American Men and Women of Science.* She was an expert on ants, and she combined this study with her missionary work overseas. After graduation from New York State Normal School in 1860, she was employed as a teacher in New York intermittently while also serving as a missionary in Siam and China from 1866 to 1899. Her scientific papers on ants and butterflies were published in prominent journals such as *Biological Bulletin* and in the series issued by the Marine Biological Laboratory and by the Academy of Natural Sciences of Philadelphia. The latter society was considered one of the most prestigious at the time. Her research centered on the reasoning power and the psychology of ants. She also published books concerned with Chinese conditions and Chinese folklore, such as *A Corner of Cathay: Studies from Life among the Chinese* (1894) and *Chinese Fairy Tales: Forty Stories Told by Almond-Eyed Folk* (1912). She prepared a dictionary entitled *A Pronouncing and Defining Dictionary of the Swatow Dialect* (1883). Her interest in social conditions carried over into her life in the United States. She was actively involved in the women's rights movement, and she wrote pamphlets on this topic in addition to her scientific papers. She was known to have written pamphlets and given speeches in Seattle in 1910 when she was over 70 years old. Altogether she would be a fitting subject for a television documentary.

Bibliography: *American Men and Women of Science* 2; Barr, Ernest S., *An Index to Biographical Fragments in Unspecialized Scientific Journals;* Herzenberg, Caroline L., *Women Scientists from Antiquity to the Present; National Union Catalog;* Rossiter, Margaret W., *Women Scientists in America.*

Fink, Kathryn Ferguson
(1917–)
biochemist

Education: B.A., University of Iowa, 1938; Ph.D. in biochemistry, University of Rochester, 1943

Employment: Research technician, Mayo Institute of Experimental Medicine, 1938–1939; research associate, Manhattan Project, University of Rochester, 1943–1946, Atomic Energy Project, 1946–1947; associate clinical professor of biophysics, School of Medicine, University of California, Los Angeles, 1948–1963, associate professor, research in biophysics and nuclear medicine, 1964–1966, professor, 1966–1967, resident professor of medicine, 1967–1974, professor of medicine, 1974–, assistant dean, 1976–

Concurrent Position: Research biochemist, Veterans Administration Hospital, 1947–1961

Married: Robert M. Fink, 1941

Kathryn Fink has been a pioneer in the field of nuclear medicine. She was completing her doctorate as part of the Manhattan Project during World War II at the University of Rochester in the 1940s. The Manhattan Project proved to be a boon to the careers of numerous women scientists, since the federal government's crash program to develop atomic power required huge staffs of scientists. Many women were able to secure employment on the project and show how competent they were. The field of nuclear medicine was a result of that earlier project.

Although she did not have a medical degree, Kathryn Fink moved to the school of medicine at the University of California, Los Angeles, as an associate professor, one of the results of the Manhattan experience. (In the Manhattan Project scientists from many disciplines were called upon to combine their expertise to reach a common goal, and today much scientific research is centered on interdisciplinary effort by teams rather than the work of an individual.) She rose through the ranks to professor and assistant dean, creating for herself a successful career at a highly rated university. She has been a member of the Society for Experimental Biology and Medicine and the American Society of Biological Chemists. She and her husband had two children, Patricia and Suzanne. One source lists her name as Kay Fink.

Bibliography: American Men and Women of Science 8–17; Debus, A. G., ed., World Who's Who in Science; Herzenberg, Caroline L., Women Scientists from Antiquity to the Present.

Fisher, Elizabeth Florette
(1873–1941)
geologist

Education: B.S., Massachusetts Institute of Technology, 1896

Employment: Instructor in geology and geography, Wellesley College, 1894–1896, associate professor of geology and mineralogy, 1906–1908, professor of geology and geography, 1908–1926; emeritus professor

Concurrent Position: Geography teacher, Harvard University, 1912–1926

*E*lizabeth Fisher was one of the few women of her era who worked as a field geologist. She began teaching at Wellesley in 1894 before she received her degree from Massachusetts Institute of Technology (MIT), a situation that was not unusual at that time due to the limited opportunities for advanced degrees for women. She rose through the ranks fairly rapidly, being promoted to professor in 1908. She also enrolled in special courses in geography at Harvard and in the summer session at Radcliffe while she was teaching. Geology was almost exclusively a male profession at the time; few women taught the subject. She started lecturing on geography in the Harvard Community Extension Courses in Boston in 1912, and for many years she was the only woman to teach these courses. She was recognized as an expert on river terraces and oil fields at a time when few women were engaged in this type of research. She retired in 1926 due to poor health. She wrote *Resources and Industries of the United States* (1919) and attended the International Geological Congress in St. Petersburg, Russia, in 1897. She was a member of American Association for the Advancement of Science, the National Geographic Society, the American Geographical Society, and the Boston Society of Natural History. Her research interests were physiography, conservation of natural resources, and oil geology. Her name was listed in the first edition of *American Men and Women of Science.* There is a photograph in the *National Cyclopedia of American Biography.*

Bibliography: *American Men and Women of Science 1–6; National Cyclopedia of American Biography;* Siegel, Patricia J. and Kay Thomas Finley, *Women in the Scientific Search.*

Fleming, Williamina Paton Stevens
(1857–1911)
astronomer

Education: Harvard College Observatory
Employment: Assistant, Harvard College Observatory, 1879–1898, curator of astronomical photographs, 1898–1911
Married: James Fleming, 1877

*W*illiamina Fleming was the first woman at the Harvard College Observatory to make significant contributions to astronomy, and she was one of the best-known astronomers in the world. As curator of astronomical photographs, she played a key role in analyzing data and preparing it for publication. She and her husband emigrated from Scotland in 1878, and after the disintegration of her marriage in 1879, she obtained a job as a maid or housekeeper in the household of Edward Pickering, director of the Harvard College Observatory. She had a son, Edward, to support, and Pickering hired her part time for clerical and computing tasks in the observatory. By 1881 she was a permanent member of the staff. In 1886 she took charge of the observatory's new project, the classification of stars on the basis of their photographed spectra. She not only administered the program but supervised the women employed as research assistants. The data were recorded on photographic plates, and then the spectra of each of hundreds of stars on each plate had to be classified.

She was the first woman to receive a corporation appointment at Harvard in 1898 when she was named curator of astronomical photographs. She made significant contributions to the discipline of astronomy, such as developing a useful classification scheme for stars by organizing them into 17 categories according to spectral characteristics. She was a vocal advocate for women to enter the profession of astronomy, and the examination of photographic plates that she supervised became a new line of women's work. Between 1885 and 1900, 21 women were hired, making the observatory a significant employer. Although the work was tedious and the pay was low, the jobs were desirable compared to the alternatives open to women at the time. In the early years Pickering published the findings but always credited Mrs. Fleming's work; later she published under her own name. She served as editor of observatory publications, particularly the *Annals*. Her own publication was *A Photographic Study of Variable Stars Forming a Part of the Henry Draper Memorial* (1907). In 1906 she was elected to the Royal Astronomical Society, one of only four women members. She was a member of the Astronomical and Astrophysical Society of America. Her name was starred in the first and second editions of *American Men and Women of Science*. There are photographs in the *Astrophysical Journal* 34 (1911): 314–317 and in *Women of Science* by G. Kass-Simon and Patricia Farnes. Background information on the observatory was published in *New England Magazine* 6 (1892): 165–176 as "Women's Work at the Harvard Observatory."

Bibliography: Abir-Am, P. G. and Dorinda Outram, eds., *Uneasy Careers and Intimate Lives; American Men and Women of Science* 1–2; Davis, Herman S., "Women Astronomers (1750–1890)"; *Dictionary of American Biography; Dictionary of Scientific Biography;* Elliott, Clark A., *Biographical Dictionary of American Science;* James, E. T., ed., *Notable American Women 1607–1950;* Kass-Simon, G. and Patricia Farnes, *Women of Science;* Mozans, H. J., *Women in Science; National Union Catalog;* Ogilvie, Marilyn B., *Women in Science;* O'Neill, Lois S., *The Women's Book of World Records and Achievements;* Rossiter, Margaret W., *Women Scientists in America;* Rossiter, Margaret W., "Women Scientists in America before 1920"; Rossiter, Margaret W., "'Women's Work' in Science, 1880–1910"; Siegel, Patricia J. and Kay Thomas Finley, *Women in the Scientific Search;* Smith, Edgar C., "Some Notable Women of Science"; Uglow, Jennifer S., *International Dictionary of Women's Biography;* Visher, Stephen S., *Scientists Starred 1903–1943 in "American Men of Science."*

Fletcher, Alice Cunningham
(1838–1923)
anthropologist

Education: Public schools
Employment: Teacher, public schools; special agent for U.S. Indian Bureau and Department of the Interior, 1883–1893; assistant, Peabody Museum, Cambridge, Massachusetts, 1886–1891, research fellow, 1891–1923

*A*lice Fletcher was recognized for her work in preserving the lands and culture of the Plains Indians. This work established her as the foremost authority on the subject. She was an early participant in several reform efforts, such as temperance and women's rights. After teaching school for several years, she began to read archaeological and ethnographic literature. In 1878 she began fieldwork by investigating the shell heaps of Florida and the Massachusetts coast. She assisted in raising funds to preserve prehistoric Serpent Mound in Ohio. She then became caught up in the Native American welfare movement of the 1870s and 1880s. She lived with the Omaha tribe in 1881 and became a spokesperson in protecting their lands from seizure by the federal government. The Omaha were afraid, with reason, that the government would dispossess them, and they turned to Alice Fletcher for assistance. During her crusade on their behalf, she won their confidence and started an extensive collection of data and relics. Her efforts also earned her the respect of Washington officials; she took care of many details in seeing that the provisions of the legislation to apportion lands among tribes were put into effect. She also worked among the Sioux, Winnebago, Pawnee, and Nez Perce. The government commissioned her to prepare the Indian Bureau's exhibit for the New Orleans Exposition of 1884. The next year she prepared a report on Indian progress for the U.S. Senate entitled "Indian Education and Civilization."

Between 1887 and 1889 she worked as a special agent of the Interior Department to implement the Dawes Act among the Winnebago of Nebraska and the Nez Perce of Idaho. In appreciation for her work in preserving the Native American relics she collected for the Peabody Museum, she was appointed an assistant there in 1886. She wrote 46 monographs about Native Americans; probably the most outstanding was *The Omaha Tribe* (1911). She made significant contributions to preserving the culture and artifacts of the tribes, and she initiated a project to preserve the songs of the Plains Indians by seeking experts to transcribe them into standard music notation. This was reported in *Indian Story and Song from North America* (1900). She still continued her interest in archaeology, and she was instrumental in establishing what became the School of American Research in Santa Fe, New Mexico.

She received many honors, including the presidency of the American Folk-Lore Society in 1905. Her name was starred in the first, second, and third editions of *American Men and Women of Science.* In a study of 20 distinguished American anthropologists in 1903 reported by Stephen Visher, Alice Fletcher was the only woman listed. Her photograph was included in the *American Anthropologist* 25 (1923): 254–258; this also gives a bibliography of her publications.

Bibliography: Abir-Am, P. G. and Dorinda Outram, eds., *Uneasy Careers and Intimate Lives; American Men and Women of Science* 1–3; *Dictionary of American Biography;* Helm, June, ed., *Pioneers of American Anthropology;* Herzenberg, Caroline L., *Women Scientists from Antiquity to the Present;* James, E. T., ed., *Notable American Women 1607–1950;* Macksey, Joan and Kenneth Macksey, *The Book of Women's Achievements;* Mozans, H. J., *Women in Science; National Union Catalog;* Ogilvie, Marilyn B., *Women in Science;* Rossiter, Margaret W., *Women Scientists in America;* Rossiter, Margaret W., "Women Scientists in America before 1920"; Rossiter, Margaret W., "'Women's Work' in Science, 1880–1910"; Siegel, Patricia J. and Kay Thomas Finley, *Women in the Scientific Search;* Uglow, Jennifer S., *International Dictionary of Women's Biography;* Visher, Stephen S., *Scientists Starred 1903–1943 in "American Men of Science."*

Flugge-Lotz, Irmgard
(1903–1974)
engineer

Education: Diplom Ingenieur, Hannover Technische Hochschule, 1927, Doktor Ingenieur, 1929

Employment: From junior research engineer to head of department of theoretical aerodynamics, Aerodynamische Versuchsanstalt, Göttingen, 1929–1938; consultant, aerodynamics and dynamics of flight, Deutsche Versuchsanstalt fur Luftfahrt, 1938–1945; chief, research group in theoretical aerodynamics, National Office for Aeronautical Research, France, 1946–1948; lecturer in engineering mechanics and research supervisor, Stanford University, 1949–1960, professor of aeronautical engineering and engineering mechanics, 1960–1968; emeritus professor

Married: Wilhelm Flugge, 1938

Irmgard Flugge-Lotz was among the world's leading authorities on fluid mechanics. She received international recognition for her many important mathematical contributions to aerodynamics and automatic control theory. In 1971 she became the only woman ever to be selected to present a von Karman Lecture, which is sponsored by the American Institute of Aeronautics and Astronautics. She also was the first woman to reach a full professorship in the engineering college at Stanford.

After she received her doctorate from the Technical University in Hannover in 1929, she obtained a position with a research institute, Aerodynamische Versuchsanstalt, in Göttingen. She was hired to perform routine tasks, such as cataloging reprints. After she developed an equation for one of her bosses, she was appointed head of a group dealing with theoretical dynamics. The work she performed in 1931 on the lifting force of wings of various shapes, known as the Lotz method, was recognized as a fundamental contribution throughout her lifetime. The only other women on the staff were "computers" who performed calculations for research engineers. After she married Wilhelm Flugge, an authority on thin shell construction, in 1938, they moved to Berlin and both worked for Deutsche Versuchsanstalt fur Luftfahrt.

There she conducted research on electronic automatic control theory that had implications for development of simple automatic flight control equipment for aircraft. Although they were known to have anti-Nazi views, they survived the war due to their scientific expertise. When Germany collapsed in 1945, the Flugges found themselves in the French zone of occupation. They worked for the National Office for Aeronautical Research in Paris for two years. Since their positions did not appear to be permanent, they moved to Stanford in 1948.

She was appointed lecturer while her husband was appointed professor. She plunged into teaching and research, however, establishing graduate research in aerodynamic theory. Although there were few graduate students who were interested in fluid dynamics, from nearby Ames Research Center she drew a large group of research engineers who were working toward advanced degrees from Stanford. She developed another new area of research in the theory of automatic controls, a topic she had first investigated in the 1940s. In 1960 she was the only woman delegate from the United States at the First Congress of the International Federation of Automatic Control in Moscow. As a result, she was appointed a full professor. After her retirement from teaching, she continued her research on problems of satellite control, heat transfer, and draft of high-speed vehicles. In addition to more than 50 technical papers, she published two books: *Discontinuous Automatic Control* (1953) and *Discontinuous and Optimal Control* (1958). The American Institute of Aeronautics and Astronautics in 1970 elected her a fellow, only the second woman to be so honored. She also was a member of the Institute of Electrical and Electronics Engineers and the Society for Industrial and Applied Mathematics.

Bibliography: American Men and Women of Science 10–12; Grinstein, Louise S. and Paul J. Campbell, eds., *Women of Mathematics;* Herzenberg, Caroline L., *Women Scientists from Antiquity to the Present;* O'Neill, Lois S., *The Women's Book of World Records and Achievements;* Sicherman, Barbara et al., *Notable American Women;* Siegel, Patricia J. and Kay Thomas Finley, *Women in the Scientific Search.*

Foot, Katharine
(1852–1944)
zoologist

Education: Private schools
Employment: No formal employment

Katharine Foot and her research partner Ella C. Strobell (q.v.) may not have been affiliated with an academic institution, yet their work was highly regarded by their contemporaries. Foot was included in a study of 150 distinguished American zoologists conducted in 1903 and reported in Stephen Visher's *Scientists Starred 1903–1943 in "American Men and Women of Science,"* and her name was starred in the first through seventh editions of *American Men and Women of Science.* Most of her papers were coauthored with Ella Strobell, and the two women probably funded their own research. Their contribution was that instead of drawing pictures of what they viewed through the microscope, the practice current at that time, they took photographs of amazing clarity. They were militant about the need to use photomicrographs in research. In one of their papers, they compared the accuracy of 200 photomicrographs to the same number of sketches of the same preparations. They also pointed out that a dozen photographs could be made in the time it took to draw one diagram. They also devised a method for making extremely thin sections of material at very low temperatures. They compiled the reprints of their papers in the monograph *Cytological Studies, 1894–1917,* which concerned the interpretation of modern studies of chromosomes. They seemed to be in the thick of scientific debates because several of their papers end with a review about the published conclusions of other scientists. Although their theories on chromosomes proved to be incorrect, their contribution to the technique of photomicrographs still is valuable today. Katharine Foot was a member of the American Society of Naturalists and American Society of Zoologists.

Bibliography: American Men and Women of Science 1–7; Herzenberg, Caroline L., *Women Scientists from Antiquity to the*

Present; Kass-Simon, G. and Patricia Farnes, *Women of Science;* Mozans, H. J., *Women in Science; National Union Catalog;* Ogilvie, Marilyn B., *Women in Science;* Rossiter, Margaret W., *Women Scientists in America;* Rossiter, Margaret W., "Women Scientists in America before 1920"; Siegel, Patricia J. and Kay Thomas Finley, *Women in the Scientific Search;* Visher, Stephen S., *Scientists Starred 1903–1943 in "American Men and Women of Science."*

Foster, Mary Louise
(1865–1960)
biochemist

Education: A.B., Smith College, 1891, A.M., 1912; Massachusetts Institute of Technology, 1893–1897; Columbia University, 1907; Ph.D. in chemistry, University of Chicago, 1914
Employment: High school chemistry teacher, 1891–1897; research chemist, C. A. Herter, 1900–1901, 1904–1907; Standard Esso Company, 1901–1904; associate professor of chemistry, Smith College, 1908–1933

Mary Foster had the distinction of being the only woman chemist of the 42 listed in the third edition of *American Men and Women of Science* to have worked for an industrial firm before 1916. She was employed as a chemist by two companies in the early 1900s. Although women scientists in general have had difficulty obtaining professional positions with corporations even to the present time, women chemists in particular were unable to secure research positions prior to World War II. She started her career in the usual pattern for a woman of her generation by teaching school after receiving her undergraduate degree from Smith College. She then broke the pattern by working for several companies as a chemist. She returned to Smith as a faculty member in 1908 and then received her advanced degree while teaching. The *American Men and Women of Science* listings state that she founded the Foster Laboratory in Madrid in 1920, but no additional information could be located on this. She also taught at Santiago College in Chile in 1932 and 1933, just prior to her retirement. She was a member of the American Association for the Advancement of Science, the American Chemical Society, and the American Society of Biological Chemists. She wrote one book, *The Life of Lavoisier* (1926). Her research centered on the effect of microorganisms on proteins, phosphatides, and absorption spectra of organic compounds.

Bibliography: *American Men and Women of Science* 3–7; Macksey, Joan and Kenneth Macksey, *The Book of Women's Achievements; National Union Catalog;* Rossiter, Margaret W., *Women Scientists in America.*

Fowler-Billings, Katharine Stevens
(1902–)
geologist

Education: A.B. in geology and biology, Bryn Mawr College, 1925; M.A., University of Wisconsin, 1926; Ph.D. in geology, Columbia University, 1930
Employment: Geologist, Sierra Leone, West Africa, 1930; Maroc Gold Company, 1931–1932; instructor in geology, Wellesley College, 1935–1938; Erskine Junior College, Boston, 1941; Tufts College, 1942–1943; geologist, New Hampshire Planning and Development Commission, 1943–1944; associate geologist, New England Museum of Natural History, 1940–1947; private research, 1947–
Married: James W. Lunn, 1929, divorced; Marland P. Billings, 1938

Katharine Fowler-Billings has been noted as one of the handful of women who has worked as a field geologist and explorer. She conducted extensive exploration of the Black Hills and the Mount Washington quadrangle. While attending the International Geological Congress in South Africa in 1929, she met and married James Lunn, also a geologist. When she was forbidden by local authorities to accompany her husband to the Gold Coast of West Africa, she went anyway. She wrote a book about her adventures in *Gold Missus: A Woman Prospector in Sierra Leone* (1938). She also found she had to disguise herself as a boy in order to be admitted to mines in the western United States due to prejudice, or in some cases, superstition against allowing women in mines. Between these adventures, she had a more prosaic life as an instructor in geology at Wellesley, Erskine Junior College, and Tufts College. She worked for the state of New Hampshire and for the New England Museum of Natural History as well as engaging in private research. She was elected a fellow of the Geological Society of America, and she has been a member of the Society of Women Geographers. Her research spanned the world: the anorthosites of the Laramie Mountains, Wyoming; iron ores and molybdenite, Sierra Leone, West Africa; and geology of the Cardigan Quadrangle of New Hampshire, Monadnock, and Mount Washington regions. She raised two children, George and Betty Jean.

Bibliography: American Men and Women of Science 7–11; Current Biography; Debus, A. G., ed., *World Who's Who in Science;* Herzenberg, Caroline L., *Women Scientists from Antiquity to the Present;* Ireland, Norma O., *Index to Scientists of the World.*

Frederick, Christine McGaffey
(1883–1970)
household efficiency specialist

Education: B.S., Northwestern University, 1906
Employment: Self-employed household equipment expert, 1910–1957; magazine editor and author, 1912–1957
Married: Justus G. Frederick, 1907

Christine Frederick was one of the first people to have commercial success in the field of home economics, operating a household equipment testing laboratory in her home. In about 1910, while living in Greenlawn, Long Island, she remodeled a few rooms of her house into the Applecroft Home Experiment Station, a model efficiency kitchen and laundry in which she tested household equipment and products. Her work contributed to standardizing the height of working surfaces in kitchens. She compiled booklets on household products, produced a film on housekeeping, and lectured on home management. She was appointed household editor for *Ladies' Home Journal* in 1912. In 1913 she expanded some of her articles into a book, *The New Housekeeping*. In 1915 she published *Household Engineering: Scientific Management in the Home*, which was used as a home economics textbook in colleges. Soon she started writing promotional literature for the products that manufacturers sent her for testing. She served as household editor for *American Weekly*, a periodical on advertising read by manufacturers and dealers. She based her book *Selling Mrs. Consumer* (1929) on a survey of the buying habits of women, one of the first such surveys conducted on this topic. She wrote numerous articles for magazines and newspapers, lectured, and gave radio talks. In 1950 she moved to California, where she taught extension courses in interior design and worked in her own consulting business until her retirement in 1957.

Bibliography: *National Union Catalog;* Rossiter, Margaret W., *Women Scientists in America;* Sicherman, Barbara et al., *Notable American Women.*

Furbish, Kate
(1834–1931)
botanical artist

Education: Public school; drawing classes, Portland, Maine, and Boston
Employment: No formal employment

Kate Furbish was recognized as one of the women amateur artists who contributed to the recording of scientific data in the nineteenth century. After inheriting an income from her father in 1873, she devoted her life to collecting, classifying, and recording in watercolor drawings the flora of Maine. Her goal was to prepare drawings of all native plants of Maine except grasses, sedges, trees, and ferns; and she was quite successful in her plan. She spent more than 35 years traveling throughout the state. The drawings comprise 16 large folio volumes that continue to be admired for both their botanical significance and their artistic value. She published several articles in the *American Naturalist* and occasionally lectured to groups. The accuracy of her paintings was highly regarded by professional botanists of the day such as Asa Gray and Merritt L. Fernald. Two of the plants she discovered were named for her. She was one of the dedicated amateurs of the nineteenth century upon whom advances in recording discoveries depended. She was a founder in 1895 and president in 1911 and 1912 of the Josselyn Botanical Society of Maine. She presented her watercolor drawings to Bowdoin College, her collection of 4,000 sheets of dried plants to the Gray Herbarium, and her collection of 182 sheets of ferns to the Portland Society of Natural History.

Bibliography: Abir-Am, P. G. and Dorinda Outram, eds., *Uneasy Careers and Intimate Lives*; Barnhart, John H., *Biographical Notes upon Botanists*; Herzenberg, Caroline L., *Women Scientists from Antiquity to the Present*; James, E. T., ed., *Notable American Women 1607–1950*; McHenry, Robert, ed., *Famous American Women*; O'Neill, Lois S., *The Women's Book of World Records and Achievements*; Siegel, Patricia J. and Kay Thomas Finley, *Women in the Scientific Search*; Uglow, Jennifer S., *International Dictionary of Women's Biography*; Vare, Ethlie Ann and Greg Ptacek, *Mothers of Invention*.

Furness, Caroline Ellen
(1869–1936)
astronomer

Education: A.B., Vassar College, 1891; Ph.D., Columbia University, 1900
Employment: High school instructor, 1891–1894; assistant, Vassar College Observatory, 1894–1903, instructor, 1903–1911, associate professor and acting director, 1911–1915, Maria Mitchell Professor of Astronomy, 1915–1936

Caroline Furness was one of the pioneer women astronomers who contributed to our knowledge of comets and minor planets. After matriculating at Vassar and teaching high school for several years, she was invited by Mary Whitney (q.v.) to return to Vassar as an assistant in the observatory. At the time Mary Whitney was carrying a heavy teaching load of eight different astronomy courses with a total of 160 students. With her own funds, she hired Caroline Furness to help with the teaching and research from 1894 through 1910. Caroline later succeeded her as professor of astronomy. They collaborated on the observation of comets and minor planets and after 1909 on variable stars. After Mary Whitney retired, Caroline Furness was named the Maria Mitchell Professor of Astronomy. During her tenure the college trained a large number of women astronomers, and the correspondence on file indicates that large observatories looked to Vassar when they wanted to hire women. Caroline emphasized the use of photography in astronomical research, and her students were actively engaged in the research. She made several trips abroad to work at the University of Groningen and to visit oriental scientific institutions throughout the world. She edited *Observations of Variable Stars Made at Vassar College (1901–1912)* in 1913. She was elected a fellow of the Royal Astronomical Society in 1922 and was also a member of the American Association for the Advancement of Science. Her name was included in the first edition of *American Men and Women of Science*.

Bibliography: *American Men and Women of Science* 1–5; Debus, A. G., ed., *World Who's Who in Science*; Herzenberg, Caroline L., *Women Scientists from Antiquity to the Present*; Kass-Simon, G. and Patricia Farnes, *Women of Science*; *National Union Catalog*; Rossiter, Margaret W., *Women Scientists in America*; Rossiter, Margaret W., "'Women's Work' in Science, 1880–1910"; Siegel, Patricia J. and Kay Thomas Finley, *Women in the Scientific Search*.

Susanna S. Phelps Gage
Eleanor Acheson McCulloch Gamble
Julia Anna Gardner
Fanny Cook Gates
Eloise B. Gerry
Eleanor Jack Gibson
Lillian E. Moller Gilbreth
Jocelyn Ruth Gill
Maria Goeppert Mayer
Gertrude Scharff Goldhaber
Winifred Goldring
Florence Laura Goodenough
Kate Gordon
Ruth Evelyn Gordon
Annie Evelyn Rathbun Gravatt
Emily L. Gregory
Emily Ray Gregory
Louisa Catherine Allen Gregory
Julia Henrietta Gulliver
Erna Gunther
Mary Jane Guthrie

Gage, Susanna S. Phelps
(1857–1915)
embryologist

Education: Ph.B., Cornell University, 1880
Employment: No formal employment
Married: Simon H. Gage, 1881

Susanna Gage's name was starred in the second edition of *American Men and Women of Science*, yet very little information on her research could be found. After receiving a degree from Cornell in 1880, she married the following year. She worked with her husband, who also was an embryologist. A perennial problem in science has been to identify the work of the women whose husbands were also scientists. In the eighteenth and nineteenth centuries especially, science was a family affair because men often funded their own research either through inheritance, business, or teaching, and their wives and daughters often assisted in the research. Susanna Gage was known to have participated in research at the Bermuda Biological Station in 1904 and at the Harvard and Johns Hopkins medical schools in 1904 and 1905. She published a few papers, such as "The Intramuscular Endings of Fibres in the Skeletal Muscles of Domestic and Laboratory Animals," which was published in the *Proceedings* of the thirteenth annual meeting of the American Society of Microscopists (1890). Her research centered on the structure of muscle, the comparative morphology of the brain, the development of the human brain, and the comparative anatomy of the nervous system. In 1917, in recognition that Susanna Gage was the first woman to take laboratory work in physics at Cornell, her husband and son gave Cornell $10,000 to be used to support research in physics. Her name was listed as Mrs. S. H. Gage in *American Men and Women of Science.*

Bibliography: American Men and Women of Science 1–2; Barr, Ernest S., *An Index to Biographical Fragments in Unspecialized Scientific Journals;* Herzenberg, Caroline L., *Women Scientists from Antiquity to the Present;* Mozans, H. J., *Women in Science; National Union Catalog;* Ogilvie, Marilyn B., *Women in Science;* Rossiter, Margaret W., *Women Scientists in America;* Rossiter, Margaret W., "'Women's Work' in Science, 1880–1910"; Siegel, Patricia J. and Kay Thomas Finley, *Women in the Scientific Search;* Visher, Stephen S., *Scientists Starred 1903–1943 in "American Men of Science."*

Gamble, Eleanor Acheson McCulloch
(1868–1933)
psychologist

Education: A.B., Wellesley College, 1889; Ph.D., Cornell University, 1898; University of Göttingen, 1906–1907
Employment: Teacher, Greek and psychology, Western Female College, 1889–1890; teacher, Greek and Latin, Plattsburgh Normal School, 1891–1895; instructor in psychology, Wellesley, 1898–1903, associate professor, 1903–1910, professor, 1910–1933

Eleanor Gamble was one of the notable faculty members of psychology of her generation. After teaching Greek, Latin, and psychology at several small schools and receiving her doctorate from Cornell, she joined the faculty of Wellesley College in 1898 as an instructor. She remained on the faculty for the remainder of her career. She was promoted in rank at seven-year intervals, which was a somewhat remarkable achievement. Many women faculty members, even those at women's colleges, experienced long delays in promotion while men faculty members advanced at regular six- and seven-year intervals. It was not until the 1970s that the practice was instituted that a person be tenured in order for faculty members to retain their positions; prior to that time people could remain on the faculty untenured for years. It is perhaps significant also that Eleanor Gamble was hired at the level of instructor, even though she had received a doctorate from a noted university. Wellesley College at that time was known for the quality of its science curriculum, just as it is today. Her area of research was the processes of memorization, and she wrote several technical articles. Her other research interest was smell intensities. She was a member of the American Psychological Association. Her name was included in the first edition of *American Men and Women of Science.*

Bibliography: *American Men and Women of Science 1–5*; Siegel, Patricia J. and Kay Thomas Finley, *Women in the Scientific Search.*

Gardner, Julia Anna
(1882–1960)
geologist

Education: A.B., Bryn Mawr College, 1905, A.M., 1907; Ph.D. in geology, Johns Hopkins University, 1911
Employment: Teacher, public school, 1906; assistant paleontologist, Johns Hopkins, 1911–1915; volunteer, Red Cross and American Friends Service Committee, in France, 1917–1919; paleontologist, U.S. Geological Survey, 1920–1924, geologist, 1924–1952

Julia Gardner was recognized as an expert in the paleontology of the Coastal Plain, and her primary interest was in the mollusks found in sedimentary and other rocks. She was one of the few women geologists whose name was starred in *American Men and Women of Science.* She had an unusual career in that she was one of the first women employed by the U.S. Geological Survey. She worked at Johns Hopkins for a few years after completing her education. She volunteered to serve in France with the Red Cross in World War I, and she was injured in the line of duty. She joined the U.S. Geological Survey in 1920 and was able to rise through the ranks, specializing in work on the Coastal Plain. The work she did was valuable to petroleum geologists because these were oil-bearing formations. Her research during the 1920s and 1930s was published as *Correlation of the Cenozoic Formations of the Atlantic and Gulf Coastal Plain and the Caribbean Region* (1943). By the 1940s her work in stratigraphic paleontology was of national and international importance, contributing especially to studies of economic geology in the western hemisphere. During World War II she worked with providing strategic and tactical information through analyses of maps, serial photographs, and other sources for use by the armed forces. One of her contributions was that she was able to identify some of the Japanese beaches from which incendiary balloons were being launched; she did it by identifying the origin of the shells in the sand ballast of the balloons. After her retirement, she immediately was rehired on a yearly contract basis for a project to prepare geological maps of the islands of the western Pacific; ill health in 1954 terminated her participation. She received the Department of the Interior's Distinguished Service Award in 1952. That same year she served as president of the Paleontological Society. She also was a member of the American Association of Petroleum

Geologists and the Geological Society of America. Her name was starred in the sixth and seventh editions of *American Men and Women of Science*. Her bibliography and photograph were published in the *Proceedings of the Geological Society of America* (1960): 87–92.

Bibliography: *American Men and Women of Science* 6–11; Arnold, Lois B., *Four Lives in Science*; Herzenberg, Caroline L., *Women Scientists from Antiquity to the Present*; Kass-Simon, G. and Patricia Farnes, *Women of Science*; Rossiter, Margaret W., *Women Scientists in America*; Sicherman, Barbara et al., *Notable American Women*; Siegel, Patricia J. and Kay Thomas Finley, *Women in the Scientific Search*; Visher, Stephen S., *Scientists Starred 1903–1943 in "American Men of Science."*

Gates, Fanny Cook
(1872–1931)
physicist

Education: A.B., Northwestern University, 1894, A.M., 1895; University of Göttingen and Zurich Polytechnic, 1897–1898; University of Chicago, 1899; McGill University, 1902–1903; Cavendish Laboratory, Cambridge University, 1905; Ph.D., University of Pennsylvania, 1909
Employment: Head, department of physics, Goucher College, 1898–1911; professor of physics and dean of women, Grinnell College, 1911–1916; dean of women, University of Illinois, 1916–1918

Fanny Gates was recognized as one of the notable women scientists at the seven women's colleges prior to 1940. She studied at first-class institutions and had research time at Cavendish Laboratory at Cambridge University. She received a fellowship from the Association of Collegiate Alumnae to study in 1897–1898 at the University of Göttingen and at Zurich Polytechnic. She did not receive a doctorate until 1909. After heading the department of physics at Goucher for 14 years, she moved

to Grinnell College in Iowa as professor of physics and dean of women. Faculty women of her generation often were assigned heavy administrative responsibilities in addition to serving as department heads, so it was not unusual to find someone with Fanny Gates' academic background working as dean of students. (After World War II, when college enrollments escalated, many of these administrative positions were assigned to administrative specialists instead of faculty members. Even in the 1930s dean of students positions were evolving into a specialty, with incumbents having credentials in counseling and similar areas.) Although she did significant work on the radioactive properties of chemical compounds at Grinnell, later at Illinois she did not have any teaching responsibilities. She was a member of both the American Physical Society and the American Mathematical Society. Her name was included in the first four editions of *American Men and Women of Science.*

Bibliography: *American Men and Women of Science* 1–4; Rossiter, Margaret W., *Women Scientists in America;* Rossiter, Margaret W., "'Women's Work' in Science, 1880–1910"; Siegel, Patricia J. and Kay Thomas Finley, *Women in the Scientific Search.*

Gerry, Eloise B.
(b. 1885)
botanist

Education: A.B., Radcliffe College, 1908, A.M., 1909; M.S., Smith College, 1909–1910; Ph.D. in plant physiology, University of Wisconsin, 1921

Employment: Expert, Forest Products Laboratory, U.S. Forest Service, 1910–1911, microscopist, 1911–1928, senior microscopist, 1928–1947, forest products technologist, 1947–1955

Concurrent Positions: Lecturer in forest products, University of Wisconsin, 1911–1955; emeritus lecturer

*E**loise Gerry* was the first woman appointed to the professional staff at the Forest Products Laboratory of the U.S. Forest Service at Madison, Wisconsin. She was one of the first women to specialize in forest products research and was an international expert on the properties of forest woods. After receiving her master's degree from Smith College in 1909, she joined the staff of the newly opened Forest Products Laboratory (usually referred to as FPL) in 1910 and spent her entire career at that installation. She joined the department as a wood microscopist and was promoted to forest products technologist in 1947. She was selected for the position because she had skills the laboratory needed, namely a highly specialized method for cutting wood specimens and preparing photomicrographs. She had developed these techniques in the course of her master's degree. She arrived at Madison just a few days after the laboratory opened, and the equipment she needed was not yet available. The botany department at the University of Wisconsin temporarily provided space and the equipment for her work. Since this was the first forest laboratory to be established, her first project was to collect wood samples from throughout the United States. After the samples were collected and analyzed, she moved to other research projects. Her first paper was published in 1914 on tyloses, the plugging of wood cells that restricts the movement of liquid. In 1916, over objections of lab administrators, she took her microtome and microscope to Mississippi and Florida to gather and analyze core samples from living trees for a project on naval stores. As a result of this research, she became a national expert in naval stores and wrote a book, *Naval Stores Handbook* (1935). During World War II she worked on projects of selecting wood suitable for packing supplies to ship to the armed services in a variety of climates all over the world. After the war her research involved foreign woods, on which she prepared 56 reports in the Foreign Wood Series of the Forest Products Laboratory. She published more than 120 papers in technical and trade journals, in FPL publications as well as those of the Forest Service and the U.S. Department of Agriculture. Concurrently she was a lecturer in forest products at the University of Wisconsin. She was elected a fellow of the American Association for the Advancement of Science, and was a member of the American Chemical Society, the American Forestry Association, the Society of American Foresters, the Forest History Society, and the International Association of Wood Anatomists. A biography that includes several photographs was published in *Journal of Forest History* 22 (1978): 192–235.

Bibliography: *American Men and Women of Science* 3–11; Barnhart, John H., *Biographical Notes upon Botanists*; Herzenberg, Caroline L., *Women Scientists from Antiquity to the Present*; *National Union Catalog*; Rossiter, Margaret W., *Women Scientists in America.*

Gibson, Eleanor Jack
(b. 1910)
psychologist

Education: A.B., Smith College, 1931, A.M., 1933; Ph.D. in psychology, Yale University, 1938

Employment: Assistant in psychology, Smith College, 1931–1933, instructor, 1933–1940, assistant professor, 1940–1949; research associate, Cornell University, 1949–1966, professor, 1966–?

Married: 1932

Eleanor Gibson was recognized as an expert in the psychology of learning. She was appointed an assistant in psychology at Smith College in 1931 but was promoted to the faculty as an instructor after completing her master's degree in 1933. The granting of her doctorate from Yale resulted in her promotion to assistant professor in 1940. She moved to Cornell as a research associate in 1949 and joined the faculty as professor in 1966. Concurrently she was a member of the Institute for Advanced Study (1958–1959) and a fellow at the Center for Advanced Study in Behavioral Science (1963–1964). The pauses in completing her graduate education may have been due to the Depression; people did not have the funds to take leaves of absences for study at other institutions, and fellowships were scarce or nonexistent. Even after completing her doctorate, she was promoted only to the rank of assistant professor, again due to the few jobs that were available. In spite of these handicaps, Eleanor Gibson assembled a solid record of research and publication that earned her

election to the National Academy of Sciences in 1971. She was a member of the American Psychological Association and received its award in 1968 and a G. Stanley Hall Award in 1970. She was also a member of the Society of Experimental Psychologists. She specialized in the psychology of learning involving general, laboratory, experimental, animal, comparative, and developmental psychology. She had two children.

Bibliography: *American Men and Women of Science* 8–12; Herzenberg, Caroline L., *Women Scientists from Antiquity to the Present*; O'Neill, Lois S., *The Women's Book of World Records and Achievements.*

Gilbreth, Lillian E. Moller
(1878–1972)
engineer, household efficiency expert, and industrial psychologist

Education: B. Litt, University of California, Berkeley, 1900, M.A., 1902; Ph.D. in psychology, Brown University, 1915
Employment: Co-owner, Gilbreth, Inc., 1904–1924; consultant, 1924–1972; visiting lecturer, Purdue University, 1924–1935, professor of management, 1935–1948, consultant on careers for women at Purdue, 1939–1948; courses for the disabled, 1948–1972; chair, department of personnel relations, Newark College of Engineering, 1941–1943; professor of management, University of Wisconsin, 1955
Married: Frank B. Gilbreth, 1904, died 1924

illian Gilbreth was one of the founders of the discipline of scientific management and a pioneer in the field of industrial psychology. She was a remarkable woman who combined a career with marriage and family. Her actual accomplishments were more remarkable than any fiction. She met and married Frank Gilbreth soon after she graduated from college. He was a self-made builder with a flair for inventing equipment and techniques for improving efficiency. She had received a master's degree in English literature, but she soon joined her husband in his industrial engineering consulting firm, Gilbreth, Inc. She obtained her doctorate in psychology in the midst of working with her husband and bearing 12 children in 17 years. The large family lived an organized life, as advocated by the parents. They used their home as a model laboratory in the effort to find the best way to carry out each task. They taught management groups at home in addition to lecturing in schools of engineering and business, consulting for industrial firms, and writing for both professional and popular magazines. They were forerunners of the science of time and motion analysis. Her major contribution to the field was injecting an appreciation of the human element in applying time and motion studies.

Lillian Gilbreth turned to college teaching when companies refused to hire their consulting firm after her husband's death in 1924. Purdue hired her as a guest lecturer, a position that Frank Gilbreth formerly had held, and later gave her a faculty appointment. According to the practice of the time, she was assigned to the home economics department, where she taught household management instead of teaching in the regular business or engineering departments. She began an intensive study of applying modern business methods in the home.

She and her husband coauthored five books on industrial efficiency. She was the sole author of *Psychology of Management* (1914). In the area of household

management she had two major publications, *The Home-Maker and Her Job* (1927) and *Management in the Home* (1954), as well as numerous articles in such popular magazines as *Good Housekeeping* and *Better Homes and Gardens*. She did significant work with people with disabilities and handicaps 50 years before the American Disabilities Act was conceived. She discussed special equipment and routines for housework in *Normal Lives for the Disabled* (1944).

She developed a model kitchen for the handicapped for the Institute of Rehabilitation Medicine at the New York University Medical Center. She received 12 honorary degrees. She continued her research past the age of 70 and was still writing and lecturing after the age of 80. In 1921 she was named an honorary member of the Society of Industrial Engineers, which did not admit women to membership. She was the first woman to receive the Hoover Medal (1966). In 1987 Purdue established a distinguished professorship of engineering in her name; the first (and current) holder of the professorship is a man. The Society of Women Engineers established a fellowship in her memory. The humorous reminiscences of the Gilbreth family were recorded by Frank Gilbreth, Jr., and Ernestine G. Carey in *Cheaper by the Dozen* (1948) and *Belles on Their Toes* (1950). There are photographs in *Current Biography*, Joan Marlow's *The Great Women*, and G. Kass-Simon's and Patricia Farnes's *Women of Science*. The Gilbreth papers are available in the special collections section of the Purdue University Libraries.

Bibliography: *Current Biography*; Debus, A. G., ed., *World Who's Who in Science*; Goff, Alice C., *Women Can Be Engineers*; Herzenberg, Caroline L., *Women Scientists from Antiquity to the Present*; Kass-Simon, G. and Patricia Farnes, *Women of Science*; McHenry, Robert, ed., *Famous American Women*; Marlow, Joan, *The Great Women*; *National Union Catalog*; O'Neill, Lois S., *The Women's Book of World Records and Achievements*; Rossiter, Margaret W.,

Women Scientists in America; Shapiro, Laura, *Perfection Salad;* Sicherman, Barbara et al., *Notable American Women;* Siegel, Patricia J. and Kay Thomas Finley, *Women in the Scientific Search;* Yost, Edna, *American Women of Science.*

Gill, Jocelyn Ruth
(1916–1984)
astronomer

Education: A.B., Wellesley College, 1938; S.M. in astronomy and astrophysics, University of Chicago, 1941; Ph.D. in astronomy, Yale University, 1959

Employment: Laboratory assistant and instructor of astronomy, Mount Holyoke College, 1940–1942; staff member, radiation laboratory, Massachusetts Institute of Technology, 1942–1945; from instructor to assistant professor of astronomy, Smith College, 1945–1952; instructor, University of California extension, 1946–1948; assistant professor, Mount Holyoke, 1952–1957; associate professor of mathematics and astronomy, Arizona State College, 1959–1960; research assistant in astronomy, Yale University, 1960–1961; staff scientist, astronomy and astrophysics, Office of Space Science and Applications, National Aeronautics and Space Administration, 1961–1963, chief of in-flight science, Manned Space Science Program Office, 1963–1966, staff scientist, Manned Flight Experiment Office, 1966–1968, program scientist, 1968–1984

Jocelyn Gill performed significant research in the National Aeronautics and Space Administration's (NASA) manned space flight program beginning in 1961. After receiving her master's degree, she was employed as a laboratory assistant and instructor of astronomy at Mount Holyoke. The beginning of World War II opened up many positions for women that hitherto had been unavailable for them. The radiation laboratory at Massachusetts Institute of Technology (MIT) hired many women to continue the work that men formerly had performed. This provided invaluable experience for women in very new areas of research. After working at MIT she taught astronomy at several schools while continuing work on her doctorate at Yale. She had several other assignments until she received an appointment with the National Aeronautics and Space Administration in 1961 with the Office of Space Science and Applications in the Washington, D.C., area. It was another case of serendipity for her.

After the former Soviet Union launched Sputnik, there was a crash program to catch up to and surpass the Russian space program. Again the U.S. program opened up many positions that women scientists with expertise in astronomy and astrophysics could fill. There simply were not enough men available in these fields. She was chief of in-flight science from 1963 to 1966 and participated in a solar eclipse flight in 1963. She also worked on the Gemini Science program. She received the Federal Women's Award in 1966 representing NASA. She was elected a fellow of the American Association for the Advancement of Science and was also a member of the American Astronomical Society and the American Association of Variable Star Observers. Her research involved motion of Neptune's satellite (Triton), celestial mechanics, and numerical analysis of satellite orbits.

Bibliography: *American Men and Women of Science* 9–14; Debus, A. G., ed., *World Who's*

Who in Science; Herzenberg, Caroline L., *Women Scientists from Antiquity to the*   *Present;* O'Neill, Lois S., *The Women's Book of World Records and Achievements.*

Goeppert-Mayer, Maria
(1906–1972)
physicist

Education: Ph.D. in physics, University of Göttingen, 1930
Employment: Assistant in physics, Johns Hopkins University, 1930–1932, associate, 1932–1936, research associate, 1936–1939; lecturer, Columbia University, 1939–1945; Sarah Lawrence College, 1941–1945; senior physicist, Argonne National Laboratory, 1946–1960; volunteer professor, Enrico Fermi Institute of Nuclear Studies, University of Chicago, 1946–1959, professor, 1959–1960; professor, school of science and engineering, University of California, San Diego at La Jolla, 1960–1972
Married: Joseph Mayer, 1930

Maria Goeppert-Mayer was a corecipient of the Nobel Prize in physics in 1963. Her professional career soared in spite of the discrimination she suffered as a married woman with respect to position and pay. She obtained her doctorate in theoretical physics in 1930 at the University of Göttingen. That same year she married Joseph Mayer and came with him to the United States, where she spent her entire postdoctoral career. Due to nepotism rules at universities at that time, Maria Goeppert-Mayer was not appointed to a faculty position with pay until 1959. Her work often was ignored, and many questioned the decision when she was a cowinner of the Nobel Prize. An examination of her papers indicates, however, that she did discover the role of spin-orbit forces in the shell model. She first was appointed an assistant in physics at Johns Hopkins and later promoted to associate and then research associate with minimal pay at each stage. One of her initial assignments was to translate scientific papers from German to English for one of the faculty members. Then she was a half-time lecturer with pay at Sarah Lawrence. She was invited to Columbia in 1942 to participate in "secret" bomb research in the Manhattan Project.

(Since there was a shortage of men scientists, many women were hired for the project.) Soon she had 20 persons working under her. She was then invited to join the staff at Los Alamos in 1946 as part of the same project. She returned to her half-time position at Sarah Lawrence when her work on the bomb was completed. The couple moved to the University of Chicago in 1946 and to her surprise she was offered an associate professorship in physics. Enrico Fermi's new Institute of Nuclear Studies at Chicago was composed of many famous scientists who had worked on the bomb project. She still did not receive a salary due to the university rule that both husband and wife, even in different departments, could not be hired by the university. Not until 1959, when the couple was being sought by the University of California, San Diego, did the University of Chicago pay her a full professor's salary. She was conducting her research at Argonne National Laboratory, where a nuclear reactor was being built. In 1960 the couple moved to the University of California, San Diego, where she was appointed professor in the school of science and engineering.

She was elected to the National Academy of Sciences in 1956 and received four honorary degrees. She was also a member of the American Academy of Arts and Sciences and the American Physical Society. One popular publication named her the Marie Curie of the Atom. She coauthored two books: *Statistical Mechanics* (1940) and *Elementary Theory of Nuclear Shell Structure* (1955). The couple had two children, Marianne and Peter. There are biographical sketches with photographs in *A Life of One's Own* (1973) by Joan Dash, Sharon McGrayne's *Nobel Prize Women in Science*, *Biographical Memoirs* of the National Academy of Sciences, and Olga Opfell's *Lady Laureates; Biographical Memoirs* includes a bibliography of her publications. Her name was listed in the various sources as either Maria Mayer or Maria Goeppert-Mayer.

Bibliography: *American Men and Women of Science* 6–11; Debus, A. G., ed., *World Who's Who in Science;* Herzenberg, Caroline L., *Women Scientists from Antiquity to the Present;* Kass-Simon, G. and Patricia Farnes, *Women of Science;* Macksey, Joan and Kenneth Macksey, *The Book of Women's Achievements;* National Academy of Sciences, *Biographical Memoirs; National Union Catalog;* O'Neill, Lois S., *The Women's Book of World Records and Achievements;* Opfell, Olga S., *The Lady Laureates;* Perl, Teri, *Math Equals;* Rossiter, Margaret W., *Women Scientists in America;* Sicherman, Barbara et al., *Notable American Women;* Siegel, Patricia J. and Kay Thomas Finley, *Women in the Scientific Search;* Uglow, Jennifer S., *International Dictionary of Women's Biography; Who Was Who in America.*

Goldhaber, Gertrude Scharff
(1911–)
physicist

Education: Ph.D. in physics, University of Munich, 1935

Employment: Research associate in physics, Imperial College, University of London, 1935–1939; research physicist, University of Illinois, 1939–1948, special research assistant professor of physics, 1948–1950; consultant, Brookhaven National Laboratory, 1948–1950, associate physicist, 1950–1958, physicist, 1958–1962, senior physicist, 1962–1979

Concurrent Positions: Consultant, Argonne National Laboratory, 1946–1950 and Los Alamos Scientific Laboratory, 1953–1979; adjunct professor, Cornell University, 1980–1982, Johns Hopkins University, 1982

Married: Maurice Goldhaber, 1939

Gertrude Goldhaber was elected to the National Academy of Sciences in 1972, the second woman physicist to be elected. She has had a long and influential career in nuclear physics. She has been involved at Brookhaven National Laboratory in both theoretical and experimental work to determine the detailed properties of nuclear energy levels and magnetic moments. After receiving a doctorate in physics from the University of Munich in 1935, she was employed as a research associate in physics at Imperial College, University of London, for five years. Moving to the United States, she was a research physicist and a special research assistant at the University of Illinois from 1939 to 1950. She was appointed to the staff at Brookhaven National Laboratory in 1950 and achieved the rank of senior physicist, working at that level from 1962 to 1979. She has held several prestigious appointments in science, such as member of the advisory panel on the nuclear data project, National

Research Council (1959–1964); chair of the panel for evaluation of nuclear data compilations, National Academy of Sciences National Research Council (1969–1971); member of the board of trustees, Fermi National Accelerator Laboratory (1972–1977); member of the research advisory committee for the National Science Foundation (1972–1974); and member of the nominating committee for the Presidential Medal of Science (1977–1979). She was elected a fellow of both the American Association for the Advancement of Science and of the American Physical Society. Her research has centered on spontaneous fission neutrons and identification of beta-rays with atomic electrons. The couple had two children, Alfred and Michael. Her name was included in the 1992–1993 edition of *American Men and Women of Science.*

Bibliography: *American Men and Women of Science* 8–18; Debus, A. G., ed., *World Who's Who in Science;* Herzenberg, Caroline L., *Women Scientists from Antiquity to the Present;* Kass-Simon, G. and Patricia Farnes, *Women of Science;* O'Neill, Lois S., *The Women's Book of World Records and Achievements.*

Goldring, Winifred
(1888–1971)
paleontologist

Education: A.B., Wellesley College, 1909, A.M., 1912; Teachers School of Science (affiliated with the Boston Society of Natural History), 1909–1911; Harvard University, 1910–1911; Columbia University, 1913; Johns Hopkins University, 1921
Employment: Assistant in geology and geography, Wellesley College, 1909–1912, instructor, 1912–1914; expert, New York State Museum, 1914–1915, assistant paleontologist, 1915–1920, associate paleontologist, 1920–1925, paleobotanist, 1925–1939, State Paleontologist, 1939–1954

Winifred Goldring was recognized for her expertise by being appointed state paleontologist of New York. Aside from the five years she taught at Wellesley College, she spent her entire career in the vicinity of Albany, New York. She began working as an "expert" at the New York State Museum and soon started her own research on the paleontology of sea lilies from the middle of the Paleozoic era. This was conducted at a time when there was a great deal of interest in paleobotany, and her collection was recognized worldwide. She received a permanent appointment as associate paleontologist in 1920. She prepared numerous handbooks, but her most important monograph was *The Devonian Crinoids of the State of New York* (1923). Her handbooks and exhibitions were widely copied and considered models for teaching. For example, her "Guide to the Geology of John Boyd Thacher Park" (1933) was a case study well suited to college courses. She made great strides in popularizing geology for the general public. In 1939 she was officially appointed state paleontologist, achieving some notoriety as the first woman to hold the post. She remained in this post until her retirement in 1954. She was the first woman elected president of the Paleontological Society in 1949. She received an honorary degree from Russell Sage College in 1937 and one from Smith College in 1957.

Bibliography: Abir-Am, P. G. and Dorinda Outram, eds., *Uneasy Careers and Intimate Lives; American Men and Women of Science* 3–10; Herzenberg, Caroline L., *Women Scientists from Antiquity to the Present;* Kass-Simon, G. and Patricia Farnes, *Women of Science; National Union Catalog;* Rossiter, Margaret W., *Women Scientists in America;* Sicherman, Barbara et al., *Notable American Women;* Siegel, Patricia J. and Kay Thomas Finley, *Women in the Scientific Search.*

Goodenough, Florence Laura
(1886–1959)
psychologist

Education: B.Pd., Pennsylvania State Normal School, Millersville, 1908; B.S., Columbia University, 1920, A.M., 1921; Ph.D. in psychology, Stanford University, 1924
Employment: Teacher, public schools, 1908–1921; research assistant, gifted children survey, Stanford, 1921–1924; psychologist, child guidance clinic, Minneapolis, 1924–1925; assistant professor, research, Institute of Child Welfare, University of Minnesota, 1925–1928, associate professor, 1928–1930, professor, 1930–1947; emeritus professor

Florence Goodenough made major contributions to the growth and usefulness of tools for the measurement and interpretation of intelligence in children. Her book, *Handbook of Child Psychology* (1931), and her creation of the Minnesota Preschool Scale for the early estimation of mental ability both were widely recognized as important contributions. Her name was starred in the sixth and seventh editions of *American Men and Women of Science*. After graduating from the Millersville State Normal School, she taught school for more than ten years while she continued her studies at Columbia University. She moved to Stanford University for her doctorate, where exciting studies of mental measurements of gifted children were being conducted. At the University of Minnesota she experimented with several methods of measurement and the Minnesota Preschool Scale, which has been widely used. In her own research and writing she stressed that IQ is not constant, and children should not be pegged at an early age at a level they cannot escape. She urged the study of the total life span; at the time she was writing, most studies stopped after adolescence. She was elected president of the National Council of Women Psychologists in 1942 and president of the Society for Research in Child Development in 1946 and 1947. She coauthored a number of books in addition to the *Handbook,* and she was sole author of *Anger in Young Children* (1931). Her research interests included human psychological development, mental tests, general psychological experimentation, and free-word association. Her biography and photograph were included in *Child Development* 30 (1959): 305–306.

Bibliography: American Men and Women of Science 4–8; Bryan, Alice I. and Edwin G. Boring, "Women in American Psychology"; Herzenberg, Caroline L., *Women Scientists from Antiquity to the Present; National Union Catalog;* Rossiter, Margaret W., *Women Scientists in America;* Sicherman, Barbara et al., *Notable American Women;* Siegel, Patricia J. and Kay Thomas Finley, *Women in the Scientific Search;* Visher, Stephen S., *Scientists Starred 1903–1943 in "American Men of Science."*

Gordon, Kate
(b. 1878)
psychologist

Education: Ph.B., University of Chicago, 1900, Ph.D., 1903
Employment: Instructor in philosophy, Mount Holyoke College, 1904–1905, associate professor of psychology, 1905–1906; instructor in educational psychology, Teachers' College, Columbia University, 1906–1907; associate professor of psychology, Bryn Mawr College, 1912–1916; assistant professor of psychology and education, Carnegie Institute of Technology, 1916–1919, associate professor, 1919–1921; lecturer in psychology, University of California, Los Angeles, 1921–1922, associate professor, 1923–1934, professor, 1934–1948; emeritus professor
Married: Ernest C. Moore

Kate Gordon had an unusual area of research in her investigations of color vision. After she received her doctorate from the University of Chicago, she moved frequently from one appointment to another. She spent three years at Mount Holyoke, two years at Columbia, five years at Bryn Mawr, and six years at Carnegie Institute of Technology. Finally, in 1921, she received an appointment at the University of California, Los Angeles, where she stayed until retiring in 1948. She had an interim appointment as a psychologist in the children's department for the California State Board of Control in 1918 and 1919. She had a remarkable career of increasingly important appointments at recognized universities. She apparently married late in life; her husband's name did not appear until the eighth edition of *American Men and Women of Science* (1949) when she would have been over 70 years old. She was a member of several scientific societies, including the American Association for the Advancement of Science, the American Psychological Association, and the American Philosophical Association. Kate Gordon's research centered on the areas of memory, attention, and the esthetics of color. Her name was included in the first edition of *American Men and Women of Science.*

Bibliography: American Men and Women of Science 1–9; Rossiter, Margaret W., *Women Scientists in America;* Siegel, Patricia J. and Kay Thomas Finley, *Women in the Scientific Search.*

Gordon, Ruth Evelyn
(1910–)
bacteriologist

Education: A.B., Cornell University, 1932, M.S., 1933, Ph.D. in bacteriology, 1934
Employment: Instructor, New York Veterinary College, Cornell University, 1934–1937; assistant bacteriologist, Division of Soil Microbiology, U.S. Department of Agriculture, 1938–1942, bacteriologist, 1950–1951; Army Medical Center, 1943–1944; bacteriologist, American Type Culture Collection, 1944–1947, curator, 1947–1951; associate research specialist, New Jersey Agricultural Experiment Station, 1951–1954; associate professor,

Waksman Institute of Microbiology, Rutgers University, 1954–1971, professor of microbiology, 1971–1981; visiting investigator, American Type Culture Collection

Ruth Gordon has been recognized for her work as a bacteriologist for the American Type Culture Collection. She first was employed as an instructor at the New York Veterinary College at Cornell University. She then had a varied career of employment with the U.S. Department of Agriculture (USDA), an army medical center, an agricultural experiment station, and academe. She was an assistant bacteriologist in the Division of Soil Microbiology, USDA, from 1938 to 1942, returning to the agency as a bacteriologist in 1950 and 1951. During World War II she was employed at the Army Medical Center. She accepted a position as a bacteriologist at the American Type Culture Collection in 1944, being promoted to curator in 1947. She became an associate research specialist at the New Jersey Agricultural Experiment Station, then moved to the faculty of Waksman Institute of Microbiology at

Rutgers, where she worked from 1954 to 1981. Ruth Gordon received the J. Roger Porter Award from the U.S. Federation for Culture Collections in 1983. She continued to be associated with the collection as a visiting investigator after her retirement. She has been a member of the American Association for the Advancement of Science, the American Society for Microbiology, the Tissue Culture Association, and the U.S. Federation for Culture Collections. Her research has involved taxonomy of aerobic, spore-forming bacteria; mycobacteria; and streptomycetes. Her name was included in the 1992–1993 edition of *American Men and Women of Science.*

Bibliography: *American Men and Women of Science* 8–18; *National Union Catalog;* O'Neill, Lois S., *The Women's Book of World Records and Achievements.*

Gravatt, Annie Evelyn Rathbun
(b. 1894)
forest pathologist

Education: A.B., Brown University, 1916, M.S., 1918
Employment: Collaborator, field assistant, assistant forest pathologist, junior pathologist, and plant pathologist, Bureau of Plant Industry, U.S. Department of Agriculture (USDA), 1916–?
Married: George Gravatt, 1924

Annie Gravatt was a scientist who served on the editorial staff of a major scientific journal, *Phytopathology,* for more than ten years. She was one of the few early women scientists specializing in forest pathology. She was appointed to the staff of the USDA's Bureau of Plant Industry in 1916 after she received her undergraduate degree. She received a master's degree two years later. She rose in

the USDA from collaborator to plant pathologist, spending her entire career with the agency. She was one of many women who found satisfying careers there. She was able to publish the results of her research under her own name, and most of them were published in *Phytopathology* and the *USDA Journal of Agricultural Research.* The USDA was the largest single employer of women scientists in the federal government in the 1920s; many women at this time sought careers in botany, and the Bureau of Plant Industry had a great deal of botanical research to be handled. She was a member of several professional societies, such as the American Association for the Advancement of Science and the American Phytopathological Society. Her areas of

research were plant physiology, damping-off of conifers, and white pine blister rust.

Bibliography: *American Men and Women of Science* 4–10; Barnhart, John H., *Biographical Notes upon Botanists; National Union Catalog.*

Gregory, Emily L.
(1840–1897)
botanist

Education: B.Lit., Cornell University, 1881; Ph.D., University of Zurich, 1886
Employment: Botany teacher, Smith College, 1881–1883; laboratory assistant, Harvard University, 1884; associate, Bryn Mawr College, 1887; assistant, University of Pennsylvania, 1888; instructor in botany, Barnard College, 1889–1897

*E*mily L. Gregory was known to be one of the first American women to be granted a doctorate from a European university. (In the latter part of the nineteenth century, women were not accepted for graduate study in American colleges. Many women sought out the universities in Germany and Switzerland, which they could attend as regular students.) After she received her doctorate from the University of Zurich, she was unable to find a salaried academic position due to prejudices against hiring women professors. She worked briefly at Bryn

Mawr and at the University of Pennsylvania and taught at Barnard College as an unpaid professor because she had an independent income. She went to Europe in the summers of 1889, 1893, 1894, and 1895 to purchase, with her own funds, the microscopes, charts, models, and books she needed for the laboratory at Barnard. Her work was regarded as superior. In *Women Scientists in America* Margaret Rossiter lists her as one of the notable women scientists at the seven major women's colleges before 1940. In 1886 she was the first woman to be elected to membership in the American Society of Naturalists, perhaps due to her doctorate. She published a textbook, *Elements of Plant Anatomy*, in 1895. A list of her other publications appears in John Harshberger's *Botanists of Philadelphia and Their Work*. In 1899 the Barnard Botanical Club dedicated a bronze tablet in her honor as the first professor of botany at Barnard.

Bibliography: Barnhart, John H., *Biographical Notes upon Botanists*; Barr, Ernest S., *An Index to Biographical Fragments in Unspecialized Scientific Journals*; Harshberger, John W., *The Botanists of Philadelphia and Their Work*; Herzenberg, Caroline L., *Women Scientists from Antiquity to the Present*; National Union Catalog; Ogilvie, Marilyn B., *Women in Science*; Rossiter, Margaret W., *Women Scientists in America*; Rudolph, Emanuel D., "Women in Nineteenth Century American Botany."

Gregory, Emily Ray
(1863–1946)
zoologist

Education: B.A., Wellesley College, 1885; Marine Biological Laboratory, Woods Hole, 1893–1895; M.A., University of Pennsylvania, 1896; Ph.D., University of Chicago, 1899; American Woman's Table, Naples Zoological Station, 1899–1900

Employment: Teacher, 1885–1888, 1893–1895; proofreader, American Academy of Political and Social Science; assistant zoologist, University of Chicago, 1897–1899; professor of biology, Wells College, 1901–1909; American College for Girls, Constantinople, 1909–1911; University of Akron, 1913–1915; substitute, Wellesley College and Sweet Briar College, 1915–1917; U.S. Treasury Department, 1919–1924

*E*mily R. Gregory's work was recognized by her contemporaries, and her name was listed in the first seven editions of *American Men and Women of Science*. Another evidence of the soundness of her research was her selection for research projects at the Naples Zoological Station, an internationally known research facility, where fellowship applications were evaluated on rigid scientific standards. She took an undergraduate degree with an emphasis in music, but switched to a zoology major after teaching in private schools for a time. She then completed her education at the University of Pennsylvania and the University of Chicago. She was employed at a variety of schools, with her longest single appointment at Wells College. Following her years at Wells, she taught for two years at the Constantinople American College for Girls and remained active in promoting that school through the American Association of University Women. She worked for the War Trade Board during World War I. The last employment she listed was with the U.S. Treasury Department from 1919 to 1924, but there is no indication what her position was there. Her career was somewhat characteristic of many women scientists of her generation. Even with degrees from three outstanding schools, it was difficult for her to secure full-time employment that allowed her time to conduct research. She was a member of the American Society of Zoologists and Biological Society of Washington. Her areas of research were the origin of the pronephric duct in selachians and the development of the excretory system in turtles.

Bibliography: *American Men and Women of Science* 1–7; Herzenberg, Caroline L., *Women Scientists from Antiquity to the Present*; Ogilvie, Marilyn B., *Women in Science*; Rossiter, Margaret W., *Women Scientists in America*; Siegel, Patricia J. and Kay Thomas Finley, *Women in the Scientific Search*.

Gregory, Louisa Catherine Allen
(1848–1920)
home economist

Education: Teachers' course, State Normal University at Normal, Illinois, 1870
Employment: Lecturer, farmers' institutes, 1870; principal, high schools, 1870–1873; dean of women and head, School of Domestic Science and Art, University of Illinois, 1874–1877, preceptress, 1878, professor, 1879–1880
Married: John M. Gregory, 1879

*L*ouisa Gregory was noted for inaugurating a short-lived home economics program at the Illinois Industrial University (later University of Illinois) from 1874 to 1880. She served as the equivalent of the dean of women and the head of the School of Domestic Science and Art. She developed a science program for women that stressed chemistry, anatomy, physiology, and botany at a time when other early university programs focused on cooking and service. In order to have a program equal in every way to that of the men students, she prepared a course in gymnastics and calisthenics to take the place of the men's military training. The home economics program was absorbed into the College of Natural Science in 1877.

She was appointed preceptress in 1878 and promoted to full professor in 1879. After she married the regent, they both resigned from the university in 1880. She received an honorary M.S. from Illinois in 1890 in recognition for her work at the university. In 1881 the women's program was integrated into the regular curriculum; in 1900 Isabel Bevier (q.v.) was hired to develop a separate home economics department. There are photographs of Louisa Gregory in Lois Arnold's *Four Lives in Science*, including one of her supervising a class of women in gymnastics costumes.

Bibliography: Arnold, Lois B., *Four Lives in Science*; Herzenberg, Caroline L., *Women Scientists from Antiquity to the Present*.

Gulliver, Julia Henrietta
(1856–1940)
philosopher

Education: A.B., Smith College, 1879, Ph.D., 1888; University of Leipzig, 1892–1893
Employment: Head, department of philosophy and biblical literature, Rockford College, 1890–1919, president, 1902–1919

Julia Gulliver was recognized as an outstanding educator when she was president of Rockford College; her name was included in the first edition of *American Men and Women of Science*. She was a member of the first class to graduate from Smith, after which she spent several years at home studying philosophy and attending lectures at Andover Theological Seminary, where her father was a professor. These studies were the basis for the doctorate at Smith; she received the second Ph.D. awarded by the college. She then spent several years as president of Rockford College, successfully putting it on a sound intellectual and financial basis. She made important additions to the stature of the faculty; she expanded the library collection and increased the size of the student body

and the endowment. Although she had some interest in the psychology of dreams, she could not be considered a scientist. She introduced courses in home economics and secretarial science into the curriculum for both practical and philosophical reasons, however. She believed women should retain their traditional influence in the home at the same time they were active participants in the community. She received an honorary degree from Smith in 1910. Her primary research interest was ethics.

Bibliography: *American Men and Women of Science* 1; James, E. T., ed., *Notable American Women 1607–1950*; Siegel, Patricia J. and Kay Thomas Finley, *Women in the Scientific Search.*

Gunther, Erna
(1896–1982)
anthropologist

Education: B.A., Barnard College, 1919; M.A., Columbia University, 1920, Ph.D. in anthropology, 1928
Employment: Assistant in anthropology, Barnard College, 1919–1921; lecturer, University of Washington, Seattle, 1923–1924, assistant professor, 1929–1941, professor and executive officer of department, 1941–1966; acting director, Washington State Museum, 1929–1930, director, 1930–1962; professor of anthropology, University of Alaska, 1966–?
Married: Leslie Spier, 1921, divorced 1932
Concurrent position: Director, Washington State Museum, 1929–1962

Erna Gunther was one of the few women who directed a state museum, a position she filled for more than 30 years. After receiving her master's degree, she accepted a position at the University of Washington as a lecturer. She then obtained her doctorate and was appointed to the faculty as assistant professor in 1929, being promoted to professor in 1941. Concurrently she was acting director and then director of the Washington State Museum from 1929 to 1962. After retiring from Washington in 1966, she accepted a position at the University of Alaska. Erna Gunther's career

was more stable than other women anthropologists and ethnologists. She secured a position where she stayed for more than 30 years and directed a museum for most of that time. Many of the other women of her generation received only short appointments at various institutions, primarily due to the shortage of jobs, especially for women, during the Depression. She was a member of the American Anthropological Association, the American Ethnological Association, and the American Folk-Lore Society. Her area of research was Native American life in the Northwest coastal area in the eighteenth century. She was the mother of two children, Robert and Christopher.

Bibliography: *American Men and Women of Science* 6–10; Debus, A. G., ed., *World Who's Who in Science*; Herzenberg, Caroline L., *Women Scientists from Antiquity to the Present; International Directory of Anthropologists*; McNeil, Barbara, ed., *Biography and Genealogy Master Index 1986–90, Cumulation*, vol.3.

Guthrie, Mary Jane
(1895–1975)
zoologist

Education: A.B., University of Missouri, 1916, A.M., 1918; Ph.D., Bryn Mawr College, 1922
Employment: Demonstrator in biology, Bryn Mawr College, 1918–1920, instructor, 1920–1921; assistant professor of zoology, University of Missouri, 1922–1926, associate professor, 1927–1937, professor, 1937–1951; research associate, Detroit Institute for Cancer Research, 1951–1960; professor, Wayne State University, 1955–1960
Concurrent Position: Researcher, Wayne State University, ca. 1951–1960

Mary Guthrie's research was recognized by her contemporaries, and her name was starred in the sixth and seventh editions of *American Men and Women of Science.* She was listed in the two previous editions before her name was starred, indicating continuing growth as a scientist. After receiving her doctorate from Bryn Mawr, she returned to the University of Missouri, where she had received her earlier education, to be appointed assistant professor. She was appointed professor before leaving the institution for a position as research associate at the Detroit Institute for Cancer Research in 1951. She had a concurrent appointment at Wayne State University for a portion of that time, but retired from both in 1960. Although she was a noted scientist, she had difficulty obtaining grants. In 1934 an official at the Rockefeller Foundation explained to her that, although she might be an outstanding scientist, as a woman she had to present

extra proof of her excellence in order to receive a grant (women were not officially excluded from the Rockefeller fellowship program). Although Mary Guthrie had the advantage of stable employment during the Depression years, she still had to face the problem of funding. She was a member of the American Association for the Advancement of Science, the American Society of Naturalists, and the American Society of Zoologists. Her area of specialization was the cytology of cytoplasm of the female reproductive system and of endocrine glands.

Bibliography: *American Men and Women of Science* 4–11; Herzenberg, Caroline L., *Women Scientists from Antiquity to the Present*; Rossiter, Margaret W., *Women Scientists in America*; Visher, Stephen S., *Scientists Starred 1903–1943 in "American Men and Women of Science"*; *Who Was Who in America*.

H

Frances Hamerstrom
Alice Hamilton
Thora Marggraff Plitt Hardy
Anna Jane Harrison
Helen Hart
Ethel Browne Harvey
Milicent Louise Hathaway
Harriet Ann Boyd Hawes
Ellen Amanda Hayes
Elizabeth Lee Hazen
Olive Clio Hazlett
Mary Hefferan
Christine Terhune Herrick
Hope Hibbard
Beatrice Alice Hicks
Alice Hamlin Hinman
(Ellen) Dorrit Hoffleit
Helen Battles Sawyer Hogg
Leonora Anita Hohl
Leta Anna Stetter Hollingsworth
Mary Emilee Holmes
Henrietta Edgecomb Hooker
Grace Murray Hopper
Cornelia C. Horsford
Dorothy Millicent Horstmann
Ethel Dench Puffer Howes
Marian Elizabeth Hubbard
Theodora Kimball Hubbard
Sally Hughes-Schrader
Emily Huntington
Zora Neale Hurston
Priscilla Butler Hussey
Ida Henrietta Hyde
Libbie Henrietta Hyman

Hahn, Dorothy Anna
(1876–1950)
chemist

Education: A.B., Bryn Mawr College, 1899; University of Leipzig, 1906–1907; Ph.D., Yale University, 1916
Employment: Professor of chemistry, Pennsylvania College for Women, 1899–1900; instructor, Mount Holyoke College, 1908–1914, associate professor, 1914–1916, professor, 1916–1941; emeritus professor

Dorothy Hahn was recognized for establishing a major research effort at Mount Holyoke in the synthesis of hydantoins. She completed this research, which resulted in 30 papers, with the assistance of undergraduate students and a very limited number of graduate students. The research required the application of both skillful organic chemical technique and the newly developed methods of ultraviolet spectrophotometry. She became actively interested in industrial chemistry, an interest that not only contributed to her awareness of important new developments but made it possible for Mount Holyoke to obtain needed facilities and scholarships. She obtained her education over a long period and in a number of laboratories, training at Bryn Mawr, Leipzig, and Yale at intervals over 17 years. She joined the Mount Holyoke faculty as an instructor in 1908 and rose through the ranks to professor, from which position she retired more than 30 years later. She inspired many of her students to continue their education in graduate school. She coauthored two books: *A Dictionary of Chemical Solubilities, Inorganic* (1921) and *The Catalytic Oxidation of Organic Compounds in the Vapor Phase* (1932). She also collaborated on a translation and enlargement of Ferdinand Henrich's *Theories of Organic Chemistry* (1922). She was a member of the American Chemical Society and the Deutsche Chemische Gesellschaft.

Bibliography: American Men and Women of Science 6–8; Herzenberg, Caroline L., *Women Scientists from Antiquity to the Present*; James, E. T., ed., *Notable American Women 1607–1950; National Union Catalog*; Rossiter, Margaret W., *Women Scientists in America*; Siegel, Patricia J. and Kay Thomas Finley, *Women in the Scientific Search.*

Hallowell, Susan Maria
(1835–1911)
botanist

Education: A.M., Colby College, 1875; summers, Harvard University, 1875–1885
Employment: Assistant, high schools, 1853–1875; professor of natural history, Wellesley College, 1875–1878, professor of botany, 1878–1902; emeritus professor

Susan Hallowell was recognized as an outstanding teacher of botany at Wellesley College. Her name was listed in the first and second editions of *American Men and Women of Science,* and she was one of the most notable women scientists at women's colleges before 1940. Following the career pattern of many women of her generation, she taught high school for a number of years before receiving her undergraduate degree at Colby College. Because American universities did not accept women in graduate programs at the time, she attended summer school at Harvard and visited botanical laboratories and museums in Europe in 1887–1888 and 1894–1895 in order to keep abreast of new developments. Many women actually enrolled in European universities during this period in order to receive advanced degrees, but she did not seem to have followed this path. She joined the faculty at Wellesley the year it was founded, 1875, and retired in 1902. Women botanists of that period often were involved with gathering and classifying specimens for botanical collections and for use in their classes. They often published little except in the form of correspondence with other botanists. Since she was visiting the laboratories of other botanists, she probably exchanged information in person or in correspondence rather than publishing the results of her research. She was a member of the Boston Society of Natural History. Her major research interest was histological and physiological botany.

Bibliography: Abir-Am, P. G. and Dorinda Outram, eds., *Uneasy Careers and Intimate Lives; American Men and Women of Science* 1–2; Barr, Ernest S., *An Index to Biographical Fragments in Unspecialized Scientific Journals;* Rossiter, Margaret W., *Women Scientists in America;* Siegel, Patricia J. and Kay Thomas Finley, *Women in the Scientific Search.*

Hamerstrom, Frances
(1907–)
wildlife biologist

Education: B.S., Iowa State University, 1935; M.S., University of Wisconsin, 1940
Employment: Game biologist, Wisconsin Department of Natural Resources, 1949–1972; adjunct professor and research associate, University of Wisconsin, Stevens Point, 1982–
Concurrent Positions: Director, Raptor Research Foundation, 1974–1976; member of science board, Wisconsin Peregrine Society, 1990–
Married: 1931

Frances Hamerstrom has been an internationally known wildlife biologist, one of the few women to pursue this profession. In addition to her scientific papers on the golden eagle and the prairie chicken, she has written magazine articles on nature study and two books for the general public: *An Eagle to the Sky* (1970) and *Strictly for Chickens* (1980). In the first book she describes how she raised one golden eagle and rehabilitated another. In the second she recounts her adventures in her work for the preservation of the greater prairie chicken. After receiving her master's degree, she worked as a game biologist for the Wisconsin Department of Natural Resources for about 20 years. She was director of the Raptor Research Foundation for three years and then joined the faculty of the University of Wisconsin, Stevens Point, as an adjunct professor in 1982. She received awards from the Wildlife Society in 1940 and 1957, the American Ornithologist's Union in 1960, and the American Museum of Natural History in 1964. She was elected a fellow of the American Ornithologists' Union and has been a member of the Wilson

Ornithological Society and the Wildlife Society. Her research has focused on ecology and behavior of raptors and hunting ethics and habits. She reared two children. Her name was included in the 1992–1993 edition of *American Men and Women of Science.*

Bibliography: *American Men and Women of Science* 10–18; *National Union Catalog.*

Hamilton, Alice
(1869–1970)
industrial toxicologist

Education: M.D., University of Michigan, 1893, A.M., 1910; University of Leipzig, 1895; University of Munich and University of Frankfurt, 1896; Johns Hopkins University, 1897; University of Chicago, 1899–1901; Pasteur Institute, Paris, 1902

Employment: Professor of pathology, Woman's Medical College of Chicago, 1897–1902; assistant pathologist, McCormick Institute for Infectious Diseases, 1902–1909; special investigator of occupational poisons, U.S. Bureau of Labor Statistics, 1911–1921; assistant professor of industrial medicine, Harvard Medical School, 1919–1935; emeritus professor

*A*lice Hamilton was a pioneer in the science of industrial toxicology, and she was an authority on hazardous industries starting in 1910, when the state of Illinois appointed her head of the new occupational disease commission. She was then hired by federal government agencies, and much of her research was done as a consultant to the Bureau of Labor Statistics. She joined Harvard Medical School as an assistant professor of industrial medicine in 1919, retiring in 1935. She insisted on a half-time appointment at Harvard so she could pursue her fieldwork. She continued to crusade for industrial safety and health legislation well into her eighties. Her books, *Industrial Poisons in the United States* (1925) and *Industrial Toxicology* (1934), are considered classics among the studies that eventually led to the passage of worker's compensation laws. She also published an autobiography, *Exploring the Dangerous Trades* (1943).

After attending a small, uncertified medical school, she entered the University of Michigan, where she obtained her M.D. in 1893. After interning in Minneapolis and Boston, she decided to specialize in bacteriology and pathology. She went to Germany for another year of training and then continued study and research at Johns Hopkins University. By this time, she had received a high level of scientific education that few people, men or women, could hope to attain. She received her first appointment as professor of pathology at the Woman's Medical College of Chicago in 1897. When this school closed in 1902, she moved to the newly opened McCormick Institute for Infectious Diseases. She studied briefly at the Pasteur Institute in Paris to prepare for her work at McCormick. Through her contacts with people at Hull House, she found that many immigrant workers had been made incurable invalids by the fumes they inhaled on their jobs in steel mills, factories, and foundries. Later she found these conditions throughout the country. This was the foundation for her campaign to establish the occupational disease commission in Illinois in 1910, the first of its kind in the United States. She was a member of the American Association for the Advancement of Science, the American Medical Association, and the American Public Health Association. Her photograph was included in *Current Biography;* her name was included in the first edition of *American Men and Women of Science.*

Bibliography: *American Men and Women of Science 1–11; Current Biography;* Herzenberg, Caroline L., *Women Scientists from Antiquity to the Present;* Kass-Simon, G. and Patricia Farnes, *Women of Science;* Mozans, H. J., *Women in Science; National Cyclopedia of American Biography; National Union Catalog;* O'Neill, Lois S., *The Women's Book of World Records and Achievements;* Rossiter, Margaret W., *Women Scientists in America;* Rossiter, Margaret W., "Women Scientists in America before 1920"; Sicherman, Barbara et al., *Notable American Women;* Siegel, Patricia J. and Kay Thomas Finley, *Women in the Scientific Search;* Yost, Edna, *American Women of Science.*

Hardy, Thora Marggraff Plitt
(b. 1902)
botanist

Education: B.A., Barnard College, 1925; M.S., University of Chicago, 1930, Ph.D. in botany, 1932

Employment: High school teacher, 1925–1929; instructor in botany, Hunter College, 1932–1933; instructor in botany and plant physiology, Vassar College, 1933–1935; junior microanalyst, National Bureau of Standards, 1935–1938; assistant microanalyst, U.S. Department of Agriculture (USDA), 1938–1939; assistant, then associate microanalyst, U.S. Fish and Wildlife Service, 1939–1946; associate microanalyst, Bureau of Animal Industry, USDA, 1946–1948, grain technologist, Production and Marketing Administration, 1948–1951; operator, Nittany Laboratory, Lamont, Pennsylvania, 1954–?

Married: 1942

Thora Hardy was employed by several federal agencies, and she had an interesting research project on fur and feathers. She was employed at Hunter College and Vassar College for several years, but although she had a doctorate from the University of Chicago, she was hired at the level of instructor. This was during the Depression, and even single women scientists had difficulty obtaining jobs. In 1935 she found her first job with a federal agency, the National Bureau of Standards. She moved to the U.S. Fish and Wildlife Service in 1939, and then the U.S. Department of Agriculture in 1938 and 1946. Although it seems incongruous that women scientists would work for the federal government, the agencies sometimes provided steady employment during the Depression. Women in these agencies were permitted to publish their research under their own names, and she published at least four papers in the *Circular* series of the USDA. As a microanalyst with the Bureau of Animal Industry, she wrote about tests on angora rabbit fur, animal fibers used in brushes, commercial fibers, and feathers from domestic and wild fowl. Later she was appointed a grain technologist with the Production and Marketing Administration. She was a member of the American Society of Plant Physiologists. Her research interests were plant microchemistry and physiology and microscopic research on commercial furs. In some of the sources consulted, she was listed as Thora Plitt.

Bibliography: *American Men and Women of Science 6–11;* Barnhart, John H., *Biographical Notes upon Botanists; National Union Catalog.*

Harrison, Anna Jane
(1912–)
chemist

Education: A.B., University of Missouri, 1933, M.A., 1937, Ph.D. in physical chemistry, 1940
Employment: Instructor in chemistry, Newcomb College, Tulane University, 1940–1942, assistant professor, 1942–1945; assistant professor, Mount Holyoke College, 1945–1947, associate professor, 1947–1950, professor, 1950–1976, department chair, 1960–1966, William R. Kenan, Jr., professor, 1976–1979; emeritus professor

*A*nna Harrison has been a distinguished chemist who was elected the first woman president of the American Chemical Society in 1978. She has been recognized by 18 academic institutions with honorary degrees, including the University of Missouri, Tulane University, and Mount Holyoke College. After receiving her doctorate from the University of Missouri, she accepted a position on the faculty at Tulane University, where she stayed six years. She moved to Mount Holyoke College in 1945 and progressed through the ranks to professor, serving as department chair from 1960 to 1966. She was named the William R. Kenan, Jr., professor in 1976, retiring in 1979. Traditionally women faculty members have advanced more slowly than men who have similar rates of research and publication; Anna Harrison, however, spent only three years as an assistant professor at Mount Holyoke and four years as an associate professor before advancing to full professorship (advancement to each level took women an average of ten years at that time). She was president of the American Association for the Advancement of Science in 1983 and 1984. Although there is a comparatively large number of early women chemists, many academic chemistry departments of Anna Harrison's generation had few or no women members, and many pioneer women chemists were assigned to home economics departments. Her area of research has been vacuum ultraviolet spectroscopy. Her name was included in the 1992–1993 edition of *American Men and Women of Science.*

Bibliography: *American Men and Women of Science* 7–18; Herzenberg, Caroline L., *Women Scientists from Antiquity to the Present*; O'Neill, Lois S., *The Women's Book of World Records and Achievements.*

Hart, Helen
(1900–1971)
plant pathologist

Education: Lawrence College, 1918–1920; B.A., University of Minnesota, 1922, A.M., 1924, Ph.D. in plant pathology, 1929
Employment: Agent, division of cereal crops and diseases, U.S. Department of Agriculture, 1923–1933; instructor in plant pathology, University of Minnesota, 1924–1933; full-time faculty member, 1933–1937; exchange assistant, Halle, 1937–1938; associate editor of the journal *Phytopathology*, 1938–1940; assistant professor of plant pathology, University of Minnesota, 1940–1944, associate professor, 1944–1947, professor, 1947–1966
Concurrent position: Editor-in-Chief, *Phytopathology*, 1944–1951

elen Hart was a leader among the group of investigators in a department famous for its research on stem rust of cereals at the University of Minnesota. She served from 1944 to 1951 as editor-in-chief of *Phytopathology*, the principal scientific journal of the American Phytopathological Society (the leading professional society in plant pathology). After receiving her master's degree, she was employed at the division of cereal crops and diseases of the U.S. Department of Agriculture for 11 years. She moved to the University of Minnesota as an instructor while she completed her doctorate. She was appointed to the faculty in 1933 and advanced from assistant professor to associate professor and full professor at three- or four-year intervals, an excellent rate for a woman scientist of her generation. She was president of the American Phytopathological Society from 1955 to 1956, the only woman to have held this office by the time of her death in 1971. She received the Elvin C. Stakman Award for her work on cereal disease in 1963. In 1965 she was elected a fellow of the American Phytopathological Society, and she was a fellow of the American Association for the Advancement of Science. She also was a member of the American Society of Plant Physiologists. Her research areas were disease resistance in crop plants, cereal rusts, and stem rust of wheat. Her photograph accompanies an obituary in *Phytopathology* 61 (1971): 1151.

Bibliography: *American Men and Women of Science* 5–10; Barnhart, John H., *Biographical Notes upon Botanists;* Herzenberg, Caroline L., *Women Scientists from Antiquity to the Present; National Union Catalog;* Rossiter, Margaret W., *Women Scientists in America.*

Harvey, Ethel Browne
(1885–1965)
cell biologist

Education: A.B., Goucher College, 1906; A.M., Columbia University, 1907, Ph.D. in zoology, 1913

Employment: Instructor in science, private school, 1908–1911; assistant in biology, Princeton University, 1912–1913; instructor in biology, private school, 1913–1914; Sarah Berliner fellow, University of California, 1914–1915; assistant in histology, medical college, Cornell University, 1915–1916; instructor in biology, Washington Square College, New York University, 1928–1931; investigator, biology department, Princeton University, 1931–1959; Marine Biological Laboratory, Woods Hole, 1959–1965

Concurrent Positions: Researcher, Oceanographic Institute, Monaco, 1920–1921; Naples Zoological Station, 1925–1926, 1933–1934, 1937

Married: Edmund Newton Harvey, 1916

thel Harvey revised the theory of cell division when she showed in the 1930s that cells of sea urchin eggs could divide after their nuclei had been removed. The popular press picked up the story and announced that she had "created life without parents." After she received her doctorate, she spent several years at the University of California and at Cornell in research. Although her husband also was a biologist who specialized in bioluminescence, they worked independently of each other. She continued her research part time while her children were young, and in 1928 she taught biology at New York University. Starting in 1931 and spanning most of her career, she was an independent investigator in the biology department at Princeton. She never was appointed to a full faculty position at the university. The only support she received for her work was office space at Princeton and a share of her husband's work space at Woods Hole. Her internationally recognized work was unsupported with the exception of one grant in 1937 from the American Philosophical Society. She spent several periods on research at the prestigious Naples Zoological Station between 1925 and 1937.

She published about 100 scientific papers and one book, *The American Arbacia and Other Sea Urchins* (1956). This volume is still a standard reference for sea urchin embryologists. In 1950 she was the second woman to be named a trustee of the Woods Hole Laboratory. Her name was starred in the sixth and seventh editions of *American Men and Women of Science.* She received numerous awards and honors, including an honorary degree from Goucher College in 1956. She was elected a fellow of the American Association for the Advancement of Science and also was a member of the American Society of Naturalists and the American Society of Zoologists. She was listed as Mrs. E. Newton Harvey in the third through sixth editions of *American Men and Women of Science,* but under her own name in later editions. The couple had two children, Edmund, Jr., and Richard. Her photograph was published in G. Kass-Simon's and Patricia Farnes' *Women of Science: Righting the Record,* and a brief biography appeared in the journal *Biological Bulletin* 9 (1967): 9–11.

Bibliography: American Men and Women of Science 3–11; Herzenberg, Caroline L., *Women Scientists from Antiquity to the Present;* James, E. T., ed., *Notable American Women 1607–1950;* Kass-Simon, G. and Patricia Farnes, *Women of Science;* Rossiter, Margaret W., *Women Scientists in America;* Rossiter, Margaret W., "Women Scientists in America before 1920"; Siegel, Patricia J. and Kay Thomas Finley, *Women in the Scientific Search;* Visher, Stephen S., *Scientists Starred 1903–1943 in "American Men of Science."*

Hathaway, Milicent Louise
(b. 1898)
physiological chemist

Education: A.B., Wells College, 1920; A.M., University of Buffalo, 1925; Ph.D., University of Chicago, 1932

Employment: Professor of science and mathematics, Cedarville College, 1920–1921, Glendale College, 1921–1922; high school teacher, 1922–1924; assistant, chemistry, University of Buffalo, 1924–1925, instructor, science survey, 1925–1929; assistant biochemist, University of Chicago, 1931–1933; assistant physiologist, college of medicine, University of Illinois, 1933–1935, associate, home economics, 1935–1937; professor of physiology and nutrition, Battle Creek College, 1937–1938; instructor, home economics, Cornell University, 1938–1941, assistant professor, 1941–1944, associate professor, 1944–1946; nutrition specialist, Bureau of Human Nutrition and Home Economics, U.S. Department of Agriculture, 1946–1962; professor of home economics, Howard University, 1962–1966

Milicent Hathaway was recognized as an expert in human nutrition, but her career followed the pattern of many women of her generation.

She had a series of positions at small colleges until she received her doctorate in 1932 from the University of Chicago. At that time Chicago was one of the top schools for nutrition in the country, but by then the country was deep into the Depression, and jobs were scarce even for single women. After several more years of insignificant jobs, she was appointed an instructor in home economics at Cornell in 1938 and rose through the ranks quite rapidly to the level of associate professor. In 1946 she accepted an appointment with the U.S. Department of Agriculture (USDA) as a nutrition specialist in the food and nutrition division of the Bureau of Human Nutrition and Home Economics, which played a key role in country's nutrition research. She remained there 17 years and then accepted a position as professor of home economics at Howard University, from which she retired in 1966. She received the Borden Award of the American Home Economics Association in 1947. She was a member of the American Institute of Nutrition, a prestigious organization, and was elected a fellow of the American Association for the Advancement of Science. She was also a member of the American Chemical Society, the American Home Economics Association, and the New York Academy of Sciences. She published papers on her research on sterols, citric acid metabolism, and human metabolism of essential vitamins and minerals.

Bibliography: *American Men and Women of Science* 6–11; Debus, A. G., ed., *World Who's Who in Science;* Hall, Diana Long, "Academics, Bluestockings, and Biologists"; Herzenberg, Caroline L., *Women Scientists from Antiquity to the Present; National Union Catalog.*

Hawes, Harriet Ann Boyd
(1871–1945)
archaeologist

Education: B.A., Smith College, 1892, M.A., 1901; American School of Classical Studies, Athens, 1896–1900
Employment: Classics teacher, private school, 1893–1896; instructor, Greek archaeology and modern Greek, Smith College, 1900–1906; lecturer on pre-Christian art, Wellesley College, 1920–1936
Married: Charles Hawes, 1906

Harriet Hawes was one of the foremost archaeologists of her generation due to her independent discoveries on the island of Crete. Initially she had rather a conventional career. After her graduation from Smith, she taught classics in a private school for several years. In 1896 she started graduate studies at the American School of Classical Studies in Athens. During her years of study there, women students could not take part in the school's excavation programs due to the social conventions of the time. Harriet Hawes used a portion of her grant money to underwrite an excavation of her own in Crete, which provided data for her thesis at Smith. Her most significant work was the discovery in 1901 of Gournia, the only well-preserved urban site of the Minoan Age to be uncovered in Crete. She received international acclaim as the first woman to direct an excavation. Her discovery was recorded in the book *Gournia, Vasiliki and Other Prehistoric Sites on the Isthmus of Hierapetra, Crete* (1908). She returned home and obtained a position teaching at Smith for six years, returning to Crete several times to conduct fieldwork. She and her husband coauthored *Crete, the Forerunner of Greece* (1909), a small volume for the general public. The couple had two children, Mary and Alexander. There is biographical material, including photographs, in her paper "Memoirs of a Pioneer Excavator in Crete" in *Archaeology* 18 (1965): 94–101, 268–276. In the photograph, she is seated at a table filled with artifacts, but she has her hat on, as any proper lady would. She returned to teaching in 1920, lecturing on pre-Christian art at Wellesley College for a few years. Although basically a classicist, Harriet Hawes used scientific methods to locate and excavate sites. Her work expanded the data available on early civilizations.

Harriet Hawes also was a social activist. She served as a volunteer nurse in Thessaly in the Greco-Turkish War in 1897 and in Florida in the Spanish-American War in 1898. During World War I she worked in a Serbian army hospital camp on Corfu and participated in relief and hospital work in France. In the 1930s she was involved in union activities in Massachusetts. She seemed to be an independent woman who enjoyed life.

Bibliography: *Dictionary of American Biography;* Herzenberg, Caroline L., *Women Scientists from Antiquity to the Present;* Ireland, Norma O., *Index to Scientists of the World;* James, E. T., ed., *Notable American Women 1607–1950;* Mozans, H. J., *Women in Science; National Union Catalog;* Ogilvie, Marilyn B., *Women in Science;* Rossiter, Margaret W., *Women Scientists in America.*

Hayes, Ellen Amanda
(1851–1930)
astronomer

Education: A.B., Oberlin College, 1878; McCormick Observatory, University of Virginia, 1887–1888

Employment: Principal of women's department, Adrian College, 1878; teacher of mathematics, Wellesley College, 1879–1883, associate professor, 1883–1888, professor, 1888–1897, professor of applied mathematics, 1897–1904, professor of astronomy, 1904–1916

*E*llen Hayes* made significant contributions in astronomical observations, and she wrote three well-received books on mathematics. She was considered an excellent teacher, but her views often clashed with those of other faculty members at Wellesley. She had such a difficult personality that she was removed as head of the mathematics department and appointed head of the department of applied mathematics (the astronomy department) as the sole member of the department. She was promoted through the ranks and achieved the level of professor in 1888, but the trustees did not name her professor emerita when she retired in 1916.

She was considered a political radical because she espoused Socialist causes. In 1912 she was the Socialist party candidate for secretary of state in Massachusetts, the first woman in Massachusetts to be nominated for a state office. Although women were unable to vote for her, she won more votes than any other Socialist candidate on the ballot. The ticket did not win the election, however. She spent her retirement writing and speaking on a variety of social causes. In her astronomical work at the McCormick Observatory, she determined the definite orbit of the newly discovered Minor Planet 267. She was the author of several books: *Lessons on Higher*

Algebra (1891, 1894), *Elementary Trigonometry* (1896), and *Calculus with Applications: An Introduction to the Mathematical Treatment of Science* (1900). She was a member of the American Association for the Advancement of Science, and her name was included in the first edition of *American Men and Women of Science.*

Bibliography: *American Men and Women of Science* 1–4; Davis, Herman S., "Women Astronomers (1750–1890)"; Grinstein, Louise S. and Paul J. Campbell, eds., *Women of Mathematics;* Rossiter, Margaret W., *Women Scientists in America;* Siegel, Patricia J. and Kay Thomas Finley, *Women in the Scientific Search.*

Hazen, Elizabeth Lee
(1885–1975)
microbiologist

Education: B.S., Mississippi University for Women, 1910; M.S., Columbia University, 1917, Ph.D. in microbiology, 1927
Employment: High school science teacher, 1910–1916; U.S. Army diagnostic laboratories, Alabama and New York, 1917–1926; instructor, College of Physicians and Surgeons, 1927–1931; researcher, New York State Department of Health, 1931–1960; guest investigator, Columbia University Mycology Laboratory, 1960–1973

*E*lizabeth Hazen was the codiscoverer of the antifungal antibiotic nystatin with Rachel Brown (q.v.). She was 42 years old when she received her doctorate, but she was recognized as an expert in the diagnosis and treatment of viral and bacterial infections. Her career started in a conventional manner—teaching school for seven years after receiving her undergraduate degree. She received her master's degree from Columbia in 1917 and a doctorate ten years later in 1927. The interval between the two degrees was spent at an army laboratory during World War I and in the research laboratories at Columbia.

After teaching at the College of Physicians and Surgeons for four years, she accepted a position in 1931 with the New York State Department of Health, Division of Laboratories and Research, as a researcher. There she was teamed with Rachel Brown, and in 1948 they discovered fungicidin, better known as nystatin (named for the New York State Department

of Health). The range of uses for this antibiotic includes combating mold in human and animal food as well as yeast infections of the vagina, intestine, skin, and mucous membranes. It was used to restore murals and manuscripts in Florence, Italy, following the 1966 flood. After they patented their discovery, they assigned the licensing fees to a foundation to administer grants and to fund their further work under the Brown-Hazen Fund.

Elizabeth Hazen was coauthor of *Laboratory Identification of Pathogenic Fungi Simplified* (1955). After she retired in 1960, she had a permanent position as a guest investigator in the Mycology Laboratory at Columbia. Together with Rachel Brown, she received the Squibb Award in Chemotherapy in 1955, the Sara Benham Award of the Mycological Society of America, and the first Chemical Pioneer Award of the American Institute of Chemists in 1975. There is biographical information in Richard Baldwin's *The Fungus Fighters: Two Women Scientists and*

Their Discovery (1981) and in *Mycologia* 68 (1976): 961–969. There are photographs of the two women in both.

Bibliography: Herzenberg, Caroline L., *Women Scientists from Antiquity to the Present*; Sicherman, Barbara et al., *Notable American Women*; Siegel, Patricia J. and Kay Thomas Finley, *Women in the Scientific Search*.

Hazlett, Olive Clio
(1890–1974)
mathematician

Education: A.B., Radcliffe College, 1912; M.S., University of Chicago, 1913, Ph.D. in mathematics, 1915
Employment: Associate in mathematics, Bryn Mawr College, 1916–1918; assistant professor, Mount Holyoke College, 1918–1924, associate professor, 1924–1925; assistant professor, University of Illinois, 1925–1929, associate professor, 1929–1959; emeritus associate professor

*O**live Hazlett** was recognized by her contemporaries as an outstanding mathematician in the area of linear algebra. She was the most prolific of all the American women working in mathematics before 1940. Her name was starred in the fourth through seventh editions of *American Men and Women of Science.* After she received her doctorate from the University of Chicago, she was employed for two years at Bryn Mawr. She accepted a position at Mount Holyoke College as an assistant instructor, advancing through the ranks to associate professor in 1924. She moved to the University of Illinois, however, in order to have the time and the library facilities to pursue her ideas. She was awarded a Guggenheim fellowship for the 1928–1929 academic year to study in Italy, Switzerland, and Germany; this was extended for the following year. In the meantime she was promoted to associate professor. In spite of her recognition as a mathematician, she remained at the level of associate professor at both universities. This was a common occurrence in mathematics departments at this time; women faculty remained at the level of assistant or associate professors, usually teaching introductory courses, long after younger men had advanced to full professorships. She was very active in professional societies during the 1920s and 1930s, serving as associate editor of the *Transactions of the American Mathematical Society* from 1923 to 1935 and as a member of the Council of the Society from 1926 to 1928. She was elected a fellow of the American Association for the Advancement of Science and was also a member of the American Mathematical Society and the New York Academy of Sciences. Her research interests were linear algebras and modular invariants. There is a photograph in G. Kass-Simon's and Patricia Farnes' *Women of Science: Righting the Record.*

Bibliography: *American Men and Women of Science* 3–11; Herzenberg, Caroline L., *Women Scientists from Antiquity to the Present*; Kass-Simon, G. and Patricia Farnes, *Women of Science*; Rossiter, Margaret W., *Women Scientists in America*; Siegel, Patricia J. and Kay Thomas Finley, *Women in the Scientific Search*; Visher, Stephen S., *Scientists Starred 1903–1943 in "American Men of Science."*

Hefferan, Mary
(1873–1948)
bacteriologist

Education: A.B., Wellesley College, 1896, A.M., 1898; Ph.D., University of Chicago, 1903
Employment: Curator, bacteriology museum, University of Chicago, 1903–1904, assistant professor and curator, 1904–1910; director, Blodgett Home for Children, 1919–?

Mary Hefferan was recognized for her work as a bacteriologist, and her name was listed in the first seven editions of *American Men and Women of Science*. After receiving her undergraduate degree from Wellesley College in 1896 and her master's degree in 1898, she received a fellowship from the University of Chicago, where she received her doctorate in 1903. She accepted a position at the university as curator of the bacteriology museum, where she remained until 1910 while she taught in the bacteriology department. Her research publications appeared in the *Journal of Infectious Diseases* and several European journals. She had a number of research interests, such as agglutinative relations of nonpathogenic organisms, red chromogenic organisms, and proteolytic enzymes. Later she worked as a bacteriologist in Grand Rapids, but changed directions in her career about the time of World War I. By 1919 she was director of the Blodgett Home for Children in Grand Rapids. She apparently stayed with her second profession, because her obituary detailed her pioneer work in social work in that city and only briefly mentions her background in science. She was not the only person who left her career in science for other pursuits, either voluntarily or due to lack of opportunities for research or advancement.

Bibliography: American Men and Women of Science 1–7; Siegel, Patricia J. and Kay Thomas Finley, *Women in the Scientific Search.*

Herrick, Christine Terhune
(1859–1944)
writer on household affairs

Education: Tutors and private schools
Employment: Author
Married: James F. Herrick, 1884, died 1893

Christine Herrick was a popular writer on household science at the turn of the century, and she helped to bring new ideas on household management to American housewives. She was the daughter of Mary V. Terhune (q.v.), a well-known author of household science books who wrote under the pseudonym Marion Harland. She was educated at home with private tutors, but spent two years at school in Europe from 1876 to 1878 due to her mother's poor health. She taught briefly at a private school for girls in Springfield, Massachusetts, before her marriage in 1884. With her background of household management, which she learned from her mother, and the encouragement of her husband, who was a newspaper editor, she published her first article, "The Wastes of the Household," in the first issue of *Good Housekeeping* magazine in May 1885. She published her first book, *Housekeeping Made Easy*, in 1888; the work had appeared serially in *Harper's Bazaar*. She also published articles in *Ladies' Home Journal* and *Demorest's Monthly*. After her husband's death in 1893, she was earning enough money from her writing to support her two sons, educating them at private preparatory schools as well as at college.

She published four additional books on household affairs and several others in collaboration with her mother. Her later magazine articles reflected a wide range of interests from field hockey to women's suffrage.

Bibliography: James, E. T., ed., *Notable American Women 1607–1950; National Cyclopedia of American Biography; National Union Catalog;* Shapiro, Laura, *Perfection Salad.*

Hibbard, Hope
(b. 1893)
zoologist

Education: A.B., University of Missouri, 1916, A.M., 1918; Ph.D. in zoology, Bryn Mawr College, 1921, Sarah Berliner fellow, 1925–1926

Employment: Demonstrator in biology, Bryn Mawr College, 1919–1920; associate professor, Elmira College, 1921–1925; preparateur, comparative anatomy techniques laboratory, University of Paris, 1926–1927; International Education Board fellow, 1927–1928; assistant professor of zoology, Oberlin College, 1928–1930, associate professor, 1930–1933, department chair, 1953–1957, professor, 1933–1961, emeritus professor

Hope Hibbard was recognized by her contemporaries for her research on cytology, and her name was starred in the seventh edition of *American Men and Women of Science,* the last edition in which this device was used. After receiving her doctorate from Bryn Mawr, she was employed as a demonstrator in biology at the school for one year. She moved to Elmira College as associate professor for five years. After spending several years abroad for further study, she was appointed an assistant professor of zoology at Oberlin College in 1928, where she stayed 34 years and advanced to professor and department chair. She had the distinction of actually working in a comparative anatomy techniques laboratory at the University of Paris. Although Oberlin College is a small private school, from the beginning it was known for its innovative curriculum and

hard-working students. It was interesting that she advanced in rank rather quickly—just three years as assistant professor before advancing to associate professor and another three before advancing to full professor. She was a member of several professional societies, including the American Association for the Advancement of Science, the American Society of Naturalists, and the American Society of Zoologists. Her research was centered on cytoplasmic inclusions and cytology.

Bibliography: *American Men and Women of Science* 4–11; Herzenberg, Caroline L., *Women Scientists from Antiquity to the Present;* Rossiter, Margaret W., *Women Scientists in America;* Visher, Stephen S., *Scientists Starred 1903–1943 in "American Men of Science."*

Hicks, Beatrice Alice
(1919–1979)
engineer

Education: B.S., Newark College of Engineering, 1939; M.S., Stevens Institute of Technology, 1949

Employment: Research assistant, Newark College of Engineering, 1939–1942; research design and manufacturing, Western Electric Company, 1942–1945; chief engineer, Newark Controls Company, 1945–1946, vice president and chief engineer, 1946–1955, president, 1955–1967; head, Rodney D. Chipp and Associates, 1967–1979

Married: Rodney C. Chipp, 1948, died 1948

Beatrice Hicks was one of the few early women scientists who owned their own company. When her father died, Beatrice Hicks became vice president and chief engineer of the family-owned Newark Controls Company. She later bought control of the company and became president. She began her career as a research assistant after receiving her chemical engineering degree from Newark College of Engineering. She accepted a position in research design and manufacturing at Western Electric Company in 1942. (During World War II many corporations hired their first women scientists and engineers in professional positions due to the shortage of available men.) It was 1945 when she moved to Newark Controls Company as chief engineer. She was promoted to vice president when her father died in 1946 and then purchased the company in 1955. She received her master's degree in physics in 1949 from Stevens Institute and took further graduate work in electrical engineering at Columbia.

Beatrice Hicks was one of the founders of the Society of Women Engineers and was the first president, serving from 1950 to 1953. She was elected to the National Academy of Engineering, and she received honorary degrees from Hobart and William Smith colleges in 1958 and Rensselaer Polytechnic Institute in 1965. She received the Society of Women Engineers Achievement Award in 1963. She was a member of the Institute of Electrical and Electronics Engineers and the American Society of Mechanical Engineers. Her research involved sensing devices under extreme environmental conditions. Her photograph was published with her biography in *Current Biography.*

Bibliography: American Men and Women of Science 14; Current Biography; Herzenberg, Caroline L., *Women Scientists from Antiquity to the Present;* Ireland, Norma O., *Index to Scientists of the World;* O'Neill, Lois S., *The Women's Book of World Records and Achievements; Who Was Who in America.*

Hinman, Alice Hamlin

(1869–1934)

psychologist

Education: A.B., Wellesley College, 1893; Ph.D., Cornell University, 1897

Employment: Teacher, private school, 1890–1892; professor of philosophy and psychology, Mount Holyoke College, 1897–1898; assistant professor, University of Nebraska, 1898–1900, lecturer, 1904–1910, substitute, 1912, 1928, instructor, nurses' training school, 1929–1934

Married: Edgar L. Hinman, 1898

*A*lice Hinman was active professionally early in her career; she was elected to the council of the American Psychological Association in 1897. Her name was included in the first edition of *American Men and Women of Science.* She was born in Constantinople, where her father, a missionary, was the founder and first president of Robert College. This may explain some of her later activities. After receiving her doctorate from Cornell, she taught philosophy and psychology at Mount Holyoke for a year. After her marriage in 1898, she moved to Lincoln, Nebraska, where her husband already was a department chair for psychology and philosophy. Alice Hinman taught sporadically at the University of Nebraska and other local schools for the rest of her life. At that time most colleges had nepotism rules that would not allow the hiring of husbands and wives on a permanent basis, even if they were not in the same department.

Her chief contribution was in her civic activities. Her notable accomplishment was serving on the board of education for the Lincoln, Nebraska, public schools from 1907 to 1919 at a time when major improvements were made in the curricula. She continued her scholarly interests and published several articles and reviews in the *American Journal of Psychology.* Her interests were in memory, hypnotism, and infant psychology; she continued to be listed in *American Men and Women of Science* until her death. The couple had one daughter, Eleanor. Her photograph was published in the *National Cyclopedia of American Biography.*

Bibliography: American Men and Women of Science 1–5; National Cyclopedia of American Biography; Rossiter, Margaret W., Women Scientists in America; Siegel, Patricia J. and Kay Thomas Finley, Women in the Scientific Search.

Hoffleit, (Ellen) Dorrit

(1907–)

astronomer

Education: A.B., Radcliffe College, 1928, M.A., 1932, Ph.D. in astronomy, 1938

Employment: Assistant, Harvard Observatory, 1929–1938, research associate, 1938–1943; mathematician, ballistic research laboratories, Aberdeen Proving Ground, 1943–1948; astronomer, Harvard Observatory, 1948–1956; director, Maria Mitchell Observatory, 1956–1978; research associate, Yale Observatory, 1956–1969, senior research astronomer, 1969–

Concurrent Positions: Lecturer, Wellesley College, 1955–1956; technical consultant, Aberdeen Proving Ground, 1948–1961

Dorrit Hoffleit has had a distinguished career working at the Yale Observatory and directing the Maria Mitchell Observatory. She has discovered 1,000 new variable stars and studied their modes of variation. She began working for the Harvard Observatory in 1929 after receiving her undergraduate degree from Radcliffe, and she continued on the staff while receiving her master's degree and doctorate. In 1943 she was hired as a mathematician in the ballistic research laboratories of Aberdeen Proving Ground; she continued there as a technical consultant from 1948 to 1961. (Many women scientists during World War II were hired by government agencies or under government contracts due to the wartime shortage of men scientists. Some continued in these positions, some continued to consult, and some went on to other work.) She returned to the Harvard Observatory as an astronomer in 1948 and moved to the Yale Observatory in 1956. From 1956 to 1978 she had a concurrent appointment as the director of the Maria Mitchell Observatory at Nantucket, Massachusetts.

In addition to her scientific papers, she has published two books: *Some Firsts in Astronomical Photography* (1950) and *Bright Star Catalogue* (1964). She was president of the American Association of Variable Star Observers from 1961 to 1963 and was editor of the journal *Meteoritics*. One of her interests has been nineteenth- and twentieth-century topics in the history of astronomy. She has written biographical sketches of Maria Mitchell (q.v.), Williamina Fleming (q.v.), and Annie Cannon (q.v.) for several reference books. In 1992 she published a history, *Astronomy at Yale, 1701–1968*. She has been a member of the American Association for the Advancement of Science, the Meteoritical Society, the International Astronomical Union, and the American Astronomical Society. Her research interests have been variable stars and stellar spectra. Her name was included in the 1992–1993 edition of *American Men and Women of Science*.

Bibliography: American Men and Women of Science 7–18; Debus, A. G., ed., *World Who's Who in Science*; Herzenberg, Caroline L., *Women Scientists from Antiquity to the Present*; Kass-Simon, G. and Patricia Farnes, *Women of Science*; Siegel, Patricia J. and Kay Thomas Finley, *Women in the Scientific Search*.

Hogg, Helen Battles Sawyer
(1905–)
astronomer

Education: A.B., Mount Holyoke College, 1926; A.M., Radcliffe College, 1928, Ph.D. in astronomy, 1931

Employment: Instructor, Smith College, 1927; Mount Holyoke College, 1930–1931; Dominion Astrophysical Observatory, British Columbia, 1931–1934; assistant, David Dunlap Observatory, Toronto, 1935–1937, research associate, 1938–1941; research associate, University of Toronto, 1941–1951, assistant professor of astronomy, 1951–1955, associate professor, 1955–1957, professor, 1957–1976; emeritus professor

Married: Frank S. Hogg, 1930, died 1950

elen Hogg's work has involved cataloging variable stars in globular clusters. She and her husband were rated one of the notable couples in science prior to 1940 in Margaret Rossiter's *Women Scientists in America.* She was employed as an instructor at Smith College the year between receiving her undergraduate degree and starting her master's. She continued her education at Radcliffe, where she received her doctorate in astronomy in 1931. She moved with her husband to Canada, where she held several positions in the observatories before joining the faculty at the University of Toronto in 1951. She rose through the ranks to professor in 1957, retiring in 1976. She was interested in bringing astronomy to the general public by serving as the columnist for the *Toronto Daily Star* from 1951 to 1981. She has been very active in professional organizations, being elected president of the American Association of Variable Stars Observers 1939–1941 and working with several Canadian astronomical societies. She received the Annie Jump Cannon Prize in 1950 and the Rittenhouse Medal in 1967.

She received honorary degrees from three universities. She was the author of *Bibliography of Individual Globular Clusters* (1947) and *Second Catalogue of Variable Stars in Globular Clusters* (1955). Her scientific papers have been published under her maiden name, Sawyer. As a mother, she raised three children. Her research interests have been globular star clusters and variable stars. Her name was included in the 1992–1993 edition of *American Men and Women of Science,* and her photograph was published in Edna Yost's *Women of Modern Science.* Her name is listed in some sources as Helen Sawyer.

Bibliography: Abir-Am, P. G. and Dorinda Outram, eds., *Uneasy Careers and Intimate Lives; American Men and Women of Science* 12–18; Debus, A. G., ed., *World Who's Who in Science;* Ireland, Norma O., *Index to Scientists of the World;* Kass-Simon, G. and Patricia Farnes, *Women of Science;* Rossiter, Margaret W., *Women Scientists in America;* Yost, Edna, *Women of Modern Science.*

Hohl, Leonora Anita
(b. 1909)
microbiologist

Education: A.B., University of California, Berkeley, 1931, A.M., University of Michigan, 1934; Ph.D. in plant physiology, University of California, Berkeley, 1939
Employment: General assistant, herbarium, University of California, Berkeley, 1931–1932, teaching assistant in botany, 1932–1933, assistant, fruit products, 1935–1940; mycologist, Roma Wine Company, 1940–1941; lecturer, home economics, University of California, Berkeley, 1941–1943; mycologist, Peerless Yeast Company and Acme Breweries, 1942–1943; instructor, food technology and assistant mycologist, experiment station, University of California, Berkeley, 1943–?

eonora Hohl was one of the few women mycologists identified as working as a scientist for companies during the 1940s, although her tenure was short-lived. She worked intermittently for

the University of California, Berkeley, for more than ten years in the 1930s while obtaining advanced degrees from the University of Michigan and the University of California. This was a fairly typical situation; many people worked for a few years to save money for further education or while waiting to find fellowships. Women scientists had an especially difficult time during the Depression finding jobs and fellowships to support their education. World War II changed the picture entirely, and Leonora Hohl obtained positions with two companies as a mycologist in the 1940s, when many women were able to secure jobs due to a shortage of available men scientists. She taught home economics for part of that time and then returned to the University of California as an instructor and a mycologist in the experiment station. She published one report in the *Bulletin* series of the experiment station in 1948. She was a member of the American Association for the Advancement of Science and the Institute of Food Technologists. Her research interests were freezing preservation of fruits and vegetables.

Bibliography: American Men and Women of Science 7–8; National Union Catalog.

Hollingsworth, Leta Anna Stetter
(1886–1939)
psychologist

Education: B.A., University of Nebraska, 1906; M.A., Columbia University, 1913, Ph.D., 1916
Employment: High school teacher, 1906–1908; clinical testing, Bellevue Hospital, 1914–1916; from instructor to professor, Teachers' College, Columbia University, 1917–1939
Married: Harry L. Hollingsworth, 1908

Leta Hollingsworth was recognized by her contemporaries for her work in clinical psychology as a faculty member at Teachers' College, Columbia University. She planned to be a writer, but she obtained a teaching certificate in order to support herself. She married in 1908 and moved with her husband to New York, where he completed his graduate degree and became a faculty member at Columbia. Finding no job market for writers or teachers in New York, she obtained further education in the subject of psychology. In 1914 she was appointed to fill New York City's first civil service position for a psychologist. She accepted a position in the psychology department of Teachers' College in 1917 and remained there the rest of her life, eventually achieving the level of professor.

Leta Hollingsworth's first area of study was the psychology of women. She measured sex differences in selected traits and types of performance to show that women could function as well as men in educational and professional pursuits. At that time men were still considered innately superior to women. These studies made her popular in feminist circles, and she and her husband marched in suffrage parades. She felt that reform in attitudes would be meaningful for women rather than just political reform. In the 1920s and 1930s she turned to the special needs of children. She published two books on her research on gifted children: *Gifted Children* (1926) and *Children above 180 I. Q.* (1942). These two texts often were cited and represented significant contributions to the field. At Teachers' College she established a guidance laboratory to carry out testing and counseling, and she consulted for school systems to obtain research data. She was instrumental in establishing in 1936 the Speyer School in the New York City School system to study exceptional children. She received an honorary degree from the University of Nebraska in 1938. Her husband wrote her biography, *Leta Stetter Hollingsworth: A Biography* (1943).

Bibliography: James, E. T., ed., *Notable American Women 1607–1950;* Siegel, Patricia J. and Kay Thomas Finley, *Women in the Scientific Search.*

Holmes, Mary Emilee
(1849–1906)
geologist

Education: A.B., Rockford College, 1868; A.M., University of Michigan, 1887, Ph.D., 1888
Employment: Instructor in natural sciences, Manitowoc, Wisconsin, 1869–1870; professor, Rockford College, 1871–1882; president, Presbyterian Home Mission Society, 1883–1906; secretary, Synodical Home Mission Society, 1883–1906

Mary **Holmes,** in 1889, became the first woman elected to membership in the Geological Society of America, and she presented a paper at the women's section of the World Congress of Geology in 1893. Her name was included in the first edition of *American Men and Women of Science.* After receiving her undergraduate degree, she taught school briefly before joining the faculty of Rockford College in 1871. She combined her interests in paleontology and zoology in her class work. After 11 years, she resigned to pursue a doctorate from the University of Michigan, which she received in 1888. Meanwhile she had shifted to working for various mission societies for the Presbyterian Church starting in 1883. She was president of the Presbyterian Home Mission Society and secretary of the Synodical Home Mission Society. She apparently continued her research, because the Geological Society of America elected her the first woman fellow for her original scientific investigation and discovery. She was active in the abolitionist movement and was editor and proprietor of "Freedmen's Bulletin" starting in 1885. She worked during the period of great social upheaval following the Civil War, and a person with strong social instincts could very well devote her life to helping the poor and homeless. She also founded the Mary Holmes Seminary in West Point, Mississippi.

Bibliography: American Men and Women of Science 1–2; Herzenberg, Caroline L., *Women Scientists from Antiquity to the Present;* Rossiter, Margaret W., *Women Scientists in America;* Siegel, Patricia J. and Kay Thomas Finley, *Women in the Scientific Search; Who Was Who in America.*

Hooker, Henrietta Edgecomb
(1851–1929)
botanist

Education: Mount Holyoke College; Ph.D., Syracuse University, 1889; Woods Hole Marine Biological Laboratory; Massachusetts Institute of Technology; University of Berlin
Employment: Teacher, public schools, 1869–1870; private school, 1870–1871; professor of botany, Mount Holyoke College, 1873–1908, department chair, 1884–1908; emeritus professor

Henrietta Hooker was a pioneer teacher of botany in a prestigious women's college, Mount Holyoke, for 35 years and as such shaped the direction of the curriculum. Her name was included in the first edition of *American Men and Women of Science.* Her career followed the pattern of many women of her generation. She taught in public and private schools for several years while taking some classes. She then accepted an appointment at Mount Holyoke in 1873 as a professor of botany. Since she served as department chair from 1884 to 1908, she had great influence in shaping the course of the botany department. Meanwhile she received her doctorate from Syracuse University in 1889. (It was not unusual for both men and women to teach in colleges before completing their formal education due to the expense and opportunities for graduate training. Higher education was expanding rapidly during this period, and there was a shortage of people with doctorates.) There were very few colleges that would accept women in graduate programs. Many had to resort to spending summers at various colleges in the United States or in foreign universities to keep up with current techniques. Although these summer sessions provided worthy information, they did not lead to advanced degrees. Henrietta Hooker supplemented her education with course work at Woods Hole, Massachusetts Institute of Technology (MIT), and the University of Berlin. She was a member of the American Association for the Advancement of Science and the Torrey Botanical Club. Her research interest was the morphology and embryology of *Cuscuta.*

Bibliography: Abir-Am, P. G. and Dorinda Outram, eds., *Uneasy Careers and Intimate Lives; American Men and Women of Science 1–4;* Herzenberg, Caroline L., *Women Scientists from Antiquity to the Present;* Rossiter, Margaret W., *Women Scientists in America;* Siegel, Patricia J. and Kay Thomas Finley, *Women in the Scientific Search.*

Hopper, Grace Murray
(1906–1992)
mathematician

Education: B.A., Vassar College, 1928; M.A., Yale University, 1930, Ph.D. in mathematics, 1934
Employment: Assistant, mathematics, Vassar College, 1931–1934, instructor, 1934–1939, assistant professor, 1939–1944, associate professor, 1944–1946; research fellow,

engineering science and applied physics, computation laboratory, Harvard University, 1946–1949; systems engineer, Univac Division, Remington Rand Corporation, 1949–1953, director, automatic programming, 1953–1959, chief engineer, 1959–1961, staff scientist, 1961–1971; professor, George Washington University, 1971–1978; special advisor to commander, Naval Data Automation Command, Department of Navy, 1967–1986; consultant, Digital Equipment Corporation, 1986–1992

Concurrent Position: Adjunct professor, Moore School of Electrical Engineering, University of Pennsylvania, 1963–1971

Married: Vincent F. Hopper, 1930, divorced 1945

*G**race Hopper's** achievements in the design of software for digital computers spanned three computer generations. She was on active duty in the U.S. Navy as a member of the Naval Reserves, until the age of 80 designing computer software. Her career started conventionally for a woman of her generation. After receiving her doctorate, she accepted a position at Vassar College in 1931 and remained there until 1946, rising through the ranks to associate professor. During World War II she took a leave of absence to join the U.S. Navy's Women Accepted for Voluntary Emergency Services (WAVES), where she spent the years 1943 through 1946 working on ordnance problems at the Harvard computer laboratory. In 1946 she resigned from Vassar to take an assistantship at Harvard to continue work on computer software. She then moved to Univac to head its automatic programming section, and she retired officially in 1971. She continued to consult for the Naval Reserves as head of the programming language section. By 1983 she was the oldest officer on active duty in the Navy when she was retired with the rank of commodore; that grade was changed to rear admiral in 1985.

Grace Hopper received numerous awards and received honorary degrees from at least ten universities in the United States and abroad. She was elected to membership in the National Academy of Engineering. She was elected a fellow of the American Association for the Advancement of Science and the Institute of Electrical and Electronics Engineers. She was a member of the Franklin Institute and the Association for Computing Machinery. She published more than 50 papers and articles on software and programming languages. There still is popular interest in her life and achievements. She was mentioned as a model for military women in Margaret Truman's novel, *Murder at the Pentagon* (1992), in which the heroine, Margit Falk, is a career officer in the U.S. Air Force. Her name was included in the 1992–1993 edition of *American Men and Women of Science.*

Bibliography: *American Men and Women of Science* 6–18; Debus, A. G., ed., *World Who's Who in Science;* Grinstein, Louise S. and Paul J. Campbell, eds. *Women of Mathematics;* Herzenberg, Caroline L., *Women Scientists from Antiquity to the Present;* Kass-Simon, G. and Patricia Farnes, *Women of Science,* O'Neill, Lois S., *The Women's Book of World Records and Achievements;* Perl, Teri, *Math Equals;* Uglow, Jennifer S., *International Dictionary of Women's Biography; Who Was Who in America.*

Horsford, Cornelia C.
(1861–1944)
archaeologist

Education: Private schools
Employment: No formal employment

Cornelia Horsford was regarded by her contemporaries as an expert on Norse archaeology. Her name was included in the first edition of *American Men and Women of Science*. She continued her father's archaeological research after his death, and financed the expeditions that she oversaw. Before the establishment of archaeology as a profession in the late nineteenth century, much of the research was conducted by private individuals, including some women. There were no courses in archaeology at the time in the United States. People learned by reading, observing, attending meetings of archaeological societies, and corresponding with other collectors. There was the American School of Classical Studies in Athens, Greece, but it did not include courses on the geographic areas in which Cornelia Horsford was interested. Although much work was being done at the time in the Mideast and Greece, her research focused on Iceland, Greenland, Vinland, and the British Isles. She set out in the mid-1890s on archaeological expeditions to Iceland and Great Britain. Most of her papers related to the Norse discovery of North America, a topic on which she conducted and directed several research projects. She was a member of several professional societies, such as the American Folk-Lore Society, the National Geographic Society, the Irish Texts Society, the Iceland Antiquity Society, and the London Viking Club, of which she was an honorary vice president. Her publications were listed in *Biographical Cyclopaedia of American Women* 13 (1904): 168–169. Her areas of research were Norse archaeology, horticulture, and the colonial history of the United States.

Bibliography: *American Men and Women of Science* 1–6; Siegel, Patricia J. and Kay Thomas Finley, *Women in the Scientific Search.*

Horstmann, Dorothy Millicent
(1911–)
epidemiologist

Education: A.B., University of California, Berkeley, 1936, M.D., 1940
Employment: Fellow, school of medicine, Yale University, 1942–1943, instructor, preventive medicine, 1943–1947; instructor, medical school, University of California, San Francisco, 1944–1945; senior fellow, University of London, 1947–1948; assistant professor, preventive medicine, medical school, Yale, 1948–1952, associate professor, 1952–1956, preventive medicine and pediatrics, 1956–1961, professor, epidemiology and pediatrics, 1961–1969, J. R. Paul professor of epidemiology and professor of pediatrics, 1969–1982; emeritus professor and senior research scientist

Dorothy Horstmann has been recognized for her research on polio and rubella; she established many of the important characteristics of polio. She secured appointments on the faculty of Yale University, where she was employed starting in 1948. She truly was fortunate in the direction her career took. In the 1940s there still was reluctance to hire women as faculty members, but she advanced in faculty rank at four-year intervals, a truly remarkable achievement that indicates the superiority and importance of her polio research. (At that time, the polio epidemic was causing public reaction much like the AIDS virus is today. The emotion was more intense, however, because the disease primarily attacked children.) She was a member of the vaccine development committee of the National Institute of Allergy and Infectious Disease from 1964 to 1967, and she received an award for contemporary leadership in polio research in 1953. She received honorary degrees from Smith College, Yale University, and the Woman's Medical College of Pennsylvania. She was elected president of the Infectious Diseases Society of America for 1974 and 1975, and she was elected to the National Academy of Sciences in 1975. She has been a fellow of the American Academy of Pediatrics, a master of the American College of Physicians, and an honorary member of the Royal Society of Medicine. She was a member of several other professional organizations. Her areas of research have been infectious disease, clinical virology, and clinical epidemiology. Her name was listed in the 1992–1993 edition of *American Men and Women of Science.*

Bibliography: *American Men and Women of Science* 8–18; Debus, A. G., ed., *World Who's Who in Science;* Herzenberg, Caroline L., *Women Scientists from Antiquity to the Present;* O'Neill, Lois S., *The Women's Book of World Records and Achievements.*

Howes, Ethel Dench Puffer
(1872–1950)
psychologist

Education: A.B., Smith College, 1891; University of Berlin and University of Freiburg, 1895–1897; Ph.D., Radcliffe College, 1902
Employment: High school teacher, 1891–1892; instructor in mathematics, Smith College, 1892–1895; assistant in psychology, Radcliffe College, 1898–1906; instructor and associate professor of philosophy, Wellesley College, 1901–1906; psychology, Simmons College, 1904–1906; director, institute for coordination of women's interests, Smith College, 1925–?, lecturer in sociology, 1928–1931
Married: Benjamin Howes, 1908

Ethel Howes' work as a psychologist was recognized by her peers in that her name was starred in the second through fifth editions of *American Men and Women of Science.* Her career followed the pattern of many women of her generation. She taught in a high school for one year and taught mathematics at Smith College for three years following her graduation from that school. After studying at the University of Berlin and the University of Freiburg, she taught psychology at Radcliffe College while completing her education there. It was not unusual for both men and women faculty members to complete their advanced degrees while teaching, even in the same college granting the degree; in some disciplines there simply were not pools of people available to fill openings. Ethel Howes later taught at Wellesley College for five years before returning to Smith as director of the institute for coordination of women's interests in 1925 and lecturer in sociology from 1928 to 1931. She was active in the woman's suffrage movement, serving as executive secretary of the National College Equal Suffrage League between 1906 and 1915. She was a member of the American Association for the Advancement of Science, the American Psychological Association, and the American Philosophical Association. Her research interest was the psychology of esthetics and symmetry. She was listed in the first edition of *American Men and Women of Science* under Ethel D. Puffer but as Ethel Howes in later editions. She had two children, Ellen and Benjamin.

Bibliography: *American Men and Women of Science* 1–5; Bryan, Alice I. and Edwin G. Boring, "Women in American Psychology"; Herzenberg, Caroline L., *Women Scientists from Antiquity to the Present*; Rossiter, Margaret W., *Women Scientists in America*; Siegel, Patricia J. and Kay Thomas Finley, *Women in the Scientific Search*; Visher, Stephen S., *Scientists Starred 1903–1943 in "American Men of Science"*; *Who Was Who in America.*

Hubbard, Marian Elizabeth
(1868–1956)
zoologist

Education: Mount Holyoke College, 1886–1889; B.S., University of Chicago, 1894; University of California, 1902–1903

Employment: Assistant in science and language, high school, 1889–1893; instructor in zoology, Wellesley College, 1894–1901, associate professor, 1902–1916, professor, 1917–1937; emeritus professor

Marian Hubbard's stature as a zoologist was supported by her inclusion in the first edition of *American Men and Women of Science*. She was chair of the zoology department at Wellesley College for 17 years, and she was a major force in rebuilding the department after a serious fire in 1914. Her career followed the pattern of many women scientists of her generation. After attending Mount Holyoke, she taught high school for several years. Upon receiving her undergraduate degree from the University of Chicago, she was appointed an instructor in zoology at Wellesley in 1894, advancing through the ranks to professor in 1917, a rather slow rate of promotion. Although she did not receive a doctorate, she conducted research at well-known institutions, such as the Woods Hole Marine Biological Laboratory, the University of California, and the San Diego Marine Biological Laboratory. She was a member of several professional societies, including the American Association for the Advancement of Science, the American Ornithologists' Union, and the American Eugenics Society. Her research interests were in heredity, and she focused on salamanders, chicks, and beetles. Her name was spelled in the various sources as Marion and Marian.

Bibliography: *American Men and Women of Science* 1–8; *National Cyclopedia of American Biography*; Siegel, Patricia J. and Kay Thomas Finley, *Women in the Scientific Search.*

Hubbard, Theodora Kimball
(1887–1935)
editor and author on landscape architecture and city planning

Education: S.B., Simmons College, 1908, M.S., 1917
Employment: Librarian, School of Landscape Architecture, Harvard University, 1911–1924, special advisor, 1924–1935; associate editor of the journal *Landscape Architecture* and contributing writer and cofounder of the journal *City Planning Quarterly*, 1924–1935
Married: Henry V. Hubbard, 1924

*T*heodora Hubbard was the author of books on landscape architecture and city planning and has been credited with establishing the landscape architecture collection of the Harvard library. After receiving her degree from Simmons College in 1908, she was employed as the librarian of the School of Landscape Architecture of Harvard starting in 1911. In 1918 and 1919, during World War I, she was a consulting librarian and chief of the reference library section of the U.S. Bureau of Industrial Housing and Transportation. She was an expert on zoning information for Secretary Hoover's Advisory Committee on Zoning. She married Henry Hubbard in 1924 and joined him as associate editor of *Landscape Architecture*, of which he was editor. The periodical was, and still is, a primary journal in the field of landscape architecture. She continued to serve as special advisor to the Harvard library.

Theodora Hubbard (as Theodora Kimball) coauthored *City Planning: A Comprehensive Analysis of the Subject...* (1913) and (as Theodora Hubbard) *An Introduction to the Study of Landscape Design* (1917). She was a co-editor of a biography of pioneer landscape architect Frederick Law Olmsted, which was published from 1922 to 1928. She was honorary librarian and a member of the American City Planning Institute, a corresponding member of the American Society of Landscape Architects, and a member of the Special Libraries Association. She was a trustee of Simmons College at one time. Her photograph and brief biography were published in *Landscape Architecture* 26 (January 1936): 51–55.

Bibliography: Barnhart, John H., *Biographical Notes upon Botanists; National Union Catalog.*

Hughes-Schrader, Sally
(b. 1895)
zoologist

Education: B.S., Grinnell College, 1917; Ph.D. in zoology, Columbia University, 1924
Employment: Instructor in zoology, Grinnell College, 1917–1919; lecturer, Barnard College, Columbia University, 1919–1921; demonstrator in biology, Bryn Mawr College, 1922–1924, instructor, 1924–1930; member of science faculty, Sarah Lawrence College, 1931–1941; member of science faculty, Columbia University, 1941–1947, research associate in cytology, department of zoology, 1947–1958; research associate in cytology, Duke University, 1959–1972; emeritus research associate in cytology

Concurrent Positions: Corporation member, Marine Biological Laboratory, Woods Hole, 1925; fellow in zoology, Duke University, 1961–1962, visiting professor, 1962–1965; emeritus visiting professor
Married: Franz Schrader, 1920

Sally Hughes-Schrader's earlier research concentrated on insects, and her name was starred in the sixth and seventh editions of *American Men and Women of Science.* Her interest shifted in the 1940s to fishes and amphibians, specifically the cranial nerves and ganglia. She had a fairly typical career for a woman scientist who was following her husband around the country, and they were considered one of the notable couples working in science prior to 1940. After receiving her undergraduate degree, she taught at Grinnell College for three years before going to Barnard and Bryn Mawr for teaching and research while she completed her doctorate. She was a member of the science faculty at Sarah Lawrence for 11 years and at Columbia for 18 years before accepting a position as a research associate in cytology at Duke in 1959. She also was a visiting professor at Duke University from 1962 to 1965. During

the summers of 1914 and 1920 she conducted research at the U.S. Department of Agriculture and the Bureau of Fisheries, respectively. She retired in 1972. She served on the editorial boards of the journals *Chromosomes* and *Biological Bulletin* beginning in 1962. She was a member of several professional societies, including the American Society of Zoologists, the Genetics Society of America, the Society for the Study of Evolution, and the American Academy of Arts and Sciences.

Bibliography: American Men and Women of Science 4–13; Debus, A. G., ed., *World Who's Who in Science;* Herzenberg, Caroline L., *Women Scientists from Antiquity to the Present;* Rossiter, Margaret W., *Women Scientists in America;* Visher, Stephen S., *Scientists Starred 1903–1943 in "American Men of Science."*

Huntington, Emily
(1841–1909)
founder of cooking school

Education: Wheaton Seminary, 1856–1858
Employment: Mission school, Massachusetts, 1859–1871; matron, Wilson Industrial School for Girls, New York City, 1872–1892; founder of kitchen garden classes for children, 1879–1880, reorganized under Kitchen Garden Association, 1880–1884, name changed to Industrial Education Association, 1884; superintendent, New York Cooking School, 1893–1909

Emily Huntington championed programs for teaching pupils in kindergarten through high school the elements of domestic science. She developed a method for teaching "housework" classes offered by the Wilson Industrial School and incorporated it into her book, *Little Lessons for Little Housekeepers*

(1875). She then introduced a method for instructing kindergarten pupils in household duties. The purpose was to teach poor children how to make their homes more comfortable and to prepare them to work as household servants. She named her system of instruction the "kitchen garden." In the late nineteenth century there was a movement in the United States to provide education and training for everyone, particularly to the thousands of immigrants who were pouring into the United States each year.

By 1879 the kitchen garden classes were taught in 14 industrial schools and missions in New York City. One of Emily Huntington's teachers developed the farm garden to instruct boys in the elements of agriculture. In 1884 the plan was incorporated into the Industrial Education Association to promote domestic and industrial training for girls and boys and to train teachers for this work. The association was responsible for the founding of Teachers' College, Columbia University.

Emily Huntington's other books included *The Cooking Garden* (1885) and *How To Teach Kitchen Garden* (1901). She was one of the original members of the Lake Placid Conference on Home Economics, first held in 1899.

Bibliography: James, E. T., ed., *Notable American Women 1607–1950*; McHenry, Robert, ed., *Famous American Women; National Union Catalog.*

Hurston, Zora Neale
(1907–1960)
anthropologist and author

Education: Howard University, 1921–1924; A.B., Barnard College, 1928
Employment: Field researcher in folklore among African Americans in the South, 1928–1932; faculty, Cookman College, 1934; drama coach, Works Progress Administration (WPA) Federal Theater Project, 1935–1936; Guggenheim fellowship in Haiti, 1938; editor, Federal Writers' Project, 1938; faculty, North Carolina College, 1939; staff, Library of Congress; author, 1927–1960
Married: Herbert Sheen, 1927, divorced 1931; Albert Price, 1939, divorced

Zora Hurston was one of the first African Americans to work as an anthropologist, and she was the first black person known to have graduated from Barnard College. She was born in Eatonville, Florida, the first incorporated all-black city in the nation. Leaving school at the age of 13, she worked as a domestic before resuming her education. She attended Howard University and in 1925 she won a scholarship to Barnard, where she studied anthropology and pursued graduate studies at Columbia. Her field studies were funded by fellowships, but she published her results in the form of plays and novels. These writings are rich sources for folklore, songs, religious cults, and games of people in the South. The reference sources conflict on the date of her birth and dates and places of employment. In the 1930s she was involved in a Federal Theater Project, a field study in Haiti, a Federal Writers' Project, and teaching in at least two colleges. She also contributed to magazines, wrote for Warner Brothers motion picture studio, and was on the staff of the Library of Congress. Her novels include *Jonah's Gourd Vine* (1934), *Mules and Men* (1935), *Their Eyes Were Watching God* (1937), and *Moses, Man of the Mountain* (1939). *Tell My Horse* (1938) is a blend of travel writing and anthropology based on her investigations in Haiti. Her work has been of lasting significance to folklorists and students of rural life in the South. There are several biographies, including Robert E. Hemenway's *Zora Neale Hurston: A Literary Biography* (1977), Lillie P. Howard's *Zora*

Neale Hurston (1980), and N. Y. Nathiri's *Zora! A Woman and Her Community* (1991).

Bibliography: *Current Biography;* Herzenberg, Caroline L., *Women Scientists from Antiquity to the Present;* Ireland, Norma O., *Index to Scientists of the World;* McHenry, Robert, ed., *Famous American Women; National Union Catalog;* Rossiter, Margaret W., *Women Scientists in America;* Sicherman, Barbara et al., *Notable American Women.*

Hussey, Priscilla Butler
(1894–1946)
entomologist

Education: A.B., University of Michigan, 1919; A.M., Smith College, 1921; Sc.D., Radcliffe College, 1923

Employment: Assistant in zoology, University of Michigan, 1917–1919; curator, department of zoology, Smith College, 1919–1921; instructor in biology, New York University, 1923–1927; assistant professor, Battle Creek College, 1927–1928; professor, Louisiana State Normal College, Natchitoches, 1928–1946

Priscilla Hussey was an entomologist who was recognized for her work in economic entomology. After receiving her doctorate, she taught five years at New York University and one year at Battle Creek College. In 1928 she became professor of biology and entomology at Louisiana State Normal College, where she stayed until retirement. These were the years of the Depression, and although she was educated at major colleges, she was unable to secure a position at a major institution. Her work was recognized, though, since her name and photograph appeared in Herbert Osborn's *Fragments of Entomological History.* She published *A Taxonomic List of Some Plants of Economic Importance* (1939). In the 1940s she compiled a card file of all insecticides prepared by commercial companies and their uses. This was a forerunner of the many handbooks on insecticides and pesticides that are published today and available in computer files, such as PESTBANK, published by Silver Platter. She was a member of several professional societies, including the American Association for the Advancement of Science, the Entomological Society of America, and the American Association of Economic Entomologists. Her research was focused on economic biology and the embryology of insects.

Bibliography: *American Men and Women of Science* 4–7; *National Union Catalog;* Osborn, Herbert, *Fragments of Entomological History.*

Hyde, Ida Henrietta
(1857–1945)
physiologist

Education: University of Illinois, 1881; A.B., Cornell University, 1891; Bryn Mawr College, 1891–1893; University of Strasbourg, 1893; Collegiate Alumnae European fellow, 1894–1895; Ph.D., University of Heidelberg, 1896; Naples Zoological Station, 1896; University of Berne, 1896; Radcliffe College, 1897; Harvard Medical School, 1897; University of Liverpool, 1904; M.D., Rush Medical College, 1911

Employment: Teacher, public schools, 1881–1888; assistant in biology, Bryn Mawr College, 1891; professor of histology and anatomy, prep school, 1897–1900; associate professor of physiology, University of Kansas, 1899–1905, professor, 1905–1925

Ida Hyde, in 1902, became the first woman to be elected a member of the American Physiological Society. She was the first woman to graduate from the University of Heidelberg and the first woman to receive a doctorate at Heidelberg. She was also the first woman to do research at Harvard Medical School. Her major contribution to physiology was the development of the microelectrode, but it has never been acknowledged officially as hers.

Some aspects of her career were typical for a woman of her generation. After teaching public school for several years, she enrolled at the University of Illinois at the age of 24. Then her career took a different course. She moved to Bryn Mawr College for further study, then went to Germany, where she received a doctorate from the University of Heidelberg in 1896. She had further study at the University of Berne, Radcliffe College, and Harvard Medical School. She taught in a prep school for four years and then accepted a position as an associate professor of physiology at the University of Kansas in 1899. After the university established a separate department of physiology in 1905, she was promoted to professor. Later she attended Rush Medical College for several summers and received an M.D. degree in 1911. She had an outstanding reputation as a teacher, and she published two textbooks: *Outlines of Experimental Physiology* (1905) and *Laboratory Outlines of Physiology* (1910). She

spent many summers at the Marine Biological Laboratory, Woods Hole, for her research. She also worked to promote equal opportunities in science for women. She was instrumental in establishing the Naples Table Association for Promoting Scientific Research by Women, an association formed to provide fellowships for American women scientists to the prestigious Naples Zoological Station. She endowed scholarships for women students of science at the University of Kansas and at Cornell. In 1945 she established the Ida H. Hyde Woman's International Fellowship of the American Association of University Women. She was a member of the American Physiological Society and the American Eugenics Society. Her research was on comparative studies of respiration and circulation and on the nervous system and sense organs. She had a long and productive life. Her name was included in the first seven editions of *American Men and Women of Science*. Photographs can be found in the *National Cyclopedia of American Biography* and in G. Kass-Simon's and Patricia Farnes' *Women of Science: Righting the Record*.

Bibliography: *American Men and Women of Science* 1–7; Herzenberg, Caroline L., *Women Scientists from Antiquity to the Present*; James, E. T., ed., *Notable American Women 1607–1950*; Kass-Simon, G. and Patricia Farnes, *Women of Science*; Mozans, H. J., *Women in Science*; *National Cyclopedia* *of American Biography; National Union Catalog;* Ogilvie, Marilyn B., *Women in Science;* O'Neill, Lois S., *The Women's Book of World Records and Achievements;* Rossiter, Margaret W., *Women Scientists in America;* Rossiter, Margaret W., "Women Scientists in America before 1920"; Siegel, Patricia J. and Kay Thomas Finley, *Women in the Scientific Search.*

Hyman, Libbie Henrietta
(1888–1969)
zoologist

Education: B.S., University of Chicago, 1910, Ph.D. in zoology, 1915
Employment: Assistant in zoology, University of Chicago, 1910–1928, associate, 1928–1931; research associate, American Museum of Natural History, 1937–1969

*L*ibbie Hyman is known for her monumental book, *The Invertebrates,* and she was elected to membership in the National Academy of Sciences in 1961. After receiving her doctorate from the University of Chicago, she had a position there as an assistant and associate in zoology until 1931, when the department head retired. She was unable to secure another university position because she was Jewish and was thought to be abrasive, according to Margaret W. Rossiter's *Women Scientists in America.* It was also extremely difficult for women scientists to find employment during the Depression years. While employed at Chicago she published several studies: *A Laboratory Manual for Elementary Zoology* (1919, 1926) and *A Laboratory Manual for Comparative Vertebrate Anatomy* (1922). Later she wrote *Comparative Vertebrate Anatomy* (1942). Since she used their library, starting in 1937 the American Museum of Natural History provided an office and laboratory but no pay for Libbie Hyman to prepare her manuscript of *The Invertebrates* in six volumes (1940–1967). During this time she supported herself from the sales of her earlier books. She received many awards, such as the gold medal of the Linnean Society of London in 1960 and the Elliot Gold Medal of the National Academy of Sciences in 1954. She received honorary

degrees from Chicago (1941), Goucher College (1958), Coe College (1959), and Upsala College (1963). She was president of the Society of Systematic Zoology from 1959 to 1963. She was also a member of the American Society of Zoologists, the American Society of Naturalists, and the American Society of Limnology and Oceanography. Her research focused on the taxonomy of free-living flatworms. Her name was starred in the fifth through seventh editions of *American Men and Women of Science.* There is a photograph in the *Biographical Memoirs* of the National Academy of Sciences.

Bibliography: *American Men and Women of Science* 5–11; Debus, A. G., ed., *World Who's Who in Science;* Herzenberg, Caroline L., *Women Scientists from Antiquity to the Present;* Kass-Simon, G. and Patricia Farnes, *Women of Science;* McHenry, Robert, ed., *Famous American Women;* Macksey, Joan and Kenneth Macksey, *The Book of Women's Achievements;* Mozans, H. J., *Women in Science;* National Academy of Sciences, *Biographical Memoirs; National Union Catalog;* O'Neill, Lois S., *The Women's Book of World Records and Achievements;* Rossiter, Margaret W., *Women Scientists in America;* Sicherman, Barbara et al., *Notable American Women;*

Siegel, Patricia J. and Kay Thomas Finley, *Women in the Scientific Search;* Visher, Stephen S., *Scientists Starred 1903–1943 in* *"American Men of Science";* Yost, Edna, *American Women of Science.*

Dorothea A. Jameson
Allene Rosalind Jeanes
(Estelle) Louise Jensen
Mary Ellen Jones

Jameson, Dorothea A.
(1920–)
psychologist

Education: B.A., Wellesley College, 1942
Employment: Research assistant, Harvard University, 1941–1947; research psychologist, color control department, Eastman Kodak Company, 1947–1957; research scientist, New York University, 1957–1962; research associate, University of Pennsylvania, 1962–1968, research professor, 1968–1972, professor of psychology, 1972–1974, professor of psychology and visual science, 1975–
Concurrent Positions: Visiting professor, University of Rochester, 1974–1975; visiting professor, Columbia University, 1974–1976
Married: Leo M. Hurvich, 1948

Dorothea Jameson has been an expert on color vision, and she combined her work in psychology with work in optics. Her career has been amazing because she did not possess any advanced degrees. She was working in new areas of color vision, however, and she was supporting her research with major grants. After receiving her undergraduate degree from Wellesley in 1942, she worked as a research assistant at Harvard for six years before accepting a position as a research psychologist at Eastman Kodak, where she worked for 10 years. After working for New York University as a research scientist for several years, she moved to the University of Pennsylvania as a research associate and then was promoted first to research professor in 1968 and then to professor of psychology in 1972. She supported her research starting in 1957 as principal investigator on grants from the National Institutes of Health (NIH) and the National Science Foundation. She was a fellow of the Center for Advanced Study in Behavioral Sciences in 1981 and 1982. She served on the national advisory eye council for NIH starting in 1985.

She received honorary degrees from the University of Pennsylvania in 1972 and from the State University of New York in 1989. She received many awards, such as the Warren Medal of the Society of Experimental Psychologists in 1971, the Distinguished Science Contribution Award of the American Psychological Association in 1972, the Helmholtz Award from the Cognitive Neuroscience Association in 1987, and the Tillyer Medal of the Optical Society of America in 1982. She was elected to membership in the National Academy of Sciences in 1975. She also has been a member of the American Academy of Arts and Sciences and the Optical Society of America. Her research has involved visual mechanisms and human perception. Her name was included in the 1992–1993 edition of *American Men and Women of Science.*

Bibliography: American Men and Women of Science 8–18; Herzenberg, Caroline L., *Women Scientists from Antiquity to the Present;* O'Neill, Lois S., *The Women's Book of World Records and Achievements.*

Jeanes, Allene Rosalind
(b. 1906)
chemist

Education: A.B., Baylor University, 1928; A.M., University of California, Berkeley, 1929; Ph.D. in organic chemistry, University of Illinois, 1938

Employment: Instructor, high school mathematics and physics, 1930; head, department of science, Athens College, 1930–1935; instructor in chemistry, University of Illinois, 1936–1937; fellow, National Institutes of Health, 1938–1940; research chemist, Northern Regional Research Laboratory, U.S. Department of Agriculture, Peoria, 1941–?

*A*llene Jeanes and her research group isolated and characterized over 100 different dextrans that have great value in research, especially in immunology and immunochemistry. After she received her master's degree, she was department head at Athens College in Alabama for several years before she enrolled in the University of Illinois, where she received her doctorate in 1938. She received one of the first Corn Industries Research Foundation fellowships at the National Institutes of Health, where she codeveloped a new technique of periodate oxidation of starches. She joined the staff at Northern Regional Research Laboratory in Peoria, a regional laboratory of the U.S. Department of Agriculture (USDA), in 1941, three months after it opened. Initially she studied the nature and structural role of the branch points in starch. During the Korean War there was a need for a blood-plasma substitute, and she and her group were able to find a chemical, dextran, that was used successfully to expand plasma volume. Her technique was used for isolating and characterizing dextrans. In 1953 she was the first woman in the Chemistry Bureau to receive the USDA Distinguished Chemist Award. In 1962 she was the first woman in the USDA to receive the Federal Woman's Award. She received the Garvan Medal in 1956. She was a member of the American Chemical Society. Her areas of research included preparation and structure of dextrans; oxidation of dextrans with periodate; and sources, structure, properties, and utility of extracellular microbial polysaccharides.

Bibliography: American Men and Women of Science 7–13; Debus, A. G., ed., World Who's Who in Science; Herzenberg, Caroline L., Women Scientists from Antiquity to the Present; Kass-Simon, G. and Patricia Farnes, Women of Science; O'Neill, Lois S., The Women's Book of World Records and Achievements.

Jensen, (Estelle) Louise
(b. 1888)
plant pathologist

Education: A.B., University of Minnesota, 1909, fellow, 1911–1912; A.M., Smith College, 1910

Employment: High school teacher, 1910–1911; xylotomist (wood expert), forest products laboratory, U.S. Department of Agriculture, Madison, Wisconsin, 1912–1913; instructor

in mycology, University of Minnesota, mycologist, Minnesota Experiment Station, 1913–1917
Married: Elvin C. Stakman, 1917

*L*ouise Jensen was one of the many wives of scientists whose work has been forgotten in the passing of years. Her career was typical for a woman of her generation. She taught high school for several years after receiving her master's degree from Smith College. She then worked for the forest products laboratory at Madison, Wisconsin, for a year before accepting a joint appointment as an instructor in mycology at the University of Minnesota and a mycologist with the Minnesota Experiment Station from 1913 to 1917. Although she did not list any employment after her marriage in 1917, Louise Jensen probably worked with her husband, E. C. Stakman, a renowned botanist at Minnesota who later had an award named in his honor. The social convention of the time was that women did not work after marriage, but many wives continued to work as unpaid or underpaid assistants in their husband's laboratories, preparing materials for the class lectures, editing and preparing manuscripts for publication, and instructing graduate students in laboratory procedures. Louise Jensen was one of the few women who continued to list herself under her maiden name in *American Men and Women of Science* after her marriage, which she did until 1938, her last listing. She was a member of the American Association for the Advancement of Science and the American Phytopathological Society. Her research interest was imperfect fungi on cereals.

Bibliography: *American Men and Women of Science* 3–7; Barnhart, John H., *Biographical Notes upon Botanists; National Union Catalog.*

Jones, Mary Ellen
(1922–)
biochemist

Education: B.S., University of Chicago, 1944; Ph.D., Yale University, 1951
Employment: Research chemist, Armour and Company, 1942–1948; fellow, biochemistry research laboratory, Massachusetts General Hospital, 1951–1957; from assistant to associate biochemist, Brandeis University, 1957–1966; from associate professor to professor, University of North Carolina, Chapel Hill, 1966–1971; professor of biochemistry, University of Southern California, 1971–1978; professor, 1978–1980, chair of biochemistry department, University of North Carolina, Chapel Hill, 1978–, Kenan professor, 1980–
Married: Paul L. Munson, 1948

*M*ary Jones has been rated a distinguished biochemist by her contemporaries, as supported by her election to the National Academy of Sciences in 1984 and her numerous awards. She worked as a research chemist for Armour and Company while obtaining her undergraduate degree from the University of Chicago. She continued her education at Yale, where she received her doctorate in 1951. She worked at Brandeis University as a biochemist for ten years before accepting a position as an associate professor at the University of North Carolina in 1966. She was promoted to professor in 1969, but she moved to the University of Southern

California in 1971. She returned to North Carolina in 1978 and was appointed Kenan professor in 1980. Mary Jones was associate editor of the *Canadian Journal of Biochemistry* from 1969 to 1974. She was co-editor of a book, *Purine and Pyrimidine Nucleotide Metabolism* (1978), which is volume 51 in the *Methods in Enzymology* series. She has received several distinguished appointments, such as member of the grants committee of the American Cancer Society (1971–1973), member of the metabolic biology study section of the National Science Foundation (1978–1981), and member of the science advisory board for the National Heart, Lung and Blood Institute, National Institutes of Health (1980–1984). She was president of the American Society of Biological Chemists in 1986. She was elected a fellow of the American Association for the Advancement of Science, and she also has been a member of the American Chemical Society. Her research has involved biosynthetic and transfer reactions, metabolic regulation of enzymes, multifunctional proteins, and pyrimidine and amino acid biosynthesis. She raised two children. Her name was listed in the 1992–1993 edition of *American Men and Women of Science.*

Bibliography: *American Men and Women of Science* 9–18; Herzenberg, Caroline L., *Women Scientists from Antiquity to the Present; National Union Catalog.*

Isabella Lugoski Karle
Annie May Hurd Karrer
Marcia Anna Keith
Ida Augusta Keller
Helen Dean King
Louisa Boyd Yeomans King
Eleanora Frances Bliss Knopf
Marian Elliott Koshland

Karle, Isabella Lugoski
(1921–)
crystallographer

Education: B.S., University of Michigan, M.S., 1942, Ph.D. in physical chemistry, 1944
Employment: Associate chemist, University of Chicago, 1944; instructor, University of Michigan, 1944–1946; physicist, Naval Research Laboratory, 1946–1959, head, x-ray analytical section, 1959–
Married: Jerome Karle, 1942

Isabella Karle, with her husband Jerome and others, developed a new mathematical technique called direct methods that has revolutionized crystallography. Jerome has been the theorist and Isabella the experimentalist. He and others developed the theory of direct methods, but she applied it and made it popular and accessible to the crystallographic world. Extremely intelligent, she received her doctorate at the age of 22, but she was unable to secure a graduate teaching assistantship in chemistry at Michigan because women had never held such a position. She was granted a fellowship by the American Association of University Women to start her graduate studies. After she received her doctorate, she and Jerome worked at the University of Chicago on the Manhattan Project and at the University of Michigan for a short time.

The couple was unable to obtain suitable employment together in a university due to nepotism rules, but the Naval Research Laboratory offered them an opportunity to work together. Isabella Karle has applied the mathematical techniques in crystallography to a variety of substances, such as DNA in human cells and solid-state peptide structures, in which she has been a leading authority. She has published more than 200 scientific papers and has received several honorary degrees. She was elected to membership in the National Academy of Sciences in 1978. Her awards include the Hillebrand Award from the American Chemical Society (1969), the Garvan Medal (1976), the Federal Woman's Award (1973), and the Pioneer Award from the American Institute of Chemists (1984). Her husband was corecipient of the Nobel Prize in chemistry in 1986. She has been president of the American Crystallographic Association in 1976 and a member of the American Physical Society and the American Chemical Society. She has had a diverse list of research interests: application of electron and x-ray diffraction to structure problems, phase determination in crystallography, elucidation of molecular formulae, peptides, and configurations and conformations of natural products and biologically active materials. Her photograph was included in G. Kass-Simon's and Patricia Farnes' *Women of Science: Righting the Record.* She and her husband raised three daughters. Her name was listed in the 1992–1993 edition of *American Men and Women of Science.*

Bibliography: American Men and Women of Science 8–18; Herzenberg, Caroline L., *Women Scientists from Antiquity to the Present*; Kass-Simon, G. and Patricia Farnes, *Women of Science*; Kundsin, Ruth B., "Successful Women in the Sciences"; O'Neill, Lois S., *The Women's Book of World Records and Achievements.*

Karrer, Annie May Hurd
(b. 1893)
plant physiologist

Education: A.B., University of Washington, Seattle, 1915, M.S., 1917; Ph.D. in plant physiology, University of California, Berkeley, 1918
Employment: Teaching assistant, University of Washington, 1915–1916; assistant plant physiologist, Bureau of Plant Industry, U.S. Department of Agriculture, 1918–1924, associate plant physiologist, 1924–1944, plant physiologist, 1944–1949
Married: Sebastian Karrer, 1923

*A*nnie Karrer's area of specialization was the improvement of cereal crops and the control of cereal diseases. She was another example of the women who had careers at the U.S. Department of Agriculture (USDA) when other federal agencies hired few women as professionals. She joined the USDA in 1918, the same year she received her doctorate from the University of California, Berkeley. Before World War I, few women scientists had doctorates, and many of the women who did earn doctorates often completed them long after they had acquired a full-time job. Annie Karrer's career, therefore, was unusual in both of those respects. She initially was hired in the Bureau of Plant Industry, the division that employed almost all of the women professionals in the USDA prior to the establishment of the division of home economics in the 1930s. The USDA permitted many women to build lists of publications and, therefore, recognition for their work among their peer professionals. Annie Karrer published 16 reports in the USDA series. She was a member of the American Association for the Advancement of Science, the American Society of Plant Physiologists, the Botanical Society of America, and the Botanical Society of Washington. Her research focused on plant physiology involved in improvement of cereal crops and control of cereal diseases. She was listed in the third edition of *American Men and Women of Science* under Annie Hurd, but under Annie Karrer in later editions.

Bibliography: *American Men and Women of Science* 3–8; Barnhart, John H., *Biographical Notes upon Botanists; National Union Catalog.*

Keith, Marcia Anna
(1859–1950)
physicist

Education: Worcester Polytechnic Institute, 1887, 1889; B.S., Mount Holyoke College, 1892; University of Berlin, 1897–1898; University of Chicago, 1901
Employment: Public school teacher, 1876–1879; science instructor, Michigan Seminary, 1883–1885; instructor in mathematics and physics, Mount Holyoke College, 1885–1889, head of physics department, 1889–1903; Lake Erie College, 1905–1906; assistant engineer, firm of Herbert Keith, 1906–1918

arcia Keith was one of the two women founders of the American Physical Society. Her career followed the pattern of many women of her generation. She taught public school for a number of years and taught in a private school before accepting a position as an instructor in mathematics and physics at Mount Holyoke. She was the first full-time instructor in the physics department at Mount Holyoke and was head of the department from 1889 to 1903. She was said to be the first to provide individual laboratory work for her students. While she was teaching at Mount Holyoke, she attended Worcester Polytechnic and finally received her undergraduate degree from Mount Holyoke in 1892. It was not unusual during this period for both men and women to obtain accredited degrees after they started academic careers. The urgency to open and expand the women's colleges meant that administrators hired instructors without academic credentials. Due to the expense of laboratory equipment, few colleges offered classes in physics, making it difficult for Marcia Keith to complete her degree.

Marcia Keith was not a research physicist. Her importance to the history of science is that she taught physics to young women and she was one of the founders of the American Physical Society. She later attended the University of Berlin and the University of Chicago. In 1905 she accepted a position at Lake Erie College for a year and then accepted a position as an assistant engineer in a consulting firm. She was a member of the American Association for the Advancement of Science and the American Physical Society. Her name was included in the first edition of *American Men and Women of Science.*

Bibliography: *American Men and Women of Science* 1–9; Herzenberg, Caroline L., *Women Scientists from Antiquity to the Present*; Ogilvie, Marilyn B., *Women in Science*; Rossiter, Margaret W., *Women Scientists in America*; Rossiter, Margaret W., "Women Scientists in America before 1920"; Siegel, Patricia J. and Kay Thomas Finley, *Women in the Scientific Search.*

Keller, Ida Augusta
(1866–1932)
plant physiologist

Education: University of Pennsylvania, 1884–1886; University of Leipzig, 1887–1889; Ph.D., University of Zurich, 1890
Employment: Assistant in botany, Bryn Mawr College, 1886–1887, lecturer, 1891–1893; teacher of chemistry, Philadelphia High School for Girls, 1893–1898, head of chemistry and biology departments, 1898–?

da Keller was recognized for her work in plant physiology, and her name was listed in the first edition of *American Men and Women of Science.* She taught at Bryn Mawr for several years after attending the University of Pennsylvania. She received her doctorate from the University of Zurich, and then returned to Bryn Mawr

for two years. She then accepted a position at the Philadelphia High School for Girls, where she later was appointed head of the chemistry and biology departments. Although it might seem strange that she did not receive a degree from the University of Pennsylvania, it was one of the colleges of that period that would allow women to attend classes but would not grant them degrees. Another incongruity was that she left Bryn Mawr to teach at a high school in Philadelphia. Although no explanation was given in our sources, it could very well have been due to family circumstances. Although the distance between Bryn Mawr and Philadelphia is not great geographically, at the turn of the century roads probably did not permit commuting. It would have been fantastic for those high school girls to have a teacher with her background in education and travel, however. Ida Keller was an active member of a number of botanical and horticultural societies in the Philadelphia area and held elective offices. In addition to a number of scientific papers that were published in the *Proceedings* of the Academy of Natural Sciences of Philadelphia, she was coauthor of a book, *Handbook of the Flora of Philadelphia and Vicinity* (1905). A list of her publications was included in John Harshberger's *Botanists of Philadelphia and Their Work*. She was a member of the American Society of Naturalists. Her research was in fertilization and in the flora of Philadelphia.

Bibliography: *American Men and Women of Science* 1–4; Harshberger, John W., *The Botanists of Philadelphia and Their Work*; *National Union Catalog*; Siegel, Patricia J. and Kay Thomas Finley, *Women in the Scientific Search.*

King, Helen Dean
(1869–1955)
geneticist

Education: B.A., Vassar College, 1892; Ph.D., Bryn Mawr College, 1899
Employment: Assistant in biology, Bryn Mawr College, 1899–1904; fellow in biology, University of Pennsylvania, 1906–1908; assistant in anatomy, Wistar Institute of Anatomy and Biology, 1908–1912, assistant professor of anatomy, 1912–1927, professor of embryology, 1927–1949

*H*elen King's outstanding contribution to science was her success in breeding pure strains of laboratory animals. Her research was obviously recognized by her contemporaries; her name was starred in the first through seventh editions of *American Men and Women of Science.* Her early work was on the effects of close inbreeding in mice, and newspapers created a sensation about her research by implying that she considered incest taboos unnecessary. Her later research was on the domestication of the Norway rat. After she received her doctorate from Bryn Mawr, she remained at the school as an assistant in biology until 1904. She accepted a fellowship in biology at the University of Pennsylvania in 1906 and then moved to the Wistar Institute in 1908. She was promoted to assistant professor in 1912 and professor of embryology in 1927. It seems strange that she was not promoted to full professor for 14 years when her name was starred in each edition of *American Men and Women of Science* during that period, but this was not unusual for a woman faculty member at that time. She served on the institute's advisory board for 24 years, and she was editor of its bibliographic service for 13 years.

She received many honors and awards. She received the Ellen Richards Prize of the Association to Aid Scientific Research for Women in 1932. She was elected a fellow of the New York Academy of Sciences. Her other memberships included the American Association for the Advancement of Science, the American Society of Naturalists, the American Society of Zoologists, and the American Association of Anatomists. In addition to developing new types of rats, Helen King's research also shed light on some important areas of heredity. Through careful inbreeding experiments with brother and sister rats, she demonstrated the capacity to improve the strain, knowledge that has been applied to other animals, such as race horses. Her research interests included sex determination in amphibians and mammals, germ cells in amphibians and mammals, parthenogenesis, growth and reproduction of the white rat, and modification of the sex ratio.

Bibliography: *American Men and Women of Science* 1–8; Herzenberg, Caroline L., *Women Scientists from Antiquity to the Present; National Union Catalog;* Ogilvie, Marilyn B., *Women in Science;* Rossiter, Margaret W., *Women Scientists in America;* Rossiter, Margaret W., "Women Scientists in America before 1920"; Siegel, Patricia J. and Kay Thomas Finley, *Women in the Scientific Search;* Visher, Stephen S., *Scientists Starred 1903–1943 in "American Men of Science."*

King, Louisa Boyd Yeomans
(1863–1948)
writer on gardening

Education: Private schools
Employment: Author
Married: Francis King, 1890, died

*L*ouisa King contributed to the popularizing of horticulture by writing garden books. She was a pioneer in the garden club movement in the United States at the turn of the century, a movement to clean up the cities and make them more attractive. This was when the profession of landscape architecture was just starting; cities were building parks and homeowners were planting gardens to set off their Victorian-style homes. She had developed an interest in gardening at her home in Alma, Michigan. Soon after 1902 she began corresponding with horticultural enthusiasts in the United States and England. By 1910 she was contributing articles to magazines such as *Garden Magazine, House Beautiful,* and *Country Life.* She published *The Well-Considered Garden*
(1915), the first of ten books she published in 15 years. It was published in various editions up to 1929. She dealt more with artistic principles of gardening than practical techniques, and she stressed massed flowers in place of the excessively formal Victorian garden. She was one of the founders in 1913 of the Garden Club of America, serving as one of the original vice presidents. She was the first president of the Woman's National Farm and Garden Association from 1914 to 1921. After her husband's death, she moved to New York State in 1927, and she started the state's first plowing contest. She had an international reputation as a gardener. She was a vice president of the Garden Club of London and a fellow of the Royal Horticultural Society. She was awarded in 1921 the

George White Medal of the Massachusetts Horticultural Society, the first given to a woman. In 1923 she received the Medal of Honor of the Garden Club of America.

Bibliography: Hollingsworth, Buckner, *Her Garden Was Her Delight;* James, E. T., ed., *Notable American Women 1607–1950; National Union Catalog;* O'Neill, Lois S., *The Women's Book of World Records and Achievements.*

Knopf, Eleanora Frances Bliss
(1883–1974)
geologist

Education: A.B., A.M., Bryn Mawr College, 1904; Ph.D. in petrology, University of California, Berkeley, 1912; Johns Hopkins University, 1917–1918

Employment: Assistant curator, geology museum, Bryn Mawr College, 1904–1905, 1908–1909, demonstrator, geology laboratory, 1905–1906; aide, U.S. Geological Survey, 1912–1917, assistant geologist, 1917–1918, associate geologist, 1918–1928, geologist, 1928–1970

Concurrent Positions: Geologist, Maryland Geological Survey, 1917–1920; research associate, department of earth sciences, Stanford University, 1951–1966

Married: Adolph Knopf, 1920

*E*leanora Knopf's contribution to science was that she introduced rock fabric analysis and structural petrology in the United States. This method was described in a book she coauthored, *Structural Petrology* (1938), which brought her recognition for her work. Her name was starred in the sixth and seventh editions of *American Men and Women of Science.* After she received her undergraduate degree at Bryn Mawr, she continued working at the school in the geology museum and the geology laboratory. She received her doctorate from the University of California, Berkeley, in 1912, taking additional studies at Johns Hopkins in the 1917–1918 academic year. She started her career with the U.S. Geological Survey as aide in 1912, being promoted to assistant geologist in 1917 and up through the ranks to geologist in 1928 before retiring in 1970. During that period the Geological Survey was hiring women geologists on a contract basis, and Eleanora Knopf accepted other work at times. She worked for the Maryland Geological Survey

before her marriage, and she had a long-term association with the department of earth sciences at Stanford from 1951 to 1966, when her husband was a faculty member there. While at Stanford she made studies of several locations in the Rocky Mountains in Montana and the Spanish peaks in Colorado. When she lived in New Haven, she was a visiting lecturer at Harvard and Yale, but she did not have formal appointments. When she moved to Stanford with her husband and family in 1951, she continued working for the U.S. Geological Survey until a few years before her death.

In 1913 she had announced her discovery of the mineral glaucophane in Pennsylvania; this was the first sighting of the substance east of the Pacific coast. One of her most important projects was at Stissing Mountain, a region on the New York–Connecticut border. In the course of her studies for this project, she decided to use structural petrology in analyzing her data, which led to the publication of her book on the topic. She was elected a fellow of the Geological Society of America. She also was a member of the American Geophysical Union. Her research interests were structural petrology applied to the study of metamorphic and sedimentary rocks and study of experimentally deformed rocks. Her husband had three children from a previous marriage, which she reared.

Bibliography: *American Men and Women of Science* 6–13; Arnold, Lois B., *Four Lives in*

Science; Debus, A. G., ed., *World Who's Who in Science;* Herzenberg, Caroline L., *Women Scientists from Antiquity to the Present;* Kass-Simon, G. and Patricia Farnes, *Women of Science; National Union Catalog;* Rossiter, Margaret W., *Women Scientists in America;* Sicherman, Barbara et al., *Notable American Women;* Siegel, Patricia J. and Kay Thomas Finley, *Women in the Scientific Search;* Visher, Stephen S., *Scientists Starred 1903–1943 in "American Men of Science."*

Koshland, Marian Elliott
(1921–)
immunologist

Education: B.A., Vassar College, 1942; M.S., University of Chicago, 1943, Ph.D. in bacteriology, 1949
Employment: Assistant, cholera project, Office of Scientific Research and Development, University of Chicago, 1943–1945; assistant, Commission on Air Borne Diseases, University of Colorado, 1943–1944; junior chemist, atomic bomb project, Manhattan district, Tennessee, 1945–1946; associate bacteriologist, Brookhaven National Laboratory, 1953–1962, bacteriologist, 1962–1965; associate research immunologist, University of California, Berkeley, 1965–1969, research immunologist, 1969–1970, professor, bacteriology and immunology, 1970– , department chair, 1983–
Concurrent Positions: Fellow, bacteriology and immunology, Harvard University, 1949–1951; visiting professor, cancer center, Massachusetts Institute of Technology, 1979, 1985–1986
Married: 1945

Marian Koshland's work in immunology was recognized by her contemporaries by her election to the National Academy of Sciences in 1981. After she received her master's degree from the University of Chicago in 1943, she worked on two projects simultaneously—a cholera project for the University of Chicago and another project with the Commission on Air Borne Diseases for the University of Colorado. These were supported by government contracts during World War II. (Scientists at this time often were moved back and forth

on projects depending on when their specific expertise was needed.) She continued on contract with an assignment as a junior chemist with the Manhattan Project. She continued in government work with the Brookhaven National Laboratory from 1953 to 1965. The gap in employment between 1946 and 1953 might be explained by her receiving her doctorate in 1949 along with her family responsibilities. She accepted a position at the University of California, Berkeley, in 1965, where she was promoted to professor of bacteriology and immunology in 1970 and department chair in 1983.

She has received many honors and awards. She was selected the R. E. Dyer Lecturer by the National Institutes of Health in 1988. She was a fellow in bacteriology and immunology at Harvard University from 1949 to 1951. She was a member of the national science board of the National Science Foundation from 1976 to 1982; this is the governing board of the foundation. She was president of the American Association of Immunologists in 1982 and 1983. She also has been a member of the American Society of Biological Chemists and the American Academy of Microbiologists. Her research includes mechanism of antibody biosynthesis, lymphokine regulation of immunoglobin gene expression, and mechanisms of lymphokine signaling of B lymphocytes. Her name was included in the 1992–1993 edition of *American Men and Women of Science*. She raised five children.

Bibliography: *American Men and Women of Science* 9–18; Herzenberg, Caroline L., *Women Scientists from Antiquity to the Present*.

L

Francesca Raimond La Monte
Christine Ladd-Franklin
Elizabeth Rebecca Laird
Rebecca Craighill Lancefield
Caroline Wormeley Latimer
Mary Frances Leach
Henrietta Swan Leavitt
Julia Southard Lee
Sarah Allen Plummer Lemmon
Elise Depew Strang L'Esperance
Ruth Mandeville Leverton
Rita Levi-Montalcini
Graceanna Lewis
Margaret Adaline Reed Lewis
Leona Woods Marshall Libby
Pearl Rubenstein Lichtenstein
Mary Johnson Bailey Lincoln
Rachel Lloyd
Christina Lochman-Balk
Helen Nina Tappan Loeblich
Edith Hirsch Luchins

La Monte, Francesca Raimond
(b. 1895)
ichthyologist

Education: B.A. and certificate of music, Wellesley College, 1918
Employment: Secretary, department of ichthyology, American Museum of Natural History, 1919–1923, 1925–1928, staff assistant, department of fishes and aquatic biology, 1928–1929, assistant curator, 1929–1935, associate curator, 1935–1962; emeritus curator

Francesca La Monte was recognized for her work as an ichthyologist at the American Museum of Natural History. Soon after receiving her undergraduate degree from Wellesley, she joined the museum in 1919 as a secretary, and she rose through the ranks to staff assistant in 1928, assistant curator in 1929, and associate curator in 1935, retiring in 1962. It was not unusual for a woman to be appointed a curator of a museum. In the nineteenth century, many women worked with fathers, husbands, or brothers as underpaid or unpaid staff in museums, arboreta, and herbaria. These positions later evolved into paid professional jobs. Francesca La Monte was a valued member of the staff at the American Museum of Natural History in that she was a member of the museum's Lerner-Cape Breton expeditions of 1936 and 1938, the Lerner-Bimini expedition of 1937, and the Chile-Peru expedition of 1940. She was co-editor of *Field Book of Fresh Water Fishes of North America* (1938), *Game Fish of the World* (1949), and *The Fisherman's Encyclopedia* (1950). She was coauthor of *Vanishing Wilderness* (1934) and author of *North American Game Fishes* (1945), *Marine Game Fishes of the World* (1952), and *Giant Fishes of the Ocean* (1966). She was a member of the fisheries committee for the 1939–1940 World's Fair in New York City. She was the museum's delegate to the International Congress of Zoologists in Italy in 1930. She was elected a fellow of the New York Academy of Sciences. Her other professional memberships included the American Association for the Advancement of Science, the American Society of Ichthyologists and Herpetologists, and the Society of Systematic Zoology. Her research interests centered on taxonomic ichthyology.

Bibliography: American Men and Women of Science 5–11; Debus, A. G., ed., World Who's Who in Science; Herzenberg, Caroline L., Women Scientists from Antiquity to the Present; National Union Catalog.

Ladd-Franklin, Christine
(1847–1930)
psychologist and logician

Education: A.B., Vassar College, 1869; Johns Hopkins University, 1878–1882, Ph.D., 1926; University of Göttingen, 1891–1892; University of Berlin, 1892, 1894, 1901
Employment: High school teacher, 1869–1878; lecturer, psychology and logic, Johns Hopkins University, 1904–1909; lecturer, psychology and logic, Columbia University, 1914–1927
Married: Fabian Franklin, 1882

*C*hristine Ladd-Franklin was one of the foremost women psychologists of the early twentieth century. She was ranked among the 50 eminent American psychologists in a study conducted in 1903 and reported by Stephen Visher in *Scientists Starred 1903–1943 in "American Men of Science"*; only two other women were included in the list. Her name was starred in the first four editions of *American Men and Women of Science.* Although she published papers on symbolic logic, today her contribution in this area is considered slight. Her emphasis on the evolutionary development of increased differentiation in color vision still has validity. She studied mathematics at Vassar because there were no laboratory facilities available for graduate study in physics. After she was graduated in 1869, she taught high school science for ten years.

While teaching she published articles on mathematics in the British journal *Educational Times* and the American journal *Analyst.* She then applied for admission to Johns Hopkins University to take advantage of their research facilities, but the administration refused to admit her. She was eventually admitted to Johns Hopkins University on a fellowship due to the recommendation of a mathematics professor who had read her papers. Although she fulfilled the requirements for a Ph.D. between 1878 and 1882, the trustees refused to grant the degree to a woman, as was the custom at that time; she finally received the degree in 1926. Nevertheless, she held a lectureship in logic

and psychology at Johns Hopkins from 1904 to 1909.

After completing her graduate studies in 1882, she married Fabian Franklin, a member of the mathematics department. Although she had been intrigued by visual problems since the mid-1880s, she found the time to study at some European universities while her husband was on sabbatical during the 1891–1892 academic year. Her work in psychology was centered on the theory of vision, particularly color vision. She published a compilation of her papers in *Colour and Colour Theories* (1929). She was invited to contribute an appendix to the English translation of Hermann von Helmholtz's classic *Handbook of Physiological Optics* (1924). Her husband changed careers to journalism in 1895, and the couple moved to New York in 1910 when he was appointed associate editor of a newspaper in that city. She spent her years in New York lecturing on logic and psychology at Columbia University.

She was a strong supporter of higher education, and she was instrumental in establishing the Sarah Berliner and other research fellowships. On several occasions she was said to have given her own money to women scientists who needed funds for research or travel. Vassar College awarded her an honorary degree in 1887. She was a member of the American Association for the Advancement of Science, the American Society of Naturalists, the American Psychological Association, the Optical Society of America, and the American Philosophical Association. Her research included the Ladd-Franklin color theory, antilogism, the doctrine of histurgy, the one-time one-place theory of judgment, and proof that a nerve when stimulated emits physical light. A list of her publications was included in Louise S. Grinstein's and Paul J. Campbell's *Women of Mathematics*; there is a photograph in the *National Cyclopedia of American Biography*. Her name was listed in some sources as Christine Ladd or as Christine Franklin. The couple had two children, one of whom, Margaret, survived childhood.

Bibliography: Abir-Am, P. G. and Dorinda Outram, eds., *Uneasy Careers and Intimate Lives*; *American Men and Women of Science* 1–4; Bryan, Alice I. and Edwin G. Boring, "Women in American Psychology"; Debus, A. G., ed., *World Who's Who in Science*; *Dictionary of American Biography*; Grinstein, Louise S. and Paul J. Campbell, eds, *Women of Mathematics*; Herzenberg, Caroline L., *Women Scientists from Antiquity to the Present*; James, E. T., ed., *Notable American Women 1607–1950*; Kass-Simon, G. and Patricia Farnes, *Women of Science*; McHenry, Robert, ed., *Famous American Women*; Macksey, Joan and Kenneth Macksey, *The Book of Women's Achievements*; *National Cyclopedia of American Biography*; Ogilvie, Marilyn B., *Women in Science*; Rossiter, Margaret W., *Women Scientists in America*; Rossiter, Margaret W., "Women Scientists in America before 1920"; Siegel, Patricia J. and Kay Thomas Finley, *Women in the Scientific Search*; Visher, Stephen S., *Scientists Starred 1903–1943 in "American Men of Science."*

Laird, Elizabeth Rebecca
(1874–1969)
physicist

Education: B.A., University of Toronto, 1896; Bryn Mawr College, 1898–1899, Ph.D., in physics and mathematics, 1901; Cambridge University, 1909; University of Wurzburg, 1913–1914; University of Chicago, 1919

Employment: Instructor in mathematics, Ontario Ladies' College, 1896–1897; assistant in physics, Mount Holyoke College, 1901–1902, instructor, 1902–1903, acting head, 1903–1904, professor, 1904–1940; emeritus professor; honorary research fellow, Yale University, 1925; physicist on radar development, University of Western Ontario, 1941–1945, honorary professor of physics, 1945–1953

Elizabeth Laird was regarded as a notable physicist by her contemporaries, and her name was included in the first edition of *American Men and Women of Science*. Margaret Rossiter's *Women Scientists in America* rated her one of the notable female scientists at the seven major women's colleges prior to 1940. She lived a very long, full life, most of which was spent teaching physics at Mount Holyoke College. After she received her undergraduate degree, she taught for two years in a ladies' college. She then applied for admission at Bryn Mawr, where she received the doctorate in physics and mathematics in 1901. She joined the faculty of Mount Holyoke College, advancing very quickly in three years from instructor to professor. She stayed at Mount Holyoke for 40 years. She received several awards and honors. She received the Sarah Berliner Research fellowship for 1913 to 1914 for study at the University of Wurzburg. After she retired, she continued her research until at least 1953. She was an honorary research fellow at Yale in 1925 and an honorary professor at the University of Western Ontario 1945–1953. She received honorary degrees from the University of Toronto (1927) and the University of Western Ontario (1954). She was elected a fellow of the American Physical Society and was a member of the American Association for the Advancement of Science, the Optical Society of America, and the History of Science Society. Her research interests included spectroscopy, thermal conductivity, spark radiation, soft x-rays, the Raman effect, and electrical properties of biological material in the microwave region.

Bibliography: *American Men and Women of Science* 1–11; Debus, A. G., ed., *World Who's Who in Science;* Herzenberg, Caroline L., *Women Scientists from Antiquity to the Present;* Rossiter, Margaret W., *Women Scientists in America;* Siegel, Patricia J. and Kay Thomas Finley, *Women in the Scientific Search.*

Lancefield, Rebecca Craighill
(1895–1981)
bacteriologist

Education: A.B., Wellesley College, 1916; A.M., Columbia University, 1918, Ph.D. in immunology and bacteriology, 1925
Employment: High school teacher, 1917; technical assistant, Rockefeller Institute, 1918–1919; department of genetics, Carnegie Institution, 1919–1921; instructor in bacteriology, University of Oregon, 1921–1922; technical assistant, Rockefeller Institute, 1922–1925, assistant, 1925–1929, associate, 1929–1942, associate member, 1942–1958, member and professor of microbiology, 1958–1965; emeritus professor
Married: Donald Lancefield, 1918

Rebecca Lancefield was recognized among microbiologists as the outstanding authority on streptococci. Both national and international organizations devoted to streptococcal problems have renamed their groups the Lancefield Society in her honor. While she was attending Wellesley College, she became interested in the biology course her roommate was taking, and she switched her major from French and English to biology. She was able to receive a scholarship offered specifically for daughters of army and navy officers to attend Columbia University. The same year she received her master's degree she was married. She and her husband later were listed as one of the notable couples in science prior to 1940; they had one daughter, Jane.

She obtained a position as a technical assistant at the Rockefeller Institute for Medical Research, working on streptococci. The group identified four distinct serological types that served to classify 70 percent of the 125 strains studied; her name was included as a coauthor of the paper reporting this work, a distinct honor so early in her career. After teaching for a year at the University of Oregon, she and her husband returned to Rockefeller, where Rebecca Lancefield remained the rest of her career. She worked with rheumatic fever research and received her doctorate in 1925. She returned to her studies of hemolytic streptococci, in which she provided a basis for understanding the clinical and epidemiological patterns of disease caused by these organisms. The research at that time was concentrated on puerperal fever, wound infections, and pneumonia that followed measles or influenza. Later research involved scarlet fever and rheumatic fever. In the mid-1920s she succeeded in obtaining two antigens in soluble form from hemolytic streptococci, one that was type specific and one that was species specific. She continued her research on streptococci until a few months before her death in 1981.

Among the honors and awards she received were the Jones Memorial Award of the Helen Hay Whitney Foundation (1960), the Research Achievement Award of the American Heart Association (1964), and the Medal of the New York Academy of Medicine (1973). As further recognition within the field, she was elected president of the American Society for Microbiology in 1943, the second woman to be elected president of the organization. She was the first woman president of the American

Association of Immunologists in 1961 and 1962. She also was a member of the American Association for the Advancement of Science and the Harvey Society. She was elected a member of the National Academy of Sciences in 1970. Rockefeller Institute granted her an honorary degree in 1973; Wellesley College granted one in 1976 on the sixtieth anniversary of her graduation. Her research was immunochemical studies of streptococci, and chemical composition and antigenic structure of hemolytic streptococci. A photograph was included in the *Biographical Memoirs* of the National Academy of Sciences.

Bibliography: *American Men and Women of Science* 4–14; Herzenberg, Caroline L., *Women Scientists from Antiquity to the Present*; National Academy of Sciences, *Biographical Memoirs*; *National Union Catalog*; O'Hern, Elizabeth M., "Women Scientists in Microbiology"; O'Neill, Lois S., *The Women's Book of World Records and Achievements*; Rossiter, Margaret W., *Women Scientists in America*.

Latimer, Caroline Wormeley
(1860–1930?)
physiologist

Education: M.D., Woman's Medical College of Baltimore, 1890; A.B., A.M., Bryn Mawr College, 1896
Employment: Instructor in biology, Goucher College, 1897–1899; literary assistant, Johns Hopkins University, 1899–1920

Caroline Latimer was another of the early women scientists who had short-term careers. After receiving her M.D. degree in 1890 and degrees from Bryn Mawr in 1896, she accepted a position as an instructor in biology at Goucher College for two years. She worked as a literary assistant for two faculty members at Johns Hopkins University until 1920. She

was associate editor of *Appleton's Medical Dictionary* in 1915. It was commonplace that at times women scientists were unable to find long-term professional employment in their chosen fields. The medical and biological sciences were popular subjects for women to pursue in the late nineteenth century. These and botany were considered appropriate for genteel women to study, but they were not always wise choices in the number of positions that were open to women. She, like many others, used her scientific background to do bibliographic research and to edit manuscripts written by other researchers. She was a member of the American Society of Naturalists. Her research interests were the presence of amylolytic ferment and its zymogen in the salivary gland, and modification of rigor mortis resulting from previous fatigue of the nerve in cold-blooded animals. She died between 1930 and 1935, according to Patricia J. Seigel and Kay Thomas Finley's *Women in Scientific Search*.

Bibliography: *American Men and Women of Science 1–2;* Siegel, Patricia J. and Kay Thomas Finley, *Women in the Scientific Search*.

Leach, Mary Frances
(1858–1939)
chemist

Education: Mount Holyoke College, 1880; B.S., University of Michigan, 1893; University of Göttingen, 1897–1898; University of Zurich, 1898–1900; Ph.D., University of Michigan, 1903
Employment: Teacher, public schools, 1878–1879, 1881–1885; high school, 1885–1891; professor of chemistry, Mount Holyoke College, 1893–1900; assistant in hygiene, University of Michigan, 1906–1907; professor of chemistry and hygiene, Western College for Women, 1907–1923

Mary Leach was a chemistry professor who taught at Western College for Women for 17 years. Her career was typical for a woman of her generation. She taught public school for two years before attending Mount Holyoke in 1880. She then continued to teach school for several years while attending the University of Michigan, where she received her undergraduate degree in 1893. She then was appointed professor of chemistry at Mount Holyoke until 1900. She attended the University of Göttingen and the University of Zurich for several years. (It was fairly typical for women scientists to attend European schools. Until very late in the nineteenth century, few American colleges would admit women to graduate programs; many went to Europe to receive the instruction they needed.) After receiving her doctorate from Michigan, she worked as an assistant in hygiene at Michigan before joining the faculty of Western College as a professor of chemistry and hygiene. Although we associate the term *hygiene* with health and personal hygiene, at the turn of the century it was centered on preserving foods correctly and analyzing products, such as patent medicines, to determine that they were safe. The subject sometimes was included in home economics curricula. She was a member of the American Association for the Advancement of Science and the American Chemical Society. Her research involved the chemistry of bacteria and the sensitizing portion of egg white. Her name was included in the first edition of *American Men of Science*.

Bibliography: *American Men and Women of Science 1–6;* Siegel, Patricia J. and Kay Thomas Finley, *Women in the Scientific Search*.

Leavitt, Henrietta Swan
(1868–1921)
astronomer

Education: Oberlin College, 1885–1888; A.B., Radcliffe College, 1892
Employment: Staff member, Harvard College Observatory, 1902–1921

Henrietta Leavitt received recognition for her discovery of the period-luminosity law, that is, the relation between a star's magnitude and its period of luminosity. Although she did not receive the honors that her coworkers Williamina Fleming (q.v.) and Annie Cannon (q.v.) did, she certainly deserved them. She took a course in astronomy during her senior year in college and developed an interest in the subject. After graduation she enrolled in another course and then spent time traveling. She began working for the Harvard College Observatory as a volunteer in 1895 and was appointed to the permanent staff in 1902. She later advanced to the head of the photographic photometry department. This work involved determining the magnitude (brightness) of a star from a photographic image. (At the turn of the century, visual photometry was superseded by photographic methods because the photographic plate is more sensitive to light of certain wavelengths than is the human eye.) She also studied color indices, which is the difference in magnitude of a star depending on the color sensitivity of photographic plates. Another of her contributions to astronomy was the discovery of 2,400 variable stars, about half of the total known at the time. Her most important scientific contribution resulted from her study of the Cepheid variable stars in the Magellanic Clouds, which resulted in her formulation of the period-luminosity law. This relation was used by later astronomers to determine the distances from the earth of similar stars within our own galaxy and in distant galaxies. The standard of photographic measurements that she evolved was accepted generally among the astronomers of the world, and it was known as the Harvard Standard. Edward Pickering, the director of the observatory, did not allow her a free rein in choosing the topics of her research, although her contemporaries commented on her scientific talent. Henrietta Leavitt conducted the research that she was assigned, usually on topics that interested the director. She was a member of the American Association for the Advancement of Science and the Astronomical and Astrophysical Society of America. She was elected an honorary member of the American Association of Variable Star Observers. Her photograph was included in G. Kass-Simon's and Patricia Farnes' *Women of Science* and in *Popular Astronomy* 30 (1922): 197–199, which provides the citations for her papers.

Bibliography: Debus, A. G., ed., *World Who's Who in Science*; *Dictionary of American Biography*; *Dictionary of Scientific Biography*; Herzenberg, Caroline L., *Women Scientists from Antiquity to the Present*; James, E. T., ed., *Notable American Women 1607–1950*; Kass-Simon, G. and Patricia Farnes, *Women of Science*; Mozans, H. J., *Women in Science*; *National Cyclopedia of American Biography*; *National Union Catalog*; Ogilvie, Marilyn B., *Women in Science*; O'Neill, Lois S., *The Women's Book of World Records and Achievements*; Rossiter, Margaret W., *Women Scientists in America*; Rossiter, Margaret W., "'Women's Work' in Science, 1880–1910"; Siegel, Patricia J. and Kay Thomas Finley, *Women in the Scientific Search*; Uglow, Jennifer S., *International Dictionary of Women's Biography*.

Lee, Julia Southard
(b. 1897)
textile chemist

Education: B.S., University of Missouri, 1926; M.S., Kansas State University, 1929; Ph.D. in organic chemistry, University of Chicago, 1936
Employment: Instructor in textiles and clothing, Purdue University, 1934–1937; associate professor, Iowa State University, 1939–1946; associate professor of home economics and chair of textiles and clothing department, Washington State University, 1946–1950; professor of home economics, New Mexico State University, 1953–?
Married: 1937

Julia Lee was recognized for her work on textile chemistry in the first half of the century. She was employed as an instructor in textiles and clothing at Purdue University while she was completing her doctorate at the University of Chicago, a common experience during the Depression years for many people who did not have independent funds. The quality of her work earned her several fellowships between 1929 and 1933, including the Ellen H. Richards fellowship from the American Home Economics Association (1930–1931) and another from Chicago (1931–1933). After receiving her doctorate in 1936, she was appointed associate professor at Iowa State for seven years. She chaired the textiles and clothing department at Washington State for five years and was professor of home economics at New Mexico State starting in 1953. A common perception has been that women who taught in home economics programs were poorly prepared in academics, but even in the early years of the profession, many women held advanced degrees from prominent universities in standard disciplines, such as chemistry, bacteriology, and biochemistry; they published their research in the prominent journals of their respective disciplines. Julia Lee published a book, *Elementary Textiles* (1953). She was a member of the American Chemical Society, the American Association of Textile Chemists and Colorists, and the American Home Economics Association. Her research involved protein fibers, x-ray studies on cellulose, and service qualities of textile materials.

Bibliography: *American Men and Women of Science* 7–11; *National Union Catalog.*

Lemmon, Sarah Allen Plummer
(1836–1923)
botanist

Education: Female College, Worchester, Massachusetts; Cooper Union
Employment: Civil War hospital nurse
Married: John G. Lemmon, 1880

Sarah Lemmon was a skilled collector and painter of plants; her name often has been mentioned as one of the early women botanizers. In the early nineteenth century few women received extensive education and few worked outside the home, but one activity acceptable during the Civil War was that of hospital nurse. This was considered more of a humanitarian effort than a career for most women, and it seems to be the case for Sarah Plummer. When she attended Cooper Union, she probably enrolled in classes in painting and drawing. In 1869 she moved to California, where she married botanist John G. Lemmon in 1880. She became interested in botany through assisting him with his work. (Research still was a family affair in the late nineteenth century.) In 1882 she discovered a new genus of plants, named *Plummera floribunda* by Asa Gray in her honor. She specialized in watercolor paintings of the flora of the Pacific slope, and her collection of sketches won a prize at the World's Exposition in New Orleans, which took place in 1884 and 1885. She

published three scientific papers and was a skilled collector and painter of plants. Apparently one of her papers, "Ferns of the Pacific Coast," originally was published in an obscure weekly journal in 1881, but it was reprinted in the *American Midland Naturalist* 33 (1944): 513–516.

Bibliography: Barnhart, John H., *Biographical Notes upon Botanists*; Bonta, Marcia M., *Women in the Field*; Herzenberg, Caroline L., *Women Scientists from Antiquity to the Present*; Mozans, H. J., *Women in Science*; *National Union Catalog*; Ogilvie, Marilyn B., *Women in Science*; Rudolph, Emanuel D., "Women in Nineteenth Century American Botany."

L'Esperance, Elise Depew Strang
(1878–1959)
pathologist

Education: M.D., Woman's Medical College of New York, 1900
Employment: Intern, New York Babies Hospital, 1900; private practice, 1901–1908; Cornell University Medical Center, 1910–1911, instructor 1912–1920, assistant professor, 1920–1932; director, Kate Depew Strang Tumor Clinic, New York Infirmary, 1933–1941; associate professor, Cornell University Medical Center, 1942–1950, professor, 1950
Married: David A. L'Esperance

Elise L'Esperance was recognized for her efforts to promote the early detection and treatment of cancer in the family clinics she established. She was a member of the last class to be graduated from the Woman's Medical College of New York in 1899, but, due to an attack of diphtheria, did not receive her degree until the next year. After serving her internship, she engaged in private practice in New York and Detroit for seven years. She became increasingly interested in pathology, and she accepted a position in 1910 at Cornell's medical college, where she served on the faculty for 20 years. Here her research focused on the pathology and treatment of malignant tumors. Elise

L'Esperance was the first woman at Cornell University Medical Center to attain the rank of assistant professor (1920) and full professor (1950). Because their mother died from cancer, Elise L'Esperance and her sister May Strang used an inheritance to open the first of three clinics in New York City devoted to the detection of cancer in 1933. The clinic offered complete physical examinations to apparently healthy women and provided referral service for any sign of cancer. Several new techniques were developed at the Strang clinics, such as the Pap smear for the diagnosis of cervical cancer. She staffed the clinic entirely with women physicians, and she conducted an extensive campaign of public education.

Later she opened other clinics where the services were expanded to men and children. Other groups in other cities built upon this model; the value of early detection became more widely accepted both by the public and the medical profession.

She returned to Cornell in 1942 as associate professor of preventive medicine, gaining the rank of clinical professor before she retired in 1950. She also worked in the fields of tuberculosis and Hodgkin's disease. She actively promoted careers in medicine for women. She was editor of the *Medical Woman's Journal* from 1936 to 1941, and she was the first editor of the *Journal* of the American Medical Women's Association, serving from 1946 to 1948. She received numerous awards, the most prestigious of which was the Albert Lasker Award of the American Public Health Association (1951). She also received the Elizabeth Blackwell Citation in 1950 for her achievements in pathology and cancer detection. She was elected a fellow of the New York Academy

of Medicine, and she was named an honorary member of the American Radiologists Society. She was president of the American Medical Women's Association in 1948. Her other memberships included the American Medical Association, the American Association of Pathologists and Bacteriologists, the American Association of Immunologists, the American Radium Society, the Harvey Society, and the American Cancer Society. She was known for the unusual hats she wore, and she is wearing one of them in a photograph in *Current Biography.*

Bibliography: *Current Biography;* Debus, A. G., ed., *World Who's Who in Science;* Herzenberg, Caroline L., *Women Scientists from Antiquity to the Present;* O'Neill, Lois S., *The Women's Book of World Records and Achievements;* Sicherman, Barbara et al., *Notable American Women;* Siegel, Patricia J. and Kay Thomas Finley, *Women in the Scientific Search.*

Leverton, Ruth Mandeville
(b. 1908)
nutritionist

Education: B.S., University of Nebraska, 1928; M.S., University of Arizona, 1932; Ph.D. in nutrition, University of Chicago, 1937
Employment: High school teacher, 1928–1930; teaching fellow in home economics, University of Arizona, 1930–1932, assistant, experiment station, 1932–1934; assistant

professor of home economics, University of Nebraska, 1937–1940; associate specialist, Bureau of Home Economics, U.S. Department of Agriculture (USDA), 1940 1941; associate professor of home economics, University of Nebraska, 1941–1949, professor, 1949–1953, director of human nutrition research, 1941–1949; professor of home economics and assistant director, agricultural experiment station, Oklahoma Agricultural and Mechanical College, 1954–1957; assistant director, human nutrition research division, USDA, 1957–1958, associate director, institute of home economics, 1958–1961, assistant director of administration, 1961–1971, science advisor, 1971–1974

Ruth Leverton was recognized by her contemporaries for her research in nutrition, and she received the Borden Award of the American Chemical Society in 1953. Her early career followed a pattern of many women of her generation; she taught school for several years after she received her undergraduate degree, and then worked as an assistant in the experiment station at the University of Arizona after receiving her master's degree. She taught for four years at the University of Nebraska following her doctorate in 1937. She was very fortunate during the Depression years not only to be employed but also to be able to continue her studies for an advanced degree. After working briefly for the U.S. Department of Agriculture, she returned to academia at Nebraska where she rose from associate professor to professor during her employment from 1941 to 1953. She accepted a position at Oklahoma Agricultural and Mechanical College as professor of home economics and assistant director of the agricultural experiment station for four years. She returned to the USDA to a position in the human nutrition

research division and the institute of home economics between 1957 and 1974, when she retired. Like many faculty members in early home economics programs, she had solid training in the sciences. She had a doctorate in nutrition from a renowned school, and she received recognition for her research. She was a Fulbright professor at the University of the Philippines in 1949 and 1950. She received an honorary degree from the University of Nebraska in 1961. She was the author of *Food Becomes You* (1952) and the coauthor of *Your Diabetes and How To Live with It* (1953). She was a member of the American Dietetic Association, the American Home Economics Association, the American Public Health Association, and the American Institute of Nutrition. Her research included human metabolism and requirements of minerals, nutritive value of Nebraska food products, and blood regeneration and prevention of anemia.

Bibliography: *American Men and Women of Science 5–13; National Union Catalog;* O'Neill, Lois S., *The Women's Book of World Records and Achievements.*

Levi-Montalcini, Rita
(1909–)
neuroembryologist

Education: M.D., University of Turin, 1936, 1940
Employment: Research associate, zoology, Washington University, St. Louis, 1947–1951, associate professor, 1951–1958, professor, 1958–1981; Cellular Biology Laboratory, Rome, 1981–

Rita Levi-Montalcini was the corecipient of the Nobel Prize in medicine and physiology in 1986. During World War II in Italy she set up a laboratory in her home because the Fascist government forbade Jews to practice medicine or science. She had to hide her experiments from the authorities, and she moved to the country to escape the bombings during the war. She was invited to join a research group in 1947 at Washington University after the director read the papers she had published. She further developed her research there, leading to the discovery of growth factors, molecules that influence the development of immature cells. Her discovery now is called nerve growth factors (NGF), and they may play a vital role in certain degenerative diseases of the central nervous system such as Alzheimer's disease.

As teenagers in Italy, she and her twin sister Paola were sent to a finishing school because their father did not believe in higher education for women. At age 20 she finally convinced her father that she would never marry, so he hired tutors in mathematics, science, Latin, and Greek to prepare her for university entrance examinations. After completing her medical degree, she continued research at the University of Turin. There she learned a new technique of staining embryonic chick neurons with chrome silver to make nerve cells stand out in the smallest detail. She continued using this technique in her private research when she was dismissed from her position at the University of Turin because her family was Jewish. She was unable to practice medicine, use the university library, or even visit friends at the university. She then set up her secret home laboratory. Since she was unable to publish her papers in Italian journals, she received international attention when they were published in Swiss and Belgian journals that could be read in the United States. After the war, she returned to the laboratory at the University of Turin until she received an invitation to emigrate.

She was at Washington University in the early stages of her discovery in 1952. In order to advance the work more quickly, she smuggled two tumor-infected mice on the plane to Rio de Janeiro to consult with a friend about the process of growing tissues in vitro. She spent the next six years on the project until she achieved success. With a National Science Foundation grant in 1961 she set up a small research unit in Rome so she could be close to her family. After a few years, when she received grants from the Italian government to establish an independent research institute, she alternated six months in Rome and six months in St. Louis. She moved to Rome in 1981 when she retired from Washington University.

In common with many women scientists, she has been known for the long hours she spent in the lab seven days a week when she was conducting her major research. She has received many awards for her work. She has been elected to the National Academy of Sciences in 1968, and she has been the only woman elected to the Papal Academy of Rome. She has been a member of the American Association for the Advancement of Science, the Society for Developmental Biology, and the American Association of Anatomists. Her research has focused on the effect of a nerve growth factor isolated from the mouse salivary gland on the sympathetic nervous system and of an antiserum to the nerve growth factor. Her autobiography is *In Praise of Imperfection: My Life and Work* (1988). The Albert P. Sloan Foundation funded a series of autobiographies written by scientists for the general public; she has been the only woman in the series. Receiving the Nobel Prize in 1986 made her a national heroine in Italy, and she frequently has been quoted in news reports relating to science and women scientists. An article in Sharon McGrayne's *Nobel Prize Women in Science* quotes her recipe for coffee ice cream.

Bibliography: American Men and Women of Science 9–16; Herzenberg, Caroline L., Women Scientists from Antiquity to the

Present; Kass-Simon, G. and Patricia Farnes, *Women of Science;* McGrayne, Sharon B., *Nobel Prize Women in Science;* O'Neill, Lois S., *The Women's Book of World Records and Achievements.*

Lewis, Graceanna
(1821–1912)
ornithologist and artist

Education: Home; boarding school
Employment: Teacher of astronomy and botany, boarding schools, 1842–1885

Graceanna Lewis was an ornithologist who was known as a painter, especially of birds and other animals. She was interested in science from an early age, but, according to the custom of the time, she acquired her scientific education informally. The boarding school she attended included astronomy, botany, and chemistry in its curriculum; she eventually taught astronomy and botany for more than 40 years. Women ornithologists started participating in scientific activities in the mid-nineteenth century at a higher level than in other sciences. Although ornithology was not considered as genteel an activity as botany, nevertheless many women were particularly active in the field. In the early 1860s when Graceanna Lewis began serious study, ornithology was practically synonymous with classification. For this reason the work of women artists was valuable as a record of data before the introduction of photography. Graceanna Lewis was a typical nineteenth-century museum ornithologist, and she exemplified early women scientists who aspired to professional employment. She prepared a number of charts on classes of birds, races of men, animals, forest leaves, wildflowers, and trees that she used for lectures on plants and animals in her classes and in her lectures before various societies. She exhibited a wax model and her Chart of the Animal Kingdom at the Centennial Exposition of 1876. This attracted the attention of several prominent naturalists of the day, even those in England. She was elected to the Academy of Natural Sciences of Philadelphia in 1870, becoming the ninth woman member. She also was a member of the Women's Anthropological Society. Deborah Warner has written her biography, *Graceanna Lewis: Scientist and Humanitarian* (1979). Her name was spelled both Grace Anna and Graceanna in various sources.

Bibliography: Abir-Am, P. G. and Dorinda Outram, eds., *Uneasy Careers and Intimate Lives;* Bonta, Marcia M., *Women in the Field;* Harshberger, John W., *The Botanists of Philadelphia and Their Work;* Herzenberg, Caroline L., *Women Scientists from Antiquity to the Present; National Cyclopedia of American Biography;* Ogilvie, Marilyn B., *Women in Science;* Rossiter, Margaret W., *Women Scientists in America;* Rossiter, Margaret W., "'Women's Work' in Science, 1880–1910."

Lewis, Margaret Adaline Reed
(1881–1970)
embryologist

Education: Woods Hole Marine Biological Laboratory, 1900; A.B., Goucher College, 1901; Bryn Mawr College, 1902–1903, 1908–1909; Columbia University, 1903–1906; University of Zurich, 1906; University of Paris and University of Berlin, 1908

Employment: Assistant in zoology, Bryn Mawr College, 1901–1902; lecturer in physiology, New York Medical College for Women, 1904–1907; lecturer, Barnard College, 1907–1909; instructor, anatomy and physiology, training school for nurses, Johns Hopkins Hospital, 1911–1912; collaborator, department of embryology, Carnegie Institution, 1915–1927, research associate, 1927–1940; member, Wistar Institute, 1940–1958; emeritus member, 1958–1964

Concurrent Positions: Preparator in zoology, Columbia University, 1903–1906; lecturer, New York Medical College, 1904–1905

Married: Warren H. Lewis, 1910

Margaret Lewis was a world-renowned authority on tumors, and she was recognized for her expertise in tissue culture. While working in Berlin she may have conducted the first known successful in vitro mammalian tissue culture experiment. She and her husband perfected the technique to develop clear solutions on special slides. This technique is known as the Lewis culture, and the medium is called the Locke-Lewis solution. In later years they studied the chemotherapy of dyes in cancer. As early as 1915 they were able to provide a reasonably complete description of a number of living cells microscopically. By 1917 they had begun to determine some physiological activities. At the Carnegie Institution Margaret Lewis added important studies of the effects of acidity on these processes. She published about 150 scientific papers, often coauthored with her husband. (They were rated as one of the notable couples in science who were working prior to 1940.) She received her undergraduate degree from Goucher College in 1901 and studied at a number of universities without receiving a graduate degree. She studied at Bryn Mawr, Columbia, and in Europe at the universities of Zurich, Paris, and Berlin. After receiving brief appointments at Bryn Mawr, New York Medical College for Women, Barnard, and Johns Hopkins, she received an appointment as a collaborator at the Carnegie Institution of Washington in Baltimore, being promoted to research associate in 1927. In 1940 she was elected a member of the Wistar Institute, where she held emeritus status from 1958 to 1964. She and her husband jointly received the Gerhard Gold Medal of the Pathological Society of Philadelphia and an honorary degree from Goucher College in 1938. She was an honorary life member of the Tissue Culture Society, and she was a member of the American Association of Anatomists. Her research involved chemotherapy of cancer, cytology of living cells in tissue cultures, the origin of epithelioid cells, and the relation of white blood cells to tumors. She was listed in the first edition of *American Men and Women of Science* as Margaret Reed. Starting in the second edition she was listed as Mrs. Warren H. Lewis, even in the sixth and seventh editions, where her name is starred.

Bibliography: American Men and Women of Science 1–9; Herzenberg, Caroline L., *Women Scientists from Antiquity to the Present*; Rossiter, Margaret W., *Women Scientists in America*; Siegel, Patricia J. and Kay Thomas Finley, *Women in the Scientific Search*; Visher, Stephen S., *Scientists Starred 1903–1943 in "American Men of Science."*

Libby, Leona Woods Marshall
(1919–)
physicist

Education: B.S., University of Chicago, 1938, Ph.D. in chemistry, 1943
Employment: Research associate, metallurgical laboratory, Manhattan Project, 1942–1944; consulting physicist, E. I. du Pont de Nemours & Company, 1944–1946; fellow, Institute for Nuclear Studies, University of Chicago, 1946–1947, research associate, 1947–1954, assistant professor, 1954–1957; fellow, Institute for Advanced Studies, New Jersey, 1957–1958; visiting scientist, Brookhaven National Laboratory, 1958–1960; associate professor of physics, New York University, 1960–1962, professor, 1962–1963; associate professor, University of Colorado, Boulder, 1963–1972; adjunct professor of engineering, University of California, Los Angeles, 1972–
Concurrent Positions: Consultant, Los Alamos Scientific Laboratory, 1951– ; consultant, Rand Corporation, 1957– , staff member, 1966– ; visiting professor of engineering, University of California, Los Angeles, 1970–1972
Married: 1943, 1966

eona Libby has been recognized for her discovery that historical climate can be measured from the isotope ratios in tree rings. She also conducted early research on neutron and proton scattering. She was a member of the Manhattan Project, the group that built the first and second Argonne reactors, the Oak Ridge reactor, and the three Hanford reactors. While obtaining her doctorate from the University of Chicago, she was a research associate in the metallurgical laboratory for a few years. Leona Libby was one of the many women scientists who secured positions funded by government contracts during World War II, and these positions provided excellent opportunities for developing expertise and working with renowned scientists. The Manhattan Project was especially valuable for women because it covered numerous sites, providing experience in many phases of physics and chemistry. Some of the women on the project, including Leona Libby, continued to work under government contracts for many years. She alternated between employment in academe and government-related projects. She was elected a fellow of the American Physical Society and the Royal Geographical Society. Her research interests included high energy nuclear physics, nuclear reactions, fundamental particles, astrophysics, and stable isotopes in tree thermometers. She raised two children.

Bibliography: *American Men and Women of Science* 12–16; Herzenberg, Caroline L., *Women Scientists from Antiquity to the Present*; Kass-Simon, G. and Patricia Farnes, *Women of Science*; O'Neill, Lois S., *The Women's Book of World Records and Achievements*.

Lichtenstein, Pearl Rubenstein
(b. 1917)
astronomer

Education: S.B., Massachusetts Institute of Technology, 1938; M.A., Radcliffe College, 1940, Ph.D. in astrophysics, 1942

Employment: Member of staff, radiation laboratory, Massachusetts Institute of Technology (MIT), 1942–1946; research associate in physics, Franklin Institute, 1946–1947; engineer, general engineering laboratory, General Electric Company (GE), 1948; research associate in astronomy, Rensselaer Polytechnic Institute, 1957–1969; assistant professor, Schenectady County Community College, 1970–1973; consultant, New York State Education Department, 1974; visiting assistant professor of physics, Union College, 1975–1976

Married: Roland M. Lichtenstein, 1946

Pearl Lichtenstein was recognized for her work on microwave propagation. After receiving her doctorate, she was a member of the staff of the radiation laboratory at MIT. During World War II, this laboratory hired women scientists due to the wartime shortage of men scientists. (Several women were assigned to this laboratory, where there was innovative research on computers, meteorology, and astronomy.) Her work on microwave propagation was an important contribution to the war effort. She worked as a research associate at Franklin Institute and then as an engineer at GE. After an interval of about 10 years, she accepted an appointment as a research associate in astronomy at Rensselaer Polytechnic Institute, where she worked for 13 years.

She later was an assistant professor at a community college for four years and a visiting professor at Union College. She was a contributing author for *Microwave Propagation* (1946). Her research was published in significant scientific journals. She was a member of the American Astronomical Society. Her research included the effects of weather on tropospheric propagation of microwaves, radio astronomy, and microwave propagation. She and her husband raised two children, Ann and Walter.

Bibliography: *American Men and Women of Science* 8–13; Debus, A. G., ed., *World Who's Who in Science;* Herzenberg, Caroline L., *Women Scientists from Antiquity to the Present.*

Lincoln, Mary Johnson Bailey
(1844–1921)
teacher, writer, and lecturer on cooking

Education: Wheaton Female Seminary, 1864

Employment: Teacher, public school, 1864; teacher, Boston Cooking School, 1879–1885; teacher, Lasell Seminary, 1885–1889; writing and lecturing, 1890–1921

Married: David A. Lincoln, 1865, died 1894

Mary Lincoln was the prominent cookbook author of her time, until Fannie Farmer's (q.v.) publications surpassed hers in popularity. Teaching in cooking schools and writing cookbooks was a profitable profession for genteel women in the late nineteenth century. There was great interest in healthful living, proper foods, and the relatively new science of nutrition. Many charitable organizations opened cooking schools to teach immigrants how to prepare food safely either as domestic workers or just for their families. Mary Lincoln's experience was somewhat typical of the period in that financial problems forced her to earn money. In the late 1870s her husband's health became impaired, and she had to supplement the family income by helping neighbors with sewing, housework, and washing. The Woman's Education Association of Boston opened the Boston Cooking School in 1879, and Mary Lincoln was hired as one of the first teachers. After teaching a few years, she published her first book, *Mrs. Lincoln's Boston Cook Book* (1883). This was written primarily as a textbook for her classes. She resigned from the school in 1885 due to family responsibilities. She taught at a public school, the Lasell Seminary, from 1885 to 1889. The course she developed for her classes she published in her *Boston School Kitchen Text-Book* (1887). She also wrote *Peerless Cook Book* (1886) and *What To Have for Luncheon* (1904), plus numerous other books. After this she devoted her time to both writing and lecturing. In 1894, the year her husband died, she started writing for *American Kitchen Magazine* (originally *New England Kitchen Magazine)*, and in 1895 she became part owner and culinary editor.

Bibliography: James, E. T., ed., *Notable American Women 1607–1950;* McHenry, Robert, ed., *Famous American Women; National Cyclopedia of American Biography; National Union Catalog;* Shapiro, Laura, *Perfection Salad.*

Lloyd, Rachel
(1839–1900)
chemist

Education: Harvard Summer School; Ph.D. in chemistry, University of Zurich, 1886
Employment: Professor, University of Nebraska, 1888–1900
Concurrent Position: Assistant chemist, Nebraska Agricultural Experiment Station, 1888–1900

Rachel Lloyd was one of the first women to become a professional chemist, and she may be the first American woman to have earned a doctorate in chemistry. She studied at private schools and at Harvard's summer schools, but apparently she did not receive an undergraduate degree. She earned a doctorate from the University of Zurich in 1886 with a dissertation on the high temperature chemistry of aromatic compounds. She made important contributions as a teacher and published several extensive papers on the synthesis of acrylic acid derivatives. In addition to her teaching competence, her important contribution was to the development of the sugar beet industry in the United States. In the Nebraska Agricultural Experiment Station she directed a detailed series of systematic experiments; these ultimately demonstrated that with careful farming the sugar beet could be a profitable crop in any part of Nebraska. During this period she was a full-time faculty member at the University of Nebraska. She was promoted to full professor in 1888, and she taught a heavy load of lecture and laboratory courses. Rachel Lloyd was head of the chemistry department at Nebraska, which, even with her doctorate, would have been an unusual appointment at the time.

Women often worked for agricultural experiment stations, but they usually were assigned work with home economics programs instead of cash crops such as sugar beets. Rachel Lloyd must have been an unusual person to have handled these assignments.

Bibliography: Siegel, Patricia J. and Kay Thomas Finley, *Women in the Scientific Search.*

Lochman-Balk, Christina
(1907–)
paleontologist

Education: A.B., Smith College, 1929, A.M., 1931; Ph.D. in geology, Johns Hopkins University, 1933

Employment: Assistant geologist, Smith College, 1929–1931; instructor, Mount Holyoke College, 1935–1940, assistant professor, 1940–1946, associate professor, 1946–1947; lecturer in physical science, University of Chicago, 1947; lecturer in life sciences, New Mexico Institute of Mining and Technology, 1954; strategic geologist, New Mexico State Bureau of Mines and Mineral Resources, 1955–1957; professor of geology, New Mexico Institute of Mining and Technology, 1957–1972; emeritus professor

Married: Robert Balk, 1947

*C*hristina *Lochman-Balk* has been a prominent geologist who held important positions at several universities. In Margaret Rossiter's *Women Scientists in America* she was rated as one of the prominent women scientists teaching at the country's seven major women's colleges prior to 1940. After receiving her doctorate, she accepted a position at Mount Holyoke in 1935, advancing to assistant professor and associate professor. She was a lecturer in physical science at University of Chicago for one year and then a lecturer in life sciences at the New Mexico Institute of Mining and Technology. She was appointed a strategic geologist for the New Mexico Bureau of Mines for two years, then returned to teaching as professor of geology at New Mexico for 16 years.

Christina Lochman-Balk has had a productive career. She graduated from Johns Hopkins, which traditionally has had a fine geology department. During the Depression she was able to secure a position at Mount Holyoke where she was promoted in rank at five- and six-year intervals, quite a good record for those times. She has succeeded in a predominantly male profession. She was elected a fellow of both the American Association for the Advancement of Science and the Geological Society of America. She also has been a member of the Paleontological Society. Her research area has been the Cambrian paleontology and stratigraphy of the United States. Her name was listed in the 1992–1993 edition of *American Men and Women of Science.* She is also listed as Christina Lochman and as Christina Balk in various sources.

Bibliography: *American Men and Women of Science* 11–18; Debus, A. G., ed., *World*

Who's Who in Science; Herzenberg, Caroline L., *Women Scientists from Antiquity to the Present;* Rossiter, Margaret W., *Women Scientists in America.*

Loeblich, Helen Nina Tappan
(1917–)
paleontologist

Education: B.S., University of Oklahoma, 1937, M.S., 1939; Ph.D. in geology, University of Chicago, 1942
Employment: Assistant geologist, University of Oklahoma, 1937–1939; instructor, Tulane University, 1942–1943; geologist, U.S. Geological Survey, 1943–1945, 1947–1959; honorary research associate in paleontology, Smithsonian Institution, 1954–1957; lecturer in geology, University of California, Los Angeles, 1958–1965, associate research geologist, 1961–1963, senior lecturer in geology, 1965–1966, vice chair of department, 1973–1975, professor of geology, 1966–1984; emeritus professor
Concurrent Position: Honorary director, Cushman Foundation of Foraminiferal Research, 1982–
Married: Alfred R. Loeblich, Jr., 1939

Helen Loeblich has been recognized for her research in micropaleontology. She has worked for several universities, the U.S. Geological Survey (USGS), and the Smithsonian Institution. After short assignments at the University of Oklahoma and Tulane, she was employed by the USGS for three years. She returned to academe when she worked as a lecturer in geology at the University of California, Los Angeles (UCLA) in 1958 and advanced to senior lecturer in geology, then professor of geology and vice chair of the department. She was named emeritus professor in 1985. Among the awards Helen Loeblich received were the Paleontological Society Medal in 1982 and both the Joseph Cushman Award and the Moore Medal in 1983. She was elected president of the Paleontological Society in 1985. She was a

fellow of the Geological Society of America, an honorary member of the Society for Sedimentary Geology, and has been a member of the American Microscopical Society. She was the coauthor of *Treatise on Invertebrate Paleontology, Part C* (1964). Her research has been on living and fossil foraminiferans, tintinnids, the camoebians, and organic-walled siliceous and calcareous phytoplankton. She raised four children: Alfred III, Karen, Judith, and Daryl. Her name was included in the 1992–1993 edition of *American Men and Women of Science.*

Bibliography: *American Men and Women of Science* 8–18; Debus, A. G., ed., *World Who's Who in Science;* Herzenberg, Caroline L., *Women Scientists from Antiquity to the Present; National Union Catalog.*

Luchins, Edith Hirsch
(1921–)
mathematician

Education: B.A., Brooklyn College, 1942; M.S., New York University, 1944; Ph.D. in mathematics, University of Oregon, 1957

Employment: Government inspector of anti-aircraft equipment, Sperry Gyroscope Company, 1942–1944; instructor in mathematics, Brooklyn College, 1944–1946, 1948–1949; assistant, applied mathematics laboratory, New York University, 1946; research fellow and research associate in mathematics, University of Oregon, 1957–1958; from research associate to associate professor in mathematics, University of Miami, 1959–1962; associate professor, Rensselaer Polytechnic Institute, 1962–1970, professor, 1970–

Married: 1942

*E*dith Luchins has been recognized for her work in Banach algebras. During World War II she worked as a government inspector at Sperry Gyroscope while she was completing her master's degree. This was not an unusual situation; women mathematicians and scientists were in great demand in government and industry to fill in for men during the war. She worked for Brooklyn College for five years and then received her doctorate from the University of Oregon. She worked for the University of Miami for four years before being appointed associate professor at Rensselaer Polytechnic in 1962. She was promoted to professor in 1970. Mathematics traditionally has been another of the male professions, and even in the 1960s a doctorate was almost a requirement for teaching at the university level. It took Edith Luchins nine years to be promoted to professor when the normal time for men was six to seven years. She was a member of the Mathematical Association of America, the American Mathematical Society, and the Society for Industrial and Applied Mathematics. Her research interests include Banach algebras, functional analysis, and mathematical psychology. She raised five children while pursuing her career.

Bibliography: American Men and Women of Science 10–17; Herzenberg, Caroline L., *Women Scientists from Antiquity to the Present;* O'Neill, Lois S., *The Women's Book of World Records and Achievements.*

Barbara McClintock
Elizabeth Florence McCoy
(Mary) Isabel McCracken
Adelia McCrea
Janet McDonald
Anita Newcomb McGee
Ruth Colvin Starrett McGuire
Anna Jane McKeag
Madge Thurlow Macklin
Grace MacLeod
Mary Alice McWhinnie
Icie Gertrude Macy-Hoobler
(Ada) Isabel Maddison
Maud Worcester Makemson
Harriet Florence Mylander Maling
Margaret Eliza Maltby
Abby Lillian Marlatt
Emilie Norton Martin
Lillien Jane Martin
Ursula Bailey Marvin
Mildred Esther Mathias
Antonia Caetana De Paiva Pereira Maury
Carlotta Joaquina Maury
Martha Dartt Maxwell
Margaret Mead
Marjorie Pettit Meinel
Dorothy Reed Mendenhall
Helen Abbot Merrill
Ynes Enriquetta Julietta Mexia
Helen Cecilia De Silver Abbott Michael
Elizabeth Cavert Miller
Harriet Mann Miller
Beatrice Mintz
Helen Swift Mitchell
Maria Mitchell
Agnes Mary Claypole Moody
Mary Blair Moody
Anne Moore
Emmeline Moore
Agnes Fay Morgan
Ann Haven Morgan
Margaretta Hare Morris
Emily L. Morton
Mary Esther Murtfeldt

M

McClintock, Barbara
(1902–1992)
geneticist

Education: B.S., Cornell University, 1923, M.A., 1925, Ph.D., 1927
Employment: Instructor in botany, Cornell University, 1927–1931, research associate, 1934–1936; fellow, National Research Council, 1931–1933; fellow, Guggenheim Foundation, 1933–1934; assistant professor of botany, University of Missouri, 1936–1941; staff member, Carnegie Institution of Washington, Cold Spring Harbor Laboratory, 1942–1967, distinguished member, 1967–1992; Andrew White Professor at Large, Cornell University, 1965–1992

Barbara McClintock received the Nobel Prize in medicine or physiology in 1983 for her pioneering work on the mechanism of genetic inheritance. She was only the third woman to win the Nobel Prize for solo work. Forty years previously her name was starred in the seventh edition of *American Men and Women of Science;* this was in 1944, the same year she was elected a member of the National Academy of Sciences. She received the National Medal of Science in 1970. In spite of her early recognition, she was relatively unknown in the scientific community for decades until she was awarded the Nobel Prize. Almost 50 years ago she performed pioneer work on the genetics of maize. This was considered interesting but not significant until other scientists' work on DNA in the 1960s supported her discoveries. Her research had been outside the mainstream because other geneticists studied drosophila while she studied maize; few were able to comprehend the significance of her research.

When she first attended Cornell as an undergraduate, she led an active social life, even playing banjo with a jazz group and being elected president of the freshmen women's class. She gradually became absorbed in her studies and retreated from social life. After she received her doctorate in 1927, she stayed at the university as an instructor in botany for five years and then worked in research for another six years. Since Cornell was not appointing women to faculty positions, she had to find other sources for income. Research positions were very scarce for women during the Depression, but she accepted an appointment as assistant professor of botany at the University of Missouri for five years. That was the last time she taught. She was one woman scientist who concentrated almost exclusively on research with very few teaching assignments. Starting in 1942 she worked at the Cold Spring Harbor Laboratory on Long Island, where she maintained a small apartment on the grounds of the laboratory. She continued to work her accustomed schedule of long hours seven days a week in the lab until just shortly before her death.

She discovered early that genes can move from one area on the chromosomes to another, a finding known as "jumping genes" that now helps molecular biologists identify, locate, and study genes. She received the Nobel Prize for this discovery more than 32 years after publishing her findings. She observed the changes in color patterns in kernels of Indian corn and correlated these changes with changes in the chromosome structure. In the 1960s, after biologists learned that the genetic material was DNA and had figured out some of the rules by which it determined inheritance, her proposed transposable elements were verified repeatedly in simpler bacterial systems with more direct biochemical techniques.

There is a question why her early work was not buried, as was the work of many women scientists when no one was accepting their theories. Fortunately she had the advantage of being elected to the National Academy of Sciences fairly early in her career, and she was active in publishing and participating in professional organizations. Her contemporaries did not reject her early work, although it was out of the mainstream and was unique. Since she tended to work independently, her reputation became hers alone.

It is difficult to say whether or not the feminist movement contributed to her recognition. Many of her most prestigious awards came after 1965: the Kimber Genetics Award (1967), the National Medal of Science (1970), the Rosenstiel Award (1978), and the Lasker Award (1981). She was elected the first woman president of the Genetics Society of America in 1945. In 1981 she was awarded a lifetime tax-free annual fellowship of $60,000 from the MacArthur Foundation. She was a member of the American Association for the Advancement of Science, the American Academy of Arts and Sciences, the American Philosophical Society, the American Society of Naturalists, and the Royal Society of England. Her research included mutation in kernels of maize (corn), transposable genetic elements, and molecular and microbial genetics. Evelyn F. Keller has published a biography, *A Feeling for the Organism: The Life and Work of Barbara McClintock* (1983). Nina Fedoroff and David Botstein edited a book discussing her research: *The Dynamic Genome: Barbara McClintock's Ideas in the Century of Genetics* (1992). There is a photograph in *Current Biography*. She was listed in the 1992–1993 edition of *American Men and Women of Science*.

Bibliography: Abir-Am, P. G. and Dorinda Outram, eds., *Uneasy Careers and Intimate Lives; American Men and Women of Science* 5–18; Herzenberg, Caroline L., *Women Scientists from Antiquity to the Present*; Kass-Simon, G. and Patricia Farnes, *Women of Science*; O'Neill, Lois S., *The Women's Book of World Records and Achievements*; Rossiter, Margaret W., *Women Scientists in America*; Vare, Ethlie Ann and Greg Ptacek, *Mothers of Invention*; Visher, Stephen S., *Scientists Starred 1903–1943 in "American Men of Science."*

McCoy, Elizabeth Florence
(b. 1903)
soil microbiologist

Education: B.S., University of Wisconsin, 1925, M.S., 1926, Ph.D. in bacteriology, 1929; National Research fellow, Rothamsted Experiment Station, England, Karlova University, Czechoslovakia, 1929–1930
Employment: Assistant professor of agricultural bacteriology, University of Wisconsin, 1930–1939, associate professor, 1939–1943, professor, 1943–?

*E*lizabeth McCoy was rated as one of the outstanding women scientists in the history of microbiology in Elizabeth O'Hern's article, "Women Scientists in Microbiology." She has been noted for her work in soil microbiology and for detecting a high-yielding strain of *Penicillium*. After she received her doctorate from the University of Wisconsin, she obtained an appointment as assistant professor of agricultural bacteriology at Wisconsin, where she was employed for the remainder of her career, being promoted to associate professor in 1939 and professor in 1943. Elizabeth McCoy was truly an outstanding scientist. These were the years of the Depression, and jobs were scarce for both men and women. She was appointed at the rank of assistant professor, almost unheard of at that time. She stayed at that level for ten years, however, before being promoted to associate professor in 1939. When she was promoted to professor, she was only the second woman to attain this rank at Wisconsin aside from faculty members in nursing and home economics. During World War II she served on several committees, such as a civilian with the Office of Scientific Research and Development. She published a book, *Anaerobic Bacteria and Their Activities in Nature and Disease* (1939). She was elected a fellow of the American Public Health Association. She was also a member of the American Association for the Advancement of Science, the American Academy of Microbiologists, and the Society for Experimental Biology and Medicine. Her research included anaerobes, serology, freshwater bacteria, water quality and waste disposal, and industrial fermentations.

Bibliography: *American Men and Women of Science* 6–12; Debus, A. G., ed., *World Who's Who in Science*; Herzenberg, Caroline L., *Women Scientists from Antiquity to the Present*; *National Union Catalog*; O'Hern, Elizabeth M., "Women Scientists in Microbiology"; O'Neill, Lois S., *The Women's Book of World Records and Achievements*; Rossiter, Margaret W., *Women Scientists in America*.

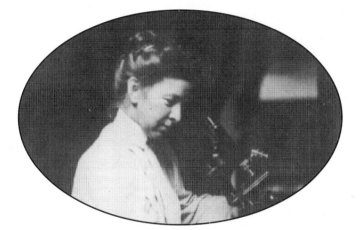

McCracken, (Mary) Isabel
(1866–1955)
entomologist

Education: A.B., Stanford University, 1904, A.M., 1905, Ph.D., 1908; University of Paris, 1913–1914

Employment: Teacher, public schools, 1890–1900; assistant in physiology and entomology, Stanford University, 1903–1904, instructor in entomology and bionomics, 1904–1909, assistant professor, 1909–1918, associate professor, 1918–1930, professor, 1930–1931; emeritus professor

Isabel McCracken was recognized by her contemporaries as an entomologist, as indicated by her inclusion in the first edition of *American Men and Women of Science*. She spent her entire academic career at Stanford University, where she enrolled at the advanced age of 34. Her career followed the pattern of many women of her generation. She taught in the public schools of Oakland, California, for more than a decade before entering college. She continued working toward her advanced degrees while she was employed by Stanford after joining the staff as an assistant in physiology and entomology in her senior year. She advanced to the level of professor a year before she retired. Her advance in rank was rather slow, especially compared to men; she was assistant professor for 10 years and associate professor for 13 years before becoming a professor. (In many colleges the women seldom were advanced above the level of assistant professors even when they possessed a doctorate.) She conducted research on a variety of topics, including bees and silkworms. Much of her research was related to her teaching, including her interest in economic entomology. After her retirement, she worked as a research associate at the California Academy of Sciences from 1931 to 1942. Her research there concentrated on her long-term interest in birds and their relationship to insects. She was elected a member of the California Academy of Sciences, and she was a member of the Entomological Society of America. Her research interests were mosquitoes in California and inheritance in beetles and silkworms.

Bibliography: *American Men and Women of Science* 1–10; *National Union Catalog;* Osborn, Herbert, *Fragments of Entomological History;* Siegel, Patricia J. and Kay Thomas Finley, *Women in the Scientific Search.*

McCrea, Adelia
(b. 1880)
botanist

Education: A.B., University of Michigan, 1919, Ph.D., 1930
Employment: Public school teacher, 1897–1899, 1904–1919; research mycologist, Parke, Davis & Company, 1919–1942

*A*delia McCrea was one of the few women in this survey who was employed by a corporation prior to World War I. She followed the pattern of many women of her generation by teaching school for a number of years before obtaining her undergraduate degree, but she broke the mold by being engaged in research for a pharmaceutical company for the remainder of her career. Corporations have had very poor records of employing women in research positions, but it varies according to discipline and geographic area. Women chemists probably had the most difficulty in finding employment, but that was only a reflection of the situation in colleges, since many companies, even through the 1960s, depended on faculty members to recommend which graduates should be hired. Industrial research was just a continuation of the academic "old boys" network. This picture has changed due to the civil rights legislation of the 1960s. When Parke, Davis was contacted about obtaining a photograph of Adelia McCrea, the library staff was delighted she was being considered for mention in a book, but they were unable to locate a photograph of her. She was a member of the American Association for the Advancement of Science, the Botanical Society of America, and the American Mycological Society. Her research interests included dermatrophytic fungi and respiratory mycoses.

Bibliography: *American Men and Women of Science* 5–11; Barnhart, John H., *Biographical Notes upon Botanists; National Union Catalog.*

McDonald, Janet
(b. 1905)
mathematician

Education: B.A., Belhaven College, 1925; M.A., Tulane University, 1929; Ph.D. in mathematics, University of Chicago, 1943

Employment: Teacher, high schools, 1925–1928; head, mathematics department, Mississippi Synodical College, 1929–1932; head, mathematics department and registrar, Hinds Junior College, 1932–1941; instructor in mathematics, University of Chicago, 1943–1944; instructor, Vassar College, 1944–1946, assistant professor, 1946–1953, associate professor, 1953–1959, professor, 1959–1971, department chair; 1962–1966, 1969–1971; emeritus professor

Concurrent Position: National Science Foundation Faculty fellow, 1959–1960

Janet McDonald was recognized by her contemporaries for her work in geometry. Her career followed the pattern of many women of her generation in that she taught high school for several years after receiving her undergraduate degree. She headed the mathematics department of a small college after she received her master's degree. In her next position she headed the mathematics department at a junior college and acted as registrar for ten years. It was not unusual during this period for faculty members to have heavy administrative duties in addition to their departmental responsibilities. These were the years of the Depression when jobs were scarce for both men and women; many people did not have the funds to continue their education. Janet McDonald returned to graduate school in 1942 to complete her doctorate at the University of Chicago. She then obtained a position at Vassar College, where she spent the remainder of her career. She quickly advanced to assistant professor, then became associate professor in eight years, and professor seven years later. This was a fairly rapid record of advancement, but she served as department chair twice. She was a member of the American Mathematical Society and the Mathematical Association of America. Her area of specialization was differential and projective geometry.

Bibliography: *American Men and Women of Science* 8–14; Debus, A. G., ed., *World Who's Who in Science*; Herzenberg, Caroline L., *Women Scientists from Antiquity to the Present.*

McGee, Anita Newcomb
(1864–1940)
military physician

Education: University of Geneva, University of Berlin, 1882–1885; M.D., George Washington University, 1892

Employment: Acting assistant surgeon, U.S. Army, as superintendent of Army Nurse Corps, 1898–1900; supervisor of nurses, with officer's rank, Japanese army, 1904; lecturer in hygiene, University of California, Berkeley, 1911

Concurrent Position: Member of corporation, Marine Biological Laboratory, Woods Hole
Married: W. J. McGee, 1888, died 1892

*A**nita McGee* was the founder of the Army Nurse Corps, and she served as acting assistant surgeon of the army during the Spanish-American War. She also served as a military physician during the Philippine insurrection and the Boxer campaign. She was an officer in the Japanese army, as superintendent of nurses, during the war with Russia in 1904. She was a fascinating woman who had a long and highly acclaimed career in military medicine. She obtained her medical degree in 1892 following her marriage in 1888, and she is mentioned in some references as a widow. The couple had two children, a daughter, Klotho, and a son, Eric. Her duties with the Japanese army included organizing and training nurses, inspecting hospitals in Japan and Manchuria, and serving as supervisor of nurses at Hiroshima and on board principal hospital ships. She received a number of decorations, including the Imperial Order of the Sacred Crown and special decorations from the emperor and empress of Japan. She was a lecturer in hygiene at the University of California, Berkeley, in 1911. The term *hygiene* at that time often meant bacteriology, but in this instance it might have been used in the medical sense of health and hygiene. She was a member of the American Association for the Advancement of Science and several military medical societies. Anita McGee had a fascinating career and she listed a number of research interests, including heredity in man. Her name was included in the first through the sixth editions of *American Men and Women of Science.*

Bibliography: *American Men and Women of Science* 1–6; McNeil, Barbara, ed., *Biography and Genealogy Master Index 1981–85, Cumulation,* vol. 4; O'Neill, Lois S., *The Women's Book of World Records and Achievements;* Rossiter, Margaret W., *Women Scientists in America;* Siegel, Patricia J. and Kay Thomas Finley, *Women in the Scientific Search; Who Was Who in America.*

McGuire, Ruth Colvin Starrett
(b. 1893)
plant pathologist

Education: A.B., Indiana University, 1914, M.A., 1916; Northwestern University, 1917; George Washington University, 1923; University of Maryland, 1930
Employment: Assistant, Indiana University, 1915–1916; high school teacher, 1916–1919; science assistant, Bureau of Plant Industry, U.S. Department of Agriculture, 1919–1923, junior plant pathologist, 1923–1925, assistant cytologist, 1925–1948, associate cytologist, 1948–?
Married: 1925, 1940

*R**uth McGuire* was a plant pathologist who specialized in sugar research. Her career followed the pattern of many women of her generation; she taught high school after receiving her master's degree from Indiana University and continued teaching while taking additional studies at Northwestern University. She was another woman scientist who was able to advance through the ranks at the U.S. Department of Agriculture (USDA) during a period when few government agencies hired women as professionals. She joined the Bureau of Plant Industry in 1919 as a science assistant and advanced to the rank of associate cytologist by 1948. In addition to the usual civil service benefits, the USDA offered additional benefits that were especially attractive to women scientists. Ruth McGuire was able to publish at least six papers before 1943, most of them in the *USDA Journal of Agricultural Research.* Her name was included in *American Men and Women of Science,* which led to additional recognition of her work. She continued further studies at two universities in the vicinity of Washington, D.C.—George Washington University and the University of Maryland. Her research involved

significant work because she specialized in sugar beets and sugarcane, both of which have been major crops in the United States. She was a member of the Botanical Society of Washington and the International Society of Sugar Cane Technologists. Her research interests were in sugarcane and beets, rubber plants, sorghum, and wild sugarcanes and grasses. She was listed in some sources as Ruth Starrett.

Bibliography: *American Men and Women of Science* 5–10; Barnhart, John H., *Biographical Notes upon Botanists; National Union Catalog.*

McKeag, Anna Jane
(1864–1947)
psychologist

Education: A.B., Wilson College, 1895; Ph.D., University of Pennsylvania, 1900
Employment: Teacher, public and private schools, 1881–1892; instructor of philosophy, Wilson College, 1892–1894, professor, 1894–1902; instructor in education, Wellesley College, 1902–1903, associate professor, 1903–1909, professor, 1909–1912; president, Wilson College, 1912–1915; professor of education, Wellesley College, 1915–1932; emeritus professor

*A*nna McKeag served as president of Wilson College from 1912 to 1915 before returning to teaching education. Her career followed the pattern of many women of her generation in that she taught school for more than ten years before entering college. She was an instructor at Wilson while she was completing her undergraduate degree and was advanced to the rank of professor while she was completing her doctorate at the University of Pennsylvania. She accepted a position at Wellesley College, where she advanced to professor in 1909. She left in 1912, however, to accept the presidency of her old school, Wilson College, a small liberal arts college for women located close to Philadelphia. She returned to Wellesley in 1915 as a professor and was elected emeritus professor in 1932. She received an honorary degree from Lafayette College in 1912. She was very active in educational psychology associations in

New England and across the nation. She presented papers at international symposia in London and Paris, and she was a collaborator on the *Journal of Educational Psychology.* She was president of the New England Association of College Teachers of Education in 1911, 1917, and 1926, and she was president of the New England Association of Colleges and Secondary Schools in 1924. Her research was in educational psychology, but she was known more for her teaching and professional activities than her research. Her name was included in the first edition of *American Men and Women of Science.*

Bibliography: *American Men and Women of Science* 1–7; Rossiter, Margaret W., *Women Scientists in America;* Siegel, Patricia J. and Kay Thomas Finley, *Women in the Scientific Search.*

Macklin, Madge Thurlow
(1893–1962)
geneticist

Education: A.B., Goucher College, 1914; M.D., Johns Hopkins University, 1919
Employment: Instructor, University of Western Ontario, 1921–1930, assistant professor,
   1930–1945; research associate, Ohio State University, 1945–1959
Married: Charles C. Macklin, 1918

Madge Macklin performed pioneering research in medical genetics, and she campaigned to include genetics in the standard medical school curriculum. Eventually she was able to convince her contemporaries of the clinical importance of the family history in diagnosis, therapy, prognosis, and prevention of disease. She demonstrated that both environment and hereditary factors are significant in specific cancers, such as those of the stomach and breast. After her marriage in 1918 and receiving her M.D. from Johns Hopkins in 1919, she moved to the University of Western Ontario, where she received a part-time appointment as an instructor in 1921 and was promoted to assistant professor in 1930. In 1945 she moved to Ohio State as a research associate, retiring in 1959. In spite of her significant work, she received only one-year appointments at Western Ontario, perhaps due to her controversial views on eugenics.

She viewed eugenics as a branch of preventive medicine in that physicians should determine which people are physically and genetically qualified to be parents of the next generation. She advocated sterilization of people with certain mental diseases. Another factor for her short appointments was that many universities did not favor hiring both husband and wife as members, although they did not specifically forbid it. Madge Macklin was not allowed to teach anything except embryology for first-year students, but she could assist her husband in his histology classes. She was meticulous in her research in preparing carefully controlled experiments and data analysis. The contributions she made in applying sound statistical techniques to genetics were of great significance. In 1945, when she was notified that her contract would not be renewed, she accepted a position at Ohio State as a National Research Council associate and as a lecturer in medical genetics. Her husband remained at Western Ontario. She received an honorary degree from Goucher College in 1938, and the Elizabeth Blackwell Medal from the American Medical Women's Association in 1957. She was elected president of the American Society of Human Genetics in 1959. The couple had three children, Carol, Margaret, and Sylva.

Bibliography: Herzenberg, Caroline L., *Women Scientists from Antiquity to the Present;* Sicherman, Barbara et al., *Notable American Women;* Siegel, Patricia J. and Kay Thomas Finley, *Women in the Scientific Search.*

MacLeod, Grace
(1878–1962)
nutritionist

Education: B.S., Massachusetts Institute of Technology, 1901; A.M., Columbia University, 1914, Ph.D., 1924

Employment: Teacher, public schools, 1901–1910; chemistry and physics teacher, Pratt Institute, 1910–1917; assistant editor of the journal *Industrial and Engineering Chemistry,* 1917–1919; instructor, assistant professor, associate professor, professor of nutrition, Teachers' College, Columbia University, 1919–1944; emeritus professor

Concurrent Position: Cooperating investigator, nutrition laboratory, Carnegie Institution, 1922–1928

Grace MacLeod was recognized by her contemporaries for her work in nutrition. Columbia University had one of the outstanding nutrition programs in the United States during the period that she and Mary Swartz Rose (q.v.) were employed. Her career followed the general pattern for a woman of her generation. She taught public school for more than ten years after receiving her undergraduate degree. She then taught chemistry and physics at Pratt for eight years while she continued work on her master's degree at Columbia. She was assistant editor of a major journal in chemistry, *Industrial and Engineering Chemistry.* She then joined the staff of Columbia University while she completed her doctorate. She rose to the level of professor during her career at that institution, which spanned the years 1919 to 1944. Although she did significant work in nutrition, she was somewhat overshadowed by Mary Swartz Rose's

accomplishments. The field of nutrition was just being recognized as a profession, and much of the credit belongs to the Columbia team. Grace MacLeod was coauthor of the revised fourth edition of Mary Swartz Rose's book, *Foundations of Nutrition* (1944). She was a member of the American Association for the Advancement of Science, the American Society of Biological Chemistry, the American Chemical Society, and the American Home Economics Association. Her research involved utilization of calcium, efficiency of proteins, energy metabolism, and availability of iron. Her photograph was included in *Mary Swartz Rose 1874–1941: Pioneer in Nutrition* (1979) by Juanith A. Eagles.

Bibliography: *American Men and Women of Science* 4–11; Herzenberg, Caroline L., *Women Scientists from Antiquity to the Present; National Union Catalog;* Rossiter, Margaret W., *Women Scientists in America.*

McWhinnie, Mary Alice
(b. 1922)
biologist

Education: B.S., De Paul University, 1944, M.S., 1946; Ph.D., Northwestern University, 1952

Employment: Assistant in biological sciences, De Paul University, 1944–1950, instructor 1950–1952, assistant professor, biology, 1952–1955, associate professor, 1955–1960, professor, 1960–?, department chair, 1966–1968

Mary McWhinnie was one of two women scientists to first winter over in Antarctica to study krill. She received numerous National Science Foundation grants to carry on her polar biology research. She spent her entire career at De Paul University, advancing through the ranks from instructor to professor. After receiving her undergraduate degree from De Paul in 1944, she was an assistant while continuing her work on her master's degree. After receiving her doctorate from Northwestern in 1952, she was advanced to assistant professor and finally to professor in 1960. She had comparatively rapid advancement, spending only five years as an associate professor before moving to professor. She also served as department chair for two years, 1966 to 1968. She received numerous grants, such as an assistantship at Woods Hole Marine Biological Laboratory in 1952, summers as a faculty fellow of the American Physiological Society in 1957, and fellow of the Lalor Foundation in 1958. She received National Science Foundation grants from 1958 to 1966 and Antarctic grants for 1962–1963, 1965, 1967, and from 1970 on. Her Antarctic research certainly set her apart from the usual pursuits of many women scientists. She was elected a fellow of the American Physiological Society. She also was a member of the American Association for the Advancement of Science and the Biophysical Society. Her research involved crustacean metabolism, with special reference to carbohydrates during the molt cycle.

Bibliography: *American Men and Women of Science 9–13;* Herzenberg, Caroline L., *Women Scientists from Antiquity to the Present;* O'Neill, Lois S., *The Women's Book of World Records and Achievements.*

Macy-Hoobler, Icie Gertrude
(1892–1984)
chemist

Education: A.B., Central College for Women, 1914; B.S., University of Chicago, 1916; A.M., University of Colorado, Boulder, 1918; Ph.D., Yale University, 1920

Employment: Assistant chemist, University of Colorado, Boulder, 1916–1917, physiological chemist, school of medicine, 1917–1918; assistant biochemist, Western Pennsylvania Hospital, 1920–1921; instructor, University of California, Berkeley, 1921–1923; director, Nutrition Research Laboratory, Merrill-Palmer School, 1923–1931; director of research laboratory, Children's Fund of Michigan and Children's Hospital of Michigan, 1931–1954; staff, Merrill-Palmer Institute of Human Development and Family Life, 1954–1957

Married: B. Raymond Hoobler, 1938, died 1943

Icie Macy-Hoobler was recognized for her research on the effect of nutrition on both mother and child. She studied the nutritional requirements of women and children and proved that malnutrition in women had a significant effect upon infant health. She was rated as one of the best physiological chemists of the first half of the twentieth century. While studying at Yale she was assigned a significant topic in 1918 on cottonseeds, which, during World War I, were being substituted for wheat flour. She found that animals that had been fed cottonseeds became ill due to gossypol, a poison present in the plant. She held a series of short-term positions at various schools while completing her advanced degrees. In 1923 she received a significant appointment in nutrition research at the Merrill-Palmer School in Detroit and then in 1931 was appointed director of two Detroit research laboratories, those at the Children's Fund of Michigan and the Children's Hospital of Michigan.

She was one of a handful of women in the United States to be director of a research laboratory. The research group was instrumental in showing the need for vitamin D and in encouraging the irradiation of milk. She studied amino acids in foods and the standardization of vitamins B and C. She was the first woman to chair a division of the American Chemical Society—the biochemistry division (1930–1931). She was active in establishing the Women's Award, later known as the Garvan Medal, which she received in 1946. She also was awarded the Borden Award in 1939, the Osborn and Mendel Award in 1952, and the Modern Medicine Award in 1955. She was a member of the American Association for the Advancement of Science, the American Chemical Society, and the American Society of Biological Chemists. Her research involved physiological chemistry and nutrition; mineral metabolism in human pregnancy, lactation, and growth; and chemistry of red blood cells in health and disease. Her photograph was published in the journal *Chemtech* 6 (1976): 738–743. Her autobiography is *Boundless Horizons: Portrait of a Pioneer Woman Scientist* (1982). There was an amusing story in her book concerning her invitation to speak at a scientific society. She was unable to eat with the group because it was held in a men's club, and she had to enter the building through the kitchen rather than the front door. A few weeks later she entered through the front door.

Bibliography: *American Men and Women of Science* 4–12; Debus, A. G., ed., *World Who's Who in Science;* Herzenberg, Caroline L., *Women Scientists from Antiquity to the Present; National Union Catalog;* O'Neill, Lois S., *The Women's Book of World Records and Achievements;* Rossiter, Margaret W., *Women Scientists in America.*

Maddison, (Ada) Isabel
(1869–1950)
mathematician

Education: Girton College, Cambridge University, 1889–1892; Bryn Mawr College, 1892–1893, Ph.D., 1896; B.Sc., University of London, 1893; University of Göttingen, 1894–1895; A.B., Trinity College, University of Dublin, 1905

Employment: Assistant secretary to president, Bryn Mawr College, 1895–1896, secretary, 1896–1904, reader in mathematics, 1896–1904, associate professor, 1904–1910, assistant to president, 1904–1926, recording dean, 1910–1926

*I*sabel Maddison was recognized for her early work on differential equations. She received her undergraduate degree at the University of London in 1893 after winning honors at both Cambridge and Oxford universities in 1892. She moved to Bryn Mawr, where she received her doctorate in 1896. This was the beginning of a lifelong association with the college. She undertook a year of further study in 1894 at the University of Göttingen as the first recipient of the Mary E. Garrett Fellowship to encourage women to study abroad. She taught and did research for a time, and she published a number of papers on differential equations prior to being named assistant to President M. Carey Thomas in 1904. This was during the school's formative years, and it comprised her most notable contribution.

Although she was named an associate professor and a reader in mathematics, after 1910 she was involved fulltime in administrative work. Although it was not unusual for faculty members to be assigned heavy administrative responsibilities in addition to their teaching and research, it was unfortunate that her brilliant research was not continued. After she retired from Bryn Mawr, she did no further research or publication. The University of Dublin, the first university in the British Isles to grant degrees to women, conferred the A.B. degree on Isabel Maddison in 1905. She had not studied at Dublin, but her work at Girton College was considered. She was a member of the American Mathematical Society and the London Mathematical Society. Her research centered on the theory of singular solutions of differential equations of the first order. Her name was listed in the first edition of *American Men and Women of Science.*

Bibliography: American Men and Women of Science 1–8; Grinstein, Louise S. and Paul J. Campbell, eds., *Women of Mathematics;* Rossiter, Margaret W., *Women Scientists in America;* Siegel, Patricia J. and Kay Thomas Finley, *Women in the Scientific Search.*

Makemson, Maud Worcester
(b. 1891)
astronomer

Education: Radcliffe College, 1908–1909; A.B., University of California, Berkeley, 1925, A.M., 1927, Ph.D. in astronomy, 1930

Employment: Newspaper reporter, *Review* (Bisbee, AZ) and *Gazette* (Phoenix, AZ), 1917–1923; public school teacher, 1925–1926; research assistant in astronomy, University of California, Berkeley, 1926–1929, instructor, 1930–1931; assistant professor, Rollins College, 1931–1932; assistant professor, Vassar College, 1932–1957, director of the observatory, 1936–1957; emeritus professor

Concurrent Positions: Research astronomer, University of California, Los Angeles, 1959–1964, lecturer in astronomy, 1960–1964; consultant, Consolidated Lockheed–California, 1961–1963, General Dynamics, Ft. Worth, 1965

Married: Thomas E. Makemson, 1912

Maud Makemson was recognized for her research on astrodynamics. In Margaret Rossiter's *Women Scientists in America* she was rated as one of the notable women scientists at the country's seven major women's colleges prior to 1940. After more than ten years as housewife, mother, and newspaper reporter, she entered the University of California in 1923 to complete her undergraduate degree, and she continued in school to obtain her doctorate. At Vassar College all professors of astronomy had been students of Maria Mitchell (q.v.) until Maud Makemson joined the faculty in 1932. She continued to work well into her seventies after she retired from Vassar. She was a research astronomer and lecturer in astronomy at the University of California, Los Angeles, from 1959 to 1964. She also consulted for Consolidated Lockheed and General Dynamics during that period. Prior to accepting the position at Vassar, she was a research assistant and instructor in astronomy at Berkeley for six years. After a brief appointment at Rollins College, she accepted a position at Vassar as an assistant professor in 1932, and she retired at the same rank in 1957. It seems incongruous that she was not promoted, since she also was director of the observatory starting in 1936. She was coauthor of *Introduction to Astrodynamics* (1961, 1967). In addition to her scientific papers, she wrote two other books: *The Morning Star Rises* (1941) and *Book of the Jaguar Priest* (1951). She was elected a fellow of the American Association for the Advancement of Science. She also was a member of the American Astronomical Society and the American Institute of Aeronautics and Astronautics. Her research centered on celestial mechanics and astrodynamics. She and her husband had three children, Lavon, Donald, and Harris.

Bibliography: *American Men and Women of Science* 6–11; *Current Biography*; Debus, A. G., ed., *World Who's Who in Science*; Herzenberg, Caroline L., *Women Scientists from Antiquity to the Present*; Ireland, Norma O., *Index to Scientists of the World*; Rossiter, Margaret W., *Women Scientists in America*.

Maling, Harriet Florence Mylander
(1919–1986?)
pharmacologist

Education: A.B., Goucher College, 1940; A.M., Radcliffe College, 1941, Ph.D. in medical science and physiology, 1944
Employment: Assistant pharmacologist, Harvard Medical School, 1944–1945, instructor, 1945–1946; assistant professor, medical school, George Washington University, 1951–1952, assistant research professor, 1952–1954; pharmacologist, National Heart and Lung Institute, National Institutes of Health, 1954–?
Married: Henry F. Maling, 1943

Harriet Maling was recognized for her work as a pharmacologist. She joined the National Institutes of Health in 1954 in pharmacological research in the area of autonomic and cardiovascular drugs. She was named the head of the division of physiology in 1962. Prior to that she worked as an assistant pharmacologist and instructor at Harvard Medical School for three years after receiving her doctorate. After a five-year break, she accepted a position at the medical school of George Washington University as assistant professor and later assistant research professor. With four children—Joan, Walter, Anne, and Charles—she was one of the many women scientists who were able to combine a career with the responsibilities of a large family, able to schedule research work around family activities. She was a member of the editorial board of the *Journal of Pharmacology and Experimental Therapeutics* from 1962 to 1965. She was a member of the American Association for the Advancement of Science, the Society for Experimental Biology and Medicine, the American Society for Pharmacology and Experimental Therapeutics, and the New York Academy of Science. In the seventeenth edition of *American Men and Women of Science* she is listed as deceased.

Bibliography: *American Men and Women of Science* 9–17; Debus, A. G., ed., *World Who's Who in Science*; Herzenberg, Caroline L., *Women Scientists from Antiquity to the Present*.

Maltby, Margaret Eliza
(1860–1944)
physicist

Education: A.B., Oberlin College, 1882, A.M., 1891; Art Students' League, 1882–1883; Massachusetts Institute of Technology, 1887–1893, B.S., 1891; Ph.D., University of Göttingen, 1895; Clark University, 1899–1900

Employment: High school teacher, 1884–1887; instructor in physics, Wellesley College, 1889–1893, department head, 1896; instructor, physics and mathematics, Lake Erie College, 1897–1898; research assistant, Physikalisch-Technische Reichsantalt, 1898–1899; instructor in chemistry, Barnard College, 1900–1903, adjunct professor of physics, 1903–1910, associate professor and department head, 1910–1931

Margaret Maltby was the first American woman to receive a degree in physics from a German university. She was the only woman included among the 150 eminent American physicists in a study in 1903 reported by Stephen Visher in *Scientists Starred 1903–1943 in "American Men of Science."* At that time, physics was almost exclusively a male profession; only two women received stars in the first seven editions of *American Men and Women of Science.* After she was graduated from Oberlin College, Margaret Maltby attended the Art Students' League for a year before returning to Ohio to teach high school for four years. She entered Massachusetts Institute of Technology in 1887 to study physics and received her undergraduate degree in 1891, the same year that Oberlin granted her a master's degree. She taught physics at Wellesley College for four years while continuing her graduate studies at Massachusetts Institute of Technology. She then was awarded a traveling fellowship to the University of Göttingen, where she received her doctorate in 1895. She returned to Wellesley as department head in 1896 before accepting a position at Lake Erie College as instructor in physics and mathematics. Her last teaching position was at Barnard College; she was an instructor in chemistry for three years, and then adjunct professor of physics until 1910, when she was promoted to associate professor and department head. She retired in 1931.

In view of her international recognition as a physicist, it seems incongruous that Barnard did not promote Margaret Maltby to professor during the years she was there. Most of her significant research occurred before she began teaching at Barnard, where her involvement in administration left her little time for research. She especially was effective in procuring scholarships for women in graduate and postdoctoral studies. For music students, she introduced what was probably the first course in the physics of music. In addition to her professional activities, she had a role in developing career opportunities for women. She was chair of the fellowship committee of the American Association of University Women (AAUW) from 1913 to 1924. This group gave funds to women for advanced study both in the United States and abroad, so she therefore influenced selection standards for disbursing the fellowships.

In 1926 the AAUW established a fellowship in her honor. She herself had received a similar fellowship from the group when she was studying for her doctorate. She was elected a fellow of the American Physical Society, and she also was a member of the American Association for the Advancement of Science. Her areas of research were measurement of high electrolytic resistances, measurement of periods of rapid electrical oscillations, conductivity of very dilute solutions of certain salts, and radioactivity. Her name was starred in the first seven editions of *American Men and Women of Science.* Her photograph was included in *American Journal of Physics* 28 (1960): 474. In this lengthy article, she was the only woman profiled along with seven men physicists.

Bibliography: *American Men and Women of Science* 1–7; Herzenberg, Caroline L., *Women Scientists from Antiquity to the Present;* James, E. T., ed., *Notable American Women 1607–1950; National Union Catalog;* Ogilvie, Marilyn B., *Women in Science;* O'Neill, Lois S., *The Women's Book of World Records and Achievements;* Rossiter, Margaret W., *Women Scientists in America;* Rossiter, Margaret W., "Women Scientists in America before 1920"; Siegel, Patricia J. and Kay Thomas Finley, *Women in the Scientific Search;* Visher, Stephen S., *Scientists Starred 1903–1943 in "American Men of Science."*

Marlatt, Abby Lillian
(1869–1943)
home economist and educator

Education: B.S., Kansas State Agricultural College, 1888, M.S. in chemistry, 1890
Employment: Head of domestic economy, Utah State Agricultural College, 1890–1894; teacher of high school home economics, 1894–1909; director of home economics department, University of Wisconsin, 1909–1935

*A*bby Marlatt was recognized for her contributions to the development of the profession of home economics. Her major contribution was in the broad type of training she insisted upon and in the high standards she maintained. Her department at the University of Wisconsin set standards that were copied by other home economics programs. After she received her master's degree from Kansas State Agricultural College, she was invited to establish a program in domestic economy at Utah State. In 1894 she accepted a position to establish a program at the Manual Training High School in Providence, Rhode Island. She took advantage of the location by enrolling in advanced studies at Clark University and Brown University. In 1909 the dean of agriculture at the University of Wisconsin invited her to revitalize a home economics program at that school. Under her management, the department rapidly expanded in number of courses, students, and faculty. She also established high academic standards for her students. Basic courses in English, foreign languages, and science were required, and technical courses including bacteriology, physiology, and journalism were introduced, greatly broadening the training available to home economics majors beyond the domestic skills courses that many colleges offered.

During World War I Marlatt served in the food conservation division of the U.S. Department of Agriculture and on several other federal committees. In 1903 she was chair of the Lake Placid Conference on Home Economics and was instrumental in continuing the conference series. After the group was established as the American Home Economics Association, she was vice president from 1912 to 1918. She also directed two fund-raising campaigns for the

association. She was a member of the American Chemical Society and the American Association for the Advancement of Science. She received honorary degrees from Kansas State in 1925 and from Utah State in 1938.

Bibliography: *American Men and Women of Science 5–7;* *Dictionary of American Biography;* Herzenberg, Caroline L., *Women Scientists from Antiquity to the Present;* James, E. T., ed., *Notable American Women 1607–1950;* McHenry, Robert, ed., *Famous American Women;* National Union Catalog; Rossiter, Margaret W., *Women Scientists in America;* Rossiter, Margaret W., "'Women's Work' in Science, 1880–1910"; Siegel, Patricia J. and Kay Thomas Finley, *Women in the Scientific Search.*

Martin, Emilie Norton
(b. 1869)
mathematician

Education: A.B., Bryn Mawr College, 1894; Ph.D., University of Göttingen, 1901
Employment: Mathematics teacher, private school, 1900–1902; instructor, Mount Holyoke College, 1903–1911, associate professor, 1911–1925, professor, 1925–?; private tutor in mathematics and Latin, 1899–1902

Emilie Martin was recognized for her work in mathematics, and her name was included in the first five editions of *American Men and Women of Science*. She studied at the University of Göttingen as a Mary E. Garrett fellow from 1897 to 1898 and received her doctorate in 1901. While completing her doctoral studies, she worked as a private tutor and as a mathematics teacher in a private school. She then received an appointment as an instructor at Mount Holyoke College in 1903, advancing to associate professor in 1911 and to professor in 1925. Her doctorate did not seem to hasten her advancement at

Mount Holyoke, however. She spent 8 years as an instructor and then was an associate professor for 15 years before being advanced to professor. (Many women faculty members received promotions less often than their male counterparts. In some universities the "glass ceiling" for women faculty was the assistant professorship.) One of Emilie Martin's publications was the index to the first ten volumes of the *Bulletin* of the American Mathematical Society in 1904. She was a member of the American Association for the Advancement of Science, the American Mathematical Society, and the Mathematical Association of America. Her research involved primitive substitution groups of degree 15 and primitive substitution groups of degree 18.

Bibliography: *American Men and Women of Science* 1 5; Siegel, Patricia J. and Kay Thomas Finley, *Women in the Scientific Search.*

Martin, Lillien Jane
(1851–1943)
psychologist

Education: A.B., Vassar College, 1880; Ph.D., University of Göttingen, 1898; University of Wurzburg, 1907; University of Bonn, 1908, 1912; University of Munich, 1914
Employment: High school science teacher, 1880–1889; vice principal, girls' high school, 1889–1894; assistant professor of psychology, Stanford University, 1899–1909, associate professor, 1909–1911, professor, 1911–1916; department head, 1915–1916; emeritus professor and consultant

*L*illien Martin was recognized by her contemporaries for her work in psychology. Her name was listed in the first edition of *American Men and Women of Science* and starred in the second through the sixth editions. She started teaching high school at age 16 in order to pay for her college education. After receiving her undergraduate degree, she taught another 14 years before deciding, at age 43, to become an experimental psychologist. She then went to the University of Göttingen for several years of study and received her doctorate in 1898. She returned to Germany for periods of research, and she received an honorary doctorate from the University of Bonn in 1913. She became better known internationally than she was at home because she published many of her research papers in German. She accepted an appointment as assistant professor at Stanford University in 1899, advancing to associate professor in 1909 and full professor in 1911. She was appointed department head in 1915, the first woman department head at Stanford. After she retired in 1916, she moved to San Francisco, where she founded mental hygiene clinics in two hospitals. The clinic at Mount Zion

Hospital probably was the first one to deal with normal preschool children. In 1929 she established what might have been the first counseling center for the elderly. She worked in many areas of psychology, but she was noted for her work in gerontology. She was a member of the American Association for the Advancement of Science and the American Psychological Association. Her research involved esthetics, the unconscious, emotions, hypnotism, and gerontology. Miriam A. DeFord wrote her biography, *Psychologist Unretired: The Life Pattern of Lillien J. Martin* (1948). Her photograph appears in *Current Biography* and the *National Cyclopedia of American Biography.*

Bibliography: *American Men and Women of Science* 1–6; Bryan, Alice I. and Edwin G. Boring, "Women in American Psychology"; *Current Biography*; Debus, A. G., ed., *World Who's Who in Science*; *Dictionary of Scientific Biography*; Herzenberg, Caroline L., *Women Scientists from Antiquity to the Present*; James, E. T., ed., *Notable American Women 1607–1950*; McHenry, Robert, ed., *Famous American Women; National Cyclopedia of American*

Biography; National Union Catalog; Ogilvie, Marilyn B., Women in Science; Rossiter, Margaret W., Women Scientists in America; Siegel, Patricia J. and Kay Thomas Finley, Women in the Scientific Search; Visher, Stephen S., Scientists Starred 1903–1943 in "American Men of Science."

Marvin, Ursula Bailey
(1921–)
planetary geologist

Education: B.A., Tufts University, 1943; M.S., Harvard University, 1946, Ph.D., 1969
Employment: Assistant silicate chemist, University of Chicago, 1947–1950; mineralogist, Union Carbide Ore Company, 1953–1958; instructor in mineralogy, Tufts University, 1958–1961; geologist, Smithsonian Astrophysical Observatory, 1961– ; coordinator, Federal Women's Program, 1974–1977
Concurrent Positions: Associate, Harvard College Observatory, 1965– ; lecturer, Tufts University, 1968–1969, lecturer, Harvard University, 1974– ; member of board of trustees, Tufts University, 1975–
Married: 1952

*U*rsula Marvin has been a prominent planetary geologist. She received her doctorate 23 years after completing the course work at Harvard because she was too busy to complete some requirements. She and her husband at one time were paid geologists who worked throughout the world, and she participated in at least one polar expedition. After receiving her master's degree from Harvard, she worked as a chemist at the University of Chicago, a mineralogist for a corporation, and an instructor in mineralogy at Tufts University. She has had concurrent positions with the Smithsonian Astrophysical Observatory, the Harvard College Observatory, and as a lecturer with Tufts and Harvard.

She has done fascinating work with analyzing lunar samples and performing geological mapping of data from the Galilean satellite. She has received numerous distinctions, such as member of the Lunar Sample Analysis Planning Team for National Aeronautics and Space Administration (1976–1978) and member of the Antarctic Search Meteorites Team (1978–1979 and 1981–1982). She was named secretary-general of the International Commission on the History of Geological Science beginning in 1989, and was an expedition member of the Geology and Paleontology of Seymour Island, Antarctica, in 1985. In 1975 and 1976 she was president of the Meteoritical Society, of which she has been also a fellow, and she served as president of the History of Earth Sciences Society in 1991. She was elected a fellow of the Geological Society of America, and she has been also a member of the Mineralogical Society of America, the American Association for the Advancement of Science, and the American Geophysical Union. Her research interests include mineralogy and petrology of meteorites and lunar samples, history of geology, and geological mapping of Galilean satellites. Her name was included in the 1992–1993 edition of *American Men and Women of Science.*

Bibliography: American Men and Women of Science 11–18; Herzenberg, Caroline L., Women Scientists from Antiquity to the Present; O'Neill, Lois S., The Women's Book of World Records and Achievements.

Mathias, Mildred Esther
(1906–)
botanist

Education: A.B., Washington University, St. Louis, 1926, M.S., 1927, Ph.D. in systematic botany, 1929

Employment: Assistant, Missouri Botanical Garden, 1929–1930; research associate, New York Botanical Garden, 1932–1936; research associate, University of California, Berkeley, 1937–1942; herbarium botanist, University of California, Los Angeles, 1947–1951, lecturer in botany, 1951–1955, from assistant professor to professor, 1955–1974; director of Los Angeles Botanical Garden, 1956–1974; emeritus professor

Concurrent Positions: Assistant specialist, experiment station, University of California, Los Angeles, 1951–1955, assistant plant systematist, 1955–1957, associate plant systematist, 1957–1962

Married: Gerald L. Hassler, 1930

Mildred Mathias has been a prominent, award-winning botanist. She received the Merit Award from the Botanical Society of America in 1973, the Liberty Hyde Bailey Medal from the American Horticultural Society in 1980, and the Medal of Honor from the Garden Club of America in 1982. After receiving her doctorate from Washington University in 1929, she was appointed an assistant at the Missouri Botanical Garden for two years and then a research associate at the New York Botanical Garden for five years. She accepted an appointment as research associate at Berkeley in 1937. Then she moved to Los Angeles in 1947 as herbarium botanist, being promoted to lecturer in

1951, to assistant professor and then professor from 1955 to 1974. She also served as director of the botanical garden from 1956 to 1974 and was a member of the experiment station staff from 1951 to 1962. She was president of the Botanical Society of America in 1984 and president of the American Society of Plant Taxonomists in 1964. She was elected a fellow of the American Association for the Advancement of Science; she also has been a member of the Society for the Study of Evolution, the American Society of Naturalists, and the American Association of Botanical Gardens and Arboretums. She was the author of *Color for the Landscape: Flowering Plants for Subtropical Climates* (1973). Her research has included classification of plants of the western United States, subtropical ornamental plants, and tropical medicinal plants. Her name was included in the 1992–1993 edition of *American Men and Women of Science*.

Bibliography: *American Men and Women of Science* 6–18; Barnhart, John H., *Biographical Notes upon Botanists;* Debus, A. G., ed., *World Who's Who in Science;* Herzenberg, Caroline L., *Women Scientists from Antiquity to the Present; National Union Catalog.*

Maury, Antonia Caetana De Paiva Pereira
(1866–1952)
astronomer

Education: B.A., Vassar College, 1887
Employment: Staff member, Harvard College Observatory, 1888–1896, 1918–1935; teacher and lecturer, physical science and astronomy, 1896–1918; curator, Draper Park Observatory Museum, 1935–1938

*A*ntonia Maury was one of the first women to receive a professional appointment at the Harvard College Observatory. She started working at Harvard in 1888 after she graduated with honors from Vassar in 1887. She did her significant research from 1888 to 1896, when she developed a new, two-dimensional system of stellar classification that included the width and sharpness of lines. It turned out that the differences in width and sharpness resulted from differences in the size and luminosity of stars. During that time she also confirmed Edward C. Pickering's discovery of a double star and then discovered a second star system. She left the observatory in 1896 due to conflicts with Director Pickering, who wanted his staff to gather data quickly under another system, while Antonia Maury wanted to develop a classification that yielded a wider range of data. (She also tended to spend time solving problems she encountered, so she was unable to meet the schedules for data that Pickering set for all of his employees.) Maury returned to the observatory in 1918 after Pickering retired. She lectured and taught at various schools in the interim. Her other significant work was on spectroscopic binaries, including some very complex systems, but she did not work steadily on this area of research. She spent time on other studies, teaching high school, giving lectures, and pursuing her interest in ornithology. After retiring from Harvard in 1935, she spent three years as curator of the Draper Park Observatory Museum.

Although Antonia Maury's contributions were not appreciated at Harvard, they have had a significant influence on scientists elsewhere. Her early studies are now widely recognized as an essential step in the development of theoretical astrophysics, and she received the Annie J. Cannon Prize of the American Astronomical Society in 1943. Although she worked chiefly as an astronomer, she also was an active ornithologist, a naturalist, and a conservationist who participated in the campaign to save the redwood forests. She was a member of the American Astronomical Society, the Royal Astronomical Society, and the National Audubon Society. Her research interests were spectra of bright northern stars and spectroscopic binaries. Her name was included in the first edition of *American Men and Women of Science,* as well as that of her sister, Carlotta Maury (q.v.). Her photograph is in *Sky and Telescope* 11 (1952): 106.

Bibliography: *American Men and Women of Science 1–8*; Davis, Herman S., "Women Astronomers (1750–1890)"; *Dictionary of Scientific Biography*; Herzenberg, Caroline L., *Women Scientists from Antiquity to the Present*; Kass-Simon, G. and Patricia Farnes, *Women of Science*; Mozans, H. J., *Women in Science*; Ogilvie, Marilyn B., *Women in Science*; O'Neill, Lois S., *The Women's Book of World Records and Achievements*; Rossiter, Margaret W., *Women Scientists in America*; Rossiter, Margaret W., "'Women's Work' in Science, 1880–1910"; Sicherman, Barbara et al., *Notable American Women*; Siegel, Patricia J. and Kay Thomas Finley, *Women in the Scientific Search*; Uglow, Jennifer S., *International Dictionary of Women's Biography*.

Maury, Carlotta Joaquina
(1874–1938)
paleontologist

Education: Radcliffe College, 1891–1894; Ph.B., Cornell University, 1896, Ph.D., 1902; Columbia University; Jardin des Plantes, Paris, 1899–1900
Employment: High school teacher, 1900–1901; assistant, department of paleontology, Columbia University, 1904–1906; paleontologist, Louisiana Geological Survey, 1907–1909; lecturer in geology, Barnard College, 1909–1912; professor of geology and zoology, University of the Cape of Good Hope, 1912–1915; paleontologist, Brazil Survey, 1918–1938

Carlotta Maury was recognized by her contemporaries for her research in paleontology and stratigraphy. After receiving her doctorate from Cornell, she was employed as an assistant at Columbia for three years and a paleontologist for the Louisiana Geological Survey for three years. She accepted a position as a lecturer in geology at Barnard in 1909 and then as a professor of geology and zoology at the University of the Cape of Good Hope in 1912. She participated in several expeditions and received a Sarah Berliner fellowship in 1917. She actively was engaged in research for much of her life and published numerous reports of her work on Antillean, Venezuelan, and Brazilian stratigraphy and fossil faunas. Many of these reports were sent to the American Museum of Natural History. She was the author of *A Comparison of the Oligocene of Western Europe and the Southern United States* (1902). She was the paleontologist for a geological expedition to Venezuela in 1910 and 1911, organized and conducted the Maury expedition to the Dominican Republic in 1916, was consulting paleontologist and stratigrapher for the Venezuelan division of the Royal Dutch Shell Petroleum Company from 1910 to 1938, and was official paleontologist to Brazil from 1918 to 1938.

She was elected a fellow of both the Geological Society of America and the American Geographical Society. She also was a member of the American Association for the Advancement of Science and a corresponding member of the Brazilian Academy of Sciences. Her research included the recent and Pleistocene eras of New York and the Gulf of Mexico; the Tertiary period of Florida and the West Indies; and stratigraphy of Venezuela. Her photograph was included in the *Proceedings* of the Geological Society of America (1938): 157–16l. She and her sister Antonia Maury (q.v.) were among several sets of sisters who were listed in the first edition of *American Men and Women of Science.*

Bibliography: *American Men and Women of Science* 1–5; Arnold, Lois B., *Four Lives in Science;* Debus, A. G., ed., *World Who's Who in Science;* Herzenberg, Caroline L., *Women Scientists from Antiquity to the Present;* Ireland, Norma O., *Index to Scientists of the World;* Kass-Simon, G. and Patricia Farnes, *Women of Science; National Cyclopedia of American Biography;* Ogilvie, Marilyn B., *Women in Science;* Rossiter, Margaret W., *Women Scientists in America;* Siegel, Patricia J. and Kay Thomas Finley, *Women in the Scientific Search.*

Maxwell, Martha Dartt
(1831–1881)
naturalist and taxidermist

Education: Oberlin College and Lawrence University
Employment: Self-employed taxidermist and owner of natural history museums
Married: James Maxwell, 1854

Martha Maxwell received international recognition for the authenticity of her natural history displays. She not only revolutionized the art of taxidermy, but she pioneered the idea of habitat grouping and the use of natural poses in museum exhibits. Natural history museums of that period set up displays consisting of row after row of stuffed birds and animals in large glass cases. (Until a few years ago the Smithsonian Institution still had a portion of their ornithology collection arranged in this stiff nineteenth-century style.)

After 1868 Martha Maxwell started gathering and mounting the birds and animals of Colorado; she sold a collection to Shaw's Garden in St. Louis in 1870. She constructed habitat displays and opened her own Rocky Mountain Museum, first in Boulder in 1874 and then in Denver in 1876. She received international acclaim for her exhibit at the Centennial Exhibition of 1876. Newspaper and magazine articles of the day called her the Colorado Huntress, but she preferred to be called the Colorado Naturalist. People flocked to see her as well as the exhibit—they were curious how this genteel woman could set off alone on camping trips to gather specimens, then bring them home to preserve them. She had a unique skill in taxidermy in giving the animals lifelike poses, and her skill at grouping animals according to their habitat made a display that was fascinating to professional naturalists as well as the general public. The purpose of her exhibits was to preserve nature; she was said to be a vegetarian.

Martha Maxwell learned her love of nature from her grandmother, and she was a member of a family of strong women. In 1842 her parents and other family members started from Pennsylvania on a trip to Oregon to convert Indians to Christianity. After several people died of malaria, a disease common at the time, the family settled halfway across the country at Baraboo, Wisconsin, in a log cabin on the edge of wilderness. Although the family was extremely poor, she attended two coeducational colleges during the early 1850s—Oberlin College in Ohio and Lawrence University at Appleton, Wisconsin. She married a local businessman, James Maxwell, in 1854, and they had a daughter, Mabel, in 1857. That same year her husband was ruined in the Panic of 1857. The family traveled overland to the Colorado goldfields in 1860. The search for gold was not successful, so her husband began driving cattle from Colorado to the Eastern markets while Martha operated a boarding house.

A chance encounter with a German taxidermist introduced her to her career. At last she had found a calling that would make her an independent, contributing member of society by preserving nature. She returned to Wisconsin without her husband in 1864 to study taxidermy for four years. For a time she took her daughter to a town colony being formed in Vineland, New Jersey, where she purchased a three-acre tract. She rejoined her husband after he convinced her to sell or lease her property in Vineland and to accompany him back to Colorado in 1868. The marriage, however, was breaking up. Her husband seemed to be content with allowing her to support herself and their daughter without his assistance. After selling a collection to Shaw's Garden, she began collecting and selling specimens for the Smithsonian Institution and then started her own museums. After the centennial exhibit, she could not find the funds to ship the collection back to Colorado. She remained on the East Coast exhibiting the collection when she could and working odd jobs. She died there in 1881 without returning to Colorado.

A Smithsonian ornithologist named a subspecies of owl in Maxwell's honor. There are two biographies: *On the Plains, and Among the Peaks; or, How Mrs. Maxwell Made Her Natural History Collection* (1878) by her sister, Mary Dartt, and *Martha Maxwell: Rocky Mountain Naturalist* (1986) by Maxine Benson. A photograph appears in Marcia Bonta's *Women in the Field: America's Pioneering Women Naturalists*.

Bibliography: Abir-Am, P. G. and Dorinda Outram, eds., *Uneasy Careers and Intimate Lives*; Bonta, Marcia M., *Women in the Field*.

Mead, Margaret
(1901–1978)
anthropologist

Education: DePauw University, 1919; B.A., Barnard College, 1923; M.A. in psychology, Columbia University, 1924, Ph.D. in anthropology, 1929

Employment: Assistant curator of ethnology, American Museum of Natural History, 1926–1942, associate curator, 1942–1964, curator, 1964–1969, director, Columbia University Research in Contemporary Cultures, 1948–1950; instructor, Columbia University, 1947–1953, adjunct professor of anthropology, 1954–1978; instructor, Vassar College, New York University, and Fordham University, among others; emeritus curator

Married: Luther Cressman, 1923; Reo Fortune, 1928; Gregory Bateson, 1936

Margaret Mead was the foremost anthropologist of the twentieth century. Through such best-selling books as *Coming of Age in Samoa* (1928), *Sex and Temperament in Three Primitive Societies* (1935), and *Male and Female* (1949), she changed anthropology from an esoteric discipline to a subject that was fascinating to the public at large. She was reared as a feminist and was active in social causes throughout her life. Her expeditions to Samoa, New Guinea, Bali, and to Native American tribes provided material for more than 1,500 books, articles, films, and occasional pieces.

Margaret Mead moved from one pioneering innovation to another in her role as anthropologist. She was the first anthropologist to study how children grow up and to compare child-rearing practices and other roles of women in various cultures. She was a founder of the culture and personality school of anthropology, which examines the ways a culture shapes an individual's personality. She was a major force, along with her third husband, Gregory Bateson, in the use of photography and eventually movies and video to document vanishing cultures. Her new methods and concepts stirred controversy and sometimes resentment among her scientific colleagues. She was able to present her ideas in easy-to-read books for the general public as well as present her data in the jargon of her discipline. A number of her books were on the best-seller lists. She was an advocate for

young people in the 1960s with her support of controversial topics such as legalized marijuana and greater sexual freedom.

She was born in Philadelphia, where her father was a faculty member at the University of Pennsylvania and her mother was a sociologist. As a child she learned to take notes on behavior of children from her paternal grandmother, who was a pioneer child psychologist. Her mother was a feminist who urged her daughters to retain their maiden names and individual identity after marriage. She attended DePauw University in 1919 for one year, but found the emphasis on social activities did not suit her. When she entered Barnard the following year, she wavered between sociology and psychology before taking a course in anthropology in her senior year. She was a campus activist and campaigned for labor unions, among other causes.

She married a divinity student, Luther Cressman, in 1923, but the marriage lasted only a few years. She received her master's degree in psychology from Columbia in 1924. The next year she spent six months studying adolescents in Samoa. This launched her career on a note of controversy that continues today. *Coming of Age in Samoa* was criticized by colleagues not only for her data-gathering methods but also for her advocacy that people were a product of their environment. (The theory popular at the time was that people inherit their traits.) In later years Margaret Mead conceded that she was too inexperienced as a field investigator at the time she made the study, but she never revised the book or returned to Samoa. Even after her death, her critics attacked her data. This first trip, however, set the pattern for subsequent journeys. She studied women and children, subjects that male anthropologists had largely ignored in their studies.

On her return to the United States in 1926 after visiting Samoa, Mead was appointed assistant curator of ethnology at the American Museum of Natural History. She was associated with the museum for the rest of her life, being appointed associate curator in 1942, curator in 1964, and emeritus curator in 1969. She conducted her next fieldwork in 1928 and 1929 on the Manus tribe of the Admiralty Islands with her second husband, Reo Fortune. In 1929 she received her doctorate from Columbia and started on a third trip, again with Reo Fortune, to study a Native-American tribe. From 1931 to 1933 the couple was investigating three contrasting tribes—the Arapesh, the Mundugumor, and the Tcambuli—to study the social conditioning of the two sexes. On this trip they developed new techniques of note-taking and of photographing their data.

Starting in 1936 she and her third husband, Gregory Bateson, engaged in fieldwork in Bali and New Guinea. She began two years as a visiting lecturer at Vassar College in 1939. Her book *And Keep Your Powder Dry* (1942) studied American character against the background of seven other cultures. During World War II she wrote pamphlets for the Office of War Information. She was a visiting lecturer at Teachers' College, Columbia University, from 1947 to 1951. During the 1950s and 1960s she lectured, wrote, taught anthropology at American universities, made several trips to New Guinea and to Bali for further research, and worked at the American Museum of Natural History, where she established a Hall of Peoples of the Pacific.

Margaret Mead was involved in an astonishing number of organizations involving all types of concerns and programs. She served at least 26 of these groups in some sort of executive capacity. In the professional organizations, she was president of the American Anthropological Association in 1960, the Society for Applied Anthropology in 1949, and the American Association for the Advancement of Science in 1975. She was elected a member of the National Academy of Sciences in 1975 and the American Philosophical Society in 1977. She also was a member of the American Academy of Arts and Sciences. Her research included personality and culture; child development; and application of psycholoanalytic theory, learning theory, ethology, and cybernetics in studies of seven oceanic cultures.

She received numerous honorary degrees and honors. One of her biographers said that describing her personality was similar to trying to inscribe the Bible on the head of a pin. Her autobiography is *Blackberry Winter: My Earlier Years* (1972). There are numerous biographies, including Jane Howard's *Margaret Mead: A Life* (1984). She and her third husband had a daughter, Mary Catherine, who wrote *With a Daughter's Eye: A Memoir of Margaret Mead and Gregory Bateson* (1984). The *American Anthropologist* 82 (1980): 261–373 was a memorial for her.

Bibliography: *American Men and Women of Science* 4–14; *Current Biography;* Debus, A. G., ed., *World Who's Who in Science;* Herzenberg, Caroline L., *Women Scientists from Antiquity to the Present; International Directory of Anthropologists;* Marlow, Joan, *The Great Women;* National Academy of Sciences, *Biographical Memoirs;* O'Neill, Lois S., *The Women's Book of World Records and Achievements;* Rossiter, Margaret W., *Women Scientists in America;* Rossiter, Margaret W., "Women Scientists in America before 1920"; Uglow, Jennifer S., *International Dictionary of Women's Biography;* Yost, Edna, *American Women of Science.*

Meinel, Marjorie Pettit
(1922–)
astronomer

Education: B.A., Pomona College, 1943; M.A., Claremont College, 1944
Employment: Rocketry, California Institute of Technology, 1944–1945; research associate, solar energy, University of Arizona, 1974–1984; technician in optics, Jet Propulsion Laboratory, California Institute of Technology, 1984–
Concurrent Positions: Consultant, Office of Technological Assessment, U.S. Congress, 1974–1980; consultant, Arizona Solar Energy Research Commission, 1975–1981
Married: Aden B. Meinel, 1944

Marjorie Meinel has been recognized for her work on solar energy. After receiving her undergraduate degree from Pomona College and her master's degree from Claremont College, she obtained employment in rocketry at the California Institute of Technology. After a lapse of several years, she was appointed a research associate in solar energy in 1974 at the University of Arizona. In 1984 she accepted a position as a technician in optics at the Jet Propulsion Laboratory at Cal Tech. She has had rather unusual experience for a woman scientist in that solar energy research is on the front line of the public interest, especially in western states with abundant sunlight year round. That research combined with collaborative work with her husband on volcanic eruptions has contributed to the current interest in global warming. Marjorie Meinel, who had seven children, came from an astronomical family; both of her parents and her husband were astronomers. (Her mother was one of the first women to receive a doctorate in astronomy from the University of Chicago.) She has been a member of the New York Academy of Sciences and the Society of Photo-Optical Instrumentation Engineers. Her research has included solar energy applications, upper atmospheric phenomena, volcanic eruptions, solar and variable stars, and astronomical optics. Her name was listed in the 1992–1993 edition of *American Men and Women of Science.*

Bibliography: American Men and Women of Science 14–18; Herzenberg, Caroline L., *Women Scientists from Antiquity to the Present;* O'Neill, Lois S., *The Women's Book of World Records and Achievements.*

Mendenhall, Dorothy Reed
(1874–1964)
research physician

Education: B.L., Smith College, 1895; Massachusetts Institute of Technology; M.D., Johns Hopkins University, 1900
Employment: Fellow, Johns Hopkins University, 1901–1902; resident, New York Infirmary for Women and Children; physician, Babies Hospital, 1903–1906; field lecturer, department of home economics, University of Wisconsin, 1914–1936; medical officer, United States Children's Bureau, 1917–1936
Married: Charles E. Mendenhall, 1906

Dorothy Mendenhall was recognized first for her early work on Hodgkin's disease and later for her pioneering efforts on child welfare. She was one of the first women to attend Johns Hopkins Medical School after the school lifted its ban on admitting women students. While working as an intern and fellow in pathology at Johns Hopkins in 1901 and 1902, she earned an international reputation for her recognition of the Reed cell, usually called the Reed-Sternberg cell, as the distinctive characteristic of Hodgkin's disease. Prior to her work, Hodgkin's disease was believed to be a form of tuberculosis. Since there were few opportunities for women to advance at Johns Hopkins, she moved to New York where in 1903 she was appointed the first resident physician at Babies Hospital.

In 1906 she moved to Madison, Wisconsin, where her husband was a faculty member. The couple had four children: Margaret, Thomas, Richard, and John. After an interval of several years to care for her family, she entered a new career field. As a field lecturer for the department of home economics at the University of Wisconsin, she began research on child welfare, particularly infant mortality, nutrition, and public health. After conducting a campaign of lectures and pamphlets, she organized Wisconsin's first infant welfare clinic in 1915. In 1917 she served as a medical officer for the U.S. Children's Bureau while her husband was on war duty in Washington, D.C. She continued working for the bureau on occasion until 1936 while maintaining her position at the University of Wisconsin. She produced numerous bulletins on nutrition and child care for both state and federal agencies. At Wisconsin she developed a correspondence course, "Nutrition Series for Mothers," in 1918. She introduced the first course in sex hygiene in the 1920s. In 1957 her family established a scholarship fund at Johns Hopkins for women medical students. In 1965 Smith College named Sabin-Reed Hall to honor both her and Florence Sabin (q.v.). There is a photograph of Dorothy Mendenhall in *Famous Wisconsin Women* 6 (1976): 48–53 and in *MS* 2 (April 1974): 98.

Bibliography: Herzenberg, Caroline L., *Women Scientists from Antiquity to the Present;* Kass-Simon, G. and Patricia Farnes, *Women of Science;* McHenry, Robert, ed., *Famous American Women;* O'Neill, Lois S., *The Women's Book of World Records and Achievements;* Sicherman, Barbara et al., *Notable American Women;* Siegel, Patricia J. and Kay Thomas Finley, *Women in the Scientific Search.*

Merrill, Helen Abbot
(1864–1949)
mathematician

Education: B.A., Wellesley College, 1886; University of Chicago; University of Göttingen; Ph.D., Yale University, 1903

Employment: Instructor, private schools, 1886–1893; instructor in mathematics, Wellesley College, 1893–1901, associate professor, 1902–1915, professor, 1915–1932, department chair, 1916–1932, emeritus professor

elen Merrill was recognized for her contributions to teaching algebra. She was a member of one of the earliest graduating classes at Wellesley College (1886). She had planned to study Latin and Greek, but she changed her mind after taking a mathematics course in her freshman year. In addition to completing her doctorate at Yale in 1903 she also studied at the University of Chicago and the University of Göttingen. After teaching in private schools for 18 years, she returned to Wellesley in 1893 as an instructor in mathematics. She was promoted to associate professor in 1902, professor in 1915, department chair in 1916, and Stimson professor in 1931, retiring in 1932. Although there was only a handful of American women who had earned doctorates in mathematics in her day, there were many women mathematicians; in fact, at Wellesley all of the mathematics teachers were women for the 50 years that Helen Merrill was associated with the school. She was a member of the Wellesley faculty during its formative years, and the department set high standards for the students. She often shared with her students subjects she had studied in graduate school, such as descriptive geometry and theory of functions. She was coauthor of two books, *A First Course in Higher Algebra* (1917) and *Mathematical Excursions* (1933). She was a member of the Mathematical Association of America and the American Mathematical Society.

Bibliography: Grinstein, Louise S. and Paul J. Campbell, eds., *Women of Mathematics; National Cyclopedia of American Biography;* Siegel, Patricia J. and Kay Thomas Finley, *Women in the Scientific Search.*

Mexia, Ynes Enriquetta Julietta
(1870–1938)
botanical explorer

Education: University of California, Berkeley, 1921–1937
Employment: Family ranch; collecting botanical specimens in Mexico and South America, 1925–1938
Married: Herman E. de Laue, 1897, died 1904; Augustin A. de Reygados, 1907

nes Mexia was a noted collector of botanical specimens in the first half of the twentieth century. Shortly after she divorced her second husband, she resumed her maiden name and moved to San Francisco, where she engaged in social work. In 1921 she was admitted as a special student at the University of California, Berkeley, where she took courses in natural sciences but did not receive a degree. She started her career at age 55 when she joined a collecting trip to Mexico in 1925. She returned with about 500 species, including a new one named in her honor. The following year she traveled alone to the western states of Mexico to collect for several institutions and to finance her expedition through the sale of specimens; she was successful in both efforts. The following years she collected in Alaska, Brazil, Peru, Ecuador, Argentina, Bolivia, and Mexico. The most distinguished scientists of the day were lavish in their praise of her skill as well as her energy. On each of her trips to these remote regions, she studied the people and animals in addition to the flora. Scientifically her collections resulted in the discovery of hundreds of new species that were deposited in prestigious institutions such as the Field Museum in Chicago and the Gray Herbarium at Harvard. Since she knew the language and customs, she was able to live and work with local citizens on her trips to South America. In only ten years she had ranged more widely and collected a greater number of plants than any other woman collector. She was said to be a generous but impulsive person who was difficult to get along with. Reports of her travels were published in the journal *Madrono* in 1929, 1932, 1935, and 1938.

Bibliography: Abir-Am, P. G. and Dorinda Outram, eds., *Uneasy Careers and Intimate Lives*; Barnhart, John H., *Biographical Notes upon Botanists*; Bonta, Marcia M., *Women in the Field*; James, E. T., ed., *Notable American Women 1607–1950*; Siegel, Patricia J. and Kay Thomas Finley, *Women in the Scientific Search*.

Michael, Helen Cecilia De Silver Abbott
(1857–1904)
chemist and botanist

Education: Woman's Medical College of Pennsylvania, 1882–1884; M.D., Medical School of Tufts University, 1903
Employment: Independent research, 1884–1900; physician, 1903–1904
Married: Arthur Michael, 1888

Helen Michael was a pioneer in analyzing the chemicals in plants. She has been credited with being the first person to express the concept of glucoside and to support it with detailed laboratory studies. She was a unique person who achieved a great deal scientifically without a university education. She entered the Woman's Medical College of Pennsylvania in 1882, but she withdrew due to poor health. The University of Pennsylvania set up a small laboratory for

her and other women to use, but she supplied much of her own equipment. She attempted, without success, to find a university in Germany and Switzerland that would accept her as a student in 1887; however, the schools would accept women only as special students, particularly if they had funds to support their own research. Her husband was a chemistry professor at Tufts University, and after their honeymoon trip—a world tour—he was appointed director of the chemistry laboratory at Clark

University. In 1891 she and her husband established a private laboratory in England for independent research, but he returned to his faculty position at Tufts in 1895. By 1900 her health was strong enough that she entered the medical school of Tufts, graduating in 1903. After receiving her M.D., she established a free hospital in Boston, but she died in 1904.

Since she had an independent income, Helen Michael was able to pursue experiments that combined chemistry and botany to study the development of glucosides in plants. She had strong support from prominent scientists, and she was elected a member of the American Philosophical Society in 1887, a member of the Franklin Institute in 1895, and a fellow of the American Association for the Advancement of Science. She also was a member of the Academy of Natural Sciences. She was a talented woman who had interests in art, literature, and philosophy. She wrote poetry and literary criticism, and she lectured on various literary subjects. Her photograph reveals a very attractive woman. Her papers were reprinted in her book *Studies in Plant and Organic Chemistry and Literary Papers* (1907); this also contains a biographical sketch and a photograph. A list of her papers also is given in *The Botanists of Philadelphia and Their Work* by John Harshberger.

Bibliography: Barnhart, John H., *Biographical Notes upon Botanists*; Harshberger, John W., *The Botanists of Philadelphia and Their Work*; Kass-Simon, G. and Patricia Farnes, *Women of Science*; *National Union Catalog*; Rossiter, Margaret W., *Women Scientists in America*; Siegel, Patricia J. and Kay Thomas Finley, *Women in the Scientific Search.*

Miller, Elizabeth Cavert
(1920–1987)
biochemist

Education: B.S., University of Minnesota, 1941; M.S., University of Wisconsin, 1943, Ph.D. in biochemistry, 1945
Employment: Fellow, Finney-Howell Foundation for Medical Research, University of Wisconsin, 1945–1947, instructor, department of oncology, 1947–1949, assistant professor, 1949–1959, associate professor, 1959–1969, professor, 1969–1987; professor of oncology, Wisconsin Alumni Research Foundation, 1980–1987
Married: James A. Miller, 1942

Elizabeth C. Miller was a biochemist who was recognized for her research on cancer. She spent her entire career at the University of Wisconsin. After she received her academic degrees at Wisconsin, she joined the faculty as an instructor in the department of oncology in 1947, then she advanced to assistant professor in 1949, associate professor in 1959, and professor in 1969. She was named professor of oncology of the Wisconsin Alumni Research Foundation in 1980. In spite of her international recognition, it seems strange that she advanced in professorial rank at ten-year intervals rather than the normal six or seven years for a man. This could be partially explained by the practices in academe in the 1940s and 1950s, when women with children (she had two, Linda and Helen) seldom advanced at the same rate as their male colleagues. Her recognition by her contemporaries was indicated by the numerous awards she received, including the National Award in Basic Science of the American Cancer Society (1977), the Founders Award of the Chemical Industry Institute of Toxicology (1978), and the Mott Award of the General Motors Cancer Research Foundation (1980). She was also elected to the National Academy of Sciences. She was a member of the American Society of Biological Chemists, the American Association for Cancer Research, and the American Academy of Arts and Sciences. Her research was on experimental chemical carcinogenesis.

Bibliography: American Men and Women of Science 9–17; Debus, A. G., ed., *World Who's Who in Science;* Herzenberg, Caroline L., *Women Scientists from Antiquity to the Present; Who Was Who in America.*

Miller, Harriet Mann
(1831–1918)
amateur ornithologist and naturalist

Education: Private schools
Employment: Author
Married: Watts T. Miller, 1854

Harriet Miller was one of several women authors who wrote on ornithology for the general public. Using the pseudonym Olive Thorne Miller, she wrote books for both adults and children. After her marriage in 1854, she devoted most of her time to her four children, Harriet, Charles, Mary, and Robert. After they had grown to adulthood, she started writing popular magazine articles and children's books and lecturing about birds and their habits. She strongly opposed the fashion of ladies wearing bird feathers on their hats. One of her most popular books, *Little Folks in Feathers and Fur, and Others in Neither (1875),* was based on research of the current literature rather than observation. One of the rooms in her home was equipped as an aviary, and there she studied her bird pets during winter. In summer she observed them in their natural surroundings. After about 1880 she moved to New York and began a more careful study of ornithology and wrote several books for adults: *Bird-Ways* (1885) was the first, followed by *In Nesting Time* (1888), *Little Brothers of the Air* (1892), *A Bird-Lover in the West* (1894), and *With the Birds in Maine* (1904). Her books enjoyed great popularity at the time they were written. She was an honorary member of several ornithological societies. She was listed in the first and second editions of *American Men and Women of Science.*

Bibliography: American Men and Women of Science 1–2; Dictionary of American Biography; Herzenberg, Caroline L., *Women Scientists from Antiquity to the Present;* Ireland, Norma O., *Index to Scientists of the World;* James, E. T., ed., *Notable American Women 1607–1950;* McHenry, Robert, ed., *Famous American Women;* Mozans, H. J., *Women in Science; National Union Catalog;* Siegel, Patricia J. and Kay Thomas Finley, *Women in the Scientific Search.*

Mintz, Beatrice
(1921–)
biologist

Education: A.B., Hunter College, 1941; New York University, 1941–1942; M.S., University of Iowa, 1944, Ph.D. in zoology, 1946

Employment: Assistant, etiology of dental caries, Guggenheim Dental Clinic, 1941–1942; assistant in zoology, University of Iowa, 1942–1946, instructor, 1946; instructor, biological science, University of Chicago, 1946–1949, assistant professor, 1949–1955, associate professor, 1955–1960; associate member, Institute for Cancer Research, Philadelphia, 1960–1965, senior member, 1965– ; professor of medical genetics, University of Pennsylvania, 1965–

Beatrice Mintz has been recognized for her research on developmental genetics, and she particularly investigated inherited susceptibility to certain tumors. After receiving her undergraduate degree, she accepted a position at the University of Iowa as assistant and instructor while she completed her doctorate. She was hired at the University of Chicago as an instructor in 1946, then promoted to assistant professor in 1949 and to associate professor in 1955. She left in 1960 to become an associate member of the Institute for Cancer Research, then senior member in 1965 with a joint appointment as professor of medical genetics at the University of Pennsylvania.

She received honorary degrees from New York Medical College (1980), Medical College of Pennsylvania (1980), and Northwestern University (1982). She has been an outstanding scientist who received numerous awards from groups such as the New York Academy of Sciences (1978) and the Genetics Society of America (1981). She was elected a member of the National Academy of Sciences in 1973, and was also elected a fellow of the American Association for the Advancement of Science and the American Academy of Arts and Sciences. She also was a member of the Genetics Society of America, the Society for Developmental Biology, the International Society of Developmental Biology, the American Institute of Biological Sciences, and the American Philosophical Society. Her research was in gene control of differentiation and disease in mammals and embryo-maternal relationships. Her name was included in the 1992–1993 edition of *American Men and Women of Science.*

Bibliography: American Men and Women of Science 8–18; Herzenberg, Caroline L., *Women Scientists from Antiquity to the Present;* O'Neill, Lois S., *The Women's Book of World Records and Achievements.*

Mitchell, Helen Swift
(b. 1895)
nutritionist

Education: B.A., Mount Holyoke College, 1917; Ph.D. in physiological chemistry, Yale University, 1921

Employment: High school instructor, 1917–1918; professor of nutrition, Battle Creek College, 1921–1935; research professor in nutrition, home economics division,

Massachusetts State College, 1935–1941; principal nutritionist, Office of Defense, Health, and Welfare, Washington, D.C., 1941–1943; chief nutritionist, Office of Foreign Relief and Rehabilitation Operations, U.S. Department of State, 1943–1944; professor of nutrition, Carnegie Institute of Technology, 1946; dean of home economics, University of Massachusetts, 1946–1960; emeritus dean

Concurrent Positions: Director of nutrition research, Battle Creek Sanitarium, 1921–1932; exchange professor, University of Hokkaido, 1960–1962

*H*elen Mitchell was recognized as an authority on nutrition. Her career followed the pattern of many women of her generation in that she taught high school for a few years after receiving her undergraduate degree. She was appointed a professor of nutrition at Battle Creek College in 1921 after receiving her doctorate, then was appointed a research professor at Massachusetts State College in 1935. During World War II she took a leave from teaching to be the chief nutritionist for a program of the Department of State after serving as principal nutritionist for the Office of Defense, Health, and Welfare. She returned to academe as a professor at Carnegie Institute of Technology for a year, then was appointed dean of home economics at the University of Massachusetts in 1946. She received an honorary degree from Massachusetts at the time of her retirement in 1960. Helen Mitchell was coauthor of the fifteenth edition of *Nutrition in Health and Disease* (1968). She was elected a fellow of the American Public Health Association, and was also a member of the American Dietetic Association, the American Home Economics Association, the American Institute of Nutrition, and the Institute of Food Technologists. Her research involved the cause and prevention of nutritional anemia and cataracts.

Bibliography: *American Men and Women of Science* 6–10; Debus, A. G., ed., *World Who's Who in Science;* Herzenberg, Caroline L., *Women Scientists from Antiquity to the Present.*

Mitchell, Maria
(1818–1889)
astronomer

Education: Private schools
Employment: Teacher, private schools, 1834–1835; librarian, Nantucket Atheneum, 1836–1847; computer, *American Ephemeris and Nautical Almanac*, U.S. Coast Survey, 1849–1868; professor of astronomy and director of the observatory, Vassar College, 1865–1888

*M*aria Mitchell was the first American woman astronomer. She was also the first woman scientist to gain international recognition, and she was one of very few scientists to be known by people outside of her field. Her interest in astronomy was influenced by her father, a skilled amateur astronomer. His skill was put to a practical use—Nantucket whalers hired him to check the accuracy of their chronometers by means of stellar observation. Maria had a flair for mathematics, and she was encouraged to continue her studies of mathematical texts after formal schooling ended. Living close to the sea and watching whaling ships setting out and returning created an environment that was conducive to studying the stars. She learned to operate the sextant at an early age. After teaching in a private school for a time, she opened her own school in 1835. In 1836 she accepted the post of librarian at the new Nantucket Atheneum; and, since the library was open only a few hours each week, the position provided her time to study. She discovered a comet in 1847 that catapulted her to international fame. Due to the slowness of the mails in reporting the discovery to the Harvard Observatory, observers in Rome and England were first declared the winner of the gold medal offered by the king of Denmark. Her right to the medal was acknowledged one year later, however. From that time forward she was honored as a leading astronomer in both the United States and Europe. In 1849 she was hired as a computer for the *American Ephemeris and Nautical Almanac,* an annual compilation of astronomical tables for mariners, and began to work for the U.S. Coast Survey. The observatory in the family home became a station for the survey, and she computed tables of the positions of planets. She had an opportunity to travel abroad in 1857 when she was asked to chaperone a young lady. With her letters of introduction from prominent Americans, she was able to visit observatories in England and on the continent.

In 1865 she received an invitation to be professor of astronomy and director of the observatory at the newly founded Vassar College. She was a member of the Vassar faculty from the day the school opened, but she was hampered in her work by the poor equipment that was available to her. She had an unorthodox method of teaching—instead of lectures, she used small classes and individual attention, and she did not mark attendance or issue grades. She stressed the mathematical basis of astronomy. She took her students to New York or to the countryside to make observations, and invited prominent women to campus to discuss current issues. She set up a program for rigorous training

and commitment to research that was a model for other women's colleges.

Maria Mitchell was honored as a leading astronomer in both the United States and Europe. She enjoyed the prestige of being "the female astronomer." She became a symbol to her contemporaries, both men and women, of the contributions women were able to make in science. She was respected by scientific colleagues, idolized by writers in popular magazines, and honored by award-giving groups. She was perhaps the only woman to have self-supporting scientific employment and international recognition in the 1850s. She was aware, however, that her calculations were sometimes questionable due to her inadequate facilities and that she might not meet her own standards for scientific creativity. She was more of an observer and a teacher than a theoretical astronomer. Through her father she gained astronomical friends at Harvard. As the first woman member in a number of male professional societies, she learned that nominal membership meant little in terms of collegiality. Although her publications indicate the breadth of her interests in observational astronomy, in the history of science, and in education, the writing did not require a mastery of theoretical astronomy.

In her later life she became a strong and vocal advocate for higher education for women, based on her Quaker background. In Nantucket the Quaker women often were responsible for civic and economic matters while their husbands were away at sea. She felt that women should be educated for their civic as well as their domestic role. On her second trip to Europe, in 1873, she again visited scientists and observatories, but her primary concern was to talk to anyone who was involved in women's education. She was a founder of the Association for the Advancement of Women (AAW) and directed its activities for several years. She was elected the first woman member of the American Academy of Arts and Sciences in 1848 and of the American Association for the Advancement of Science in 1850. She received honorary degrees from Hanover College (1853), Rutgers Female College (1870), and Columbia University (1887). A crater on the moon was named for her. Her research was centered on sunspots and the surfaces of Jupiter and Saturn. One biography is *Sweeper in the Sky* (1949) by Helen Wright.

Bibliography: Abir-Am, P. G. and Dorinda Outram, eds., *Uneasy Careers and Intimate Lives*; Davis, Herman S., "Women Astronomers (1750–1890)"; Debus, A. G., ed., *World Who's Who in Science; Dictionary of American Biography; Dictionary of Scientific Biography*; Herzenberg, Caroline L., *Women Scientists from Antiquity to the Present*; James, E. T., ed., *Notable American Women 1607–1950*; Kass-Simon, G. and Patricia Farnes, *Women of Science;*

McHenry, Robert, ed., *Famous American Women;* Macksey, Joan and Kenneth Macksey, *The Book of Women's Achievements*; Mozans, H. J., *Women in Science; National Cyclopedia of American Biography; National Union Catalog*; Ogilvie, Marilyn B., *Women in Science*; O'Neill, Lois S., *The Women's Book of World Records and Achievements*; Rossiter, Margaret W., *Women Scientists in America*; Rossiter, Margaret W., "Women Scientists in America before 1920"; Rossiter, Margaret W., "'Women's Work' in Science, 1880–1910"; Siegel, Patricia J. and Kay Thomas Finley, *Women in the Scientific Search*; Smith, Edgar C., "Some Notable Women of Science"; Uglow, Jennifer S., *International Dictionary of Women's Biography.*

Moody, Agnes Mary Claypole
(1870–1954)
zoologist

Education: Ph.B., Buchtel College, 1892; M.S., Cornell University, 1894; Ph.D., University of Chicago, 1896
Employment: Instructor in zoology, Wellesley College, 1896–1898; assistant in histology and embryology, Cornell University, 1898–1900; instructor, zoology and geology, California Institute of Technology, 1900–1903; lecturer in sociology, Mills College, 1918–1923
Married: Robert Moody, 1903

Agnes Moody was one of the leading zoologists of her day. She was ranked among the 150 eminent American zoologists in 1903 in a study reported by Stephen Visher. Agnes Moody and her twin sister, Edith Claypole (q.v.), both were listed in the first edition of *American Men and Women of Science*, as was her mother-in-law, Mary Blair Moody (q.v.). Agnes Moody's name was also starred in the first through the seventh editions. After receiving her doctorate from the University of Chicago in 1896, she was employed as an instructor in zoology at Wellesley for three years. She then accepted

an appointment as an assistant in histology and embryology at Cornell for three years. She moved to the California Institute of Technology as instructor in zoology and geology in 1900; her father already was teaching there.

There was a lull in employment after she was married in 1903, but in 1918 she was appointed a lecturer in sociology at Mills College, where she remained until 1923. Her husband was a professor of anatomy at the University of California, San Francisco. One source indicates that she was the first woman to teach in the laboratory and recitation courses that Cornell required of all students. She apparently continued independent research after her marriage because she listed the same research interests up to and including the eighth edition of *American Men and Women of Science*. She was a member of the American Association for the Advancement of Science. Her research included social anthropology, histology of Cayuga Lake lamprey, and embryology of Anurida maritime. There is a photograph of Agnes and her sister in Margaret Rossiter's *Women Scientists in America*. She is listed under either Moody or Claypole in various sources.

Bibliography: *American Men and Women of Science* 1–8; Herzenberg, Caroline L., *Women Scientists from Antiquity to the Present*; Mozans, H. J., *Women in Science*; *National Cyclopedia of American Biography*; Ogilvie, Marilyn B., *Women in Science*; Rossiter, Margaret W., *Women Scientists in America*; Rossiter, Margaret W., "'Women's Work' in Science, 1880–1910"; Siegel, Patricia J. and Kay Thomas Finley, *Women in the Scientific Search*; Visher, Stephen S., *Scientists Starred 1903–1943 in "American Men of Science."*

Moody, Mary Blair
(1837–1919)
physician

Education: M.D., University of Buffalo, 1876
Employment: Founder and senior physician, Women's and Children's Dispensary, Buffalo, 1882–1886; book reviewer of one publication and associate editor of another

Mary Moody, in 1894, became the first woman elected to membership in the Association of American Anatomists, which was founded in 1886. Her name was listed in the first edition of *American Men and Women of Science* as was her daughter-in-law's, Agnes C. Moody (q.v.). She was educated at the University of Buffalo, where she received her M.D. in 1876. She founded and was the senior physician at the Women's and Children's Dispensary in Buffalo from 1882 to 1886. Apparently she moved to New Haven, Connecticut, prior to 1906. She was associated with two publications, serving as a book reviewer for the *Buffalo Medical and Surgical Journal* and as associate editor of the *Bulletin* of the Buffalo Natural Field Club. The latter might have been concerned with the environment, since she was a member of the American Forestry Association. After moving to New Haven, it is uncertain whether she continued to practice medicine or pursued her varied interests of household economics and the rearing and education of children. She was one of the people selected for inclusion in *American Men and Women of Science* for reasons that are not clear to us today. Perhaps she was selected on the basis of her membership in the anatomy society, because, although medicine was a curriculum that was considered appropriate for genteel women, many women found difficulty in obtaining jobs in the field. Mary Moody was a member of the American Society of Naturalists, the Association of American Anatomists, the American Medical Association, the American Forestry Association, and the American Association for the Advancement of Science. Her research was flora of California and bird life in the United States.

Bibliography: *American Men and Women of Science* 1–2; Herzenberg, Caroline L.,

Women Scientists from Antiquity to the Present; Rossiter, Margaret W., *Women Scientists in America;* Siegel, Patricia J. and Kay Thomas Finley, *Women in the Scientific Search.*

Moore, Anne
(1872–1937)
physiologist

Education: A.B., Vassar College, 1896, A.M., 1897; Ph.D., University of Chicago, 1901
Employment: Assistant in biology, Vassar College, 1898–1899; head, department of biology, California State Normal School, San Diego, 1901–1905

*A*nne Moore did significant work on the effects of electrolytic solutions on muscle tissue, and she wrote *Physiology of Man and Other Animals* (1909). After she received her master's degree from Vassar, she was employed there as an assistant in biology for two years. She returned to school to obtain her doctorate from the University of Chicago before being appointed head of the department of biology at California State, a position she held from 1901 to 1905. Nothing is known of her scientific work after that date, although she continued to be listed in *American Men and Women of Science* until 1938 (sixth edition), the year following her death. Later in life she seems to have turned away from science to become a drama critic and to work with the Civic Repertory Theater. She wrote two books of poems, *Children of God and Winged Things* (1921) and *A Misty Sea* (1937). She did not list any professional memberships in *American Men and Women of Science.* Her research included the poisonous effects of a pure sodium chloride solution, the power of sodium sulfate to neutralize ill effects of sodium chloride, and the effects of electrolytes and nonconductors upon rigor mortis. Her name was included in the first through the sixth editions of *American Men and Women of Science.*

Bibliography: *American Men and Women of Science* 1–6; Ogilvie, Marilyn B., *Women in Science;* Siegel, Patricia J. and Kay Thomas Finley, *Women in the Scientific Search.*

Moore, Emmeline
(1872–1963)
aquatic biologist

Education: A.B., Cornell University, 1905; A.M., Wellesley College, 1906; Ph.D., Cornell University, 1914
Employment: Teacher, public schools, 1895–1903; instructor in biology, normal school, 1906–1910; substitute professor of botany, Huguenot College, South Africa, 1911; instructor and assistant professor, Vassar College, 1914–1919; research biologist and later director of biological survey, New York Conservation Commission, 1919–1944

*E*mmeline Moore was recognized by her contemporaries as an aquatic biologist. She was one of the few women to be appointed the director of a state biological survey. Her career followed the pattern of many women in that she taught public school for several years before receiving her undergraduate degree. She was appointed an instructor in biology at a normal school in 1906 after receiving her master's degree from Wellesley. She substituted as a botany professor in a college in South Africa in 1911 before returning to Cornell to complete her doctorate in 1914. She was appointed instructor and then assistant professor at Vassar in 1914, but joined the New York biological survey in 1919. (Several women scientists were engaged in research on fish culture and several worked for the biological surveys in various states, some on a part-time and some on a full-time basis.) Moore diverged from the usual pattern of employment for women of her generation in that she eventually was appointed director of the survey. She retired in 1944. She received the Walker Prize of the Boston Society of Natural History in both 1909 and 1915. She was the first woman president of the American Fisheries Society in 1928 and was a member of the American Association for the Advancement of Science and the Ecological Society of America. Her research concentrated on fish foods, fish pathology, and pollution of waters.

Bibliography: American Men and Women of Science 4–5; Herzenberg, Caroline L., *Women Scientists from Antiquity to the Present;* Rossiter, Margaret W., *Women Scientists in America.*

Morgan, Agnes Fay
(1884–1968)
biochemist and nutritionist

Education: B.S., University of Chicago, 1904, M.S., 1905, Ph.D. in chemistry, 1914; University of Montana, 1907–1908

Employment: Instructor in chemistry, Hardin College, 1905–1907; instructor in chemistry, University of Washington, 1910–1913; assistant professor of nutrition, University of California, Berkeley, 1915–1919, associate professor, 1919–1923, professor, 1923–1928, professor of home economics and biochemistry, 1938–1954, department chair, 1923–1954; emeritus professor

Concurrent Positions: Biochemist, experiment station, University of California, Berkeley, 1938–1954; emeritus biochemist
Married: Arthur I. Morgan, 1908

Agnes Fay Morgan was recognized as one of the pioneers in the development of home economics as a scientific discipline and as one of the pioneers in nutrition research. After she received her master's degree, she accepted a position as instructor in chemistry at Hardin College in 1905, where she stayed for three years. She attended the University of Montana, married in 1908, and then taught at the University of Washington. After receiving her doctorate in 1914, she accepted a position as assistant professor of nutrition at the University of California, Berkeley, in 1915 in the new department of Household Science and Arts. She rapidly advanced to associate professor in 1919 and to professor in 1923, when she also was appointed the department chair. She held a concurrent appointment in the experiment station at Berkeley as a biochemist from 1938 to 1954.

The home economics department at Berkeley under Agnes Morgan had one of the outstanding programs in the country due to her emphasis on research. She was the first to make chemistry an integral part of the home economics curriculum. Between 1951 and 1954 she was department chair for both the Berkeley and Davis campuses of the university. She founded Iota Sigma Pi, a national society for women in chemistry. Although she had a fine record of research and teaching, she was proudest of her administrative skills in establishing this department and in playing a major role in the growth of the science of home economics. She was recognized for her pioneering work on the biochemistry of vitamins, which has had a lasting influence on research today. Among her research activities, she was the first to produce graying of hair through vitamin deficiency and the first to note certain supplementary effects of vitamin D.

Morgan received the Garvan Medal in 1949 for her work on vitamins, and she received the Borden Award in 1954. In 1961 the university named the home economics building in her honor. She received an honorary degree from the University of California in 1959. She published *Experimental Food Study* (1927, 1940). During World War II she was a civilian with the Office of Scientific Research and Development, and she worked for the U.S. Department of Agriculture. She was elected a fellow of the American Institute of Nutrition and was a member of the American Association for the Advancement of Science and the American Society of Biological Chemists. Her research included the effect of heat on the biological value of proteins and the mechanism of action of vitamins. Her photograph was published in *Chemtech* 6 (1976): 738–743. She and her husband had one son, Arthur.

Bibliography: *American Men and Women of Science* 3–11; Debus, A. G., ed., *World Who's Who in Science*; Herzenberg, Caroline L., *Women Scientists from Antiquity to the Present*; Kass-Simon, G. and Patricia Farnes, *Women of Science*; *National Union Catalog*; O'Neill, Lois S., *The Women's Book of World Records and Achievements*; Rossiter, Margaret W., *Women Scientists in America*; Rossiter, Margaret W., "'Women's Work' in Science, 1880–1910"; Sicherman, Barbara et al., *Notable American Women*; Siegel, Patricia J. and Kay Thomas Finley, *Women in the Scientific Search*.

Morgan, Ann Haven
(1882–1966)
zoologist and ecologist

Education: A.B., Cornell University, 1906, Ph.D., 1912
Employment: Assistant in zoology, Mount Holyoke College, 1906–1907, instructor, 1907–1909; assistant and instructor, Cornell University, 1909–1911; associate professor, Mount Holyoke College, 1912–1913, professor, 1914–1947, department chair, 1916–1947

Ann Morgan was recognized for her pioneering research on ecology and conservation. Her name was starred in the fifth, sixth and seventh editions of *American Men and Women of Science,* and her photograph was published in the 20 March 1933 issue of *Time* magazine as one of the three women whose names were starred in the fifth edition. Her books have continued to be popular. These include *Field Book of Ponds and Streams: An Introduction to the Life of Fresh Water* (1930), the source for information on collecting and preserving specimens for many amateur naturalists, and *Field Book of Animals in Winter* (1939). Her students nicknamed her Mayfly Morgan after the subject of her thesis.

In the 1940s and 1950s she concentrated on reforming the science curriculum to include the topics of ecology and conservation in both schools and colleges. She gave lectures and workshops for teachers of geography, zoology, and sociology. Her last book, *Kinships of Animals and Man: A Textbook of Animal Biology* (1955),

written for an introductory course in zoology, synthesized her work on this topic. After she received her undergraduate degree, she was employed as an assistant in zoology at Mount Holyoke, where she stayed the rest of her career, aside from the time she spent at Cornell. She received her doctorate from Cornell and returned to Mount Holyoke as an associate professor, being advanced to professor in 1914, and serving as department chair from 1916 to 1947, when she retired.

She was a member of the American Association for the Advancement of Science, the American Society of Naturalists, the American Society of Zoologists, and the Entomological Society of America. Her research included freshwater biology, respiration and ecology of aquatic insects, biology of mayflies, habits and conditions of hibernating animals, and conservation. Her name originally was Anna, but she shortened it to Ann on her thesis in 1912. There is a photograph in Marcia Bonta's *Women in the Field.*

Bibliography: *American Men and Women of Science* 3–11; Bonta, Marcia M., *Women in the Field; National Union Catalog;* Rossiter, Margaret W., *Women Scientists in America;* Sicherman, Barbara et al., *Notable American Women;* Siegel, Patricia J. and Kay Thomas Finley, *Women in the Scientific Search;* Visher, Stephen S., *Scientists Starred 1903–1943 in "American Men of Science."*

Morris, Margaretta Hare
(1797–1867)
entomologist

Education: No formal education
Employment: No formal employment

Margaretta Morris and Charlotte Taylor (q.v.) were the earliest known American women field entomologists. Margaretta Morris was acquainted with a number of scientists and prepared illustrations for botanical papers. In the leading scientific journals of the day she published her studies of the Hessian fly and the 17-year locust, which represent an important contribution, particularly for agriculture. In her studies of the Hessian fly, she based her observations on insects raised for the study. She delineated their life history and concluded that eggs were laid in the grain rather than the stalk. She also described the main predator on Hessian flies. She was said to have investigated fungi as an enemy of plants. The papers she sent to various societies always were read by male members; no genteel female would have considered reading a paper before an all-male audience. Apparently her work was respected enough that she had no trouble finding men willing to present her papers. At the time Margaretta Morris was alive, there were few educational opportunities for women beyond grammar school and there were no opportunities for advanced instruction in science. Nonetheless, throughout the second half of the nineteenth century and well into the twentieth, women entomologists were active in fieldwork, laboratory studies, teaching, and writing. Although Lucy Say (q.v.) was the first woman naturalist to become a member of the Academy of Natural Sciences of Philadelphia, Margaretta Morris became the first practicing woman naturalist (and second woman) to be elected to membership when she was appointed an honorary member in the late 1850s. A list of her publications was included in Clark Elliott's *Biographical Dictionary of American Science.*

Bibliography: Bonta, Marcia M., *Women in the Field;* Elliott, Clark A., *Biographical Dictionary of American Science;* Herzenberg, Caroline L., *Women Scientists from Antiquity to the Present;* Rossiter, Margaret W., *Women Scientists in America;* Siegel, Patricia J. and Kay Thomas Finley, *Women in the Scientific Search.*

Morton, Emily L.
(b. 1841)
entomological artist and amateur collector

Education: Unknown
Employment: Unknown

Emily Morton, like Margaretta Morris (q.v.), was recognized for her contributions to entomology. She was another of the gifted amateurs who built extensive collections and contributed to the work of other collectors by drawing and coloring the plates for their publications. There was no information available on her background or how she supported herself. She and her sister lived in the family home at New Windsor, New York. Her story probably is typical of how women of her generation educated themselves in the science of entomology. She became interested in insects as a small child. When she was 13 years old, a relative gave her a scientific work on insects, complete with Latin names. Later she accumulated a few more books. One set was nine volumes of the agricultural reports of the state of New York. Scattered throughout the volumes were articles by Asa Fitch, the State Entomologist, and she devoured these articles. Later she found that the Astor Library in New York City (later New York Public Library) had entomological books she could read, but not borrow, on her trips to the city. She became acquainted with other collectors through articles and advertisements in the journal *Canadian Entomologist.* Later she made an extensive collection of Lepidoptera and succeeded in hybridizing several types. She sold eight of them to an English collector, the only money she ever made from her collection. She was not known to have published any articles on her research, and it is difficult to identify in which books her drawings were published. Her collection was dispersed among the American Museum of Natural History, the Boston Society of Natural History, and private collectors in about 1904. A short biography with a photograph was published in *Entomological News* 28 (1917): 96–101, and she was mentioned in the Entomological Society of Washington *Proceedings* 23 (1921): 92. The photograph probably was taken sometime in the 1880s; it is a profile view, which might have been popular at the time.

Bibliography: See journal references mentioned in above text.

Murtfeldt, Mary Esther
(1848–1913)
entomologist and botanist

Education: Rockford College, 1859–1862
Employment: Assistant to C. V. Riley, 1868–1877; assistant to state entomologist of Missouri, 1876–1878; field agent, division of entomology, U.S. Department of Agriculture, 1880–1893; acting state entomologist, Missouri, 1888–1896; staff contributor on entomology and botany for the *St. Louis Republic,* 1896–1913
Concurrent position: Field agent, U.S. Department of Agriculture, 1880–1893

Mary Murtfeldt was both an entomologist and a botanist who was acting state entomologist for Missouri for eight years. She attended Rockford College, but she was unable to complete her college education due to poor health. A childhood illness, perhaps polio, forced her to remain on crutches. She developed an interest in entomology after her father became editor of *Colman's Rural World* in 1868. Through him, she met C. V. Riley, the state entomologist of Missouri. She worked as Riley's assistant for several years before being appointed to a position in the agency. In 1888 she was appointed the acting state entomologist; this lasted until 1896. Concurrently she was a field agent for the U.S. Department of Agriculture (USDA) in Missouri from 1880 to 1893. In her position with the USDA, she attended scientific meetings and presented numerous papers. She left the state agency in 1896 to accept a position as staff contributor on entomology and botany for the local paper. Knowledgeable in both fields, she did significant work on the relationship of insects to the pollination of plants. One of her important findings was the pollination of yucca. She specialized in moths and made an outstanding collection. She also contributed articles on Tortricidae to scientific journals. She published two books: *Outlines of Entomology: Prepared for the Use of Farmers and Horticulturists...* (1891) and *Stories of Insect Life* (1899). She was elected a fellow of the American Association for the Advancement of Science. She also was a member of the Entomological Society of America and the American Association of Economic Entomologists. Her photograph is on file at the National Archives, and it was included in Herbert Osborn's *Fragments of Entomological History.*

Bibliography: American Men and Women of Science 2; Barr, Ernest S., *An Index to*

Murtfeldt, Mary Esther

Biographical Fragments in Unspecialized Scientific Journals; Bonta, Marcia M., *Women in the Field;* Herzenberg, Caroline L., *Women Scientists from Antiquity to the Present;* Mozans, H. J., *Women in Science;* Ogilvie, Marilyn B., *Women in Science;* Osborn, Herbert, *Fragments of Entomological History;* Rossiter, Margaret W., *Women Scientists in America;* Rossiter, Margaret W., "'Women's Work' in Science, 1880–1910."

Nellie Ward Nance
Mary Frances Winston Newson
Margaret Morse Nice
Mary Louise Nichols
Dorothy Nickerson
Margaret Lewis Nickerson
Dorothy Virginia Nightingale
(Amalie) Emmy Noether
Naomi Norsworthy
Ann Hero Northrup
Mary Alice (Peloubet) Norton
Zelia Maria Magdalena Nuttall

Nance, Nellie Ward
(b. 1893)
plant pathologist

Education: A.B., George Washington University, 1931, M.A., 1938
Employment: Personnel worker, U.S. Department of Agriculture, 1922–1930, senior science aide, 1930–1936, junior pathologist, 1936–1943, assistant pathologist, 1943–1950, plant pathologist, 1950–?

Nellie Nance was a plant pathologist who was recognized for her work for the U.S. Department of Agriculture (USDA). Her career was a typical one for many women of her generation. She began working for the USDA in 1922. She started taking courses at George Washington at some point, receiving an undergraduate degree in 1931. This qualified her for a scientific assignment in the agency, and she advanced through the ranks of senior science aide, junior pathologist, and finally assistant pathologist and plant pathologist after she received her master's degree. She was just one of the many women who found opportunities to advance in her career in the federal agencies; at the time, the USDA employed the largest number of women in professional positions. In addition to the usual civil service benefits and the opportunities for advancement, USDA women were permitted to publish their research in their own names. (In academic, corporate, and other agency laboratories, publications were issued under the name of the department head or the chief scientist, sometimes with an acknowledgment to the contributors in a footnote.) Nellie Nance was a member of the American Phytopathological Society and the Botanical Society of Washington. Her research interests were listed as epidemiology and history of plant diseases.

Bibliography: American Men and Women of Science 7–11; Barnhart, John H., Biographical Notes upon Botanists; National Union Catalog.

Newson, Mary Frances Winston
(1869–1959)
mathematician

Education: A.B., University of Wisconsin, 1889; Bryn Mawr College, 1891–1892; University of Chicago, 1892–1893; Ph.D. in mathematics, University of Göttingen, 1896
Employment: High school teacher, 1889–1891, 1896–1897; professor, mathematics department, Kansas State Agricultural College, 1897–1900; assistant professor, Washburn College, 1913–1921; professor, Eureka College, 1921–1934, chair, division of science and mathematics, 1934–1942
Married: Henry B. Newson, 1900, died 1910

Mary Newson, in 1896, became the first American woman to receive a doctorate in mathematics from a European university and the second American woman to earn a doctorate from the University of Göttingen. When she did not receive a fellowship to attend Göttingen, Christine Ladd-Franklin (q.v.)

gave her $500 from her own funds to pay for her travel and expenses. During her last year at Göttingen, she was awarded a fellowship from the Association of Collegiate Alumnae. She taught high school for several years after receiving her undergraduate degree in 1889, the usual pattern for women of her generation; however, she continued her advanced studies at Bryn Mawr and the University of Chicago before entering Göttingen to complete her doctorate. She was appointed a professor of mathematics at Kansas State in 1897, but she resigned from teaching when she married in 1900. Her husband, a member of the mathematics faculty at the University of Kansas, died of a heart attack in 1910, leaving her with no job, no pension, no insurance benefits, and three children. Fortunately she was able to move in with her parents for a time. In 1913 she finally found work at nearby Washburn College and then received an appointment as

professor at Eureka College in 1921, serving as chair of the division of science and mathematics from 1934 to 1942. She was recognized as an outstanding and dedicated teacher. In 1970 her three children started a fund to establish an annual lecture at Eureka College called the Mary Winston Newson Memorial Lecture on International Relations. Her name was listed in the first edition of *American Men and Women of Science;* in the third to the sixth editions, she was listed as Mrs. H. B. Newson. She was a member of the American Mathematical Society and the Mathematical Association of America. Her area of research was differential equations.

Bibliography: *American Men and Women of Science* 1–6; Grinstein, Louise S. and Paul J. Campbell, eds., *Women of Mathematics;* Rossiter, Margaret W., *Women Scientists in America;* Siegel, Patricia J. and Kay Thomas Finley, *Women in the Scientific Search.*

Nice, Margaret Morse
(1883–1974)
ornithologist

Education: B.A., Mount Holyoke College, 1906; Clark University, 1907–1909, A.M. in
   psychology, 1915
Employment: Independent researcher, 1915–1974
Married: L. Blaine Nice, 1909

Margaret Nice was an internationally known ornithologist, although she did not have a faculty appointment, was not formally associated with a museum, and had small amounts of grant money. From all appearances she might have been considered just another academic spouse following her husband around the country, spending her spare time bird-watching; but she was more than that—she adapted the techniques of scientific investigation from

psychology to a new area of research, that of bird behavior. After receiving her master's degree, she continued her study of ornithology and published *The Birds of Oklahoma* (1924), coauthored with her husband. She was the sole author of the two-part *Studies in the Life History of the Song Sparrow* (1937, 1943). This established her reputation as one of the world's foremost ornithologists and bird behaviorists. Initially she was interested in languages as a student at Mount Holyoke College, where she received her undergraduate degree in 1906. At that time ornithology was taught in the zoology department and consisted of identifying dead species. Her interest shifted to psychology at Clark University, where she received her master's degree in 1915. She published 18 articles on child psychology from observations of her own children between 1915 and 1933. For a time she lived the life of a typical housewife, but she became bored and frustrated. In 1919 she and her husband bought a car, which gave her increased mobility and the opportunity for fieldwork. Her career took off when she started corresponding with fellow ornithologists.

Margaret Nice was at the center of a network of women ornithologists whose scientific correspondence also served as a support system. She and her husband followed their particular scientific interests, but the entire family helped her with her observations; for instance, the children would climb trees to observe nests for her. She published about 250 papers and other works between 1920 and 1965. Her skill in languages also contributed to the discipline, because she reviewed a large number of the leading European publications. She was active in ornithological and conservation organizations; she was an associate editor of the journal *Bird-Banding* from 1935 to 1942 and from 1946 to 1971. When the family lived in Columbus, Ohio, the local ornithology club was an all-male group; they invited her husband to join, but ignored her. By that time, however, her work was known nationally and internationally. She published one bird book for the general public, *The Watcher at the Nest* (1939). Although it was not a financial success, it has been reprinted in paperback and still is read. In later life, she increasingly turned her attention to educating the public about conservation and nature with lectures and talks on the radio.

Margaret Nice was awarded the Brewster Medal of the American Ornithologists' Union in 1942. She was the first woman president of the Wilson Ornithological Society (1938–1939), and she was elected a fellow of the American Ornithologists' Union. She received an honorary degree from Mount Holyoke in 1955 and one from Elmira College in 1962. Her research interests included birds of Oklahoma; life history studies of birds, particularly mourning doves, warblers, and song sparrows; and speech development of children. She and her husband had five daughters: Janet, Constance, Eleanor, Barbara, and Marjorie. There is a photograph in Marcia Bonta's *Women in the Field*. Her autobiography is *Research Is a Passion with Me* (1979). She was listed in the third edition of *American Men and Women of Science* as Mrs. L. B. Nice, but as Margaret Nice in succeeding editions.

Bibliography: Abir-Am, P. G. and Dorinda Outram, eds., *Uneasy Careers and Intimate Lives; American Men and Women of Science* 3–13; Bonta, Marcia M., *Women in the Field;* Herzenberg, Caroline L., *Women Scientists from Antiquity to the Present;* Rossiter, Margaret W., *Women Scientists in America;* Sicherman, Barbara et al., *Notable American Women;* Siegel, Patricia J. and Kay Thomas Finley, *Women in the Scientific Search.*

Nichols, Mary Louise
(1873–1953)
zoologist

Education: University of Pennsylvania, 1890–1893; Marine Biological Laboratory, Woods Hole, 1895–1897, 1900; University of Pennsylvania, 1895–1901, Ph.D., 1901
Employment: Teacher of zoology, Philadelphia Normal School, 1893–1902, zoology and geography, 1902–1916; head, department of science, public school, 1916–1935

Mary Nichols was recognized by her contemporaries as a zoologist; her name was included in the first edition of *American Men and Women of Science.* After receiving a certificate from the University of Pennsylvania in 1893, she taught zoology and geography at the local normal school while working toward her doctorate, which she received in 1901. In 1916 she was appointed head of the department of science in a girls' high school in Philadelphia; she remained there until she retired in 1935. She studied for several years at Woods Hole, probably in the summers, and she published a number of scientific papers dealing with diverse topics of her research. Her career reflects the opportunities that were available to women scientists of her era. Although it now seems strange that a woman with a doctorate from a distinguished university would teach high school, family responsibilities might explain this employment. An additional factor was that she was teaching students whose families could afford their continuing education, and presumably the students would be motivated to learn. She was a member of the American Association for the Advancement of Science, the American Genetic Association, and the American Eugenics Society. Her research included development of the pollen of Saracenia and habits of the mining bee.

Bibliography: American Men and Women of Science 1–9; Siegel, Patricia J. and Kay Thomas Finley, *Women in the Scientific Search.*

Nickerson, Dorothy
(b. 1900)
physicist

Education: Unknown
Employment: Assistant, Munsell Research Laboratory, assistant manager, Munsell Color Company, 1921–1926; color technologist, U.S. Department of Agriculture, 1927–1964; consultant, 1965–1974
Concurrent Position: Trustee, Munsell Color Foundation, 1942–1979

Dorothy Nickerson specialized in color standards for agricultural products. She was employed by a corporation that specialized in color technology starting in 1921, rising to the level of assistant manager. She joined the U.S. Department of Agriculture (USDA) in 1927 as a color technologist in the bureau of agricultural economics. She left the USDA in 1964 to form a consulting firm, retiring in

1974. She served as a U.S. expert on color rendering for the International Commission on Illumination from 1956 to 1967. The color of foods would be an important factor in agricultural economics; in developing new strains of vegetables, for example, not only the shape and taste of tomatoes is important in marketing but also the color. Dorothy Nickerson received several awards, such as the Superior Service Award from the USDA (1951), the Distinguished Achievement Award of the Instrument Society of America (1964), the gold certificate of the American Horticultural Council (1957), and the Gold Medal of the Illuminating Engineering Society (1970). She was elected president of the International Society of Color Council in 1954. She was a member of the American Association for the Advancement of Science, the Optical Society of America, and the Illuminating Engineering Society. She listed herself in *American Men and Women of Science* as a physicist, a psychophysicist, and a color scientist.

Bibliography: *American Men and Women of Science* 6–16.

Nickerson, Margaret Lewis
(b. 1870)
zoologist

Education: A.B., Smith College, 1893; A.M., Radcliffe College, 1897; M.D., University of Minnesota, 1904
Employment: Instructor, histology and embryology, medical department, University of Minnesota, 1898–1906; physician, public schools, 1912–?
Married: Winfield S. Nickerson

Margaret Nickerson was a zoologist whose name was starred in the first through fifth editions of *American Men and Women of Science.* Her husband's name also was starred. Her name was included in a study of 150 eminent American zoologists in 1903 reported by Stephen Visher in *Scientists Starred 1903–1943 in "American Men of Science."* After receiving her master's degree from Radcliffe in 1897, she accepted a position as an instructor of histology and embryology in the medical department at the University of Minnesota in 1898, working there until 1906. She received her M.D. from Minnesota in 1904. She attended Radcliffe as a fellow of the Association of Collegiate Alumnae. After a gap of several years, she was employed as a physician in public schools starting in 1912. There was no indication of her research interests or publications in the sources that were checked; she did not list memberships in professional societies. Possibly she worked with her husband while both were employed at Minnesota. In *Women Scientists in America*, Margaret Rossiter mentions a controversy over the awarding of stars in the first seven editions of *American Men and Women of Science;* the correspondence files of the publication indicate that Margaret Nickerson was not considered a star performer after the first edition, but her name continued to be starred in all the later editions in which she was listed.

Bibliography: *American Men and Women of Science* 1–5; Herzenberg, Caroline L., *Women Scientists from Antiquity to the Present;* Rossiter, Margaret W., *Women Scientists in America;* Siegel, Patricia J. and Kay Thomas Finley, *Women in the Scientific Search;* Visher, Stephen S., *Scientists Starred 1903–1943 in "American Men of Science."*

Nightingale, Dorothy Virginia
(1902–)
organic chemist

Education: A.B., University of Missouri, 1922, A.M., 1923; University of Chicago, 1924–1927, Ph.D. in organic chemistry, 1928

Employment: Instructor in chemistry, University of Missouri, 1923–1939, assistant professor, 1939–1948, associate professor, 1948–1958, professor, 1958–1972; emeritus professor

Concurrent Positions: Research associate, University of California, Los Angeles, 1946–1947; civilian with Office of Scientific Research and Development, 1942–1945

Dorothy Nightingale has been recognized for her work in organic synthetic reactions. She joined the faculty at the University of Missouri as instructor in chemistry in 1923 after receiving her master's degree there. She received her doctorate in organic chemistry in 1928, but she was not promoted to assistant professor until 1939. She became associate professor in 1948 and professor in 1958, retiring in 1972 after 50 years with the institution. During World War II she took a leave from the university to work as a civilian with the Office of Scientific Research and Development. There was a long interval between receiving her doctorate and being promoted to assistant professor, but this could be explained by the shortage of jobs during the Depression. The university was very slow in promoting her to associate and full professor when the significance of her research is considered, however. She received the Garvan Medal of the American Chemical Society in 1959 for her work in organic synthetic reactions. She was a member of the American Chemical Society. Her research includes chemiluminescence of organomagnesium halides, alkylations and acylations in the presence of aluminum chloride, action of nitrous acid on alicyclic amines, and reactions of nitroparaffins with alicyclic ketones. Her name was listed in the 1992–1993 edition of *American Men and Women of Science.*

Bibliography: American Men and Women of Science 5–18; Herzenberg, Caroline L., Women Scientists from Antiquity to the Present; O'Neill, Lois S., The Women's Book of World Records and Achievements.

Noether, (Amalie) Emmy
(1882–1935)
mathematician

Education: University of Erlangen, 1900–1902, 1904–1907, Ph.D., 1907; University of Göttingen, 1903–1904

Employment: Unpaid instructor, University of Erlangen, 1908–1915; lecturer, University of Göttingen, 1915–1922, associate professor, 1922–1933; visiting professor, Bryn Mawr College, 1933–1935; lecturer, Institute for Advanced Study, Princeton University, 1933–1935

Emmy Noether generally is considered one of the greatest mathematicians of the twentieth century. Her work in abstract algebra has inspired so many mathematicians that they speak of the "Noether School" of mathematics. Since the University of Erlangen was not accepting women students, Emmy Noether received permission to audit lectures, perhaps because her father was a faculty member in mathematics. Since she planned to be a teacher of English and French, she studied mathematics and foreign languages. After two years, she attended the University of Göttingen for a time, concentrating on mathematics, before returning to Erlangen when it changed its policy. She received her doctorate in 1907. She worked as an unpaid instructor at Erlangen until 1915, when she accepted a position as an unpaid lecturer at Göttingen. It was still virtually impossible for women with doctorates to find employment in Germany in the 1920s. For this reason Emmy Noether was listed as an unofficial faculty member at Göttingen, but eventually she did receive a small salary.

In 1933 she and the other Jewish faculty members were dismissed from their positions, and she emigrated to the United States, having received offers from Somerville College, Oxford University, and Bryn Mawr College. She decided to accept the latter invitation partly due to Bryn Mawr's reputation for eminent women mathematicians. She lectured and did research at both Bryn Mawr and the Institute for Advanced Study at Princeton University beginning in 1933. Within two years she died of cancer. Her most important achievement was devising mathematical formulations for several concepts found in Einstein's general theory of relativity. As a mathematician, she was one of the earliest figures in twentieth-century theoretical physics. She was instrumental in discounting the idea that women were incapable of theoretical advances. In addition, she profoundly changed the appearance of algebra in her work on abstract algebra. She wrote some 45 research papers on these topics. There are several biographies, including *Emmy Noether, 1882–1935* (1981) by Auguste Dick and *Emmy Noether: A Tribute to Her Life and Work* (1981), edited by James W. Brewer and Martha K. Smith.

Bibliography: *Dictionary of Scientific Biography*; Grinstein, Louise S. and Paul J. Campbell, eds., *Women of Mathematics*; Herzenberg, Caroline L., *Women Scientists from Antiquity to the Present*; Kass-Simon, G. and Patricia Farnes, *Women of Science*; Macksey, Joan and Kenneth Macksey, *The Book of Women's Achievements*; *National Union Catalog*; Ogilvie, Marilyn B., *Women in Science*; O'Neill, Lois S., *The Women's Book of World Records and Achievements*; Perl, Teri, *Math Equals*; Rossiter, Margaret W., *Women Scientists in America*; Siegel, Patricia J. and Kay Thomas Finley, *Women in the Scientific Search*; Uglow, Jennifer S., *International Dictionary of Women's Biography*.

Norsworthy, Naomi
(1877–1916)
psychologist

Education: Diploma, Trenton State Normal School, 1896; B.S., Columbia University, 1901, Ph.D., 1904
Employment: Teacher, public schools, 1896–1899; assistant in psychology, Teachers' College, Columbia University, 1901–1902, tutor, 1902–1904, instructor, 1904–1909, adjunct professor, 1909–1916

Naomi Norsworthy was recognized for her contributions to psychology as the first woman faculty member at Teachers' College, Columbia University, and her name appeared in the first edition of *American Men and Women of Science*. Although she had a short career, she made important contributions to the study of the feebleminded. Her career followed the pattern of many women scientists of her generation. After receiving a diploma from a normal school, she taught in the public schools for three years. She received an appointment as an assistant in psychology in 1901 after receiving her undergraduate degree from Columbia. She was a tutor for several years while completing her doctorate in 1904. She then rejoined the Columbia faculty as an instructor, being promoted to adjunct professor in 1909. She died in 1916. She was joint author of *How To Teach* (1917) and *The Psychology of Childhood* (1918). She was a member of the American Psychological Association. Her research involved the effect of special training in school on the general ability of children, mental defects in children, and a statistical study of character.

Bibliography: American Men and Women of Science 1–2; Dictionary of American Biography; National Union Catalog; Rossiter, Margaret W., Women Scientists in America; Siegel, Patricia J. and Kay Thomas Finley, Women in the Scientific Search.

Northrup, Ann Hero
(1875–1949)
chemist

Education: A.B., Vassar College, 1896, A.M., 1897
Employment: Instructor in chemistry, Pratt Institute, 1898–1903; acting professor, Newcomb College, Tulane University, 1904–1905, professor, 1905–1926
Married: Elliott J. Northrup, 1914

Ann Northrup was recognized by her contemporaries as a contributing member of the chemistry profession. After she received her master's degree from Vassar, she was appointed an instructor in chemistry at Pratt Institute in 1898. She accepted a position as an acting professor at Newcomb College in 1904, then was promoted to professor in 1905. She and her husband, a law professor at Tulane, both were faculty members. Since Newcomb was the women's college of Tulane, apparently the couple was able to retain their professorships because they worked for different departments. For a number of years it was virtually impossible for a woman to receive a faculty appointment, even if her husband were in another department. After the couple left Tulane in 1926, they moved to Europe, where Ann Northrup translated three important books by eminent German chemists. She long had an interest in the German language. She must have been a rather interesting person, since a resolution of the Newcomb faculty at the time of her death mentions that her individuality made her a unique figure on the faculty. She was a member of the American Chemical Society, and her name was listed in the first and second editions of *American Men and Women of Science* as Ann Hero.

Bibliography: American Men and Women of Science 1–2; Siegel, Patricia J. and Kay Thomas Finley, Women in the Scientific Search.

Norton, Mary Alice (Peloubet)
(1860–1928)
home economics educator

Education: A.B., Smith College, 1882; Massachusetts Institute of Technology, 1894–1896; Boston Normal School of Household Arts, 1896; A.M., Smith College, 1897

Employment: Lecturer, Boston Young Women's Christian Association school of domestic science, 1895–1900; lecturer, Boston Cooking School, 1898–1900; teacher of high school domestic science, 1896–1900; assistant professor of home economics, School of Education, University of Chicago, 1900–1913; dietitian, Cook County public institutions, 1913–1914; secretary of American Home Economics Association, 1915–1918; editor of the *Journal of Home Economics,* 1915–1921; professor of home economics, Constantinople Women's College, 1921–1924; interim head, home economics department, Indiana University, 1924–1925

Married: Lewis M. Norton, 1883, died 1893

Mary Norton was one of the women instrumental in forming the American Home Economics Association and developing home economics into a profession. She received her undergraduate degree from Smith College in 1882 and married the following year. Her husband was a chemistry professor at Massachusetts Institute of Technology (MIT). After he died in 1893, she taught at two Boston cooking schools starting in 1895. She enrolled in MIT in 1894 on the advice of Ellen Richards (q.v.) to find employment in the new field of sanitary science applied to the home. She enrolled in additional training at the normal school and then received her master's degree from Smith in 1897.

She assisted Ellen Richards and Marion Talbot (q.v.) to prepare the book *Home Sanitation: A Manual for Housekeepers* (1887). She taught high school domestic science for a few years before accepting a position as assistant professor of home economics at the University of Chicago in 1901. There she worked with Marion Talbot again. She played a key role in the development of that institution's worldwide reputation for outstanding education in the growing field of home economics. She resigned in 1913, protesting the appointment of a new head of the School of Education. She published a book entitled *Food and Dietetics* in 1906. She was one of the founders of the American Home Economics Association and served as secretary from 1915 to 1918. She was editor of the association's journal for seven years. She returned to teaching when she was invited to form a department of home economics at the Constantinople Women's College in 1921, and then served as interim head of the home economics department at Indiana University for one year. While pursuing her career she raised five children—Margaret, John, Grace, Louise, and Lewis.

Bibliography: Dictionary of American Biography; James, E. T., ed., *Notable American Women 1607–1950; National Union Catalog;* Siegel, Patricia J. and Kay Thomas Finley, *Women in the Scientific Search.*

Nuttall, Zelia Maria Magdalena
(1857–1933)
archaeologist

Education: Private schools
Employment: Honorary special assistant, Peabody Museum, Cambridge, Massachusetts, 1887–1933; honorary professor of archaeology, National Museum of Mexico, 1908–1933
Concurrent Positions: Field director, Crocker archaeological researches, Mexico and California, 1904–?; advisory council, department of anthropology, University of California; science mission to Russia, 1904
Married: Alphonse L. Pinart, 1880, divorced 1888

Zelia Nuttall was recognized as one of the archaeologists who showed the extent and significance of the pre-Columbian history of Mexico. Since her family lived abroad for several years, she was well versed in several languages. She acquired her interest in Mexico as a child because her mother had been born there. She educated herself in archaeology by reading, observing, and traveling. Her husband was a French archaeologist who came to California on an expedition to the Pacific coast. The couple had one daughter, Nadine, and later divorced, with Zelia retaining custody of her daughter and resuming her maiden name. She made her first trip to Mexico in 1884 and 1885; this resulted in her first publication, a paper on terra-cotta heads from San Juan Teotihuacan. In 1902 she settled permanently in Mexico with occasional trips to Europe and the United States.

She made two important contributions to archaeology in her ability to discover forgotten documents and to understand the significance of artifacts that were uncovered in excavations. In Florence she found evidence for the manuscript that was named for her, the Codex Nuttall. While searching for unrelated material in the National Archives of Mexico she found new information on the voyages of Sir Francis Drake. She followed up on this discovery by searching libraries and archives in the United States, Britain, and the continent. She was the first to recognize and demonstrate that the culture of Mexico is much older than had been thought. Although she had no special background in archaeology, she was named an honorary special assistant at Harvard's Peabody Museum in 1887 after her first paper was published in 1886. She also was an honorary professor of archaeology at the National Museum of Mexico and was field director of the Crocker archaeological researches. She developed a vast collection of native plants, including medicinals, in her garden in Mexico City.

She had a vivid mind, a command of many languages, and a positive approach to her work. She had copied hundreds of documents in museums and libraries to back her theories on pre-Columbian Mexico. She was elected a fellow of the American Anthropological Association, and was a member of the American Association for the Advancement of Science, the American Ethnology Society, the American Geographical Society, and the American Philosophical Society. Her research included ancient and colonial history, calendar systems, religions, and languages of the inhabitants of Mexico and Central America; ancient manuscripts and picture writings; documents relating to expeditions of Sir Francis Drake and John Hawkins; and the botany of Mexico. Her name was listed in the first edition of *American Men and Women of Science.* There is a biography with photograph in *American Anthropologist* 35 (1933): 475–482.

Bibliography: *American Men and Women of Science* 1–5; Helm, June, ed., *Pioneers of*

American Anthropology; Herzenberg, Caroline L., *Women Scientists from Antiquity to the Present;* James, E. T., ed., *Notable American Women 1607–1950;* Mozans, H. J., *Women in Science;* Rossiter, Margaret W., *Women Scientists in America;* Rossiter, Margaret W., "'Women's Work' in Science, 1880–1910"; Siegel, Patricia J. and Kay Thomas Finley, *Women in the Scientific Search.*

Eunice Rockwood Oberly
Ida Helen Ogilvie
Ruth Eliza Okey

Oberly, Eunice Rockwood
(1878–1921)
librarian

Education: A.B., Vassar College, 1900
Employment: Bibliographer, Bureau of Animal Industry, U.S. Department of Agriculture, 1900–1908; librarian, Bureau of Plant Industry, 1908–1921

Eunice Oberly was recognized for her contributions as a bibliographer by the establishment of a prize in her name. At the time of her death, her associates at the U.S. Department of Agriculture (USDA) and the American Phytopathological Society established the Eunice Rockwood Oberly Memorial Prize to be administered by the American Library Association for contributions to scientific bibliography. After receiving her undergraduate degree from Vassar, she joined the staff of the Bureau of Animal Industry at the USDA as a bibliographer. Later she was appointed librarian for the Bureau of Plant Industry when several libraries were consolidated. The Plant Industry library, which contained few books, was a service for the purpose of indexing and cataloging botanical literature and making it readily available to employees; the files were used extensively by outsiders as well. Eunice Oberly instituted a column in the journal *Phytopathology* on the literature of plant diseases in 1914; it was continued after her death by library staff members. She was the author of the pamphlet "Check List of Publications of the Department of Agriculture on the Subject of Plant Pathology, 1837–1918." The Oberly Prize first was awarded in 1924, and currently it is presented in alternate years at the annual meeting of the American Library Association. The recipients often are scientists rather than librarians. There is a biography, including a photograph, in *Phytopathology* 15 (1925): 61–66.

Bibliography: Barnhart, John H., *Biographical Notes upon Botanists; National Union Catalog.*

Ogilvie, Ida Helen
(1874–1963)
geologist

Education: A.B., Bryn Mawr College, 1900; University of Chicago, 1901; Ph.D., Columbia University, 1903
Employment: Lecturer in geology, Barnard College, 1903–1905, tutor, 1905–1910, instructor, 1910–1912, assistant professor, 1912–1916, associate professor, 1916–1938, professor, 1938–1941; emeritus professor; farm owner and operator
Concurrent Position: Director, Women's Agricultural Camp, 1917–1920

*I*da Ogilvie was the founder of Barnard's department of geology, which in 1903 was one of the first in an American women's college. After she received her doctorate from Columbia, she was appointed a lecturer in geology at Barnard in 1903 and then advanced to tutor in 1905, instructor in 1910, assistant professor in 1912, associate professor in 1916, and professor in 1938. She was remembered as a superb lecturer, but she published few papers. In addition to her teaching and administrative duties, she conducted geological studies in Maine, New York, California, and Mexico. During World War I she was involved in the Women's Land Army, and she continued her interest in agriculture as a subject for research after returning to Barnard. She had an interest in cattle breeding, as well as petrology, paleontology, and glacial problems. She was the third woman elected a fellow of the Geological Society of America. She also was a member of the American Association for the Advancement of Science, the Ecological Society of America, and the New York Academy of Sciences. Her research interests were glaciology of the Adirondacks, British Columbia, and Maine; and geology of the Ortiz Mountains, New Mexico. Her name was listed in the first edition of *American Men of Science.*

Bibliography: *American Men and Women of Science* 1–10; Kass-Simon, G. and Patricia Farnes, *Women of Science;* Rossiter, Margaret W., *Women Scientists in America;* Siegel, Patricia J. and Kay Thomas Finley, *Women in the Scientific Search.*

Okey, Ruth Eliza
(b. 1893)
biochemist and nutritionist

Education: B.S., Monmouth College, 1914; M.S., University of Illinois, 1915, Ph.D. in chemistry, 1918

Employment: Instructor in physiological chemistry, University of Illinois, 1918–1919; assistant professor of household science, University of California, Berkeley, 1919–1926; assistant professor of home economics, University of Iowa, 1921–1922; associate professor and associate biochemist, experiment station, University of California, Berkeley, 1926–1944, professor and biochemist, 1944–1956, chair, department of nutrition and home economics, 1956–1960; emeritus professor

Ruth Okey had a strong science background that she brought to the home economics department at the University of California, Berkeley. After she received her doctorate from the University of Illinois, she accepted an appointment as an instructor in physiological chemistry at Illinois in 1918. She was hired as an assistant professor of household science at the University of California, Berkeley, in 1919, and later at the University of Iowa in 1921. She returned to California to accept a position as associate professor and associate biochemist of the experiment station at Berkeley in 1926. She was promoted to professor in 1944, became chair of the nutrition and home economics department in 1956, and was appointed emeritus professor in 1961. For a number of years she had formal research responsibilities as a biochemist with the agricultural experiment station. She received the Borden Award in 1961. She was a member of the American Association for the Advancement of Science, the American Chemical Society, the American Society of Biological Chemists, the Society for Experimental Biology and Medicine, the American Home Economics Association, the American Dietetic Association, and the American Institute of Nutrition. Her research interests included emodin-containing drugs; insulin metabolism; and fat and cholesterol metabolism.

Bibliography: *American Men and Women of Science* 3–11; Herzenberg, Caroline L., *Women Scientists from Antiquity to the Present; National Union Catalog;* Rossiter, Margaret W., *Women Scientists in America;* Siegel, Patricia J. and Kay Thomas Finley, *Women in the Scientific Search.*

Mary Esther Trueblood Paine
Katherine Evangeline Hilton Van Winkle Palmer
Miriam Augusta Palmer
Anna Helene Palmie
Barbara Frances Palser
Maria Parloa
Elsie Worthington Clews Parsons
Edith Marion Patch
Ruth Patrick
Flora Wambaugh Patterson
Nellie Maria de Cottrell Payne
Cecelia Helena Payne-Gaposchkin
Louise Pearce
Annie Smith Peck
Elizabeth Gifford Peckham
Florence Peebles
Mary Engle Pennington
Mary Locke Petermann
Almira Hart Lincoln Phelps
Martha Austin Phelps
Melba Newell Phillips
Eliza Lucas Pinckney
Dorothy Riggs Pitelka
Margaret Pittman
Judith Graham Pool
Gene Stratton Porter
Mary Proctor

Paine, Mary Esther Trueblood
(1872–1939)
mathematician

Education: Ph.B., Earlham College, 1893; Ph.M., University of Michigan, 1896; University of Göttingen, 1900–1901
Employment: Instructor of mathematics, Earlham College, 1897–1899; instructor, Mount Holyoke College, 1902–1910; head, extension department of mathematics, University of California, Berkeley, 1914–1939
Married: Robert Paine, 1911

Mary Paine was considered by her contemporaries to be one of the most competent women mathematicians in the country. After receiving degrees from Earlham College and the University of Michigan, she accepted a position as instructor of mathematics at Earlham in 1897. She received a fellowship from the Woman's Educational Association to study at the University of Göttingen in 1900 and 1901. She moved to Mount Holyoke in 1902, where she held a position as instructor until 1910. Her scholarly work there centered on the history and philosophy of mathematics. She was married in 1911 and was appointed head of the extension department of mathematics at the University of California, Berkeley, in 1914. She was a member of the Mathematical Association of America and the American Mathematical Society. Her research included the directive force of philosophy in the development of mathematical thought, the period of germination (preceding Francis Bacon), and the history of the role played in mathematics by the idea of infinity. She was listed in the first and second editions of *American Men and Women of Science* as Mary Trueblood.

Bibliography: *American Men and Women of Science* 1–2; Siegel, Patricia J. and Kay Thomas Finley, *Women in the Scientific Search.*

Palmer, Katherine Evangeline Hilton Van Winkle
(b. 1895)
paleontologist

Education: B.S., University of Washington, Seattle, 1918; Ph.D. in paleontology, Cornell University, 1925
Employment: Assistant geologist, University of Oregon, 1918; assistant professor, history of geology and paleontology, University of Washington, Seattle, 1922; faculty, geology department, Cornell University, 1918–1935, lecturer, 1942–1946; curator of paleontology, Oberlin College, 1928–1929; technical expert, zoology, New York State Museum, 1945–1946; special technical expert, McGill University, 1950–1951; director, Paleontological Research Institute, Ithaca, New York, 1951–1978; director emeritus
Concurrent Position: Secretary-treasurer, Cushman Foundation, 1954–1971
Married: Ephraim L. Palmer, 1921

Katherine Palmer was a notable paleontologist who was director of the Paleontological Research Institute. After receiving her undergraduate degree from the University of Washington, she was appointed an assistant in geology at the University of Oregon in 1918. The same year she was appointed to the faculty of the geology department of Cornell, where she continued to teach until 1946. She had several interim appointments at the University of Washington, Oberlin College, and the New York State Museum. She worked as a special technical expert at McGill University in 1950 and then assumed the position of director of the Paleontological Research Institute in Ithaca, New York, in 1951, being elected director emeritus in 1978. Another interim appointment was with the Cushman Foundation from 1954 to 1971. She received

grants from several sources, including the National Science Foundation, and received numerous honors and awards. She received an honorary degree from Tulane University and was a fellow of both the Paleontology Society and the Geological Society of America. She was elected president of the American Malacological Union in 1960. She was also a member of the American Association for the Advancement of Science and the American Association of Petroleum Geologists. Her research interests were paleontology, stratigraphy, and conchology. She and her husband had two children, Laurence and Robin.

Bibliography: American Men and Women of Science 6–15; Debus, A. G., ed., World Who's Who in Science; Herzenberg, Caroline L., Women Scientists from Antiquity to the Present.

Palmer, Miriam Augusta
(b. 1878)
entomologist

Education: A.B., University of Kansas, 1903, A.M., 1904; M.S., Colorado Agricultural College, 1925, D.Sc., 1959
Employment: Delineator, experiment station, Colorado State College, 1904–1947, instructor in zoology and physiology, 1904–1922, assistant professor of entomology, 1922–1927, associate professor, 1927–1947

Miriam Palmer was recognized for her work on aphididae; she was a world authority on the subject. She was coauthor of *Aphididae of Colorado* (1931–1936) and author of *Aphids of the Rocky Mountain Region* (1952), which was issued as publication number five of the Thomas Say Foundation. She spent her career at Colorado State College both teaching and working for the experiment station. After receiving her master's degree from the University of Kansas, she joined the Colorado state experiment station as a delineator and as an instructor in zoology and physiology in the college. (A delineator

illustrated scientific papers prepared by the department or the entomology section of the experiment station. This seems to be a common assignment for women at this period; several women worked for the U.S. Department of Agriculture and other state experiment stations with the job title of either delineator or artist.) Miriam Palmer was promoted to assistant professor of entomology in 1922 and associate professor in 1927, retiring in 1947. She received an honorary degree from the university in 1959. She was elected a fellow of the Entomological Society of America, and was also a member of the American Association for the Advancement of Science and the Society of Systematic Zoology. Her research was on the taxonomy of aphidae. Her photograph was included in Herbert Osborn's *Fragments of Entomological History.*

Bibliography: *American Men and Women of Science* 5–11; Bonta, Marcia M., *Women in the Field; National Union Catalog;* Osborn, Herbert, *Fragments of Entomological History.*

Palmie, Anna Helene
(1863–1946)
mathematician

Education: Ph.B., Cornell University, 1890, fellow, 1890–1891; University of Chicago, 1896; University of Göttingen, 1898–1899
Employment: Instructor in German and mathematics, high school, 1891–1892; instructor in mathematics, College for Women, Western Reserve University, 1892–1893, associate professor, 1893–1895, professor, 1895–1928; emeritus professor

*A*nna Palmie was another early member of the American Mathematical Society, joining in 1897. She received her Ph.B. degree from Cornell in 1890, but she stayed another year on a fellowship. She then taught high school German and mathematics for two years. She accepted a position as instructor in mathematics in the women's college of Western Reserve in 1892 and was promoted to associate professor the following year and professor in 1895. She took additional course work at the University of Chicago and the University of Göttingen between 1896 and 1899. She retired in 1928. The rate of her advancement in academic rank was unmatched for faculty at this time; perhaps

the women's college, called the Flora Stone Mather College at that time, was entirely separate from the university. She may have advanced rapidly because she was a superior mathematician and teacher, and the administration would have been unable to replace her. It was not due to her membership in the American Mathematical Society, because she did not join until 1897, after she had been named professor. Her name was listed in the first seven editions of *American Men and Women of Science.*

Bibliography: *American Men and Women of Science* 1–7; Siegel, Patricia J. and Kay Thomas Finley, *Women in the Scientific Search.*

Palser, Barbara Frances
(1916–)
botanist

Education: A.B., Mount Holyoke College, 1938, A.M., 1940; Ph.D. in botany, University of Chicago, 1942
Employment: Instructor in botany, University of Chicago, 1942–1945, assistant professor, 1945–1951, associate professor, 1951–1960, professor, 1960–1965; associate professor of

botany, Rutgers University, 1965–1966, professor, 1966–1982, director, graduate program in botany, 1972–1979

Concurrent Positions: Editor, *Botanical Gazette,* 1959–1965; visiting professor, Duke University, 1962; visiting research fellow, University of Melbourne, 1984–1985

Barbara Palser's research has been recognized by her contemporaries by her appointment as editor of the *Botanical Gazette.* After receiving her doctorate from the University of Chicago, she accepted an appointment as an instructor in botany at the same institution, and she was promoted to assistant professor in 1945, associate professor in 1951, and professor in 1960. She accepted an appointment as associate professor of botany at Rutgers in 1965, was promoted to professor in 1966 and named director of the graduate program in botany in 1972. She retired from Rutgers around 1979 and later was a visiting research fellow at the University of Melbourne. She received the Merit Award of the Botanical Society of America in 1985, and was awarded an honorary degree from Mount Holyoke College in 1978. She was president of the Botanical Society of America in 1976 and of the Torrey Botanical Club in 1968. She has been a member of the International Society of Plant Morphologists and the American Institute of Biological Sciences. Her research interests were anatomy and morphology of Pteridophytes, histological responses to growth-regulating substances, floral morphology and anatomy of angiosperms, and experimental anatomy. Her name was listed in the 1992–1993 edition of *American Men and Women of Science.*

Bibliography: American Men and Women of Science 7–18.

Parloa, Maria
(1843–1909)
home economics educator

Education: Maine Central Institute, 1871–1872
Employment: School teacher and owner, cooking school, 1877–1887; teacher, Boston Cooking School, 1879–1887; writer and lecturer, 1887–1909

Maria Parloa was a pioneer in home economics teaching. She was involved in the sessions that led to the formation of the American Home Economics Association, but she died about the time the organization was formed. She had supported herself as a hotel cook before she enrolled in the normal school, where she took teacher training. In 1872 she published *The Appledore Cook Book,* based on her experience as a cook. In 1878 she published a book on outdoor cooking, *Camp Cookery.* She opened her own cooking school in 1877, and she also was one of two teachers at the new Boston Cooking School, which opened in 1879. (The cooking schools served as important steps in the development of the profession of home economics.) She then published her textbook, *First Principles of Household Management and Cookery* (1879). She requested Ellen Richards (q.v.) to develop material on the chemistry of cooking and cleaning for her classes. She published *Miss Parloa's New Cook Book and Marketing Guide* (1881) and moved her school to New York City in 1883. She then published *Practical Cookery* (1884). She ceased teaching about 1887 and moved to Roxbury, Massachusetts, to concentrate on writing and lecturing. Beginning in 1891, she was a regular contributor to the *Ladies' Home Journal,* of which she was a part owner. She returned to New York City in 1898 to work with teacher training. She was a charter member of the Lake Placid conferences, which later became the American Home Economics Association.

Bibliography: Barr, Ernest S., *An Index to Biographical Fragments in Unspecialized Scientific Journals;* Herzenberg, Caroline L., *Women Scientists from Antiquity to the Present;* James, E. T., ed., *Notable American Women 1607–1950; National Union Catalog;* Shapiro, Laura, *Perfection Salad.*

Parsons, Elsie Worthington Clews
(1875–1941)
anthropologist and sociologist

Education: A.B., Barnard College, 1896, A.M., 1897, Ph.D., 1899
Employment: High school teacher, 1897; fellow, Barnard College, 1899–1902, lecturer in sociology, 1902–1905; independent research, field trips, and writing, 1900–1941
Married: Herbert Parsons, 1900

Elsie Parsons was recognized as one of the leading women anthropologists of this century. She was born into a wealthy family, but instead of spending her time on charitable work, she devoted her life first to sociology and then to anthropology. Her husband was a lawyer who at one time was a member of Congress; he supported her in her chosen career. They had six children, but only four survived childhood: Elsie, John, Herbert, and McIlvaine. She received all three degrees from Barnard College, and after marriage continued to teach at Barnard. Based on her lectures to her sociology classes, Elsie Parsons wrote *The Family* (1906), in which she brought sociological arguments to the feminine cause of equal opportunities for women. That was the first of more than 20 books. Her next was a study of sexual practices associated with various religions, *Religious Chastity* (1913), which she wrote under a pseudonym. Her other major books of this period were *The Old Fashioned Woman* (1913) and *Fear and Conventionality* (1914).

The direction of her research changed around 1915 when, on a trip to the Southwest with her husband, she first saw Native Americans in their environment. She then shifted from sociology to anthropology. Annually she made extended field trips to the pueblos, living with and interviewing the people there. These studies resulted in numerous books and scientific papers. Her major publication was the encyclopedic *Pueblo Indian Religion* (1939). She then extended her study of folklore to other groups such as the Gullahs of the Carolina coastal islands. One of her last research projects was investigating the degree of Spanish influence on twentieth-century Native American cultures. This work also resulted in several publications.

Since she was able to finance her own research, she could choose topics to study and could support unpopular causes, such as pacifism during World War I. She was a soft-spoken person who was very firm in her opinions, but able to substitute discussion for argument. She was elected president of the American Folklore Society (1918–1920), the American Ethnological Association (1923–1925), and the American Anthropological Association (1940–1941). A list of her publications was included in the *Journal of American Folklore* 56 (1943): 45–56. Her name was starred in the fourth through seventh editions of *American Men and Women of Science.*

Bibliography: *American Men and Women of Science 4–7;* Debus, A. G., ed., *World Who's Who in Science;* Herzenberg, Caroline L., *Women Scientists from Antiquity to the* *Present;* James, E. T., ed., *Notable American Women 1607–1950;* McHenry, Robert, ed., *Famous American Women;* Macksey, Joan and Kenneth Macksey, *The Book of Women's Achievements;* Rossiter, Margaret W., *Women Scientists in America;* Siegel, Patricia J. and Kay Thomas Finley, *Women in the Scientific Search;* Visher, Stephen S., *Scientists Starred 1903–1943 in "American Men of Science."*

Patch, Edith Marion
(1876–1954)
entomologist

Education: B.S., University of Minnesota, 1901; M.S., University of Maine, 1910; Ph.D., Cornell University, 1911

Employment: Instructor, high schools, 1901–1903; instructor in entomology, University of Maine, 1903–1904, head entomologist, experiment station, 1904–1937; emeritus entomologist

Edith Patch was recognized for her work in entomology by being named to head a state agency. She was known internationally as an authority on aphids. She was head of the Department of Entomology at the Maine Agricultural Experiment Station in Orono from 1904 to 1937. Since the station was affiliated with the University of Maine, she became the second woman to be appointed to the university faculty. Although she was interested in natural history, in college at the University of Minnesota she majored in English. She taught high school for two years while seeking a job in entomology. She received a position at the University of Maine in 1903 teaching entomology and agricultural English to prepare her for developing a department of entomology at the university in 1904. She continued her graduate education with a master's degree from Maine in 1910 and a doctorate from Cornell in 1911. In 1924 she was appointed head of the Maine experiment station, the first woman in the country to head such a facility. Her technical publications included 15 books and nearly 100 papers. In 1930 she was elected the first woman president of the Entomological Society of America. The University of Maine awarded her an honorary degree in 1937. After she retired, she wrote a number of nature books for children. One new genus and several species of insects were named in her honor. She also was a member of the American Association for the Advancement of Science, the American Society of Naturalists, and the American Association of Economic Entomologists. Her research was on economic and ecological entomology and the life histories and ecology of migratory aphids. A photograph was included in Marcia Bonta's *Women in the Field* and in Herbert Osborn's *Fragments of Entomological History.*

Bibliography: *American Men and Women of Science* 2–8; Bonta, Marcia M., *Women in the Field;* Herzenberg, Caroline L., *Women Scientists from Antiquity to the Present;* Mozans, H. J., *Women in Science; National Union Catalog;* Ogilvie, Marilyn B., *Women in Science;* Osborn, Herbert, *Fragments of Entomological History;* Rossiter, Margaret W., *Women Scientists in America.*

Patrick, Ruth
(1907–)
limnologist

Education: B.S., Coker College, 1929; M.S., University of Virginia, 1931, Ph.D. in botany, 1934

Employment: Assistant, Coker College, 1929; assistant, research, Temple University, 1934; assistant curator, Academy of Natural Sciences, Philadelphia, 1939–1947, chair, department of limnology, 1947–1973, curator of limnology, 1947–?, Francis Boyer research chair, 1973–, chair of board, 1973–1976,

Concurrent Positions: Curator, Leidy Micros. Society, 1939–1947; lecturer, University of Pennsylvania, 1952–1970, adjunct professor, 1970–; trustee, Coker College, 1941–; member of board, E. I. du Pont de Nemours and Company, 1972–; with American Philosophical Society expedition to Mexico, 1947; leader, Catherwood Expedition to Amazon River, 1955

Married: Charles Hodge, 1931

Ruth Patrick's invention of a device called the diatometer made it possible for the first time to determine accurately the presence of pollution in fresh water. She and Rachel Carson (q.v.) were the two women biologists largely responsible for ushering in the current concern with ecology. Ruth Patrick has specialized in limnology, the scientific study of freshwater ecosystems. Her specific expertise has been on diatoms, a family of microscopic one-celled algae that is the basic food for many organisms in the freshwater ecology. She was employed as an assistant at Coker College and Temple University before receiving her doctorate from the University of Virginia in 1934. She then was appointed an assistant curator at the Academy of Natural Sciences in Philadelphia and promoted to chair of the limnology department and curator of limnology in 1947. She was elected to a research chair in 1973. Her field trips took her as far as the Amazon. She received many honors, including honorary degrees from Swarthmore College, Drexel

University, the University of Massachusetts, and Princeton University. She was elected to membership in the National Academy of Sciences in 1970. In 1975 she was awarded the $150,000 John and Alice Tyler Ecology Award. She was the first woman elected chair of the board of the Academy of Natural Sciences and the first woman director at Du Pont. She was elected president of the Phycological Society of America (1954–1957) and of the American Society of Naturalists (1975–1977). She also was a member of the Botanical Society of America, the American Society of Limnology and Oceanography, the American Institute of Biological Sciences, the Ecological Society of America, and the American Society of Plant Taxonomists. She wrote *Groundwater Contamination in the United States* (1983, 1987). Her research included taxonomy, ecology, and physiology of diatoms; the biodynamic cycle of rivers; and forces that determine the diversity of ecosystems.

Bibliography: *American Men and Women of Science* 6–17; Barnhart, John H., *Biographical Notes upon Botanists*; Bonta, Marcia M., *Women in the Field*; Herzenberg, Caroline L., *Women Scientists from Antiquity to the Present*; O'Neill, Lois S., *The Women's Book of World Records and Achievements*.

Patterson, Flora Wambaugh
(1847–1928)
vegetable pathologist and mycologist

Education: Antioch College, 1860; Cincinnati Wesleyan College, 1865, A.M., 1883; Radcliffe College, 1892–1895; A.M., University of Iowa, 1895

Employment: Assistant, Gray Herbarium, Harvard University, 1895; private school instructor, 1896; assistant pathologist in charge of the herbarium, U.S. Department of Agriculture, 1896–1901, mycologist in charge of pathological collections, Bureau of Plant Industry, 1901–1923

Married: Edwin Patterson, 1869

Flora Patterson was the second woman scientist who was employed by the U.S. Department of Agriculture (USDA); the first was Effie (Southworth) Spalding (q.v.). Patterson's husband was injured in an accident, requiring her to support him and their two sons. She had received some college education at Antioch and at Cincinnati Wesleyan College prior to her marriage; and when she was forced to support her family, she completed her master's degree from Cincinnati in 1883 and another from the University of Iowa in 1895. She worked as an assistant at the Gray Herbarium and in a private school before obtaining a position at the USDA in 1896, where she remained until retiring in 1923. One benefit of working for the USDA was that women were permitted to publish their research under their own names. Flora Patterson published a dozen or so papers in addition to the publications she prepared in the USDA series. She was coauthor of "Mushrooms and Other Common Fungi" (Bulletin 175, 1915) with Vera Charles (q.v.). She was a member of the American Association for the Advancement of Science, the American Phytopathological Society, and the Botanical Society of America. Her research included fungal diseases of plants and insects and systematic mycology. She wrote the chapter on plant pathology in Catherine Filene's *Careers for Women* (1920). Her papers are listed in *Mycologia* 21 (1929): 1–4 and

Phytopathology 18 (1928): 877–879; her photograph is included in the former. Her photograph also is on file at the National Archives. Her name was listed in the first edition of *American Men and Women of Science.*

Bibliography: *American Men and Women of Science* 1–4; Baker, Gladys L., "Women in the U.S. Department of Agriculture";

Barnhart, John H., *Biographical Notes upon Botanists;* Herzenberg, Caroline L., *Women Scientists from Antiquity to the Present; National Union Catalog;* Ogilvie, Marilyn B., *Women in Science;* Rossiter, Margaret W., *Women Scientists in America;* Rudolph, Emanuel D., "Women in Nineteenth Century American Botany"; Siegel, Patricia J. and Kay Thomas Finley, *Women in the Scientific Search.*

Payne, Nellie Maria de Cottrell
(b. 1900)
entomologist and agricultural chemist

Education: B.S., Kansas State College, 1920, M.S., 1921; Ph.D. in entomology, University of Minnesota, 1925

Employment: Assistant zoologist and entomologist, Kansas State, 1918–1921; instructor in chemistry and math, Lindenwood College, 1921–1922; assistant entomologist, University of Minnesota, 1922–1925, lecturer, 1933–1937; National Research Foundation fellow, University of Pennsylvania, 1925–1927; scientific staff, *Biological Abstracts,* 1927–1933; assistant research entomologist, American Cyanamid Company, 1937–1943, entomologist, 1943–1944, zoologist, 1944–1957; literature chemist, Velsicol Chemical Corporation, 1957–1971; consultant

Concurrent Positions: Research investigator, University of Vienna and University of Berlin, 1930–1931

Nellie Payne was recognized for her research in entomology. She had a varied career, involving both academic and corporate appointments. She was employed as an assistant zoologist and entomologist while she was working toward both her bachelor and master's degrees at Kansas State. She taught one year in chemistry and mathematics at Lindenwood College, then received an appointment as assistant entomologist while she completed her doctorate at the University of Minnesota. After positions as a fellow at the University of Pennsylvania and a member of the scientific staff of the major index *Biological Abstracts,* she returned to Minnesota as a lecturer for five years. She was appointed entomologist and zoologist in research at American Cyanamid in 1937. In 1957 she accepted a position as a

literature chemist at Velsicol Chemical, then became a consultant starting in 1971. She described herself as an entomologist and an agricultural chemist in *American Men and Women of Science.* The term *agricultural chemist* was used synonymously with *biochemist* through the 1960s. Nellie Payne seemed to be interested in indexing and abstracting throughout her career.

She worked for *Biological Abstracts* for about six years and then for a corporation in the 1960s. One of her consultancies was with the information center of the Entomological Society of America. (Prior to the 1960s many companies would hire women as literature chemists instead of placing them in research laboratories, but the equal opportunity in employment legislation opened up many positions for women scientists in industry. Today corporations hire both men and women scientists in their information centers in an effort to keep abreast of both the internal and external research data that are pouring out.) She was elected a fellow of the American Association for the Advancement of Science, the Entomological Society of America, and the American Institute of Chemists. She also was a member of the American Chemical Society, the Biometric Society, the American Society of Zoologists, and the New York Academy of Sciences.

Her research included hydroid pigments, hibernation and low temperature effect in insects, and mathematics of population growth. Her photograph was included in Herbert Osborn's *Fragments of Entomological History.*

Bibliography: *American Men and Women of Science* 4–12; *National Union Catalog;* Osborn, Herbert, *Fragments of Entomological History.*

Payne-Gaposchkin, Cecelia Helena
(1900–1979)
astronomer

Education: A.B., Newnham College, Cambridge University, 1923; Ph.D. in astronomy, Radcliffe College, 1925
Employment: National Research fellow, Harvard University, 1925–1927, astronomer, Harvard College Observatory, 1927–1938, Phillips astronomer, 1938–1967, Phillips professor of astronomy and chair of department, Harvard University, 1956–1967; member of staff, Smithsonian Astrophysical Observatory, 1967–1979; emeritus professor
Married: Sergei I. Gaposchkin, 1934

Cecelia Payne-Gaposchkin, an authority on variable stars and galactic structure, was the first woman to achieve the rank of full professor at Harvard. After receiving her undergraduate degree from Cambridge in 1923, she won a National Research Fellowship to study at Radcliffe and to work at the Harvard College Observatory. In 1925 she was the first scholar at Radcliffe to receive a doctorate in astronomy. She continued working at the Observatory and was appointed a permanent member of the staff in 1927. She was promoted to Phillips astronomer in 1938 and then Phillips professor of astronomy and chair of the department at Harvard in 1956. After she retired in 1967, she became a staff member at the Smithsonian Astrophysical Observatory. When Cecelia Payne-Gaposchkin received her doctorate in astronomy in 1925, it changed the career pattern for women astronomers. When

doctoral degrees became part of the career pattern, the possibilities for women to broaden their research opportunities became more promising because they were branching out into areas other than variable stars and stellar spectra, the traditional areas for women. Later in her career Payne-Gaposchkin examined galactic structure and novae.

Early in her career she developed new techniques for ascertaining stellar magnitudes from photographic plates. She applied these techniques to a large collection of photographic plates dating back to 1890 that was stored at the observatory. In the mid-1930s she concentrated on the study of variable stars. The research team made several million observations over the entire sky. She collaborated with her husband and other staff members in her research and also worked independently in some areas. She received the Annie J. Cannon Prize of the

American Astronomical Society in 1935. In addition to her scientific publications, she was the author of several books, including *Variable Stars* (1938), *Stars in the Making* (1952), *Variable Stars and Galactic Structure* (1954), and *Galactic Novae* (1957). She was a member of the American Astronomical Society, the American Philosophical Society, the American Academy of Arts and Sciences, and the Royal Astronomical Society. She and her husband had three children, Edward, Katherine, and Peter. There are photographs in *Current Biography* and in P.B. Abir-Am's and Dorinda Outram's *Uneasy Careers and Intimate Lives.* Her name was starred in the fourth through the seventh editions of *American Men and Women of Science.* She was listed under Gaposchkin and Payne-Gaposchkin in the sources.

Bibliography: Abir-Am, P. G. and Dorinda Outram, eds., *Uneasy Careers and Intimate Lives; American Men and Women of Science 4–13; Current Biography;* Debus, A. G., ed., *World Who's Who in Science;* Herzenberg, Caroline L., *Women Scientists from Antiquity to the Present;* Kass-Simon, G. and Patricia Farnes, *Women of Science;* O'Neill, Lois S., *The Women's Book of World Records and Achievements;* Rossiter, Margaret W., *Women Scientists in America;* Siegel, Patricia J. and Kay Thomas Finley, *Women in the Scientific Search;* Visher, Stephen S., *Scientists Starred 1903–1943 in "American Men of Science."*

Pearce, Louise
(1885–1959)
pathologist

Education: A.B., Stanford University, 1907; Boston University school of medicine, 1907–1908; M.D., Johns Hopkins University school of medicine, 1912; intern, Johns Hopkins Hospital, 1912

Employment: Fellow, Rockefeller Institute for Medical Research, 1913–1923, associate member, 1923–1951

*L*ouise Pearce was one of the foremost American women scientists of her day. She was one of the principal figures in developing the drug tryparsamide to control African sleeping sickness. She went herself to the Belgian Congo in 1920 to supervise tests of the drug on humans. She spent her entire career at the Rockefeller Institute for Medical Research after receiving her M.D. from Johns Hopkins, and her work included the biology of infectious and inherited diseases, such as syphilis and smallpox. In her study of syphilis in rabbits, she found that it closely resembled the human variety. The observations were therefore valuable to students of immunity and to physicians engaged in treating syphilitic patients. She and her collaborators found a tumor in rabbits that was capable of being grown. The Brown-Pearce tumor, for years the only known transplantable tumor of the rabbit, was studied by cancer laboratories worldwide.

The breeding program and studies led the research team to isolate a virus similar to human smallpox when an epidemic of rabbit pox nearly destroyed the carefully developed rabbit colony. In the 1930s the team enlarged its breeding program for rabbits, and by 1940 more than two dozen hereditary diseases and deformities were represented in the rabbit colony. Unfortunately many of Louise Pearce's files were destroyed after her death, and she had not completed writing up the results of all of her research. She did much to advance the cause of women in medicine and science. She served as a member of the board of the Woman's Medical College of Philadelphia from 1941 to 1946 and as president from 1946 to 1951. She was twice decorated by the Belgian government for her work on sleeping sickness.

Bibliography: Herzenberg, Caroline L., *Women Scientists from Antiquity to the Present;* Rossiter, Margaret W., *Women Scientists in America;* Sicherman, Barbara et al., *Notable American Women;* Siegel, Patricia J. and Kay Thomas Finley, *Women in the Scientific Search.*

Peck, Annie Smith
(1850–1935)
archaeologist and explorer

Education: A.B., University of Michigan, 1878, A.M., 1881; studied German and music in Hanover, Germany, 1884; American School of Classical Studies, Athens, 1885
Employment: Schoolteacher, 1872–1874, 1878–1881; professor of Latin and elocution, Purdue University, 1881–1883; Latin teacher, Smith College, 1886–1887; lecturer on classic art and archaeology, 1888–1935; explorer, 1888–1935

Annie Peck was known for her success at climbing mountains, but the popular press usually did not mention her successes as an archaeologist. She was the first woman student to be admitted to the American School in Athens in 1885. The same year she started training herself as a mountain climber in both Europe and the United States; her first important climb was Mount Shasta in 1888. Her career started in a prosaic manner following the pattern of many women of her generation. She taught school for a number of years while obtaining her undergraduate and master's degrees from the University of Michigan. In 1881 she obtained a position as professor of Latin and elocution at Purdue and left to study German and music in Germany in 1884. After completing the course at the American School, she was employed as a Latin teacher at Smith for a year and then spent the rest of her life as a lecturer on classic art and architecture and as an explorer. She received international fame when she climbed the Matterhorn in 1895. Her other firsts were Mount Sorato in Bolivia in 1904, Mount Huascaran in Peru in 1908, and Mount Coropuna in Peru in

1911. Although her mountain climbing has been emphasized in biographies, she had a solid background in classics, and she contributed scientific data by measuring the mountains she explored. Her climbing costume shocked people because she wore knickerbockers, a tunic, and a felt hat tied by a veil; at that time women did not wear slacks or jeans. It is amazing how she succeeded in many of her climbs without oxygen. She continued mountain climbing until she reached her eighty-second birthday, and was a founder of the American Alpine Club. There is an extensive biography in *Women of the Four Winds* (1985) by Elizabeth F. Olds, and photographs are included in Joan Marlow's *The Great Women* and in the *National Cyclopedia of American Biography.*

Bibliography: Herzenberg, Caroline L., *Women Scientists from Antiquity to the Present;* James, E. T., ed., *Notable American Women 1607–1950;* McHenry, Robert, ed., *Famous American Women;* Macksey, Joan and Kenneth Macksey, *The Book of Women's Achievements;* Marlow, Joan, *The Great Women; National Cyclopedia of American Biography.*

Peckham, Elizabeth Gifford
(1854–1940)
arachnologist and entomologist

Education: B.A., Vassar College, 1876, A.M., 1889; Ph.D., Cornell University, 1916
Employment: Author
Married: George W. Peckham, 1880, died 1914

Elizabeth Peckham was recognized by her contemporaries for her research on spiders and wasps. She coauthored the majority of her husband's publications, but she was one of the few scientists' wives who received credit for her individual research. (It always has been a problem to determine how much independent research the wives of scientists conducted. In the eighteenth and nineteenth centuries science was a family endeavor. Women worked with husbands, fathers, or brothers either in home laboratories or in museums and colleges with minimum or no salaries.) Elizabeth Peckham had a solid educational background, with an undergraduate degree from Vassar in 1876, a master's degree in 1889, and a doctorate from Cornell in 1916. She received her doctorate after she was widowed in 1914. At the time, Cornell had one of the preeminent programs in entomology in the nation. She was listed as the first author of *Wasps Social and Solitary* (1905). Many of the couple's publications appeared in a series issued by the Geological and Natural History Survey of Wisconsin and by the Wisconsin Academy of Sciences, Arts, and Letters. Her research interests were hymenoptera and arachnology. The couple had three children. She was listed in the first three editions of *American Men and Women of Science,* but as Mrs. George W. Peckham. Her photograph was included in Herbert Osborn's *Fragments of Entomological History.*

Bibliography: American Men and Women of Science 1–3; Bonta, Marcia M., *Women in the Field*; Herzenberg, Caroline L., *Women Scientists from Antiquity to the Present*; National Union Catalog; Ogilvie, Marilyn B., *Women in Science*; Osborn, Herbert, *Fragments of Entomological History*; Siegel, Patricia J. and Kay Thomas Finley, *Women in the Scientific Search.*

Peebles, Florence
(1874–1958)
zoologist

Education: A.B., Goucher College, 1895; Woods Hole Marine Laboratory, 1895–1897; Bryn Mawr College, 1895–1897, Ph.D., 1900; University of Halle and University of Munich, 1898–1899; American Woman's Table, Naples Zoological Station, 1898, 1901, 1907–1913; University of Bonn, 1905; University of Wurzburg, 1911; University of Freiburg, 1913
Employment: Assistant in biology, Bryn Mawr College, 1897–1898; instructor, Goucher College, 1899–1902, associate professor, 1902–1906; lecturer, Bryn Mawr, 1913; professor of biology, Newcomb College, Tulane University, 1915–1917; associate professor of physiology, Bryn Mawr, 1917–1919; professor of biology, California Christian College, 1928–1935; biologist, Chapman College, 1935–?

Florence Peebles was recognized for her work on problems of tissue determination during regeneration and development, focusing on external influences. Her name was starred in the first seven editions of *American Men and Women of Science*. She was appointed an assistant in biology at Bryn Mawr in 1897 while she was completing her doctorate, which she received in 1900. This was interspersed with further work at the Universities of Halle and Munich and at the Naples Zoological Station. She received an appointment at Goucher College in 1899 as an instructor, being promoted to associate professor in 1902. She continued taking advanced work at the Universities of Bonn, Wurzburg, and Freiburg and at the Naples Zoological Station interspersed with lecturing at Bryn Mawr in 1913. Between 1898 and 1927 she worked five times at the Naples Zoological Station, and ten times at the Woods Hole Marine Laboratory between 1895 and 1924. Since she was recognized as an important contributor to scientific literature, she received support from fellowships for many of these sessions. She held a position at Newcomb College in 1915, returning to Bryn Mawr in 1917. After retiring in 1928, she established a bacteriology department at California Christian College in 1928, then moved to Chapman College in 1935 to found a biology laboratory. She received an honorary degree from Goucher in 1954. She was a member of the American Association for the Advancement of Science and the American Society of Naturalists. Her research included the morphology of regeneration, growth and development, and the embryology of chicks. Her photograph was included in G. Kass-Simon's and Patricia Farnes' *Women of Science*.

Bibliography: *American Men and Women of Science* 1–10; Herzenberg, Caroline L., *Women Scientists from Antiquity to the Present*; Kass-Simon, G. and Patricia Farnes, *Women of Science*; Ogilvie, Marilyn B., *Women in Science*; Rossiter, Margaret W., *Women Scientists in America*; Siegel, Patricia J. and Kay Thomas Finley, *Women in the Scientific Search*; Visher, Stephen S., *Scientists Starred 1903–1943 in "American Men of Science."*

Pennington, Mary Engle
(1872–1952)
chemist

Education: Certificate of proficiency, University of Pennsylvania, 1892, Ph.D., 1895, fellow in botany, 1895–1897; fellow in physiological chemistry, Yale University, 1897–1898
Employment: Research, University of Pennsylvania, 1898–1901; director of chemical laboratory, Woman's Medical College of Pennsylvania, 1898–1906, lecturer, 1898–1906; owner, Philadelphia Chemical Laboratory, 1901–1905; director, bacteriological laboratory, Philadelphia Health Department, 1904–1907; bacteriological chemist, Bureau of Chemistry, U.S. Department of Agriculture, 1907–1908, chief, Food Research Laboratory, 1908–1919; director of research and development department, American Balsa Company, 1919–1922; owner, consulting firm, 1922–1952

Mary Pennington was a chemist and authority on food refrigeration. Her name was starred in the second through the seventh editions of *American Men and Women of Science*. Although she completed the requirements for a B.S. at the University of Pennsylvania, she was given a certificate of proficiency instead of a degree because she was a woman. She then continued working on her doctorate, which she received in 1895. She studied an additional two years and then moved to Yale for another year of study in physiological chemistry. Since there were no positions available in Philadelphia, she opened her own laboratory for chemical analysis, the Philadelphia Chemical Laboratory. She was appointed a lecturer at the Woman's Medical College of Pennsylvania. Next she became director of the laboratory for the Philadelphia Health Department, where she developed methods for preserving dairy products and standards for milk inspection that later were employed throughout the country.

She was appointed a bacteriological chemist with the Bureau of Chemistry of the U.S. Department of Agriculture (USDA) in 1907 by taking the civil service exam as M. E. Pennington and accepting the job before the officials knew she was a woman. She used the same strategy when she was made chief of the Food Research Laboratory of USDA in 1908. She conducted a series of studies that led to methods of processing, storing, and shipping food that greatly increased its quality and availability. During World War I she devised standards for railroad refrigerator cars that were used nationally. In 1919 she accepted a position as director of research and development at American Balsa Company, where she continued her work on the chemistry and bacteriology of foods and food processing. In her consulting office in New York City starting in 1922, she specialized on food handling, storage, and transportation for the next 30 years. She also did original research on frozen foods; one popular article referred to her as the Ice Lady.

She was awarded the Garvan Medal in 1940. She was the first woman member of the American Society of Refrigerating Engineers and was the first woman elected to the American Poultry Historical Society's Hall of Fame. She was a member of the American Association for the Advancement of Science, the American Chemical Society, the American Society of Biological Chemists, and the Society of American Bacteriologists. Her research interests included bacteriological chemistry; chemico-bacteriology of milk; chemistry, bacteriology, and histology of fresh foods; and food refrigeration. Her photograph was published in *Chemtech* 6 (1976): 738–743.

Bibliography: *American Men and Women of Science* 1–8; Baker, Gladys L., "Women in the U.S. Department of Agriculture"; Barnhart, John H., *Biographical Notes upon Botanists*; Goff, Alice C., *Women Can Be Engineers*; Harshberger, John W., *The Botanists of Philadelphia and Their Work*; Herzenberg, Caroline L., *Women Scientists from Antiquity to the Present*; Macksey, Joan and Kenneth Macksey, *The Book of Women's Achievements*; Mozans, H. J., *Women in Science*; Ogilvie, Marilyn B., *Women in Science*; O'Neill, Lois S., *The Women's Book of World Records and Achievements*; Rossiter, Margaret W., *Women Scientists in America*; Rossiter, Margaret W., "Women Scientists in America before 1920"; Sicherman, Barbara et al., *Notable American Women*; Siegel, Patricia J. and Kay Thomas Finley, *Women in the Scientific Search*; Vare, Ethlie Ann and Greg Ptacek, *Mothers of Invention*; Visher, Stephen S., *Scientists Starred 1903–1943 in "American Men of Science"*; Yost, Edna, *American Women of Science*.

Petermann, Mary Locke
(1908–1976)
biochemist

Education: A.B., Smith College, 1929; Ph.D. in physiological chemistry, University of Wisconsin, 1939

Employment: Alumni Foundation fellow, University of Wisconsin, 1939–1942; professional assistant, Committee on Medical Research, 1942–1944; Rockefeller Foundation fellow, Finney Howell, 1944–1945; research chemist, Memorial Hospital, New York, 1945–1946; fellow, Finney Howell, 1946–1948; associate, Sloan-Kettering Institute for Cancer Research, 1946–1960, associate member, 1960–1963, member, 1963–1976; associate professor of biochemistry, Sloan-Kettering Division, medical college, Cornell University, 1952–1966, professor, 1966–1976

Mary Petermann was the first person to isolate and characterize animal ribosomes, and in 1963 she became the first woman appointed a member of the Sloan-Kettering Institute for Cancer Research in New York City. After receiving her doctorate in physiological chemistry at the University of Wisconsin in 1939, she held several fellowships. She was appointed an associate at Sloan-Kettering in 1946, then promoted to associate member in 1960 and member in 1963. Concurrently she was appointed associate professor of biochemistry at the medical college of Cornell University in 1952, being promoted to professor in 1966. She was awarded an honorary degree by Smith College in 1966. Among the awards she received were the Sloan Award in cancer research in 1963 and the Garvan Medal in 1966. She was the author of *The Physical and Chemical Properties of Ribosomes* (1964). She was elected a fellow of the New York Academy of Sciences, and was a member of the American Society of Biological Chemists, the Harvey Society, and the Biophysical Society. Among the fellowships she received were the Wisconsin Alumni Foundation fellow (1939–1942), the Rockefeller Foundation fellow (1944–1945), and the Finney Howell fellow (1946–1948). Her research included the physical chemistry of proteins, electrophoresis, plasma proteins, and ribosomes.

Bibliography: *American Men and Women of Science* 7–13; Debus, A. G., ed., *World Who's Who in Science;* Herzenberg, Caroline L., *Women Scientists from Antiquity to the Present; National Union Catalog;* O'Neill, Lois S., *The Women's Book of World Records and Achievements.*

Phelps, Almira Hart Lincoln
(1793–1884)
science author and educator

Education: Public schools, private academies

Employment: Teacher, public schools, 1813–1817; teacher, Troy Female Seminary, 1823–1831; principal of various schools for young ladies, 1838–1856

Married: Simeon Lincoln, 1817, died 1823; John Phelps, 1831, died 1849

lmira Phelps was an early educator who wrote popular science textbooks. Her *Familiar Lectures on Botany* (1829) went through numerous editions and sold thousands of copies. She was greatly influenced in her teaching by her sister, Emma Willard, who developed a model boarding school for girls called the Troy Female Seminary. She taught in various public schools and opened a boarding school for a time before her marriage to Simeon Lincoln, a newspaper editor. After he died in 1823 of yellow fever, she returned to teaching at her sister's school. *Familiar Lectures* launched Almira Phelps's career as the author of popular texts on chemistry, geology, botany, and natural philosophy. These included *Chemistry for Beginners* (1834) and *Familiar Lectures on Natural Philosophy* (1837). After she married John Phelps in 1831, the couple operated a series of schools, with Mr. Phelps acting as business manager and Almira as principal. Her best work was done at the female institute at Ellicott's Mills, Maryland, where much of the course of study, especially in the sciences, was of collegiate quality. The school trained homemakers and teachers, the only careers open to young ladies at the time. She was elected in 1859 as the second woman member of the American Association for the Advancement of Science; the first woman was the astronomer Maria Mitchell (q.v.). Although the early editions of

Familiar Lectures adhered to the strict Linnaean system of classification, by the fifth edition she was including the natural system that currently was being used. She had three children in her first marriage and two in her second. She retired in 1856 and died in 1884. Her biography is *Almira Hart Lincoln Phelps: Her Life and Work* (1936) by Emma L. Bolzau. Her photograph is included in Lois Arnold's *Four Lives in Science.*

Bibliography: Abir-Am, P. G. and Dorinda Outram, eds., *Uneasy Careers and Intimate Lives; Appleton's Cyclopaedia of American Biography;* Arnold, Lois B., *Four Lives in Science;* Barnhart, John H., *Biographical Notes upon Botanists; Dictionary of American Biography;* Elliott, Clark A., *Biographical Dictionary of American Science;* James, E. T., ed., *Notable American Women 1607–1950;* Herzenberg, Caroline L., *Women Scientists from Antiquity to the Present;* Kass-Simon, G. and Patricia Farnes, *Women of Science;* McHenry, Robert, ed., *Famous American Women;* Mozans, H. J., *Women in Science; National Cyclopedia of American Biography; National Union Catalog;* Ogilvie, Marilyn B., *Women in Science;* Rossiter, Margaret W., *Women Scientists in America;* Rudolph, Emanuel D., "Women in Nineteenth Century American Botany"; Siegel, Patricia J. and Kay Thomas Finley, *Women in the Scientific Search.*

Phelps, Martha Austin
(1870–1933)
chemist

Education: B.S., Smith College, 1892; Ph.D., Yale University, 1898
Employment: High school teacher, 1892–1896; analyst, Rhode Island Experiment Station, 1900–1901; teacher, high school, 1901–1903; chemistry and physics teacher, Wilson College, 1903–1904; analyst, U.S. Bureau of Standards, 1908–1909
Married: Isaac K. Phelps, 1904

Martha Phelps was among the first women scientists employed by the Bureau of Standards. Her name was included in the first three editions of *American Men and Women of Science*. Her career followed the pattern of many women scientists of her generation. After receiving her undergraduate degree from Smith in 1892, she worked as a high school teacher for several years before returning to school at Yale, where she received her doctorate in 1898. She worked for a few years at the Rhode Island experiment station and, in what seems surprising today, taught high school again before accepting a position as a chemistry and physics teacher at Wilson College for two years. After her marriage in 1904, she worked for the Bureau of Standards starting in 1908. She and her husband published a number of articles in the *American Journal of Science* on the quantitative analysis of several elements. These include the double ammonium phosphates in the analysis of magnesium, zinc, and cadmium; gravimetric determination of phosphoric acid; and salts of manganese in analysis.

Bibliography: *American Men and Women of Science 1–3*; Herzenberg, Caroline L., *Women Scientists from Antiquity to the Present*; Siegel, Patricia J. and Kay Thomas Finley, *Women in the Scientific Search*.

Phillips, Melba Newell
(1907–)
physicist

Education: A.B., Oakland City College, 1926; A.M., Battle Creek College, 1928; Ph.D. in physics, University of California, Berkeley, 1933

Employment: High school teacher, 1926–1927; instructor, Battle Creek College, 1928–1930; research associate, University of California, Berkeley, 1933–1934, instructor, 1934–1935; research fellow, Bryn Mawr College, 1935–1936; fellow, Institute for Advanced Study, 1936–1937; instructor of physics, Connecticut College, 1937–1938; instructor, Brooklyn College, 1938–1944, assistant professor, 1944–1952; lecturer in physics and associate director, academic year institute, Washington University, St. Louis, 1957–1962; professor of physics, University of Chicago, 1962–1972; emeritus professor

Concurrent Positions: Visiting professor, State University of New York, Stony Brook, 1972–1975; lecturer, University of Minnesota, 1941–1944; member, theoretical group, radio research laboratory, Harvard University, 1944; acting executive officer, American Association of Physics Teachers, 1975–1977

Melba Phillips has been recognized for her work in teaching physics more than for her research. She has had a remarkable career, starting at tiny Oakland City College and retiring as a professor of physics at the University of Chicago. Her career followed the pattern of many women scientists in that she taught high school after receiving her undergraduate degree. She then was an instructor at Battle Creek College for three years after receiving her master's degree from that institution. She worked as an instructor at Berkeley after receiving her doctorate in 1933. Jobs were difficult to find during the Depression, but she was appointed an instructor at Connecticut College for two years. She was appointed an instructor at Brooklyn College in 1938, being promoted to assistant professor in 1944. She was a lecturer in physics at Washington University in 1957, but left in 1962 to join the University of Chicago as a professor, retiring in 1972. After retiring she was a visiting lecturer at the State University of New York at Stony Brook for four years. She has received several awards, including the Oerstad Medal of the American Association of Physics Teachers in 1974 and the Compton Award of the American Institute of Physics in 1981. The American Association of Physics Teachers established in her honor the Melba Newell Phillips Award, of which she was the first recipient in 1982. She was president of this association from 1966 to 1967. She was elected a fellow of the American Physical Society, and she has been a member of the American Association for the Advancement of Science. Her research includes theory of complex spectra and theory of light nuclei. Her name was listed in the 1992–1993 edition of *American Men and Women of Science.*

Bibliography: *American Men and Women of Science* 6–18; Herzenberg, Caroline L., *Women Scientists from Antiquity to the Present;* Kass-Simon, G. and Patricia Farnes, *Women of Science;* Rossiter, Margaret W., *Women Scientists in America.*

Pinckney, Eliza Lucas
(1723–1793)
agronomist

Education: No formal education
Employment: No formal employment
Married: Charles Pinckney, 1744, died 1758

Eliza Pinckney often is mentioned as one of the pioneer women agriculturists in the United States in the eighteenth century. She was noted for her success in the cultivation of indigo on the family's South Carolina plantation. While her father was away acting as lieutenant governor of Antigua, she experimented with growing indigo to break South Carolina's dependence on the single crop of rice. She experimented with various plants that he sent her from the West Indies, including ginger, figs, cotton, and alfalfa. She was able to develop a superior indigo plant that rivaled the quality of the French product when the blue dye was extracted. For more than three decades, South Carolina thrived on the income derived from her blue dye cakes, freeing itself from both British exports and ties to the French-controlled Caribbean. Eliza married Charles Pinckney in 1744 and moved to Charleston, South Carolina. At his plantation she experimented with the cultivation of silkworms. After her husband's death in 1758, she managed the plantation while her sons were at school in England. Her sons, Charles and Thomas, became heroes of the American Revolution. Both continued their mother's tradition of experimental agriculture, and Charles was one of the first planters to grow cotton. Charles represented South Carolina at the Constitutional Convention, served on the special mission to France, and was the candidate of the Federalist party for president in 1804 and 1808. Thomas was governor of the state in 1787 and later minister to Great Britain and special commissioner to Spain.

Bibliography: Abir-Am, P. G. and Dorinda Outram, eds., *Uneasy Careers and Intimate Lives*; Herzenberg, Caroline L., *Women Scientists from Antiquity to the Present*; James, E. T., ed., *Notable American Women 1607–1950*; Macksey, Joan and Kenneth Macksey, *The Book of Women's Achievements*; Rossiter, Margaret W., *Women Scientists in America*; Vare, Ethlie Ann and Greg Ptacek, *Mothers of Invention*.

Pitelka, Dorothy Riggs
(1920–)
zoologist

Education: B.A., University of Colorado, 1941; fellow, University of California, Berkeley, 1943–1945, Ph.D. in zoology, 1948

Employment: Assistant in zoology, University of California, Berkeley, 1941–1943, 1945–1946, lecturer, 1949–1952, assistant research zoologist, 1953–1960, associate research zoologist, 1960–1966, research zoologist, 1966–1984, adjunct professor of zoology, 1971–1984; emeritus research zoologist and emeritus adjunct professor of zoology

Concurrent Position: Fellow, University of Paris, 1957–1958

Married: Frank A. Pitelka, 1943

Dorothy Pitelka has been recognized for her research on protozoa. She spent her entire career at the University of California, Berkeley, after receiving her doctorate in 1948. She was first appointed lecturer in 1949, after which she was promoted to assistant research zoologist in 1953, associate research zoologist in 1960, and research zoologist in 1966. She was named adjunct professor of zoology in 1971 and then emeritus research zoologist and emeritus adjunct professor of zoology in 1985. In addition to her scientific papers she published *Electron-Microscopic Structure of Protozoa* (1963). She served on the editorial boards of three journals: *Journal of Protozoology, Journal of Morphology,* and *Transactions of the American Microscopical Society.* She was elected president of the Society of Protozoologists, serving from 1964 to 1967. She has been a member of the American Association for the Advancement of Science, the American Society for Cell Biology, the American Association of Cancer Research, and the Tissue Culture Association. Her research has included ultrastructure, function, and carcinogenesis in mammary glands; epithelial cell differentiation in cell culture; interactions of epithelium and stroma; and the ultrastructure and morphogenesis of protozoa. She is the mother of three children, Louis, Wenzel, and Kazl Helen. Her name was included in the 1992–1993 edition of *American Men and Women of Science.*

Bibliography: *American Men and Women of Science* 6–18; Debus, A. G., ed., *World Who's Who in Science*; Herzenberg, Caroline L., *Women Scientists from Antiquity to the Present; National Union Catalog.*

Pittman, Margaret
(1901–)
bacteriologist

Education: A.B., Hendrix College, 1923; M.S., University of Chicago, 1926, Ph.D. in bacteriology, 1929

Employment: Principal, Galloway Woman's College, 1923–1925; fellow, influenza commission, Metropolitan Life Insurance Company, 1926–1928; assistant, Rockefeller Institute for Medical Research, 1928–1934; assistant bacteriologist, New York State Department of Health, 1934–1936; associate bacteriologist, U.S. Public Health Service, 1936–1941, bacteriologist, 1941–1947, senior bacteriologist, 1948–1954, principal bacteriologist, 1954–1958, bacteriologist and chief, laboratory of bacterial products, division of biological standards, 1958–1971, guest worker, 1971–1972; guest worker and consultant, center for biological evaluation and research, Food and Drug Administration, 1972–1975

Concurrent Positions: Consultant, World Health Organization, 1958–1959, 1962, 1969, 1971–1973; U.S. Pharmacopeia Panels, 1966–1975; guest lecturer, Howard University, 1967–1970

M*argaret Pittman* has been famous for her work standardizing the pertussis vaccine for whooping cough. She has been involved internationally on standardizing vaccines for whooping cough, cholera, and typhoid. After several jobs that involved short-term employment, she joined the U.S. Public Health Service in 1936, where she advanced quickly through the ranks to chief of the laboratory of bacterial products in 1958. After her official retirement from the National Institutes of Health in 1971, she continued to consult and work for the Food and Drug Administration. She was a consultant for the World Health Organization numerous times and was active on the U.S. Pharmacopeia Panels.

She has received numerous awards and honors, such as the Superior Service Award in 1963 and the Distinguished Service Award in 1968 from the Department of Health, Education, and Welfare; the Federal Woman's Award (1970); and the Alice Evans Award from the American Society for Microbiology (1990). She has been a member of the American Association for the Advancement of Science, the American Academy of Microbiology, the Society for Experimental Biology and Medicine, and the International Association of Biological Standardization. Her research has included work on pneumococcus, meningococcus, tetanus toxoid, pertussis, and vaccine standards. Her name was included in the 1992–1993 edition of *American Men and Women of Science.*

Bibliography: American Men and Women of Science 6–18; Debus, A. G., ed., *World Who's Who in Science;* Herzenberg, Caroline L., *Women Scientists from Antiquity to the Present;* O'Neill, Lois S., *The Women's Book of World Records and Achievements;* Rossiter, Margaret W., *Women Scientists in America.*

Pool, Judith Graham
(1919–1975)
physiologist

Education: B.S., University of Chicago, 1939, Ph.D. in physiology, 1946

Employment: Assistant in physiology, University of Chicago, 1940–1942; instructor in physics, Hobart and William Smith colleges, 1943–1945; assistant in physiology and pharmacology, toxicity laboratory, University of Chicago, 1946; research associate, Stanford Research Institute, 1950–1953; research fellow, school of medicine, Stanford University, 1953–1956, research associate, 1957–1960, senior research associate, 1960–1970, senior scientist, 1970–1972, professor of medicine, 1972–1975

Concurrent Position: Fulbright research scholar, Norway, 1958–1959

Married: Ithiel de Sola Pool, 1938, divorced 1953; Maurice D. Sokolow, 1972, divorced 1975

Judith Pool was renowned for her work in blood coagulation, which resulted in major contributions to the treatment of hemophilia. She developed the method of isolating the antihemophilic factor in blood, a method that is used for transfusions to correct bleeding in hemophiliac patients. Her procedure has since become a standard. She did not receive credit, however, for her participation as a graduate student in the development of the microelectrode, which generally is referred to as the Ling-Gerard electrode. After teaching physics for three years at Hobart and William Smith colleges, she returned to the University of Chicago and completed the requirements for her doctorate in 1946. She joined the Stanford Research Institute as a research associate in 1950, then moved to the school of medicine at Stanford University in 1953, quickly moving up to senior scientist in 1970 and professor of medicine in 1972, just three years prior to her death. Among her many awards and honors, the National Hemophilia Foundation renamed its awards the Judith Graham Pool Research Fellowships. She was president of the Association for Women in Science in 1971, and was a member of the American Association for the Advancement of Science, the American Physiological Society, and the Society for Experimental Biology and Medicine. Her research included cellular physiology, plasma proteins, and blood coagulation. She had three children, Jonathan, Jeremy, and Lorna. A photograph is included in *Thrombosis and Haemostasis* 35 (1976): 269–271.

Bibliography: *American Men and Women of Science* 8–13; Debus, A. G., ed., *World Who's Who in Science*; Herzenberg, Caroline L., *Women Scientists from Antiquity to the Present*; Kass-Simon, G. and Patricia Farnes, *Women of Science*; Sicherman, Barbara et al., *Notable American Women*; Siegel, Patricia J. and Kay Thomas Finley, *Women in the Scientific Search.*

Porter, Gene Stratton
(1863–1924)
nature writer and novelist

Education: Public schools

Employment: Author

Married: Charles D. Porter, 1886

*G*ene *Stratton Porter* (born Geneva Grace Stratton) was one of the most influential popularizers of the nature movement in the early twentieth century. She was self-taught as an expert in ornithology. Growing up in a rural area, as a child she was fascinated with nature. After their marriage her husband, Charles Porter, discovered oil on farmland he owned and built a 14-room house that Gene designed and called Limberlost Cabin. She continued her nature studies from her home, which was located close to a wild swamp area. In about 1895 she began contributing a column on nature photography to *Recreation* magazine. Later she started a similar column in *Outing,* and wrote numerous articles for other popular magazines. She began writing novels with conservation themes, some of which were autobiographical, as well as studies of wildlife and nature.

Her books and articles were enhanced by the photographs she developed and printed, as was the custom of photographers at that time. Her novels often were set in the Limberlost area of northern Indiana. Titles include *Freckles* (1904) and *Girl of the Limberlost* (1909). These novels stressed her belief that virtue stemmed from contact with wild nature,

representing the urban nostalgia for living close to nature. Her nature studies include *Birds of the Bible* (1909) and *Moths of the Limberlost* (1912). Her nature books were designed for the general public and were illustrated with excellent photographs and drawings. They were popular due to her reputation as a novelist. Many of her novels were popular in the Midwest and still are available in reprint editions. When the Limberlost Swamp was reclaimed for cultivation in 1913, Mrs. Porter moved to northern Indiana and built a second cabin of 20 rooms. She and her family moved to California in 1922 to start a film company that produced movie versions of her stories to be used in schools and churches. She died in Los Angeles in 1924 as a result of a traffic accident. The couple had one daughter, Jeannette. Her biography is *Gene Stratton-Porter: Novelist and Naturalist* (1990) by Judith R. Long.

Bibliography: *Dictionary of American Biography;* James, E. T., ed., *Notable American Women 1607–1950;* McHenry, Robert, ed., *Famous American Women; National Union Catalog;* O'Neill, Lois S., *The Women's Book of World Records and Achievements.*

Proctor, Mary
(b. 1862)
astronomer

Education: College of Preceptors, London; Columbia University
Employment: Teacher, private school; lecturer on popular astronomy, New York City Board of Education and elsewhere

*M*ary *Proctor's* chief contribution to science was in popularizing astronomy, especially for children. She developed an interest in astronomy as a child by assisting her father, a noted astronomer, with his observations and writing. She attended college in London and attended classes at Columbia

University after the family emigrated to the United States. As an adult she contributed articles on mythology and astronomy to journals such as *Popular Astronomy, Scientific American,* and *Popular Science News.* She wrote a book for children entitled *Stories of Starland* (1898), which was used as a supplementary reader in public schools at the time. She arranged to give a series of six lectures on astronomy for children at the World's Fair in Chicago in 1893, and prepared illustrations suitable for kindergarten students who, she surmised, would be her audience. She was amazed when she arrived for the first lecture in the children's area to find the hall filled with adults. She had to give an impromptu presentation that day and revise her talks daily for the remaining five days. The Chicago press gave her talks very favorable reviews. She then became a popular lecturer on the subject. She gave lectures under the auspices of the board of education of New York City, and also she traveled throughout the country and Canada giving presentations. She was a member of the American Association for the Advancement of Science and the British Astronomical Society. Her name was listed in the first three editions of *American Men and Women of Science.*

Bibliography: *American Men and Women of Science 1–3; National Cyclopedia of American Biography; National Union Catalog;* Siegel, Patricia J. and Kay Thomas Finley, *Women in the Scientific Search.*

Edith Hinkley Quimby

Quimby, Edith Hinkley
(1891–1982)
radiological physicist

Education: B.S., Whitman College, 1912; M.A., University of California, Berkeley, 1916
Employment: High school teacher, 1912–1914; assistant in physics, University of California, 1914–1915; assistant physicist, Memorial Hospital, New York, 1919–1932, associate physicist, 1932–1942; associate professor of radiological physics, college of physicians and surgeons, Columbia University, 1942–1954, professor, 1954–1960; emeritus professor of radiology; special lecturer
Concurrent Position: Assistant professor, medical college, Cornell University, 1941–1942
Married: Shirley L. Quimby, 1915

*E*dith Quimby was a pioneer in the new field of radiation physics. When she started working at Memorial Hospital in 1919, commercial radium had been in production in the United States for only six years. She was one of the scientists who brought the field to maturity; between 1920 and 1940 she published more than 50 papers describing the results of her research. She not only prepared data on radiation hazards and radiation safety, but also developed training courses in medical physics.

Her career followed the pattern of many women scientists of her generation in that she taught high school for several years after receiving her undergraduate degree in 1912. She enrolled in advanced courses at the University of California and received her master's degree in 1916. She accepted a position as an assistant physicist at Memorial Hospital, where she began her career in radiation physics. She was promoted to associate physicist in 1932, but she accepted a position as associate professor of radiological physics at the college of physicians and surgeons in 1942. She was promoted to professor in 1954 and named emeritus professor in 1960. She received many awards, such as a medal from the American Cancer Society (1957), the Janeway Medal (1960) of the Radium Society (date unavailable), the gold medal of the Radiological Society of North America (1941), and the gold medal of the American College of Radiologists (1963). She was president of the American Radium Society in 1954, was elected a fellow of the American Physical Society and of the American College of Radiology, and was a member of the American Roentgen Ray Society. Her research included applications of x-rays and rays from radioactive substances to medicines, radiation hazards and radiation safety, and development of medical physics training courses. Her photograph appears in Edna Yost's *Women of Modern Science* and in *Current Biography*.

Bibliography: *American Men and Women of Science* 9–12; *Current Biography*; Kass-Simon, G. and Patricia Farnes, *Women of Science*; Macksey, Joan and Kenneth Macksey, *The Book of Women's Achievements*; McNeil, Barbara, ed., *Biography and Genealogy Master Index 1986–90, Cumulation*, vol. 3; Yost, Edna, *Women of Modern Science*.

Estelle Rosemary White Ramey
(Marie) Gertrude Rand
Janet Lorraine Cooper Rapp
Mary Jane Rathbun
Sarah Ratner
Dixy Lee Ray
Mina Spiegel Rees
Gladys Amanda Reichard
(Clarice) Audrey Richards
Ellen Henrietta Swallow Richards
Dorothea Klumpke Roberts
Edith Adelaide Roberts
Lydia Jane Roberts
Daisy Maude Orleman Robinson
Julia Bowman Robinson
Winifred Josephine Robinson
Sarah Tyson Heston Rorer
Flora Rose
Mary Davies Swartz Rose
Augusta Rucker
Dorothea Rudnick
Caroline Thomas Rumbold
Elizabeth Shull Russell
Jane Anne Russell

Ramey, Estelle Rosemary White
(1917–)
endocrinologist

Education: M.A., Columbia University, 1940; Ph.D. in physiology, University of Chicago, 1950

Employment: Instructor, Queens College, New York, 1938–1941; lecturer, University of Tennessee, 1942–1947; instructor in physiology, University of Chicago, 1951–1954, assistant professor, 1954–1958; assistant professor, school of medicine, Georgetown University, 1956–1960, associate professor, 1960–1966, professor of physiology, 1966–1987, professor of biophysics, 1980–1987; emeritus professor of biophysics

Concurrent Positions: U.S. Public Health Service fellow, 1950–1951; visiting professor and lecturer at several universities

Married: James T. Ramey, 1941

Estelle Ramey has been recognized for her research in endocrinology. She was employed as an instructor at Queens College while she was completing her master's degree at Columbia University in 1940. After teaching at the University of Tennessee for six years, she returned to school to obtain her doctorate from the University of Chicago in 1950 and continued teaching there for several years. She accepted a position at Georgetown University in the medical school as assistant professor in 1956, and was promoted to associate professor in 1960 and professor in 1966. She was named professor of biophysics in 1980 and emeritus professor in 1987. In addition to the major scientific associations, she also has been involved in several programs concerning women scientists. She was president of the Association for Women in Science from 1972 to 1974 and a founder of its Education Foundation. She was a member of the Committee for Women Veterans, the U.S. Veterans Administration, and the President's Advisory Committee on Women. She has received honorary degrees from several universities. She was the coauthor of *Electrical Studies on the Unanesthetized Brain* (1960). She has been a member of several professional societies, including the American Physiological Society, the American Chemical Society, the Endocrine Society, the American Diabetes Association, and the American Academy of Neurology. Her research has centered on endocrinology metabolism chiefly in the field of adrenal function and insulin action. She and her husband had two children, James and Drucilla. Her name was included in the 1992–1993 edition of *American Men and Women of Science.*

Bibliography: American Men and Women of Science 9–18; Debus, A. G., ed., *World Who's Who in Science;* Herzenberg, Caroline L., *Women Scientists from Antiquity to the Present; National Union Catalog.*

Rand, (Marie) Gertrude
(1886–1970)
psychologist

Education: A.B., Cornell University, 1908; scholar, Bryn Mawr College, 1908–1909, fellow, 1909–1911, M.A. and Ph.D. in psychology, 1911
Employment: Fellow, Bryn Mawr College, 1911–1913, reader in experimental psychology, 1913–1914, associate in experimental and applied psychology, 1914–1924, demonstrator, 1924–1927; associate professor, research in ophthalmology, Wilmer Institute, school of medicine, Johns Hopkins University, 1928–1932, physiological optics, 1932–1936, associate director, research laboratory of physiological optics, 1936–1943; research associate, ophthalmology, Knapp Foundation, college of physicians and surgeons, Columbia University, 1943–1957
Married: Clarence E. Ferree, 1918, died 1942

Gertrude Rand was a leading researcher in the field of physiological optics. She developed the Ferree-Rand perimeter in collaboration with her husband while they were working at Bryn Mawr. It maps the retina for its perceptual abilities, and it became an important tool for diagnosing vision problems. At the Knapp Foundation she collaborated in developing the Hardy-Rand-Rittler color plates for testing color vision. She started collaborating with her husband while she was a graduate student at Bryn Mawr, and they continued working together for the rest of his life. After they were married in 1918, she continued to use her maiden name professionally. They moved to Johns Hopkins in 1928, where she first taught in the area of research ophthalmology, then physiological optics before becoming associate director of the research laboratory of physiological optics in 1936.

Besides their academic work, the couple served as consultants for industries and agencies concerned with lighting technology. After her husband's death, she moved to Columbia University, where she returned to her earlier work in color perception. In 1952 she became the first woman elected a fellow of the Illuminating Engineering Society, and the society awarded her the Gold Medal for 1963. She was the first to win the Edgar Y. Tillyer Medal of the Optical Society of America for outstanding research in vision (1959). She received an honorary degree from Wilson College in 1943. She also was a member of the American Association for the Advancement of Science and the American Psychological Association. Her research included color blindness; spatial orientation; and central and peripheral light and color sensitivity. There is a photograph and list of publications in the *Journal of the Optical Society of America* 49 (1959): 937–941.

Bibliography: American Men and Women of Science 8–11; Herzenberg, Caroline L., *Women Scientists from Antiquity to the Present; National Cyclopedia of American Biography;* Rossiter, Margaret W., *Women Scientists in America;* Sicherman, Barbara et al., *Notable American Women;* Siegel, Patricia J. and Kay Thomas Finley, *Women in the Scientific Search.*

Rapp, Janet Lorraine Cooper
(b. 1921)
animal nutritionist

Education: B.Sc., Rutgers University, 1943; M.S., University of Illinois, 1945, Ph.D. in entomology, 1948

Employment: Assistant in botany, University of Illinois, 1944–1947; instructor in biology, Doane College, 1948–1949, assistant professor of chemistry, 1951–1952; assistant director of research, Archem Corporation, 1949–1952; director, J-B Lab, 1952–1953; research nutritionist, Feed Service Corporation, 1953–?

Married: 1944

Janet Rapp was recognized for her work in animal nutrition, and she was one of the few women who could be identified as working in ruminant nutrition. She was an early member of the American Society of Animal Science. After receiving her doctorate in entomology at the University of Illinois, she was employed as an instructor in biology at Doane College in 1948 and as an assistant professor of chemistry for two years beginning in 1951. Concurrently she was assistant director of research at Archem Corporation, starting in 1949. She accepted a position at director of J-B Lab in 1952 and moved to Feed Service Corporation as a research nutritionist in 1953. The only information that could be found about these companies is that they were located in Crete, Nebraska. She had a diverse career in entomology, biology, chemistry, and nutrition, which reflects the interdisciplinary nature of most research, including that of animal nutrition. It also could reflect the number of jobs that were available in the geographic area in which she lived. She was a member of the American Chemical Society and the American Society of Animal Science. Her research interests were the chloride ion in insect hemolymph, molasses-urea-alcohol feeds, and ruminant nutrition. She was the mother of three children.

Bibliography: American Men and Women of Science 8–12; National Union Catalog.

Rathbun, Mary Jane
(1860–1943)
marine zoologist

Education: Ph.D., George Washington University, 1917

Employment: Clerk, U.S. Fish Commission, 1884–1887; copyist and aide, division of marine invertebrates, U.S. National Museum, 1887–1898, second assistant curator, 1898–1907, assistant curator, 1907–1914, honorary associate zoologist, 1915–1939

Mary Rathbun was recognized internationally for her research on Crustacea. She began her career assisting her brother Richard Rathbun in his work at the Fish Commission and the division of marine invertebrates at the National Museum. They worked together in sorting and studying the huge collections of marine fauna being brought in by Fish Commission ships. Gradually she took over much of the research while he was burdened with administrative responsibilities. She was involved in classifying the major collections of that time: the decapods of the Harriman Alaska expedition, crabs of the gulf of Siam, crabs of the Sealark expedition, decapods of the Albatross East Pacific expedition, and fossil decapods of America. Largely self-educated, she published 158 papers on decapod Crustacea, primarily shrimps and crabs. The study on which she received her doctorate was "The Grapsoid Crabs of America" (Bulletin 97). She relinquished her salary in 1914 so an assistant could be hired; however, she continued working until 1939. She received an honorary M.A. degree from the University of Pittsburgh in 1916. One of her most significant contributions was fixing the nomenclature for many of the decapod Crustacea. Another contribution was the large collection of data she compiled, which has been a rich source for scientists since that time. She was a member of the American Association for the Advancement of Science, the American Society of Naturalists, and the natural history societies of several countries. Her name was listed in the first edition of *American Men and Women of Science*, and starred in the third through sixth editions.

Bibliography: American Men and Women of Science 1–6; Herzenberg, Caroline L., *Women Scientists from Antiquity to the Present*; James, E. T., ed., *Notable American Women 1607–1950*; Mozans, H. J., *Women in Science*; Ogilvie, Marilyn B., *Women in Science*; Rossiter, Margaret W., *Women Scientists in America*; Rossiter, Margaret W., "Women Scientists in America before 1920"; Siegel, Patricia J. and Kay Thomas Finley, *Women in the Scientific Search*; Visher, Stephen S., *Scientists Starred 1903–1943 in "American Men of Science."*

Ratner, Sarah
(1903–)
biochemist

Education: A.B., Cornell University, 1924; A.M., Columbia University, 1927, Ph.D. in biochemistry, 1937

Employment: Assistant, pediatrics, Long Island College of Medicine, 1926–1930; assistant biochemist, college of physicians and surgeons, Columbia University, 1930–1931, teaching assistant, 1932–1934, Macy research fellow, department of biochemistry, 1937–1939, instructor, 1939–1943, associate, 1943–1946, assistant professor, 1946; assistant professor, pharmacology, college of medicine, New York University, 1946–1953, associate professor, 1953–1954; associate member, division of nutrition and physiology, Public Health Research Institute of the City of New York, Inc., 1954–1957, member, division of biochemistry, 1957–

Concurrent Positions: Editor, *Journal of Biological Chemistry*, 1959–; editor, *Analytical Biochemistry*, 1974–; research professor, college of medicine, New York University; Fogarty scholar in residence, National Institutes of Health, 1978–1979

Sarah Ratner has been one of the leading researchers in the biochemistry of amino acids and protein metabolism. She discovered arginosuccinic acid and developed a sensitive color test to study its formation in brain tissue, leading to a better understanding of a defect that causes mental retardation in children. She was employed for 17 years at the college of physicians and surgeons of Columbia University starting in 1930 as an assistant biochemist and advancing to assistant professor in 1946. A portion of this time was spent in completing her doctorate, which she received in 1937. Her slow advancement could be due to working during the years of the Depression, when both assistantships and permanent positions were scarce. She accepted a position as an assistant professor of pharmacology at the college of medicine at New York University, being promoted to associate professor in 1953. She then accepted a position at the Public Health Research Institute of the City of New York in 1954.

She has received numerous awards, such as the Neuberg Medal (1959), the Garvan Medal (1961), and the L & B Freedman Foundation Award (1975). She was elected to membership in the National Academy of Sciences in 1974 and was awarded honorary degrees by the University of North Carolina

(1981), Northwestern University (1982), and the State University of New York, Stony Brook (1984). She was elected a fellow of the Harvey Society and of the New York Academy of Sciences. She has been a member of the American Academy of Arts and Sciences, the American Society of Biological Chemists, and the American Chemical Society. Her research has included metabolism and chemistry of amino acids; application of isotopes to intermediary metabolism; and enzymatic mechanisms of arginine biosynthesis and urea formation and other nitrogen-transferring reactions. Her name was listed in the 1992–1993 edition of *American Men and Women of Science.*

Bibliography: *American Men and Women of Science* 6–18; Debus, A. G., ed., *World Who's Who in Science;* Herzenberg, Caroline L., *Women Scientists from Antiquity to the Present;* Kass-Simon, G. and Patricia Farnes, *Women of Science;* O'Neill, Lois S., *The Women's Book of World Records and Achievements.*

Ray, Dixy Lee
(1914–1994)
zoologist and public official

Education: B.A., Mills College, 1937, M.A., 1938; Ph.D. in biological sciences, Stanford University, 1945

Employment: Public school teacher, 1938–1942; instructor in zoology, University of Washington, Seattle, 1945–1947, assistant professor, 1947–1957, associate professor, 1957–1963; director, Pacific Science Center, 1963–1973; member of the Atomic Energy Commission, 1972–1973, chair 1973–1974; Department of State, 1975; governor of Washington State, 1977–1981

Concurrent Position: Guggenheim fellow, 1952–1953

Dixy Ray received recognition for her work as a scientist as well as her work as a public official. Her career followed the pattern of many women of her generation in that she taught public school for five years after receiving her master's

degree in 1938. She accepted a position as instructor in zoology at the University of Washington in 1945 after completing her doctorate, then advanced to assistant professor in 1947 and associate professor in 1957. From 1963 to 1973 she was director of the Pacific Science Center, which quickly developed into an important institution for encouraging public interest in and the understanding of science. Even before she entered public service full time, she was involved in many national and international projects: she was a consultant for the division of biological and medical sciences, National Science Foundation (1960–1963); a visiting professor at the International Indian Ocean Expedition, Stanford University (1964); a member of the committee on oceanography, National Science Foundation (1958–1963); and a member of the President's Task Force on Oceanography (1969).

She was appointed to the Atomic Energy Commission in 1972, and she was the first woman to be promoted to chair of the commission, serving from 1973 to 1974. After working briefly for the Department of State, she was elected the first woman governor of Washington State in 1977. (She was only the second woman governor who was not preceded in office by a husband.) After leaving that office she spoke and wrote about environmental issues. Two of her recent books are *Trashing the Planet* (1990) and *Environmental Overkill* (1993). She was a member of the American Association for the Advancement of Science. Her photograph appears in *Current Biography*.

Bibliography: *American Men and Women of Science 8–13; Current Biography;* Herzenberg, Caroline L., *Women Scientists from Antiquity to the Present;* McHenry, Robert, ed., *Famous American Women; National Union Catalog;* O'Neill, Lois S., *The Women's Book of World Records and Achievements.*

Rees, Mina Spiegel
(1902–)
mathematician

Education: A.B., Hunter College, 1923; A.M., Columbia University, 1925; Ph.D. in mathematics, University of Chicago, 1931

Employment: Instructor in mathematics, Hunter College, 1926–1932, assistant professor, 1932–1940, associate professor, 1940–1943, professor of mathematics and dean of faculty, 1953–1961; dean of graduate studies, City University of New York, 1961–1968, president of graduate studies, 1969–1972, provost, graduate division, 1968–1969; emeritus professor of mathematics; emeritus professor of graduate school

Concurrent Positions: Principal technical aide, applied mathematics panel, National Defense Research Committee, 1943–1946; head of mathematics division, Office of Naval Research, 1946–1949, director of mathematics science division, 1949–1952, deputy science director, 1952–1953

Married: Leopold Brahdy, 1955

Mina Rees has been honored for setting up programs for large-scale support for mathematical research by the federal government. She established the program in mathematics at the Office of Naval Research (ONR) (1946–1952) and was the deputy science director there from 1952 to 1953. When the National Science Foundation was established in 1950, her ONR program was used as the model for funding mathematical research. She was employed by Hunter College for 35 years, starting as an instructor in mathematics in 1926 and rising through the ranks to assistant professor in 1932, associate professor in 1940, and professor of mathematics and dean of faculty in 1953. In 1943 she took a leave from Hunter to work for the Office of Scientific Research and Development during World War II. At this time she laid the groundwork for her model program in funding mathematical research. She accepted a position as dean of graduate studies at City University of New York in 1961 and was promoted to president of graduate studies in 1969, retiring in 1972. She has received many honorary degrees, honors, and awards. Among the latter were the President's Certificate of Merit (1958) and the first Award for Distinguished Service to Mathematics of the Mathematical Association of America (1962). She was elected president of the American Association for the Advancement of Science in 1972 and was a fellow of both the American Association for the Advancement of Science and the New York Academy of Sciences.

She has been a member of the American Mathematical Society, the Mathematical Association of America, and the Society for Industrial and Applied Mathematics. Her areas of research are linear algebra, numerical analysis, and the history of computers. A bibliography of her papers is included in *Women of Mathematics,* and her name was listed in the 1992–1993 edition of *American Men and Women of Science* and her photograph in *Current Biography.*

Bibliography: *American Men and Women of Science* 5–18; *Current Biography;* Grinstein, Louise S. and Paul J. Campbell, eds., *Women of Mathematics;* Herzenberg, Caroline L., *Women Scientists from Antiquity to the Present;* Ireland, Norma O., *Index to Scientists of the World;* O'Neill, Lois S., *The Women's Book of World Records and Achievements.*

Reichard, Gladys Amanda
(1893–1955)
anthropologist

Education: A.B., Swarthmore College, 1919; A.M., Columbia University, 1920, Ph.D. in anthropology, 1925
Employment: Elementary school teacher, 1909–1915; instructor, anthropology, Barnard College, 1923–1928, assistant professor, 1928–1941, associate professor, 1941–1951, professor, 1951–1955
Concurrent Position: Guggenheim fellowship, Hamburg, Germany, 1926–1927

ladys Reichard was known for her expertise in Navajo language and culture, but she studied other tribes. She was head of what was for many years the only undergraduate department of anthropology in a women's college in the United States. Like many women of her generation, she taught public school for a number of years before receiving her undergraduate degree from Swarthmore. She started her career at Barnard in 1923 as an instructor in anthropology, advancing through the ranks to assistant professor in 1928, associate professor in 1941, and professor in 1951, retiring in 1955.

Starting about 1923, she spent summers each year on the reservations learning languages, learning to weave, and observing daily life by living with families from time to time. In 1934 she made the first attempt to teach native speakers to write the Navajo language. (One factor that often was not mentioned in the biographies of women anthropologists was that, since Navajo society traditionally is matriarchal, women anthropologists were more successful than men in working with these tribes.) In addition to scientific articles, she published a number of books, including *Social Life of the Navajo Indians* (1928), *Melanesian Design* (1933), *Spider Woman*

(1934), *Navajo Shepherd and Weaver* (1936), Handbook of American Indian Languages (1938), *Navajo Religion: A Study of Symbolism* (1950), and *Navajo Grammar* (1951). The latter grammar was controversial in that she did not accept a method of transcription that was newer than the one she developed. She was a member of the American Ethnological Society, the American Folklore Society, and the American Association for the Advancement of Science. A list of her papers and her photograph are included in *American Anthropologist* 58 (1956): 913–916.

Bibliography: Herzenberg, Caroline L., *Women Scientists from Antiquity to the Present; International Directory of Anthropologists; National Union Catalog;* Rossiter, Margaret W., *Women Scientists in America;* Sicherman, Barbara et al., *Notable American Women.*

Richards, (Clarice) Audrey
(b. 1887)
forest pathologist

Education: A.B., Miami University, Ohio, 1912, M.A., 1914; Ph.D. in botany, University of Wisconsin, 1922

Employment: Public school teacher, 1906–1909; assistant in botany, Miami University, Ohio, 1912–1914; assistant, Ohio Biological Survey, 1915; assistant botanist, University of Wisconsin, 1915–1917; forest pathologist, Bureau of Plant Industry, U.S. Department of Agriculture, 1917–1929, pathologist in charge, Madison branch, 1929–1943, forest pathologist, 1943–1947, senior pathologist, 1947–1952

*A*udrey Richards was recognized for her research as a forest pathologist. Her career followed the pattern of many women of her generation; she taught at public schools before completing her undergraduate degree at Miami University, Ohio, in 1912. After receiving her master's degree in 1914, she worked for the Ohio Biological Survey for one year and then worked on her doctorate at the University of Wisconsin. She started her long career with the U.S. Department of Agriculture at the forestry laboratory at Madison, Wisconsin. She first was employed as a forest pathologist in 1917, promoted to pathologist in charge in 1929, returned to the rank of forest pathologist in 1943, and was promoted to senior pathologist in 1947.

Although she was appointed pathologist in charge of the Madison branch, she never was named chief, as her male predecessors had been; however, women scientists at the Madison branch seem to have had opportunities for research and publication that many other women scientists of that period did not have. She was a member of the American Association for the Advancement of Science, the Botanical Society of America, the American Phytopathological Society, and the Forest Products Research Society. Her research included fungi-causing defects in wood and wood products, evaluation of wood preservatives, and the physiology of wood-inhibiting fungi. Among her scientific papers was one published by the American Wood Preservers' Association on "Defects in Cross Ties Caused by Fungi" in a report entitled "Railroad Tie Decay" (1939). One reference source lists her name as Clarissa Richards.

Richards, Ellen Henrietta Swallow
(1842–1911)
chemist and home economist

Education: A.B., Vassar College, 1870; B.S., Massachusetts Institute of Technology, 1873; M.A., Vassar College, 1873; D.Sc., Smith College, 1910
Employment: Public school teacher, 1867; tutor, 1868–1875; instructor, Woman's Laboratory, Massachusetts Institute of Technology (MIT), 1876–1884, instructor, sanitary chemistry, 1884–1911
Married: Robert H. Richards, 1875

*E*llen Richards is recognized as the founder of the home economics movement, the discipline of dietetics, and the disciplines of environmental engineering and sanitary chemistry, which refers to standards for foods and pharmaceuticals. She was among the few American women scientists actually to have founded a discipline. She was listed in the first edition of *American Men and Women of*

Science as Mrs. Robert H. Richards. Her name was starred in the first three editions, but her husband's was not. She received a B.S. degree from Massachusetts Institute of Technology in 1873 and an M.A. from Vassar College that same year. She continued graduate study for two years, but she was not awarded a degree, perhaps because the heads of the departments did not want a woman to be the first person to receive a doctorate in chemistry. When she had applied for admission at MIT, the college president was reluctant to admit her in spite of her qualifications. He solved the problem by admitting her as a special student so her name would not appear on the class lists. She married Robert H. Richards, head of MIT's metallurgical and mining engineering department. She often assisted him with his work, and she was elected the first woman member of the American Institute of Mining and Metallurgical Engineers in 1879.

In order to encourage women to pursue scientific study, Ellen Richards established a Woman's Laboratory at MIT in 1876. This provided classes in chemical analysis, industrial chemistry, mineralogy, and biology. She also carried on consulting work for private industry by testing and analyzing products. From 1878 to 1879 she investigated for the state board of health the adulteration of staple groceries. This work was the basis for her manual *The Chemistry of Cooking and Cleaning* (1882) and of *Food Materials and Their Adulterations* (1885). The first Massachusetts Food and Drug Act was passed on the basis of her pioneer research in public health.

MIT was admitting women into the regular programs by 1878, and she closed the Woman's Laboratory in 1884 and was appointed an instructor in sanitary chemistry as the first woman faculty member. She remained at the level of instructor for the remainder of her career. She wrote *Air, Water, and Food for Colleges* (1900) for use in MIT's courses. Starting about 1890 Ellen Richards increasingly concentrated on what became known as the home economics movement. She consulted

on several of the early bulletins on nutrition issued by the U.S. Department of Agriculture. She helped organize a school of housekeeping at the Woman's Educational and Industrial Union in Boston in 1899. This later was incorporated into Simmons College as the department of home economics after the founding of that institution. In 1899 she helped to inaugurate the first of a series of summer conferences at Lake Placid, New York, to organize the new field of home economics. The purpose was to develop courses of study for public schools as well as for colleges and women's clubs. In 1908 the Lake Placid conference group organized the American Home Economics Association with Ellen Richards as president from 1908 to 1910. She assumed the financial responsibility for the association's *Journal of Home Economics.*

She and her husband seemed to have maintained a mutually supportive marriage. They met when she was a student doing research in metallurgy and he was a faculty member. After she was graduated, he proposed marriage one day while they were both working in the same laboratory. He did not seem to be jealous of her accomplishments and, in fact, supported her at each phase. He talked about her career and wrote about her work. He probably was responsible for preserving the records of her contributions by saving her reports, correspondence, and other papers.

Ellen Richards applied her theories of healthful living and safe environments to her home. She completely remodeled the house, replacing lead water pipes, designing a more efficient furnace and water heater with her husband, and checking the sanitary drains. She was among the first to have a gas stove and a vacuum cleaner in her home. She replaced the dusty drapes and carpets with sheer window curtains and scatter rugs, both of which were easier to keep clean. Although they did not have children, they often had college students living with them to earn their room and board by housekeeping.

She wrote at least a dozen books in addition to those mentioned above. She received an honorary degree from Smith College in 1910 and was a member of the American Chemical Society, the American Public Health Association, and the Boston Society of Natural History. Her research was on water and sanitary problems, food in relation to health, and the therapeutic value of certain foods in diets of the insane. Her biography is *The Life of Ellen H. Richards* (1912), by Caroline L. Hunt. Some sources list her as Ellen Swallow. A photograph is included in Margaret Rossiter's *Women Scientists in America* and in G. Kass-Simon's and Patricia Farnes' *Women of Science*.

Bibliography: Abir-Am, P. G. and Dorinda Outram, eds., *Uneasy Careers and Intimate Lives; American Men and Women of Science 1–3*; Debus, A. G., ed., *World Who's Who in Science; Dictionary of American Biography*; Herzenberg, Caroline L., *Women Scientists from Antiquity to the Present*; James, E. T., ed., *Notable American Women 1607–1950*; Kass-Simon, G. and Patricia Farnes, *Women of Science*; McIIenry, Robert, ed., *Famous American Women*; Macksey, Joan and Kenneth Macksey, *The Book of Women's Achievements*; Marlow, Joan, *The Great Women; National Union Catalog*; Ogilvie, Marilyn B., *Women in Science*; O'Neill, Lois S., *The Women's Book of World Records and Achievements*; Rossiter, Margaret W., *Women Scientists in America*; Rossiter, Margaret W., "Women Scientists in America before 1920"; Rossiter, Margaret W., "'Women's Work' in Science, 1880–1910"; Shapiro, Laura, *Perfection Salad*; Siegel, Patricia J. and Kay Thomas Finley, *Women in the Scientific Search*; Uglow, Jennifer S., *International Dictionary of Women's Biography*; Vare, Ethlie Ann and Greg Ptacek, *Mothers of Invention*; Visher, Stephen S., *Scientists Starred 1903–1943 in "American Men and Women of Science"*; Yost, Edna, *American Women of Science*.

Roberts, Dorothea Klumpke
(1861–1942)
astronomer

Education: B.S., University of Paris, 1886; Matt D., 1893
Employment: Assistant, Paris Observatory, 1887–1901; director, Bureau of Measurements, Paris Observatory, 1891–1901; independent research, 1901–1934
Married: Isaac Roberts, 1901, died 1904

Dorothea Roberts was recognized for her work in charting and cataloging stars. She was a U.S. citizen, but she spent most of her career in France. She was the first woman to receive a doctorate from the University of Paris. At the Paris Observatory she was placed in charge of the Bureau of Measurements to chart and catalog stars down to the eleventh magnitude. Her paper on charting, which she presented during the World's Columbia Exposition in Chicago in 1893, earned her an award from the Academié des Sciences in 1893 and from the Société Astronomique de France in 1897. She published *Isaac Roberts Atlas of 52 Regions* (1929) and a supplement (1932), which reported her husband's work on celestial photography. (He was a prominent Welsh astronomer.) For this she received another prize from the Academié des Sciences in 1932. In 1934 she was elected Chevalier of the Legion of Honor by the French government for her contributions to French astronomy. In 1974 the Astronomical Society of the Pacific established the Dorothea Klumpke Roberts Award for her work in popularizing astronomy. Her skills in English, French, and German made her a popular lecturer. She often was asked to translate the scientific memoirs of astronomers who attended conferences in Paris. She was a member of the American Astronomical Society, the American Association for the Advancement of Science, the International Astronomical Union, and numerous other professional societies. Her photograph is included in *Mercury* 10 (1981): 139–140.

Bibliography: Davis, Herman S., "Women Astronomers (1750–1890)"; *National Union Catalog;* Ogilvie, Marilyn B., *Women in Science;* Rossiter, Margaret W., *Women Scientists in America;* Siegel, Patricia J. and Kay Thomas Finley, *Women in the Scientific Search;* Uglow, Jennifer S., *International Dictionary of Women's Biography.*

Roberts, Edith Adelaide
(b. 1881)
botanist

Education: A.B., Smith College, 1905; M.S., University of Chicago, 1911, Ph.D. in plant physiology, 1915

Employment: Instructor and associate professor of botany, Mount Holyoke College, 1915–1917; extension worker with women, U.S. Department of Agriculture, 1917–1919; associate professor of botany, Vassar College, 1919–1921, professor, 1921–1950; emeritus professor

*E**dith Roberts** was recognized by her contemporaries for her research in plant physiology. She was a faculty member at Vassar College for more than 30 years. After completing her doctorate from the University of Chicago in 1915, she joined the faculty of Mount Holyoke for three years, then accepted a position with the U.S. Department of Agriculture (USDA) as an extension worker with women for three years. The sources do not mention the specific work she did for the USDA. Since this was during World War I, it is possible she was involved in gardening projects for women during wartime when women managed farms for the men who were in service. She was appointed an associate professor of botany at Vassar College in 1919 and promoted to professor in 1921, retiring in 1950. After retirement she worked in the department of food technology at Massachusetts Institute of Technology. She was the author of two books: *American Plants for American Gardens: Plant Ecology, the Study of Plants in Relation to Their Environment* (1929) and *American Ferns: How To Know, Grow and Use Them* (1935). She was a member of the Botanical Society of America and the American Association for the Advancement of Science. Her areas of research were plant physiology and ecology, germination of seeds, and propagation of native plants.

Bibliography: *American Men and Women of Science* 3–13; Barnhart, John H., *Biographical Notes upon Botanists*; Macksey, Joan and Kenneth Macksey, *The Book of Women's Achievements*; *National Union Catalog*.

Roberts, Lydia Jane
(1879–1965)
nutritionist and home economics educator

Education: Mount Pleasant Normal School, 1909; B.S., University of Chicago, 1917, M.S., 1919, Ph.D. in home economics, 1928
Employment: Schoolteacher, 1899–1915; assistant professor of home economics, University of Chicago, 1919–1928, associate professor, 1928–1930, professor and department chair, 1930–1944; chair, home economics department, University of Puerto Rico, 1944–1952

Lydia Roberts was a specialist in the nutrition of children. She entered the University of Chicago at age 36 to begin her formal training in nutrition. Her book, *Nutrition Work with Children* (1927), was a classic in its field and served as her dissertation. When Katharine Blunt (q.v.) resigned as department chair, Lydia Roberts was chosen to replace her. Her career followed the pattern of many women of her generation in that she taught public school for a number of years before starting her college education. She entered the University of Chicago and received her undergraduate degree in 1917, her master's degree in 1919, and her doctorate in home economics in 1928. She accepted an appointment as assistant professor at Chicago, being promoted to associate professor in 1928 and to professor and department chair in 1930. After retiring in 1944 she accepted a position as chair of the home economics department at the University of Puerto Rico until retiring again in 1952. While she was chair at Chicago, she continued Katharine Blunt's program by offering a curriculum that had a strong scientific basis. The experimental program she started at the University of Puerto Rico became a model for the rest of the island. She was a member of the American Association for the Advancement of Science. Her research was nutrition and related health problems of children.

Bibliography: *American Men and Women of Science* 5–11; Herzenberg, Caroline L., *Women Scientists from Antiquity to the Present*; *National Union Catalog*; Rossiter, Margaret W., *Women Scientists in America*; Sicherman, Barbara et al., *Notable American Women*; Siegel, Patricia J. and Kay Thomas Finley, *Women in the Scientific Search*.

Robinson, Daisy Maude Orleman
(1869–1942)
biologist and physician

Education: M.D., George Washington University, 1890; University of Zurich, 1892–1894; M.S., George Washington University, 1894

Employment: Schoolteacher, 1885–1887; medical examiner, U.S. Pension Bureau, 1890–1893; surgeon and associate principal, private school, 1895–1904; lecturer, New York Polyclinic Medical School; vice president, North West Dispensary, New York; president, woman's auxiliary board, New York Polyclinic; regional consultant, U.S. Public Health Service; lecturer and diagnostician, division of social hygiene, New York State Department of Health

Married: Andrew R. Robinson

Daisy Robinson was recognized for her work in military medicine, but she had a varied career. It started in a conventional manner with her teaching public schools for a few years. She received an M.D. degree from George Washington University in 1890, attended the University of Zurich for three years, and then received a master's degree from George Washington in 1894. She worked as physician for the U.S. Pension Bureau for four years, hence her interest in communicable diseases. She served as a physician for the French army during World War I and transferred to the U.S. Army when the United States entered the war, receiving decorations from both nations. After the war she worked for the U.S. Public Health Service, where she served for a short time as the acting Surgeon-General. She also worked at the New York State Department of Health in addition to working with a dispensary in New York. She had a private practice in dermatology. She was elected a fellow of the American Public Health Association and was also a member of the American Medical Association. Her research included injurious effects of roentgen rays; diagnosis and treatment of herpes zoster, cancer, gonorrhea, and syphilis; and treatment of leprosy by x-rays. Her name was listed in the first edition of *American Men and Women of Science*. One source lists her as graduating from Columbia University, but she actually graduated from George Washington University, which at the time she attended was called Columbian College (or University).

Bibliography: American Men and Women of Science 1–6; Siegel, Patricia J. and Kay Thomas Finley, *Women in the Scientific Search*.

Robinson, Julia Bowman
(1919–1985)
mathematician

Education: San Diego State University; A.B., University of California, Berkeley, 1940, M.A., 1941, Ph.D. in mathematics, 1948

Employment: Junior mathematician, Rand Corporation, 1949–1950; lecturer in mathematics, University of California, Berkeley, 1960–1964, 1966–1967, 1969–1970, 1975, professor of mathematics, 1976–1985

Married: Raphael Robinson, 1941

Julia Robinson, in 1976, was the first woman mathematician elected to the National Academy of Sciences, and in 1982 she became the first woman elected president of the American Mathematical Society. She entered San Diego State University at the age of 16, but she transferred in her senior year to the University of California, Berkeley. She was married just before the Japanese attack on Pearl Harbor, and during World War II she worked for the Berkeley Statistical Laboratory on government contracts. Her husband was a member of the mathematics faculty while she was a graduate student at Berkeley. When they married, the nepotism rule did not apply. She was discouraged at being unable to have children, but she took up mathematics again and received her doctorate in 1948. While she was working for the Rand Corporation in 1949 and 1950, she wrote an important paper on game theory. She became involved in campaigning for Adlai Stevenson in 1952 and 1956 and worked in politics for the next half-dozen years. She had poor health for much of her life due to rheumatic fever in childhood, but after surgery in 1961 she was able to lead a fairly normal life. She taught only one graduate course per quarter at Berkeley due to her health. She was internationally known for her work in logic, and she was promoted from lecturer to professor at Berkeley on the basis of that work. She received an honorary degree from Smith College in 1979. In 1983 she was awarded a MacArthur Fellowship of $60,000 per year for five years. She also was a member of the American Academy of Arts and Sciences and the Association for Symbolic Logic. Her research was on number theoretical decision problems and on recursive functions. A list of her publications was included in *Women of Mathematics* by Louise S. Grinstein and Paul J. Campbell.

Bibliography: *American Men and Women of Science* 13–15; Grinstein, Louise S. and Paul J. Campbell, eds., *Women of Mathematics;* Herzenberg, Caroline L., *Women Scientists from Antiquity to the Present;* O'Neill, Lois S., *The Women's Book of World Records and Achievements;* Perl, Teri, *Math Equals.*

Robinson, Winifred Josephine
(b. 1867)
botanist

Education: B.S., B.Pd., University of Michigan, 1899; A.M., Columbia University, 1904, Ph.D., 1912

Employment: Instructor in botany, training department, Michigan State Normal College, 1893–1895; instructor in biology, Vassar College, 1900–1907, botanist, 1909–1913, assistant professor, 1913–1914; dean of Women's College, University of Delaware, 1914–1938; dean emeritus

Concurrent Position: Research fellow, New York Botanical Garden, 1903

Winifred Robinson was recognized for her research in botany. Her career followed the pattern of many women of her generation. She was hired as an instructor in botany at Michigan State Normal College for three years before she received her undergraduate degree from the University of Michigan. She was appointed an instructor in biology at Vassar College in 1900 and continued teaching there while she completed her graduate degrees at Columbia University in 1912. She accepted a position as dean of the Women's College at the University of Delaware in

1914, retiring in 1938. Women scientists often accepted these administrative positions because there were limited opportunities for positions in teaching and research for them. (Starting about the turn of the century, many colleges established separate women's colleges when the pressure to admit women students no longer could be ignored.) After she accepted the position as college dean, Winifred Robinson still listed her research interest in plant morphology and taxonomy of Hawaiian ferns. She received honorary degrees from the University of Delaware and from Michigan State. She was a member of the American Association for the Advancement of Science, the American Society of Naturalists, and the Torrey Botanical Club.

Bibliography: American Men and Women of Science 3–10; Barnhart, John H., *Biographical Notes upon Botanists; National Union Catalog.*

Rorer, Sarah Tyson Heston
(1849–1937)
cookbook author and dietitian

Education: East Aurora Academy, New York, 1869; New Century Club cooking school, Philadelphia, 1879
Employment: Director, New Century Club cooking school, 1880–1883; owner, Philadelphia Cooking School, 1883–1903; director, school of domestic science of the Chautauqua
Married: William A. Rorer, 1871

Sarah Rorer was a pioneer teacher of cooking, a cookbook author, and a dietitian. Following the pattern of many early women in this field, she attended the New Century Club cooking school before becoming its director in 1880. By 1897 her own school, the Philadelphia Cooking School, conducted classes for ladies, cooks, and young girls, as well as offering a two-year normal course to prepare teachers of domestic arts. She also gave lectures on suitable diets for the sick to students at Woman's Medical College, nurses at the Woman's Hospital, and to students at the University of Pennsylvania. She published a book on the subject, *Mrs. Rorer's Diet for the Sick* (1914). Many graduates of her cooking school became hospital dietitians. She became nationally known when she published *Mrs. Rorer's Philadelphia Cook Book* (1886). She published about 40 books and pamphlets on cooking during her lifetime, and for five years starting in 1885 she published a monthly publication, *Table Talk.* Then came *Mrs. Rorer's New Cook Book* in 1902. At the World's Columbia Exposition in Chicago in 1893 she had charge of the "corn kitchen." She was editor and part owner of the magazine *Household News* from 1893 to 1897, when it was absorbed by the *Ladies' Home Journal.* She continued as domestic editor for the Journal until 1911 and was an editor for *Good Housekeeping.* She closed her cooking school in 1903. She later became director of the school of domestic science of the Chautauqua in Pennsylvania. She and her husband had three children, William, Anne, and James.

Bibliography: James, E. T., ed., *Notable American Women 1607–1950; National Cyclopedia of American Biography; National Union Catalog;* Shapiro, Laura, *Perfection Salad.*

Rose, Flora
(1874–1959)
home economist

Education: B.S., Kansas State College, 1904; A.M., Columbia University, 1909; Ped. D.,
New York State College for Teachers, 1931; Sc.D., Kansas State College, 1937
Employment: Instructor, Kansas State College, 1903–1906; lecturer in home economics,
Cornell University, 1907–1911, professor, college of home economics, 1911–1940,
codirector of college of home economics, 1911–1945; emeritus professor

Flora Rose was recognized for her research in nutrition. She was codirector of the college of home economics at Cornell starting in 1911, and after Martha Van Rensselaer's (q.v.) death in 1932, she continued as director of the program. The two were instrumental in persuading the New York legislature to create the college of home economics. They were the first women faculty members at Cornell to be promoted to full professors. Their names often are mentioned together in biographical sources, with Martha Van Rensselaer receiving the prominent attention. By the time these two women were involved in the home economics movement, there was additional funding available to land grant institutions for home economics departments.

The U.S. Department of Agriculture had several programs specifically for vocational education in public schools and for agricultural extension services for adults, including housewives. This opened up an unprecedented number of jobs for women in home economics and nutrition, and the schools expanded rapidly in the number of students and faculty in addition to the amount of research funds that were made available. Flora Rose received her undergraduate degree and her doctorate from Kansas State with a master's degree from Columbia. She was an instructor at Kansas State for four years before she was appointed a lecturer in home economics at Cornell in 1907. She was promoted to professor and codirector of the college of home economics in 1911. She specialized in the study of weight control, and she coauthored several books on foods and nutrition, including *The New Butterick Cook-Book* (1924) and *A Manual of Home-Making* (1928). She was a member of the American Association for the Advancement of Science. Her research included weight and how to control it, nutrition, and homemaking.

Bibliography: *American Men and Women of Science* 6–10; Herzenberg, Caroline L., *Women Scientists from Antiquity to the Present; National Union Catalog;* O'Neill, Lois S., *The Women's Book of World Records* and *Achievements;* Rossiter, Margaret W., *Women Scientists in America;* Rossiter, Margaret W., "'Women's Work' in Science, 1880–1910."

Rose, Mary Davies Swartz
(1874–1941)
chemist and nutritionist

Education: Litt.B., Denison University, 1901; diploma in home economics, Mechanics Institute, 1902; B.S., Columbia University, 1906; Ph.D. in physiological chemistry, Yale University, 1909

Employment: High school teacher, 1899–1905; assistant in nutrition, Teachers' College, Columbia University, 1906–1907, instructor in nutrition and dietetics, 1909–1910, assistant professor, 1911–1918, associate professor, 1918–1923, professor, 1923–1940

Married: Anton R. Rose, 1910

Mary Swartz Rose was a pioneer in the field of nutrition. She was appointed an assistant professor of nutrition at Teachers' College a year after the department was established, and the department became a national university center for training teachers of nutrition. She published more than 40 scientific papers and two widely used textbooks, *A Laboratory Hand-Book for Dietetics* (1912) and *The Foundations of Nutrition* (1927). She also wrote popular books for mothers, *Feeding the Family* (1916) and *Teaching Nutrition to Boys and Girls* (1932). After receiving a certificate from Denison University in 1901 and a diploma in home economics from the Mechanics Institute in Rochester, New York, in 1902, she taught high school home economics for five years. She then enrolled in Teachers' College, Columbia University, where she received her undergraduate degree in 1906, remaining another year as an assistant in the household arts department. Since there were no graduate programs in nutrition at the time, she enrolled in Yale, where she received her doctorate in physiological chemistry in 1909. She met Anton Rose when both were graduate students at Yale; they were married in 1910 and had one son, Richard. She returned to Teachers' College to become the first full-time instructor in nutrition and dietetics. She organized a program in which students could secure a solid grounding in the scientific aspects of nutrition as well as in the best methods for teaching the subject. She was promoted to assistant professor in 1911, associate professor in 1918, and professor in 1923.

A charter member of the American Institute of Nutrition, she was its president in 1937 and 1938 and associate editor of its publication, *Journal of Nutrition,* from 1928 to 1936. The American Dietetic Association elected her an honorary member in 1919. Teachers' College established a scholarship and the Greater New York Dietetic Association established a lectureship in her name. She also was a member of the American Association for the Advancement of Science, the American Society of Biological Chemists, the Society of Experimental Biology and Medicine, the American Home Economics Association,

and the American Public Health Association. Her research centered on nutrition and dietetics, including the vitamin content of food, protein comparison, effects of nutrients on anemia, metabolism, and trace elements in the diet. Her biography is *Mary Swartz Rose: Pioneer in Nutrition* (1979) by Juanith A. Eagles and others. She was listed as Mrs. Anton R. Rose in the fourth and fifth editions of *American Men and Women of Science.* Many sources refer to her as Mary Swartz Rose.

Bibliography: *American Men and Women of Science* 4–7; Herzenberg, Caroline L., *Women Scientists from Antiquity to the Present;* James, E. T., ed., *Notable American Women 1607–1950;* McHenry, Robert, ed., *Famous American Women; National Union Catalog;* Rossiter, Margaret W., *Women Scientists in America;* Rossiter, Margaret W., "Women Scientists in America before 1920"; Rossiter, Margaret W., "'Women's Work' in Science, 1880–1910"; Siegel, Patricia J. and Kay Thomas Finley, *Women in the Scientific Search.*

Rucker, Augusta
(b. 1873)
zoologist and physician

Education: A.B., University of Texas, 1896, A.M. in zoology, 1899; M.D., Johns Hopkins University, 1911
Employment: Tutor in biology, University of Texas, 1897–1899, instructor, 1899–1900, zoologist, 1900; practicing physician, 1911–?

*A*ugusta Rucker was listed in the first eight editions of *American Men and Women of Science* as both a zoologist and a physician. She was employed as a tutor while she received her undergraduate and master's degrees in zoology at the University of Texas. She taught for one year at Texas and then made an abrupt change in career after 1900, when she went on to attend Johns Hopkins and

receive a medical degree. She listed herself as a practicing physician both at the New York Infirmary for Women and Children and at Ruptured and Crippled Hospital. She was noted for her outstanding work in treating patients. At the turn of the century the medical profession was a popular career choice for women. Several medical schools for women had been established in the late nineteenth century, and schools that previously had been all-male began accepting women students. Medicine was one of the few professions open to women that allowed them to work independently, and it was considered an appropriate career for a genteel woman, especially if she treated women and children. There was a burgeoning interest in health and nutrition at this period, and many new medical procedures and new pharmaceuticals were being introduced. Augusta Rucker was a member of the American Association for the Advancement of Science and a fellow of the Texas Academy. Her research was the anatomy of Koenenia and its position among the Arachnida. Her name was listed in the first edition of *American Men and Women of Science.*

Bibliography: *American Men and Women of Science* 1–8; Siegel, Patricia J. and Kay Thomas Finley, *Women in the Scientific Search.*

Rudnick, Dorothea
(1907–)
embryologist

Education: Ph.B., University of Chicago, 1928, Ph.D. in zoology, 1931

Employment: Fellow, Yale University, 1931–1934; research fellow, University of Rochester, 1934–1937; assistant instructor in genetics, Storrs experiment station, University of Connecticut, 1937–1939; instructor in zoology, Wellesley College, 1939–1940; assistant professor of biology, Albertus Magnus College, 1940–1948, professor, 1948–1977; research associate, Yale University, 1940–1971, associate fellow, 1969–1977; emeritus professor

Concurrent Positions: Guggenheim fellow, 1952–1953; U.S. Public Health Service special fellow, 1965–1966

Dorothea Rudnick has been recognized for her research in embryology. Because Albertus Magnus is a small liberal arts college with very limited laboratory facilities, she maintained a lab at nearby Yale University, where she conducted studies on the embryology of the chick and rat. Due to her heavy teaching and administrative responsibilities, this work was done of necessity during weekends or summers. After receiving her doctorate from the University of Chicago in 1931, she was a fellow at Yale and then at the University of Rochester. In 1937 she accepted a position as assistant instructor at the University of Connecticut and as instructor in zoology at Wellesley in 1939. She was appointed assistant professor of biology at Albertus Magnus in 1940, advanced to professor in 1948, and retired in 1977. During the Depression years when both assistantships and faculty positions were scarce, the quality of her work enabled her to continue her research in a continuous series of jobs at several institutions. For several years she served as editor of the symposia of the Society for the Study of Growth and Development. She was a member of the American Society of Zoologists, the American Association of Anatomists, the Society for Developmental Biology, the Tissue Culture Association, and the International Institute of Embryology. Her research included experimental embryology of the chick and rat; developmental genetics of the chick;

and enzymatic development in the liver, brain, and retina of the chick. Her photograph was included in Edna Yost's *Women of Modern Science.*

Bibliography: *American Men and Women of Science* 9–14; Ireland, Norma O., *Index to Scientists of the World;* Yost, Edna, *Women of Modern Science.*

Rumbold, Caroline Thomas
(1877–1949)
plant pathologist

Education: B.L., Smith College, 1901; A.M., Washington University, St. Louis, 1903, Ph.D., 1911

Employment: Science aide, Bureau of Plant Industry, U.S. Department of Agriculture, 1903–1905; assistant in botany, University of Missouri, 1908–1910; fellow, Missouri Botanical Garden, 1910–1911; expert and collaborator, Bureau of Plant Industry, U.S. Department of Agriculture, 1911–1917, assistant pathologist, 1917–1919, plant pathologist, 1919–1924; assistant pathologist, Office of Forest Pathology, Madison, Wisconsin, 1924–1929, associate pathologist, 1929–1942

*C*aroline *Rumbold* was one of the few women scientists identified as working in the area of forest pathology. She worked for the Department of Agriculture for a total of 26 years. After receiving her master's degree from Washington University, St. Louis, in 1903, she accepted a position as a science aide at the U.S. Department of Agriculture (USDA). She returned to the St. Louis area, where she was an assistant in botany at the University of Missouri and a fellow at the Missouri Botanical Garden while completing her doctorate at Washington University,

which she received in 1911. She returned to the USDA in 1911 as an expert and collaborator, and moved up the ranks to assistant pathologist in 1917 and plant pathologist in 1919. She moved to the forestry laboratory at Madison, Wisconsin, as an assistant pathologist in 1924, was promoted to associate pathologist in 1929, and retired in 1942. She was one of many women scientists who found opportunities for advancement in government agencies that were not available in other work situations, and as part of the USDA she could publish research under her own name. During the

1930s she published at least four lengthy papers in the *USDA Journal of Agricultural Research*. She was a member of the American Association for the Advancement of Science, the American Phytopathological Society, and the American Society of Plant Physiologists. Her research included fungal disease of trees, the injection of chemicals into chestnut trees, and the blue stain of wood.

Bibliography: American Men and Women of Science 3–9; Barnhart, John H., *Biographical Notes upon Botanists; National Union Catalog.*

Russell, Elizabeth Shull
(1913–)
geneticist

Education: A.B., University of Michigan, 1933; A.M., Columbia University, 1934; Ph.D. in zoology, University of Chicago, 1937

Employment: Assistant, zoology, University of Chicago, 1935–1937; investigator, Jackson Laboratory, 1937–1940, research associate, 1946–1957, senior staff scientist, 1957–1982, emeritus senior scientist, 1982–1988

Concurrent Position: Guggenheim fellow, 1958–1959

Married: 1936

Elizabeth Russell has been recognized for her research on the pigmentation of mice. She spent much of her career at Jackson Laboratory, which is known internationally for its research in breeding mice to represent specific genetic conditions. After receiving her master's degree from Columbia in 1934, she joined the University of Chicago as an assistant in zoology while she completed her doctorate. She accepted an appointment at Jackson Laboratory as an investigator in 1937. She did not list any employment between 1940 and 1946, possibly due to family responsibilities; she and her husband had four children. She returned to Jackson in 1946 as a research associate, was promoted to senior staff scientist in 1957, emeritus senior scientist in 1982, and retired in 1988.

When a fire in 1947 destroyed the buildings at the laboratory, it also destroyed the mice that were bred there for scientific research throughout the world. She was in charge of rebuilding the stock of mice at that time, and she was able to accomplish the task within ten years. Elizabeth Russell was a pioneer in mouse genetics, and she identified several types of anemia. She also conducted significant research on muscular dystrophy. She received honorary degrees from several universities, and she was elected to the National Academy of Sciences in 1972. She was a member of the American Academy of Arts and Sciences, the Genetics Society of America, the American Society of Naturalists, and the Society for Developmental Biology. Her research included mammalian physiological genetics, the action of deleterious genes, mouse anemias and hemoglobins, coat color, muscular dystrophy, and genetic effects on aging. Her photograph is included in Edna Yost's *Women of Modern Science.* Her name is listed in the 1992–1993 edition of *American Men and Women of Science.*

Bibliography: American Men and Women of Science 7–18; Herzenberg, Caroline L., *Women Scientists from Antiquity to the Present;* O'Neill, Lois S., *The Women's Book of World Records and Achievements;* Yost, Edna, *Women of Modern Science.*

Russell, Jane Anne
(1911–1967)
endocrinologist

Education: B.A., University of California, Berkeley, 1932, Ph.D. in biochemistry, 1937
Employment: Technical assistant in biochemistry, University of California, Berkeley, 1932–1933, assistant, institute of experimental biology, 1934–1937; research associate, pharmacology, Washington University, St. Louis, 1936; research fellow in medicine, school of medicine, Yale University, 1938–1939, fellow, 1939–1941, instructor, physiological chemistry, 1941–1950; assistant professor of biochemistry, Emory University, 1950–1953, associate professor, 1953–1965, professor, 1965–1967
Married: Alfred E. Wilhelmi, 1940

Jane Russell was recognized for her research in endocrinology. After receiving her undergraduate degree at the University of California, Berkeley, she continued as an assistant while she completed her doctorate in biochemistry in 1937. She spent a year in 1936 collaborating with Carl and Gerty Cori (q.v.) at Washington University, St. Louis. She was appointed a research fellow in Yale's school of medicine in 1938, a fellow in 1939, and an instructor in physiological chemistry in 1941. She accepted a position as assistant professor of biochemistry at Emory in 1950, and she was promoted to associate professor in 1953 and professor in 1965, two years before her death. She was appointed to significant committees in the National Institutes of Health, the National Science Foundation, and the National Research Council, and she was a consultant for the National Science Board. She received the Ciba Award in 1945, and she shared the Upjohn Award of the Endocrine Society with her husband in 1961. She received little recognition for her work at Yale, however, and she remained at the rank of instructor before moving to Emory. She was a member of the American Physiological Society and the Endocrine Society. Her research included endocrine control of intermediate metabolism; adrenal cortex, anterior pituitary, growth hormone, and insulin in carbohydrate and protein metabolism; the metabolic aspects of shock; and the use of isotopic tracers in metabolism.

Bibliography: *American Men and Women of Science* 6–11; Herzenberg, Caroline L., *Women Scientists from Antiquity to the Present*; Sicherman, Barbara et al., *Notable American Women*; Siegel, Patricia J. and Kay Thomas Finley, *Women in the Scientific Search*.

Florence Rena Sabin
Ruth Sager
Grace Adelbert Sandhouse
Lucy Way Sistare Say
Berta Vogel Scharrer
Charlotte Angas Scott
Florence Barbara Seibert
Ellen Churchill Semple
Kate Olivia Sessions
Lydia White Shattuck
Jennie Maria Arms Sheldon
Althea Rosina Sherman
Lora Mangum Shields
Milicent Washburn Shinn
Odette Louise Shotwell
Sofia Simmonds
Dorothy Martin Simon
Charlotte Emma Moore Sitterly
Annie Trumbull Slosson
Maud Caroline Slye
Helen Edith Fox Smart
Elizabeth Hight Smith
Erminnie Adelle Platt Smith
Isabel Seymour Smith
Margaret Keiver Smith
Julia Warner Snow
Anna Louise Sommer
Effie Almira Southworth Spalding
Thressa Campbell Stadtman
Louise Stanley
Genevieve Stearns
Frances Stern
Nettie Maria Stevens
Matilda Coxe Evans Stevenson
Sara Yorke Stevenson
Lucille Farrier Stickel
Hazel Katherine Stiebeling
Alice Mary Stoll
Isabelle Stone
Ella Church Strobell
F. Agnes Naranjo Stroud-Lee
Betty J. Sullivan
Beatrice Marcy Sweeney

Sabin, Florence Rena
(1871–1953)
anatomist

Education: B.S., Smith College, 1893; M.D., Johns Hopkins University, 1900
Employment: Schoolteacher, 1894–1895; assistant in zoology, Smith College, 1896; intern, Johns Hopkins Hospital, 1901, assistant in anatomy, 1902, associate in anatomy, 1903–1905, associate professor, 1905–1917, professor of histology, 1917–1925; member, Rockefeller Institute, 1925–1938; emeritus member

Florence Sabin is regarded as the outstanding woman scientist in the medical field in the first half of this century. After she received her undergraduate degree from Smith in 1893, she taught school for two years to earn money to continue her education. She entered the medical school at Johns Hopkins in the fourth class the school offered, and she received her degree in 1900. As a student, she had shown great interest in research, and she published her first paper, as a second-year student, on the nuclei of cochlear and vestibular nerves. Choosing to continue in research, she was appointed an assistant in anatomy in 1902, an associate in 1903, an associate professor in 1905, and a professor of histology in 1917. When the research director retired, everyone assumed she would be named director, but a man was appointed to the position. She accepted a position as a member of the Rockefeller Institute in 1925, becoming an emeritus member in 1938. Here she conducted significant research on tuberculosis. After she retired, she became involved in reforming the public health legislation in Colorado and the city of Denver, and she developed a second career in public health and social issues.

She was the first woman faculty member at Johns Hopkins when she was appointed in 1902, and she was the first woman to become full professor in 1917. She was the first woman elected a member of the Rockefeller Institute, the first woman president of the American Association of Anatomists (1924–1926), and the first woman elected to the National Academy of Sciences (1925). Her major areas of research were the origin of the lymphatic vessels, the study of red and white corpuscles, and the pathogenesis of tuberculosis. Her first research efforts were in a controversial field, the origin of lymphatic vessels. By using the approach of injecting lymphatic channels with India ink, she demonstrated that the vessels derived from the venous system. This work caused considerable controversy but ultimately was acclaimed as a highly significant contribution. Other important contributions included the development of supravital staining techniques for living cells and the identification of the monocyte as a definitive type of white blood cell.

She received honorary degrees from a dozen universities. Among her honors and awards were the National Achievement Award (1932), the M. Carey Thomas Prize (1935), the Trudeau Medal of the National Tuberculosis Association (1945), and the Lasker Award (1951). A bronze statue was placed in her honor in Statuary Hall in Washington, D.C. In addition to her papers, she was the author of *An Atlas of the Medulla and Mid-Brain* (1901) and *Biography of Franklin Paine Mall* (1934). She was a member of the American Association for the Advancement of Science, the American Physiological Society, the Society for Experimental Biology and Medicine, the Harvey Society, and the National Tuberculosis Association. She was an honorary member of the New York Academy of Sciences. There are photographs in *Current Biography* and *Biographical Memoirs* of the National

Academy of Sciences. Her name was listed in the first edition and starred in the first through seventh editions of *American Men and Women of Science*.

Bibliography: *American Men and Women of Science* 1–8; Bryan, Alice I. and Edwin G. Boring, "Women in American Psychology"; *Current Biography*; Debus, A. G., ed., *World Who's Who in Science*; *Dictionary of American Biography*; *Dictionary of Scientific Biography*; Herzenberg, Caroline L., *Women Scientists from Antiquity to the Present*; Kass-Simon, G. and Patricia Farnes, *Women of Science*; McHenry, Robert, ed., *Famous American Women*; Macksey, Joan and Kenneth Macksey, *The Book of Women's Achievements*; Mozans, H. J., *Women in Science*; National Academy of Sciences, *Biographical Memoirs*; Ogilvie, Marilyn B., *Women in Science*; O'Neill, Lois S., *The Women's Book of World Records and Achievements*; Rossiter, Margaret W., *Women Scientists in America*; Rossiter, Margaret W., "Women Scientists in America before 1920"; Sicherman, Barbara et al., *Notable American Women*; Siegel, Patricia J. and Kay Thomas Finley, *Women in the Scientific Search*; Visher, Stephen S., *Scientists Starred 1903–1943 in "American Men of Science"*; Yost, Edna, *American Women of Science*.

Sager, Ruth
(1918–)
geneticist

Education: B.S., University of Chicago, 1938; M.S., Rutgers University, 1944; Ph.D. in genetics, Columbia University, 1948

Employment: Fellow, Rockefeller Institute, 1949–1951, assistant biochemist, 1951–1955; research associate in zoology, Columbia University, 1955–1960, senior research associate, 1960–1965; professor of biology, Hunter College, 1966–1975; professor of cellular genetics, Harvard medical school; chief, division of genetics, Farber Cancer Institute, 1975–

Concurrent Position: Guggenheim research fellow, 1972–1973

Married: 1973

Ruth Sager has pioneered the development of experimental material for the analysis of non-chromosome heredity, called non-Mendelian inheritance or cytoplasmic inheritance. Her work has changed the way biologists think about cell heredity. There was a long delay in recognizing her achievements, however; she remained a professor at Hunter for ten years before she was invited to head the cancer institute at Harvard. She received her doctorate in genetics from Columbia in 1948 and became a Merck research fellow for three years. She was appointed assistant biochemist at the Rockefeller Institute in 1951. In 1955 she returned to Columbia as a research associate and was promoted to senior research associate in 1960. She accepted a position at Hunter College as a professor of biology in 1966, and she continued in that role for ten years. She was appointed professor of cellular genetics at Harvard medical school and chief of the division of genetics of the Farber Cancer Institute in 1975.

Although she was working in an unpopular area of research, cytoplasmic inheritance, it seems incongruous that there was a long delay in recognizing her achievements. Along with other women who are profiled in this volume, she received renown only after the rise of the new feminism in the 1970s. She was elected to the National Academy of Sciences in 1977. Among her honors and awards, she has received the Gilbert Morgan Smith Medal of the National Academy of Sciences in 1988 and the Schneider Memorial Lectureship from the University of Texas in 1990.

She has coauthored two books: *Cell Heredity* (1961) and *Cytoplasmic Genes and Organelles* (1972). She has been a member of the American Society for Cell Biology, the Genetics Society of America, the American Academy of Arts and Sciences, the American Society of Biological Chemists, the American Association of Cancer Research, and the American Society of Human Genetics. Her research includes organelle genetics and biogenesis, mammalian cell genetics, genetic mechanisms of carcinogenesis, tumor suppressor genes, and breast cancer. Her name was listed in the 1992–1993 edition of *American Men and Women of Science.* Her photograph appeared in *Current Biography.*

Bibliography: *American Men and Women of Science* 9–18; *Current Biography;* Debus, A. G., ed., *World Who's Who in Science;* Herzenberg, Caroline L., *Women Scientists from Antiquity to the Present;* Kass-Simon, G. and Patricia Farnes, *Women of Science;* McHenry, Robert, ed., *Famous American Women;* O'Neill, Lois S., *The Women's Book of World Records and Achievements.*

Sandhouse, Grace Adelbert
(1896–1940)
entomologist

Education: A.B., University of Colorado, 1920, A.M., 1923; Cornell University, 1924–1925
Employment: Senior scientific aide, Federal Horticulture Board, U.S. Department of Agriculture, 1925–1926; junior entomologist, Bureau of Entomology and Plant Quarantine, U.S. Department of Agriculture, 1926–1928, assistant entomologist, 1928–1937, associate entomologist, 1937–1940

Grace Sandhouse was recognized for her research on bees and sawflies. Her publication, "The North American Bees of the Genus Osmia (Hymenoptera: Apoida)" (1939), was issued as Memoir number one of the Entomological Society of America. After receiving her master's degree from Cornell University, she joined the U.S. Department of Agriculture (USDA) in 1925 as a senior scientific aide for the Federal Horticulture Board. She then was promoted to junior entomologist in 1926, assistant entomologist in 1928, and associate entomologist in 1937.

She died in 1940. Along with other women scientists of that era, she enjoyed the advantage of advancing through the ranks at USDA and publishing her own research at a time when other agencies and other employers were not offering these opportunities. She published several papers in the *Proceedings* of the U.S. National Museum. She was a member of the American Association for the Advancement of Science and the Entomological Society of America. Her research was Aculeate Hymenoptera and taxonomy of Apoidea. A bibliography of her publications and a photograph were published in the *Proceedings* of the Entomological Society of America 42 (1940): 186–189. There also was a photograph in Herbert Osborn's *Fragments of Entomological History.*

Bibliography: *American Men and Women of Science* 5–7; Bonta, Marcia M., *Women in the Field; National Union Catalog;* Osborn, Herbert, *Fragments of Entomological History.*

Say, Lucy Way Sistare
(1801–1885)
artist

Education: No formal education
Employment: No formal employment
Married: Thomas Say, 1827, died 1834

*L*ucy Say's contribution to the development of science was as an artist. In the days before photography, drawings were the primary method for illustrating scientific publications. The wife of naturalist Thomas Say, she provided the majority of the illustrations for his book, *American Conchology* (1830–1834). They married when both were residents of New Harmony, a commune in southern Indiana that was a scientific and cultural center. She was a superb illustrator, and she provided numerous plates for most of his publications. One source states that at New Harmony she trained schoolchildren to assist her in coloring the illustrations by hand, the method used at the time to provide color plates. After her husband's death in 1834, she stayed at New Harmony to assist in publishing the final volumes of his book. She moved back to New York City to live with her sister, but returned to New Harmony from time to time to visit friends and discuss her husband's work. She probably was the first woman to join an American scientific society. In 1841 she was elected an associate member of the Academy of Natural Sciences of Philadelphia; one author speculated this was due to her contributing her husband's entomological cabinet and library to the academy's museums. She continued collecting specimens throughout her life, and for many years she corresponded with various naturalists about identifying them. One of the former leaders of the New Harmony commune provided an annuity of $300 for her in his will. It is not known how she supported herself in the intervening years. Her photograph is included in her husband's biographies, *Thomas Say: Early American Naturalist* (1931) by H. B. Weiss and G. M. Ziegler and *Thomas Say: New World Naturalist* (1992) by Patricia T. Stroud.

Bibliography: Herzenberg, Caroline L., *Women Scientists from Antiquity to the Present;* James, E. T., ed., *Notable American Women 1607–1950;* Ogilvie, Marilyn B., *Women in Science;* Rossiter, Margaret W., *Women Scientists in America.*

Scharrer, Berta Vogel
(1906–)
neuroendocrinologist

Education: Ph.D. in zoology, University of Munich, 1930
Employment: Assistant, Research Institute of Psychiatry, University of Munich, 1932–1934; guest investigator, Neurological Institute, Frankfurt, 1934–1937; guest investigator, department of anatomy, University of Chicago, 1937–1938; guest investigator, Rockefeller Institute, 1938–1940; senior instructor, Western Reserve University, 1940–1946; instructor and assistant professor, University of Colorado, 1946–1954; professor of anatomy, Albert Einstein Medical College, 1955–1978; emeritus professor
Concurrent Position: Guggenheim fellow, 1947–1948
Married: Ernst Scharrer, 1934, died 1965

Berta Scharrer and her husband, Ernst, pioneered the research on neurosecretion that helped to create a new discipline in physiology, that of neuroendocrinology. (Neurosecretion is the theory that nerves secrete hormones into the blood.) Among the most important of the couple's findings was the discovery that, in both mammals and insects, there were two completely analogous neuroendocrine organ systems, each of which controlled a variety of non-nervous processes. Berta Scharrer has concentrated on invertebrates while her husband studied vertebrates; therefore they produced few joint publications.

After receiving her doctorate from the University of Munich in 1930, she was appointed an assistant in the Research Institute of Psychiatry in Munich in 1932 and a guest investigator in the Neurological Institute in Frankfurt in 1934. After moving to the United States, she was appointed a guest investigator in the department of anatomy at the University of Chicago in 1937; she held a similar appointment at Rockefeller Institute in 1938. She accepted a position as a senior instructor at Western Reserve in 1940, and she was appointed an instructor and then assistant professor at the University of Colorado in 1946. She was appointed professor of anatomy at the Albert Einstein Medical College in 1955 and then emeritus professor in 1978. Due to nepotism rules at most institutions, she was unable to obtain a full-time faculty appointment until the couple joined the Einstein Medical College. In several interviews, Berta Scharrer said the situation was to her advantage because she could concentrate on research without the burden of administrative responsibilities and pressure to publish. She has received several awards, and she received honorary degrees from eight universities. Among her honors were the Kraepelin Gold Medal Award (1978), the Koch Award (1980), the Henry Gray Award (1982), the Schleiden Medal (1983), and the National Medal of Science from the National Science Foundation (1983). She was elected to the National Academy of Sciences in 1967 and elected president of the American Association of Anatomists for the 1978–1979 term. She was an honorary member of the American Society of Zoologists and the International Society of Neuroendocrinology. She has been a member of the American Academy of Arts and Sciences and several German and other European scientific academies. Her research has included neuroendocrinology and neurosecretion, comparative endocrinology, ultrastructure, and neuroimmunology. Her name was listed in the 1992–1993 edition of *American Men and Women of Science.*

Bibliography: American Men and Women of Science 8–18; Debus, A. G., ed., *World*

Who's Who in Science; Herzenberg, Caroline L., *Women Scientists from Antiquity to the Present;* Kass-Simon, G. and Patricia Farnes, *Women of Science;* O'Neill, Lois S., *The Women's Book of World Records and Achievements.*

Scott, Charlotte Angas
(1858–1931)
mathematician

Education: Girton College, Cambridge University, 1876–1880; B.S., University of London, 1882, D.Sc. in mathematics, 1885
Employment: Lecturer in mathematics, Girton College, 1880–1884; associate professor, mathematics department, Bryn Mawr College, 1885–1888, professor, 1888–1925

*C*harlotte Scott probably was the most recognized woman mathematician of her time. Her name was listed in the first edition and starred in the first through the fourth editions of *American Men and Women of Science.* In a study of 93 eminent American mathematicians in 1903, she was one of only three women included, as reported by Stephen Visher in *Scientists Starred 1903–1943 in "American Men of Science."* Although she placed eighth in the exams as an undergraduate, she did not graduate because Cambridge University did not grant degrees to women. She received a doctorate from the University of London in 1885, however, after continuing her studies at that university while she was a resident lecturer at Girton College. She was invited to come to the United States to develop the mathematics department at the newly opened Bryn Mawr College. At the time, she was one of the few women in the world who had been granted a doctorate in mathematics. She was instrumental in organizing the American Mathematical Society in 1894 and 1895 and was the only woman to be a charter member. She maintained contacts with many European societies. She was an expert in algebraic geometry, and published more than 30 papers on this subject. She was the author of a highly respected textbook, *An*

Introductory Account of Certain Modern Ideas and Methods in Plane Analytical Geometry (1894, 1924, 1961). The analytical geometry in the title was not the subject that is taught today to high school seniors and college freshmen; instead it was an introduction to projective algebraic geometry with prerequisites of Cartesian geometry and differential calculus. Her research included the theory of plane algebraic curves, singularities, intersections, systems of curves, transformation, and the nature of circuits. As early as her teaching days at Girton, she experienced a loss of hearing that gradually grew worse, hindering both her social and professional life; in later life she was completely deaf. While living in the United States she enjoyed gardening, but when she returned to England after retiring, she started betting on horses as a diversion, using her knowledge of mathematical statistics as an aid.

Bibliography: *American Men and Women of Science* 1–4; Elliott, Clark A., *Biographical Dictionary of American Science;* Grinstein, Louise S. and Paul J. Campbell, eds., *Women of Mathematics;* Herzenberg, Caroline L., *Women Scientists from Antiquity to the Present;* James, E. T., ed., *Notable American Women 1607–1950;* Kass-Simon, G. and Patricia Farnes, *Women of Science;* Mozans, H. J., *Women in*

Science; O'Neill, Lois S., *The Women's Book of World Records and Achievements*; Rossiter, Margaret W., *Women Scientists in America*; Rossiter, Margaret W., "Women Scientists in America before 1920"; Siegel, Patricia J. and Kay Thomas Finley, *Women in the*

Scientific Search; Uglow, Jennifer S., *International Dictionary of Women's Biography*; Visher, Stephen S., *Scientists Starred 1903–1943 in "American Men of Science."*

Seibert, Florence Barbara
(1897–1991)
biochemist

Education: A.B., Goucher College, 1918; Ph.D. in physiological chemistry, Yale University, 1923

Employment: Chemist, Hammersley Paper Mill, 1918–1920; instructor in pathology, University of Chicago, assistant, Sprague Memorial Institute, 1924–1928, assistant professor and associate biochemist, 1928–1932; assistant professor, Henry Phipps Institute, University of Pennsylvania, 1932–1937, associate professor, 1937–1955, professor, 1955–1959; emeritus professor

Concurrent Positions: Guggenheim fellow, Upsala, 1937–1938; visiting lecturer, various schools, 1946–1948; director, cancer research laboratory, Mound Park Hospital Foundation, 1964–1966

Florence Seibert was recognized as the person who purified the tuberculin PPD that is used worldwide in skin tests to detect tuberculosis. A case of polio in childhood left her partially lame, thus preventing her from pursuing a career as a physician. The main focus of her research was tuberculosis, but later she investigated the chemistry of cancer. She was one of the few early women physiological chemists who worked for a private company. After receiving her undergraduate degree, she worked as a chemist for a paper mill, possibly due to the shortage of male chemists during World War I. She returned to school to continue her graduate studies at Yale, where she received her doctorate in 1923. She joined the faculty of the University of Chicago as an instructor in pathology in 1924 and was promoted to assistant professor in 1928. She accepted a position as assistant professor at the University of Pennsylvania in 1932, being promoted to associate professor in 1937 and professor in 1955, just four years before she was named emeritus professor. Later she was director of the cancer research laboratory at Mound Park Hospital Foundation, serving from 1964 to 1966. She received a number of awards for her work: the Trudeau Medal from the National Tuberculosis Association (1938), the Garvan Medal (1942), the Gimbal Award (1945), the Scott Award (1947), and the Elliot Memorial Award (1962). She was a member of the American Association for the Advancement of Science, the American Cancer Society, and the American Association of Blood Banks. Her research included intravenous therapy and blood transfusions, the standard tuberculin PPD-S, and the isolation of specific pleomorphic bacteria to give some immunity in cancer. Her name was included in the 1992–1993 edition of *American Men and Women of Science* with the notation that she was deceased.

Bibliography: *American Men and Women of Science 9–18; Current Biography;* Hall, Diana Long, "Academics, Bluestockings, and Biologists"; Herzenberg, Caroline L., *Women Scientists from Antiquity to the Present;* Mozans, H. J., *Women in Science;* O'Neill, Lois S., *The Women's Book of World Records and Achievements;* Rossiter, Margaret W., *Women Scientists in America;* Yost, Edna, *American Women of Science.*

Semple, Ellen Churchill
(1863–1932)
geographer

Education: A.B., Vassar College, 1882, A.M., 1891; University of Leipzig, 1891–1892, 1895
Employment: Founder and teacher, Semple Collegiate School, 1893–1895; lecturer on anthropology, University of Chicago, various years, 1906–1920; lecturer, Clark University, 1921–1923, professor, 1923–1932
Concurrent Positions: Lecturer, Oxford University, 1912, 1922; Wellesley College, 1914–1915; University of Colorado, 1916; Columbia University, 1918

llen Semple was recognized by her contemporaries as one of the outstanding geographers of her time. After attending the University of Leipzig, she and her sister opened a private school in which she taught history. She combined this experience with her interest in geography in her book *American History and Its Geographic Conditions* (1903). This attracted attention from her contemporaries and resulted in invitations to teach at the University of Chicago. Her second book was *Influences of Geographic Environment, on the Basis of Ratzel's System of Anthropo-Geography* (1911), viewed as one of the most scholarly books on geography at that time. A third book, published shortly before her death, was *The Geography of the Mediterranean Region: Its Relation to Ancient History* (1931).

After she received her undergraduate degree from Vassar in 1882, she returned home to teach in a private school. She opened her own school in 1893 after returning from Europe. Throughout her career she rode into the backcountry of Kentucky to study the influence of geographic isolation on the life of the people there. Her papers on her research received favorable reviews. She taught anthropo-geography at the University of Chicago various years between 1906 and 1920. She also lectured at Oxford University, Wellesley College, the University of Colorado, and Columbia University. In 1921 she joined the new graduate department of geography at Clark University and was promoted to professor in 1923. Her scholarship was highly regarded by her contemporaries. She received the Cullum Medal of the American Geographical Society (1914) and the gold medal of the Geographic Society of Chicago (1932). She received an honorary degree from the University of Kentucky in 1923, and in 1921 she was the first woman to be elected president of the Association of American Geographers. She also was a member of the American Geographical Society. Her biography and photograph were included in *Annals* of the Association of American Geographers 23 (1933): 229–240. Her name was listed in the first four editions of *American Men and Women of Science.*

Bibliography: *American Men and Women of Science 1–4;* Debus, A. G., ed., *World Who's*

Who in Science; Dictionary of American Biography; Herzenberg, Caroline L., *Women Scientists from Antiquity to the Present;* James, E. T., ed., *Notable American Women 1607–1950;* O'Neill, Lois S., *The Women's Book of World Records and Achievements;*

Rossiter, Margaret W., *Women Scientists in America before 1920;* Rossiter, Margaret W., *Women Scientists in America;* Siegel, Patricia J. and Kay Thomas Finley, *Women in the Scientific Search.*

Sessions, Kate Olivia
(1857–1940)
horticulturist and nursery owner

Education: Ph.B. in chemistry, University of California, Berkeley, 1881
Employment: Teacher and high school principal, 1882–1885; owner of a plant nursery, 1885–1940; owner of a retail flower shop, 1885–1909; supervisor of agriculture, grammar schools, 1915–1918

Kate Sessions was the founder of Balboa Park in San Diego. She was famous for the new varieties of plants she introduced into the San Diego area and into the horticultural trade in general. In her world travels, she brought back such new plants as queen palm, flame eucalyptus, camphor trees, various acacias, and many vines, aloes, and succulents. She received the Ph.B. degree from the University of California, Berkeley, in 1881 with a major in chemistry. After working as a teacher in Oakland, she moved in 1882 to San Diego as an instructor and principal of what is now San Diego High School.

In 1885 she left teaching to open the first of her plant nurseries. In 1892 she leased 30 acres in the San Diego city park to use as a plant nursery on the condition that she plant 100 trees there annually and donate 300 more to the city; this was the beginning of Balboa Park. At various times she owned nurseries in Coronado, Mission Hills, and Pacific Beach; she also owned a retail flower shop in San Diego. She published about 250 popular articles in the magazine *California Garden,* and she founded Arbor Day celebrations in San Diego. She sold her retail flower shop in 1909 but continued to operate a nursery business until her death. Between 1915 and 1918 she served as supervisor of agriculture for the San Diego grammar schools. In 1939 she conducted classes for adults, "Gardening Practice and Landscape Design," for the University of California Extension Division. In 1956 an elementary school was named in her honor as was a memorial park in the town of Pacific Beach in 1957.

Bibliography: Barnhart, John H., *Biographical Notes upon Botanists;* James, E. T., ed., *Notable American Women 1607–1950;* O'Neill, Lois S., *The Women's Book of World Records and Achievements;* Siegel, Patricia J. and Kay Thomas Finley, *Women in the Scientific Search;* Uglow, Jennifer S., *International Dictionary of Women's Biography.*

Shattuck, Lydia White
(1822–1889)
botanist, chemist, and naturalist

Education: Graduated, Mount Holyoke Seminary, 1851; Anderson School of Natural
  History, 1873
Employment: Teacher, public schools, 1837–1846; teacher, Mount Holyoke Seminary,
  1851–1889; professor emeritus
Concurrent Position: Member, Woods Hole Biological Laboratory Corporation, 1889

*L*ydia Shattuck was considered one of
the most knowledgeable American
women working in botanical and
natural history studies. She was recognized
as an outstanding science teacher at Mount
Holyoke, but her own scientific background
was developed largely from wide reading
and association with scientists at other
institutions. Typically women botanists of
her generation concentrated on
classification of plants and setting up
collections, and she excelled at both. Her
correspondence with other scientists is the
major record of her research and
observations. Her career was typical of
many women of her generation. She taught
public school for about ten years, and
entered Mount Holyoke Seminary at the
age of 26. After she was graduated, she
taught at the school for many years. She
trained her students in all aspects of science:
botany, chemistry, physiology, physics,
mathematics, and astronomy. She
developed her interests in botany through
travel, including a trip to Hawaii. The
school built an impressive herbarium and
botanical garden under her direction. After
Mount Holyoke became a college in 1888,
she was named professor emeritus when
she retired in 1889. She was elected a
member of the Woods Hole Biological
Laboratory Corporation in 1889. In the
1890s the college named a chemistry and
physics building in her memory. When this
building was demolished in 1954, the name
was transferred later to a physics building.

Bibliography: Abir-Am, P. G. and
Dorinda Outram, eds., *Uneasy Careers and
Intimate Lives;* Barnhart, John H.,
Biographical Notes upon Botanists; Elliott,
Clark A., *Biographical Dictionary of
American Science;* Herzenberg, Caroline L.,
*Women Scientists from Antiquity to the
Present;* James, E. T., ed., *Notable American
Women 1607–1950; National Union Catalog;*
Rossiter, Margaret W., *Women Scientists in*

America; Rudolph, Emanuel D., "Women in Nineteenth Century American Botany"; Siegel, Patricia J. and Kay Thomas Finley, *Women in the Scientific Search.*

Sheldon, Jennie Maria Arms
(1852–1938)
entomologist

Education: Massachusetts Institute of Technology, 1877–1879; laboratory school of the Boston Society of Natural History, 1879–1880
Employment: Special teacher, public schools, 1878–1897; staff member, museum of Boston Society of Natural History, 1890–1904; curator of museum, Pocumtuck Valley Memorial Association, 1912–?, president, 1929–?
Married: George Sheldon, 1897

*J*ennie Sheldon was recognized as an entomologist when she coauthored an important book on insects. Her career was fairly typical for women scientists of her generation when there were limited opportunities for science education. Women learned by working with and assisting the experts, and they often taught subjects on which they had very little academic background. They retired from outside employment after marriage but continued to work on a volunteer basis, and many produced high levels of research due to their interest and perseverance. Jennie Sheldon attended the Massachusetts Institute of Technology for two years and the laboratory school of the Boston Society of Natural History as a special student for one year. Meanwhile she was a special teacher in zoology and geology in the Boston schools from 1878 until she married in 1897. She also lectured during the summers of 1886, 1887, and 1888 at Saratoga. She was an assistant to Alpheus Hyatt at the Natural History laboratory for

25 years, perhaps on a volunteer basis after 1904. They were coauthors of the book *Insecta* (1890). After her marriage she continued to study in Deerfield, Massachusetts, and to publish articles on the clays of the Connecticut Valley, invertebrates, and historical subjects. She published another book, *Concretions from the Champlain Clays of the Connecticut Valley* (1900). She was a member of the American Association for the Advancement of Science and the Boston Society of Natural History. She worked to establish the Naples Table for Promoting Laboratory Research by Women.

Bibliography: *American Men and Women of Science* 2–5; Herzenberg, Caroline L., *Women Scientists from Antiquity to the Present*; Mozans, H. J., *Women in Science; National Union Catalog*; Ogilvie, Marilyn B., *Women in Science*; Siegel, Patricia J. and Kay Thomas Finley, *Women in the Scientific Search.*

Sherman, Althea Rosina
(1853–1943)
ornithologist

Education: A.B., Oberlin College, 1875, A.M., 1882; Art Institute in Chicago and Art Students' League in New York

Employment: Teacher, public schools, 1875–1879; instructor in drawing, Carleton College, 1882–1887; supervisor of drawing, public schools, 1892–1895

Althea Sherman was an expert on the birds of Iowa, and she included her drawings in the papers she published. Although she planned to be a professional artist, she returned home in 1895 to care for her elderly parents. After they died she launched her career as an ornithologist at the age of 50. She established her research studies and published extensively in ornithological journals from her home in National, Iowa. After receiving her undergraduate degree from Oberlin College, she taught in public schools for five years before returning to Oberlin for her master's degree. She was employed as an instructor in drawing at Carleton College for six years and supervisor of drawing in public schools for another four years.

The research project that she established in Iowa was the nesting biology of birds. She used her talent for drawing in her detailed field notes on the life histories of many bird species nesting at what she called her "Iowa dooryard." She was particularly interested in cavity-nesting birds, such as woodpeckers, of which very little information was available at the time. Many of the studies of nesting biology reported by other ornithologists involved only two or three seasons of observations, while hers represented 35 years of study. One of her best-known projects was on the chimney swift. In order to attract this species, in 1915 she had a 28-foot tower built on her property. There was an artificial chimney inside, with windows and observation holes permitting unobstructed viewing of different parts of the chimney.

From 1918, when the swifts first came to nest, to 1936 she filled more than 400 pages of notes. In order to keep abreast of current ornithological research, she attended scientific meetings, where she presented papers and exhibited her bird art. The quality of her research was supported by her election to membership in the American Ornithologists' Union in 1912. There were very few women members at the time in that predominantly male organization. Her book, *Birds of an Iowa Dooryard,* was published posthumously in 1952. A biography, a bibliography of her papers, and several photographs are included in *Iowa Bird Life* 13 (1943): 19–35. Margaret Nice (q.v.) also published an article about her in *Iowa Bird Life* 22 (1952): 51–55. There are photographs also in P. G. Abir-Am's and Dorinda Outram's *Women in the Field* and *Uneasy Careers and Intimate Lives.*

Bibliography: Abir-Am, P. G. and Dorinda Outram, eds., *Uneasy Careers and Intimate Lives; American Men and Women of Science* 3–8; Bonta, Marcia M., *Women in the Field;* Herzenberg, Caroline L., *Women Scientists from Antiquity to the Present; National Union Catalog;* Rossiter, Margaret W., *Women Scientists in America.*

Shields, Lora Mangum
(1912–)
biologist

Education: B.S., University of New Mexico, 1940, M.S., 1942; Ph.D. in botany, University of Iowa, 1947
Employment: Associate professor of biology, New Mexico Highlands University, 1947–1954, professor and department head, 1954–1978, director, Environmental Health Division, 1971–1978; researcher and visiting professor, Navajo Community College, Shiprock, New Mexico, 1978–
Concurrent Positions: Research grants from agencies including Atomic Energy Commission, National Institutes of Health, National Science Foundation, March of Dimes Birth Defects Foundation, and Minority Biomedical Research Support
Married: 1931

*L*ora Shields has been recognized for her research on the effects of nuclear bomb testing in the Southwest and the health hazards from mining uranium. After she received her doctorate from the University of Iowa, she was appointed associate professor of biology at New Mexico Highland University in 1947. She was promoted to professor and department head in 1954 and named director of the Environmental Health Division in 1971. A Native American, she has been examining the health and environment of New Mexico and New Mexicans since the 1970s. She was appointed researcher and visiting professor at Navajo Community College in 1978. She has received research grants from some of the agencies that recently declassified data regarding the effects of nuclear testing on humans, such as the Atomic Energy Commission. Her research has focused on nuclear effects on vegetation, serum lipids in Spanish- and Anglo-Americans, birth anomalies in the Navajo uranium district, plant nitrogen sources and leaf nitrogen content, and streptococcal disease among the Navajos. She has been a member of the American Association for the Advancement of Science and the Ecological Society of America. She is the mother of one child. Her name was listed in the 1992–1993 edition of *American Men and Women of Science.*

Bibliography: *American Men and Women of Science* 9–18; Herzenberg, Caroline L., *Women Scientists from Antiquity to the Present*; O'Neill, Lois S., *The Women's Book of World Records and Achievements.*

Shinn, Milicent Washburn
(1858–1940)
psychologist

Education: A.B., University of California, Berkeley, 1880, Ph.D., 1898
Employment: Teacher, public schools, 1875–1876, 1881–1882; editor *San Francisco Commercial Herald,* 1879–1881; editor, *Overland Monthly,* 1883–1894

*M*ilicent Shinn was recognized for her detailed and systematic observations of the physical and mental development of a child. After teaching public school for years, she received an undergraduate degree from the University of California in 1880, about the time she became a member of the editorial staff of a San Francisco paper. She returned to teaching again before becoming editor of the *Overland Monthly* in 1883. She contributed poetry and prose in addition to editorial content for both of the newspapers with which she was involved. She was considered an excellent writer. In 1894 she sold her interest in the *Overland Monthly* to concentrate on making a careful and detailed record of the physical and mental development of a niece. At the same time she enrolled in the University of California graduate school. When published, her detailed notes were the basis for her thesis for a doctorate in psychology; for some years hers were among the few systematic observations published in English, and they attracted international scientific and popular attention. She later published the reports in a popular form as *The Biography of a Baby* (1900). She was involved in educational sessions held during the Columbian Exposition of 1893 and a child study program held in San Francisco in 1894. She did no further work in psychology. She retired to the family ranch and became involved in community efforts on prohibition, forest conservation, and women's suffrage. She was a member of the American Association for the Advancement of Science. Her research included development of the senses in infancy, development of instinctive movement, primary education, and development of memory and association in infancy. Her name was listed in the first six editions of *American Men and Women of Science;* her first name sometimes is spelled Milicent and sometimes Millicent in various references.

Bibliography: *American Men and Women of Science* 1–6; Herzenberg, Caroline L., *Women Scientists from Antiquity to the Present;* James, E. T., ed., *Notable American Women 1607–1950;* Rossiter, Margaret W., *Women Scientists in America;* Siegel, Patricia J. and Kay Thomas Finley, *Women in the Scientific Search;* Vare, Ethlie Ann and Greg Ptacek, *Mothers of Invention.*

Shotwell, Odette Louise
(1922–)
organic chemist

Education: B.S., Montana State University, 1944; M.S., University of Illinois, 1946, Ph.D. in organic chemistry, 1948

Employment: Assistant, inorganic chemistry, University of Illinois, 1944–1948; chemist, Northern Regional Research Laboratory, U.S. Department of Agriculture (USDA), 1948–1977, research leader, mycotoxin analysis and chemical research, 1975–1984, research leader, mycotoxin research, 1985–1989

Concurrent Positions: Consultant, Bureau of Veterinary Medicine, Food and Drug Administration, 1981–1986; consultant, Canadian Health and Welfare Department, 1983–1989; collaborator, Northern Center for Agricultural Utilization Research, USDA, 1990–

*O*dette Shotwell has made significant contributions to environmental science, and she has been recognized for her work in developing a cancer-producing toxin from molds. After receiving her doctorate from the University of Illinois, she joined the Northern Regional Research Laboratory of the U.S. Department of Agriculture in Peoria in 1948. She was promoted to research leader in mycotoxin analysis and chemical research in 1975 and research leader in mycotoxin research in 1985 before retiring in 1989. She has continued to work for the agency, now called the Northern Center for Agricultural Utilization Research, as a collaborator since 1990. Among the awards she has received have been the Harvey W. Wiley Award (1982) and the Outstanding Handicapped Federal Employee Award (1969). She was elected a fellow of the Association of Official Analytical Chemists, and she also has been a member of the American Association for the Advancement of Science, the American Chemical Society, the American Oil Chemists' Society, and the American Association of Cereal Chemists. Her research has included synthetic organic chemistry; the chemistry of natural products including isolation, purification, and characterization; microbial insecticides; and mycotoxins. Her name was included in the 1992–1993 edition of *American Men and Women of Science*.

Bibliography: *American Men and Women of Science* 8–18; Herzenberg, Caroline L., *Women Scientists from Antiquity to the Present*; O'Neill, Lois S., *The Women's Book of World Records and Achievements*.

Simmonds, Sofia
(1917–)
biochemist

Education: B.A., Columbia University, 1938; Ph.D. in biochemistry, Cornell University, 1942

Employment: Assistant biochemist, medical college, Cornell University, 1941–1942, research associate, 1942–1945; instructor, physiological chemistry, school of medicine, Yale University, 1945–1946, microbiologist, 1946–1949, assistant professor, 1949–1950, assistant professor, biochemistry and microbiology, 1950–1954, associate professor, 1954–1962, biochemist, 1962–1969, molecular biophysicist and biochemist, 1969–1975, professor; 1975–1988, associate dean and dean of undergraduate studies, 1988, lecturer and dean of undergraduate studies, 1990–1991, emeritus professor

Concurrent Position: Director of undergraduate studies, department of molecular biophysics and biochemistry, Yale University, 1973–1985

Married: 1936

*S*ofia Simmonds has been recognized for her research on bacteria amino acid metabolism. In the past 20 years she has had many administrative responsibilities in the Yale medical school, some of which continued after her retirement. After receiving her undergraduate degree from Columbia in 1938, she attended Cornell University, where she received her doctorate in biochemistry in 1942. She continued working there as a research associate until 1945. She accepted an appointment as instructor of physiological chemistry in the school of medicine at Yale in 1945, advanced to microbiologist in 1946, assistant professor in 1949, assistant professor of biochemistry and microbiology in 1950, associate professor in 1954, biochemist in 1962, molecular biophysicist and biochemist in 1969, and professor in 1975. She was named associate dean and dean of undergraduate studies in 1988 at the same time that she was named emeritus professor. She continued to work as lecturer and dean of undergraduate studies in 1990 and 1991. She received the Garvan Medal in 1969. She has been a member of the American Society of Biological Chemists and the American Chemical Society. Her research has included amino acid metabolism, transmethylation in animals, and amino acid and protein metabolism in microorganisms. Her name was listed in the 1992–1993 edition of *American Men and Women of Science.*

Bibliography: *American Men and Women of Science* 8–18; Herzenberg, Caroline L., *Women Scientists from Antiquity to the Present;* O'Neill, Lois S., *The Women's Book of World Records and Achievements.*

Simon, Dorothy Martin
(1919–)
physical chemist

Education: A.B., Southwest Missouri State College, 1940; Ph.D. in chemistry, University of Illinois, 1945

Employment: Assistant in chemistry, University of Illinois, 1941–1945; research chemist, E. I. Du Pont de Nemours & Company, 1945–1946; chemist, Clinton Laboratory, 1947; associate chemist, Argonne National Laboratory, 1948–1949; aeronautical research scientist, Lewis Laboratory, National Advisory Committee on Aeronautics, 1949–1953, assistant chief, chemical branch, 1954–1955; Rockefeller fellow, Cambridge University, 1953–1954; group leader in combustion, Magnolia Petroleum Company, 1955–1956; principal scientist and technical assistant to president, research and advanced development division, Avco Corporation, 1956–1962, director of corporate research, 1962–1964, vice president, defense and industrial products group, 1964–1968, corporate vice president and director of research, 1968–1981

Concurrent Positions: Marie Curie lecturer, Pennsylvania State University, 1962; member, NASA Space Systems and Technology Advisory Committee, 1978–; member, committee of sponsored research, Massachusetts Institute of Technology, 1972–; member, President's Committee on the National Medal of Science, 1978–1981

Married: 1946

*D*orothy Simon has had a distinguished career as a researcher and administrator. She has been an international expert in the field of combustion, and she has been vice president of research for a major company since 1968. After receiving her doctorate from the University of Illinois in 1945, she worked for E. I. Du Pont de Nemours, Clinton Laboratory, Argonne National Laboratory, the National Advisory Committee on Aeronautics (the predecessor of NASA), and Magnolia Petroleum Company, all before 1956. She was named assistant to a division president of Avco Corporation in 1956 and rose to corporate vice president and director of research in 1968.

She served on prestigious national and international committees. She served on the boards of directors of five corporations, and she was a trustee for two universities. She received the Rockefeller Public Service Award in 1953 and the Society of Women Engineers' Achievement Award in 1956. She was elected a fellow of the American Institute of Aeronautics and Astronautics and a fellow of the American Institute of Chemists. She also has been a member of the American Association for the Advancement of Science, the American Chemical Society, and the Combustion Institute. Her research has included combustion, aerothermo chemistry, and research management and strategic planning. Her name was listed in the 1992–1993 edition of *American Men and Women of Science.*

Bibliography: *American Men and Women of Science* 8–18; Herzenberg, Caroline L., *Women Scientists from Antiquity to the Present;* Kass-Simon, G. and Patricia Farnes, *Women of Science;* O'Neill, Lois S., *The Women's Book of World Records and Achievements.*

Sitterly, Charlotte Emma Moore
(1898–1990)
astronomer

Education: A.B., Swarthmore College, 1920; Ph.D. in astronomy, University of California, Berkeley, 1931

Employment: Computer, Princeton Observatory, 1920–1925, 1928–1929, assistant spectroscopist, 1931–1936, research associate, 1936–1945; computer, Mount Wilson Observatory, 1925–1928; physicist, atomic physics division, National Bureau of Standards, 1945–1968; Office of Standard Reference Data, 1968–1970; U.S. Naval Research Laboratory, 1971–1978

Concurrent Positions: Member, committee on line spectra of the elements, National Research Council; member, commission on standard wavelengths and spectral tables, International Astronomical Union, 1950–1964; and numerous other similar committees; consultant, 1928–1990

Married: Bancroft W. Sitterly, 1937

Charlotte Sitterly was recognized for her work on major projects concerning atomic spectra, atomic energy levels, and spectroscopic data for more than 50 years. After receiving her undergraduate degree from Swarthmore in 1920, she was employed as a computer for the Princeton Observatory and the Mount Wilson Observatory for nine years. Returning to Princeton, she was promoted to assistant spectroscopist in 1931 and research associate in 1936. She accepted a position as a physicist at the National Bureau of Standards in 1945, then moved to the Office of Standard Reference Data in 1968 and to the Naval Research Laboratory in 1971, retiring in 1978. She received the Annie J. Cannon Prize in 1937, the Silver Medal in 1951 and the Gold Medal in 1960 of the U.S. Department of Commerce, and the Federal Women's Award in 1961.

Her expertise was recognized very early because her name was starred in the sixth and seventh editions of *American Men and Women of Science.* She authored or coauthored eight books, including *The Infrared Solar Spectrum* (1947), *Atomic Energy Levels* (1949–1958), and *An Ultraviolet Multiplet Table* (1950–1962). She was elected a fellow of the American Physical Society and the Optical Society of America. She also was a member of the American Association for the Advancement of Science and the American Astronomical Society. Her research has been identification of lines in solar and sunspot spectra, analysis of atomic spectra, and compilation of spectroscopy data derived from analysis of optical spectra. Her name was listed in the 1992–1993 edition of *American Men and Women of Science;* she was listed under Charlotte Moore in the fifth through seventh editions and as Charlotte Sitterly in later editions.

Bibliography: *American Men and Women of Science* 5–18; Debus, A. G., ed., *World Who's Who in Science;* Herzenberg, Caroline L., *Women Scientists from Antiquity to the Present;* O'Neill, Lois S., *The Women's Book of World Records and Achievements;* Rossiter, Margaret W., *Women Scientists in America;* Visher, Stephen S., *Scientists Starred 1903–1943 in "American Men of Science";* *Who Was Who in America.*

Slosson, Annie Trumbull
(1838–1926)
entomologist

Education: Public schools
Employment: No formal employment
Married: Edward Slosson, 1867

*A*nnie Slosson was an entomologist who popularized natural history. She collected unusual insects in her winter home in Florida and her summer home in New Hampshire to give to specialists for analysis. Her ability to discover strange insects seems to have been unusual, but she had the leisure time to explore random habitats. She also was very knowledgeable of which species were rare or unusual. Her own interest seemed to be

in the descriptions of the habitats or peculiarities of the insects she studied. Many new species were named in her honor. She started her collections late in her forties when she wanted to know which bugs infested her garden. She supported herself by writing popular magazine stories and books, primarily on New England village themes, and she also contributed articles on entomology to scientific journals. A typical popular paper she wrote was published in *Harpers* 75 (1887): 303 as "Aunt Randy: An Entomological Sketch." One source speculates that she was elected a member of the New York Entomological Society in 1893 because she was the primary financial backer of their journal. The members often met in her home in New York until she persuaded the American Museum of Natural History to let the group meet in the museum. For many years she was one of the group's few women members. There is a brief biography and a photograph in the *Journal* of the New York Entomological Society 34 (1926): 360–365. Her photograph is also included in Herbert Osborn's *Fragments of Entomological History*, and it is on file at the National Archives.

Bibliography: Bonta, Marcia M., *Women in the Field*; Herzenberg, Caroline L., *Women Scientists from Antiquity to the Present*; Mozans, H. J., *Women in Science; National Union Catalog*; Ogilvie, Marilyn B., *Women in Science*; Osborn, Herbert, *Fragments of Entomological History*; Rossiter, Margaret W., *Women Scientists in America*.

Slye, Maud Caroline
(1879–1954)
pathologist

Education: A.B., Brown University, 1899; University of Chicago, 1906, 1908–1911
Employment: Professor, psychology and pedagogy, Rhode Island State Normal School, 1899–1905; member of staff, Sprague Memorial Institute, University of Chicago, 1911–1944, instructor in pathology, 1919–1922, assistant professor, 1922–1926, associate professor and director of Cancer Laboratory, 1926–1944; emeritus professor

aud Slye was recognized by her contemporaries as a pioneer in the study of the inheritance of cancer in mice and how it related to human cancers. The popular press called her the American Curie for her contributions. She was a remarkable woman who held a prestigious directorship, although she did not have a doctorate. After receiving her undergraduate degree from Brown in 1899, she was appointed a professor of psychology and pedagogy at the Rhode Island State Normal School for seven years. She accepted an appointment as member of the staff at the new Sprague Memorial Institute in 1911, retiring in 1944. During this time she held a joint appointment as a faculty member at the University of Chicago, rising to the rank of associate professor and director of the Cancer Laboratory in 1926. Her theories on cancer later were proven to be incorrect. At first she theorized that susceptibility to cancer was limited to the presence of a single recessive character, but she later modified her ideas to agree that more than one gene was involved. A tireless worker, she raised and kept pedigrees on over 150,000 mice during her career. She received many honors for her contributions to cancer research, including a gold medal from the American Medical Association (1914), a gold medal from the American Radiological Society (1922), and the Ricketts Prize of the University of Chicago (1915). Brown University granted her an honorary degree in 1937. In addition to her scientific papers, she wrote two books of poetry: *Songs and Solaces* (1934) and *I in the Wind* (1936). Her work was discussed in detail in Bernard Jaffe's *Outposts of Science: A Journey to the Workshops of Our Leading Men of Research* (1935). She was a member of the American Medical Association and the New York

Academy of Sciences. There is also a photograph in *Current Biography*.

Bibliography: *American Men and Women of Science 6–8*; *Current Biography*; Herzenberg, Caroline L., *Women Scientists from Antiquity to the Present*; Kass-Simon, G. and Patricia Farnes, *Women of Science*; O'Neill, Lois S., *The Women's Book of World Records and Achievements*; Rossiter, Margaret W., *Women Scientists in America*; Sicherman, Barbara et al., *Notable American Women*; Siegel, Patricia J. and Kay Thomas Finley, *Women in the Scientific Search*.

Smart, Helen Edith Fox
(b. 1891)
bacteriologist and plant pathologist

Education: A.B., University of Michigan, 1918
Employment: Junior pathologist, Bureau of Plant industry, U.S. Department of Agriculture, 1918–1928, assistant pathologist, 1928–1936, assistant bacteriologist, Bureau of Agricultural Chemistry and Engineering, 1936–1943, associate marketing specialist, War Food Administration, 1943–1947, associate pathologist, Bureau of Plant Industry, Soils, and Agriculture, 1947–?
Married: Bernard J. Smart, 1927

Helen Smart was recognized by her contemporaries for her work in bacteriology. She began employment with the U.S. Department of Agriculture (USDA) just after receiving her undergraduate degree at the University of Michigan in 1918 and continued with the department for many years. She rose through the ranks from junior pathologist to assistant pathologist in 1928, assistant bacteriologist in 1936, associate marketing specialist in 1943, and associate pathologist in 1947. Although there was a ten-year period before she received her first promotion, she received a promotion during the Depression. This was quite an accomplishment, since jobs were scarce for both men and women, and married women especially found it impossible to find employment. Helen Smart retained her job, even though she was married. She was another of the many women who found opportunities for advancement in the bureaus at the USDA. She published at least one paper in the *USDA Journal of Agricultural Research*. Her research involved bacteriology of foods, microbiology of frozen foods, and storage diseases of fruits and vegetables. She was listed in some references under her maiden name, Helen Fox.

Bibliography: *American Men and Women of Science 4–8*; Barnhart, John H., *Biographical Notes upon Botanists*; *National Union Catalog*.

Smith, Elizabeth Hight
(1877–1933)
plant pathologist

Education: A.B., Smith College, 1900; M.S., Massachusetts College, 1905
Employment: Assistant in botany, Mount Holyoke College, 1901; high school teacher, 1902–1904; assistant in plant pathology, experiment station, University of California, Berkeley, 1905–1910, instructor, 1910–1915, assistant professor, 1915–1922

*E*lizabeth Smith was noted for her work as a plant pathologist. She was almost 30 years old when she started her college education. After receiving her undergraduate degree from Smith College in 1900, she was employed as an assistant botanist at Mount Holyoke for one year before teaching high school for two years. She continued her education and received a master's degree from Massachusetts College in 1905. She became an assistant plant pathologist at the experiment station of the University of California, Berkeley, in 1905. In 1910, she obtained a position as instructor. She was then assistant professor from 1915 until 1922. Although women scientists had difficulty finding jobs at any time in those days, women in academe had an added hurdle to overcome, seldom being promoted above the level of assistant

professor. In land grant institutions, however, women had the option of remaining staff members in the experiment station. Elizabeth Smith continued working for the experiment station until her death in 1933. She published one bulletin for the agricultural experiment station while a graduate student at Massachusetts College and four while employed at Berkeley. She was a member of the American Phytopathological Society. Her research was on diagnosis of plant disease.

Bibliography: *American Men and Women of Science* 3–6; Barnhart, John H., *Biographical Notes upon Botanists*; Herzenberg, Caroline L., *Women Scientists from Antiquity to the Present; National Union Catalog*; Rossiter, Margaret W., *Women Scientists in America.*

Smith, Erminnie Adelle Platt
(1836–1886)
geologist and ethnologist

Education: Graduate, Troy Female Seminary, New York, 1853; Universities of Strasbourg, Heidelberg, and Freiburg
Employment: Staff, Bureau of American Ethnology, Smithsonian Institution, 1880–1882
Married: Simeon H. Smith, 1855

*E*rminnie Smith was recognized by her contemporaries as an effective popularizer of science. She was the first woman to be elected a fellow of the

New York Academy of Sciences, and she was an early member of the American Association for the Advancement of Science. After her marriage, she continued her childhood interest in geology by independent study. While she was in Europe to supervise her sons' schooling for four years, she studied German and crystallography at several universities and completed the two-year mineralogy course at the school of mines in Freiburg. Back in the United States, she set up one of the country's largest private mineralogy collections in her home and started giving lectures on geological and cultural subjects. She founded the Aesthetic Society in Jersey City in 1876 and served as the first president. This was a group of women who met monthly to discuss papers on science, literature, and art. The club was typical of those that were established all over the country to encourage women to educate themselves because they were denied admittance to most universities. In 1880 she began a study of the Iroquois culture and language, and she was the first woman to carry out fieldwork in ethnography. Under the sponsorship of the Smithsonian Institution, she compiled an Iroquois-English dictionary, which remains unpublished in the Smithsonian archives. She published *Myths of the Iroquois* (1883). In 1883 Vassar College founded a geological prize in her honor.

Bibliography: *Appleton's Cyclopaedia of American Biography;* Debus, A. G., ed., *World Who's Who in Science; Dictionary of American Biography;* Elliott, Clark A., *Biographical Dictionary of American Science;* Helm, June, ed., *Pioneers of American Anthropology;* Herzenberg, Caroline L., *Women Scientists from Antiquity to the Present;* James, E. T., ed., *Notable American Women 1607–1950;* Rossiter, Margaret W., *Women Scientists in America;* Rossiter, Margaret W., "'Women's Work' in Science, 1880–1910"; Siegel, Patricia J. and Kay Thomas Finley, *Women in the Scientific Search.*

Smith, Isabel Seymour
(1864–1948)
botanist

Education: A.B., Oberlin College, 1901; M.S., University of Chicago, 1905, Ph.D., 1922
Employment: High school teacher, 1891–1895; assistant in botany, Oberlin College, 1897–1902; instructor in biology, Illinois College, 1903–1905, assistant professor, 1905–1909, professor, 1909–1927, dean of women, 1927–1948; assistant curator of herbarium, Oberlin College, 1928–1934; emeritus professor
Concurrent Position: Marine Biological Laboratory, Woods Hole, 1903, 1910

*I*sabel Smith was noted for her research on the trees of Illinois. After teaching high school for five years, she was appointed an assistant in botany at Oberlin in 1897 while she completed her undergraduate degree in 1901. She was in her late thirties at that time. She accepted a position as instructor in biology at Illinois College where she stayed until retiring in 1927. While teaching at Illinois College, she also served as dean of women for a time. (It was fairly common practice at that period for teaching faculty also to have sometimes heavy administrative responsibilities.) Interspersed with obtaining her master's degree and doctorate from the University of Chicago, she was promoted to assistant professor in 1905, professor in 1909, and emeritus professor in 1927. She then returned to Oberlin where she was assistant curator of the herbarium until 1934. Her career was fairly typical for a woman of her generation: teaching school for a time, and completing an undergraduate degree later in life than the average college graduate. She completed all three of her academic degrees while she was working. She was a member of the Botanical Society of America. Her research included nutrition of the egg in Zamia; native trees of Morgan County, Illinois; and herbarium work in flowering plants and fungi. Her name was listed in the first seven editions of *American Men and Women of Science.*

Bibliography: *American Men and Women of Science* 1–7; Siegel, Patricia J. and Kay Thomas Finley, *Women in the Scientific Search.*

Smith, Margaret Keiver
(1856–1934)
psychologist

Education: Diploma, Oswego Normal School, New York, 1883; Stoy's School and University of Jena, 1885–1887; University of Göttingen, 1896–1897; Ph.D., University of Zurich, 1900

Employment: Schoolteacher, 1887–1896; director of psychology and geography, State Normal School, New Paltz, New York, 1901–1909; supervisor of education of a family, 1909–1918; with department of languages, State Normal School, New Paltz, 1918–1934

Margaret Smith was involved in the beginnings of the discipline of child development and family studies. After receiving her diploma from the Oswego Normal School in 1883, she studied in Europe for two years. Then, beginning in 1887, she was a schoolteacher for ten years before returning to Germany to study at the University of Göttingen. She then received her doctorate from the University of Zurich in 1900. Her employer from 1909 to 1918, when she supervised a program on education of a family, could not be identified; it may have been a state extension program of some type. She then accepted a position with the department of languages at the normal school in New Paltz in 1918. At the time she was starting her career, the profession of psychology was in its infancy, and many people attended the European schools. Her career was typical for women scientists of her time—teaching in public school for a number of years before graduating from college and obtaining employment in her field of interest. She was a member of the American Psychological Association. Her research included psychology of rhythm and work, retarded development in a child, and the psychological value of Latin as a subject of instruction. Her name was listed in the first edition of *American Men and Women of Science.*

Bibliography: *American Men and Women of Science* 1–5; Siegel, Patricia J. and Kay Thomas Finley, *Women in the Scientific Search.*

Snow, Julia Warner
(1863–1927)
botanist

Education: B.S., Cornell University, 1888, M.S., 1889; Ph.D., University of Zurich, 1893
Employment: Science teacher, American College for Girls, Constantinople, 1894–1896; assistant in botany, University of Michigan, 1897–1898, instructor, 1898–1900; teacher, Rockford College, 1900–1901; assistant, Smith College, 1901–1902, instructor, 1902–1906, associate professor, 1906–1927

Julia Snow was recognized for her research on freshwater algae. After receiving degrees from Cornell University in 1888 and 1889, she took advanced work and received her doctorate from the University of Zurich in 1893, one of the first American women to receive a doctorate from a German university. She accepted a position as a science teacher at the American College for Girls at Constantinople in 1894 for three years and then had short-term appointments at the University of Michigan and at Rockford College.

She spent summers between 1898 and 1901 as a participant in the U.S. Fish Commission's biological survey of Lake Erie, studying plankton and microscopic forms of freshwater algae as part of the project. She was appointed an assistant at Smith College in 1901, and then was promoted to instructor in 1902 and associate professor in 1906, where she remained until 1927. She was fond of travel and became an authority on the art and architecture of China and India. In the 1890s she traveled alone through Russia, an unprecedented undertaking for a woman in her early thirties at that time. She was a member of the American Association for the Advancement of Science and the Botanical Society of America. Her name was listed in the first edition of *American Men and Women of Science.*

Bibliography: American Men and Women of Science 1–4; Barnhart, John H., *Biographical Notes upon Botanists;* Herzenberg, Caroline L., *Women Scientists from Antiquity to the Present;* Mozans, H. J., *Women in Science; National Union Catalog;* Ogilvie, Marilyn B., *Women in Science;* Rossiter, Margaret W., *Women Scientists in America;* Siegel, Patricia J. and Kay Thomas Finley, *Women in the Scientific Search.*

Sommer, Anna Louise
(b. 1889)
plant nutritionist

Education: B.S., University of California, Berkeley, 1920, M.S., 1921, Ph.D. in plant nutrition, 1924
Employment: Teaching fellow in botany, University of California, Berkeley, 1922–1924, plant nutritionist, 1924, assistant, 1924–1926; research fellow, University of Minnesota, 1926–1929; associate professor of plant nutrition and associate soil chemist, Alabama Polytechnic, 1930–1948, professor of soils and soil chemist, 1948–1949

*A*nna Sommer was one of the few women identified in this study as a soil chemist, which was usually considered a male profession. It is significant that she was promoted to professor only a year prior to her retirement, although she had received her doctorate from University of California, Berkeley. After receiving her doctorate in 1924, she continued working for the school for three years as a plant nutritionist and an assistant. She was appointed a research fellow at University of Minnesota in 1926 for three years. She then accepted a position as an associate professor of plant nutrition and associate soil chemist at Alabama Polytechnic in Auburn, Alabama. She remained an associate professor for 18 years before being promoted to professor in 1948. One reason for the delay in promotion could be explained by the shortage of jobs

during the Depression in the 1930s, but during World War II many women scientists had opportunities to gain promotions and increase their career opportunities. Even today, agriculture schools tend to be male dominated and traditional, although the number of women agriculture students has been increasing for the past ten years. Anna Sommer was a member of the American Association for the Advancement of Science, the American Society of Plant Physiologists, and the Soil Science Society of America. Her research centered on inorganic nutrition of plants and soil fertility.

Bibliography: *American Men and Women of Science* 4–10; Barnhart, John H., *Biographical Notes upon Botanists; National Union Catalog.*

Spalding, Effie Almira Southworth
(1860–1947)
plant pathologist

Education: B.S., University of Michigan, 1885; fellow, Bryn Mawr College, 1885–1887; fellow, Barnard College, Columbia University, 1893–1895; M.S., University of Southern California, 1923
Employment: Assistant pathologist, Bureau of Plant Industry, U.S. Department of Agriculture, 1888–1893; assistant professor of botany, University of Southern California, 1920–1926
Married: Volney M. Spalding, 1896, died 1918

*E*ffie Spalding was the first woman scientist who was employed by the U.S. Department of Agriculture (USDA). After receiving her undergraduate degree from the University of Michigan in 1885, she was a fellow at Bryn Mawr for three years. She was appointed assistant pathologist at the Bureau of Plant Industry, USDA, in 1888. She resigned in 1893 to attend Barnard College, but she left in 1895 without completing her degree. She received her master's degree from the University of Southern California in 1923

while teaching there. Her name was not included in *American Men and Women of Science* until the fourth edition.

She was the first of what proved to be a long line of women scientists who worked for the Bureau of Plant Industry, which accounted for the majority of the women scientists employed by the federal government until the 1920s, when the USDA established a home economics department. (Since the bureau permitted women to publish their research under their own names, they received recognition for their work and were listed in *American Men and Women of Science.*) Effie Spalding was the cotranslator of *The True Grasses* (1890). Unfortunately little biographical information could be located for her. Her research included fungi, mycology, and changes in form and growth of cacti in relation to water supply.

Bibliography: American Men and Women of Science 4–8; Baker, Gladys L., "Women in the U.S. Department of Agriculture"; Barnhart, John H., *Biographical Notes upon Botanists;* Harshberger, John W., *The Botanists of Philadelphia and Their Work;* Herzenberg, Caroline L., *Women Scientists from Antiquity to the Present;* National Union Catalog; Rossiter, Margaret W., "'Women's Work' in Science, 1880–1910"; Rudolph, Emanuel D., "Women in Nineteenth Century American Botany."

Stadtman, Thressa Campbell
(1920–)
biochemist

Education: B.S., Cornell University, 1940, M.S., 1942; Ph.D. in microbiology, University of California, 1949

Employment: Research assistant, nutrition, agricultural experiment station, Cornell University, 1942–1943; research associate, food microbiology, University of California, 1943–1946; research assistant, Harvard medical school, 1949–1950; biochemist, National Heart, Lung, and Blood Institute, National Institutes of Health, 1950

Concurrent Positions: Fellow, Oxford University, 1954–1955; institute of cell chemistry, Munich, 1960–1961; institute of biological and physical chemistry, France, 1961

Married: 1943

*T*hressa Stadtman has been recognized for her work in microbiology at the National Institutes of Health (NIH) since 1950. The quality of her work is seen by her election to the National Academy of Sciences in 1981 and her research at several European institutes. After receiving her master's degree from Cornell in 1942, she worked for the agricultural experiment station at Cornell for two years and in food microbiology at the University of California for four years. After receiving her doctorate from the University of California in 1949, she joined Harvard medical school as a research assistant the same year. In 1950 she accepted an appointment at the National Heart, Lung, and Blood Institute, where she stayed until retirement.

She originally worked in bacteriology, but she switched to microbiology after joining NIH. Among the honors she has received are the Hillebrand Award in 1979 and the Rose Award in 1987. She was a Whitney fellow at Oxford University and had a Rockefeller grant at the University of Munich. She was also a French government fellow. She has been a member of the American Society of Biological Chemists, the American Chemical Society, and the American Society of Microbiology. Her research has included amino acid intermediary metabolism, one-carbon metabolism, methane formation, microbial biochemistry, and selenium biochemistry. Her name was listed in the 1992–1993 edition of *American Men and Women of Science.*

Bibliography: American Men and Women of Science 9–18; Herzenberg, Caroline L., *Women Scientists from Antiquity to the Present.*

Stanley, Louise

(1883–1954)

chemist and home economist

Education: A.B., Peabody College, 1903; B.Ed., University of Chicago, 1906; A.M.,
Columbia University, 1907; Ph.D., Yale University, 1911
Employment: From instructor to professor and department chair, home economics,
University of Missouri, 1917–1923; chief, Bureau of Home Economics, U.S. Department
of Agriculture, 1923–1950; consultant for home economics, Office of Foreign Agricultural
Relations, 1950–1953

*L*ouise Stanley was the first woman to
direct a bureau in the U.S.
Department of Agriculture (USDA).
Her career coincided with the emergence of
home economics as a promising profession.
For many women it offered employment
opportunities and the chance to combine
scientific interest with education programs.
After receiving her master's degree from
Columbia University in 1907 and her
doctorate from Yale in 1911, she obtained
an appointment as an instructor in the
department of home economics at the
University of Missouri in 1917. She rose
through the ranks to professor and
department chair.

In 1923 she was the highest ranking
woman scientist in the federal government
when she was appointed as the first chief of
the Bureau of Home Economics, USDA, the
only woman bureau chief in the agency. She
retired in 1950. During her tenure, research
in nutrition led to the four basic diet plans
for families at different economic levels. She
directed the first national survey of rural
housing and the first survey of consumer
purchasing. Under her direction, the bureau
also conducted time and motion studies of
housekeeping methods and worked toward
standardizing clothing sizes. She was the
official representative of the USDA to the
American Standards Association, and was

the first woman to hold such an
appointment.

A specialist in home economics
education, during World War II she
developed programs for Latin American
countries. She received an honorary degree
in 1940 from the University of Missouri,
which dedicated the home economics
building in her name in 1961. She was the
author of *Foods, Their Selection and
Preparation* (1935). She was a member of the
American Chemical Society and the
American Home Economics Association.
Her research included food chemistry,
organic and inorganic phosphorus, purin
enzymes, and temperatures for baking.
There is a photograph in *Yearbook of
Agriculture* (1962).

Bibliography: *American Men and Women of
Science* 3–8; Baker, Gladys L., "Women in
the U.S. Department of Agriculture";
Herzenberg, Caroline L., *Women Scientists
from Antiquity to the Present; National Union
Catalog;* O'Neill, Lois S., *The Women's Book
of World Records and Achievements;* Rossiter,
Margaret W., *Women Scientists in America;*
Rossiter, Margaret W., "Women Scientists
in America before 1920"; Sicherman,
Barbara et al., *Notable American Women;*
Siegel, Patricia J. and Kay Thomas Finley,
Women in the Scientific Search.

Stearns, Genevieve
(b. 1892)
biochemist

Education: B.S., Carleton College, 1912; M.S., University of Illinois, 1920; Ph.D. in biochemistry, University of Michigan, 1928

Employment: High school teacher, 1912–1918; assistant, chemistry, University of Illinois, 1918–1920; research associate, child welfare research station, University of Iowa, 1920–1925; assistant, biochemistry, University of Michigan, 1926–1927; research associate, pediatrics, University of Iowa, 1927–1930, research assistant professor, 1930–1931, research associate professor, 1931–1943, research professor, 1943–1954, research professor, orthopedics, 1954–1958; emeritus research professor

Concurrent Position: Fulbright professor, Women's College, Ain Shams University, Cairo, 1960–1961

Genevieve Stearns was recognized for her research on infant nutrition. She was a corecipient of the Borden Award from the American Home Economics Association in 1942 and the Borden Award from the American Institute of Nutrition in 1946. In addition to her scientific publications on nutritional requirements, she was a contributing author to the book *Infant Metabolism* (1956). Among her awards, she was a Fulbright professor at the Women's College in Cairo, Egypt, 1960–1961. Her work has centered for more than 35 years on infant and child nutrition.

Her career followed the pattern of many women of her generation. After receiving her undergraduate degree from Carleton College in 1912, she was a high school teacher until 1918. She returned to school to receive her master's degree from the University of Illinois in 1920, working at the child welfare research station at the University of Iowa until 1925. She returned to school to receive her doctorate from the University of Michigan in 1928 while continuing to the work in pediatrics at Iowa. She was promoted to research assistant professor in 1930, research associate professor in 1931, research professor in 1943, and research professor in orthopedics in 1954. She was named emeritus research professor in 1958. Although there was a long gap between her promotions in 1931 and 1943, the Depression of the 1930s not only reduced the number of jobs that were available both to men and to women, but also reduced salaries and opportunities for promotion for those who retained their jobs. She was elected a fellow of the American Institute of Nutrition. She also has been a member of the American Society of Biological Chemists and the American Chemical Society. Her research included requirements of minerals, vitamins A and D during growth; chemistry of human growth; and metabolic disturbances of bone and cartilage.

Bibliography: *American Men and Women of Science* 6–11; Debus, A. G., ed., *World Who's Who in Science;* Herzenberg, Caroline L., *Women Scientists from Antiquity to the Present; National Union Catalog.*

Stern, Frances
(1873–1947)
social worker and dietitian

Education: Garland Kindergarten Training School, Boston, 1897; Massachusetts Institute of Technology, 1909–1912

Employment: Secretary and research assistant for Ellen Richards; industrial health inspector, State Board of Labor and Industries, 1912–1915; teacher, Simmons College School of Social Work, Tufts College Medical School, Massachusetts Institute of Technology, and State Teachers College, Framingham; Red Cross in France, 1918–1922; established Boston Dispensary Food Clinic, 1922–

Frances Stern was recognized as an early teacher of nutrition and dietetics. She graduated in 1897 from the Garland Kindergarten Training School in Boston. By chance she obtained a position as the secretary and research assistant of Ellen Richards (q.v.), the founder of home economics, at Massachusetts Institute of Technology (MIT). Her contact with Mrs. Richards stimulated her desire for further scientific knowledge about the relation of food to sociological problems. She enrolled in courses in food chemistry and sanitation at MIT in 1909. She developed a visiting housekeeping program for the Boston Association for the Relief and Control of Tuberculosis and later a similar program for the Boston Provident Association. In 1912 she obtained a position as an industrial health inspector for the State Board of Labor and Industries. During World War I she worked as a member of the Division of Home Conservation of the U.S. Food Administration and, in the U.S. Department of Agriculture, as an investigator of the adequacy of food for the industrial worker. After serving with the Red Cross in France from 1918 to 1922, she studied economics and politics as a special student at the London School of Economics. She returned to Boston to establish the Boston Dispensary Food Clinic. In her clinic she worked with immigrants on adapting their native foods to products that were available in this country. In 1925 she set up a Nutrition Education Department to train American and foreign doctors, dentists, social workers, and nurses in dietetics. She taught nutrition or dietetics at various schools, such as Simmons College, Tufts College Medical School, MIT, and the State Teachers College at Framingham. She coauthored the book *Food for the Worker* (1917) to show the need for unifying science, social work, income, and nutrition. Her other books were *Food and Your Body* (1932), *How To Teach Nutrition to Children* (1942), and *Diabetic Care in Pictures* (1946). She was the sole author of *Applied Dietetics* (1936). She was a member of the American Public Health Association, the American Home Economics Association, and the American Dietetic Association.

Bibliography: James, E. T., ed., *Notable American Women 1607–1950; National Union Catalog.*

Stevens, Nettie Maria
(1861–1912)
geneticist

Education: Normal School, Westfield, Massachusetts, 1892; A.B., Stanford University, 1899, A.M., 1900; Ph.D., Bryn Mawr College, 1903; Naples Zoological Station, 1901, 1905; University of Wurzburg, 1901, 1908–1909
Employment: Schoolteacher, 1883–1892; public librarian, 1893–1895; schoolteacher, 1895–1896; research fellow in biology, Bryn Mawr College, 1903–1904, reader in experimental morphology, 1904–1905, associate in experimental morphology, 1905–1912

Nettie Stevens was one of the first American women to achieve recognition for her contributions to scientific research. Working independently at separate institutions, she and biologist Edmund B. Wilson were the first to demonstrate that sex was determined by a particular chromosome. Prior to their research, most biologists thought that external influences such as food and temperature determined the sex of offspring. She was the first person to establish that chromosomes exist as paired structures in body cells and the first to ascertain that certain insects have supernumerary chromosomes. Although she received recognition for her work during her lifetime, in recent years textbooks have given primary emphasis to Wilson's work.

Between 1883 and 1896 she taught school and worked as a public librarian. At the age of 31 she entered the Normal School at Westfield, Massachusetts, and four years later transferred as an undergraduate to Stanford University. She received an A.B. degree in 1899 and her A.M. in 1900. During 1901 she studied at the Naples Zoological Station and at the University of Wurzburg. She received her doctorate from Bryn Mawr in 1903. She continued at Bryn Mawr as a research fellow in biology, a reader in experimental morphology in 1904, and an associate in experimental morphology from 1905 to her death in 1912. She received the Ellen Richards Prize for study at the Naples Zoological Station in 1905, and in 1908 and 1909 she again studied at Wurzburg. Although she had a very short research career, she published about 40 papers. Her name was listed in the first edition and starred in the second edition of *American Men and Women of Science.* There are extensive discussions of her work, biographical information, and photographs in the journal *Isis* 69 (1978): 162–172 and in *Proceedings* of the American Philosophical Society 125 (1981): 292–311. There is a brief biography in *Science* 36 (1912): 468–470.

Bibliography: American Men and Women of Science 1–2; Herzenberg, Caroline L., *Women Scientists from Antiquity to the Present;* Kass-Simon, G. and Patricia Farnes, *Women of Science;* McHenry, Robert, ed., *Famous American Women;* Rossiter, Margaret W., *Women Scientists in America;* Rossiter, Margaret W., "Women Scientists in America before 1920"; Siegel, Patricia J. and Kay Thomas Finley, *Women in the Scientific Search;* Uglow, Jennifer S., *International Dictionary of Women's Biography;* Visher, Stephen S., *Scientists Starred 1903–1943 in "American Men of Science."*

Stevenson, Matilda Coxe Evans
(1849–1915)
anthropologist

Education: Private school
Employment: Ethnologist, Bureau of American Ethnology, Smithsonian Institution, 1890–1915
Married: James Stevenson, 1872, died 1888

Matilda Stevenson was recognized for her research as one of the early ethnologists. She became interested in Native Americans when she accompanied her husband, a government geologist, on archaeological surveys for the Bureau of American Ethnology, including an 1879 expedition party that stayed six months at the Zuni pueblo in New Mexico. Later, as she aided her husband in the preparation of reports and herself published a paper on the Zuni, she began to contribute significant research on all phases of pueblo culture. She was the first to concentrate on data on domestic and womanly matters. She made valuable studies of the child life of the Zuni, including their customs, habits, games, and ordinary activities.

She was one of the pioneer ethnologists who used observation and collection of data in the field. She prepared numerous reports, most of which were published in the *Annual Reports* of the bureau, on the life of the Zuni and other pueblo tribes. After her husband's death, she was appointed to the staff of the Bureau of American Ethnology to complete his notes and catalog exhibits. She played a key role in opening opportunities for women anthropologists. She was the founder and first president of the Women's Anthropological Society in 1885; this merged with the American Anthropological Association in 1899. She was elected a fellow of the American Association for the Advancement of Science. Her research included philosophy, religion, and sociology of the Pueblo Indians; and comparative study of the pueblos of the Southwest. There is a photograph in the *National Cyclopedia of American Biography* and in *American Anthropologist* 18 (1916): 552–559. Her name was listed in the first two editions of *American Men and Women of Science.*

Bibliography: *American Men and Women of Science* 1–2; Debus, A. G., ed., *World Who's Who in Science;* Helm, June, ed., *Pioneers of American Anthropology;* Herzenberg, Caroline L., *Women Scientists from Antiquity to the Present;* James, E. T., ed., *Notable American Women 1607–1950;* McHenry, Robert, ed., *Famous American Women; National Cyclopedia of American Biography; National Union Catalog;* Rossiter, Margaret W., *Women Scientists in America;* Rossiter, Margaret W., "Women Scientists in America before 1920"; Rossiter, Margaret W., "'Women's Work' in Science, 1880–1910"; Siegel, Patricia J. and Kay Thomas Finley, *Women in the Scientific Search.*

Stevenson, Sara Yorke
(1847–1921)
archaeologist

Education: Private school
Employment: Secretary, department of archaeology, University of Pennsylvania, 1894–1902, president, 1902–1905; curator, Egyptian section, American Exploration Society, 1894–1905, secretary, 1894–1901, trustee, Philadelphia Museum, 1894–1901, curator, 1906; lecturer, Pennsylvania Museum and school of industrial art
Married: Cornelius Stevenson, 1870

ara Stevenson was a civic leader in Philadelphia who was instrumental in the creation and development of a department of archaeology at the University of Pennsylvania starting in 1892. She also helped establish the Free Museum of Science and Art, now the university museum, which opened in 1899. She was instrumental in securing funds to build the museum. She helped organize the American Exploration Society in Philadelphia. She collected, cataloged, labeled, and installed artifacts for both museums. She was sent to Rome in 1897 on a special archaeological mission for the University of Pennsylvania and to Egypt in 1898 in connection with archaeological work in the Nile valley for the Exploration Society and the city of Philadelphia. She was vice president of the jury for ethnology at the 1893 Columbian exposition and a director of the National Export exposition in 1899. In 1894 she was the first woman to receive an honorary degree from the University of Pennsylvania. She also received an honorary degree from Temple University. She was a member of the American Philosophical Society and the American Archaeological Institute. Her other civic work included working with a home for Native American boys and girls and helping indigent gentlewomen find work. A drawing of her is included in the *National Cyclopedia of American Biography*. She was listed as Mrs. Cornelius Stevenson in the first three editions of *American Men and Women of Science*.

Bibliography: *American Men and Women of Science 1–3*; *Dictionary of American Biography*; Mozans, H. J., *Women in Science*; *National Cyclopedia of American Biography*; Rossiter, Margaret W., *Women Scientists in America*; Siegel, Patricia J. and Kay Thomas Finley, *Women in the Scientific Search*.

Stickel, Lucille Farrier
(1915–)
zoologist

Education: B.A., Eastern Michigan University, 1936; M.S., University of Michigan, 1938, Ph.D. in zoology, 1949
Employment: Biologist, Patuxent Wildlife Research Center, U.S. Fish and Wildlife Service, 1943–1947, 1961–1972, director, 1972–1980
Married: 1941

Lucille Stickel has been recognized for developing original methods for determining pesticide residue levels in wildlife. In her work in the pioneering field of pesticide research, she has studied the significance of residues in animal brain tissue as indications of lethal levels, a method still used today. Although she did important work 20 years ago, her research still is significant today. Pesticide residues are a problem not only for fish and wildlife but also for people who eat fish, swim in lakes and rivers, and drink water drawn from lakes and rivers. She joined the Patuxent Wildlife Research Center at Laurel, Maryland, as a biologist in 1943 several years after receiving her master's degree from the University of Michigan. She returned to the Center as a biologist in 1961 after receiving her doctorate from the University of Michigan in 1949. She was promoted to director in 1972. She received the Federal Woman's Award for the Department of the Interior in 1968, the Aldo Leopold Award in 1974, and an honorary degree from Eastern Michigan University in 1974. Although there was a long break in her employment, she was able to continue a productive career. She has participated in a number of conferences and published papers on pesticide residues. Her research has included vertebrate population ecology and the ecology and pharmacotoxicology of environmental pollution.

Bibliography: American Men and Women of Science 9–14; Herzenberg, Caroline L., *Women Scientists from Antiquity to the Present*; O'Neill, Lois S., *The Women's Book of World Records and Achievements*; Vare, Ethlie Ann and Greg Ptacek, *Mothers of Invention.*

Stiebeling, Hazel Katherine
(b. 1896)
food chemist and nutritionist

Education: B.S., Columbia University, 1919, M.A., 1924, Ph.D. in chemistry, 1928
Employment: School supervisor in home economics, 1915–1928; supervising teacher for home economics, Kansas State Teachers College, Emporia, 1919–1923; instructor in nutrition, Columbia University, 1924–1926; senior food economist, Bureau of Home Economics, U.S. Department of Agriculture (USDA), 1930–1944, assistant chief, 1943–1944, chief, 1944–1954, director of research in human nutrition and home economics, 1954–1957, director of institute of home economics, 1957–1960, deputy administrator of Agricultural Research Service, 1960–1963

Hazel Stiebeling was noted for her work in establishing nutritional menus based on various levels of income. Joining the USDA's Bureau of Home Economics shortly after it was established in 1927, she was promoted to assistant bureau chief in 1943 and chief in 1944. Although there were changes in the name of the bureau, she continued as head until 1960, when she was appointed deputy administrator of the Agricultural Research Service, retiring in 1963. Prior to joining the USDA, she had been a school supervisor in home economics, a supervising teacher for home economics at Kansas State, and an instructor in nutrition at Columbia University. She had received all three of her academic degrees from Columbia, the B.S. in 1919, the M.A. in 1924, and the Ph.D. in 1928. It has been a common belief that people who taught in home economics programs were weak in their subjects, but

Hazel Stiebeling earned degrees in chemistry in rigorous programs at Columbia, and many of her contemporaries had similar educational backgrounds. She received the Borden Award in 1943, the distinguished service award from the USDA in 1952, and the president's Gold Medal Award for distinguished federal civilian service in 1959. She was a member of the American Statistical Association, the American Home Economics Association, and a fellow of the American Institute of Nutrition. Her research involved composition and nutritive values of food, energy metabolism, and food consumption habits of population groups. She received several honorary degrees. Her photograph was published in *Current Biography*.

Bibliography: *American Men and Women of Science* 5–11; Baker, Gladys L., "Women in the U.S. Department of Agriculture"; *Current Biography; Herzenberg, Caroline L., Women Scientists from Antiquity to the Present;* Ireland, Norma O., *Index to Scientists of the World;* Mozans, H. J., *Women in Science; National Union Catalog;* Yost, Edna, *American Women of Science.*

Stoll, Alice Mary
(1917–)
biophysicist

Education: B.A., Hunter College, 1938; M.S., Cornell University, 1948

Employment: Assistant, allergy, metabolism, and infrared spectrophotography, New York hospital and medical college, Cornell University, 1938–1943, temperature regulation, 1946–1948, physiological research associate, environmental thermal radiation, medical college, instructor, school of nursing, 1948–1953; physiologist, medical research laboratory, U.S. Naval Air Development Center, 1953–1956, special technical assistant, 1956–1960, head, thermal laboratory, 1960–1964, head, biophysical and bioastronautical division, 1964–1970, head, biophysical laboratory, crew systems department, 1970–1982

Concurrent Positions: Consultant, Arctic aero-medical laboratory, Ladd Air Force Base, Alaska, 1952–1953; U.S. Naval Reserves, 1943–1946

*A*lice Stoll has been a pioneer in bioengineering with the U.S. Navy in carrying out biophysical and bioastronautical research. She has been recognized for her development of fire-resistant fibers and fabrics. She had a unique history of employment at the U.S. Naval Air Development Center in studying the biophysical effects of temperature on humans. During this period the armed services were developing supersonic planes that made many physiological demands on crews as well as planes. Her work involved assuring that crews can withstand the extremely cold temperature at high altitudes, the physiological stress of breaking the sound barrier at supersonic speeds, and the constant danger of fire in a closed environment. She had a solid background for this work. After receiving her master's degree in 1948, she was appointed a physiological research associate in environmental thermal radiation at the Cornell medical college. She accepted an appointment at the Navy lab as a physiologist in the medical research laboratory in 1953. She then rose to head of the thermal laboratory in 1960, head of the biophysical and bioastronautical division in 1964, and head of the biophysical laboratory in the crew systems department in 1970. She received the Federal Civil Service Award in

1965 and the Achievement Award of the Society of Women Engineers in 1969. She was elected a fellow of the American Association for the Advancement of Science and of the Aerospace Medical Association. She has been a member of the Biophysical Society, the American Physiological Society, and the American Society of Mechanical Engineers. Her research has involved environmental thermal radiation, temperature regulation and special instrumentation, biophysics of and engineering guidelines for thermal safety, and heat transfer and thermal protection principles.

Bibliography: *American Men and Women of Science* 9–14; Herzenberg, Caroline L., *Women Scientists from Antiquity to the Present;* O'Neill, Lois S., *The Women's Book of World Records and Achievements.*

Stone, Isabelle
(b. 1868)
physicist

Education: A.B., Wellesley College, 1890; M.S., University of Chicago, 1896, Ph.D., 1897
Employment: High school teacher, 1897–1898; instructor in physics, Vassar College, 1898–1906; head, School for American Girls, Rome, 1907–1914; professor of physics, Sweet Briar College, 1918–1923; head, the Missus Stone's School for Girls, 1923–?

Isabelle Stone was the first woman to receive a doctorate from the University of Chicago (1897). She went to the University of Chicago after receiving her undergraduate degree from Wellesley College in 1890. She worked for one year as a teacher in the Bryn Mawr preparatory school and then accepted a position as an instructor in physics at Vassar College until 1906. It seems incongruous that, although she had a doctorate from a major university, she was hired as an instructor at Vassar. At that time, many schools, especially women's colleges, were expanding their science programs, and teachers with appropriate academic credentials were in demand. She and her sister operated the School for American Girls in Rome from 1907 to 1914 and then moved it to Washington, D.C., in 1923 as the Misses Stone's School for Girls. Between 1918 and 1923 she was a professor of physics at Sweet Briar College. In addition to her heavy administrative responsibilities, she conducted research on thin films. Some of this work was carried out at Columbia University, where she also studied the colors of platinum films. She was one of the founders of the American Physical Society. Her research included electrical resistance of thin films, color in platinum films, and properties of thin films when deposited in a vacuum. Her name was listed in the first seven editions of *American Men and Women of Science.*

Bibliography: *American Men and Women of Science* 1–7; Herzenberg, Caroline L., *Women Scientists from Antiquity to the Present;* Ogilvie, Marilyn B., *Women in Science;* Rossiter, Margaret W., *Women Scientists in America;* Rossiter, Margaret W., "Women Scientists in America before 1920"; Siegel, Patricia J. and Kay Thomas Finley, *Women in the Scientific Search; Who Was Who in America.*

Strobell, Ella Church
(1862–1920)
geneticist

Education: Private schools
Employment: No formal employment

Ella Strobell was recognized for her research on chromosomes early in the twentieth century. She and her collaborator, Katharine Foot (q.v.), did not seem to be affiliated with an academic or research institution; they might have funded their own research. Between 1894 and 1917 the two women published at least 23 papers that were at the center of debates over sex determination by chromosomes. Their contribution to science was the use of photomicrographs at a time when everyone else was drawing diagrams of what they saw through the microscope. Although their theory on chromosomes was not correct, their work gave the field of biology a fundamental change in its technology—photomicrographs were remarkable for their clarity and detail. More than that, they represent the first systematic attempts to remove the subjectivity of the observer from the material observed. In one of their early papers they pointed out that a dozen photographs of a variety of features could be taken in the time required to reproduce any one of them by a careful drawing. They further point out that a photograph can be kept in a form that is suitable for frequent reference. (Today no one draws diagrams in place of taking photographs.) The two women also devised a method for making extremely thin sections of material at low temperatures; although their specific technique no longer is used, they were among the first to develop the procedure. Ella Strobell was a member of the American Society of Zoologists. Very little is known about her life; she attended private schools and lived in New York City. She was listed in the first two editions of *American Men and Women of Science;* however, Katharine Foot's name was starred and hers was not.

Bibliography: American Men and Women of Science 1–2; Herzenberg, Caroline L., *Women Scientists from Antiquity to the Present;* Kass-Simon, G. and Patricia Farnes, *Women of Science;* Ogilvie, Marilyn B., *Women in Science;* Rossiter, Margaret W., "Women Scientists in America before 1920"; Siegel, Patricia J. and Kay Thomas Finley, *Women in the Scientific Search.*

Stroud-Lee, F. Agnes Naranjo
(1922–)
radiation biologist

Education: B.S., University of New Mexico, 1945; Ph.D., University of Chicago, 1966
Employment: Research technician, hematology, Los Alamos Scientific Laboratory, 1945–1946; associate cytologist, Argonne National Laboratory, 1946–1969; director, Department of Tissue Culture, Pasadena Foundation for Medical Research, 1969–1970; senior research cytogeneticist, Scientific Data Analysis Section, Jet Propulsion

Laboratory, 1970–1975; staff cytogeneticist, health research division, Los Alamos Scientific Laboratory, 1975–1979; consultant, radiobiology and cytogenetics
Married: 1950, 1966

*A*gnes Stroud-Lee has been recognized for her research in radiobiology. She received numerous honors and awards, including the Morrison Prize of the New York Academy of Sciences (1955) and the NASA Certificate of Recognition (1976). During her career she worked at several of the major research centers in radiobiology, such as Los Alamos and Argonne National laboratories. After receiving her undergraduate degree from the University of New Mexico in 1945, she was employed at Los Alamos for one year before receiving an appointment as associate cytologist at Argonne, where she worked until 1969. During this time she received her doctorate from the University of Chicago, (1966). She accepted an appointment at the Jet Propulsion Laboratory as a senior research cytogeneticist in 1970. She returned to Los Alamos in 1975 as a staff cytogeneticist in the health research division. In 1979 she left

to consult in radiobiology and cytogenetics. She has been a member of the Radiation Research Society, the American Society for Cell Biology, the Biophysical Society, and the Tissue Culture Association. Her research has included automation of chromosome analysis by computers, effects of radiation on animal tumors, effects of ionizing radiation in vitro and in vivo, and mammalian radiation biology. She was listed in the sources under Stroud, Stroud-Schmink, and Stroud-Lee. She is a Native American, a member of the Tewa tribe of the Santa Clara Indian Pueblo, and she has one child.

Bibliography: American Men and Women of Science 9–17; Herzenberg, Caroline L., *Women Scientists from Antiquity to the Present;* O'Neill, Lois S., *The Women's Book of World Records and Achievements.*

Sullivan, Betty J.
(1902–)
cereal chemist

Education: B.S., University of Minnesota, 1922, Ph.D. in biochemistry, 1935
Employment: Laboratory assistant, Russell Miller Milling Company, 1922–1924, 1926–1927, chief chemist, 1927–1947, director of research, 1947–1958; vice president and director of research, Peavey Company, 1958–1967; vice president, Experience, Inc., 1967–1969, president, 1969–1973, board chair, 1973–1975, director, 1975–

*B*etty Sullivan has been recognized as an authority on the chemistry of wheat proteins and the chemistry and biochemistry of baking. In 1948 she became the first woman to receive the Osborne Medal of the American Association of Cereal Chemists, and she received the Garvan Medal of the American Chemical Society in 1954. She started

working for the Russell Miller Milling Company in 1922 just after she received her undergraduate degree. She moved up to chief chemist in 1927, received her doctorate in 1935, and advanced to director of research in 1947. She accepted a position as vice president and director of research for Peavey Company in 1958. She moved to Experience, Inc., as vice president in 1967, then president in 1969, board chair in 1973, and director in 1975. She published about 40 papers on the determination of moisture in wheat and flour and on the role of certain amino acids in relation to the processing of flour. She was president of the American Association of Cereal Chemists in 1943 and 1944. She has been a member of the American Chemical Society and the American Association for the Advancement of Science. Her research has included chemistry of wheat gluten. She was one of the few women chemists who could be identified as holding significant positions in industry prior to World War II; chemists in particular seemed to have few opportunities for advancement during the time of her career. Her photograph was included in *Chemtech* 6 (1976): 738–743. Her name was listed in the 1992–1993 edition of *American Men and Women of Science.*

Bibliography: *American Men and Women of Science* 6–18; Herzenberg, Caroline L., *Women Scientists from Antiquity to the Present;* O'Neill, Lois S., *The Women's Book of World Records and Achievements;* Rossiter, Margaret W., *Women Scientists in America.*

Sweeney, Beatrice Marcy
(1914–)
botanist

Education: A.B., Smith College, 1936; Ph.D. in biology, Radcliffe College, 1942
Employment: Laboratory assistant in endocrinology, Mayo Clinic, 1942; fellow, University of Minnesota, 1942–1943; junior research biologist, Scripps Institute, California, 1947–1955, assistant research biologist, 1955–1960, associate research biologist, 1960–1961; research staff biologist, Yale University, 1961–1962, lecturer in biology, 1962–1967; lecturer in biology, University of California, Santa Barbara, 1967–1969, associate professor, 1969–1971, professor, 1971–1982, associate provost, College of Creative Studies, 1978–1981; emeritus professor
Married: 1937, 1962

Beatrice Sweeney has been recognized for her research in biological rhythms. Her career exhibited a pattern similar to many women scientists who followed their husbands from job to job. Her longest appointment was with the Scripps Institute in California, where she advanced from junior research biologist in 1947 to associate research biologist in 1960. She then was on the research staff at Yale starting in 1961. She moved to the University of California, Santa Barbara, in 1967 as a lecturer in biology and was promoted to associate professor in 1969, professor in 1971, and associate provost of the College of Creative Studies in 1978, retiring in 1981. Her work was recognized by the Botanical Society of America, which awarded her the Darbaker Award in 1984. She was president of the American Society for Photobiology (1979) and of the Phycological Society of America (1986). She was the author of *Rhythmic Phenomena in Plants* (1969).

She published an autobiographical sketch (with photograph) in *Annual Reviews of Plant Physiology* 38 (1987): 1–9, in which she urged women scientists to continue to combine their careers in science with raising a family. She was elected a fellow of the American Association for the Advancement of Science and has been a member of the American Society of Plant Physiologists, the Society of General Physiologists, and the

Society for the Study of Biological Rhythms. Her research has included photosynthesis, bioluminescence, and circadian rhythms in marine dinoflagellates. She is the mother of four children. One source lists her name as Eleanor Beatrice Sweeney. She was listed in the 1992–1993 edition of *American Men and Women of Science.*

Bibliography: *American Men and Women of Science* 7–18; Barnhart, John H., *Biographical Notes upon Botanists;* Herzenberg, Caroline L., *Women Scientists from Antiquity to the Present; National Union Catalog.*

Marion Talbot
Mignon Talbot
Helen Brooke Taussig
Olga Taussky
Charlotte De Bernier Scarbrough Taylor
Mary Virginia Hawes Terhune
Giuliana C. Tesoro
Caroline Burling Thompson
Laura Thompson
Josephine Elizabeth Tilden
Mary Lua Adelia Davis Treat

Talbot, Marion
(1858–1948)
home economist

Education: A.B., Boston University, 1880, A.M., 1882; B.S., Massachusetts Institute of Technology (MIT), 1888

Employment: Instructor in domestic science, Wellesley College, 1890–1892; dean of undergraduate women and assistant professor of sanitary science, University of Chicago, 1892–1895, associate professor, 1895–1904, professor and head, department of household administration, 1904–1925, dean of women, 1899–1925; acting president, Constantinople Womans' College, 1927–1928 and 1931–1932

Marion Talbot was recognized for her pioneer work in the new disciplines of sanitary science and home economics. She studied under Ellen Richards (q.v.) at MIT, and she collaborated on editing *Home Sanitation: A Manual for Housekeepers* (1887). She and Ellen Richards shared in their efforts to establish the emerging field of home economics and to make education more available to women.

Although it was difficult for women to be accepted in colleges during the 1870s, Marion Talbot succeeded in obtaining an undergraduate degree from Boston University in 1880, a master's degree in 1882, and a B.S. from MIT in 1888. She was employed at Wellesley College as an instructor in domestic science for three years before receiving an invitation to join the faculty at the University of Chicago as dean of undergraduate women and assistant professor of sanitary science in

1892. She advanced to associate professor in 1895 and to professor and head of the department of household administration in 1904. She played a key role in establishing the department as one of the major home economics departments in the country. She was appointed dean of women for the university in 1899, retiring in 1925. After retirement she was acting president of the Constantinople Womans' College for two terms.

Although she was a prominent scientist who was listed in the first edition of *American Men and Women of Science,* she was burdened with extensive administrative duties as dean of women during much of her career. Her experience in supervising the women's student housing and recreational facilities at the University of Chicago resulted in a book, *Food as a Factor in Student Life* (1894), with Ellen Richards as coauthor. She also wrote *The Education of*

Women (1910), *The Modern Household* (1912), and an autobiography (with photographs) entitled *More Than Lore: Reminiscences of Marion Talbot, Dean of Women, University of Chicago, 1895–1925* (1936). She was an early member of the American Home Economics Association, and she received honorary degrees from three academic institutions. She also was a member of the American Association for the Advancement of Science and the American Public Health Association. Her research included house sanitation, the modern household, and education of women.

Bibliography: *American Men and Women of Science* 1–8; Hall, Diana Long, "Academics, Bluestockings, and Biologists"; Herzenberg, Caroline L., *Women Scientists from Antiquity to the Present*; James, E. T., ed., *Notable American Women 1607–1950*; Macksey, Joan and Kenneth Macksey, *The Book of Women's Achievements*; *National Cyclopedia of American Biography*; *National Union Catalog*; Rossiter, Margaret W., *Women Scientists in America*; Rossiter, Margaret W., "Women Scientists in America before 1920"; Rossiter, Margaret W., "'Women's Work' in Science, 1880–1910"; Shapiro, Laura, *Perfection Salad*; Siegel, Patricia J. and Kay Thomas Finley, *Women in the Scientific Search.*

Talbot, Mignon
(1869–1950)
geologist

Education: A.B., Ohio State University, 1892; Ph.D., Yale University, 1904
Employment: High school teacher, 1896–1902; head, department of geology, Mount Holyoke College, 1904–1908, professor of geology, 1908–1935; emeritus professor

Mignon Talbot was among the first women to enter the field of geology, and she spent her entire career at Mount Holyoke. Her work was primarily in the area of paleontology. Her career followed the pattern of many women of her generation. She taught high school after receiving her undergraduate degree from Ohio State in 1892. She continued her graduate education and received her doctorate from Yale in 1904. She accepted an appointment as head of the department of geology at Mount Holyoke in 1904 and was promoted to professor of geology in 1908, retiring in 1935. She was listed among the notable women scientists at the seven major women's colleges in America prior to 1940 in Margaret Rossiter's *Women Scientists in America*. She published few technical papers, but she put her efforts into building a department. After a fire in the science hall in 1916 destroyed the interior, she had to restock the collections of books as well as fossils and minerals from scratch. She included field trips in training her students. However, she believed that laboratories, offices, or museums were environments more proper for women than most field locales. She was elected a fellow of the Geological Society of America. She also was a member of the American Association for the Advancement of Science and the Paleontological Society. Her name was listed in the first eight editions of *American Men and Women of Science*.

Bibliography: *American Men and Women of Science* 1–8; Herzenberg, Caroline L.,

Women Scientists from Antiquity to the Present; Ireland, Norma O., *Index to Scientists of the World;* Kass-Simon, G. and Patricia Farnes, *Women of Science;* Rossiter, Margaret W., *Women Scientists in America.*

Taussig, Helen Brooke
(1898–1986)
endocrinologist

Education: Radcliffe College, 1917–1919; A.B., University of California, 1921; M.D., Johns Hopkins University, 1927

Employment: Fellow, medicine, Johns Hopkins Hospital, 1927–1928, intern, pediatrics, 1928–1930; physician in charge, cardiac clinic, Harriet Lane Home, 1930–1963; associate professor of pediatrics, Johns Hopkins University, 1946–1959, professor, 1959–1963; emeritus professor

Helen Taussig originated the idea for the "blue-baby" operation, first tried in 1945 as the Blalock-Taussig procedure, which involves treating babies within the first few days of birth. In 1962 she was the first physician to alert the United States to the dangers of thalidomide, a medicine routinely given to pregnant women to control nausea that was found to cause deformities in the limbs of numerous newborns. She was the first to demonstrate that changes in the heart and lungs could be diagnosed by x-ray and fluoroscope. In recognition for her achievements, she received 20 honorary degrees plus numerous awards, including the Lasker Award (1954), the Gold Heart Award (1963), and the Medal of Freedom (1964).

She was elected to the National Academy of Sciences in 1973; however, Dr. Blalock had already been elected in 1946, the year after the two introduced the Blalock-Taussig procedure. In addition to many scientific papers, she was the author of *Congenital Malformations of the Heart* (1947, 1960). She was elected a master of the American College of Physicians and was the first woman president of the American Heart Association. She also was a member of the American Pediatric Society and the Society for Pediatric Research. Her research centered on congenital malformations of the heart. After she received her M.D. degree from Johns Hopkins in 1927 and completed her internship, she spent her entire career as physician in charge of the cardiac clinic at the Harriet Lane Home and as a member of the faculty of Johns Hopkins medical school from 1946 until retiring in 1963.

Bibliography: *American Men and Women of Science* 9–16; Debus, A. G., ed., *World Who's Who in Science;* Herzenberg, Caroline L., *Women Scientists from Antiquity to the Present;* Kass-Simon, G. and Patricia Farnes, *Women of Science;* McHenry, Robert, ed., *Famous American Women;* Macksey, Joan and Kenneth Macksey, *The Book of Women's Achievements; National Union Catalog;* O'Neill, Lois S., *The Women's Book of World Records and Achievements;* Uglow, Jennifer S., *International Dictionary of Women's Biography.*

Taussky, Olga
(1906–)
mathematician

Education: Ph.D. in mathematics, University of Vienna, 1930; Bryn Mawr College, 1934–1935; M.A., Cambridge University, 1937

Employment: Assistant, University of Göttingen, 1931–1932; assistant, University of Vienna, 1932–1934; lecturer, University of London, 1937–1943; scientific officer, Ministry of Aircraft Production, England, 1943–1946; research, Department of Scientific and Industrial Research, 1946–1947; mathematician, National Bureau of Standards, 1947–1957; research associate, California Institute of Technology, 1957–1971, professor, 1971

Concurrent Positions: Member, Institute for Advanced Study, Princeton University, 1948; Fulbright visiting professor, University of Vienna, 1965

Married: John Todd, 1938

Olga Taussky was the first woman appointed to a position with the mathematics department at the California Institute of Technology. Her area of specialization has been algebraic number theory and integral matrices. When she enrolled in the University of Vienna, she first majored in chemistry, but quickly dropped that study to concentrate on mathematics, graduating in 1930. She received an appointment as an assistant at the University of Göttingen, where she edited several books. She received a fellowship at Bryn Mawr in 1934–1935 and another at Girton College in 1935–1936. During World War II she worked for a government agency in England. She joined her husband at the National Bureau of Standards in 1947 and they then moved to the California Institute of Technology in 1957. She received an honorary degree from the University of Southern California in 1988 and one from the University of Vienna in 1980. She was the co-editor of *Hilbert's Collected Papers in Number Theory* (1932) and editor of *Ternary Quadratic Forms and Norms* (1982). A list of her publications was included in *Women of Mathematics* by Louise S. Grinstein and Paul J. Campbell. She was elected a fellow of the American Association for the Advancement of Science. She has been a member of the American Mathematical Society and the Mathematical Society of America. Her research has involved algebraic number theory, integral matrices, matrices in algebra and analysis, and topological algebra. Her name was listed in the 1992–1993 edition of *American Men and Women of Science.*

Bibliography: American Men and Women of Science 10–18; Debus, A. G., ed., *World Who's Who in Science;* Grinstein, Louise S. and Paul J. Campbell, eds., *Women of Mathematics;* Herzenberg, Caroline L., *Women Scientists from Antiquity to the Present.*

Taylor, Charlotte De Bernier Scarbrough
(1806–1861)
entomologist

Education: Private schools
Employment: Author
Married: James Taylor, 1829

Charlotte Taylor and Margaretta H. Morris (q.v.) generally are recognized as the first two American women entomologists. Charlotte Taylor's biography in the *National Cyclopedia of American Biography* states that she was the only woman entomologist in the world at that time. She published her papers in popular rather than scientific journals. There were few formal opportunities for study in this field in the United States; probably she was self-taught. She read widely and possessed contemporary agricultural and zoology works. The family had great wealth, so she was able to purchase the books and equipment she needed. During the 1830s she began a serious study of insects, but she did not start publishing until about 15 years later. Living in Savannah, she studied the insect parasites of the cotton plant. During the 1850s she started publishing her findings in a number of American periodicals, notably in *Harper's New Monthly Magazine;* there were 19 articles in this journal alone. She also wrote on wheat parasites, silkworms, and spiders. Her entomological work involved the use of powerful magnifying glasses, although she probably did not have a compound microscope. Her articles were illustrated with drawings that her daughters assisted in preparing. The insect drawings were accurate, but the plant drawings were not reliable. Since her papers were published in general literary journals rather than scientific publications, they have been largely neglected by investigators. She had two daughters and one son. At the approach of the Civil War, she moved to England to the Isle of Man and did not return to the United States.

Bibliography: Bonta, Marcia M., *Women in the Field; Dictionary of American Biography;* Elliott, Clark A., *Biographical Dictionary of American Science; National Cyclopedia of American Biography;* O'Neill, Lois S., *The Women's Book of World Records and Achievements;* Siegel, Patricia J. and Kay Thomas Finley, *Women in the Scientific Search.*

Terhune, Mary Virginia Hawes
(1830–1922)
writer on household affairs

Education: Private schools
Employment: Author
Married: Edward P. Terhune, 1856

Mary Terhune was a popular novelist and writer on household affairs who wrote under the pseudonym Marion Harland. Her daughters, Christine T. Herrick (q.v.) and Virginia T. Van de Water, also wrote on household topics. Her son, Albert Payson Terhune, also was a writer, primarily of dog stories. She began writing novels in her teens and continued after her marriage. In 1854 her first novel, *Alone,* was published privately, but two years later it appeared in a commercial edition that sold more than 100,000 copies. She published her second novel in 1856, *The Hidden Path.* After her marriage she wrote primarily antebellum plantation romances. In her forties she shifted to writing books on cooking and housekeeping, and she published about 25 books concerning domestic science. She enjoyed virtually a second career writing on these subjects. Her books include *Common Sense in the Household* (1871), *The Dinner Year-Book* (1878), *Eve's Daughters* (1882), and *Every Day Etiquette* (1905). She contributed articles on homemaking to numerous magazines and at one time edited two magazines, the *Home-Maker* and *Housekeeper's Weekly.* Her syndicated columns on women's affairs, written for the *Philadelphia North American* from 1900 to 1910 and for the *Chicago Tribune* from 1911 to 1917, were reprinted in 25 daily newspapers. She lectured for the Chautauqua Association from 1891 to 1894. In addition to novels, she published books on travel, biography, and colonial history. Her autobiography is *Marion Harland's Autobiography: The Story of a Long Life* (1910).

Bibliography: James, E. T., ed., *Notable American Women 1607–1950;* McHenry, Robert, ed., *Famous American Women; National Union Catalog;* Shapiro, Laura, *Perfection Salad.*

Tesoro, Giuliana C.
(1921–)
polymer chemist

Education: Ph.D. in organic chemistry, Yale University, 1943
Employment: Research chemist, Calco Chemical Company, 1943–1944; research chemist, Onyx Oil and Chemical Company, 1944–1946, head, organic synthesis department, 1946–1955, assistant director of research, 1955–1957, associate director, 1957–1958; assistant director of organic research, central research laboratory, J. P. Stevens & Company, Inc., 1958–1968; senior chemist, Textile Research Institute, 1968–1969; senior chemist, Burlington Industries, Inc., 1969–1971, director, chemical research, 1971–1972; research professor, Polytechnic Institute, 1982–
Concurrent Positions: Visiting professor, Massachusetts Institute of Technology, 1972–1976, adjunct professor and senior research scientist, 1976–1982; member, committee on military personnel supplies, National Research Council, 1979–1982, committee on toxic combustion products, 1984–1989
Married: 1943

Giuliana Tesoro has been recognized internationally as an expert on the science and technology of polymers. She has made important contributions to developments in polymer flammability and flame retardants, and she has held high-level positions in several textile companies. After receiving her doctorate in

1943, she worked summers for Calco Chemical Company before accepting a position as research chemist at Onyx Oil and Chemical Company in 1944. She was promoted to head of the organic synthesis department in 1946, assistant director of research in 1955, and associate director in 1957. She was appointed assistant director of organic research for J. P. Stevens & Company, then moved to the Textile Research Institute for two years. She accepted a position as senior chemist at Burlington Industries in 1969 and was appointed director of chemical research in 1971. She was appointed research professor at Polytechnic Institute in 1982.

She has been a member of several committees of the National Academy of Sciences and the National Research Council concerning toxic materials and fire safety.

She was president of the Fiber Society in 1974, and has been a member of the American Chemical Society, the American Association of Textile Chemists and Colorists, the American Institute of Chemists, and the American Association for the Advancement of Science. Her research has involved synthesis of pharmaceuticals, textile chemicals, chemical modification of fibers, and polymer flammability and flame retardants. She is the mother of two children. Her name was listed in the 1992–1993 edition of *American Men and Women of Science.*

Bibliography: *American Men and Women of Science* 8–18; Herzenberg, Caroline L., *Women Scientists from Antiquity to the Present;* O'Neill, Lois S., *The Women's Book of World Records and Achievements.*

Thompson, Caroline Burling
(1869–1921)
biologist

Education: B.S., University of Pennsylvania, 1898, Ph.D., 1901
Employment: Teacher, private schools, 1892–1894; instructor in zoology, Wellesley College, 1901–1903, 1905–1909, associate professor, 1909–1916, professor, 1916–1921

Caroline Thompson was recognized for her research on termites, and she was known for the excellence of her original methods of teaching. She carried this originality into her research. In her work with termites, she demonstrated that scientific views of their behavior were inadequate, and she led the research into new and productive directions. In her first paper on termites in 1916 she demonstrated that there was very little differentiation between the brains of the different castes of a particular breed and none between the sexes. She was a collaborator of the Bureau of Entomology of the U.S. Department of Agriculture starting in 1917. She examined other social animals, such as the honey bee. Her career followed the pattern of many women of her generation in that she taught private school for several years before completing her undergraduate schooling at the University of Pennsylvania. She received an appointment as an instructor in zoology in 1901 at Wellesley College after receiving her doctorate from the University of Pennsylvania. She continued to teach at Wellesley until her death in 1921, being promoted to associate professor in 1909 and professor in 1916. She was a member of the American Association for the Advancement of Science, the American Society of Zoologists, the American Society of

Naturalists, and the Boston Society of Natural History. Her research involved comparative morphology of nemertean worms, and the morphology of insects, especially termites. There is a brief biography in *Science* 55 (13 January 1922): 40–41. Her name was included in the first three editions of *American Men and Women of Science.*

Bibliography: *American Men and Women of Science* 1–3; Siegel, Patricia J. and Kay Thomas Finley, *Women in the Scientific Search.*

Thompson, Laura
(1905–)
anthropologist

Education: B.A., Mills College, 1927; Radcliffe College, 1928; Ph.D. in anthropology, University of California, Berkeley, 1933
Employment: Assistant ethnologist, Bishop Museum, Honolulu, 1929; field study, Fiji Islands, 1933–1934; research anthropologist, Institute of Pacific Relations, 1937; anthropologist, University of Hawaii, 1938; social scientist, community survey, Territory of Hawaii, 1940; coordinator, committee on human development, University of Chicago, 1941–1947; research associate, Institute for Ethnic Affairs, 1946–1954; professor of anthropology, City College of New York, 1954–1956; visiting professor, University of North Carolina, 1957–1958; visiting professor, North Carolina State College, 1959–1960; professor, University of Southern Illinois, 1961–1962; professor, San Francisco State College, 1962–1963; consulting anthropologist
Concurrent Positions: Consultant, Guam, 1938; consultant, U.S. Office of Indian Affairs, 1942–1944
Married: Sam Duker, 1963

*L*aura Thompson has been recognized for her research on Native Americans. She has conducted field research in Fiji, Germany, Guam, Hawaii, Iceland, and in the United States with the Papago, Navajo, Zuni, Sioux, and Hopi people. She has consulted for the Hutterite communities in Pennsylvania in tracing their early history in Germany before emigrating to the United States. In addition to her scientific papers she has published six books relating to her research: *Fijian Frontier* (1940), *The Hopi Way* (1944), *Guam and Its People* (1947), *Culture in Crisis* (1950), *Personality and Government* (1951), and *Toward a Science of Mankind* (1961). She has had numerous appointments since receiving her doctorate in anthropology from the University of California, Berkeley, in 1933. She was a member of the faculty at City College of New York, the University of Southern Illinois, and San Francisco State College. Starting in 1963 she worked as a consulting anthropologist.

She received grants from the Viking Fund, received a Wenner-Gren fellowship to study in New York and Iceland, and received Rockefeller Foundation grants in 1951 and 1952. She was the founder of the Society for Applied Anthropology, and she was elected a fellow of the American Anthropological Association. She also has been a member of the New York Academy of Sciences and the American Association for the Advancement of Science. Her research has included comparative interdisciplinary research in small communities, especially among Native Americans and Lower Saxons of West

Germany; human ecology; and ecosystem approach toward population control.

Bibliography: *American Men and Women of Science* 7–13; Debus, A. G., ed., *World*

Who's Who in Science; Herzenberg, Caroline L., *Women Scientists from Antiquity to the Present; International Directory of Anthropologists.*

Tilden, Josephine Elizabeth
(1869–1957)
botanist

Education: B.S., University of Minnesota, 1895, M.S., 1897
Employment: Instructor in botany, University of Minnesota, 1898–1902, assistant professor, 1902–1910, professor, 1910–1937

Josephine Tilden was an expert on algae, and her book, *Minnesota Algae* (1910), still was a widely used technical reference at the time of her death in 1957. She wrote another book, *The Algae and Their Life Relations* (1935–1937), which represents the first American effort to summarize the known characteristics of these important marine and freshwater plants. She had an important role in developing standard methods for drawing algae for publication. She spent her entire career at the University of Minnesota. Born in Davenport, Iowa, she received her undergraduate degree from Minnesota in 1895 and her master's degree in 1897. She was appointed instructor in botany at the school in 1898, promoted to assistant professor in 1902 and professor in 1910, retiring in 1937. At the time she was employed, this rate of advancement would have been unusual for a woman faculty member. The "glass ceiling" often stopped a woman's progress at the level of assistant professor. Her promotion to professor would be an indication of the recognition she had received for her research and teaching. She was honored by being selected as a delegate to the First Pan-Pacific Scientific Congress of 1920 and to the succeeding congresses in 1923 and 1926. She was a member of the American Society for the Advancement of Science, the American Society of Naturalists, the American Geographical Society, the Botanical Society of America, and the Torrey Botanical Club. Her research focused on algae and on the phycology in Pacific Ocean countries. Her name was listed in the first edition of *American Men and Women of Science.*

Bibliography: *American Men and Women of Science* 1–10; Rudolph, Emanuel D., "Women in Nineteenth Century American Botany"; Siegel, Patricia J. and Kay Thomas Finley, *Women in the Scientific Search.*

Treat, Mary Lua Adelia Davis
(b. 1830)
botanist and entomologist

Education: Public schools
Employment: Author
Married: Joseph Treat, 1863, died ca. 1878

Mary Treat wrote popular books and articles on natural history that were highly regarded during her lifetime. Only after her marriage did she begin a serious study of nature. She and her husband were living in Vineland, New Jersey, where there was interest in fruit culture. The community was unfortunately infested with insect pests, which prompted the Treats to begin studying and writing about insects. At that time textbooks on the natural sciences were rare, and she based her research on self-directed investigations. She corresponded with naturalists of the period to identify many of the specimens she found; as a result, numerous plants and animals were named in her honor. She asked many of her correspondents in return to send her plants and insects to examine. While on a trip to Florida she rediscovered a water lily that the artist James Audubon had depicted in his white American swan portrait. Botanists previously had dismissed the lily as a figment of Audubon's imagination, but Mary Treat discovered acres of the plant. As a naturalist, she easily moved from writing articles about birds at the same time she was studying insects and plants. The marriage broke up about 1870, and Mary Treat supported herself by writing about nature. Her books include *Chapters on Ants* (1879), *Injurious Insects of the Farm and Garden* (1882), *Home Studies in Nature* (1885), and *My Garden Pets* (1887). Her work was respected by her male contemporaries. Unlike many of the people writing about nature for both adults and children during that period, she made her writing as accurate as possible. Although her productive writing period lasted only 30 years, she was able to earn enough from book royalties to support herself through old age. There is a brief biography and list of her publications in John Harshberger's *Botanists of Philadelphia and Their Work.* Her photograph is on file at the National Archives.

Bibliography: Barnhart, John H., *Biographical Notes upon Botanists;* Bonta, Marcia M., *Women in the Field;* Harshberger, John W., *The Botanists of*

Philadelphia and Their Work; Herzenberg, Caroline L., *Women Scientists from Antiquity to the Present;* Mozans, H. J., *Women in Science; National Union Catalog;* Rossiter, Margaret W., *Women Scientists in America; Who Was Who in America.*

Martha Van Rensselaer
Florence Wilhemina Van Straten
Birgit Vennesland
Marjorie Jean Young Vold
Hilda Geiringer Von Mises

Van Rensselaer, Martha
(1864–1932)
home economist

Education: Chamberlain Institute, 1884; A.B., Cornell University, 1909
Employment: Public school teacher, 1884–1893; county school commissioner, 1884–1899; head, extension program for farm wives, Cornell University, 1900–1903, resident instruction in homemaking, 1903–1907, codirector, department of home economics, 1907–1925, codirector, New York State College of Home Economics, 1925–1932, professor, 1911–1932

*M*artha *Van Rensselaer* taught the first accredited home economics courses at Cornell University. Her early career followed the pattern of many women of her generation in that she taught in various public and private schools in New York State and served as a county school commissioner for many years. She became interested in the agricultural extension program at Cornell, and after she joined the program, she completed her undergraduate degree at Cornell in 1909. In 1900 Cornell's dean of agriculture invited her to organize an extension program for farm wives, and in 1903 the dean instituted home economics instruction on a resident and accredited basis.

In 1907 a department of home economics was formed within the college of agriculture with Martha Van Rensselaer and Flora Rose (q.v.) as codirectors. Their courses became a four-year degree program, with a strong emphasis on research. The two women shared administrative responsibilities, with Martha Van Rensselaer concentrating on administration and extension work and Flora Rose on resident instruction and research. In 1911, by faculty vote, the two women were promoted to the rank of professor. In 1919 the Cornell trustees upgraded the department to a school within the college of agriculture. This was confirmed in 1925 by the state legislature when it established the New York State College of Home Economics with Van Rensselaer and Rose as codirectors. The state legislature in 1929 and 1930 appropriated the funds to build a new home economics building at Cornell, which was named Van Rensselaer Hall.

She was very active professionally, as president of the American Home Economics Association (1914–1916), homemaking editor of the journal *Delineator* (1920–1926), and assistant director of the

White House Conference on Child Health and Protection (1930). She was chair of the home economics section of the Association of Land-Grant Colleges and Universities in 1928 and 1929. She was a member of the American Association of University Women committee to welcome Madame Curie on her visit to New York City in 1921. On campus she was affectionately known as Miss Van.

Bibliography: Herzenberg, Caroline L., *Women Scientists from Antiquity to the Present;* James, E. T., ed., *Notable American Women 1607–1950; National Union Catalog;* O'Neill, Lois S., *The Women's Book of World Records and Achievements;* Rossiter, Margaret W., *Women Scientists in America;* Rossiter, Margaret W., "'Women's Work' in Science, 1880–1910."

Van Straten, Florence Wilhemina
(b. 1913)
meteorologist

Education: B.S., New York University, 1933, M.S., 1937, Ph.D. in chemistry, 1939
Employment: Assistant instructor in chemistry, New York University, 1933–1942; aerology engineer, U.S. Department of the Navy, 1946–1948, head, technical requirements section, Naval Weather Service, 1948–1962; consultant and writer
Concurrent Position: U.S. Naval Reserve, 1942–1946

Florence Van Straten was recognized for her work as a meteorologist. She had taught at New York University as an assistant instructor in chemistry while completing her doctorate in chemistry from that university in 1939. She continued teaching there until she joined the U.S. Navy's Women Accepted for Voluntary Service (WAVES) and launched her career in meteorology, the study of the physical processes that combine to produce weather. While she was in the WAVES during World War II, she received a Certified Meteorologists diploma, which provided her entry into what had been solely a male profession. (The science of meteorology really did not develop until World War II when there was a crushing need for accurate information to deploy troops and supplies all over the world.) She was in the first group of 25 WAVES selected for training to see if women could be used successfully to overcome the shortage of available men meteorologists. Twenty-two of these women completed the course. Her responsibility as an aerology engineer (meteorologist) was to advise commanders of the Pacific fleet on weather conditions for planning strategy.

She continued working for the Naval Weather Service as a civilian until 1962, forecasting weather for the launching of long-range missiles. One study she initiated was to investigate the pattern of radioactive fallout in case of an atomic attack on the United States. She received the Navy's Meritorious Civilian Service Award in 1956 after ten years of civilian service. After she left her civilian job with the Navy, she turned to consulting and writing. When she entered college, she had planned to major in English; however, when she was invited to substitute in teaching a chemistry class, she found she could obtain a graduate assistantship if she received a B.S. in chemistry. She was a member of the American Association for the Advancement of Science, the American Meteorological

Society, and the American Geophysical Union. Her research included metal gas catalysis, the upper atmosphere, and atmospheric physics. Her photograph was included in Edna Yost's *Women of Modern Science*.

Bibliography: *American Men and Women of Science* 9–11; Yost, Edna, *Women of Modern Science*.

Vennesland, Birgit
(1913–)
enzymologist

Education: B.S., University of Chicago, 1934, Ph.D. in biochemistry, 1938
Employment: Assistant biochemist, University of Chicago, 1938–1939; research fellow, Harvard University medical school, 1939–1941; instructor, University of Chicago, 1941–1944, assistant professor, 1944–1948, associate professor, 1948–1957, professor, 1957–1968; director, Max Planck Institute of Cell Biology, 1968–1970, director, Vennesland Research Institute, Max Planck Society, 1970–1981; adjunct professor, biochemistry and biophysics, University of Hawaii, 1987– ; emeritus professor
Concurrent Position: Civilian with Office of Scientific Research and Development, 1944

Birgit Vennesland was one of the first chemists to use radioactive carbon 11 to study carbohydrate metabolism. She has served on several study teams for the National Science Foundation and the Public Health Service. After receiving her doctorate in biochemistry from the University of Chicago in 1938 and working as a research fellow at Harvard University medical school for two years, she returned to Chicago as an instructor in 1941. She was promoted to assistant professor in 1944, associate professor in 1948, and professor in 1957. It seems unaccountable that there was such a long gap before she was promoted to professor. She left Chicago for a position at another prestigious institute in Germany, being appointed a director at the Max Planck Institute of Cell Biology in 1968 and then director of the Vennesland Research Institute of the Max Planck Society in 1970, retiring in 1981.

She received the Hales Award (1950) and the Garvan Medal (1964), as well as an honorary degree from Mount Holyoke College (1960). She was elected a fellow of the New York Academy of Sciences and the American Association for the Advancement of Science, and she has been a member of the American Chemical Society, the American Society of Biological Chemists, and the American Society of Plant Physiologists. Her research has included carboxylation reactions in animals and plants, mechanisms of hydrogen transfer in pyridine nucleotide dehydrogenases, and enzymology and mechanism of photosynthesis. Her name was listed in the 1992–1993 edition of *American Men and Women of Science*.

Bibliography: *American Men and Women of Science* 7–18; Debus, A. G., ed., *World Who's Who in Science*; Herzenberg, Caroline L., *Women Scientists from Antiquity to the Present*; O'Neill, Lois S., *The Women's Book of World Records and Achievements*.

Vold, Marjorie Jean Young
(1913–)
colloid chemist

Education: B.S., University of California, Berkeley, 1934, Ph.D. in chemistry, 1936
Employment: Junior research associate, chemistry, Stanford University, 1937–1941; research associate, University of Southern California, 1941–1943; research chemist, Union Oil Company, 1942–1946; research associate and lecturer in chemistry, University of Southern California, 1945–1958, adjunct professor, 1958–1973; emeritus professor of chemistry
Concurrent Positions: Civilian with the Office of Naval Research; Guggenheim fellow, University of Utrecht, 1953–1954; professor of physical chemistry, Indian Institute of Science, Bangalore, 1955–1957
Married: Robert D. Vold, 1936

Marjorie Vold has been recognized for her research in colloid chemistry. Although she was employed as a lecturer in chemistry and adjunct professor at the University of Southern California (USC) for almost 30 years, her research record has been outstanding. She received the University Medal from the University of California, Berkeley, in 1934 and the Garvan Medal in 1967. After receiving her doctorate in chemistry from Berkeley in 1936, she was appointed junior research associate in chemistry at Stanford in 1937. This was late in the Depression, and jobs still were scarce for both men and women. In 1941 she was appointed research associate at USC and she also worked at Union Oil Company until 1946. She then returned to USC, where she remained until retiring. In addition to her scientific papers, she was coauthor of

An Introduction to the Physical Sciences (1961) and *Colloid Chemistry* (1964). She has been a member of the American Chemical Society, the International Association of Colloid-Interface Scientists, and the American Association for the Advancement of Science. Her research has included association colloids, gels and other colloidal solids, and computer simulation of colloidal processes. She and her husband had three children, Mary, Robert, and Wylda. Her name was listed in the 1992–1993 edition of *American Men and Women of Science.*

Bibliography: *American Men and Women of Science* 7–18; Debus, A. G., ed., *World Who's Who in Science;* Herzenberg, Caroline L., *Women Scientists from Antiquity to the Present; National Union Catalog;* O'Neill, Lois S., *The Women's Book of World Records and Achievements.*

Von Mises, Hilda Geiringer
(1893–1973)
mathematician

Education: Ph.D., University of Vienna, 1917
Employment: Staff, *Jahrbuch uber die Fortschritte der Mathematik,* 1918–1920; assistant, Institute of Applied Mathematics, University of Berlin, 1921–1927; staff, University of

Berlin, 1927–1933; research associate, Institute of Mechanics, University of Brussels, 1933–1934; professor of mathematics, University of Istanbul, 1934–1939; lecturer, Bryn Mawr College, 1939–1944; professor and chair, mathematics department, Wheaton College, Massachusetts, 1944–1959; research fellow in mathematics, Harvard University, 1955–1959; emeritus professor

Married: Felix Pollaczek, divorced; Richard M. E. Von Mises, 1943, died 1953

Hilda Von Mises was a distinguished mathematician in her own right, although her second husband was mathematician Richard Von Mises. She developed her fundamental Geiringer equations for plane plastic distortions while on the staff at the University of Berlin and continued to produce significant work during the remainder of her career. After receiving her doctorate from the University of Vienna in 1917, she was on the staff of a review journal for three years. It was impossible for a woman mathematician to find a teaching position in the 1920s in Germany, but she was appointed an assistant at the University of Berlin in 1921 and a member of the staff starting in 1927. Meanwhile she and her first husband had a daughter, Magda, before their divorce. She was forced to flee Germany in 1933 with her child along with other Jewish professionals.

She first went to the University of Brussels and then to the University of Istanbul. She received an appointment as a lecturer at Bryn Mawr in 1939. She then was appointed professor and chair of the mathematics department of Wheaton College in Massachusetts in 1944. This placed her closer to her second husband, Richard M. E. Von Mises, who was teaching at Harvard. She had known him since her days at the University of Berlin in the 1920s. After his death in 1953, she spent several years as a research fellow at Harvard, editing his work for publication and developing her own theories. She was recognized for her work in probability theory. She received an honorary degree from Wheaton in 1960, and in 1956 the University of Berlin named her professor emerita. The University of Vienna made a special presentation on the occasion of the fiftieth anniversary of her graduation. She was elected a fellow of the American Academy of Arts and Sciences. There is a list of her publications in Louise S. Grinstein and Paul J. Campbell's *Women of Mathematics*. She used the name Hilda Geiringer professionally, although most references list her under Hilda Von Mises.

Bibliography: Grinstein, Louise S. and Paul J. Campbell, eds., *Women of Mathematics*; Sicherman, Barbara et al., *Notable American Women*; Siegel, Patricia J. and Kay Thomas Finley, *Women in the Scientific Search*.

W

Salome Gluecksohn Waelsch
Mary Morris Vaux Walcott
Louise Baird Wallace
Mary Elizabeth Warga
Margaret Floy Washburn
Betty Monaghan Watts
Katharine Way
Cynthia Westcott
Anna Johnson Pell Wheeler
Ruth Wheeler
Sarah Frances Whiting
Mary Watson Whitney
Mary Alice Willcox
Anna Wessels Williams
Lucy Wilson
Lucy Langdon Williams Wilson
Evelyn Maisel Witkin
Elizabeth Armstrong Wood
Ruth Goulding Wood
Helen Bradford Thompson Woolley
Mary Raphael Schenck Woolman
Helen Wright
Mabel Osgood Wright
Dorothy Maud Wrinch
Chien-Shiung Wu

Waelsch, Salome Gluecksohn
(1907–)
geneticist

Education: Ph.D. in zoology, University of Freiburg, 1932
Employment: Assistant, department of experimental cell research, University of Berlin, 1932–1933; research associate and lecturer, zoology, Columbia University, 1936–1953, college of physicians and surgeons, 1953–1955; from associate professor to professor of anatomy, Albert Einstein college of medicine, 1955–1963, chair of genetics department, 1963–1976, professor of genetics, 1958–1988; distinguished emeritus professor
Married: Heinrich B. Waelsch, 1943

Salome Waelsch has had a distinguished career due to her research on the role of genes in normal and abnormal cell differentiation and on genetically controlled congenital abnormalities. After receiving her doctorate from the University of Freiburg in 1932, she worked briefly at the University of Berlin before fleeing to the United States in 1933. She was one of the many Jewish scientists who were forced to leave Germany during that period. She obtained a position as a research associate and lecturer in zoology at Columbia University in 1936 and transferred to a similar position in the college of physicians and surgeons in 1953.

She joined the Albert Einstein college of medicine and rose from associate professor to professor of anatomy between 1955 and 1963. In 1958 she was promoted to professor of genetics, and she served as chair of the genetics department from 1963 to 1976. She was named distinguished emeritus professor in 1988. She was elected to membership in the National Academy of Sciences in 1979, and has been a member of the American Academy of Arts and Sciences, the American Association of Anatomists, the Genetics Society of America, the Society for Developmental Biology, and the American Society of Zoologists. Her research has included developmental and mammalian genetics, and the role and control of genes in differentiation. She and her husband had two children, Naomi and Peter. Her name was listed in the 1992–1993 edition of *American Men and Women of Science.*

Bibliography: American Men and Women of Science 9–18; Debus, A. G., ed., *World Who's Who in Science;* Herzenberg, Caroline L., *Women Scientists from Antiquity to the Present.*

Walcott, Mary Morris Vaux
(1860–1940)
naturalist

Education: Friends Select School, Philadelphia, 1879
Employment: Artist/Author
Married: Charles D. Walcott, 1914

Mary Walcott was a naturalist who was famous for her watercolors of wildflowers, and she has been called the Audubon of American wildflowers. Her major work was *North American Wild Flowers* (1925) in five volumes, published by the Smithsonian Institution, of which her husband was secretary. The volumes contained 400 of her watercolors of native flowers with brief descriptions of each. Although she had no formal training in art or science, her watercolors were widely accepted. She also was active in geography, mineralogy, glaciology, exploration, and horticulture. She developed her interest in wildflowers as an amateur naturalist during family vacations to the Canadian Rockies, when a botanist urged her to paint flowers instead of the landscapes she had been doing since childhood. After her marriage, she and her husband continued to vacation in the Rockies and she continued with her watercolors. Her husband was a geologist and paleontologist, and she accompanied him on many of his expeditions. She was also invited to lecture before many groups. A member of the Society of Friends, she was active in social causes. After the death of her brother in 1927, Mary Walcott was appointed by President Coolidge to complete her brother's term on the Board of Indian Commissioners. She was reappointed by President Hoover, serving until 1932. She was elected president of the Society of Women Geographers in 1933. She was a member of the American Association for the Advancement of Science. She was an ardent mountain climber and was a member of several alpine clubs; Mount Mary Vaux in British Columbia was named for her. Her estate was bequeathed to the Smithsonian for the support of scientific research. Her research was on wildflowers, particularly North American pitcher plants.

Bibliography: *American Men and Women of Science* 6–7; Barnhart, John H., *Biographical Notes upon Botanists*; Herzenberg, Caroline L., *Women Scientists from Antiquity to the Present*; James, E. T., ed., *Notable American Women 1607–1950*; *National Union Catalog*; Rossiter, Margaret W., *Women Scientists in America*; Siegel, Patricia J. and Kay Thomas Finley, *Women in the Scientific Search*.

Wallace, Louise Baird
(1867–1968)
zoologist

Education: A.B., Mount Holyoke College, 1898; Woods Hole Biological Laboratory, 1891–1903; Naples Zoological Station, 1901; A.M., University of Pennsylvania, 1904, Ph.D., 1908

Employment: Assistant zoologist, Mount Holyoke College, 1893–1896; assistant, Smith College, 1896–1899; instructor, Mount Holyoke, 1899–1903, associate professor, 1904–1912; professor of biology, Constantinople College, 1912–1925, dean of faculty, 1913–1924, vice president, 1924–1925; professor of zoology, Mount Holyoke College, 1927–1928; professor of zoology, Spelman College, 1928–1931

*L*ouise Wallace was recognized for her research on spiders. She had a varied career of about 20 years on the Mount Holyoke faculty along with heavy administrative responsibilities as dean of faculty and vice president of Contantinople College. Her career was typical of many women of her generation in that she attended classes at Woods Hole starting in 1891 and worked as an assistant at both Mount Holyoke and Smith before completing her undergraduate degree at Mount Holyoke in 1898. She was then hired as an instructor there while she continued classes at Woods Hole and conducted research at the Naples Zoological Station. After receiving her master's degree from the University of Pennsylvania, she was promoted to associate professor in 1904 and then received her doctorate in 1908. She accepted a position as professor of biology at Constantinople College in 1912, where she was appointed dean of the faculty in 1913 and vice president in 1924. She returned to Mount Holyoke in 1927 and then accepted a position at Spelman College in 1928, where she worked for four years. At a time when both men and women completed their advanced degrees while teaching in colleges, it was not unusual that Louise Wallace spent ten years in completing her education. (During this period there was a spurt in education on all levels. Many of the women's colleges were still forming, and many schools were coeducational. There was a demand for faculty members in all disciplines nationwide.) Louise Wallace's scientific papers were concerned with toadfish and spiders. She received an honorary degree from Mount Holyoke in 1919. She was a member of the American Society of Zoologists. Her research included auxiliary glands of Batrachus, and spermatogenesis and oogenesis of the spider. Her name was listed in the first edition of *American Men and Women of Science.*

Bibliography: *American Men and Women of Science* 1–10; Siegel, Patricia J. and Kay Thomas Finley, *Women in the Scientific Search.*

Warga, Mary Elizabeth
(b. 1904)
physicist

Education: B.S., University of Pittsburgh, 1926, scholar, Allegheny Observatory, 1926–1928, M.S., 1928, Ph.D. in spectroscopy, 1937

Employment: Industrial assistant, Mellon Institute, 1928–1930, industrial fellow, 1930–1933; industrial fellow, University of Pittsburgh, 1934–1936, from instructor to professor of physics and director of spectroscopy laboratory, 1936–1962, adjunct professor of physics, 1962–1972, emeritus professor of physics and engineering; executive secretary, Optical Society of America, 1959–1972; emeritus executive secretary

Mary Warga, after a distinguished career in teaching and research, was selected as executive secretary of the Optical Society of America. During her first few years in this position, she still directed the spectroscopy laboratory at the University of Pittsburgh, but in 1962 she reduced her teaching load to adjunct professor of physics, probably due to the increased burden of society work. After receiving her master's degree from the University of Pittsburgh in 1928, she received several fellowships before being appointed instructor of physics in 1936. She rose through the ranks to professor of physics and director of the spectroscopy laboratory after receiving her doctorate in spectroscopy in 1937. She retired from teaching and the association in 1973. She was very fortunate in her career choice because she seemed to have been employed all during the Depression years. She received a distinguished service award from the Optical Society of America when she retired in 1973. She was a member of the governing board of the American Institute of Physics beginning in 1960 and served as secretary of the Joint Council on Quantum Electronics. She was elected a fellow of the Optical Society of America, the American Institute of Physics, and the American Association for the Advancement of Science. She was a member of the American Association of Physics Teachers, the American Chemical Society, and the Society for Applied Spectroscopy. Her research involved ultraviolet, visible, and infrared optical emission spectroscopy; and optical absorption and upper atmosphere spectroscopy.

Bibliography: *American Men and Women of Science* 6–12; Debus, A. G., ed., *World Who's Who in Science;* Herzenberg, Caroline L., *Women Scientists from Antiquity to the Present.*

Washburn, Margaret Floy
(1871–1939)
psychologist

Education: A.B., Vassar College, 1891, A.M., 1893; Ph.D., Cornell University, 1894
Employment: Professor of psychology and ethics, Wells College, 1894–1900; warden, Sage College, Cornell University, 1900–1902, lecturer, psychology, 1901–1902; assistant professor, University of Cincinnati, 1902–1903; associate professor of philosophy in charge of psychology, Vassar College, 1903–1908, professor of psychology, 1908–1937; emeritus professor

argaret Washburn was recognized for her motor theory of consciousness, that is, all thoughts and perceptions produce some form of motor reaction. Her most important publication was *The Animal Mind* (1908), which analyzed the large literature of animal psychology. The book *Movement and Mental Imagery* (1916) presents her theory of consciousness. Her name was included in a study of 50 eminent American psychologists in 1903 as reported by Stephen Visher in *Scientists Starred 1903–1943 in "American Men of Science."* She was elected president of the American Psychological Association in 1921, the second woman to be elected. In 1931 she was the second woman to be elected to the National Academy of Sciences.

After receiving her doctorate from Cornell University in 1894, she was appointed a professor of psychology and ethics at Wells College for seven years before returning to Cornell as a lecturer in psychology. She was appointed assistant professor at the University of Cincinnati for one year. She accepted a position as associate professor of philosophy in charge of psychology at Vassar College in 1903, was promoted to professor in 1908, and became emeritus professor in 1937. She published over 200 scientific papers in her career. She had her students assist with much of her experimental work and then listed them as coauthors when she published the results. She was criticized for this practice because most faculty members merely appropriated their students' work without crediting them. Although she supported educational equality for women, she was not involved in organized efforts for women's rights. She was strongly in favor of coeducation in place of single-sex colleges.

She published an autobiographical article in *A History of Psychology in Autobiography* 2 (1932): 333–358; she also included anecdotes about some of her contemporaries in psychology. Her research involved space perception of the skin, after images, comparative psychology, and psychology of affective processes. There is a photograph in the *Biographical Memoirs* of the National Academy of Sciences and one in the

National Cyclopedia of American Biography. Her name was listed in the first edition of *American Men and Women of Science* and starred in the first six editions.

Bibliography: *American Men and Women of Science* 1–6; Bryan, Alice I. and Edwin G. Boring, "Women in American Psychology"; *Dictionary of American Biography;* Herzenberg, Caroline L., *Women Scientists from Antiquity to the Present;* James, E. T., ed., *Notable American Women 1607–1950;* National Academy of Sciences, *Biographical Memoirs; National Cyclopedia of American Biography; National Union Catalog;* Ogilvie, Marilyn B., *Women in Science;* O'Neill, Lois S., *The Women's Book of World Records and Achievements;* Rossiter, Margaret W., *Women Scientists in America;* Rossiter, Margaret W., "'Women's Work' in Science, 1880–1910"; Siegel, Patricia J. and Kay Thomas Finley, *Women in the Scientific Search;* Visher, Stephen S., *Scientists Starred 1903–1943 in "American Men of Science."*

Watts, Betty Monaghan
(b. 1907)
food chemist

Education: B.S., Wilson College, 1928; Ph.D. in biological sciences, Washington University, St. Louis, 1932
Employment: Assistant zoologist, Washington University, St. Louis, 1928–1932; physiologist, medical school, 1933–1936; instructor, household science, and later, assistant professor, home economics, University of California, Berkeley, 1937–1943; associate professor, Washington State College, 1943–1946; professor, home economics, Syracuse University, 1946–1951; professor, food and nutrition, Florida State University, 1951–1968, distinguished professor, 1965–1968; emeritus distinguished professor
Concurrent Position: Civilian with Office of Scientific Research and Development, 1944
Married: Hilary Watts, 1936, died 1956

Betty Watts was an expert on the flavor and color of plant and animal tissues used as food, a very specialized area of food chemistry that is becoming more important each year. (The current controversy over genetically engineered crops and animals touches on the premise that this food will look the same and taste the same as "pure" food; but consumers are wary of the latent effects on humans.) Betty Watts conducted research on food irradiation, which is still a controversial topic. She first was employed as a zoologist and physiologist at Washington University in St. Louis. She accepted a position in the home economics department at the University of California, Berkeley, in 1937 and then at Washington State in 1943. She was a professor of home economics at Syracuse University in 1946. She then accepted a position as professor of food and nutrition at Florida State in 1951, was named distinguished professor in 1965, and was named emeritus distinguished professor in 1968. Although the general impression has been that home economics faculty members lack strong educational backgrounds, Betty Watts had a doctorate in biological sciences from Washington University, St. Louis. She was a member of the research advisory committee on human nutrition of the U.S. Department of Agriculture, beginning in 1964. She received several awards, including the

Vibrans Award of the American Meat Institute Foundation (1958) and the Borden Award (1964). She was a member of the American Association for the Advancement of Science, the American Home Economics Association, the Institute of Food Technologists, and the American Oil Chemists' Society. Her research included lipid oxidations, meat pigments, enzymatic deterioration in meats and vegetables, and food preservation by radiation and freeze drying. She and her husband had one son, Jeremy.

Bibliography: American Men and Women of Science 6–12; Debus, A. G., ed., *World Who's Who in Science;* Herzenberg, Caroline L., *Women Scientists from Antiquity to the Present.*

Way, Katharine
(1903–)
physicist

Education: B.S., Columbia University, 1932; Ph.D. in physics, University of North Carolina, 1938

Employment: Research fellow, Bryn Mawr College, 1938–1939; instructor in physics, University of Tennessee, 1939–1941, assistant professor, 1941–1942; physicist, Naval Ordnance Laboratory, 1942, Manhattan Project, Oak Ridge National Laboratory, 1942–1948; physicist, National Bureau of Standards, 1949–1953; director, nuclear data project, National Research Council, 1953–1963; director, Oak Ridge National Laboratory, 1964–1968; adjunct professor of physics, Duke University, 1968–1988

Concurrent Positions: Editor, *Nuclear Data Tables,* 1965–1973; editor, *Atomic Data,* 1969–1973; editor, *Atomic Data and Nuclear Data Tables,* 1973–1982; director, surgery and bioengineering, National Institutes of Health study section, 1981–1985

Katharine Way's notable contribution to science has been the vast project of compiling and editing the *Atomic Data and Nuclear Data Tables* and its preceding publications, *Nuclear Data Tables* and *Atomic Data.* These are the publications on which nuclear physicists commonly depend; however, computer technology now allows physicists to access the data in other formats. She was in on the ground floor of the entire project during World War II when she was involved in the Manhattan Project at the Naval Ordnance Laboratory, the Oak Ridge National Laboratory, and the National Bureau of Standards. The Manhattan Project started as a crash program to develop the atomic bomb and then spun off into building nuclear reactors at Argonne National Laboratory and other installations.

While she was director of the nuclear data project for the National Research Council (NRC), she was also an adjunct professor of physics at Duke University from 1968 to 1988. One of her responsibilities for the NRC was to serve as editor of the three successive data publications listed above. She left the project in 1982 after accepting a position with the National Institutes of Health, where she worked from 1981 to 1985. She received her doctorate in physics from the University of North Carolina in 1938. She was elected a fellow of the American Physical Society and of the American Association for the Advancement of Science. Her research has included nuclear fission, radiation shielding, and nuclear constants. Her name was listed in the 1992–1993 edition of *American Men and Women of Science.*

Bibliography: *American Men and Women of Science* 7–18; Herzenberg, Caroline L., *Women Scientists from Antiquity to the* *Present*; O'Neill, Lois S., *The Women's Book of World Records and Achievements.*

Westcott, Cynthia
(1898–1983)
plant pathologist

Education: B.A., Wellesley College, 1920; Ph.D. in plant pathology, Cornell University, 1932

Employment: High school science teacher, 1920–1921; assistant in plant pathology, Cornell University, 1921–1923, instructor, 1923–1925, research assistant, 1925–1931; research assistant in seed laboratory, New Jersey Experiment Station, 1931–1933; private practice in plant pathology, 1933–?

Concurrent Position: Plant pathologist, U.S. Department of Agriculture, 1943–1945

Cynthia Westcott was one of the first consulting plant pathologists. She established a private practice as the Plant Doctor when she was unable to find a full-time professional position. She supported herself by maintaining the gardens of her wealthy customers, by lectures to women's clubs, and by her writing. After teaching high school for two years, she went to Cornell University, where she worked as an assistant and instructor for about ten years while completing work on her doctorate, which she received in 1932. She obtained a position in the seed laboratory at the New Jersey Experiment Station for three years before setting up her own business. Since the turn of the century, women routinely found employment in seed testing at the experiment stations, and many of these were dead-end jobs. According to her autobiography, Cynthia Westcott was able to support herself by operating her business and writing books, and she loved it. During World War II she worked as a plant pathologist for the U.S. Department of Agriculture because she was unable to

obtain the supplies she needed for her business. Her books include *The Plant Doctor: The How, Why and When of Disease and Insect Control in Your Garden* (1937), *The Gardener's Bug Book* (1946), *Plant Disease Handbook* (1950), and *Anyone Can Grow Roses* (1952). The publishers of some of these titles are still issuing revised editions. She was a member of the American Association for the Advancement of Science, the American Phytopathological Society, and the American Association of Economic Entomologists. Her research included rose diseases, diseases of ornamentals in New Jersey, and garden diseases and pests. Her autobiography is *Plant Doctoring Is Fun* (1957).

Bibliography: *American Men and Women of Science* 6–10; Barnhart, John H., *Biographical Notes upon Botanists*; Herzenberg, Caroline L., *Women Scientists from Antiquity to the Present*; McNeil, Barbara, ed., *Biography and Genealogy Master Index 1986–90, Cumulation,* vol. 3; *National Union Catalog*; Rossiter, Margaret W., *Women Scientists in America.*

Wheeler, Anna Johnson Pell
(1883–1966)
mathematician

Education: A.B., University of South Dakota, 1903; M.A., University of Iowa, 1904; A.M., Radcliffe College, 1905; University of Göttingen, 1906–1907; Ph.D. in mathematics, University of Chicago, 1910

Employment: Instructor in mathematics, Mount Holyoke College, 1911–1914, associate professor, 1914–1918; associate professor, Bryn Mawr College, 1918–1925, department chair, 1924–1948, professor, 1925–1927, nonresearch professor, 1929–1932, professor, 1932–1948; emeritus professor

Married: Alexander Pell, 1907, died 1921; Arthur L. Wheeler, 1925, died 1932

Anna Pell Wheeler was recognized as a distinguished research mathematician; her work primarily was in the area of linear algebra of infinitely many variables. She was only the second woman to receive a doctorate in mathematics at the University of Chicago, and was one of only three women mathematicians whose names were starred in the first seven editions of *American Men and Women of Science*. In 1903 she graduated from the University of South Dakota after only three years and then obtained a master's degree from both the University of Iowa in 1904 and Radcliffe in 1905. She received a fellowship to study for a year at the University of Göttingen; one stipulation of the fellowship was that she remain single. She was married in Göttingen to Alexander Pell, one of her mathematics professors at South Dakota with whom she remained in contact, when the fellowship was completed. They returned to South Dakota for two years, and she taught classes. She returned to Göttingen to complete her course work, but she had a conflict with her major professor. She received her doctorate from the University of Chicago in 1910; her husband was then teaching at Armour Institute of Technology. Since the college did not want to hire women faculty members on a full-time basis, she taught parttime at the University of Chicago.

When her husband suffered a paralytic stroke, she substituted for him at Armour, but she was unable to obtain a position there. She accepted a position at Mount Holyoke in 1911 in order to support them, but she did not have time for her research. She moved to Bryn Mawr as an associate professor in 1918, serving as department chair from 1924 to 1948. She was promoted to professor in 1925, the year she married Arthur Wheeler, a classics professor. They moved to Princeton, New Jersey, but she continued to teach at Bryn Mawr on a part-time basis. When her husband died in 1932, she returned to full-time work at Bryn Mawr, retiring in 1948. In addition to her teaching and research, she was active professionally in mathematical associations. She was an editor of the *Annals of Mathematics* from 1927 to 1945. She received honorary degrees from two colleges and was a member of the American Mathematical Society, the Mathematical Association of America, and the American Association for the Advancement of Science. Her research included integral equations and functions of infinitely many variables. Her photograph was included in G. Kass-Simon and Patricia Farnes' *Women of Science*. She was listed as Mrs. Alexander Pell in the third edition and Mrs. Arthur L. Wheeler in the fourth through seventh editions of *American Men and Women of Science*.

Bibliography: American Men and Women of Science 3–10; Grinstein, Louise S. and Paul J. Campbell, eds., *Women of Mathematics;*

Herzenberg, Caroline L., *Women Scientists from Antiquity to the Present*; Kass Simon, G. and Patricia Farnes, *Women of Science*; Ogilvie, Marilyn B., *Women in Science*; Rossiter, Margaret W., *Women Scientists in America*; Rossiter, Margaret W., "Women Scientists in America before 1920"; Sicherman, Barbara et al., *Notable American Women*; Siegel, Patricia J. and Kay Thomas Finley, *Women in the Scientific Search*; Visher, Stephen S., *Scientists Starred 1903–1943 in "American Men of Science."*

Wheeler, Ruth
(1877–1948)
physiological chemist and nutritionist

Education: A.B., Vassar College, 1899; Ph.D., Yale University, 1913

Employment: High school science teacher, 1899–1905; chemistry teacher, Pratt Institute, 1905–1910; teacher, dietetics and nutrition, University of Illinois, 1913, associate in household science, 1913–1915, associate professor, 1915–1918; professor of home economics and department head, Goucher College, 1918–1921; head, department of nutrition, college of medicine, University of Iowa, 1921–1926; professor of physiology and nutrition, Vassar College, 1926–1944

Concurrent position: Director, Vassar Summer Institute of Euthenics, 1928–1942

Ruth Wheeler was one of the early researchers in the discipline of nutrition. She was a charter member of the American Home Economics Association when it was formed in 1908 and was president of the American Dietetic Association from 1924 to 1926. After she received her undergraduate degree from Vassar in 1899, she followed the pattern of many women of her generation by teaching high school for six years. She obtained a position at Pratt Institute as a chemistry teacher for six years before receiving her doctorate from Yale in 1913. She had observed the new discipline of nutrition and decided to obtain further work in physiological chemistry. She was appointed an associate in household science at the University of Illinois in 1913 and promoted to associate professor in 1915. She was invited to join Goucher College as professor of home economics and department head in 1918 and moved to a similar position in the department of nutrition at the University of Iowa in 1921. This was a new department at Iowa, and she continued to insist on a balanced program of teaching, research, and service. One of her innovations was the internship leading to a master's degree. She was appointed professor of physiology and nutrition at Vassar in 1926, retiring in 1944. Concurrently she was director of the Vassar Summer Institute of Euthenics, a broad-based program aimed at improving human relations, starting in 1928. During and long after World War I, she was chair of the committee on nutrition of the American Red Cross and published *American Red Cross Textbook on Food and Nutrition* (1927). She also was the author of *Talks to Nurses on Dietetics and Dietotherapy* (1926). She was a member of the American Society of Biological Chemists, the American Institute of Nutrition, and the American Association for the Advancement of Science. Her research involved dietetics and nutrition.

Bibliography: *American Men and Women of Science* 3–8; Herzenberg, Caroline L., *Women Scientists from Antiquity to the Present;* James, E. T., ed., *Notable American Women 1607–1950; National Union Catalog;* Rossiter, Margaret W., *Women Scientists in America;* Rossiter, Margaret W., "Women Scientists in America before 1920"; Siegel, Patricia J. and Kay Thomas Finley, *Women in the Scientific Search.*

Whiting, Sarah Frances
(1847–1927)
physicist

Education: B.A., Ingham University, 1865; University of Berlin, 1888–1889; Edinburgh University, 1896–1897
Employment: Teacher of classics and mathematics, Ingham University and Brooklyn Heights Seminary, 1865–1876; professor of physics, Wellesley College, 1876–1912, director of Whitin Observatory, 1900–1916

*S*arah Whiting established the departments of physics and astronomy at Wellesley College; she probably was the first person to introduce laboratory experiments for women. At the time, she was one of the few women in the United States who was capable of setting up these departments. Since American colleges were not admitting women as students, Wellesley had been unable to find a teacher for their science course. She had taught mathematics for about 12 years at a private school. By special arrangement, she audited physics courses at Massachusetts Institute of Technology in order to learn the subject matter and how to use the instruments. Since another of her responsibilities was to select and order equipment for the new physics department, she visited many schools and institutions in the area to see what was available to order. The instruments were made in Germany, but the companies did not issue catalogs.

She had a heavy schedule of classes because physics was required of all candidates for a degree until 1893. She had to demonstrate and conduct experiments herself because she did not have an assistant until 1885. One anecdote that indicates her capabilities was when the school planned to install electric lights in the library. The trustees were afraid the glare would harm the students' eyes, but Sarah Whiting obtained some Edison bulbs and demonstrated how they gave a steady light better than the arc lamps and gas lights currently in use. Although she introduced the course in astronomy in 1880, the school did not establish an observatory until 20 years later with a gift from a Wellesley trustee, Mrs. John C. Whitin. Whiting had acquired some instruments over the years, but she designed and equipped the new observatory with the same zeal as she had set up the physics department. She acquired her own instruction from the faculty at the Harvard College Observatory. She made several trips to England and Europe over the years to study new techniques and view new equipment. She was a member of the American Astronomical Society and the American Physical Society. She was awarded an honorary degree from Tufts University in 1905. There is a biography and photograph in *Popular Astronomy* 35 (1927): 538–545.

Bibliography: *American Men and Women of Science* 4; Elliott, Clark A., *Biographical Dictionary of American Science*; Herzenberg, Caroline L., *Women Scientists from Antiquity to the Present*; James, E. T., ed., *Notable American Women 1607–1950*; Kass-Simon, G. and Patricia Farnes, *Women of Science*; Ogilvie, Marilyn B., *Women in Science*; O'Neill, Lois S., *The Women's Book of World Records and Achievements*; Rossiter, Margaret W., *Women Scientists in America*; Siegel, Patricia J. and Kay Thomas Finley, *Women in the Scientific Search*; Uglow, Jennifer S., *International Dictionary of Women's Biography*.

Whitney, Mary Watson
(1847–1921)
astronomer

Education: A.B., Vassar College, 1868, A.M., 1872; Harvard University, 1872; University of Zurich, 1874–1876

Employment: High school teacher, 1872–1874; assistant, Vassar Observatory, 1881–1888, professor of astronomy and director of observatory, 1889–1910; emeritus professor

Mary Whitney was recognized as one of the pioneer women astronomers in the United States, and her name was listed in the first three editions of *American Men and Women of Science*. She was a member of the second class graduated from Vassar in 1868. After teaching school for two years, she went to the University of Zurich to study mathematics and celestial mechanics. She also received a master's degree from Vassar and studied mathematics at Harvard. She was invited to be Maria Mitchell's (q.v.) assistant in the observatory in 1881, succeeding Mitchell in 1888 as director of the Vassar Observatory and professor of astronomy. She had a heavy teaching load,

with 160 students in eight classes. With her own funds, she hired Caroline Furness (q.v.) in 1894 to assist her, and later Furness succeeded her.

Since Mitchell devoted her energy to obtaining necessary equipment and to teaching, it was left to Mary Whitney to establish scientific work at Vassar. The Vassar research, which was concentrated on calculating orbits and making observations of minor planets, was published as 102 articles and other publications in the major astronomical journals during the time of her chairmanship. This was a significant accomplishment for a small college. Sometime in the 1890s she upgraded the equipment by purchasing a Repsold machine for making accurate measurements of stars on photographic plates. This allowed research on plates borrowed from other observatories. She resigned in 1910 due to illness. She was a member of the American Astronomical Society, the American Mathematical Society, and the American Association for the Advancement of Science. Her research involved observations of comets, asteroids, and variable stars. There is a biography with photographs in *Popular Astronomy* 30 (1922): 597–608.

Bibliography: Abir-Am, P. G. and Dorinda Outram, eds., *Uneasy Careers and Intimate Lives; American Men and Women of Science* 1–3; Davis, Herman S., "Women Astronomers (1750–1890)"; *Dictionary of American Biography;* Elliott, Clark A., *Biographical Dictionary of American Science;* Herzenberg, Caroline L., *Women Scientists from Antiquity to the Present;* James, E. T., ed., *Notable American Women 1607–1950;* Kass-Simon, G. and Patricia Farnes, *Women of Science;* McHenry, Robert, ed., *Famous American Women;* Macksey, Joan and Kenneth Macksey, *The Book of Women's Achievements;* Mozans, H. J., *Women in Science;* Ogilvie, Marilyn B., *Women in Science;* Rossiter, Margaret W., *Women Scientists in America;* Siegel, Patricia J. and Kay Thomas Finley, *Women in the Scientific Search;* Uglow, Jennifer S., *International Dictionary of Women's Biography.*

Willcox, Mary Alice
(1856–1953)
zoologist

Education: Newnham College, Cambridge University, 1880–1883; Naples Zoological Station, 1898; Ph.D., University of Zurich, 1898
Employment: High school teacher, 1876–1879; professor of zoology and physiology, Wellesley College, 1883–1910; emeritus professor

Mary Willcox was recognized for her research on mollusks. Although she was an American, she attended Newnham College of Cambridge University for her undergraduate education. Cambridge was not granting degrees to women, although they were allowed to attend the school at that time. She taught high school for four years before going to England to attend school. She was appointed professor of zoology and physiology at Wellesley College in 1883. In 1898 she performed research at the Naples Zoological Station, which was internationally known as a research institution. The people who did research there had to provide their own funds, but many American women were able to use fellowships and gifts to pay for their stay. She received her doctorate from the University of Zurich in 1898 after attending classes since 1896. She returned to Wellesley, where she remained on the faculty until 1910. After she retired, she became involved in social issues, such as the League of Women Voters and the Federation of Women's Clubs. She was a member of the National Audubon Society and the Boston Society of Natural History. Her research involved comparative anatomy of mollusks and of acmaeidae. Her name was spelled both Wilcox and Willcox in the various sources; she was listed in the first edition of *American Men and Women of Science.*

Bibliography: *American Men and Women of Science* 1–8; Rossiter, Margaret W., *Women Scientists in America;* Siegel, Patricia J. and Kay Thomas Finley, *Women in the Scientific Search.*

Williams, Anna Wessels
(1863–1954)
bacteriologist

Education: Diploma, New Jersey State Normal School, Trenton, 1883; M.D., Woman's Medical College, New York, 1891
Employment: Public school teacher, 1883–1885; instructor in pathology, New York Infirmary, 1891–1893, assistant to department chair, pathology and hygiene, 1891–1895, consulting pathologist, 1902–1905; assistant, diagnostic laboratory, New York City Department of Health, 1894, assistant bacteriologist, 1895–1905, assistant director, 1905–1934

*A*nna Williams gained national recognition for her work on infectious diseases. At the diagnostic laboratory of the New York City Department of Health, she made significant contributions on effective immunization for diphtheria, streptococcal and pneumococcal infections, and scarlet fever. She also contributed to the development of a rabies vaccine. In the first year of her research she isolated a strain of the diphtheria bacillus that made possible the widespread immunization of children and almost complete eradication of the disease.

She continued to contribute significant work. She also played a significant role in building the diagnostic laboratory into a nationally known laboratory and the first municipal laboratory to apply bacteriology to the problems of public health. After receiving her diploma from the New Jersey State Normal School, she taught public school for several years to earn funds to obtain her M.D. in 1891 from the Woman's Medical College of New York. She had convinced her family to allow her to become a physician after a sister almost died from diphtheria because the doctors knew of no treatments. After working as a pathologist for the New York Infirmary for several years, she was initially a volunteer with the diagnostic laboratory in 1894 while working as a consulting pathologist. She joined the staff in 1895 and was appointed assistant director in 1905, a position she held until retiring in 1934.

In spite of the pleas of her coworkers, the mayor decided she had to leave at the regulation retirement age. She was coauthor of a book for lay readers entitled *Who's Who among the Microbes* (1929). In addition to her scientific papers, she was coauthor of *Pathogenic Microorganisms Including Bacteria and Protozoa* (1905) and was the author of *Streptococci in Relation to Man in Health and Disease* (1932). She was a member of the American Public Health Association.

Bibliography: Abir-Am, P. G. and Dorinda Outram, eds., *Uneasy Careers and Intimate Lives; National Union Catalog;* Rossiter, Margaret W., *Women Scientists in America;* Sicherman, Barbara et al., *Notable American Women;* Siegel, Patricia J. and Kay Thomas Finley, *Women in the Scientific Search.*

Wilson, Lucy
(b. 1888)
physicist

Education: A.B., Wellesley College, 1909; Ph.D. in optics, Johns Hopkins University, 1917
Employment: Assistant, physics, Mount Holyoke College, 1909–1911, instructor, 1911–1914; instructor, physics and psychology, Wellesley College, 1917–1920, assistant professor of physics, 1920–1924, associate professor, 1924–1935, professor, 1935–1954, acting dean of college, 1938–1939, dean of students, 1939–1954

Lucy Wilson was recognized for her research in physics. After receiving her undergraduate degree from Wellesley in 1909, she was employed as an assistant in physics and then instructor at Mount Holyoke for five years. She continued her education at Johns Hopkins, receiving her doctorate in 1917. She was appointed an instructor in physics and psychology at Wellesley in 1917. Although it seems strange to have the combination of physics and psychology in her position at Wellesley, she was involved in research on theories of vision at the time, a topic that could be applicable to either area. She was promoted through the ranks to assistant professor in 1920, associate professor in 1924, and professor in 1935. (In the 1920s Wellesley had the most women physicists teaching as assistant professor or higher than any academic institution.) Starting in 1939, Lucy Wilson shifted to the administrative assignment of dean of students in addition to her teaching and research, retiring from both positions in 1954. She was a member of the American Physical Society, the Optical Society of America, and the American Association for the Advancement of Science. Her research involved theories of vision, optics in pure physics, and x-ray spectroscopy.

Bibliography: *American Men and Women of Science* 5–10; Kass-Simon, G. and Patricia Farnes, *Women of Science;* Rossiter, Margaret W., *Women Scientists in America.*

Wilson, Lucy Langdon Williams
(1865–1937)
anthropologist and geographer

Education: State Normal School, Vermont, 1878; State Normal School, Philadelphia, 1881; Ph.D., University of Pennsylvania, 1897; Cornell University, University of Chicago, Harvard University; Woods Hole Marine Biological Laboratory
Employment: Public school teacher and principal, 1882–1934; lecturer, education, Temple University, 1934–1936
Married: William P. Wilson, 1894

Lucy L. Wilson gained recognition for her use of the laboratory method in teaching natural sciences, primarily at the elementary school level. She listed herself as a biologist in the first edition of *American Men and Women of Science* but as an anthropologist and a geographer in the second, third, and fourth editions. After attending normal schools in Vermont and Philadelphia, she taught school and served as a principal from 1882 to 1934. She received a doctorate from the University of Pennsylvania in 1897 and took further studies at several other universities. After she retired, she was a lecturer on education at Temple University. She studied teaching methods in Europe and South America and regularly lectured at seminars and congresses. She also lectured at international conferences, winning a gold medal at the 1900 Paris Exposition. She was the author of eight books describing her methods and those she had studied. These works include *Nature Study: A Manual for Teachers* (1897), *Domestic Science* (1906), and

The New Schools in New Russia (1928). From 1915 to 1917 she excavated a pueblo and other prehistoric remains in New Mexico. She was a member of the American Anthropological Association, the American Geographical Society, and the American Association for the Advancement of Science. Her research involved anthropogeography and American archaeology. She and her husband had one son, David.

Bibliography: *American Men and Women of Science* 1–4; *National Cyclopedia of American Biography*; Siegel, Patricia J. and Kay Thomas Finley, *Women in the Scientific Search*.

Witkin, Evelyn Maisel
(1921–)
geneticist

Education: B.A., New York University, 1941; M.A., Columbia University, 1943, Ph.D. in zoology, 1947

Employment: Research associate, bacterial genetics, Carnegie Institution, Cold Spring Harbor, 1946–1949, member of staff, genetics, 1949–1955; associate professor of medicine, college of medicine, State University of New York, Downstate Medical Center, Brooklyn, 1955–1969, professor, 1969–1971; professor, biological science, Douglass College, Rutgers University, 1971–1979; Barbara McClintock professor of genetics, Waksman Institute of Microbiology, 1979–

Concurrent Positions: American Cancer Society fellow, 1947–1949; research associate, Carnegie Institution, 1955–1971, fellow, 1956

Married: 1943

*E*velyn Witkin has had the distinction of being appointed the Barbara McClintock (q.v.) professor of genetics at the Waksman Institute of Microbiology. She has been recognized for her work on mutation in bacteria. While completing her doctorate in zoology from Columbia University, she was employed as a research associate in bacterial genetics at the Carnegie Institution in 1946, becoming a member of the staff in 1949. She was a research associate of the Carnegie

Institution from 1955 to 1971. She was appointed an associate professor of medicine in the college of medicine of the State University of New York in 1955 and promoted to professor in 1969. She was appointed a professor of biological science at Rutgers University in 1971 and the Barbara McClintock professor of genetics at the Waksman Institute in 1979. She was elected a member of the National Academy of Sciences in 1977 and received an honorary degree from New York Medical

College in 1978. She has been a member of the American Society for Microbiology, the Genetics Society of America, the American Society of Naturalists, the Radiation Research Society, and the American Academy of Arts and Sciences. Her research has involved mechanism of spontaneous and induced mutation in bacteria, genetic effects of radiation, and enzymatic repair of DNA damage. Her name was listed in the 1992–1993 edition of *American Men and Women of Science.*

Bibliography: *American Men and Women of Science* 9–18; Herzenberg, Caroline L., *Women Scientists from Antiquity to the Present;* O'Neill, Lois S., *The Women's Book of World Records and Achievements.*

Wood, Elizabeth Armstrong
(1912–)
crystallographer

Education: B.A., Barnard College, 1933; M.A., Bryn Mawr College, 1934, Ph.D. in geology, 1939
Employment: Demonstrator in geology, Bryn Mawr College, 1934–1935, 1937–1938; assistant, Barnard College, 1936–1937, lecturer, 1938–1941, research assistant, 1941–1942, National Research Council fellow, 1942–1943; technical staff, crystal research, Bell Telephone Laboratories, 1943–1967
Married: Ira E. Wood, 1947

Elizabeth Wood has been recognized for her research on x-ray crystallography and the physical properties of crystals. She was the author of two books, *Crystal Orientation Manual* (1963) and *Crystals and Light: An Introduction to Optical Crystallography* (1964), which still are classics in the field. She received her undergraduate degree from Barnard in 1933. After earning her master's degree at Bryn Mawr in 1934, she was employed there as a demonstrator in geology while she did further graduate work. In 1938 she returned to Barnard as a lecturer, and in 1939 she received her doctorate in geology from Bryn Mawr. She was promoted to research assistant at Barnard in 1941. She joined the technical staff in crystal research at Bell Labs in 1943, retiring in 1967.

Her work in crystallography at Bell came at the very beginning of the discipline of solid-state chemistry and physics. Bell was one of the significant participants in the development of lasers and other solid-state devices, and the basis of this new electronics research was growing the crystals used in the devices. All of this is now routine production work, but in the 1950s and 1960s it was the threshold of the new generation of electronics. Elizabeth Wood was still working when these developments began. She was elected president of the American Crystallographic Association in 1957. She received an honorary degree from Wheaton College, Massachusetts, in 1963 and Western College in 1965. She was a fellow of the Mineralogical Society of America and the American Physical Society. Her research has included geology and petrology of igneous and metamorphic rocks, optical mineralogy, x-ray crystallography, and the physical properties of crystals.

Bibliography: *American Men and Women of Science* 8–11; Debus, A. G., ed., *World Who's Who in Science;* Herzenberg, Caroline L., *Women Scientists from Antiquity to the Present;* Kass-Simon, G. and Patricia Farnes, *Women of Science; National Union Catalog.*

Wood, Ruth Goulding
(b. 1875)
mathematician

Education: B.L., Smith College, 1898; Ph.D., Yale University, 1901; University of Göttingen, 1908–1909
Employment: Instructor in mathematics, Mount Holyoke College, 1901–1902; instructor, Smith College, 1902–1909, associate professor, 1909–1914, professor, 1914–1935; emeritus professor

Ruth Wood was recognized for her work on non-Euclidean geometry. She graduated from Smith College in 1898 and spent 33 years on the faculty, except for a one-year position at Mount Holyoke College. After receiving her doctorate from Yale in 1901, she accepted a position as an instructor in mathematics at Mount Holyoke for one year. She then returned to Smith as an instructor in 1902. She was promoted to associate professor in 1909 after taking postgraduate study at the University of Göttingen. She then became professor in 1914, retiring in 1935. Even at women's colleges, women faculty members were often retained indefinitely at the level of assistant professor, but Ruth Wood advanced quite rapidly in professorial rank, perhaps because she received a doctorate from Yale and took postgraduate study at the University of Göttingen. There was a shortage of teachers at the college level in all disciplines, especially in science and mathematics, but other women with similar credentials did not receive such quick promotions. She was a member of the American Mathematical Society. Her area of research was non-Euclidean geometry. Her name was listed in the first six editions of *American Men and Women of Science.*

Bibliography: *American Men and Women of Science* 1–6; Siegel, Patricia J. and Kay Thomas Finley, *Women in the Scientific Search.*

Woolley, Helen Bradford Thompson
(1874–1947)
psychologist

Education: Ph.B., University of Chicago, 1897, Ph.D., 1900
Employment: Instructor and professor of psychology, Mount Holyoke College, 1901–1905; experimental psychologist, Bureau of Education, Philippine Islands, 1905–1906; instructor in philosophy, University of Cincinnati, 1910–1912; director, Vocation Bureau, Cincinnati public schools, 1911–1921; psychologist and assistant director, Merrill-Palmer School, 1921–1926; professor of education and director, bureau of child development, Teachers' College, Columbia University, 1926–1930
Married: Paul G. Woolley, 1905, died 1932

elen Woolley was a pioneer in the study of child development. She organized one of the first nursery schools in the country at Merrill-Palmer School, which was a laboratory for the study of child development. After she received her doctorate from the University of Chicago in 1900, she undertook further studies at the Universities of Berlin and Paris before she accepted a position in the psychology department at Mount Holyoke in 1901. When she was married in 1905, she and her husband spent several years in the Orient, where she worked in the Philippine Bureau of Education for a time. They returned to the United States to live in Cincinnati, where she taught at the University of Cincinnati for three years. She obtained a position as a psychologist with the public schools and director of the Vocation Bureau. Here she made extensive studies of the mental and physical characteristics of children who left school at age 14. The Ohio child labor law had been enacted in 1910, and she compared those students who remained in school and those who left. This study was the basis of the monograph *Mental and Physical Measurements of Working Children* (1914) and was instrumental in the passage of a compulsory school attendance and child labor law in Ohio in 1921.

She accepted a position as assistant director and psychologist at the Merrill-Palmer School in Detroit in 1921, and she helped develop the Merrill-Palmer Scale of Mental Tests. She then moved to Teachers' College, Columbia University, in 1926 as professor of education and director of the bureau of child development. After she and her husband separated in 1926, she became ill. Although she returned to work in 1928, even with the help of an assistant director she was unable to continue her teaching and administrative work. She officially retired in 1930. She was elected president of the National Vocational Guidance Association in 1921. She also was a member of the American Psychological Association and the American Association for the Advancement of Science. Her research involved the psychology of adolescence and of young childhood; comparison by physical and mental measurements and industrial and home life of working and school adolescents; and mental development and tests, educational methods, personality, and social behavior of young children. She was listed in the first edition of *American Men and Women of Science* as Helen Thompson and in the second to fourth editions as Mrs. Paul G. Woolley. Her name was starred in the third to seventh editions.

Bibliography: *American Men and Women of Science* 1–7; Bryan, Alice I. and Edwin G. Boring, "Women in American Psychology"; Herzenberg, Caroline L., *Women Scientists from Antiquity to the Present*; James, E. T., ed., *Notable American Women 1607–1950*; Rossiter, Margaret W., *Women Scientists in America*; Rossiter, Margaret W., "Women Scientists in America before 1920"; Siegel, Patricia J. and Kay Thomas Finley, *Women in the Scientific Search*; Visher, Stephen S., *Scientists Starred 1903–1943 in "American Men of Science."*

Woolman, Mary Raphael Schenck
(1860–1940)
home economist and textile specialist

Education: University of Pennsylvania, 1883–1884; diploma, Teachers' College, Columbia University, 1895, B.S., 1897

Employment: Assistant in domestic science, Teachers' College, Columbia University, 1892, instructor of sewing, 1893–1897, adjunct professor of household arts education, 1897–1903, professor, 1903–1912; acting head, home economics department, Simmons College, 1912–1914

Married: Franklin C. Woolman, 1883

Mary Woolman was one of the pioneers in home economics education, and her significant work was in vocational education. She made significant contributions to the discipline of textile chemistry. The family moved to New York City in 1891, and by this time her husband was a semi-invalid. While she was working as a copyeditor, by chance a faculty member from Teachers' College asked her to review a book on sewing instructions that had been written for the college. Her critique was so negative that she was asked to prepare one of her own. Her ideas were so innovative that, although she lacked a college degree, she was appointed an assistant in domestic science in 1892 and an instructor of sewing the following year. She continued her college education while teaching, receiving a diploma from Teachers' College in 1895 and a B.S. degree in 1897. In 1897 she was also appointed adjunct professor of

household arts education, and in 1903 she became a professor, one of the first women to achieve this rank at Columbia. She organized the department of domestic art and introduced the study of textiles.

In 1902 she was granted a half-time leave to establish the Manhattan Trade School for Girls to train girls for employment in factories and workrooms. This was incorporated into the city school system in 1910. In 1912 she moved to Boston to become acting head of the home economics department of Simmons College for two years. After 1914 she lectured, attended classes, and participated in associations. She was a founding member of the American Home Economics Association. Her books include *A Sewing Course* (1900), *The Making of a Trade School* (1910), and *Textile Problems for the Consumer* (1935).

Bibliography: James, E. T., ed., *Notable American Women 1607–1950; National Union Catalog.*

Wright, Helen
(1914–)
astronomer and author

Education: A.B., Vassar College, 1937, M.A., 1939; graduate courses, University of California
Employment: Assistant in astronomy department, Vassar College, 1937–1939; Mount Wilson Observatory, 1937; junior astronomer, U.S. Naval Observatory, 1942–1943; author
Married: John F. Hawkins, 1946, divorced

Helen Wright has been contributing to the literature of science by writing about science and scientists since the 1940s. She was the author of a biography of Maria Mitchell, *Sweeper in the Sky: The First Woman Astronomer in America* (1949), and she wrote the biographical sketch of Maria Mitchell that was published in *Notable American Women 1607–1950*. After receiving her undergraduate degree from Vassar College in 1937, she was an assistant in astronomy at Vassar and at Mount Wilson Observatory while completing her master's degree, which she received in 1939. She accepted a position as a junior astronomer at the U.S. Naval Observatory for two years before concentrating on her writing. She has written books on astronomy, biology, physical sciences, medicine, geology, mathematics, archaeology, engineering, and physics, to name a few disciplines. Her books include *Readings in the Physical Sciences* (1948), *Great Adventures in Medicine* (1952), *Palomar, The World's Largest Telescope* (1952), and *The Great Explorers* (1957), *Explorer of the Universe: A Biography of George Ellery Hale* (1966). She has been a member of the International Astronomical Union, the American Astronomical Society, and the History of Science Society. Her research includes studies in the history of science, the history of telescopes, and science in the nineteenth-century United States. Her photograph is in *Current Biography*.

Bibliography: Debus, A. G., ed., *World Who's Who in Science; Current Biography;* Herzenberg, Caroline L., *Women Scientists from Antiquity to the Present;* Ireland, Norma O., *Index to Scientists of the World; National Union Catalog*.

Wright, Mabel Osgood
(1859–1934)
nature writer and bird protectionist

Education: Private schools
Employment: Author
Married: James O. Wright, 1884

Mabel Wright contributed to the popularization of science by writing both magazine articles and books. It is not known how she became interested in nature, but sometime after 1884 she began writing popular nature studies for newspapers. The first was "A New England May Day," published in the

New York Evening Post in 1893. She published her first nature book, *The Friendship of Nature*, in 1894; this was a collection of articles that had previously appeared in newspapers. The book *Birdcraft: A Field Book of Two Hundred Song, Game, and Water Birds* (1895) was considered by ornithologist Frank M. Chapman as one of the first modern bird manuals. All of her books showed a deep respect for nature and a concern for accurate description. Her next books reflected her concern about preserving the natural heritage. These were *Citizen Bird*, coauthored with Elliott Coues (1897), and *Gray Lady and the Birds* (1907). She was associated with Chapman's magazine, *Bird-Lore*, until her death. Another nature book was *Flowers and Ferns in Their Haunts* (1901). She published several novels in addition to her nature books; they are romances that give some indication of the social changes that were taking place in her lifetime. She helped to establish the Connecticut Audubon Society in 1898, and she served as its president for many years. She was elected a member of the American Ornithologists' Union in 1901. She pioneered bird protection by constructing a bird sanctuary near her Connecticut home.

Bibliography: Herzenberg, Caroline L., *Women Scientists from Antiquity to the Present*; James, E. T., ed., *Notable American Women 1607–1950*; *National Cyclopedia of American Biography*; *National Union Catalog*; Siegel, Patricia J. and Kay Thomas Finley, *Women in the Scientific Search*.

Wrinch, Dorothy Maud
(1894–1976)
biochemist

Education: Cambridge University, 1913–1918, 1920–1923, 1930–1935; M.Sc., University of London, 1920, D.Sc., 1921; M.A., Oxford University, 1924, D.Sc., 1929, research fellow 1931–1934; University of Vienna, 1931–1932; University of Paris, 1933–1934
Employment: Lecturer in pure mathematics, University College, University of London, 1918–1920; lecturer in mathematics and director, studies for women, member, faculty of physical sciences, Oxford University, 1923–1939; research fellow, Somerville College, Oxford, 1939–1941; lecturer in chemistry, Johns Hopkins University, 1939–1941; visiting professor, natural sciences, Amherst College and Mount Holyoke College, 1941–1942; Rockefeller research fellow, 1935–1941; lecturer in physics, Smith College, 1941–1954, visiting professor, 1954–1971
Married: John W. Nicholson, 1922, marriage dissolved, 1938; Otto C. Glaser, 1941, died 1950

Dorothy Wrinch received in 1929 the first D.Sc. that Oxford University awarded a woman. She was a talented person whose interests spanned mathematical physics, molecular biology, philosophy, and sociology. From 1936 to 1939 she developed an important contribution to science—the first theory of protein structure, or the cyclol theory. It was the first concept to focus on molecular biology. She received so much publicity about this discovery that part of the scientific world turned against her, since she was attacking accepted chemical theories of proteins and she was a woman. In addition to the degree from Oxford, she also received a doctorate from the University of London and attended Cambridge and the Universities of Vienna and Paris. She alternated between teaching at London and Oxford. Her husband became increasingly incapacitated due to alcoholism, and the marriage was dissolved in 1938.

She and their daughter Pamela moved to the United States, where she accepted a position as a lecturer in chemistry at Johns Hopkins in 1939. She supported them by lectureships and fellowships at numerous schools on the East Coast. She was never able to secure a permanent faculty appointment, partially due to her theories on molecular biology and partially due to the popular presses' calling her the Woman Einstein. Several years after she married Otto Glaser in 1941, she secured a visiting professorship at Smith College, where she worked until she retired in 1971. Her *Fourier Transforms and Structure Factor* (1946) was considered a solid contribution to knowledge. Her other books were *Chemical Aspects of the Structure of Small Peptides: An Introduction* (1960) and *Chemical Aspects of*

Polypeptide Chain Structure and the Cyclol Theory (1965). She was elected a fellow of the American Physical Society and was a member of the American Chemical Society and the American Crystallographic Association. There are photographs in P.G. Abir-Am's and Dorinda Outram's *Uneasy Careers and Intimate Lives* and G. Kass-Simon's and Patricia Farnes' *Women of Science: Righting the Record.*

Bibliography: Abir-Am, P. G. and Dorinda Outram, eds., *Uneasy Careers and Intimate Lives; American Men and Women of Science* 7–8; Debus, A. G., ed., *World Who's Who in Science;* Herzenberg, Caroline L., *Women Scientists from Antiquity to the Present;* Ireland, Norma O., *Index to Scientists of the World;* Kass-Simon, G. and Patricia Farnes, *Women of Science; National Union Catalog;* Rossiter, Margaret W., *Women Scientists in America.*

Wu, Chien-Shiung

(1912–)

nuclear physicist

Education: B.S., National Central University, China, 1934; Ph.D. in physics, University of California, Berkeley, 1940

Employment: Lecturer, University of California, Berkeley, 1942–1944; assistant professor, Smith College, 1942–1943; instructor, Princeton University, 1943–1944; senior scientist, Manhattan Project, Columbia University, 1944–1947, associate, 1947–1952, from associate professor to professor, 1952–1972, Pupin professor of physics, 1972–1981

Concurrent Position: Member, advisory committee to director, National Institutes of Health, 1975–1982

Married: Luke C. Yuan, 1942

Chien-Shiung Wu has been one of the top women in elementary particle physics in the world for a number of years. She experimentally established nonconservation of parity in beta decay in 1957 and conservation of vector current in beta decay in 1963. She was elected a member of the National Academy of Sciences in 1958. She has achieved a

continuous record of outstanding work and significant appointments in her career.

After receiving her doctorate from the University of California, Berkeley, in 1940, she was employed briefly at Berkeley, Smith, and Princeton. In the nation's top 20 research universities at the time, not one had a woman physics professor, but she was hired as Princeton's first woman instructor due to the shortage of men physicists during World War II. The Manhattan Project gave a boost to her career, as it did many women scientists of the period. In 1944 she was appointed a senior scientist on the project at Columbia, where she helped develop sensitive radiation detectors for the atomic bomb project. She was one of the few scientists asked to remain at Columbia after the Manhattan Project was completed, and she was appointed an associate in 1947. She advanced from associate professor to professor in 1952 and then to Pupin professor of physics in 1972, retiring in 1981.

Her research has been marked by precise and careful experimentation on delicate matters such as spin correlations. It was said she always chose to do the significant and important experiments. She became known as someone whose work could be believed. She received honorary degrees from eight universities, and a number of awards both in the United States and China, including the National Science Medal (1975) and the Wolf Prize in Physics (1978). She was the first living scientist with an asteroid named after her (1990). She was president of the American Physical Society in 1975, was elected a fellow of the American Association for the Advancement of Science, and has been a member of the American Academy of Arts and Sciences. She was coauthor of *Beta Decay* (1965). There are photographs in Sharon McGrayne's *Nobel Prize Women in Science,* G. Kass-Simon's and Patricia Farnes' *Women of Science,* and Edna Yost's *Women of Modern Science.* Although there is a lengthy biography in McGrayne's book, Chien-Shiung Wu did not receive a Nobel Prize. She and her husband had a son, Vincent. Her name was listed in the 1992–1993 edition of *American Men and Women of Science.*

Bibliography: *American Men and Women of Science* 10–18; Debus, A. G., ed., *World Who's Who in Science;* Herzenberg, Caroline L., *Women Scientists from Antiquity to the Present;* Kass-Simon, G. and Patricia Farnes, *Women of Science;* McGrayne, Sharon B., *Nobel Prize Women in Science; National Union Catalog;* O'Neill, Lois S., *The Women's Book of World Records and Achievements;* Yost, Edna, *Women of Modern Science.*

Rosalyn Sussman Yalow
Anne Sewell Young

Yalow, Rosalyn Sussman
(1921–)
medical physicist

Education: A.B., Hunter College, 1941; M.S., University of Illinois, 1942, Ph.D. in physics, 1945

Employment: Assistant in physics, University of Illinois, 1941–1943, instructor, 1944; assistant engineer, Federal Telecommunications Laboratory, 1945–1946; lecturer and assistant professor, physics, Hunter College, 1946–1950; physicist, assistant chief, chief, radioimmunoassay service, Veterans Administration Hospital, 1950–1970, nuclear medical service, 1970–1980; research professor, Mount Sinai school of medicine, 1968–1974, distinguished service professor, 1974–1979; department chair, Montefiore hospital and medical center, 1980–1985; distinguished professor at large, Albert Einstein college of medicine, 1979–1985; emeritus professor

Concurrent Position: Consultant, radioisotope unit, U.S. Veterans Administration Hospital, 1947–1950

Married: Aaron Yalow, 1943

Rosalyn Yalow was a corecipient of the Nobel Prize in 1977, the second woman to receive a Nobel Prize in medicine and the first American-born woman to receive a Nobel Prize in science. In 1976 she was the first woman and first nuclear physicist to win the Albert Lasker Medical Research Award for her discovery of radioimmunoassay. She and her collaborators were pioneers in the new science of neuroendocrinology, a discipline that eventually allowed doctors to diagnose conditions caused by minute changes in hormones. The work of Rosalyn Yalow and her colleagues was a spectacular combination of immunology, isotope research, mathematics, and physics.

As a child she was encouraged by her parents to be independent and to think for herself. They encouraged her to seek an excellent education in whatever field she chose. She graduated from high school at the age of 15 and entered Hunter College. She chose physics because, in the late 1930s, physics, particularly nuclear physics, was the most exciting field. Although she wanted to go to medical school after graduating, she was unable to enter because she was Jewish and did not have the tuition money. Graduate schools started admitting women science students during World War II, however, because there were not enough men students to keep their doors open. She was offered an assistantship in physics at the University of Illinois, where she was the first woman permitted in the engineering school since 1917 (during World War I). She could at first teach only pre-med students instead of engineering students; but as more men faculty left for wartime work, she taught men engineers. She met her future husband, Aaron Yalow, at this time, and they were married in 1943.

After receiving her doctorate, she was unable to find a position in nuclear physics. She became the first woman engineer at the Federal Telecommunications Laboratory for a year, returning to Hunter to teach when the engineering job folded. She turned to medical physics, and she set up one of the first radioisotope labs in the United States when she was hired in 1947 at the Veterans Administration Hospital in the Bronx. At the time, the Veterans Administration thought that radioisotopes would be a cheap alternative to radium for cancer treatment. She initiated studies in using radioactive isotopes as tracers in chemical and physiological processes. With her engineering experience, she was able to design equipment; this was helpful because no commercial instrumentation existed at the time. Within two years she had prepared eight publications on her work.

In 1950 she started her long collaboration with Solomon Berson, a physician at the VA hospital. They were an ideal team because their talents complemented each other; they alternated first authorships of papers. They invented the radioimmunoassay (RIA) by accident as an offshoot of their insulin research. Insulin, which was obtained from the pancreas of swine and cattle at that time, was almost but not quite the same as human insulin. Their research indicated that the human immune system produced antibodies to fight foreign insulins. The result was that today manufactured insulin is genetically engineered to be precisely the same as human insulin. They called their system radioimmunoassay because they used radioactively tagged substances to measure antibodies produced by the immune system. Their later research concentrated on all of the hormones. Today RIA is used to measure the concentration of hundreds of hormones, enzymes, vitamins, viruses, and drugs within the human body. They did not patent their discovery, although commercial laboratories have realized enormous sums from performing RIA. Although Berson accepted a position at Mount Sinai school of medicine in 1968, they continued their work together until he died in 1972.

As a woman it was virtually impossible for Rosalyn Yalow to be considered for prestigious appointments after her research partner died. She was determined to succeed on her own, however, and she did. The lab published 60 papers between 1972 and 1976, and she won a dozen medical awards in her own right. She taught at Mount Sinai school of medicine, Montefiore hospital and medical center, and Albert Einstein college of medicine during these years. She was awarded the Nobel Prize in 1977.

The independent streak of her childhood turned to aggressiveness in college and in her first jobs, but she succeeded in her teaching and her research. In later life she became unpopular among contemporaries when her aggressiveness turned to verbal and written attacks on people. She retired from the VA hospital in 1991 and started a public service career as a science activist. She received honors and awards too numerous to list. She was elected to the National Academy of Sciences in 1975. She was elected president of the Endocrine Society (1978–1979) and fellow of the New York Academy of Sciences. She has been a member of the American Academy of Arts and Sciences, the Radiation Research Society, the American College of Radiology, the Biophysical Society, the American Diabetes Association, and the American Physiological Society. She and her husband had two children, Benjamin and Elanna. There are photographs in Sharon McGrayne's *Nobel Prize Women in Science* and Olga Opfell's *Lady Laureates*. Her name was listed in the 1992–1993 edition of *American Men and Women of Science.*

Bibliography: *American Men and Women of Science* 8–18; Herzenberg, Caroline L., *Women Scientists from Antiquity to the Present*; McGrayne, Sharon B., *Nobel Prize Women in Science*; O'Neill, Lois S., *The Women's Book of World Records and Achievements*; Opfell, Olga S., *The Lady Laureates*; Perl, Teri, *Math Equals*; Uglow, Jennifer S., *International Dictionary of Women's Biography.*

Young, Anne Sewell

(1871–1961)

astronomer

Education: B.L., Carleton College, 1892, M.S., 1897; University of Chicago, 1898, 1902; Ph.D. in astronomy, Columbia University, 1906

Employment: Instructor in mathematics, Whitman College, 1892–1893, professor, 1893–1895; high school principal, 1898–1899; from instructor to professor of astronomy, Mount Holyoke College, 1899–1936; emeritus professor

Concurrent Position: Director, Williston Observatory, 1899–1936

*A*nne Young was recognized for her research in astronomy. She conducted an active program at Mount Holyoke on sunspot observations, asteroid positions, comet orbits, and variable stars. After receiving her undergraduate degree from Carleton College in 1892, she was an instructor and then professor of mathematics at Whitman College for four years. She returned to Carleton for her master's degree and was a high school principal for a year. She was appointed an instructor at Mount Holyoke in 1899 and rose through the ranks to professor, being named emeritus professor in 1936. She had a concurrent position as director of the Williston Observatory. She was well grounded in research and published papers in astronomical journals before joining the faculty at Mount Holyoke. She had taken additional studies at the University of Chicago before receiving her doctorate in astronomy from Columbia in 1906; she also spent many summers at Yerkes Observatory. In 1900 she started a program of daily sunspot observations at Mount Holyoke, and after 1907 these observations were sent to the University of Zurich as part of a worldwide cooperative project. She was elected president of the American Association of Variable Star Observers (1923). One of her contributions to the profession was that she promoted popular interest in astronomy by writing a monthly column on astronomy for a local paper and by providing a series of open nights at the observatory for the public. She was elected a fellow of the American Astronomical Society, and she also was a member of the American Association for the Advancement of Science. Her research involved observations of variable stars, measurement of astronomical photographs, and reduction of occultation observations. There is a photograph in *Women of Science: Righting the Record* by G. Kass-Simon and Patricia Farnes.

Bibliography: American Men and Women of Science 2–10; Herzenberg, Caroline L., Women Scientists from Antiquity to the Present; Kass-Simon, G. and Patricia Farnes, Women of Science; Mozans, H. J., Women in Science; Ogilvie, Marilyn B., Women in Science; Rossiter, Margaret W., Women Scientists in America.

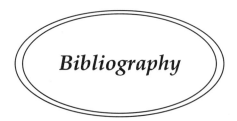

Bibliography

Abir-Am, P. G. and Dorinda Outram, eds. *Uneasy Careers and Intimate Lives: Women in Science 1789–1979*. New Brunswick, NJ: Rutgers University Press, 1987.

American Men and Women of Science [formerly *American Men of Science*]. 1st–18th eds. New York: Bowker, 1906–1992/93.

Appleton's Cyclopaedia of American Biography. Rev. ed. 12 vols. New York: D. Appleton, 1900–1931.

Arnold, Lois B. *Four Lives in Science: Women's Education in the Nineteenth Century*. New York: Schocken Books, 1984.

Baker, Gladys L. "Women in the U.S. Department of Agriculture." *Agricultural History* 50 (1976): 190–201.

Barnhart, John H. *Biographical Notes upon Botanists*. 3 vols. Boston: G. K. Hall, 1965.

Barr, Ernest S. *An Index to Biographical Fragments in Unspecialized Scientific Journals*. University: University of Alabama Press, 1973.

Bonta, Marcia M. *Women in the Field: America's Pioneering Women Naturalists*. College Station: Texas A & M University Press, 1991.

Bryan, Alice I. and Edwin G. Boring. "Women in American Psychology: Prolegomenon." *Psychological Bulletin* 41 (1944): 447–454.

Current Biography. New York: H. W. Wilson, 1940–.

Davis, Herman S. "Women Astronomers (1750–1890)." *Popular Astronomy* 6(4) (1898): 211–228.

Debus, A. G., ed. *World Who's Who in Science*. Chicago: Marquis Who's Who, 1968.

Dictionary of American Biography. New York: Scribner's, 1928–.

Dictionary of Scientific Biography. 16 vols. New York: Scribner's, 1970–1980.

Elliott, Clark A. *Biographical Dictionary of American Science: The Seventeenth through the Nineteenth Centuries*. Westport, CT: Greenwood, 1979.

Goff, Alice C. *Women Can Be Engineers*. Youngstown, OH: Privately published, 1946.

Grinstein, Louise S. and Paul J. Campbell, eds. *Women of Mathematics: A Biobibliographic Sourcebook*. New York: Greenwood, 1987.

Hall, Diana Long. "Academics, Bluestockings, and Biologists: Women at the University of Chicago, 1892–1932." *Annals of the New York Academy of Sciences* 323 (1979): 300–330.

Harshberger, John W. *The Botanists of Philadelphia and Their Work*. Philadelphia: Davis, 1899.

Helm, June, ed. *Pioneers of American Anthropology: The Uses of Biography*. American Ethnological Society Monograph 43. Seattle: University of Washington Press, 1966.

Bibliography

Herzenberg, Caroline L. *Women Scientists from Antiquity to the Present: An Index.* West Cornwall, CT: Locust Hill, 1986.

Hollingsworth, Buckner. *Her Garden Was Her Delight.* New York: Macmillan, 1962.

International Directory of Anthropologists. 3d ed. Washington: American Anthropological Association, 1950.

Ireland, Norma O. *Index to Scientists of the World, from Ancient to Modern Times: Biographies and Portraits.* Boston: Faxon, 1962.

James, E. T., ed. *Notable American Women 1607–1950: A Biographical Dictionary.* 3 vols. Cambridge: Harvard University Press, 1971.

Kass-Simon, G. and Patricia Farnes. *Women of Science: Righting the Record.* Bloomington: Indiana University Press, 1990.

Kundsin, Ruth B. "Successful Women in the Sciences: An Analysis of Determinants." *Annals of the New York Academy of Sciences* 208 (1973): 3–255.

McGrayne, Sharon B. *Nobel Prize Women in Science: Their Lives, Struggles, and Momentous Discoveries.* Secaucus, NJ: Carol, 1993.

McHenry, Robert, ed. *Famous American Women: A Biographical Dictionary from Colonial Times to the Present.* New York: Dover, 1983.

Macksey, Joan and Kenneth Macksey. *The Book of Women's Achievements.* New York: Stein and Day, 1976.

McNeil, Barbara, ed. *Biography and Genealogy Master Index* (1981–85 and 1986–90). Detroit: Gale Research Inc.

Marlow, Joan. *The Great Women.* New York: A & W, 1979.

Mozans, H. J. *Women in Science.* Reprint of 1913 ed. Cambridge, MA: MIT Press, l979.

National Academy of Sciences. *Biographical Memoirs.* Washington, 1932–.

National Cyclopedia of American Biography. Clifton, NJ: J. T. White, 1893–.

National Union Catalog. New York: Rowman & Littlefield, 1956–.

Ogilvie, Marilyn B. *Women in Science: Antiquity through the Nineteenth Century: A Biographical Dictionary with Annotated Bibliography.* Cambridge, MA: MIT Press, 1986.

O'Hern, Elizabeth M. "Women Scientists in Microbiology." *Bioscience* 23 (1973): 539–543.

O'Neill, Lois S. *The Women's Book of World Records and Achievements.* Garden City, NY: Anchor/Doubleday, 1979.

Opfell, Olga S. *The Lady Laureates: Women Who Have Won the Nobel Prize.* Metuchen, NJ: Scarecrow, 1978.

Osborn, Herbert. *Fragments of Entomological History, Including Some Personal Recollections of Men and Events.* 2 vols. Columbus, OH: Privately published, 1937–1946.

Perl, Teri. *Math Equals.* Menlo Park, CA: Addison-Wesley, 1978.

Rossiter, Margaret W. "Women Scientists in America before 1920." *American Scientist* 62 (May/June 1974): 312–323.

———. *Women Scientists in America: Struggles and Strategies to 1940.* Baltimore: Johns Hopkins University Press, 1982.

———. "'Women's Work' in Science, 1880–1910." *Isis* 71 (1980): 381–398.

Rudolph, Emanuel D. "Women in Nineteenth Century American Botany: A Generally Unrecognized Constituency." *American Journal of Botany* 69(8) (1982): 1346–1355.

Shapiro, Laura. *Perfection Salad: Women and Cooking at the Turn of the Century.* New York: Farrar, Straus & Giroux, 1986.

Sicherman, Barbara, et al. *Notable American Women: The Modern Period: A Biographical Dictionary.* Cambridge, MA: Harvard University Press, 1980.

Siegel, Patricia J. and Kay Thomas Finley. *Women in the Scientific Search: An American Bio-Bibliography 1724–1979.* Metuchen, NJ: Scarecrow, 1985.

Smith, Edgar C. "Some Notable Women of Science," *Nature* 127 (27 June 1931): 976–977.

Uglow, Jennifer S. *International Dictionary of Women's Biography.* New York: Continuum, 1985.

Vare, Ethlie Ann and Greg Ptacek. *Mothers of Invention: From the Bra to the Bomb: Forgotten Women & Their Unforgettable Ideas.* New York: Morrow, 1988.

Visher, Stephen S. *Scientists Starred 1903–1943 in "American Men of Science."* Baltimore: Johns Hopkins University Press, 1947.

Who Was Who in America. Chicago: Marquis – Who's Who, 1607/1896– .

Yost, Edna. *American Women of Science.* Rev. ed. Philadelphia: Lippincott, 1955.

———. *Women of Modern Science.* New York: Dodd, Mead, 1959.

Illustration Credits

Illustration Credits

324 Forest Products Laboratory, USDA Forest Service, Madison, Wisconsin.

325 MIT Museum.

328 Courtesy Special Collections, Vassar College Libraries.

333 Division of Rare and Manuscript Collections, Cornell University Library.

334 Columbia University, Columbiana Collection.

337 Forest Products Laboratory, USDA Forest Service, Madison, Wisconsin.

352 Mount Holyoke College Library/Archives.

360 National Archives. Photo RG-7-H-633.

385 University of Chicago Archives.

394 National Archives. Photo RG-7-H-561.

399 Division of Rare and Manuscript Collections, Cornell University Library.

415 Courtesy Special Collections, Vassar College Libraries.

425 Columbia University, Columbiana Collection.

Jacket Illustrations (clockwise)

Coutesy Department of Library Services, American Museum of Natural History. Neg. 337676.

Coutesy Department of Library Services, American Museum of Natural History. Neg. 2A 5176.

National Archives. Photo RG-16-ES-633.

Forest Products Laboratory, USDA Forest Service, Madison, Wisconsin.

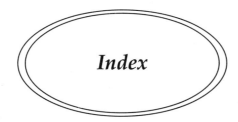

Index

Index

Index

Index

Index

Index

Index

Index

Index

Physicists, 313, 416–417
  in corporate research, 68–69
  employed after marriage, 68, 135–136, 213,
    428–429, 433–434
  in first edition of *American Men and Women of*
    Science, 129–130, 191, 201–202, 234, 377
  government employment of, 213, 270–271, 412,
    433–434
  nuclear, 135–137, 213, 412, 428–429
  in spectroscopy, 409–410, 420
  starred in *American Men and Women of Science*,
    30, 234
  in teaching, 9–10, 191, 304–305
Physiologists, 16–17, 63, 177, 204, 257, 308
  plant, 81–82, 96–97, 101, 190, 192
  in poison research, 40–41
Physiology and Calisthenics for Schools and Families, 25
Physiology of Man and Other Animals, 257
Phytopathology, 140, 154, 281, 295
Pickering, Edward, 116, 117, 205, 240
The Piegan Indians, 89
Pinckney, Charles, 305
Pinckney, Eliza Lucas, 305–306
Pioneer Award, American Institute of Chemists, 189
Pitelka, Dorothy Riggs, 306
Pittman, Margaret, 307
Plains Indians, 118
Planetary geologists, 238
Plant Anatomy, 105
Plant Book for Dumbarton Oaks, 111
Plant Disease Handbook, 413
The Plant Doctor: The How, Why and When of Disease
  and Insect Control in Your Garden, 413
Plant Doctoring is Fun, 413
Plant nurseries, 351
Plant pathologists
  government employment of, 6–7, 23–24, 41–42,
    58, 84, 140–141, 153–154, 184–185, 267,
    294–295, 324–325, 337–338, 362, 363, 367–368,
    413
  in sugar research, 226–227
Plant physiologists, 81–82, 96–97, 101, 190, 192,
    328–329
Plant Quarantine Act (1912), 58
Plant Science Bulletin, 105
Plant World, 75
Plants, Viruses, and Insects, 105
Poisons research, 16, 40, 151, 176
Polio research, 171
Polish Countrysides, 34
Polymer research, 26–27, 390–391
Pool, Judith Graham, 308
Popular Astronomy, 46, 205, 309, 417, 418
Popular Flora of Denver, Colorado, 95
Popular Science News, 309
Porter, Charles, 309
Porter, Gene Stratton, 308–309
Practical Cookery, 290
A Practical Course in Botany, 8
Practical Microscopy, 33
Presidential Certificate of Merit, 9, 323

Preventive Medicine and Public Health, 17
Priestley, Joseph, 32
Prisoners of Poverty Abroad, 53
The Problem of the Poor, 53
Proceedings, American Philosophical Society, 372
Proceedings, American Society of Microscopists, 127
Proceedings, California Academy of Science, 96
Proceedings, Entomological Society of Washington,
    112, 346
Proceedings, Geological Society of America, 129
Proceedings, Indiana Academy of Science, 29
Proceedings, U.S. National Museum, 45, 345
Proceedings, Washington Academy of Sciences, 112
Proctor, Mary, 309–310
A Pronouncing and Defining Dictionary of the Swatow
  Dialect, 114
Protein structure theory, 427
Psychiatrists, 3
Psychologist Unretired: The Life Pattern of Lillien J.
  Martin, 237
Psychologists
  in child development, 356, 365, 424
  clinical, 166–167
  consciousness theory of, 410
  employed after marriage, 131–132, 133, 139, 163,
    200–201, 318, 423–424
  in esthetics, 172, 237
  in first edition of *American Men and Women of*
    Science, 17, 52, 139, 163, 172, 200, 227, 237,
    274, 356, 365, 411, 424
  industrial, 132–133
  in intelligence research, 131–132, 138, 274
  in memory research, 128, 139, 356
  in personality research, 52, 90
  starred in *American Men and Women of Science*,
    52, 90, 138, 171, 200, 237, 411, 424
  in visual mechanisms, 183, 200, 318
Psychology of Management, 133
Publications in Botany, 36
Pueblo Indian Religion, 291
Purine and Pyrimidine Nucleotide Metabolism, 186

The Quadrupeds of North America, 16
Quartermaster Corps, 81–82
Quimby, Edith Hinkley, 313

R. E. Dyer Lecturer, National Institutes of Health,
    195–196
Race: Science and Politics, 26
Rachel Carson at Work: The House of Life, 57
Racial discrimination, 92
Radcliffe College, 5, 44
Radiation Laboratory, MIT, 11
Radiation research, 379, 400, 433, 434
  See also Nuclear research
Radioimmunoassay (RIA) discovery, 433, 434
Ramey, Estelle Rosemary White, 317
Rand, (Marie) Gertrude, 318
Rapp, Janet Lorraine Cooper, 319
Rat breeding, 192, 193
Rathbun, Mary Jane, 319–320

Index

Index